THE CENTURY
POLITICAL SCIENCE SERIES

A Book of Readings Selected and Edited by

HILLMAN M. BISHOP and SAMUEL HENDEL

Department of Political Science, The City College of New York

BASIC ISSUES *of*
AMERICAN
DEMOCRACY

FOURTH EDITION

New York: APPLETON-CENTURY-CROFTS, INC.

To the Students of
THE CITY COLLEGE

PREFACE

The teacher who knows this book will understandably seek, in the first instance, to determine what changes have been made in assembling materials for our *fourth* edition.

We have extended our treatment of civil rights to include a discussion of the "lawfulness" of the desegregation decisions and of the moral, sociological, and psychological arguments for and against desegregation; added Professor Schumpeter's view to "What Is Democracy?" and substituted H. B. Mayo's "Defense of Democracy" for that appearing in the *third* edition; supplemented the decision in the *Dennis* case with that in the *Yates* case; and altered the materials concerned with the Loyalty-Security program to focus on its fundamental premises and on the distinction sometimes made between its application to sensitive and non-sensitive agencies.

With respect to the American party system, we have raised more sharply the issues involved in the demand for "A More Responsible Two-Party System"; and, with respect to Congress, introduced discussions of the case for and against cloture and on the values and vices of Congressional investigations.

In the foreign policy section, we have presented a debate between Bertrand Russell and Sidney Hook (with a third position by John H. Herz) on the political implications of the development of atomic weapons and reproduced the discussion on "coexistence" between Nikita S. Khrushchev and George F. Kennan which first appeared in the pages of *Foreign Affairs*.

The basic premises and objectives reflected in the earlier editions of this book remain unchanged. It is our belief that it is desirable to devote considerable attention to the study of fundamental values and persistent issues of our democracy in the introductory, and frequently terminal, American Government and related courses. This view finds support in the statement by Professor Francis O. Wilcox, Chairman of the American Political Science Association's Committee on Undergraduate Instruction who, in the *American Political Science Review,* wrote:

> [It] must be apparent that we have neglected to give adequate attention to the concept of democracy. We speak at great length about the electoral process, the legislature in action, the Constitution, the courts and the executive, but nowhere do we pause to ponder the real meaning of democracy. Yet here, it seems to me, is the all-important question. What is democracy? What are its weaknesses? Wherein lies its strength? What are its chances to survive? What is the real nature of the alternatives to democracy? It is infinitely more important for a student to think about these questions than it is for him to know the steps a bill must go through before it can become a law.

In the years since 1948, when the *first* edition of this book appeared, this viewpoint has commanded increasing approval from the political science profession.

A second conviction that guided our selection of materials is that in dealing with controversial issues it is desirable, within limits of space, to present the most persuasively reasoned or authoritative statements obtainable. We agree with John Stuart Mill that full justice can be done to arguments only if they are presented by persons "who actually believe them; who defend them in earnest, and do their utmost for them," and that the "beliefs we have the most warrant for, have no safeguard to rest on, but a standing invitation to the whole world to prove them unfounded." And it is noteworthy that these principles of selection have meant the inclusion of materials representing some of the truly great names in political science.

Inevitably in making selections out of the vast literature of political discourse, some painful choices proved necessary. (To those who may be disappointed because of particular omissions we can only express the hope that compensation will be found in some of the additions and substitutions.) It should be noted, too, that since material on one side of a controversy was not ordinarily written in reply to that on another, direct and sharp conflict will not invariably be found. Notwithstanding these reservations, we believe that there is no other book of readings that gives as much emphasis to, and with as great consistency presents, diverse positions on the fundamental values and problems of American government and democracy.

What purposes are served by the emphasis of *Basic Issues?* We believe that this book contributes to a realization of the following: (*a*) It requires the student to analyze conflicting viewpoints, to weigh evidence and arguments, to make value judgments and reach his own conclusions. This experience, and skills developed in the classroom, may assist him in deciding between alternative policies which confront him as a citizen. (*b*) It increases interest in political discussion and may encourage active participation in public affairs outside the classroom. (*c*) It compels the student to re-examine the foundations of his beliefs and brings "clearer perception and livelier impression" to those to which he adheres; particularly, we think, it heightens his understanding of the meaning and value of democracy.

This volume, we suggest, may be adapted to the primary political science course, or to one semester of an integrated social science course, in a number of ways. At some colleges, for purposes of day-to-day classroom discussion, assignments consist of selections from these readings; in addition, students are required to read particular chapters in a standard textbook. While many of the textbook chapters are not discussed in the classroom, knowledge of this largely descriptive, factual material is tested in periodic examinations. At other colleges, instructors prefer to rely upon a standard textbook, supplemented at appropriate points with required reading from this volume. (Teachers and students should note that throughout this book authors' footnotes are numbered, whereas those of the editors are marked by asterisks or other symbols.)

We are indebted to the authors, editors, and publishers who graciously granted permission to reproduce the material of this volume. Our obligation to members of the Department of Political Science at The City College of New York, past and present, is considerable. Special mention must be made, however, of Mr. Marvin E. Gettleman and of Professor Bernard E. Brown (now at Vanderbilt University) who collaborated in the editing of the *fourth* and *second* editions, respectively, and of Mr. Stanley Feingold. Their assistance and suggestions were of particular value. Finally, we are grateful for the many comments received from professional colleagues all over the country.

SAMUEL HENDEL
HILLMAN M. BISHOP

CONTENTS

Contents

SOURCES OF READINGS

(Bracketed numbers refer to pages in this volume. A selection marked with an * is new to *Basic Issues;* one marked with a † has been substantially revised for this edition.)

BOOKS, ARTICLES, SPEECHES

(Book titles are italicized; article titles are quoted)

BLACK, Charles L., Jr.   "The Lawfulness of the Segregation Decisions" [217] *

BRYCE, James   *The American Commonwealth* [297]
BURNHAM, James   *Congress and the American Tradition* [339] *
BURNS, James M.   *Congress on Trial* [280]
CARDOZO, Benjamin N.   *The Nature of the Judicial Process* [258]
COHEN, Morris R.   "Is Judicial Review Necessary?" [249]
                                "Why I Am Not a Communist" [408]
COOK, Eugene, and   "The School Segregation Cases: Opposing the
    POTTER, William I.   Opinion of the Supreme Court" [208] *
COMMAGER, Henry Steele   *Majority Rule and Minority Rights* [68]
FARRAND, Max   *Records of the Federal Convention* [42]
FINER, Herman   *The Theory and Practice of Modern Govern-
                                    ment* [308]
FISCHER, John   "Unwritten Rules of American Politics" [266]
GARRISON, Lloyd K.   "Congressional Investigations: Are They a
                                    Threat to Civil Liberties?" [349] *
GELLHORN, Walter   *Security, Loyalty and Science* [175] *
GROUP FOR THE ADVANCE-   *Emotional Aspects of School Desegregation*
    MENT OF PSYCHIATRY   [237] *
HACKER, Louis M.   "The Limits of Intervention" [357]
HAZLITT, Henry   *A New Constitution Now* [313]
HERRING, Pendleton   *The Politics of Democracy* [303]
HERZ, John H.   "Balance System and Balance Policies in a Nu-
                                    clear and Bipolar Age" [499] *
HOOK, Sidney   *Political Power and Personal Freedom* [162] *
                                "A Foreign Policy for Survival" [489] *
                                "A Free Man's Choice" [492] *
                                "Bertrand Russell Retreats" [496] *
JAVITS, Jacob J.   *Proposed Amendments to Rule XXII of the
                                    Standing Rules of the Senate* [327] *
KENNAN, George F.   "Peaceful Coexistence: A Western View" [471] *
KHRUSHCHEV, Nikita S.   "On Peaceful Coexistence" [455] *
LASKI, Harold J.   "Democracy" [10]
                                Karl Marx: An Essay [414]
                                The American Presidency [301]
LENIN, V. I.   *State and Revolution* [382]
LERNER, Max   "State Capitalism and Business Capitalism"
                                    [367]
LINDBLOM, Charles E.   "Empirical Problems and Particular Goals"
                                    [364]
LIPPMANN, Walter   *The Phantom Public* [2]

CASES

BASIC ISSUES OF
AMERICAN DEMOCRACY

He who knows only his own side of the case, knows little of that. His reasons may be good, and no one may have been able to refute them. But if he is equally unable to refute the reasons on the opposite side; if he does not so much as know what they are, he has no ground for preferring either opinion. The rational position for him would be suspension of judgment, and unless he contents himself with that, he is either led by authority, or adopts, like the generality of the world, the side to which he feels most inclination. Nor is it enough that he should hear the arguments of adversaries from his own teachers, presented as they state them, and accompanied by what they offer as refutations. That is not the way to do justice to the arguments, or bring them into real contact with his own mind. He must be able to hear them from persons who actually believe them; who defend them in earnest, and do their very utmost for them. He must know them in their most plausible and persuasive form; he must feel the whole force of the difficulty which the true view of the subject has to encounter and dispose of; else he will never really possess himself of the portion of truth which meets and removes that difficulty.

JOHN STUART MILL—*On Liberty*

Democracy and Public

Opinion

THE NATURE and meaning of democracy have been subjects of con-siderable controversy. Dispute is in part engendered by confusion between the democratic ideal and the reality. To the early Greeks, democracy simply meant rule by the people; a term derived from *dēmos*-people and *kratein*-to rule. But, as Walter Lippmann makes clear, a false conception of democracy may lead to widespread dis-illusionment.

Further difficulty arises from the fact that radically different régimes have laid claim to the name and sanction of democracy. One result of this apparent confusion might be to push aside the whole question as a mere matter of semantics. This would be unfortunate; for disagreement over the nature and meaning of democracy may derive from deep-lying differences over values that manifest themselves in the institutions de-signed to realize these values.

The ensuing section raises several issues. Apart from a general dis-cussion of the nature and meaning of democracy, it considers spe-cifically the relationship of the people and their representatives and the implications to be drawn from the increasing resort to polls to ascertain public opinion. Should the representative simply reflect the public's views of desirable policy or should he, as Burke insisted, refuse to sacri-fice "his unbiased opinion, his mature judgment, his enlightened con-science . . . to any man, or any set of men living"?

(For the views of the Founding Fathers on democracy see next section. See also "Democracy Evaluated.")

WHAT IS DEMOCRACY?

❧✧❧

The Phantom Public

WALTER LIPPMANN *

THE UNATTAINABLE IDEAL

A false ideal of democracy can lead only to disillusionment and to meddlesome tyranny. If democracy cannot direct affairs, then a philosophy which expects it to direct them will encourage the people to attempt the impossible. . . .

The private citizen today has come to feel rather like a deaf spectator in the back row, who ought to keep his mind on the mystery off there, but cannot quite manage to keep awake. He knows he is somehow affected by what is going on. Rules and regulations continually, taxes annually and wars occasionally, remind him that he is being swept along by great drifts of circumstance.

Yet these public affairs are . . . for the most part invisible. They are managed, if they are managed at all, at distant centers, from behind the scenes, by unnamed powers. As a private person he does not know for certain what is going on, or who is doing it, or where he is being carried. No newspaper reports his environment so that he can grasp it; no school has taught him how to imagine it; his ideals, often, do not fit with it; listening to speeches, uttering opinions and voting do not, he finds, enable him to govern it. He lives in a world which he cannot see, does not understand and is unable to direct. . . .

There is then nothing particularly new in the disenchantment which the private citizen expresses by not voting at all, by voting only for the head of the ticket, by staying away from the primaries, by not reading speeches and documents, by the whole list of sins of omission for which he is denounced. I shall not denounce him further. My sympathies are with him, for I believe that he has been saddled with an impossible task and that he is asked to practice an unattainable ideal. I find it so myself for,

---

* Newspaper columnist. Formerly Editor of *New York World*. Author of *Public Opinion, A Preface to Politics, The Good Society, The Public Philosophy* and numerous other books. The selection is from Walter Lippmann, *The Phantom Public* (New York, The Macmillan Co., 1927), *passim*. By permission.

2

although public business is my main interest and I give most of my time to watching it, I cannot find time to do what is expected of me in the theory of democracy; that is, to know what is going on and to have an opinion worth expressing on every question which confronts a self-governing community. And I have not happened to meet anybody, from a President of the United States to a professor of political science, who came anywhere near to embodying the accepted ideal of the sovereign and omnipotent citizen. . . .

The actual governing is made up of a multitude of arrangements on specific questions by particular individuals. These rarely become visible to the private citizen. Government, in the long intervals between elections, is carried on by politicians, officeholders and influential men who make settlements with other politicians, officeholders, and influential men. The mass of people see these settlements, judge them, and affect them only now and then. They are altogether too numerous, too complicated, too obscure in their effects to become the subject of any continuing exercise of public opinion.

Nor in any exact and literal sense are those who conduct the daily business of government accountable after the fact to the great mass of the voters. They are accountable only, except in spectacular cases, to the other politicians, officeholders and influential men directly interested in the particular act. Modern society is not visible to anybody, nor intelligible continuously and as a whole. One section is visible to another section, one series of acts is intelligible to this group and another to that.

Even this degree of responsible understanding is attainable only by the development of fact-finding agencies of great scope and complexity. These agencies give only a remote and incidental assistance to the general public. Their findings are too intricate for the casual reader. They are also almost always much too uninteresting. Indeed the popular boredom and contempt for the expert and for statistical measurement are such that the organization of intelligence to administer modern affairs would probably be entirely neglected were it not that departments of government, corporations, trade unions and trade associations are being compelled by their own internal necessities of administration, and by compulsion of other corporate groups, to record their own acts, measure them, publish them and stand accountable for them. . . .

It may be objected at once that an election which turns one set of men out of office and installs another is an expression of public opinion which is neither secondary nor indirect. But what in fact is an election? We call it an expression of the popular will. But is it? We go into a polling booth and mark a cross on a piece of paper for one or two, or perhaps three or four names. Have we expressed our thoughts on the public policy of the United States?—Presumably we have a number of thoughts on this and that with many buts and ifs and ors. Surely the cross on a piece of paper does not express them. It would take us hours to express our thoughts, and calling a vote the expression of our mind is an empty fiction.

A vote is a promise of support. It is a way of saying: I am lined up with these men, on this side. I enlist with them. I will follow. . . . The public does not select the candidate, write the platform, outline the policy any more than it builds the automobile or acts the play. It aligns itself for or against somebody who has offered himself, has made a promise, has produced a play, is selling an automobile. The action of a group as a group is the mobilization of the force it possesses. . . .

I do not wish to labor the argument any further than may be necessary to establish the theory that what the public does is not to express its opinions but to align itself for or against a proposal. If that theory is accepted, we must abandon the notion that democratic government can be the direct expression of the will of the people. We must abandon the notion that the people govern. Instead we must adopt the theory that, by their occasional mobilizations as a majority, people support or oppose the individuals who actually govern. We must say that the popular will does not direct continuously but that it intervenes occasionally. . . .

The attempt has been made to ascribe some intrinsic moral and intellectual virtue to majority rule. It was said often in the nineteenth century that there was a deep wisdom in majorities which was the voice of God. Sometimes this flattery was a sincere mysticism, sometimes it was the self-deception which always accompanies the idealization of power. In substance it was nothing but a transfer to the new sovereign of the divine attributes of kings. Yet the inherent absurdity of making virtue and wisdom dependent on 51 per cent of any collection of men has always been apparent. The practical realization that the claim was absurd has resulted in a whole code of civil rights to protect minorities and in all sorts of elaborate methods of subsidizing the arts and sciences and other human interests so they might be independent of the operation of majority rule.

The justification of majority rule in politics is not to be found in its ethical superiority. It is to be found in the sheer necessity of finding a place in civilized society for the force which resides in the weight of numbers. I have called voting an act of enlistment, an alignment for or against, a mobilization. These are military metaphors, and rightly so, I think, for an election based on the principle of majority rule is historically and practically a sublimated and denatured civil war, a paper mobilization without physical violence.

Constitutional democrats, in the intervals when they were not idealizing the majority, have acknowledged that a ballot was a civilized substitute for a bullet. "The French Revolution," says Bernard Shaw, "overthrew one set of rulers and substituted another with different interests and different views. That is what a general election enables the people to do in England every seven years if they choose." . . . Hans Delbrück puts the matter simply when he says that the principle of majority rule is "a purely practical principle. If one wants to avoid a civil war, one lets those rule who in any case would obtain the upper hand if there should be a struggle; and they are the superior numbers." . . .

To support the Ins when things are going well; to support the Outs when they seem to be going badly, this, in spite of all that has been said about tweedledum and tweedledee, is the essence of popular government. Even the most intelligent large public of which we have any experience must determine finally who shall wield the organized power of the state, its army and its police, by a choice between the Ins and Outs. A community where there is no choice does not have popular government. It is subject to some form of dictatorship or it is ruled by the intrigues of the politicians in the lobbies.

Although it is the custom of partisans to speak as if there were radical differences between the Ins and the Outs, it could be demonstrated, I believe, that in stable and mature societies the differences are necessarily not profound. If they were profound, the defeated minority would be constantly on the verge of rebellion. An election would be catastrophic, whereas the assumption in every election is that the victors will do nothing to make life intolerable to the vanquished and that the vanquished will endure with good humor policies which they do not approve.

In the United States, Great Britain, Canada, Australia and in certain of the Continental countries an election rarely means even a fraction of what the campaigners said it would mean. It means some new faces and perhaps a slightly different general tendency in the management of affairs. The Ins may have had a bias toward collectivism; the Outs will lean toward individualism. The Ins may have been suspicious and non-cooperative in foreign affairs; the Outs will perhaps be more trusting or entertain another set of suspicions. The Ins may have favored certain manufacturing interests; the Outs may favor agricultural interests. But even these differing tendencies are very small as compared with the immense area of agreement, established habit and unavoidable necessity. In fact, one might say that a nation is politically stable when nothing of radical consequence is determined by its elections. . . .

The test of whether the Ins are handling affairs effectively is the presence or absence of disturbing problems. . . . It is my opinion that for the most part the general public cannot back each reformer on each issue. It must choose between the Ins and the Outs on the basis of a cumulative judgment as to whether the problems are being solved or aggravated. The particular reformers must look for their support normally to the ruling insiders.

EDUCATION FOR DEMOCRACY

Education has furnished the thesis of the last chapter of every optimistic book on democracy written for one hundred and fifty years. Even Robert Michels, stern and unbending antisentimentalist that he is, says in his "final considerations" that "it is the great task of social education to raise the intellectual level of the masses, so that they may be enabled, within the limits of what is possible, to counteract the oligarchical tendencies" of all collective action. . . .

The usual appeal to education as the remedy for the incompetence of democracy is barren. It is, in effect, a proposal that school teachers shall by some magic of their own fit men to govern after the makers of laws and the preachers of civic ideals have had a free hand in writing the specifications. The reformers do not ask what men can be taught. They say they should be taught whatever may be necessary to fit them to govern the modern world.

The usual appeal to education can bring only disappointment. For the problems of the modern world appear and change faster than any set of teachers can grasp them, much faster than they can convey their substance to a population of children. If the schools attempt to teach children how to solve the problems of the day, they are bound always to be in arrears. The most they can conceivably attempt is the teaching of a pattern of thought and feeling which will enable the citizen to approach a new problem in some useful fashion. But that pattern cannot be invented by the pedagogue. It is the political theorist's business to trace out that pattern. In that task he must not assume that the mass has political genius, but that men, even if they had genius, would give only a little time and attention to public affairs. . . .

At the root of the effort to educate a people for self-government there has, I believe, always been the assumption that the voter should aim to approximate as nearly as he can the knowledge and the point of view of the responsible man. He did not, of course, in the mass, ever approximate it very nearly. But he was supposed to. It was believed that if only he could be taught more facts, if only he would take more interest, if only he would read more and better newspapers, if only he would listen to more lectures and read more reports, he would gradually be trained to direct public affairs. The whole assumption is false. It rests upon a false conception of public opinion and a false conception of the way the public acts. No sound scheme of civic education can come of it. No progress can be made toward this unattainable ideal.

This democratic conception is false because it fails to note the radical difference between the experience of the insider and the outsider; it is fundamentally askew because it asks the outsider to deal as successfully with the substance of a question as the insider. He cannot do it. No scheme of education can equip him in advance for all the problems of mankind; no device of publicity, no machinery of enlightenment, can endow him during a crisis with the antecedent detailed and technical knowledge which is required for executive action. . . .

The fundamental difference which matters is that between insiders and outsiders. Their relations to a problem are radically different. Only the insider can make decisions, not because he is inherently a better man but because he is so placed that he can understand and can act. The outsider is necessarily ignorant, usually irrelevant and often meddlesome, because he is trying to navigate the ship from dry land. That is why excellent automobile manufacturers, literary critics and scientists often talk such nonsense about politics. Their congenital excellence, if it exists, reveals itself only in their own activity. The aristocratic theorists work from the fallacy of supposing that a sufficiently excellent square peg will also fit a round hole. In short, like the democratic theorists, they miss the essence of the matter, which is, that competence exists only in relation to function; that men are not good, but good for something; that men cannot be educated, but only educated for something. . . .

Democracy, therefore, has never developed an education for the public. It has merely given it a smattering of the kind of knowledge which the responsible man requires. It has, in fact, aimed not at making good citizens but at making a mass of amateur executives. It has not taught the child how to act as a member of the public. It has merely given him a hasty, incomplete taste of what he might have to know if he meddled in everything. The result is a bewildered public and a mass of insufficiently trained officials. The responsible men have obtained their training not from the courses in "civics" but in the law schools and law offices and in business. The public at large, which includes everybody outside the field of his own responsible knowledge, has had no coherent political training of any kind. Our civic education does not even begin to tell the voter how he can reduce the maze of public affairs to some intelligible form. . . .

Education for citizenship, for membership in the public, ought, therefore to be distinct from education for public office. Citizenship involves a radically different relation to affairs, requires different intellectual habits and different methods of action. The force of public opinion is partisan, spasmodic, simple-minded and external. It needs for its direction . . . a new intellectual method which shall provide it with its own usable canons of judgment. . . .

THE RÔLE OF THE PUBLIC

If this is the nature of public action, what ideal can be formulated which shall conform to it?

We are bound, I think, to express the ideal in its lowest terms, to state it not as an ideal which might conceivably be realized by exceptional groups now and then or in some distant future but as an ideal which normally might be taught and attained. In estimating the burden which a public can carry, a sound political theory must insist upon the largest factor of safety. It must understate the possibilities of public action. . . .

We cannot, then, think of public opinion as a conserving or creating force directing society to clearly conceived ends, making deliberately toward socialism or away from it, toward nationalism, an empire, a league of nations or any other doctrinal goal. . . .

The work of the world goes on continually without conscious direction from public opinion. At certain junctures problems arise. It is only with the crises of some of these problems that public opinion is concerned. And its object in dealing with a crisis is to help allay that crisis.

I think this conclusion is inescapable. For though we may prefer to believe that the aim of popular action should be to do justice or promote the true, the beautiful and the good, the belief will not maintain itself in the face of plain experience. The public does not know in most crises what specifically is the truth or the justice of the case, and men are not agreed on what is beautiful and good. Nor does the public rouse itself normally at the existence of evil. It is aroused at evil made manifest by the interruption of a habitual process of life. And finally, a problem ceases to occupy attention not when justice, as we happen to define it, has been done but when a workable adjustment that overcomes the crisis has been made. . . .

Thus we strip public opinion of any implied duty to deal with the substance of a problem, to make technical decisions, to attempt justice or impose a moral precept. And instead we say that the ideal of public opinion is to align men during the crisis of a problem in such a way as to favor the action of those individuals who may be able to compose a crisis. The power to discern those individuals is the end of the effort to educate public opinion. The aim of research designed to facilitate public action is the discovery of clear signs by which these individuals may be discerned.

The signs are relevant when they reveal by coarse, simple and objective tests which side in a controversy upholds a workable social rule, or which is attacking an unworkable rule, or which proposes a promising new rule. By following such signs the public might know where to align itself. In such an alignment it does not, let us remember, pass judgment on the intrinsic merits. It merely places its force at the disposal of the side which, according to objective signs, seems to be standing for human adjustments according to a clear rule of behavior and against the side which appears to stand for settlement in accordance with its own unaccountable will.

Public opinion, in this theory, is a reserve of force brought into action during a crisis in public affairs. Though it is itself an irrational force, under favorable institutions, sound leadership and decent training the power of public opinion might be placed at the disposal of those who stood for workable law as against brute assertion. In this theory, public opinion does not make the law. But by canceling lawless power it may establish the condition under which law can be made. It does not reason, investigate, invent, persuade, bargain or settle. But, by holding the aggressive party in check, it may liberate intelligence. Public opinion in its highest ideal will defend those who are prepared to act on their reason against the interrupting force of those who merely assert their will. . . .

These in roughest outline are some of the conclusions, as they appear to me, of the attempt to bring the theory of democracy into somewhat truer alignment with the nature of public opinion. I have conceived public opinion to be, not the voice of God, nor the voice of society, but the voice of the interested spectators of action. I have, therefore, supposed that the opinions of the spectators must be essentially different from those of the actors, and that the kind of action they were capable of taking was essentially different too. It has seemed to me that the public had a function and must have methods of its own in controversies, qualitatively different from those of the executive men; that it was a dangerous confusion to believe that private purposes were a mere emanation of some common purpose. . . .

It is a theory which puts its trust chiefly in the individuals directly concerned. They initiate, they administer, they settle. It would subject them to the least possible interference from ignorant and meddlesome outsiders, for in this theory the public intervenes only when there is a crisis of maladjustment, and then not to deal with the substance of the problem but to neutralize the arbitrary force which prevents adjustment. It is a theory which economizes the attention of men as members of the public, and asks them to do as little as possible in matters where they can do nothing very well. It confines the effort of men, when they are a public, to a part they might fulfill, to a part which corresponds to their own greatest interest in any social disturbance; that is, to an intervention which may help to allay the disturbance, and thus allow them to return to their own affairs.

For it is the pursuit of their special affairs that they are most interested in. It is by the private labors of individuals that life is enhanced. I set no great store on what can be done by public opinion and the action of masses.

I have no legislative program to offer, no new institutions to propose. There are, I believe, immense confusions in the current theory of democracy which frustrate and pervert its action. I have attacked certain of the confusions with no conviction except that a false philosophy tends to stereotype thought against the lessons of experience. I do not know what the lessons will be when we have learned to think of public opinion as it is, and not as the fictitious power we have assumed it to be. It is enough if with Bentham we know that "the perplexity of ambiguous discourse . . . distracts and eludes the apprehension, stimulates and inflames the passions."

Equality and Democracy

HAROLD J. LASKI *

No definition of democracy can adequately comprise the vast history
which the concept connotes. To some it is a form of government, to others
a way of social life. Men have found its essence in the character of the
electorate, the relation between government and the people, the absence
of wide economic differences between citizens, the refusal to recognize
privileges built on birth or wealth, race or creed. Inevitably it has changed
its substance in terms of time and place. What has seemed democracy
to a member of some ruling class has seemed to his poorer fellow citizen a
narrow and indefensible oligarchy. Democracy has a context in every
sphere of life; and in each of those spheres it raises its special problems
which do not admit of satisfactory or universal generalization.

The political aspect of democracy has the earliest roots in time. For
the most part it remained a negative concept until the seventeenth century. Men protested against systems which upon one ground or another
excluded them from a share in power. They were opposed to an oligarchy
which exercised privileges confined to a narrow range of persons. They
sought the extension of such privileges to more people on the ground
that limitation was not justifiable. They felt and argued that exclusion
from privilege was exclusion from benefit; and they claimed their equal
share in its gains.

That notion of equality points the way to the essence of the democratic
idea—the effort of men to affirm their own essence and to remove all barriers to that affirmation. All differentials by which other men exercise authority or influence they do not themselves possess hinder their own self-
realization. To give these differentials the protection of the legal order is to
prevent the realization of the wishes and interests of the mass of men. The
basis of democratic development is therefore the demand for equality, the
demand that the system of power be erected upon the similarities and not
the differences between men. Of the permanence of this demand there can
be no doubt; at the very dawn of political science Aristotle insisted that its
denial was the main cause of revolutions. Just as the history of the state
can perhaps be most effectively written in terms of the expanding claims
of the common man upon the results of its effort, so the development of
the realization of equality is the clue to the problem of democracy. . . .

It is because political equality, however profound, does not permit the

* Late Professor of Political Science at London School of Economics and Political Science. The selection is from Harold J. Laski, "Democracy," *Encyclopaedia
of Social Sciences* (New York, The Macmillan Co., 1942). By permission.

full affirmation of the common man's essence that the idea of democracy has spread to other spheres. The discovery that men may be politically equal without attaining a genuine realization of their personalities was seen by not a few during the Puritan revolution, and the demand for economic equality was loudly and ably voiced there by Winstanley and his followers. It was only, however, with the French Revolution that economic equality may be said to have become a permanent part of the democratic creed. From that time, particularly in the context of socialist principles, it has been increasingly insisted that in the absence of economic equality no political mechanisms will of themselves enable the common man to realize his wishes and interests. Economic power is regarded as the parent of political power. To make the diffusion of the latter effective, the former also must be widely diffused. To divide a people into rich and poor is to make impossible the attainment of a common interest by state action. Economic equality is then urged as the clue upon which the reality of democracy depends. . . .

The case for democracy is built upon the assumption that in its absence men become the tools of others, without available proof that the common good is inherently involved in this relationship. The case at bottom is an ethical one. It postulates that the right to happiness is inherent in man as a member of society and that any system which denies that right cannot be justified. The main argument in its favor is the important one that in any social order where it has not been accepted a rational analysis finds it difficult to justify the distribution of benefits which occurs. . . .

SOCIALISM AND DEMOCRACY

Democratic government during the nineteenth century may be said to have been successful so long as it confined its activities to the purely political field. While it occupied itself with matters of religious freedom, formal political equality, the abrogation of aristocratic privilege, its conquests were swift and triumphant. But the attainment of these ends did not solve any of the major social and economic issues. The masses still remained poor; a small number of rich men still exercised a predominant influence in the state. With the grant of the franchise to the workers therefore a movement toward collectivism was inevitable. Political parties had to attract their support; the obvious method was to offer the prospect of social and economic legislation which should alleviate the workers' condition. And from the early days of the French Revolution there had appeared the portent of socialism with its insistence that only in the rigorous democratization of economic power could a solution to the social problem be found. Incoherent at first, the development of trade unions and the growth of doctrines like that of Marx made what seemed visionary utopianism into a movement. By the eighties of the nineteenth century socialism could represent itself as the natural and logical outcome of democratic theory. It could outbid the older parties on ground which universal suffrage had made the inevitable territory of conflict. In the opening years of the twentieth century the central theme of debate had become the power of the state to satisfy the economic wants of the working class. . . .

If the hypothesis of self-government is valid in the political sphere it must be valid in the economic sphere also; whence is born the insistence upon constitutional government in industry. Not only must the state interfere to this end in the general details of economic life, but it cannot realize its end if the operation of the profit making motive is admitted in any industry of basic importance to the community. The new ideals of democracy therefore foreshadow a functional society in which the older conception of liberty of contract has no place. Any state in which the economic sphere is left largely uncontrolled is necessarily a class society tilted to the advantage of the rich; it lacks that necessary basis of unity which enables men to compose their differences in peace. The claim for the sovereignty of the state no longer rests upon the strong basis provided by the old liberal hypothesis of a society equal in fact because formally equal in political power. Largely the new democratic theory accepts a quasi-Marxian interpretation of the state while refusing to draw therefrom the inference that revolution is its only satisfactory corrective. . . .

[The new democratic theory] regards the right of men to share in the results of social life as broadly equal; and it regards differences of treatment as justifiable only in so far as they can be shown to be directly relevant to the common good. It takes its stand firmly on the need for a close economic equality on the ground that the benefits a man can obtain from the social process are, at least approximately and in general, a function of his power of effective demand, which in turn depends upon the property he owns. It is thus hostile to all economic privilege as being in its nature fatal to the end at which a democratic society must aim. For the new democratic theory liberty is necessarily a function of equality. . . .

One final remark may be made. It is not the view of modern democratic theory that a political man can be constructed whose interest in the public business of the community is assured. It does believe that increased educational opportunity will increase that interest; a belief which further emphasizes the need for equality. It does argue further that the main result of inequality is so to depress the moral character of those at the base of the social pyramid as to minimize their power to get attention for their experience. Again therefore it sees in equality the path to the end democracy seeks to serve.

The Role of the People

R. M. MACIVER *

Democracy cannot mean the rule of the majority or the rule of the masses. This was the manner in which democracy was interpreted by the Greek philosophers, at a time before there was any representative system or any party system—and this fact may help to explain why they on the whole disapproved of it. The meaning of democracy was then obscure. Even today, with all our experience of democracy, it is often misunderstood. Democracy is not a way of governing, whether by majority or otherwise, but primarily a way of determining who shall govern and, broadly, to what ends. The only way in which the people, *all the people,* can determine who shall govern is by referring the question to public opinion and accepting on each occasion the verdict of the polls. Apart from this activity of the people there is no way of distinguishing democracy from other forms of government.

Any kind of government can claim to rest on "the will of the people," whether it be oligarchy or dictatorship or monarchy. One kind of government alone rests on the constitutional exercise of the will of the people. Every other kind prevents the minority—or the majority—from freely expressing opinion concerning the policies of government, or at the least from making that opinion the free determinant of government. Quite possibly in Russia, at the time of writing, a larger proportion of the people approves and supports its government than may be found in democratic countries to support their governments. But that fact is quite irrelevant to the question of democracy. In the Soviet Union, under these conditions, there is no free exercise of opinion on matters of policy, nor any constitutional means by which the changing currents of opinion can find political expression. It would therefore be the sheerest confusion to classify the Soviet system as democratic.

The growth of democracy has always been associated with the free discussion of political issues, with the right to differ concerning them, and with the settlement of the difference, not *by force majeure* but by resort to the counting of votes. It has always been associated with the growing authority of some assembly of the people or of the people's representatives,

* Professor Emeritus of Political Philosophy and Sociology at Columbia University. Author of *Leviathan and the People, The More Perfect Union* and others. From R. M. MacIver, *The Web of Government* (New York, The Macmillan Co., 1947), pp. 198–199. By permission.

such as the Greek *ecclesia,* the Roman *comitia,* the English parliament. The right to differ did not end with the victory of the majority but was inherent in the system. It was a necessary condition of democracy everywhere that opposing doctrines remained free to express themselves, to seek converts, to form organizations, and so to compete for success before the tribunal of public opinion. Any major trend of opinion could thus register itself in the character and in the policies of government. . . .

THE FUNCTION OF THE PUBLIC *

There are those who condemn democracy because, they say, the people are unfit to rule. And there are those who, in a more friendly spirit, deplore the plight of democracy because the people simply cannot undertake the task it imposes on them, the task of coping with all the complex issues of modern government. In one of his earlier books, *The Phantom Public,* Walter Lippmann put forward the plaint that the democratic man was baffled and disenchanted. He could not make his sovereign voice heard concerning a thousand tangled affairs, and how could he? How could he have an effective opinion about the situation in China today and about the sewers of Brooklyn tomorrow, and the next day about the effects of subsidies to agriculture, and the next day about some deal with Yugoslavia, and so on without end? He gave it up. He was disillusioned about democracy. He could not live up to its demands.

If any "man in the street" holds these views about his democratic obligations it is quite proper he should be disillusionized. But not, we hope, about democracy. Only about his illusions about democracy. Representative democracy, the only kind that has any meaning under modern conditions, does not put any such impossible strain on the citizen. The people, let us repeat, do not and cannot govern; they control the government. In every live democracy they decide the broad march of politics. They decide whether there is to be more social legislation or less, more collectivization or somewhat more play for private enterprise, more dependence on an international system of security or more self-sufficiency and relative isolation, and so forth. They decide these issues, not one at a time but by voting for an administration favorable to one or another "platform." They decide them partly—and in the last resort—at the polls, and partly by the continuously manifested indications of public sentiment. To make decisions easier there is in every community a sense of alternative directions, marked respectively left and right, and a sway of opinion in one or the other direction. . . .

* From R. M. MacIver: *The Ramparts We Guard,* copyright, 1950, by Robert M. MacIver, and used with the permission of The Macmillan Co., pp. 27–30, 49–51.

This incessant activity of popular opinion is the dynamic of democracy. It decides between the larger alternatives of policy-making and in that way has an impact on a thousand issues. Mr. Lippmann, in the book referred to, was clearly off the beam when he suggested that it is not the business of the public to decide the substantive policies of government but merely to see that the government abides by the rules, like a referee who watches the players but takes no part in the game. The great changes in the socio-economic policies of Western European countries in the nineteenth and twentieth centuries—the whole trend toward social legislation and the control of economic power—were due to the swelling currents of public opinion, responsive to changing conditions. Or we may cite the more recent experience of the United States, where a new manifestation of public opinion, opposed by most of the prestige-bearers and of the well-to-do, carried to power and maintained in power the party of the "New Deal."

That is how the citizens of a democracy make their citizenship effective. Not as individuals deciding for themselves the successive problems of politics, each in speculative detachment registering his opinion on every issue. Not merely as units casting their separate votes every few years as election time comes round—the citizens of a democracy are *continuously* engaged in a massive give-and-take of creative opinion-making. Certainly not as experts who must willy-nilly do the job of the administration, that is, by finding the answers to the very specific questions that the administration must face from day to day. No business is run that way, and no government can be. Executive jobs are for executives, whether in business or in government. The public—or the workers or the shareholders—may very well entertain an opinion on whether the management is doing well or badly, but that is a different matter altogether.

We observe in passing that in a democracy there are two stages of decision-making before the *proper* job of the expert begins. First, there is the primary function of policy-making, the choice between directions, the function of the people. Second, there is the delineation of policy by the legislators and the heads of the government—in accordance with the "mandate" thus entrusted to them. Third, there is the implementation of policy. At this third stage the expert finds his place. It is here, and here alone, that he belongs. He is the technician or the craftsman in the art of government.

It is an eminently logical system. The representatives of the people have the authority. They are presumably—they always become at least—more conversant with the ways of governing than are the lay citizens, but they are not experts. They mark out the lines of advance and the experts build the roads. The logic is admirable, but as in all human affairs it is subject to distortion. These three functions are not clear-cut and separable in practice. The limits of each in relation to the others must be discretionary and flexible. Which means also that there may be conflict, confusion, and encroachment between the participants. The legislator may not let the expert do his proper job or, more commonly, he permits the expert to follow his own devices into the area of policy-making. The cabinet officers may ignore the spirit of their mandate, particularly in the screened-off sector of foreign policy. The expert may become a worshipper of routine, a jealous guardian of the secrets of office, a bureaucrat in the less honorable sense of the word.

Such things happen everywhere, and perhaps there is no safeguard except the vigilance of the public, as it becomes better educated in the ways of democracy and armed with fuller knowledge of its practical operation. What indeed appears throughout, as we study democracy at work, is that the defects and shortcomings it exhibits are due not to any inherent weakness in its principle but to the greater responsibilities it imposes on those who carry it out. These responsibilities are in themselves reasonable and never excessive, but interest and pride and office are always at hand, to deflect, to distort, and to betray. The ever-active democratic process checks these tendencies. How effectively it does so is in the keeping of the public, who have the authority and the means to control those whom they entrust with the business of governing. . . .

DEMOCRACY AND FREE EXPRESSION

Democracy constitutionally guarantees certain fundamental rights to all citizens. Apart from these rights—the right to think and believe after one's own mind and heart, the right to express one's opinions and to organize for their furtherance, the right to vote according to one's opinions, and so forth—democracy cannot exist. But the rights in question are not the same thing as a form of government. They may properly be made a *test* of its existence but they do not constitute it. [Former] Secretary of State George C. Marshall applied this test when the Western Powers were in dispute with Soviet Russia regarding the implementation of a pledge made under the Yalta agreement of 1945. The allied plenipotentiaries pledged themselves to use "democratic means" for the solution of the problems of the occupied countries of Europe, and again at the Berlin Conference they gave directions "for the eventual reconstruction of German political life on a democratic basis." But when it came to performance the Soviet Union and the Western Powers were completely opposed, the former claiming that its own restrictive and high-handed methods were in accordance with the democratic pledge.

General Marshall insisted that the essence of democracy was the recognition that "human beings have certain inalienable rights—that is, rights that may not be given or taken away," and that until these rights were granted and guaranteed the pledge was not fulfilled. These rights included "the right of every individual to develop his mind and his soul in the ways of his own choice, free of fear and coercion—provided only that he does not interfere with the rights of others." "To us," he said, "a society is not free if law-abiding citizens live in fear of being denied the right to work or being deprived of life, liberty and the pursuit of happiness."

The argument was just, in the light of the whole history of what the world has known as democracy. For our purpose of definition, however, we must look beyond the possession of such rights to the constitutional order that gives and guards the assurance. This constitutional order, in any of its varieties, *is* democracy. Now then we must ask: what kind of order is it that can *constitutionally* assure these rights? We find that both historically and logically it is an order that, to establish the right of opinion, gives free opinion itself a politically creative role. In other words, the government must be dependent on, and responsive to, the changes of public opinion. More closely, each successive administration is voted into office by an election or series of elections at which the people freely express their effective preference for one group of candidates over another group or other groups. In order that this process may be constitutionally possible the law must bind the relations of men in the areas to which it applies but must not bind their opinions in any areas. (We shall not pause here to examine the apparent but not genuine exceptions to this principle that fall under laws relating to libel, slander, incitement to violence, and so forth.) In a democracy those who oppose the policies of the government lose no civil rights and those who support its policies acquire thereby no civil rights. In a democracy minority opinion remains as untrammeled as majority opinion.

The importance of the creative role assigned to public opinion under democracy lies primarily in the fact that if opinion is free then the whole cultural life of man is free. If opinion is free, then belief is free and science is free and art and philosophy and all the variant styles and modes in which men manifest and develop their values and tastes and ways of living—always up to the limit where they endeavor by oppression or violence to deprive their fellowmen of these same prerogatives. Democracy alone assures the citadel of human personality against the deadly invasions of power. If only we could comprehend what this means we would never let our disappointments with the defects and weaknesses that the workings of democracy may reveal blind us to the intrinsic superiority of democracy over all other systems of government. . . .

"POLITICAL" AND "ECONOMIC" DEMOCRACY *

Some recent writers draw a distinction between "political democracy" and "economic democracy." They regard "economic democracy" as either the complement or the fulfillment of "political democracy." Sometimes they treat "political democracy" as less important than "economic democracy." Not infrequently they refer to the Soviet system as embodying this superior form of democracy. Mr. Harold Laski, who follows this line, writes: "If the hypothesis of self-government is valid in the political sphere it must be valid in the economic sphere also." Now when Mr. Laski speaks of "economic democracy" he is not speaking of *democracy* in any sense. He does not mean that the workers should elect by ballot the managers and the executive boards of industrial corporations or banks and decide what policies they should pursue in the conduct of their business. He certainly can offer no evidence that these democratic procedures are applied in Soviet Russia. Moreover, the economic program he is concerned about is one he wants the state to implement. His program is a *political* one. He wants democratic countries to adopt a collectivist system. But he should not identify a collectivist system with democracy, whether "economic" or "political." A democracy may approve a collectivist program or may reject it. It is still a democracy, and either way it is taking action "in the economic sphere." "The economic sphere" can never be separated from "the political sphere." What policy a democracy follows in this sphere depends on the conditions, and immediately on public opinion.

Mr. Laski, like many others, is apt to identify democracy with the things he would like democracy to do. In some of his writings he suggests that if a democracy should adopt a "revolutionary" socialist program it might meet such resistance from the propertied classes that democracy itself would come to an end and dictatorship take its place. It is indeed possible, but where the democratic spirit prevails, as in England, the United States, the self-governing British Dominions, and the Scandinavian countries, it seeks to avoid such drastic alternatives; it prefers to move to its goals by steps, not by one convulsive act. The point, however, is that should such a convulsion take place Mr. Laski's socialist program would be achieved at the price of democracy. Nor could it reasonably be argued that "economic democracy" had taken the place of "politial democracy." There might be greater economic equality, but we have no ground, either in logic or in history, for assuming that collectivist equality, arrived at on such terms, would become the boon companion of democracy.

* R. M. MacIver, *The Web of Government* (New York, The Macmillan Co., 1947), pp. 206–208. By permission.

Competition for Political Leadership

JOSEPH A. SCHUMPETER *

Our chief troubles about the classical theory [of democracy] † centers in the proposition that "the people" hold a definite and rational opinion about every individual question and that they give effect to this opinion—in a democracy—by choosing "representatives" who will see to it that that opinion is carried out. Thus the selection of the representatives is made secondary to the primary purpose of the democratic arrangement which is to vest the power of deciding political issues in the electorate. Suppose we reverse the roles of these two elements and make the deciding of issues by the electorate secondary to the election of the men who are to do the deciding. To put it differently, we now take the view that the role of the people is to produce a government, or else an intermediate body which in turn will produce a national executive or government. And we define: *the democratic method is that institutional arrangement for arriving at political decisions in which individuals acquire the power to decide by means of a competitive struggle for the people's vote.*

Defense and explanation of this idea will speedily show that, as to both plausibility of assumptions and tenability of propositions, it greatly improves the theory of the democratic process.

First of all, we are provided with a reasonably efficient criterion by which to distinguish democratic governments from others. We have seen that the classical theory meets with difficulties on that score because both the will and the good of the people may be, and in many historical instances have been, served just as well or better by governments that cannot be described as democratic according to any accepted usage of the term. Now we are in a somewhat better position partly because we are resolved to stress a *modus procedendi* the presence or absence of which it is in most cases easy to verify.[1]

For instance, a parliamentary monarchy like the English one fulfills the requirements of the democratic method because the monarch is prac-

---

* Late Professor of Economics at Harvard University. Former Austrian Minister of Finance. Author of *The Theory of Economic Development, Business Cycles, Imperialism and Social Classes*. The selection is from *Capitalism, Socialism, and Democracy*, 3rd ed. (New York, Harper & Brothers, 1950), pp. 269–273. By permission.

† The author defines the classical theory of democracy as ". . . that institutional arrangement for arriving at political decisions which realizes the common good by making the people itself decide issues through the election of individuals who are to assemble to carry out its will."

[1] See however the fourth point below.

tically constrained to appoint to cabinet office the same people as parliament would elect. A "constitutional" monarchy does not qualify to be called democratic because electorates and parliaments, while having all the other rights that electorates and parliaments have in parliamentary monarchies, lack the power to impose their choice as to the governing committee: the cabinet ministers are in this case servants of the monarch, in substance as well as in name, and can in principle be dismissed as well as appointed by him. Such an arrangement may satisfy the people. The electorate may reaffirm this fact by voting against any proposal for change. The monarch may be so popular as to be able to defeat any competition for the supreme office. But since no machinery is provided for making this competition effective the case does not come within our definition.

Second, the theory embodied in this definition leaves all the room we may wish to have for a proper recognition of the vital fact of leadership. The classical theory did not do this but attributed to the electorate an altogether unrealistic degree of initiative which practically amounted to ignoring leadership. But collectives act almost exclusively by accepting leadership—this is the dominant mechanism of practically any collective action which is more than a reflex. Propositions about the working and the results of the democratic method that take account of this are bound to be infinitely more realistic than propositions which do not. . . .

Third, however, so far as there are genuine group-wise volitions at all —for instance the will of the unemployed to receive unemployment benefit or the will of other groups to help—our theory does not neglect them. On the contrary we are now able to insert them in exactly the role they actually play. Such volitions do not as a rule assert themselves directly. Even if strong and definite they remain latent, often for decades, until they are called to life by some political leader who turns them into political factors. This he does, or else his agents do it for him, by organizing these volitions, by working them up and by including eventually appropriate items in his competitive offering. The interaction between sectional interests and public opinion and the way in which they produce the pattern we call the political situation appear from this angle in a new and much clearer light.

Fourth, our theory is of course no more definite than is the concept of competition for leadership. This concept presents similar difficulties as the concept of competition in the economic sphere, with which it may be usefully compared. In economic life competition is never completely lacking, but hardly ever is it perfect. Similarly, in political life there is always some competition, though perhaps only a potential one, for the allegiance of the people. To simplify matters we have restricted the kind of competition for leadership which is to define democracy to free competition for a free vote. The justification for this is that democracy seems to imply a recognized method by which to conduct the competitive struggle, and that the electoral method is practically the only one available for communities of any size. But though this excludes many ways of securing leadership which should be excluded,[2] such as competition by military insurrection, it does not exclude the cases that are strikingly analogous to the economic phenomena we label "unfair" or "fraudulent" competition or restraint of competition. And we cannot exclude them because if we did we should be left with a completely unrealistic ideal.[3] Between this ideal case which does not exist and the cases in which all competition with the established leader is prevented by force, there is a continuous range of variations within which the democratic method of government shades off into the autocratic one by imperceptible steps. But if we wish to understand and not to philosophize, this is as it should be. The value of our criterion is not seriously impaired thereby.

Fifth, our theory seems to clarify the relation that subsists between democracy and individual freedom. If by the latter we mean the existence of a sphere of individual self-government the boundaries of which are historically variable—*no* society tolerates absolute freedom even of conscience and of speech, *no* society reduces that sphere to zero—the question clearly becomes a matter of degree. We [believe] that the democratic method does not necessarily guarantee a greater amount of individual freedom than another political method would permit in similar circumstances. It may well be the other way round. But there is still a relation between the two. If, on principle at least, everyone is free to compete for political leadership [4] by presenting himself to the electorate, this will in most cases though not in all mean a considerable amount of freedom of discussion *for all*. In particular it will normally mean a considerable amount of freedom of the press. This relation between democracy and freedom is not absolutely stringent and can be tampered with. But, from the standpoint of the intellectual, it is nevertheless very important. At the same time, it is all there is to that relation.

Sixth, it should be observed that in making it the primary function of the electorate to produce a government (directly or through an inter-

[2] It also excludes methods which should not be excluded, for instance, the acquisition of political leadership by the people's tacit acceptance of it or by election *quasi per inspirationem*. The latter differs from election by voting only by a technicality. But the former is not quite without importance even in modern politics; the sway held by a party boss *within his party* is often based on nothing but tacit acceptance of his leadership. Comparatively speaking, however, these are details which may, I think, be neglected in a sketch like this.

[3] As in the economic field, *some* restrictions are implicit in the legal and moral principles of the community.

[4] Free, that is, in the same sense in which everyone is free to start another textile mill.

mediate body) I intended to include in this phrase also the function of
evicting it. The one means simply the acceptance of a leader or a group
of leaders, the other means simply the withdrawal of this acceptance.
This takes care of an element the reader may have missed. He may have
thought that the electorate controls as well as installs. But since electorates normally do not control their political leaders in any way except by
refusing to reelect them or the parliamentary majorities that support them,
it seems well to reduce our ideas about this control in the way indicated
by our definition. Occasionally, spontaneous revulsions occur which upset a government or an individual minister directly or else enforce a certain course of action. But they are not only exceptional, they are, as we
[believe], contrary to the spirit of the democratic method.

Seventh, our theory sheds much-needed light on an old controversy.
Whoever accepts the classical doctrine of democracy and in consequence
believes that the democratic method is to guarantee that issues be decided
and policies framed according to the will of the people must be struck
by the fact that, even if that will were undeniably real and definite, decision by simple majorities would in many cases distort it rather than
give effect to it. Evidently the will of the majority is the will of the majority and not the will of "the people." The latter is a mosaic that the
former completely fails to "represent." To equate both by definition is
not to solve the problem. Attempts at real solutions have however been
made by the authors of the various plans for Proportional Representation.

These plans have met with adverse criticism on practical grounds. It
is in fact obvious not only that proportional representation will offer opportunities for all sorts of idiosyncrasies to assert themselves but also that
it may prevent democracy from producing efficient governments and thus
prove a danger in times of stress.[5] But before concluding that democracy
becomes unworkable if its principle is carried out consistently, it is just
as well to ask ourselves whether this principle really implies proportional
representation. As a matter of fact it does not. If acceptance of leadership is the true function of the electorate's vote, the case for proportional
representation collapses because its premises are no longer binding. The
principle of democracy then merely means that the reins of government
should be handed to those who command more support than do any of
the competing individuals or teams. And this in turn seems to assure the
standing of the majority system within the logic of the democratic method,
although we might still condemn it on grounds that lie outside of that
logic.

[5] The argument against proportional representation has been ably stated by Professor F. A. Hermens in "The Trojan Horse of Democracy," *Social Research* (November, 1938).

Topic 2

PUBLIC-OPINION POLLS IN A DEMOCRACY

The Pollsters' False Premises

LINDSAY ROGERS *

Public-opinion polling, if not a major, is a large and important American industry whose tycoons and their academic acolytes have been far from reticent in boasting of achievements. "The speed with which sampling referenda can be completed for the entire nation," writes Dr. George Gallup, "is such that public opinion on any given issue can be reported within forty-eight hours if the occasion warrants. Thus the goal has nearly been reached when public opinion can be 'ascertainable at all times.' " . . .

I concede that polls on a wide variety of questions have become a significant feature of journalism in the United States and in other countries, and that they are a new kind of reporting which gives the reading public data that it did not previously possess and that are sometimes worthy of analysis. But the data conceal more than they reveal and will have different meanings for different analysts. And for the pollsters to maintain that percentages of "yeses," "noes," "no opinion," "never heard of it," disclose public opinion on the policy that they have inquired about, and to which many respondents may not have given a moment's thought before they were interrogated, is to advertise a mouthwash as a cure for anemia. If the pollsters sold their product in bottles instead of as news, the Federal Trade Commission would long since have been after them.

Why the misbranding? It results, I think, from two great sins of omission of which the pollsters are guilty. They have never attempted to define what it is they are measuring. . . . And this is the second great omission—that in the now enormous literature on polling methods and the data that have been secured, one never—well almost never—finds any reasoned statement of premises concerning the nature of the political society in

* Formerly Professor of Public Law at Columbia University. Author of *The American Senate, Crisis Government,* and other works. The selection is reprinted from *The Pollsters* by Lindsay Rogers, by permission of Alfred A. Knopf, Inc. Copyright, 1949, by Alfred A. Knopf, Inc.

23

which public opinion should be the ruler. When, as if by accident, premises are articulated, they prove to be false. They have to be, because, if they were not, the pollsters would not be able to make the exaggerated claims that they do about the meaning of the data they present for consideration. They would see that they are talking nonsense when they speak of "implementing democracy," "making it more articulate," and "speeding up its processes." Moreover, they do not bother to say how they define "democracy," which may be anything from a non-snobbish sentimental interest in the underdog to the system that Stalin and the Politburo impose on Russia. . . .

Most men and women do not study public questions and endeavor to form rational opinions. They have neither time nor interest. What they learn from newspapers or the radio gives them incomplete, ofttimes unintentionally, and sometimes intentionally, distorted information. People follow the "pictures" in their heads, which Lippmann called "stereotypes." There is in fact and need be no public opinion on an issue until it has already been shaped and has its advocates and opponents. Even then people will really concern themselves only if they are directly interested. The Reciprocal Trade Agreements policy, for example, may affect importers and exporters. In the long run it may be of vital importance to the economy of the nation as a whole. Apart from those who feel an immediate self-interest, there are few people—mostly persistent students of public affairs—who know of or care one way or the other about the Reciprocal Trade Agreements.

As Doob wisely remarks, "What is discouraging about democracy in the modern world and what elsewhere has helped give rise to alternate forms of government is the increasing complexity of the affairs with which government must deal. If the forces of democracy have enabled information to be spread at an arithmetically increasing rate, it can be said without much exaggeration that technology and social changes have increased at a geometrical rate the amount of information which needs to be known for the electorate to be intelligent and reasonably expert." The Athenians could choose members of administrative bodies by lot because then any intelligent citizen had sufficient knowledge of the matters that must be dealt with. This is no longer true. . . .

"The task of government, and hence of democracy as a form of government, is not to express an imaginary popular will, but to effect adjustments among the various special wills and purposes which at any given time are pressing for realization." And to do this, I might add, after full discussion in the country and mature deliberation in the representative assembly. . . . The pollsters overlook the really vital role of representative assemblies in focusing attention on political issues. If there were no Congress, with its clash of personalities, parties, and sections, could questions be asked, for example, about the Taft-Hartley Act or the Marshall Plan? If they were, "no opinion" would be by far the most frequent reply. . . .

There are few questions suitable for mass answers by yes or no. This the pollsters must ignore when they talk about sample referenda implementing democracy and making it articulate. A man may say that he is in favor of a protective tariff, but would it be worth while to ask him? No one in his senses would propose that a series of tariff schedules should be submitted for rejection or acceptance at the polls, yet the schedules determine whether there is to be any tariff protection and if so, how much. A man can be for or against the Taft-Hartley Act, but what would this mean? Few who know anything about the statute would say that all its provisions are good or that all are bad.

How, in the postwar period, could any issue of foreign policy have been put to the electorate for decision? The Marshall Plan? Its essence lay in the amounts of money, the strings attached to its use, and the concern of our government in respect of the ancillary measures to be taken by receiving states. Policy toward Russia? What questions could be put to an electorate? In an age when 531 representatives and senators who are paid so well for their time that they do not have to have other means of livelihood, and who are staffed for the investigation of the merits of proposed legislation, have to throw up their hands and say there are many details on which they cannot pass and which they must leave to administrative determination, it is absurd to suggest that counting the public pulse can give any light or leading save on the simplest kind of a proposition. And on such simple propositions the wishes of the public can usually be known without the assistance of a poll.

Harold J. Laski writes:

> If it [a referendum] is confined to obtaining answers to questions of principle, then, in the absence of concrete details, the questions are devoid of real meaning. If it is enlarged to consider the full amplitude of a complicated statute, then it is useless to pretend that a mass judgment upon its clauses is in any way a valid one. . . .

The public's lack of information on certain important issues suggests that in many cases even the pollsters should have viewed their percentages with suspicion and should have boldly declared that there was no opinion for them to try to measure. . . . After the Atlantic Charter had been discussed for some little while, 60 per cent of the population had "never heard of it" and 95 per cent could not name a single one of its provisions. A later poll disclosed eight in ten admitting that they had not read or heard about the Charter. Only one citizen in ten could name the Four Freedoms. Slightly more than one half of the people thought that Lend-Lease operated in reverse, but a majority of these believed that the return was "good will and co-operation" rather than substantial amounts of goods. At the time, polling organizations were telling us what "public opinion" was on the kind of peace settlement that was desirable (1944); and when there was a good deal of discussion of schemes for a new world organization, more than one half of the population thought we had joined the old League of Nations. The same year, seven out of ten did not know that the Senate must approve treaties by a two-thirds vote. . . . In 1946, 31 per cent of a sample had never heard of the Bill of Rights; 36 per cent had heard of it but could not identify it; and 12 per cent gave confused or contradictory answers. . . . And what of opinion on the Taft-Hartley Act? One poll disclosed 61 per cent claiming to have heard of the law, but of this "informed group" 75 per cent could not mention any specific provision that they considered particularly good, and 85 per cent could not pick out a provision that they thought particularly bad. . . .

A premise the pollsters do not make articulate is that if there is a majority public opinion, it should prevail, and presumably at once. They have never bothered to examine what majority rule means in the government the founding fathers proposed, which was accepted, and which, in its main outlines, no section of opinion save the Communists has since challenged. That system is not majority rule pure and simple, which is what the pollsters seem to assume it is. Our arrangements are fashioned as much to protect minorities as they are to enable majority opinion to prevail. Moreover . . . we endeavor to make the arrangements work in a federal system of government. . . . Under the American system of government we take many fateful decisions by less than a majority and sometimes prevent the larger part from having its way against the smaller part. . . .

From the grimness of the contemporary world it is sometimes useful to turn back to a piece of political literature that is still pertinent and suggestive and that deserves rereading. . . . [In 1774, Edmund] Burke made a speech that has been frequently quoted by those who have concerned themselves with the relations between representatives and their constituencies. Burke referred to the fact that his successful colleague at the election (Bristol returned two members to the House of Commons) had declared that "the topic of instructions has occasioned much altercation and uneasiness in this city," and had expressed himself "in favour of the coercive authority of such instructions." That view Burke vehemently repudiated.

> Certainly, gentlemen, [he declared], it ought to be the happiness and glory of a representative to live in the strictest union, the closest correspondence, and the most unreserved communication with his constituents. Their wishes ought to have great weight with him; their opinion high respect; their business unremitted attention. It is his duty to sacrifice his repose, his pleasures, his satisfaction, to theirs; and above all, ever, and in all cases, to prefer their interest to his own. But his unbiased opinion, his mature judgment,

his enlightened conscience, he ought not to sacrifice to you; to any man, or to any set of men living. These he does not derive from your pleasure; no, nor from the law and the constitution. They are a trust from Providence, for the abuse of which he is deeply answerable. Your representative owes you, not his industry only, but his judgment; and he betrays, instead of serving you, if he sacrifices it to your opinion.

Burke said that his colleague had declared that "his will ought to be subservient to yours." If that were all, there would be no objection.

If government were a matter of will upon any side, yours, without question, ought to be superior. But government and legislation are matters of reason and judgment, and not of inclination; and what sort of reason is that, in which the determination precedes the discussion; in which one set of men deliberate, and another decide; and where those who form the conclusion are perhaps three hundred miles distant from those who hear the arguments?

Of course it was the right of all men to deliver opinions, and those expressed by constituents would be "weighty and respectable." A representative ought always to be glad to hear them and he ought always most seriously to consider them. "But *authoritative* instructions, *mandates* issued, which the member is bound blindly and implicitly to obey, to vote, and to argue for, although contrary to the clearest conviction of his judgment and conscience—these are things utterly unknown to the laws of this land, and which arise from a fundamental mistake of the whole order and tenor of our constitution."

Then follows the passage that has been quoted most frequently:

Parliament is not a *congress* of ambassadors from different and hostile interests; which interests each must maintain, as an agent and advocate, against other agents and advocates; but parliament is a *deliberative* assembly of *one* nation, with *one* interest, that of the whole; where, not local purposes, not local prejudices ought to guide, but the general good, resulting from the general reason of the whole. You choose a member indeed; but when you have chosen him, he is not a member of Bristol, but he is a member of *parliament*. If the local constituent should have an interest, or should form an hasty opinion, evidently opposite to the real good of the rest of the community, the member for that place ought to be as far, as any other, from any endeavour to give it effect. . . .

The principles on which Burke insisted are more frequently ignored than honored. He himself stated them in too extreme a form. He was indifferent to the value of discussion, which is indispensable in any community that seeks to govern itself rather than to permit itself to be ruled. As Sir Ernest Barker has suggested, "Burke regarded himself and his fellow members in the light of 'publick-Counsellors,' or as we may say in the language of that book of Ecclesiastes which he knew and quoted, 'leaders of the people by their counsels and by their knowledge of learning meet for the people wise and eloquent instruction.' He remained something of a scholar of

Trinity House, 'damned absolute'; something of a professor who even in the House of Commons was apt to speak *ex cathedra."*

On the other hand, too many men have thought too exclusively of staying in a legislature or holding onto their seals of office. They have hesitated to express their convictions and have been content to follow rather than to lead public opinion. In Burke, wrote Lord Morley, "there was none of that too familiar casuistry, by which public men argue themselves out of their consciences in a strange syllogism, that they can best serve the country in Parliament; that to keep their seats they must follow their electors; and that, therefore, in the long run they serve the country best by acquiescing in ignorance and prejudice." In other public men who do not thus deceive themselves, hesitation and softness may result from the fact that they are tired; that swimming with the tide requires much less exertion than going against the tide; that plaudits are usually more pleasant than criticism. I could select innumerable illustrations of what I mean, but one will suffice. . . .

In November 1936 Stanley Baldwin told the House of Commons "that not once but on many occasions, in speeches and in various places, when I have been speaking and advocating as far as I am able the democratic principle, I have stated that a democracy is always two years behind the dictator. I believe that to be true." So far as British rearmament was concerned, Mr. Baldwin had made it true as he proceeded to explain to the House with what he himself described as "an appalling frankness." In order to win an election he had deceived Great Britain on Germany's rearmament program.

"Supposing I had gone to the country and said that Germany was rearming and that we must rearm, does anybody think that this pacific democracy would have rallied to that cry at that moment? I cannot think of anything that would have made the loss of the election from my point of view more certain." But the consequences of the policy were far more appalling than the frankness of the statement. To be sure, Mr. Baldwin's successor as Prime Minister had time in which he could have retrieved the error at least partially. But until the war came in September 1939, and Churchill, Eden, and others entered the Cabinet, there had been in the British executive little of that "energy" which in *The Federalist* papers Alexander Hamilton described as "a leading character in the definition of good government."

Energy is not to be found in those who do no more than follow—in those who look upon a legislative assembly as a congress of ambassadors. In Burke's day the sentiment of a constituency had to be ascertained from its leading members. Now legislators quail under a deluge of telegrams or letters, and not only keep their ears to the ground, but wonder whether they would not be wise to use the acousticon of public-opinion polls. . . .

Party first, mandated representatives, sectional and special interests—this is the setting in which free peoples, in Burke's phrase, now expect their governments to be contrivances of human wisdom to provide for human wants. It would be comforting to accept the sales patter of the pollsters and agree that what they call "public-opinion polls" really do "implement democracy." For reasons already given, I think that even to talk in such a fashion discloses reasoning that is fantastically muddled. To do more than talk—to permit the pollsters' pronouncements to influence policy would be disastrous politically. . . .

The great problem, Lord Acton once said, is not to discover "what governments prescribe but what they ought to prescribe." We cannot wait to obtain the prescription from the perfectionists who, as someone remarked, are people who have no solution for any difficulty but are, nevertheless, able to find a difficulty in any proposed solution. The great question so far as public opinion is concerned is not what it wants, but what it ought to want. . . .

During pre-Munich days, for example, the "essential wisdom" of the British people was latent because the nation had no leadership. Every people, it is cynically and untruthfully said, have as good a government as they deserve. But a government may have no better an electorate than it deserves because it fails to give leadership. In the days of Baldwin and Chamberlain, British politicians congratulated themselves on being able to catch buses they were supposed to be driving. Later, as Bertrand Russell said, the British people were magnificent.

"In a multitude of counsellors there is wisdom," wrote Huxley, "but only in a few of them." *Vox populi* cannot help democratic governments to decide what they ought to do. Political and intellectual leaders must propose alternative policies. They must educate the electorate, and if the leadership and education are effective, then the people will demonstrate their "essential wisdom." "It is the few," said Guicciardini, "which commonly give the turn to affairs" and to which "any general temper in a nation" may be traced.

True it is that in a free state public opinion rules, but this is no reason for more than interest in the yeses and noes that may be disclosed by sampling. A baker can ask a sample of consumers whether it wants the loaf of bread sliced or unsliced, and, if the answer is two to one for sliced, can decide to distribute loaves in that proportion. A housing authority *should* ask a sample whether it prefers flats or single dwellings. The British Broadcasting Corporation can ask its listeners whether they prefer jazz or classical music, but the directors of the BBC have a duty that goes beyond satisfying what the public says is its taste. They should endeavor to change that taste for the better.

"Shall income taxes be reduced?" can be asked of a sample, but the

Secretary of the Treasury and congressional committees on appropriations should take note of the answers only for the purpose of endeavoring to change those answers if they do not agree with them.

> It is the business of a statesman to lead [wrote the London *Times*], and with his ear perpetually to the ground he is in no posture of leadership. The honest leader determines his course by the light of his own conscience and the special knowledge available to him, not by ascertaining the views of his necessarily less well-informed followers, in order that he may meekly conform. Having decided for himself what is right, he has then to convince the rank and file, knowing that if he fails to win or hold their support they will dismiss him and transfer their trust to another. That, and that only, is the sanction for the ultimate control of public opinion over policy. By no other means can the general will be formulated and elicited. A leader, in war or peace, who hesitates to take his political life in his hands will not be followed; neither social surveys nor any other mechanical device can be manipulated as an insurance by a politician playing for safety. Democracy implies and demands leadership in the true sense, and flounders without it.

The United States has been fortunate in that it had leadership at critical times. The chief incidents are well known. Jefferson made the Louisiana Purchase without consulting Congress. "A John Randolph," he wrote, "would find means to protract the proceeding on it by Congress until the ensuing spring, by which time new circumstances would change the mind of the other party." Public opinion approved Jefferson's acquisition. President Monroe announced what for a century was the basis of American foreign policy in a message to Congress—the Monroe Doctrine. Abraham Lincoln took courageous action that he admitted was beyond his legal power as President but that he thought was not beyond the constitutional competence of Congress, which would be called upon to approve it. . . .

Franklin Roosevelt made his "New Deal" and took his decisions on the transfer of destroyers in return for the use of British bases and of convoying before he was sure of congressional or public approval. Even if a sample poll had shown majority criticism, and its findings had had support from other quarters, the decisions should have stood and the President could have waited for the "essential wisdom" of the people to manifest itself. The polls did show support for the President, and this was better than if they had shown lack of support, which might have caused a little but only temporary embarrassment.

What of leadership now? What foreign policies should we have? What, domestically, should be our program? Answers to these questions are not my present subject. The pollsters will not be able to discover what our policies should be from samples in which each respondent says "yes" or "no" or "don't know." That method may be suitable for predicting election results, and should work *if the sample is properly chosen.* But the method is not suitable for measuring public opinion on the foreign or domestic proposals that statesmen may make. Each member of the electorate casts a ballot that is the equal of every other ballot. But who are the people who favor certain policies? How influential are they? Whom do they represent? How well are they organized? How much do they care? . . . In politics it is not the accumulation of facts but insight that will find the highroad if and when it is found.

The facts that the pollsters accumulate and endeavor to explain they create themselves. Bernard Shaw once declared that he was unable to see a great deal of difference between the controversies of the schoolmen over how many angels could stand on the point of a needle and the discussions of the physicists over the number of electrons in an atom. There is a difference: the physicist proposes to do something with his answer when he gets it, and he knows that it will be accepted by all other physicists. The pollsters get answers—yeses and noes—that are frequently suspect on their faces, that are not the same answers as other pollsters get, and that sometimes cancel each other out.

Since they must maintain that their work is important, the pollsters use a false premise: that our political system must accept and act on their answers. . . . So far as the pollers of public opinion are concerned, the light they have been following is a will-o'-the-wisp. They have been taking in each other's washing, and have been using statistics in terms of the Frenchman's definition: a means of being precise about matters of which you will remain ignorant.

Do the Polls Serve Democracy?

JOHN C. RANNEY *

Most of the current controversy over public opinion polls has centered about the question of their accuracy: the reliability of the sample taken, the impartiality of the sponsorship, the honesty of the interviewer and the person interviewed, the fairness of the questions, the measurement of intensities or gradations of feeling, and the validity of the analysis or interpretation. These are all, admittedly, important questions; but they tend to ignore or to beg one which is both more important and more theoretical: Assuming that the polls were to attain a miraculously perfect and unchallengeable accuracy, would they, even then, contribute significantly to the working of democracy?

One's first inclination is to take it for granted that the answer is "Yes."

* Late Professor of Government at Smith College. The selection is from John C. Ranney, "Do the Polls Serve Democracy?" *Public Opinion Quarterly,* Vol. 10 (Fall, 1946), pp. 349–360. By permission.

No principle, in democratic theory, has been more fundamental than the belief that political decisions ought to be made by the people as a whole or in accordance with their desires. Yet no principle, in democratic practice, has proved more difficult of precise application. In theory, even when doubts are entertained as to the rationality, the objectivity, and the capacity of the ordinary citizen, modern democratic writers have continued to find the essence of democracy in popular participation in policy-making.[1] But in practice, it has long been apparent that our electoral system, as a reflection of popular wishes and as a channel for popular activity, leaves a good deal to be desired.

Various improvements have been suggested, ranging from the initiative and the referendum to proportional or functional representation. But none of these devices, except by placing an intolerable strain on the voter, has solved the problem of how to reflect simultaneously the great diversity of his interests and attitudes on different issues.[2] The result, under our present system, is that even if one assumes that the voter does anything more than choose between the personalities of rival candidates, an election approximates what has been called "plebiscitary democracy." It is a way of approving or disapproving in the most general terms the policies of the party or individual in office and of renewing or transferring this exceedingly vague mandate for the coming term of office.

Such a check and consultation is much better than none at all. Notwithstanding its resemblance to some of the dictatorial plebiscites, it permits, in a free society, the expression of at least the major discontents. But consultations which are so sweeping and which occur at such rare intervals are only the thinnest caricature of the democratic belief that the health of the community depends upon the personal, active, and continuous political participation of the body of its citizens.

[1] For some recent statements on this subject, see Carl L. Becker, *Modern Democracy* (New Haven, 1941), p. 7; James Bryce, *Modern Democracies* (New York, 1924), Vol. 1, p. 20; Francis Coker, *Recent Political Thought* (New York and London, 1934), p. 293; Carl J. Friedrich, *The New Belief in the Common Man* (Boston, 1942), pp. 31, 221; Harold J. Laski, "Democracy," *Encyclopaedia of the Social Sciences* (New York, 1932), Vol. 3, pp. 80, 84; John D. Lewis, "The Elements of Democracy," *American Political Science Review,* Vol. 34, p. 469 (June, 1940); A. D. Lindsay, *The Modern Democratic State* (London, New York, Toronto, 1943), Vol. 1, pp. 267–268; Charles E. Merriam, *The New Democracy and the New Despotism* (New York, 1939), pp. 11–12; Francis Graham Wilson, *The Elements of Modern Politics* (New York and London, 1936), pp. 189–190, 247.

[2] John Dickinson, "Democratic Realities and the Democratic Dogma," *American Political Science Review,* Vol. 24, p. 300 (May, 1930); Pendleton Herring, *The Politics of Democracy* (New York, 1940), p. 329; E. E. Schattschneider, *Party Government* (New York, 1942), p. 33. For the weaknesses of such devices as the initiative and referendum, see Harold F. Gosnell, "The Polls and Other Mechanisms of Democracy," *Public Opinion Quarterly,* Vol. 4, p. 225 (June, 1940); A. Lawrence Lowell, *Public Opinion and Popular Government* (New York, 1913), pp. 152–235; William B. Munro, "Initiative and Referendum," *Encyclopaedia of the Social Sciences,* Vol. 4, pp. 50–52.

It is here that the polls are supposed to make their great contribution. By separating the issues from one another, by stating them simply and clearly, and by covering the electorate completely and continuously, they avoid the most obvious obscurities, strains, and distortions of the older procedures. If to these virtues one might add unchallengeable accuracy, the well-known dream of Bryce would be realized: the will of the majority of the citizens could be ascertained at all times; representative assemblies and elaborate voting machinery would be unnecessary and obsolete.

ATTACKS ON THE POLLS

Not everyone has rejoiced over this possibility. Anyone who agrees with Hamilton, for example, that the people are turbulent and changing, seldom judging or determining right, is hardly likely to welcome a device to make the voice of the people (which decidedly is not the voice of God) more audible than ever. Nor is this attitude likely to surprise or disturb the genuine democrat.

What should disturb him, however, is the fact that there are many people who consider themselves good democrats and who nevertheless consider the polls a menace to democracy. The objections of this second group deserve more systematic attention than they have yet received.

THE DESTRUCTION OF LEADERSHIP

The first and most frequent of these objections is that the polls destroy political courage and leadership. Every adequate government, it is maintained, requires these qualities in its officials. They can exist, however, only where there is freedom and flexibility and where the statesman is not bound, either in form or in fact, by rigid instructions from the voters. The government official, whether Congressman or administrator, has access to information which is beyond the reach of the ordinary voter, and he has something more than the ordinary voter's leisure in which to consider it. To subject his judgment to the ill-informed and hasty judgment of the electorate is to commit the political crime of rendering a decision before considering the evidence on which it ought to be based. It is true that the polls have no official standing and cannot bind any office-holder. But, the charge runs, the official who wants to keep his job will abandon his duty of analyzing and judging proposed policies in favor of the simpler, and safer, device of deciding as the polls tell him to decide.[3]

---

[3] For a concise statement of this position, see Eric F. Goldman, "Poll on the Polls," *Public Opinion Quarterly,* Vol. 8, pp. 461–467 (Winter, 1944–45), and the literature there cited.

So far as the legislator is concerned, there are several weaknesses in this argument. Simply as a matter of fact, it would be extremely difficult to show that the polls have had a decisive effect in determining the voting habits of any substantial number of representatives.[4] It is one of the dubious advantages of the American system that it is extremely difficult to allocate responsibility; and even in those cases in which responsibility can be fixed, the ordinary voter is only too likely to be ignorant of the voting record of his representative. The average Congressman on the average issue need not worry too much about the opinion of his constituents in the mass. What he does need to worry about is the opinion of specific organizations and individuals inside his constituency, especially the political machines and the organized pressure groups. Any Congressman who is concerned with political realities knows that it is more important to appease a well-disciplined minority, which can deliver the votes on election day, than to gratify an unorganized and casual majority, the intensity of whose convictions and the efficacy of whose action is far less likely to be decisive. If the polls exert any influence at all, therefore, they tend to moderate or deflate rather than to reinforce the special pressures already influencing legislators.

The absence of scientific methods for measuring opinion, moreover, has never prevented politicians from trying to guess what it is. The representative, if such there be, who follows the polls slavishly would have his ear well to the ground under any circumstances. It is hard to see how democracy is undermined or its moral fibre destroyed simply by providing him with more reliable methods of judgment. It can hardly be urged that so long as a representative is going to vote according to public opinion anyway, the more distorted his picture of it, the better. Nor would it be easy to show that, among those restrained by the polls, the idealists seriously outnumber those who would otherwise follow the dictates of selfish and limited interests.

Finally, it should be remembered that public opinion is not so definite and rigid as the argument implies. In some instances, changes have been both rapid and extreme, and political leaders have often been in a strategic position to influence or shape it. In addition, men of intelligence and foresight who understand the probable effects of an unfortunate policy or the

[4] More Congressmen would be influenced by the polls, and the argument strengthened, if there were more general confidence in their accuracy and if the returns were published by Congressional districts. For evidence of the influence of polls on legislators, see L. E. Gleeck, "96 Congressmen Make Up Their Minds," *Public Opinion Quarterly,* Vol. 4, pp. 3–24 (March, 1940); George W. Hartman, "Judgments of State Legislators Concerning Public Opinion," *Journal of Social Psychology,* Vol. 21, pp. 105–114 (February, 1945); Martin Kriesberg, "What Congressmen and Administrators Think of the Polls," *Public Opinion Quarterly,* Vol. 9, pp. 333–337 (Fall, 1945); George F. Lewis, Jr., "The Congressmen Look at the Polls," *Ibid.,* Vol. 4, pp. 229–231 (June, 1940).

misconceptions on which it is based can anticipate the ultimate revulsion of public feeling and act accordingly. Voters, it should be remembered, do not always show great tolerance for the Congressman who excuses his own past mistakes with the plea that most of the electorate, at the time, shared his way of thinking.

Although the argument concerning the destruction of leadership is usually made with the legislator in mind, it actually has somewhat more factual strength in the case of the policy-making administrator. Surveys indicate that he is more likely to pay attention to the results of the polls, and he is also more likely to have expert or specialized personal knowledge as an alternative basis for decision. There is a possibility, at least, that his interest in the polls may indicate a tendency to subordinate his own well-informed judgment to the opinion of the electorate; and there is a further possibility that he may become so dependent upon it that he will take no action at all when that opinion is confused or divided or simply non-existent.

On the other hand, the administrator is, if anything, subject to even greater and more numerous pressures than is the Congressman. For him, therefore, the polls may be even more important as a basis for resisting minority pressures in the public interest. Moreover, like the legislator, he has considerable power to influence public opinion, although his methods are somewhat different; and a precise knowledge of what that opinion is can be an important help in enlightening or changing it.

The factual basis, or lack of basis, for the argument that the polls destroy leadership is less important, however, than two of the argument's theoretical implications.

The first of these is that government officials, whether legislators or administrators, constitute something of an expert body, possessing unusual intelligence, information, and skill, and that to this body the voter, because of his personal inadequacy, should delegate his power.

This argument, however, proves too much. If expertness is to be the criterion for the right to participate in government, the ordinary Congressman would himself have difficulty in qualifying. Even the policy-making administrator, in an age of increasingly voluminous and technical legislation, is likely to be an expert only in the most attenuated sense of the term. To be sure, both he and the legislator must make use of the knowledge and experience of the expert, especially in determining the technical means to achieve broader and predetermined objectives. But when it comes to determining the objectives themselves—and it is with objectives rather than with means that the polls are primarily concerned—the democratic theorist who would free leaders from the restraint of a less well-informed public opinion is, consciously or unconsciously, on the road to what, since the days of Plato, has been the radically undemocratic position of urging rule by some elite.

The second theoretical implication is the even stranger one that ignorance of what the people want and feel is a positive advantage in a democracy. Yet few defenses of democracy have been more persuasive than the one which insists that democracy alone provides the government with adequate information about the desires and attitudes of the people and that, even if these prove to be ignorant or irrational, it is only on the basis of such information that a government can act intelligently. Legislation cannot be separated from the practical problem of administration and enforcement; and it is of fundamental importance, in framing and administering laws with intelligence, to understand, as one of the vital factors in the situation, the state of public feeling. This is not to say that opinion is the only factor to be considered. It is saying that it is an essential element in the rational analysis of any political situation. People will not refrain from having opinions and acting upon them simply because they are not asked what they are. Yet statesmen, whether legislators or administrators, are unlikely to have direct personal knowledge of these feelings; and the weaknesses of elections, the press, and other methods of identifying them have been obvious for decades. Here, therefore, if anywhere, the polls, far from being a menace to democracy, give substance and meaning to what has always, in theory, been one of its outstanding advantages.[5]

In short, so far as this first set of criticisms is concerned, the polls are neither, in fact, so destructive of leadership and courage as critics suggest nor, in theory, so incompatible with the traditional meaning of democracy. On the contrary, the unstated assumptions of the critics tend logically to a conclusion which is itself basically undemocratic.

THE POLLS AS A BRAKE ON PROGRESS

A second set of charges is remarkable for the way in which it parallels Hamilton's way of thinking for purposes which are quite un-Hamiltonian. Its authors agree that the intelligence and judgment of the people is to be distrusted—not because of their radicalism, however, but because of their conservatism and complacency. Far from being a source of turbulence and unrest and a menace to private property and traditional ways of doing things, the people are so conventional and so contented with things as they are that they constitute a formidable brake upon progress, slow to see the need for drastic social changes and slow to take the necessary steps, always

---

[5] The use already made of the polls by such governmental agencies as the Department of Agriculture indicates their value in making this theoretical advantage of democracy into a real one. See Friedrich, *op. cit.,* pp. 117, 217–221.

doing too little and always doing it too late. Public opinion polls, by giving publicity to these attitudes, increase their force. In addition, the attention and deference paid them intensify both the complacency of the people and their confidence in their own mystical rightness. What the people need, however, is to develop some realization of their own shortcomings and some willingness to leave to the expert those matters of which he alone can judge.[6]

Here, as in the case of the first set of criticisms, it would be difficult to prove that the people are actually more conservative than their representatives. Some observers, in fact, contend that the polls have repeatedly shown the people to be far readier than Congress to accept progressive ideas.[7] But even if the people proved, as a regular matter, to be a hindrance to progress, certain theoretical difficulties would remain. It is undoubtedly true that the process of modern government is too technical and complex to be directed in detail by the ordinary citizen and that the skill and knowledge of the expert must be tapped in a responsible fashion. Yet this argument is too easily confused with the very different argument that the "responsible" expert must be given the power to introduce, according to his own judgment, drastic social changes. There is, to begin with, a certain lack of logic in an argument which speaks of ultimate responsibility to the public while maintaining that "trained intelligence" must none the less be free to introduce the drastic changes which the uninformed public is not prepared to accept. And the more one tries to avoid this dilemma by limiting responsibility to the voter in favor of government by a disinterested, wise, and public-spirited elite, the more the criticism becomes one, not of the polls as a hindrance to the operation of democracy, but of democracy as a hindrance to progress.

The defense of democracy, which is as old as Aristotle, does not need to be elaborated here. But it is essential to point out, as Plato himself came to recognize, that no government, however well intentioned, can force a community to move in directions in which it does not want to move, or to move much more rapidly than it would otherwise move, without resorting to instruments of force and tyranny which are incompatible with both the spirit and the practice of democracy.

THE POLLS AS A MISCONCEPTION OF DEMOCRACY

The third, and by far the most valid, criticism which can be made of the polls is that they represent a fundamental misconception of the nature of democracy. Bryce's picture of a society in which the will of the majority of

---

[6] Robert S. Lynd, "Democracy in Reverse," *Public Opinion Quarterly,* Vol. 4, pp. 218–220 (June, 1940). See also Lindsay, *op. cit.,* p. 234.

[7] William A. Lydgate, *What America Thinks* (New York, 1944), pp. 2–8.

the citizens would be ascertainable at all times is neither a very profound nor a very realistic picture of democratic society. Democracy is not simply the ascertaining and the applying of a "will of the people"—a somewhat mystical entity existing in and of itself, independent, unified, and complete. It is the whole long process by which the people and their agents inform themselves, discuss, make compromises, and finally arrive at a decision.

The people are not the only element in this process, and they are not necessarily the agent which is best suited to each part of the task. In general, the executive and the administrative services are best fitted to see policy as a whole and to prepare a coherent program as well as to handle the technical details of legislation. The legislature provides a forum in which the different interests within the country can confront one another in a regularized way, as the people cannot, and acquire something of the mutual understanding and comprehensive outlook which is essential for the satisfactory adjustment of interests. The people themselves, finally, can express better than any other agency what it is they need and want.

None of these functions, it is true, belongs exclusively to any one agency, nor can any be separated rigidly from the others. The process of discussion and adjustment is a continuous one, carried on on all levels. There is a constant interweaving and interpenetration of talk and action subject to no precise demarcation but in which it is none the less essential that each agency refrain from functions which are beyond its competence. In this process the operation of the polls may be positively harmful, not in interfering with "government by experts" as more frequently charged, but in emphasizing the content of the opinion rather than the way in which it is formed and in focussing attention on the divergency of opinion rather than upon the process of adjusting and integrating it.

To say this is not to urge a restriction on popular participation but to emphasize its real nature and function. Popular participation in government is thin and meaningless if it is nothing more than the registering of an opinion. It becomes meaningful to the extent that the opinion is itself the product of information, discussion, and practical political action. There is something not only pathetic but indicative of a basic weakness in the polls' conception of democracy in the stories of those who tell interviewers they could give a "better answer" to the questions if only they had time to read up a bit or think things over. It is precisely this reading up and thinking over which are the essence of political participation and which make politics an educational experience, developing the character and capacity of the citizens.[8]

---

[8] To some, this is the greatest justification of democracy. C. Delisle Burns, *Democracy* (London, 1929); Coker, *op. cit.;* John Dewey, *The Public and Its Problems* (New York, 1927); John Stuart Mill, *Considerations on Representative Government* (New York, 1862); Alexis de Tocqueville, *Democracy in America* (New York, 1838).

The polls, however, except as their publication tends to stimulate political interest, play almost no part in this process. They make it possible for the people to express their attitude toward specific proposals and even to indicate the intensity of their feeling on the subject; and they can distinguish the attitudes of different social and economic groups from one another. But they provide no mechanism on the popular level for promoting discussion, for reconciling and adjusting conflicting sectional, class, or group interests, or for working out a coherent and comprehensive legislative program.

In fact, far less perfect instruments for discovering the "will" of the voters are often much more effective in arousing popular participation. The initiative and the referendum, for all their weaknesses, stir opponents and advocates of measures to unusual activity and stimulate a large proportion of the voters, rather than a small selected sample, to consider and discuss the issues. Similarly, the privately-conducted British Peace Ballot proved to be an educational experience for the entire British people. Even the much maligned *Literary Digest* Poll performed a greater service in arousing thought and discussion than did its more accurate competitors.

In short, the polls are not concerned with, and provide no remedy for, the gravest weaknesses in the democratic process. If one thinks of democracy in practical terms of discussion and political activity rather than of a disembodied "will," the great need is to get rid of the obstacles to popular education, information, debate, judgment, and enforcement of responsibility. To do this, there must be a multiple effort directed against a multiplicity of evils. To mention only a few of these, the political education in most of our schools, handicapped as they are by conventional schoolboards and the fear of controversy, is wretchedly inadequate. In too many cities the sources of information are insufficient, the news itself distorted, and the free competition of ideas seriously restricted.[9] In general, our facilities for discussion—clubs, unions, pressure organizations, forums, round-tables, and the radio—provide no adequate successor to the town meeting in the sense of active and responsible personal participation.[10] More fundamen-

[9] The development of the one-newspaper pattern is particularly unfortunate. Oswald Garrison Villard, *The Disappearing Daily* (New York, 1944), pp. 3, 5, 10–12. See also Morris L. Ernst, *The First Freedom* (New York, 1946), xii and *passim* for a survey not only of the newspaper but of book publishing, the radio, and the motion picture.

[10] On the need for new devices for discussion, see Harwood L. Childs, *An Introduction to Public Opinion* (New York, 1940), p. 137; Coker, *op. cit.,* p. 373; Harold D. Lasswell, *Democracy through Public Opinion* (Menasha, Wisconsin, 1941), pp. 80–95; Merriam, *On the Agenda of Democracy* (Cambridge, 1941), pp. 21–22; Joseph R. Starr, "Political Parties and Public Opinion," *Public Opinion Quarterly,* Vol. 3, pp. 436–448 (July, 1939). For a more optimistic picture, see Friedrich, *Constitutional Government,* p. 546.

tally, the undemocratic character of much of our economic and social life is a real hindrance to the growth of political democracy.

Moreover, even if our political education were magnificent, the channels of information completely clear, the facilities for discussion abundant, and the spirit of democracy universal, the obscurity and confusion in our political system, resulting from its checks and balances and its lack of party discipline, would make it almost impossible for the ordinary voter to understand what is going on, to pass judgment intelligently, and to place responsibility. Yet any government in which the people are to share must at a minimum be comprehensible. Obscurity and anonymity kill democracy. These defects, however, are present in our government, and about them the polls can do very little.

SUMMARY

The chief advantage of the polls is that, in an age of increasing strain upon traditional democratic procedures, they have made a constructive technical contribution by reflecting sensitively and flexibly the currents of public feeling, by making this information available to political leaders in a way which is neither rigid nor mandatory, and by testing the claims of special interests to represent the desires of the people as a whole. These are services performed by no other agency, and they should not be underestimated.

But if, in a democracy, the health of the community depends upon the personal, active, and continuous political participation of the body of its citizens, this contribution is a limited and even a minor one. Even when used with the greatest accuracy and intelligence, the polls cannot achieve any fundamental improvement until our political system itself is simplified, until the lines of responsibility are clarified, and until devices are discovered for increasing the direct participation of the people, not simply in the registration of their aims, but in the deliberative procedure which is the real heart of democracy.

Some Fundamental Constitutional Principles

THE CONSTITUTIONAL CONVENTION of 1787 met behind closed doors and very early adopted a rule "that nothing spoken in the House be printed, or otherwise published, or communicated without leave." This made it possible for the Framers to speak with greater frankness than one would find in speeches intended for the general public. The debates over suffrage, the term of office, and method of electing congressmen reveal the attitude of the Founding Fathers toward democracy and representative government.

Apart from Benjamin Franklin, few members of the Convention had the great faith in the ultimate wisdom of the people which was characteristic of Jefferson. Many delegates made reference to their assumption that men in politics were usually motivated by self-interest and ambition. Although accepting Hamilton's dictum that "Real liberty is neither found in despotism or the extremes of democracy, but in moderate governments," they rejected, however, Hamilton's conclusion that "the rich and well born" should be given a permanent check on the turbulence and follies of democracy.

While it is something of an exaggeration to call Madison "the Father of the Constitution," it is certainly true that among the delegates he was the most widely read and profound student of political institutions. No other member contributed more to the success of the Convention. "The principal task of modern legislation," said Madison, "is the regulation of the various and conflicting economic interests." Assuming that "justice" should be the aim of government, Madison concluded that since human beings are most likely to be biased by self-interest, no body of men should be allowed to judge in its own cause. In writing to Jefferson about the Constitution, Madison asked: "If two individuals are under the bias of interest or enmity against a third, the rights of the latter could never be safely referred to the majority of the three. Will two thousand individuals be less apt to oppress one thousand, or two hundred thousand one hundred thousand?" Madison's answer to this question was the same as that given later by de Tocqueville and Lippmann—that in a completely democratic form of government the civil rights and the economic interests of the minority would be at the mercy of the majority. Jefferson's greater faith in the majority is supported by Commager's "In Defense of Majority Rule."

Although the American Constitution has been changed by amendments and modified by more than a century and a half of political practice, it still embodies, to a considerable extent, the philosophy of the Founding Fathers. The great object of the Constitution, said Madison in Number 10 of *The Federalist,* is to secure the public good and private rights against the power of popular majorities "and at the same time preserve the spirit and form of popular government." The ideal of Madison was representative government which would, to a much greater extent than under the Articles of Confederation, be independent of the people and yet sufficiently controlled by the people so that it would not serve the interests of the representatives at the expense of general welfare.

Topic 3

DEBATES IN THE CONSTITUTIONAL CONVENTION

Excerpts from the Debates in the Constitutional Convention of 1787

DEBATE ON THE HOUSE OF REPRESENTATIVES *

Resolution: 4. first clause; "that the members of the first branch of the National Legislature ought to be elected by the people of the several states." [under consideration]

Mr. Sherman [Roger Sherman of Connecticut] opposed the election by the people, insisting that it ought to be by the State Legislatures. The people, he said, immediately should have as little to do as may be about the Government. They want information and are constantly liable to be misled.

* This selection is taken from James Madison's Journal of the Debates as reprinted in Max Farrand, ed., *Records of the Federal Convention* (New Haven, Yale University Press, 1927), Vol. I, pp. 48–50. By permission of Yale University Press. The Journal of the Debates was originally published in 1840, after all the members of the Convention had died, as part of *The Papers of James Madison.* Farrand's notations indicating additions and corrections made by Madison in his manuscript in later years have been omitted. The spelling has been modernized and most abbreviations spelled out.

Mr. Gerry [Elbridge Gerry of Massachusetts].* The evils we experience flow from the excess of democracy. The people do not want virtue; but are the dupes of pretended patriots. In Massachusetts it has been fully confirmed by experience that they are daily misled into the most baneful measures and opinions by the false reports circulated by designing men, and which no one on the spot can refute. One principal evil arises from the want of due provision for those employed in the administration of Government. It would seem to be a maxim of democracy to starve the public servants. He mentioned the popular clamor in Massachusetts for the reduction of salaries and the attack made on that of the Governor though secured by the spirit of the Constitution itself. He had he said been too republican heretofore: he was still however republican, but had been taught by experience the danger of the levelling spirit.

Mr. Mason [George Mason of Virginia, author of the Virginia Declaration of Rights] † argued strongly for an election of the larger branch by the people. It was to be the grand depository of the democratic principle of the Government. It was, so to speak, to be our House of Commons— It ought to know and sympathize with every part of the community; and ought therefore to be taken not only from different parts of the whole republic, but also from different districts of the larger members of it, which had in several instances particularly in Virginia, different interests and views arising from difference of produce, of habits &c. &c.

He admitted that we had been too democratic but was afraid we should incautiously run into the opposite extreme. We ought to attend to the rights of every class of the people. He had often wondered at the indifference of the superior classes of society to this dictate of humanity and policy, considering that however affluent their circumstances, or elevated their situations, might be, the course of a few years, not only might but certainly would distribute their posterity throughout the lowest classes of Society. Every selfish motive therefore, every family attachment, ought to recommend such a system of policy as would provide no less carefully for the rights—and happiness of the lowest than of the highest orders of Citizens.

Mr. Wilson [James Wilson of Pennsylvania, member of the first Supreme Court] contended strenuously for drawing the most numerous branch of the Legislature immediately from the people. He was for raising the federal pyramid to a considerable altitude, and for that reason wished to give it as broad a basis as possible. No government could long subsist without the confidence of the people. In a republican Government this confidence was peculiarly essential. He also thought it wrong to increase the weight

* Gerry refused to sign the Constitution and opposed its adoption.
† Mason also refused to sign the Constitution and opposed its adoption.

of the State Legislatures by making them the electors of the national Legislature. All interference between the general and local Governments should be obviated as much as possible. On examination it would be found that the opposition of States to federal measures had proceeded much more from the Officers of the States, than from the people at large.

Mr. Madison [James Madison of Virginia] considered the popular election of one branch of the national Legislature as essential to every plan of free Government. He observed that in some of the States one branch of the Legislature was composed of men already removed from the people by an intervening body of electors. That if the first branch of the general legislature should be elected by the State Legislatures, the second branch elected by the first—the Executive by the second together with the first; and other appointments again made for subordinate purposes by the Executive, the people would be lost sight of altogether; and the necessary sympathy between them and their rulers and officers, too little felt. He was an advocate for the policy of refining the popular appointments by successive filtrations, but thought it might be pushed too far. He wished the expedient to be resorted to only in the appointment of the second branch of the Legislature, and in the Executive and judiciary branches of the Government. He thought too that the great fabric to be raised would be more stable and durable if it should rest on the solid foundation of the people themselves, than if it should stand merely on the pillars of the Legislatures.

Mr. Gerry did not like the election by the people. The maxims taken from the British constitution were often fallacious when applied to our situation which was extremely different. Experience he said had shown that the State Legislatures drawn immediately from the people did not always possess their confidence. He had no objection however to an election by the people if it were so qualified that men of honor and character might not be unwilling to be joined in the appointments. He seemed to think that the people might nominate a certain number out of which the State Legislatures should be bound to choose.

Mr. Butler [Pierce Butler of South Carolina] thought an election by the people an impracticable mode.

On the question for an election of the first branch of the national Legislature, by the people; Massachusetts aye, Connecticut divided, New York aye, New Jersey no, Pennsylvania aye, Delaware divided, Virginia aye, North Carolina aye, South Carolina no, Georgia aye. (Ayes—6; noes—2; divided—2.)

HAMILTON'S PLAN FOR THE CONSTITUTION *

Monday, June 18, In Committee of the Whole

On motion of Mr. Dickinson to postpone the first Resolution in Mr. Patterson's plan, [New Jersey Plan] in order to take up the following, viz: *"that the articles of confederation ought to be revised and amended so as to render the Government of the U.S. adequate to the exigencies, the preservation and the prosperity of the union."* The postponement was agreed to by 10 States, Pennsylvania divided.

Mr. Hamilton. [Alexander Hamilton of New York] Yet, I confess, I see great difficulty of drawing forth a good representation. What, for example, will be the inducements for gentlemen of fortune and abilities to leave their houses and business to attend annually and long? It cannot be the wages; for these, I presume, must be small. Will not the power, therefore, be thrown into the hands of the demagogue or middling politician, who, for the sake of a small stipend and the hopes of advancement, will offer himself as a candidate, and the real men of weight and influence, by remaining at home, add strength to the state governments?

I am at a loss to know what must be done—I despair that a republican form of government can remove the difficulties. Whatever may be my opinion, I would hold it however unwise to change that form of government. I believe the British government forms the best model the world ever produced, and such has been its progress in the minds of the many, that this truth gradually gains ground. This government has for its object *public strength* and *individual security*. It is said with us to be unattainable. If it was once formed it would maintain itself.

All communities divide themselves into the few and the many. The first are the rich and well born, the other the mass of the people. The voice of the people has been said to be the voice of God; and however generally this maxim has been quoted and believed, it is not true in fact. The people are turbulent and changing; they seldom judge or determine right. Give therefore to the first class a distinct, permanent share in the government. They will check the unsteadiness of the second, and as they cannot receive any advantage by a change, they therefore will ever maintain good government. Can a democratic assembly, who annually revolve in the mass

* The selections from Hamilton's speech originally appeared in *Secret Proceedings and Debates of the Convention Assembled at Philadelphia, in the year 1787, for the purpose of forming the Constitution of the United States of America. From Notes taken by the late Robert Yates, Esq. Chief Justice of New York, and copied by John Lansing, Jun, Esq.* Reprinted in Farrand, *Records*, Vol. I, pp. 298–301. Farrand's *Records* contain three other versions of Hamilton's speech. The first paragraph below is from Madison's Journal as reprinted in Farrand, *Records*, Vol. I, p. 282.

of the people, be supposed steadily to pursue the public good? Nothing but a permanent body can check the imprudence of democracy. Their turbulent and uncontrolling disposition requires checks.

The senate of New York, although chosen for four years, we found to be inefficient. Will, on the Virginia plan, a continuance of seven years do it? It is admitted that you cannot have a good executive upon a democratic plan. See the excellency of the British executive— He is placed above temptation— He can have no distinct interests from the public welfare. Nothing short of such an executive can be efficient. The weak side of a republican government is the danger of foreign influence. This is unavoidable, unless it is so constructed as to bring forward its first characters in its support. I am therefore for a general government, yet would wish to go the full length of republican principles.

Let one body of the legislature be constituted during good behavior or life.

Let one executive be appointed who dares execute his powers. It may be asked is this a republican system? It is strictly so, as long as they remain elective.

And let me observe, that an executive is less dangerous to the liberties of the people when in office during life, than for seven years.

It may be said this constitutes an elective monarchy? Pray what is a monarchy? May not the governors of the respective states be considered in that light? But by making the executive subject to impeachment, the term monarchy cannot apply. These elective monarchs have produced tumults in Rome, and are equally dangerous to peace in Poland; but this cannot apply to the mode in which I would propose the election. Let electors be appointed in each of the states to elect the executive.

[Yate's notes indicate that here Hamilton produced his plan for the federal "legislature"] to consist of two branches—and I would give them the unlimited power of passing *all laws* without exception. The assembly to be elected for three years by the people in districts—the senate to be elected by electors to be chosen for that purpose by the people, and to remain in office during life. The executive to have the power of negativing all laws— to make war or peace, with the advice of the senate—to make treaties with their advice, but to have the sole direction of all military operations, and to send ambassadors and appoint all military officers, and to pardon all offenders, treason excepted, unless by advice of the senate. On his death or removal, the president of the senate to officiate, with the same powers, until another is elected. Supreme judicial officers to be appointed by the executive and the senate. The legislature to appoint courts in each state, so as to make the state governments unnecessary to it.

All state laws to be absolutely void which contravene the general laws.

An officer to be appointed in each state to have a negative on all state laws. All the militia and the appointment of officers to be under the national government.

I confess that this plan and that from Virginia are very remote from the idea of the people. Perhaps the Jersey plan is nearest their expectation. But the people are gradually ripening in their opinions of government—they begin to be tired of an excess of democracy—and what even is the Virginia plan, but *pork still, with a little change of the sauce.*

DEBATE ON THE SENATE *

Tuesday, June 26, In Convention

The duration of the second branch under consideration.

Mr. Gorham [Nathaniel Gorham of Massachusetts] moved to fill the blank with "six years," one third of the members to go out every second year.

Mr. Wilson seconded the motion. . . .

Mr. Madison. In order to judge of the form to be given to this institution, it will be proper to take a view of the ends to be served by it. These were first to protect the people against their rulers: secondly to protect [the people] against the transient impressions into which they themselves might be led. A people deliberating in a temperate moment, and with the experience of other nations before them, on the plan of Government most likely to secure their happiness, would first be aware, that those charged with the public happiness, might betray their trust. An obvious precaution against this danger would be to divide the trust between different bodies of men, who might watch and check each other. In this they would be governed by the same prudence which has prevailed in organizing the subordinate departments of Government where all business liable to abuses is made to pass through separate hands, the one being a check on the other.

It would next occur to such a people, that they themselves were liable to temporary errors, through want of information as to their true interest, and that men chosen for a short term, and employed but a small portion of that in public affairs, might err from the same cause. This reflection would naturally suggest that the Government be so constituted, as that one of its branches might have an opportunity of acquiring a competent knowledge of the public interests. Another reflection equally becoming a people on such an occasion, would be that they themselves, as well as a numerous body of Representatives, were liable to err also, from fickleness and passion. A necessary fence against this danger would be to select a portion of

* The following extracts from Madison's Journal of the Debates are reprinted from Farrand, *Records,* Vol. I, pp. 421–426.

enlightened citizens, whose limited number, and firmness might seasonably interpose against impetuous counsels. It ought finally to occur to a people deliberating on a Government for themselves, that as different interests necessarily result from the liberty meant to be secured, the major interest might under sudden impulses be tempted to commit injustice on the minority. In all civilized Countries the people fall into different classes having a real or supposed difference of interests. There will be creditors and debtors, farmers, merchants and manufacturers. There will be particularly the distinction of rich and poor. It was true as had been observed (by Mr. Pinckney) we had not among us those hereditary distinctions of rank which were a great source of contests in the ancient Governments as well as the modern States of Europe, nor those extremes of wealth or poverty which characterize the latter.

We cannot, however, be regarded even at this time, as one homogeneous mass, in which everything that affects a part will affect in the same manner the whole. In framing a system which we wish to last for ages, we should not lose sight of the changes which ages will produce. An increase of population will of necessity increase the proportion of those who will labor under all the hardships of life, and secretly sigh for a more equal distribution of its blessings. These may in time outnumber those who are placed above the feelings of indigence. According to the equal laws of suffrage, the power will slide into the hands of the former. No agrarian attempts have yet been made in this Country, but symptoms of a leveling spirit, as we have understood, have sufficiently appeared in certain quarters to give notice of the future danger.

How is this danger to be guarded against on republican principles? How is the danger in all cases of interested coalitions to oppress the minority to be guarded against? Among other means by the establishment of a body in the Government sufficiently respectable for its wisdom and virtue, to aid, on such emergencies, the preponderance of justice by throwing its weight into the scale. Such being the objects of the second branch in the proposed Government he thought a considerable duration ought be given to it. He did not conceive that the term of nine years could threaten any real danger; but in pursuing his particular ideas on the subject, he should require that the long term allowed to the 2d. branch should not commence till such a period of life as would render a perpetual disqualification to be re-elected little inconvenient either in a public or private view. He observed that as it was more than probable we were now digesting a plan which in its operation would decide forever the fate of Republican Government we ought not only to provide every guard to liberty that its preservation could require, but be equally careful to supply the defects which our own experience had particularly pointed out.

Mr. Sherman. Government is instituted for those who live under it. It ought therefore to be so constituted as not to be dangerous to their liberties. The more permanency it has the worse if it be a bad Government. Frequent elections are necessary to preserve the good behavior of rulers. They also tend to give permanency to the Government, by preserving that good behavior, because it ensures their re-election. In Connecticut elections have been very frequent, yet great stability and uniformity both as to persons and measures have been experienced from its original establishment, to the present time; a period of more than 130 years. He wished to have provisions made for steadiness and wisdom in the system to be adopted; but he thought six or four years would be sufficient. He should be content with either. . . .

Mr. Gerry wished we could be united in our ideas concerning a permanent Government. All aim at the same end, but there are great differences as to the means. One circumstance He thought should be carefully attended to. There were not 1/1000 part of our fellow citizens who were not against every approach toward Monarchy. Will they ever agree to a plan which seems to make such an approach? The Convention ought to be extremely cautious in what they hold out to the people. Whatever plan may be proposed will be espoused with warmth by many out of respect to the quarter it proceeds from as well as from an approbation of the plan itself. And if the plan should be of such a nature as to rouse a violent opposition, it is easy to foresee that discord and confusion will ensue, and it is even possible that we may become a prey to foreign powers.

He did not deny the position of Mr. Madison that the majority will generally violate justice when they have an interest in so doing; but did not think there was any such temptation in this Country. Our situation was different from that of Great Britain: and the great body of lands yet to be parcelled out and settled would very much prolong the difference. Notwithstanding the symptoms of injustice which had marked many of our public Councils, they had not proceeded so far as not to leave hopes, that there would be a sufficient sense of justice and virtue for the purpose of Government. He admitted the evils arising from a frequency of elections: and would agree to give the Senate a duration of four or five years. A longer term would defeat itself. It never would be adopted by the people. . . .

On the question for 9 years; ⅓ to go out triennially: Massachusetts no, Connecticut no, New York no, New Jersey no, Pennsylvania aye, Delaware aye, Maryland no, Virginia aye, North Carolina no, South Carolina no, Georgia no. (Ayes—3; noes—8.)

On the question for 6 years; ⅓ to go out biennially: Massachusetts aye, Connecticut aye, New York no, New Jersey no, Pennsylvania aye, Delaware aye, Maryland aye, Virginia aye, North Carolina aye, South Carolina no, Georgia no. (Ayes—7; noes—4.)

DEBATE ON SUFFRAGE *

Tuesday, August 7th, In Convention

"Article IV. Section 1. (Constitution) taken up."

Article IV, Section 1. "The members of the House of Representatives shall be chosen every second year, by the people of the several States comprehended within this Union. The qualifications of the electors shall be the same, from time to time, as those of the electors in the several States, of the most numerous branch of their own legislatures."

Mr. Gouverneur Morris [of Pennsylvania] moved to strike out the last member of the section beginning with the words "qualifications" of "Electors" in order that some other provision might be substituted which would restrain the right of suffrage to freeholders.

Mr. Fitzsimmons [Thomas Fitzsimmons of Pennsylvania] seconded the motion.

Mr. Williamson [Hugh Williamson of North Carolina] was opposed to it.

Mr. Wilson. This part of the Report was well considered by the Committee, and he did not think it could be changed for the better. It was difficult to form any uniform rule of qualifications for all the States. Unnecessary innovations he thought too should be avoided. It would be very hard and disagreeable for the same persons, at the same time, to vote for representatives in the State Legislature and to be excluded from a vote for those in the National Legislature. . . .

Col. Mason. The force of habit is certainly not attended to by those gentlemen who wish for innovations on this point. Eight or nine States have extended the right of suffrage beyond the freeholders. What will the people there say, if they should be disfranchised? A power to alter the qualifications would be a dangerous power in the hands of the Legislature. . . .

Mr. Dickinson [John Dickinson of Delaware] had a very different idea of the tendency of vesting the right of suffrage in the freeholders of the Country. He considered them as the best guardians of liberty; and the restriction of the right to them as a necessary defense against the dangerous influence of those multitudes without property and without principle, with which our Country like all others, will in time abound. As to the unpopularity of the innovation it was in his opinion chimerical. The great mass of our Citizens is composed at this time of freeholders, and will be pleased with it.

Mr. Ellsworth [Oliver Ellsworth of Connecticut, Chief Justice of the United States 1796–1800]. How shall the freehold be defined? Ought not every man who pays a tax to vote for the representative who is to levy and dispose of his money? Shall the wealthy merchants and manufacturers, who

* The following extracts from Madison's Journal of the Debates are reprinted from Farrand, *Records*, Vol. II, pp. 201–206.

will bear a full share of the public burdens be not allowed a voice in the imposition of them. Taxation and representation ought to go together.

Mr. Gouverneur Morris. He had long learned not to be the dupe of words. The sound of Aristocracy therefore, had no effect on him. It was the thing, not the name, to which he was opposed, and one of his principal objections to the Constitution as it is now before us, is that it threatens this Country with an Aristocracy. The aristocracy will grow out of the House of Representatives. Give the votes to people who have no property, and they will sell them to the rich who will be able to buy them. We should not confine our attention to the present moment. The time is not distant when this Country will abound with mechanics and manufacturers who will receive their bread from their employers. Will such men be the secure and faithful Guardians of liberty? Will they be the impregnable barrier against aristocracy?— He was as little duped by the association of the words, "Taxation and Representation"— The man who does not give his vote freely is not represented. It is the man who dictates the vote. Children do not vote. Why? Because they want prudence, because they have no will of their own. The ignorant and the dependent can be as little trusted with the public interest. He did not conceive the difficulty of defining "freeholders" to be insuperable. Still less that the restriction could be unpopular. $\frac{9}{10}$ of the people are at present freeholders and these will certainly be pleased with it. As to Merchants etc. if they have wealth and value the right they can acquire it. If not they don't deserve it.

Col. Mason. We all feel too strongly the remains of ancient prejudices, and view things too much through a British medium. A Freehold is the qualification in England, and hence it is imagined to be the only proper one. The true idea in his opinion was that every man having evidence of attachment to and permanent common interest with the Society ought to share in all its rights and privileges. Was this qualification restrained to freeholders? Does no other kind of property but land evidence a common interest in the proprietor? Does nothing besides property mark a permanent attachment? Ought the merchant, the monied man, the parent of a number of children whose fortunes are to be pursued in their own Country, to be viewed as suspicious characters, and unworthy to be trusted with the common rights of their fellow Citizens?

Mr. Madison. The right of suffrage is certainly one of the fundamental articles of republican Government, and ought not to be left to be regulated by the Legislature. A gradual abridgment of this right has been the mode in which Aristocracies have been built on the ruins of popular forms. Whether the Constitutional qualification ought to be a freehold would with him depend much on the probable reception such a change would meet with in States where the right was now exercised by every description of people. In several of the States a freehold was now the qualification. Viewing the subject in its merits alone, the freeholders of the Country would be the safest depositories of Republican liberty. In future times a great majority of the people will not only be without landed, but any other sort of property. These will either combine under the influence of their common situation; in which case, the rights of property and the public liberty, will not be secure in their hands; or which is more probable, they will become the tools of opulence and ambition, in which case there will be equal danger on another side. The example of England has been misconceived (by Col. Mason). A very small proportion of the Representatives are there chosen by freeholders. The greatest part are chosen by the Cities and boroughs, in many of which the qualification of suffrage is as low as it is in any one of the U.S. and it was in the boroughs and Cities rather than the Counties, that bribery most prevailed, and the influence of the Crown on elections was most dangerously exerted.

Doctor Franklin. [Benjamin Franklin of Pennsylvania] It is of great consequence that we should not depress the virtue and public spirit of our common people; of which they displayed a great deal during the war, and which contributed principally to the favorable issue of it. He related the honorable refusal of the American seamen who were carried in great numbers into the British Prisons during the war, to redeem themselves from misery or to seek their fortunes, by entering on board the Ships of the Enemies to their Country; contrasting their patriotism with a contemporary instance in which the British seamen made prisoners by the Americans, readily entered on the ships of the latter on being promised a share of the prizes that might be made out of their own Country. This proceeded, he said, from the different manner in which the common people were treated in America and Great Britain. He did not think that the elected had any right in any case to narrow the privileges of the electors. He quoted as arbitrary the British Statute setting forth the danger of tumultuous meetings, and under that pretext, narrowing the right of suffrage to persons having freeholds of a certain value; observing that this Statute was soon followed by another under the succeeding Parliament subjecting the people who had no votes to peculiar labors and hardships. He was persuaded also that such a restriction as was proposed would give great uneasiness in the populous States. The sons of a substantial farmer, not being themselves freeholders, would not be pleased at being disfranchised, and there are a great many persons of that description.

Mr. Mercer. [John Francis Mercer of Maryland] The Constitution is objectionable in many points, but in none more than the present. He objected to the footing on which the qualification was put, but particularly to the *mode of election* by the people. The people can not know and judge of the characters of Candidates. The worse possible choice will be made. He quoted the case of the Senate in Virginia as an example in point— The people in Towns can unite their votes in favor of one favorite; and by that means always prevail over the people of the Country, who being dispersed will scatter their votes among a variety of candidates.

Mr. Rutledge [John Rutledge of South Carolina] thought the idea of restraining the right of suffrage to the freeholders a very ill advised one. It would create division among the people and make enemies of all those who should be excluded.

On the question for striking out as moved by Mr. Gouverneur Morris, from the word "qualifications" to the end of article III: New Hampshire no, Massachusetts no, Connecticut no, Pennsylvania no, Delaware aye, Maryland divided, Virginia no, North Carolina no, South Carolina no, Georgia not present. (Ayes—1; noes—7; divided—1; absent 1.)

Topic 4

THE CONTROL OF MAJORITY "FACTIONS"

❦

The Union as a Safeguard Against Domestic Faction

The Federalist, No. 10

JAMES MADISON

Among the numerous advantages promised by a well-constructed Union, none deserves to be more accurately developed than its tendency to break and control the violence of faction. The friend of popular governments never finds himself so much alarmed for their character and fate, as when he contemplates their propensity to this dangerous vice. He will not fail, therefore, to set a due value on any plan which, without violating the principles to which he is attached, provides a proper cure for it. The instability, injustice, and confusion introduced into the public councils have, in truth, been the mortal diseases under which popular governments have everywhere perished; as they continue to be the favorite and fruitful topics from which the adversaries to liberty derive their most specious declamations.

The valuable improvements made by the American constitutions on the popular models, both ancient and modern, cannot certainly be too much admired; but it would be an unwarrantable partiality, to contend that they have as effectually obviated the danger on this side, as was wished and expected. Complaints are everywhere heard from our most considerate and virtuous citizens, equally the friends of public and private faith, and of public and personal liberty, that our governments are too unstable; that the public good is disregarded in the conflicts of rival parties; and that measures are too often decided, not according to the rules of justice, and the rights of the minor party, but by the superior force of an interested and overbearing majority. However anxiously we may wish that these complaints had no foundation, the evidence of known facts will not permit us to deny that they are in some degree true.

It will be found, indeed, on a candid review of our situation, that some of the distresses under which we labor have been erroneously charged on the operation of our governments; but it will be found, at the same time, that other causes will not alone account for many of our heaviest misfortunes; and, particularly, for that prevailing and increasing distrust of public engagements, and alarm for private rights, which are echoed from one end of the continent to the other. These must be chiefly, if not wholly, effects of the unsteadiness and injustice with which a factious spirit has tainted our public administrations.

By a faction, I understand a number of citizens, whether amounting to a majority or a minority of the whole, who are united and actuated by some common impulse of passion, or of interest, adverse to the rights of other citizens, or to the permanent and aggregate interests of the community.

There are two methods of curing the mischiefs of faction: the one, by removing its causes; the other, by controlling its effects. There are again two methods of removing the causes of faction: the one, by destroying the liberty which is essential to its existence; the other, by giving to every citizen the same opinions, the same passions, and the same interests.

It could never be more truly said than of the first remedy, that it was worse than the disease. Liberty is to faction what air is to fire, an aliment without which it instantly expires. But it could not be less folly to abolish liberty, which is essential to political life, because it nourishes faction, than it would be to wish the annihilation of air, which is essential to animal life, because it imparts to fire its destructive agency.

The second expedient is as impracticable as the first would be unwise. As long as the reason of man continues fallible, and he is at liberty to exercise it, different opinions will be formed. As long as the connection subsists between his reason and his self-love, his opinions and his passions will have a reciprocal influence on each other; and the former will be objects to which the latter will attach themselves. The diversity in the faculties of men, from which the rights of property originate, is not less an insuperable obstacle to a uniformity of interests. The protection of these faculties is the first object of government. From the protection of different and unequal faculties of acquiring property, the possession of different degrees and kinds of property immediately results; and from the influence of these on the sentiments and views of the respective proprietors, ensues a division of the society into different interests and parties.

The latent causes of faction are thus sown in the nature of man; and we see them everywhere brought into different degrees of activity, according to the different circumstances of civil society. A zeal for different opinions concerning religion, concerning government, and many other points, as well of speculation as of practice; an attachment to different leaders ambitiously contending for pre-eminence and power; or to persons of other descriptions whose fortunes have been interesting to the human passions, have, in turn, divided mankind into parties, inflamed them with mutual animosity, and rendered them much more disposed to vex and oppress each other, than to co-operate for their common good. So strong is this propensity of mankind to fall into mutual animosities, that where no substantial occasion presents itself, the most frivolous and fanciful distinctions have been sufficient to kindle their unfriendly passions and excite their most violent conflicts. But the most common and durable source of factions has been the various and unequal distribution of property. Those who hold and those who are without property have ever formed distinct interests in society. Those who are creditors, and those who are debtors, fall under a like discrimination. A landed interest, a manufacturing interest, a mercantile interest, a moneyed interest, with many lesser interests, grow up of necessity in civilized nations, and divide them into different classes, actuated by different sentiments and views. The regulation of these various and interfering interests forms the principal task of modern legislation, and involves the spirit of party and faction in the necessary and ordinary operations of the government.

No man is allowed to be a judge in his own cause, because his interest would certainly bias his judgment and, not improbably, corrupt his integrity. With equal, nay, with greater reason, a body of men are unfit to be both judges and parties at the same time; yet what are many of the most important acts of legislation, but so many judicial determinations, not indeed concerning the rights of single persons, but concerning the rights of large bodies of citizens? And what are the different classes of legislators, but advocates and parties to the causes which they determine? Is a law proposed concerning private debts? It is a question to which the creditors are parties on one side and the debtors on the other. Justice ought to hold the balance between them. Yet the parties are, and must be, themselves the judges; and the most numerous party, or, in other words, the most powerful faction, must be expected to prevail. Shall domestic manufacturers be encouraged, and in what degree, by restrictions on foreign manufactures? are questions which would be differently decided by the landed and the manufacturing classes, and probably by neither with a sole regard to justice and the public good. The apportionment of taxes on the various descriptions of property is an act which seems to require the most exact impartiality; yet there is, perhaps, no legislative act in which greater opportunity and temptation are given to a predominant party, to trample on the rules of justice. Every shilling with which they overburden the inferior number, is a shilling saved to their own pockets.

It is in vain to say that enlightened statesmen will be able to adjust these clashing interests, and render them all subservient to the public good. Enlightened statesmen will not always be at the helm. Nor, in many cases, can such an adjustment be made at all, without taking into view indirect and remote considerations, which will rarely prevail over the immediate interest which one party may find in disregarding the rights of another or the good of the whole. The inference to which we are brought is, that the *causes* of faction cannot be removed, and that relief is only to be sought in the means of controlling its *effects*.

If a faction consists of less than a majority, relief is supplied by the republican principle, which enables the majority to defeat its sinister views by regular vote. It may clog the administration, it may convulse the society; but it will be unable to execute and mask its violence under the forms of the Constitution. When a majority is included in a faction, the form of popular government, on the other hand, enables it to sacrifice to its ruling passion or interest both the public good and the rights of other citizens. To secure the public good and private rights against the danger of such a faction, and at the same time to preserve the spirit and the form of popular government, is then the great object to which our inquiries are directed. Let me add that it is the great desideratum, by which alone this form of government can be rescued from the opprobrium under which it has so long labored, and be recommended to the esteem and adoption of mankind.

By what means is this object attainable? Evidently by one of two only. Either the existence of the same passion or interest in a majority at the same time must be prevented; or the majority, having such coexisting passion or interest, must be rendered, by their number and local situation, unable to concert and carry into effect schemes of oppression. If the impulse and the opportunity be suffered to coincide, we well know that neither moral nor religious motives can be relied on as an adequate control. They are not found to be such on the injustice and violence of individuals, and lose their efficacy in proportion to the number combined together; that is, in proportion as their efficacy becomes needful.

From this view of the subject it may be concluded that a pure democracy, by which I mean a society consisting of a small number of citizens, who assemble and administer the government in person, can admit of no cure for the mischiefs of faction. A common passion or interest will, in almost every case, be felt by a majority of the whole; a communication and concert result from the form of government itself; and there is nothing to check the inducements to sacrifice the weaker party or an obnoxious individual. Hence it is that such democracies have ever been spectacles of turbulence and contention; have ever been found incompatible with personal security, or the rights of property; and have in general been as short in their lives as they have been violent in their deaths. Theoretic politicians, who have patronized this species of government, have erroneously supposed that by reducing mankind to a perfect equality in their political rights, they would at the same time be perfectly equalized and assimilated in their possessions, their opinions, and their passions.

A republic, by which I mean a government in which the scheme of representation takes place, opens a different prospect, and promises the cure for which we are seeking. Let us examine the points in which it varies from pure democracy, and we shall comprehend both the nature of the cure and the efficacy which it must derive from the Union.

The two great points of difference between a democracy and a republic are: first, the delegation of the government, in the latter, to a small number of citizens elected by the rest; secondly, the greater number of citizens, and greater sphere of country, over which the latter may be extended.

The effect of the first difference is, on the one hand, to refine and enlarge the public views, by passing them through the medium of a chosen body of citizens, whose wisdom may best discern the true interests of their country, and whose patriotism and love of justice will be least likely to sacrifice it to temporary or partial considerations. Under such a regulation, it may well happen that the public voice, pronounced by the representatives of the people, will be more consonant to the public good than if pronounced by the people themselves, convened for the purpose. On the other hand, the effect may be inverted. Men of factious tempers, of local prejudices, or of sinister designs, may, by intrigue, by corruption, or by other means, first obtain the suffrages, and then betray the interests of the people. The question resulting is, whether small or extensive republics are more favorable to the election of proper guardians of the public weal; and it is clearly decided in favor of the latter by two obvious considerations.

In the first place, it is to be remarked that, however small the republic may be, the representatives must be raised to a certain number, in order to guard against the cabals of a few; and that, however large it may be, they must be limited to a certain number, in order to guard against the confusion of a multitude. Hence, the number of representatives in the two cases not being in proportion to that of the two constituents, and being proportionally greater in the small republic, it follows that if the proportion of fit characters be not less in the large than in the small republic, the former will present a greater option, and consequently a greater probability of a fit choice.

In the next place, as each representative will be chosen by a greater number of citizens in the large than in the small republic, it will be more difficult for unworthy candidates to practice with success the vicious arts, by which elections are too often carried; and the suffrages of the people, being more free, will be more likely to centre in men who possess the most attractive merit and the most diffusive and established characters.

It must be confessed that in this as in most other cases, there is a mean, on both sides of which inconveniences will be found to lie. By enlarging too much the number of electors, you render the representative too little acquainted with all their local circumstances and lesser interests; as by reducing it too much, you render him unduly attached to these, and too little fit to comprehend and pursue great and national objects. The federal Constitution forms a happy combination in this respect; the great and aggregate interests being referred to the national, the local and particular to the State legislatures.

The other point of difference is, the greater number of citizens and extent of territory which may be brought within the compass of republican than of democratic government; and it is this circumstance principally which renders factious combinations less to be dreaded in the former than in the latter. The smaller the society, the fewer probably will be the distinct parties and interests composing it; the fewer the distinct parties and interests, the more frequently will a majority be found of the same party; and the smaller the number of individuals composing a majority, and the smaller the compass within which they are placed, the more easily will they concert and execute their plans of oppression. Extend the sphere, and you take in a greater variety of parties and interests; you make it less probable that a majority of the whole will have a common motive to invade the rights of other citizens; or if such a common motive exists, it will be more difficult for all who feel it to discover their own strength, and to act in unison with each other. Besides other impediments, it may be remarked that where there is a consciousness of unjust or dishonorable purposes, communication is always checked by distrust in proportion to the number whose concurrence is necessary.

Hence it clearly appears that the same advantage which a republic has over a democracy, in controlling the effects of faction, is enjoyed by a large over a small republic—is enjoyed by the Union over the States composing it. Does the advantage consist in the substitution of representatives, whose enlightened views and virtuous sentiments render them superior to local prejudices, and to schemes of injustice? It will not be denied that the representation of the Union will be most likely to possess these requisite endowments. Does it consist in the greater security afforded by a greater variety of parties, against the event of any one party being able to outnumber and oppress the rest? In an equal degree does the increased variety of parties, comprised within the Union, increase this security? Does it, in fine, consist in the greater obstacles opposed to the concert and accomplishment of the secret wishes of an unjust and interested majority? Here, again, the extent of the Union gives it the most palpable advantage.

The influence of factious leaders may kindle a flame within their particular States, but will be unable to spread a general conflagration through the other States. A religious sect may degenerate into a political faction in a part of the confederacy; but the variety of sects dispersed over the entire face of it must secure the national councils against any danger from that source. A rage for paper money, for an abolition of debts, for an equal division of property, or for any other improper or wicked project will be less apt to pervade the whole body of the Union than a particular member of it; in the same proportion as such a malady is more likely to taint a particular county or district, than an entire State.

In the extent and proper structure of the Union, therefore, we behold a republican remedy for the diseases most incident to republican government. And according to the degree of pleasure and pride we feel in being republicans, ought to be our zeal in cherishing the spirit and supporting the character of federalists.

PUBLIUS

Topic 5

"SINCE ANGELS DO NOT GOVERN MEN"

❧❧❧

Separation of Powers

The Federalist, No. 47

JAMES MADISON *

One of the principal objections inculcated by the more respectable adversaries of the Constitution, is its supposed violation of the political maxim that the legislative, executive, and judiciary departments ought to be separate and distinct. In the structure of the federal government, no regard, it is said, seems to have been paid to this essential precaution in favor of liberty. The several departments of power are distributed and blended in such a manner as at once to destroy all symmetry and beauty of form, and to expose some of the essential parts of the edifice to the danger of being crushed by the disproportionate weight of other parts.

No political truth is certainly of greater intrinsic value, or is stamped with the authority of more enlightened patrons of liberty, than that on which the objection is founded. The accumulation of all powers, legislative, executive, and judiciary, in the same hands, whether of one, a few, or many, and whether hereditary, self-appointed, or elective, may justly be pronounced the very definition of tyranny. Were the federal Constitution, therefore, really chargeable with the accumulation of power, or with a mixture of powers, having a dangerous tendency to such an accumulation, no further arguments would be necessary to inspire a universal reprobation of the system. I persuade myself, however, that it will be made apparent to everyone that the charge cannot be supported, and that the maxim on which it relies has been totally misconceived and misapplied. In order to form correct ideas on this important subject, it will be proper to investigate the sense in which the preservation of liberty requires that the three great departments of power should be separate and distinct.

The oracle who is always consulted and cited on this subject is the celebrated Montesquieu. If he be not the author of this invaluable precept in the science of politics, he has the merit at least of displaying and recom-

* Many editions of *The Federalist* credit Hamilton with the authorship of Numbers 47 and 51. Recent research has established that both were written by Madison.

mending it most effectually to the attention of mankind. Let us endeavor, in the first place, to ascertain his meaning on this point.

The British Constitution was to Montesquieu what Homer has been to the didactic writers on epic poetry. As the latter have considered the work of the immortal bard as the perfect model from which the principles and rules of the epic art were to be drawn, and by which all similar works were to be judged, so this great political critic appears to have viewed the Constitution of England as the standard, or to use his own expression, as the mirror of political liberty, and to have delivered, in the form of elementary truths, the several characteristic principles of that particular system. That we may be sure, then, not to mistake his meaning in this case, let us recur to the source from which the maxim was drawn.

On the slightest view of the British Constitution we must perceive that the legislative, executive, and judiciary departments are by no means totally separate and distinct from each other. The executive magistrate forms an integral part of the legislative authority. He alone has the prerogative of making treaties with foreign sovereigns, which, when made, have, under certain limitations, the force of legislative acts. All the members of the judiciary department are appointed by him, can be removed by him on the address of the two Houses of Parliament, and form, when he pleases to consult them, one of his constitutional councils. One branch of the legislative department forms also a great constitutional council to the executive chief; as, on another hand, it is the sole depositary of judicial power in cases of impeachment, and is invested with the supreme appellate jurisdiction in all other cases. The judges, again, are so far connected with the legislative department as often to attend and participate in its deliberations, though not admitted to a legislative vote.

From these facts, by which Montesquieu was guided, it may clearly be inferred that in saying "There can be no liberty where the legislative and executive powers are united in the same person or body of magistrates," or, "if the power of judging be not separated from the legislative and executive powers," he did not mean that these departments ought to have no *partial agency* in, or no *control* over, the acts of each other. His meaning, as his own words import, and still more conclusively as illustrated by the example in his eye, can amount to no more than this, that where the *whole* power of one department is exercised by the same hands which possess the *whole* power of another department, the fundamental principles of a free constitution are subverted. This would have been the case in the Constitution examined by him if the King, who is the sole executive magistrate, had possessed also the complete legislative power, or the supreme administration of justice; or if the entire legislative body had possessed the supreme judiciary or the supreme executive authority.

This, however, is not among the vices of that Constitution. The magistrate in whom the whole executive power resides cannot of himself make a law, though he can put a negative on every law; nor administer justice in person, though he has the appointment of those who do administer it. The judges can exercise no executive prerogative, though they are shoots from the executive stock; nor any legislative function, though they may be advised with by the legislative councils. The entire legislature can perform no judiciary act; though by the joint act of two of its branches the judges may be removed from their offices, and though one of its branches is possessed of the judicial power in the last resort. The entire legislature, again, can exercise no executive prerogative, though one of its branches constitutes the supreme executive magistracy, and another, on the impeachment of a third, can try and condemn all the subordinate officers in the executive department.

The reasons on which Montesquieu grounds his maxim are a further demonstration of his meaning. "When the legislative and executive powers are united in the same person or body," says he, "there can be no liberty, because apprehensions may arise lest *the same* monarch or Senate should *enact* tyrannical laws to *execute* them in a tyrannical manner." Again: "Were the power of judging joined with the legislative, the life and liberty of the subject would be exposed to arbitrary control, for the *judge* would then be the *legislator*. Were it joined to the executive power, the *judge* might behave with all the violence of *an oppressor*." Some of these reasons are more fully explained in other passages; but briefly stated as they are here, they sufficiently establish the meaning which we have put on this celebrated maxim of this celebrated author.

If we look into the constitutions of the several States, we find that, notwithstanding the emphatical and in some instances the unqualified terms in which this axiom has been laid down, there is not a single instance in which the several departments of power have been kept absolutely separate and distinct. . . .

[Here the author examines the constitutions of the original thirteen states, excepting those of Rhode Island and Connecticut which were formed prior to the American Revolution.]

What I have wished to evince is, that the charge brought against the proposed Constitution, of violating a sacred maxim of free government, is warranted neither by the real meaning annexed to that maxim by its author nor by the sense in which it has hitherto been understood in America.

PUBLIUS

Checks and Balances

The Federalist, No. 51

JAMES MADISON

To what expedient, then, shall we finally resort, for maintaining in practice the necessary partition of power among the several departments, as laid down in the Constitution? The only answer that can be given is, that as all these exterior provisions are found to be inadequate, the defect must be supplied, by so contriving the interior structure of the government as that its several constituent parts may, by their mutual relations, be the means of keeping each other in their proper places. Without presuming to undertake a full development of this important idea, I will hazard a few general observations, which may perhaps place it in a clearer light, and enable us to form a more correct judgment of the principles and structure of the government planned by the Convention.

In order to lay a due foundation for that separate and distinct exercise of the different powers of government, which to a certain extent is admitted on all hands to be essential to the preservation of liberty, it is evident that each department should have a will of its own; and consequently should be so constituted that the members of each should have as little agency as possible in the appointment of the members of the others. Were this principle rigorously adhered to, it would require that all the appointments for the supreme executive, legislative, and judiciary magistracies should be drawn from the same fountain of authority, the people, through channels having no communication whatever with one another.

Perhaps such a plan of constructing the several departments would be less difficult in practice than it may in contemplation appear. Some difficulties, however, and some additional expense would attend the execution of it. Some deviations, therefore, from the principle must be admitted. In the constitution of the judiciary department in particular, it might be inexpedient to insist rigorously on the principle: first, because peculiar qualifications being essential in the members, the primary consideration ought to be to select that mode of choice which best secures these qualifications; secondly, because the permanent tenure by which the appointments are held in that department must soon destroy all sense of dependence on the authority conferring them.

It is equally evident that the members of each department should be as little dependent as possible on those of the others, for the emoluments annexed to their offices. Were the executive magistrate, or the judges, not independent of the Legislature in this particular, their independence in every other would be merely nominal.

But the great security against a gradual concentration of the several powers in the same department consists in giving to those who administer each department the necessary constitutional means and personal motives to resist encroachments of the others. The provision for defence must in this, as in all other cases, be made commensurate to the danger of attack. Ambition must be made to counteract ambition. The interest of the man must be connected with the constitutional rights of the place. It may be a reflection on human nature, that such devices should be necessary to control the abuses of government. But what is government itself, but the greatest of all reflections on human nature? If men were angels, no government would be necessary. If angels were to govern men, neither external nor internal controls on government would be necessary. In framing a government which is to be administered by men over men, the great difficulty lies in this: you must first enable the government to control the governed; and in the next place oblige it to control itself. A dependence on the people is, no doubt, the primary control on the government; but experience has taught mankind the necessity of auxiliary precautions.

This policy of supplying, by opposite and rival interests, the defect of better motives, might be traced through the whole system of human affairs, private as well as public. We see it particularly displayed in all the subordinate distributions of power, where the constant aim is to divide and arrange the several offices in such a manner as that each may be a check on the other—that the private interest of every individual may be a sentinel over the public rights. These inventions of prudence cannot be less requisite in the distribution of the supreme powers of the State.

But it is not possible to give to each department an equal power of self-defence. In republican government, the legislative authority necessarily predominates. The remedy for this inconveniency is to divide the legislature into different branches; and to render them, by different modes of election and different principles of action, as little connected with each other as the nature of their common functions and their common dependence on the society will admit. It may even be necessary to guard against dangerous encroachments by still further precautions. As the weight of the legislative authority requires that it should be thus divided, the weakness of the executive may require, on the other hand, that it should be fortified. An absolute negative on the legislature appears at first view to be the natural defence with which the executive magistrate should be armed. But perhaps it would be neither altogether safe nor alone sufficient. On ordinary occasions it might not be exerted with the requisite firmness, and on extraordinary occasions it might be perfidiously abused. May not this defect of an absolute negative be supplied by some qualified connection between this weaker department and the weaker branch of the stronger department, by which the latter may be led to support the constitutional rights of the former, without being too much detached from the rights of its own department?

If the principles on which these observations are founded be just, as I persuade myself they are, and they be applied as a criterion to the several State constitutions, and to the federal Constitution, it will be found that if the latter does not perfectly correspond with them, the former are infinitely less able to bear such a test.

There are, moreover, two considerations particularly applicable to the federal system of America, which place that system in a very interesting point of view.

First. In a single republic all the power surrendered by the people is submitted to the administration of a single government, and the usurpations are guarded against by a division of the government into distinct and separate departments. In the compound republic of America, the power surrendered by the people is first divided between two distinct governments, and then the portion allotted to each subdivided among distinct and separate departments. Hence a double security arises to the rights of the people. The different governments will control each other, at the same time that each will be controlled by itself.

Second. It is of great importance in a republic not only to guard the society against the oppression of its rulers, but to guard one part of the society against the injustice of the other part. Different interests necessarily exist in different classes of citizens. If a majority be united by a common interest, the rights of the minority will be insecure. There are but two methods of providing against this evil: the one by creating a will in the community independent of the majority, that is, of the society itself; the other by comprehending in the society so many separate descriptions of citizens as will render an unjust combination of a majority of the whole very improbable, if not impracticable.

The first method prevails in all governments possessing an hereditary or self-appointed authority. This, at best, is but a precarious security; because a power independent of the society may as well espouse the unjust views of the major as the rightful interests of the minor party, and may possibly be turned against both parties. The second method will be exemplified in the federal republic of the United States. Whilst all authority in it will be derived from and dependent on the society, the society itself will be broken into so many parts, interests and classes of citizens, that the rights of individuals, or of the minority, will be in little danger from interested combinations of the majority.

In a free government the security for civil rights must be the same as that for religious rights. It consists in the one case in the multiplicity of interests, and in the other in the multiplicity of sects. The degree of security in both cases will depend on the number of interests and sects; and this may be presumed to depend on the extent of country and number of people comprehended under the same government. This view of the subject must particularly recommend a proper federal system to all the sincere and considerate friends of republican government, since it shows that in exact proportion as the territory of the Union may be formed into more circumscribed confederacies, or States, oppressive combinations of a majority will be facilitated; the best security under republican forms, for the rights of every class of citizens, will be diminished; and, consequently, the stability and independence of some member of the government, the only other security, must be proportionally increased.

Justice is the end of government. It is the end of civil society. It ever has been and ever will be pursued until it be obtained, or until liberty be lost in the pursuit. In a society under the forms of which the stronger faction can readily unite and oppress the weaker, anarchy may as truly be said to reign as in a state of nature, where the weaker individual is not secured against the violence of the stronger; and as in the latter state even the stronger individuals are prompted by the uncertainty of their condition to submit to a government which may protect the weak as well as themselves; so, in the former state, will the more powerful factions or parties be gradually induced, by a like motive, to wish for a government which will protect all parties, the weaker as well as the more powerful.

It can be little doubted that if the State of Rhode Island was separated from the confederacy, and left to itself, the insecurity of rights under the popular form of government within such narrow limits would be displayed by such reiterated oppressions of factious majorities that some power altogether independent of the people would soon be called for by the voice of the very factions whose misrule had proved the necessity of it.

In the extended republic of the United States, and among the great variety of interests, parties, and sects which it embraces, a coalition of a majority of the whole society could seldom take place on any other principles than those of justice and the general good; whilst there being thus less danger to a minor from the will of a major party, there must be less pretext, also, to provide for the security of the former, by introducing into the government a will not dependent on the latter; or, in other words, a will independent of the society itself. It is no less certain than it is important, notwithstanding the contrary opinions which have been entertained, that the larger the society, provided it lie within a practical sphere, the more duly capable it will be of self-government. And happily for the *republican cause,* the practicable sphere may be carried to a very great extent, by a judicious modification and mixture of the *federal principle.*

PUBLIUS

Topic 6

MAJORITY RULE AND MINORITY RIGHTS

❧

In Defense of Majority Rule

HENRY STEELE COMMAGER *

It was in America that the doctrine of majority rule was first successfully
asserted and effectuated; it was in America that the principle of limited
government was first institutionalized and that machinery for maintaining
it was first fashioned.

These statements may require some elaboration. What we have here are
two fundamental—perhaps the two most fundamental—principles of American politics: the principle that men make government, and the principle
that there are limits to the authority of government. The philosophical
origins of the first principle may be found in the natural-rights philosophy
of the seventeenth century—in the notion that all rights inhered originally
in men and that men, living in a state of nature, came together for mutual
self-protection and set up government, and that the governments thus instituted derive all their just powers from the consent of the governed. . . .

The second great basic principle—that governments are limited, that
there are things no government may do, rights no government may impair,
powers no government may exercise—traces its philosophical origins deep
into the past but again derives authority from American experience with
Parliamentary and royal pretensions. It held, simply enough, that as government was instituted to secure certain rights, its jurisdiction was strictly
limited to the fields assigned to it, and that if it over-stepped the bounds
of its jurisdiction its acts were not law. In the great words of Samuel Adams,
addressed to Shelburne and Rockingham and Camden, "in all free states
the constitution is fixed; it is from thence that the legislative derives its
authority; therefore it cannot change the constitution without destroying its
own foundations." . . .

[The] generation [of the American Revolution], more conscious of the
dangers than of the potentialities of government, more concerned with pro-

* Professor of History at Amherst College. Author of *The American Mind*. Co-
author of *The Growth of the American Republic*, *The Heritage of America* and other
works. Contributor to many journals and periodicals. The selection is from Henry
Steele Commager, *Majority Rule and Minority Rights* (New York, Oxford University
Press, 1943), Chs. I and III. By permission of author and publisher.

tection against governmental tyranny than with the promotion of majority welfare, devised cunning mechanisms for putting limitations upon government. When we contemplate the ingenuity of the Fathers in setting up their system of checks and balances we are deeply impressed, almost dismayed. That the limits of governmental authority might not be misunderstood, that authority was described—for the first time—in written constitutions, and to these constitutions were added bills of rights. But this was merely elementary. There were, in addition, the checks and balances of the federal system, of the tripartite division of powers, of the bicameral legislatures, of frequent elections, and of impeachment. And atop all this there developed— I would not say there was established—the practice of judicial review.

But in their laudable zeal to give reality to John Dickinson's description of a free people—"Not those over whom government is reasonably and equitably exercised, but those who live under a government so constitutionally checked and controlled, that proper provision is made against its being otherwise exercised"—the framers of our constitutions confused, it would seem, jurisdiction with power, and the confusion has persisted down to our own day. They failed properly to distinguish between the authority government should have, and the manner in which government might exercise that authority which it did have. They set up limits on the jurisdiction of government, enumerating things no government could do; and this was eminently proper and in harmony with the philosophy of the Revolutionary era. But they went farther. So fearful were they of governmental tyranny that even where they granted to government certain necessary powers they put obstacles in the way of the effective exercise of those powers. They set up not only boundaries to government but impediments in government. Thus they not only made it difficult for government to invade fields denied to it, but they made it difficult for government to operate at all. They created a system where deadlock would be the normal character of the American government—a situation from which political parties rescued us.

So here we have two institutions which are—or would appear to be— fundamentally contradictory. We have first the institutionalization of the principle that men can alter, abolish, and institute governments, can, in short, make government conform to their will. But over against this we have the institutionalization of the principle that governments are limited— that there are things not even a majority may require government to do because they are outside the jurisdiction of any government. If the majority may use government to do its will, is that not an attack upon the inalienable rights of men over against government? if there are limits upon what governments may do, is that not a challenge to or even a denial of the principle of majority rule? Here is a paradox not yet resolved in our political philosophy or our constitutional system.

This paradox is presented in most familiar form in Jefferson's First Inaugural Address: "All, too, will bear in mind this sacred principle, that
though the will of the majority is in all cases to prevail, that will to be rightful must be reasonable; that the minority possess their equal rights which
equal law must protect, and to violate would be oppression." And throughout our history runs this theme of majority will and minority rights.
Jefferson, as we shall see, emphasized majority will, and so did Jefferson's
successors, Jackson and Lincoln—Jackson, who brushed aside judicial interposition, Lincoln, who reminded us that

> A majority . . . is the only true sovereign of a free people. Whoever
> rejects it does, of necessity, fly into anarchy or to despotism. Unanimity is
> impossible; the rule of a minority, as a permanent arrangement, is wholly
> inadmissible; so that, rejecting the majority principle, anarchy or despotism
> in some form is all that is left.

But the emphasis since the Civil War has been increasingly on minority
rights—an emphasis so marked, between Reconstruction and the New Deal,
that it is no great exaggeration to say that tenderness for the minority
became the distinguishing characteristic of the American constitutional system.

Underlying this distinction are, of course, the assumptions that majority
will and minority rights are antithetical, that majority rule constantly threatens minority rights, and that the principal function of our constitutional
system is to protect minority rights against infringement.

So plausible are these assumptions that there has developed, in course of
time, the theory of the "tyranny of the majority"—a theory which derived
much support abroad as well as here from the misleading observations of
Tocqueville. Tocqueville, who leaned heavily for material and authority on
that pillar of conservatism, Joseph Story, confessed that "the very essence
of democratic government consists in the absolute sovereignty of the majority," and concluded from this that the prospects for American democracy were bleak indeed. His analysis of the consequences that flow from
the tyranny of the majority has given comfort, ever since, to those who
fear democracy. So persuasive is this theory of the tyranny of the majority
that many Americans have come to believe that our constitutional system
is not, in fact, based upon the principle of majority rule. And they have
found support and consolation in the curious notion that ours is a "republican" form of government, and that a republic is the very opposite of
a democracy.

The fear of the tyranny of the majority has haunted many of the most
distinguished and respectable American statesmen and jurists since the
days of the founding of the Republic; it persists today, after a century and
a half of experience. It was first formulated, in elaborate and coherent
fashion, by John Adams in his famous *Defense of the Constitutions of*

Government of the United States of America (1786). The people, Adams urges, are not to be trusted, nor are their representatives, without an adequate system of checks and balances:

> If it is meant by the people . . . a representative assembly, . . . they are not the best keepers of the people's liberties or their own, if you give them all the power, legislative, executive and judicial. They would invade the liberties of the people, at least the majority of them would invade the liberties of the minority, sooner and oftener than any absolute monarch. . . .

[And in No. 51 of *The Federalist,* the warning was given that]

> It is of great importance in a republic not only to guard the society against the oppression of its rulers, but to guard one part of the society against the injustice of the other part. Different interests necessarily exist in different classes of citizens. If a majority be united by a common interest, the rights of the minority will be insecure. . . . Justice is the end of government. It is the end of civil society. . . . In a society under the forms of which the stronger faction can readily unite and oppress the weaker, anarchy may as truly be said to reign as in a state of nature where the weaker individual is not secured against the violence of the stronger. . . .

Confronted by these different interpretations of the American constitutional system, of democracy and of republicanism, we may turn with some confidence to Thomas Jefferson. On these questions he is, indubitably, our leading authority. He helped to create and to establish the new political systems in America, and he furnished them with a good part of their political philosophy. He never wrote a formal treatise on the subject (as did his old friend John Adams), but in his public papers and his private letters we can find the most comprehensive and consistent statement of the nature of American democracy that has come down to us from the generation of the founders.

And it must be observed, first, that Jefferson was by no means unaware of the dangers inherent in majority rule. . . . [To him] majority rule is neither anarchy nor absolutism, but government within self-imposed restraints. And we search in vain through the voluminous writings of Jefferson for any expression of distrust of the virtue or the wisdom of the people. What we do find, on the contrary, from the beginning to the end of Jefferson's career, is an unterrified and unflinching faith in majority rule.

"I am not among those who fear the people," he wrote to Kercheval in 1816; "they and not the rich, are our dependence for continued freedom." . . . Writing to Madison [he said], . . . "After all, it is my principle that the will of the majority should prevail." And to another Virginia friend, Colonel Carrington, went the same reassurance:

> I am persuaded myself that the good sense of the people will always be found to be the best army. They may be led astray for a moment, but will soon correct themselves. The people are the only censors of their governors; and even their errors will tend to keep these to the true principles of their institution.

That the people, if led astray, would "soon correct themselves" was a fixed conviction and one which, *mirabile dictu,* found confirmation in their tenacious support of his own administration. Thus to John Tyler in 1804:

> No experiment can be more interesting than that we are now trying, and which we trust will end in establishing the fact that man may be governed by reason and truth. . . . The firmness with which the people have withstood the late abuses of the press, the discernment that they have manifested between truth and falsehood, show that they may safely be trusted to hear everything true and false, and to form correct judgment between them. . . .

This was the consistent note—that the people may—and must—be trusted. "No government can continue good," he assured John Adams, "but under the control of the people"; and again, to that doughty opponent of judicial pretensions, Spencer Roane, "Independence can be trusted nowhere but with the people in the mass. They are inherently independent of all but the moral law." "I know of no safe depository of the ultimate powers of the society," he told William Jarvis, "but the people themselves; and if we think them not enlightened enough to exercise their control with a wholesome discretion, the remedy is not to take it from them, but to inform their discretion by education." And recalling Hume's argument that "all history and experience" confounded the notion that "the people are the origin of all just power," Jefferson burst out with uncharacteristic violence: "And where else will this degenerate son of science, this traitor to his fellow men, find the origin of just powers, if not in the majority of the society? Will it be in the minority? Or in an individual of that minority?" And we hear an echo of that question which the First Inaugural submits to the contemporary world: "Sometimes it is said that man can not be trusted with the government of himself. Can he, then, be trusted with the government of others? Or have we found angels in the forms of kings to govern him? Let history answer this question." For himself, Jefferson knew the answer. His devotion to the people was not that of the benevolent despot, the party boss, or the dictator, but of the good citizen, and his whole career is a monument to the sincerity of his confession to Du Pont de Nemours. "We both love the people," he said, "but you love them as infants, whom you are afraid to trust without nurses; and I as adults whom I freely leave to self-government."

To all of this many of Jefferson's contemporaries could have subscribed without reservation: he, assuredly, had no monopoly on faith in popular government. "We of the United States," as he explained simply, "are constitutionally and conscientiously democrats." But in one respect Jefferson went farther than most of his contemporaries, went so far, indeed, that his argument sounds bizarre and almost alien to our ears. That was his advocacy of what we may call the doctrine of the continuing majority. It was easy enough for most Americans to subscribe to the compact theory of government—the compact made, of course, by the original majority—

just as it is easy for us to subscribe, now, to the doctrine that we are, all of us, bound by the compact made at Philadelphia in 1787 and ratified by the majority of that time. And just as we have invested that Constitution with sacrosanctity, so—in England, in France, in America of the eighteenth century—there was a tendency to regard the original compact, the product of the Golden Age of the past, with reverence and to invest it with a peculiar sanctity. Such an attitude was foreign to Jefferson. His conviction, however, that each new majority must write its own fundamental law has sometimes been regarded as merely an amusing exaggeration, a whimsey to be indulged along with the whimsey that a little rebellion, now and then, is an excellent thing. But there can be no doubt of Jefferson's sincerity in the matter, nor of his persuasion that the issue was one of fundamental importance.

This problem is more fundamental, and more complex, than might appear at first glance—this problem of the original *versus* the continuing majority. All of us seem to agree that we are bound by the original majority—by the majority of 1787, or that which decreed our state constitutions. But what if the will of the present majority conflicts with that of the original majority? Is majority will valid only for some past generation? The easy answer is that the present majority can, if it chooses, change the original compact by constitutional amendment or by substituting an entirely new constitution. But it takes more than a majority to amend a constitution or to write a new one, and under our present system a determined minority can, if it will, effectively veto any change in the federal document and in most state documents. Not only this, but the courts have pretty consistently held that the current majority may not even interpret the original constitution to accommodate it to felt needs. . . .

Jefferson, as we know, entertained no reverence for the constitutional dogmas of the past. His attitude, set forth in the famous letter to Samuel Kercheval, of July 1816, is too familiar to justify quotation in full:

> Let us [not] weakly believe that one generation is not as capable as another of taking care of itself, and of ordering its own affairs. Let us . . . avail ourselves of our reason and experience, to correct the crude essays of our first and unexperienced, although wise, virtuous and well-meaning counsels. And lastly, let us provide in our Constitution for its revision at stated periods. What these periods should be, nature herself indicates. . . . Each generation is as independent of the one preceding, as that was of all which had gone before. It has, then, like them, a right to choose for itself the form of government it believes most promotive of its own happiness . . . and it is for the peace and good of mankind that a solemn opportunity of doing this every nineteen or twenty years should be provided by the Constitution. . . .

"The People," a distinguished contemporary statesman has said in a phrase already classic, "have no right to do wrong." It is at least suggestive that Eamon de Valera, who has fought pretty consistently for his people and who regards himself as a democrat, should have found it necessary to invoke the techniques of totalitarianism to prevent the people from "doing wrong." And it is a characteristic of almost every anti-democratic philosophy that it purports to serve the welfare of the people but refuses to trust the judgment of the people on questions affecting their welfare. . . .

Our constitutional system, as has already been observed, is one of checks and balances: these have already been noted. It is sometimes forgotten that our political system is one of checks and balances too. Anyone who has followed the slow and tortuous course of a major public issue—the poll tax, for example, or neutrality, through the arena of public opinion, into the party conventions and caucuses, into the halls of Congress and the rooms of appropriate committees, knows how much of delay, of balance, of compromise, is implicit in our political machinery. A good part of our politics, indeed, seems to be concerned with reconciling majority and minority will, class hostilities, sectional differences, the divergent interests of producer and consumer, of agriculture and labor, of creditor and debtor, of city and country, of tax-payer and tax-beneficiary, of the military and the civilian. In small issues as in great, the result is generally a compromise. Democracy, in short, whether from instinct or from necessity, furnishes its own checks and balances—quite aside from such as may be provided in written constitutions.

Indeed it might plausibly be argued that it is one of the major advantages of democracy over other forms of government that it alone can indulge in the luxury of tolerating minority and dissenting groups because it alone has developed the technique for dealing with them. It is sometimes charged as a criticism of democracy that it cannot act speedily and effectively in an emergency—as can totalitarian or despotic governments. The charge is not sound—as witness the efficiency of our own democracy in the spring of 1933 or the winter of 1941–2—but it is true that in a democracy it requires a real emergency to produce prompt and effective action.

But there is this to be said of the checks and balances of democratic politics—that they are natural, not artificial; that they are flexible rather than rigid; that they can yield to public opinion and to necessity. They do, sometimes, enable the majority to ride down the minority; they do, far more frequently, enable the minority to delay and defeat the majority. But the responsibility in all this is with the people themselves—where it belongs. Where they indulge their apathy, their carelessness, their blindness, they pay the price, and it is right that they should pay the price. As the fault is theirs, so, too, the remedy. Where issues appear sufficiently important the majority can have its way even against the recalcitrance of minorities who take refuge in the labyrinths of our party and our legislative systems. But against minorities entrenched in the judiciary there is no effective appeal except through the complicated and slow process of constitutional amendment. Here it is true today as it was in 1801 that the minority can "retire into the judiciary as a stronghold," and "from that battery" beat down the works of republicanism. . . .

This is the crucial objection to judicial nullification of majority will in any field: that "education in the abandonment of foolish legislation is itself a training in liberty." If our democracy is less educated in this respect than we might wish, if our legislatures are less alert to constitutional principles than might seem desirable, a heavy responsibility rests upon the courts. For these, by taking over to themselves the peculiar guardianship of the Constitution and of civil liberties, have discouraged the people's active and intelligent interest in these matters. Judges—and liberals—have ignored what Professor Chafee finely says, that "the victories of liberty of speech must be won in the mind before they are won in the courts." For in the long run only an educated and enlightened democracy can hope to endure. . . .

Our own experience, I believe, justifies Jefferson's faith that men need no masters—not even judges. It justifies us, too, in believing that majority will does not imperil minority rights, either in theory or in operation. It gives us firm basis for a belief that the people themselves can be trusted to realize that the majority has a vital interest in the preservation of an alert and critical minority and that, conversely, the minority can have no rights fundamentally inimical to the commonwealth. It justifies us in the belief that only in a democracy where there is free play of ideas, where issues are freely fought out in the public forum,—where, in short, the safety valves of public discussion and experimentation and reconsideration are always open— can there be assurance that both majority and minority rights will be served. It is the glory of democracy that it—and it alone—can tolerate dissent. It is the strength of democracy that dissent, where tolerated, is helpful rather than harmful.

The Tyranny of the Majority

ALEXIS DE TOCQUEVILLE *

I hold it to be an impious and an execrable maxim that, politically speaking, a people has a right to do whatsoever it pleases, and yet I have asserted that all authority originates in the will of the majority. Am I, then, in contradiction with myself? . . .

* Noted French statesman and critic. Author of *The Old Government and the Revolution* and other works on political and social subjects. The selection is from Alexis de Tocqueville, *Democracy in America* (Henry Reeve translation, 1835), Vol. I, Chs. XIII–XV.

A majority taken collectively may be regarded as a being whose opinions, and most frequently whose interests, are opposed to those of another being, which is styled a minority. If it be admitted that a man, possessing absolute power, may misuse that power by wronging his adversaries, why should a majority not be liable to the same reproach? Men are not apt to change their characters by agglomeration; nor does their patience in the presence of obstacles increase with the consciousness of their strength. And for these reasons I can never willingly invest any number of my fellow creatures with that unlimited authority which I should refuse to any one of them. . . .

I am of opinion that some one social power must always be made to predominate over the others; but I think that liberty is endangered when this power is checked by no obstacles which may retard its course, and force it to moderate its own vehemence.

Unlimited power is in itself a bad and dangerous thing; human beings are not competent to exercise it with discretion, and God alone can be omnipotent, because his wisdom and his justice are always equal to his power. But no power upon earth is so worthy of honor for itself, or of reverential obedience to the rights which it represents, that I would consent to admit its uncontrolled and all-predominant authority. When I see that the right and the means of absolute command are conferred on a people or upon a king, upon an aristocracy or a democracy, a monarchy or a republic, I recognize the germ of tyranny, and I journey onward to a land of more hopeful institutions.

In my opinion the main evil of the present democratic institutions of the United States does not arise, as is often asserted in Europe, from their weakness, but from their overpowering strength; and I am not so much alarmed at the excessive liberty which reigns in that country as at the very inadequate securities which exist against tyranny.

When an individual or a party is wronged in the United States, to whom can he apply for redress? If to public opinion, public opinion constitutes the majority; if to legislature, it represents the majority, and implicitly obeys its injunctions; if to the executive power, it is appointed by the majority, and remains a passive tool in its hands; the public troops consist of the majority under arms; the jury is the majority invested with the right of hearing judicial cases; and in certain States even the judges are elected by the majority. However iniquitous or absurd the evil of which you complain may be, you must submit to it as well as you can. . . .

I do not say that tyrannical abuses frequently occur in America at the present day, but I maintain that no sure barrier is established against them, and that the causes which mitigate the government are to be found in the circumstances and the manners of the country more than in its laws. . . .

In America, the majority raises very formidable barriers to the liberty of opinion: within these barriers an author may write whatever he pleases, but he will repent it if he ever step beyond them. Not that he is exposed to the terrors of an *auto-da-fé,* but he is tormented by the slights and persecutions of daily obloquy. His political career is closed forever, since he has offended the only authority which is able to promote his success. . . .

Monarchical institutions have thrown an odium upon despotism; let us beware lest democratic republics should restore oppression, and should render it less odious and less degrading in the eyes of the many, by making it still more onerous to the few.

The Constitution: "Road or Gate"?

MARBURY v. MADISON established the power of the Supreme Court to declare Acts of Congress unconstitutional and unenforceable. The Constitution explicitly provided for the exercise of similar power by the Court with respect to state legislation. Thus the limits of both federal and state power have been determined, in the final analysis, by the Supreme Court except in those rare instances where the Constitution has been changed by amendment. That the Court has enjoyed considerable discretion in defining those limits is illustrated by the cases in this section.

McCulloch v. Maryland, in which Chief Justice Marshall gave elastic scope to Congressional power generally under the Constitution, is not merely of historic interest but proved of great importance in helping to sustain much of the New Deal legislation and continues as the foundation of broad federal authority.

On the other hand, the Schechter case, in which the Supreme Court unanimously invalidated the National Industrial Recovery Act, reflects a restricted view of delegated congressional power. This was one of several blows to New Deal legislation which led President Roosevelt in 1937 to seek to reorganize the Supreme Court. Wickard v. Filburn, decided in the decade of the 40's, is representative of sweeping extensions of federal power over the economy upheld by the Court in its greatly expanded view of Congressional prerogative under the Constitution.

[For further discussion, see "Judicial Review Evaluated."]

Topic 7

FOUNDATION OF JUDICIAL REVIEW

The Judicial Power

MARBURY *V*. MADISON

1 Cranch 137 (1803)

[On March 2, 1801, two days before the close of his term, President John Adams appointed William Marbury, among others, as a justice of the peace in the District of Columbia. Through some inadvertence the commission was left on the desk of the Secretary of State when President Adams' term expired at midnight, March 3rd. Upon Thomas Jefferson's accession to the presidency, he directed his Secretary of State, James Madison, to refuse delivery of the commission. Marbury applied to the Supreme Court, sitting as a court of original jurisdiction, for a writ of mandamus to compel delivery of the commission. This specific writ was sought under section 13 of the Judiciary Act of 1789.]

The following opinion of the court was delivered by the CHIEF JUSTICE [Marshall]. . . .

The first object of inquiry is, 1st. Has the applicant a right to the commission he demands? . . . Mr. Marbury, then, since his commission was signed by the President and sealed by the Secretary of State, was appointed; and as the law creating the office gave the officer a right to hold for five years, independent of the executive, the appointment was not revocable, but vested in the officer legal rights, which are protected by the laws of his country. To withhold his commission, therefore, is an act deemed by the court not warranted by law, but violative of a vested legal right.

This brings us to the second inquiry, which is, 2d. If he has a right, and that right has been violated, do the laws of his country afford him a remedy? . . .

It is then the opinion of the court,

1st. That by signing the commission of Mr. Marbury, the President of the United States appointed him a justice of peace for the county of Washington, in the District of Columbia; and that the seal of the United States, affixed thereto by the Secretary of State, is conclusive testimony of the verity of the signature, and of the completion of the appointment; and that the appointment conferred on him a legal right to the office for the space of five years.

2dly. That, having this legal title to the office, he has a consequent right to the commission; a refusal to deliver which is a plain violation of that right, for which the laws of his country afford him a remedy.

It remains to be inquired whether, 3dly. He is entitled to the remedy for which he applies. This depends on,

1st. The nature of the writ applied for; and, 2dly. The power of this court.

[As to the 1st, in light of the facts, this was held to be] a plain case for a mandamus, either to deliver the commission, or a copy of it from the record; and it only remains to be inquired, whether it can issue from this court.

[The Court then decided that the portion of Section 13 of the Judiciary Act of 1789 which provided that "The Supreme Court . . . shall have power to issue . . . writs of mandamus in cases warranted by the principles and usages of law, to any persons holding office, under the authority of the United States," was in conflict with the constitution as an attempt to enlarge the original jurisdiction of the Supreme Court beyond that provided by Article III, Section 2 of the Constitution of the United States which reads in part as follows: "In all cases affecting ambassadors, other public ministers and consuls, and those in which a State shall be Party, the Supreme Court shall have *original jurisdiction.*"]

[Chief Justice Marshall continued:] The question, whether an act, repugnant to the constitution, can become the law of the land, is a question deeply interesting to the United States; but, happily, not of an intricacy proportioned to its interest. It seems only necessary to recognize certain principles, supposed to have been long and well established, to decide it. That the people have an original right to establish, for their future government, such principles as, in their opinion shall most conduce to their own happiness, is the basis on which the whole American fabric has been erected. The exercise of this original right is a very great exertion; nor can it, nor ought it, to be frequently repeated. The principles, therefore, so established, are deemed fundamental; and as the authority from which they proceed is supreme, and can seldom act, they are designed to be permanent.

This original and supreme will organizes the government, and assigns to different departments their respective powers. It may either stop here, or establish certain limits not to be transcended by those departments. The government of the United States is of the latter description. The powers of the legislature are defined and limited; and that those limits may not be mistaken, or forgotten, the constitution is written. To what purpose are powers limited, and to what purpose is that limitation committed to writing, if these limits may, at any time, be passed by those intended to be restrained? The distinction between a government with limited and unlimited powers is abolished, if those limits do not confine the persons on whom they are imposed, and if acts prohibited and acts allowed, are of equal obligation. It is a proposition too plain to be contested, that the constitution controls any legislative act repugnant to it; or that the legislature may alter the constitution by an ordinary act.

Between these alternatives, there is no middle ground. The constitution is either a superior paramount law, unchangeable by ordinary means, or it is on a level with ordinary legislative acts, and, like other acts, is alterable when the legislature shall please to alter it. If the former part of the alternative be true, then a legislative act, contrary to the constitution, is not law; if the latter part be true, then written constitutions are absurd attempts, on the part of the people, to limit a power, in its own nature, illimitable.

Certainly, all those who have framed written constitutions contemplate them as forming the fundamental and paramount law of the nation, and consequently, the theory of every such government must be, that an act of the legislature, repugnant to the constitution, is void. This theory is essentially attached to a written constitution, and is, consequently, to be considered, by this court, as one of the fundamental principles of our society. It is not, therefore, to be lost sight of, in the further consideration of this subject.

If an act of the legislature, repugnant to the constitution, is void, does it, notwithstanding its invalidity, bind the courts, and oblige them to give it effect? Or, in other words, though it be not law, does it constitute a rule as operative as if it was a law? This would be to overthrow, in fact, what was established in theory; and would seem, at first view, an absurdity too gross to be insisted on. It shall, however, receive a more attentive consideration.

It is, emphatically, the province and duty of the judicial department, to say what the law is. Those who apply the rule to particular cases, must of necessity expound and interpret that rule. If two laws conflict with each other, the courts must decide on the operation of each. So, if a law be in opposition to the constitution; if both the law and the constitution apply to a particular case, so that the court must either decide that case, conformably to the law, disregarding the constitution; or conformably to the constitution, disregarding the law; the court must determine which of these conflicting rules governs the case; this is of the very essence of judicial duty. If then, the courts are to regard the constitution, and the constitution is superior to any ordinary act of the legislature, the constitution, and not such ordinary act, must govern the case to which they both apply.

Those, then, who controvert the principle, that the constitution is to be considered, in court, as a paramount law, are reduced to the necessity of maintaining that courts must close their eyes on the constitution, and see only the law. This doctrine would subvert the very foundation of all written constitutions. It would declare that an act which, according to the principles and theory of our government, is entirely void, is yet, in practice, completely obligatory. It would declare, that if the legislature shall do what is expressly forbidden, such act, notwithstanding the express prohibition, is in reality effectual. It would be giving to the legislature a practical and real omnipotence, with the same breath which professes to restrict their powers within narrow limits. It is prescribing limits, and declaring that those limits may be passed at pleasure. That it thus reduces to nothing, what we have deemed the greatest improvement on political institutions, a written constitution, would of itself, be sufficient, in America, where written constitutions have been viewed with so much reverence, for rejecting the construction.

But the peculiar expressions of the constitution of the United States furnish additional arguments in favor of its rejection. The judicial power of the United States is extended to all cases arising under the constitution. Could it be the intention of those who gave this power, to say, that in using it, the constitution should not be looked into? That a case arising under the constitution should be decided, without examining the instrument under which it arises? This is too extravagant to be maintained. In some cases, then, the constitution must be looked into by the judges. And if they can open it at all, what part of it are they forbidden to read or to obey?

There are many other parts of the constitution which serve to illustrate this subject. It is declared, that "no tax or duty shall be laid on articles exported from any state." Suppose, a duty on the export of cotton, of tobacco, or of flour; and a suit instituted to recover it. Ought judgment to be rendered in such a case? ought the judges to close their eyes on the constitution, and only see the law?

The constitution declares "that no bill of attainder or *ex post facto* law shall be passed." If, however, such a bill should be passed, and a person should be prosecuted under it; must the court condemn to death those victims whom the constitution endeavors to preserve?

"No person," says the constitution, "shall be convicted of treason, unless on the testimony of two witnesses to the same overt act, or on confession in open court." Here, the language of the constitution is addressed especially to the courts. It prescribes, directly for them, a rule of evidence not to be departed from. If the legislature should change that rule, and declare one witness, or a confession out of court, sufficient for conviction, must the constitutional principle yield to the legislative act?

From these, and many other selections which might be made, it is apparent, that the framers of the constitution contemplated that instrument as a rule for the government of courts, as well as of the legislature. Why otherwise does it direct the judges to take an oath to support it? This oath certainly applies in an especial manner, to their conduct in their official character. How immoral to impose it on them, if they were to be used as the instruments, and the knowing instruments, for violating what they swear to support!

The oath of office, too, imposed by the legislature, is completely demonstrative of the legislative opinion on this subject. It is in these words: "I do solemnly swear, that I will administer justice, without respect to persons, and do equal right to the poor and to the rich; and that I will faithfully and impartially discharge all the duties incumbent on me as ――, according to the best of my abilities and understanding, agreeably to the constitution and laws of the United States." Why does a judge swear to discharge his duties agreeably to the constitution of the United States, if that constitution forms no rule for his government? if it is closed upon him, and cannot be inspected by him? If such be the real state of things, this is worse than solemn mockery. To prescribe, or to take this oath, becomes equally a crime.

It is also not entirely unworthy of observation, that in declaring what shall be the supreme law of the land, the constitution itself is first mentioned; and not the laws of the United States, generally, but those only which shall be made in pursuance of the constitution, have that rank.

Thus, the particular phraseology of the constitution of the United States confirms and strengthens the principle, supposed to be essential to all written constitutions, that a law repugnant to the constitution is void; and that courts, as well as other departments, are bound by that instrument.

The rule must be discharged.

Critique of Marbury v. Madison

EAKIN *v.* RAUB

12 Sergeant and Rawle (Pennsylvania Supreme Court) 330 (1825).

GIBSON, J. (dissenting) . . .

I am aware, that a [judicial] right to declare all unconstitutional acts void . . . is generally held as a professional dogma; but, I apprehend, rather as a matter of faith than of reason. I admit that I once embraced the same doctrine, but without examination, and I shall therefore state the arguments that impelled me to abandon it, with great respect for those by whom it is still maintained. But I may premise, that it is not a little remarkable, that although the right in question has all along been claimed by the judiciary, no judge has ventured to discuss it, except Chief Justice Marshall (in Marbury *v.* Madison, 1 Cranch, 176), and if the argument of a jurist so distinguished for the strength of his ratiocinative powers be found inconclusive, it may fairly be set down to the weakness of the position which he attempts to defend. . . .

The Constitution and the right of the legislature to pass the act, may be in collision. But is that a legitimate subject for judicial determination? If it be, the judiciary must be a peculiar organ, to revise the proceedings of the legislature, and to correct its mistakes; and in what part of the Constitution are we to look for this proud pre-eminence? Viewing the matter in the opposite direction, what would be thought of an act of assembly in which it should be declared that the Supreme Court had, in a particular case, put a wrong construction on the Constitution of the United States, and that the judgment should therefore be reversed? It would doubtless be thought a usurpation of judicial power. But it is by no means clear, that to declare a law void which has been enacted according to the forms prescribed in the Constitution, is not a usurpation of legislative power. It is an act of sovereignty; and sovereignty and legislative power are said by Sir William Blackstone to be convertible terms. It is the business of the judiciary to interpret the laws, not scan the authority of the lawgiver; and without the latter, it cannot take cognizance of a collision between a law and the Constitution. So that to affirm that the judiciary has a right to judge of the existence of such collision, is to take for granted the very thing to be proved. And, that a very cogent argument may be made in this way, I am not disposed to deny; for no conclusions are so strong as those that are drawn from the *petitio principii.*

But it has been said to be emphatically the business of the judiciary, to ascertain and pronounce what the law is; and that this necessarily involves a consideration of the Constitution. It does so: but how far? If the judiciary will inquire into anything besides the form of enactment, where shall it stop? There must be some point of limitation to such an inquiry; for no one will pretend that a judge would be justifiable in calling for the election returns, or scrutinizing the qualifications of those who composed the legislature. . . .

In theory, all the organs of the government are of equal capacity; or, if not equal, each must be supposed to have superior capacity only for those things which peculiarly belong to it; and, as legislation peculiarly involves the consideration of those limitations which are put on the law-making power, and the interpretation of the laws when made, involves only the construction of the laws themselves, it follows that the construction of the constitution in this particular belongs to the legislature, which ought therefore to be taken to have superior capacity to judge of the constitutionality of its own acts. But suppose all to be of equal capacity in every respect, why should one exercise a controlling power over the rest? That the judiciary is of superior rank, has never been pretended, although it has been said to be co-ordinate. It is not easy, however, to comprehend how the power which gives law to all the rest, can be of no more than equal rank with one which receives it, and is answerable to the former for the observance of its statutes. . . .

Everyone knows how seldom men think exactly alike on ordinary subjects; and a government constructed on the principle of assent by all its parts, would be inadequate to the most simple operations. The notion of a complication of counter checks has been carried to an extent in theory, of which the framers of the Constitution never dreamt. When the entire sovereignty was separated into its elementary parts, and distributed to the appropriate branches, all things incident to the exercise of its powers were committed to each branch exclusively. The negative which each part of the legislature may exercise, in regard to the acts of the other, was thought sufficient to prevent material infractions of the restraints which were put on the power of the whole; for, had it been intended to interpose the judiciary as an additional barrier, the matter would surely not have been left in doubt. The judges would not have been left to stand on the insecure and ever shifting ground of public opinion as to constructive powers; they would have been placed on the impregnable ground of an express grant. . . .

But the judges are sworn to support the Constitution, and are they not bound by it as the law of the land? In some respects they are. In the very few cases in which the judiciary, and not the legislature, is the immediate organ to execute its provisions, they are bound by it in preference to any act of assembly to the contrary. In such cases, the Constitution is a rule to the courts. But what I have in view in this inquiry, is the supposed right of the judiciary to interfere, in cases where the Constitution is to be carried into effect through the instrumentality of the legislature, and where that organ must necessarily first decide on the constitutionality of its own act.

The oath to support the Constitution is not peculiar to the judges, but is taken indiscriminately by every officer of the government, and is designed rather as a test of the political principles of the man, than to bind the officer in the discharge of his duty: otherwise it were difficult to determine what operation it is to have in the case of a recorder of deeds, for instance, who, in the execution of his office, has nothing to do with the Constitution. But granting it to relate to the official conduct of the judge, as well as every other officer, and not to his political principles, still it must be understood in reference to supporting the Constitution, only as far as that may be involved in his official duty; and, consequently, if his official duty does not comprehend an inquiry into the authority of the legislature, neither does his oath.

It is worthy of remark here, that the foundation of every argument in favor of the right of the judiciary, is found at last to be an assumption of the whole ground in dispute. Granting that the object of the oath is to secure a support of the Constitution in the discharge of official duty, its terms may be satisfied by restraining it to official duty in the exercise of the ordinary judicial powers. Thus, the Constitution may furnish a rule of construction,

where a particular interpretation of a law would conflict with some constitutional principle; and such interpretation, where it may, is always to be
avoided. But the oath was more probably designed to secure the powers of
each of the different branches from being usurped by any of the rest: for
instance, to prevent the House of Representatives from erecting itself into
a court of judicature, or the Supreme Court from attempting to control the
legislature; and, in this view, the oath furnishes an argument equally plausible against the right of the judiciary. But if it require a support of the Constitution in anything beside official duty, it is in fact an oath of allegiance to
a particular form of government; and, considered as such, it is not easy to
see why it should not be taken by the citizens at large, as well as by the
officers of the government. It has never been thought that an officer is under
greater restraint as to measures which have for their avowed end a total
change of the Constitution, than a citizen who has taken no oath at all. The
official oath, then, relates only to the official conduct of the officer, and
does not prove that he ought to stray from the path of his ordinary business
to search for violations of duty in the business of others; nor does it, as
supposed, define the powers of the officer.

But do not the judges do a positive act in violation of the Constitution,
when they give effect to an unconstitutional law? Not if the law has been
passed according to the forms established in the Constitution. The fallacy
of the question is, in supposing that the judiciary adopts the acts of the
legislature as its own; whereas the enactment of a law and the interpretation of it are not concurrent acts, and as the judiciary is not required to
concur in the enactment, neither is it in the breach of the Constitution
which may be the consequence of the enactment. The fault is imputable to
the legislature, and on it the responsibility exclusively rests. . . .

For these reasons, I am of opinion that it rests [ultimately] with the
people, in whom full and absolute sovereign power resides, to correct abuses
in legislation, by instructing their representatives to repeal the obnoxious
act. What is wanting to plenary power in the government, is reserved by
the people for their own immediate use; and to redress an infringement of
their rights in this respect, would seem to be an accessory of the power thus
reserved. It might, perhaps, have been better to vest the power in the
judiciary; as it might be expected that its habits of deliberation, and the
aid derived from the arguments of counsel, would more frequently lead to
accurate conclusions. On the other hand, the judiciary is not infallible; and
an error by it would admit of no remedy but a more distinct expression of
the public will, through the extraordinary medium of a convention; whereas,
an error by the legislature admits of a remedy by an exertion of the same
will, in the ordinary exercise of the right of suffrage,—a mode better calculated to attain the end, without popular excitement.

Topic 8

THE BASES OF NATIONAL POWER

"It Is a Constitution We Are Expounding"

McCULLOCH *v.* MARYLAND

4 Wheaton 316 (1819)

Error to the Court of Appeals of the State of Maryland.

[Congress in 1816 passed an act to incorporate the Bank of the United States, and in the following year the bank established a branch in Baltimore. In 1818 the state of Maryland required all banks not chartered by the state to pay an annual tax of $15,000 or to pay a stamp tax on each bank note issued. McCulloch, the cashier of the Baltimore branch of the Bank of the United States, issued bank notes in violation of the state law whereupon the state of Maryland brought suit against him. The state courts decided in favour of Maryland. McCulloch appealed the case to the United States Supreme Court on a writ of error.]

MARSHALL, Chief Justice, delivered the opinion of the court. . . .

The first question made in the cause is, has congress power to incorporate a bank? . . . The power now contested was exercised by the first congress elected under the present constitution. The bill for incorporating the Bank of the United States did not steal upon an unsuspecting legislature, and pass unobserved. Its principle was completely understood, and was opposed with equal zeal and ability. After being resisted, first in the fair and open field of debate, and afterwards in the executive cabinet, with as much persevering talent as any measure has ever experienced, and being supported by arguments which convinced minds as pure and as intelligent as this country can boast, it became a law.

The original act was permitted to expire; but a short experience of the embarrassments to which the refusal to revive it exposed the government, convinced those who were most prejudiced against the measure of its necessity, and induced the passage of the present law. It would require no ordinary share of intrepidity to assert, that a measure adopted under these circumstances, was a bold and plain usurpation, to which the constitution gave no countenance. These observations belong to the cause: but they are not made under the impression that, were the question entirely new, the law would be found irreconcilable with the constitution.

87

In discussing this question, the counsel for the state of Maryland have deemed it of some importance, in the construction of the constitution, to consider that instrument not as emanating from the people, but as the act of sovereign and independent states. The powers of the general government, it has been said, are delegated by the states, who alone are truly sovereign; and must be exercised in subordination to the states, who alone possess supreme dominion. It would be difficult to sustain this proposition.

The convention which framed the constitution was, indeed, elected by the state legislatures. But the instrument, when it came from their hands, was a mere proposal, without obligation, or pretensions to it. It was reported to the then existing congress of the United States, with a request that it might "be submitted to a convention of delegates, chosen in each state by the people thereof, under the recommendation of its legislature, for their assent and ratification." This mode of proceeding was adopted; and by the convention, by congress, and by the state legislatures, the instrument was submitted to the *people*. They acted upon it, in the only manner in which they can act safely, effectively, and wisely, on such a subject, by assembling in convention. . . . From these conventions, the constitution derives its whole authority. The government proceeds directly from the people; is "ordained and established" in the name of the people; and is declared to be ordained, "in order to form a more perfect union, establish justice, insure domestic tranquility, and secure the blessings of liberty to themselves and to their posterity." . . . The government of the Union, then, is emphatically and truly, a government of the people. In form, and in substance, it emanates from them. Its powers are granted by them, and are to be exercised directly on them, and for their benefit.

This government is acknowledged by all, to be one of enumerated powers. The principle, that it can exercise only the powers granted to it, would seem too apparent, to have required to be enforced by all those arguments, which its enlightened friends, while it was depending before the people, found it necessary to urge; that principle is now universally admitted. But the question respecting the extent of the powers actually granted, is perpetually arising, and will probably continue to arise, as long as our system shall exist. In discussing these questions, the conflicting powers of the general and state governments must be brought into view, and the supremacy of their respective laws, when they are in opposition, must be settled.

If any one proposition could command the universal assent of mankind, we might expect that it would be this—that the government of the Union, though limited in its powers, is supreme within its sphere of action. This would seem to result, necessarily, from its nature. It is the government of all; its powers are delegated by all; it represents all, and acts for all. Though any one state may be willing to control its operations, no state is willing to allow others to control them. The nation, on those subjects on which it can act, must necessarily bind its component parts. But this question is not left to mere reason: the people have, in express terms, decided it, by saying, "this constitution, and the laws of the United States, which shall be made in pursuance thereof," "shall be the supreme law of the land," and by requiring that the members of the state legislatures, and the officers of the executive and judicial departments of the state, shall take the oath of fidelity to it. The government of the United States, then, though limited in its powers, is supreme; and its laws, when made in pursuance of the constitution, form the supreme law of the land, "anything in the constitution or laws of any state, to the contrary notwithstanding."

Among the enumerated powers, we do not find that of establishing a bank or creating a corporation. But there is no phrase in the instrument which, like the articles of confederation, excludes incidental or implied powers; and which requires that everything granted shall be expressly and minutely described. Even the 10th amendment, which was framed for the purpose of quieting the excessive jealousies which had been excited, omits the word "expressly," and declares only that the powers "not delegated to the United States, nor prohibited to the states, are reserved to the states or to the people"; thus leaving the question, whether the particular power which may become the subject of contest, has been delegated to the one government, or prohibited to the other, to depend on a fair construction of the whole instrument.

The men who drew and adopted this amendment had experienced the embarrassments resulting from the insertion of this word in the articles of confederation, and probably omitted it, to avoid those embarrassments. A constitution, to contain an accurate detail of all the subdivisions of which its great powers will admit, and of all the means by which they may be carried into execution, would partake of the prolixity of a legal code, and could scarcely be embraced by the human mind. It would, probably, never be understood by the public. Its nature, therefore, requires, that only its great outlines should be marked, its important objects designated, and the minor ingredients which compose those objects, be deduced from the nature of the objects themselves. That this idea was entertained by the framers of the American constitution, is not only to be inferred from the nature of the instrument, but from the language. Why else were some of the limitations, found in the 9th section of the 1st article, introduced? It is also, in some degree, warranted, by their having omitted to use any restrictive term which might prevent its receiving a fair and just interpretation. In considering this question, then, we must never forget, that it is a *constitution* we are expounding.

Although, among the enumerated powers of government, we do not find the word "bank," or "incorporation," we find the great powers, to lay and collect taxes; to borrow money; to regulate commerce; to declare and conduct war; and to raise and support armies and navies. . . . A government, intrusted with such ample powers, on the due execution of which the happiness and prosperity of the nation so vitally depends, must also be intrusted with ample means for their execution. The power being given, it is the interest of the nation to facilitate its execution. It can never be their interest, and cannot be presumed to have been their intention, to clog and embarrass its execution, by withholding the most appropriate means.

Throughout this vast republic, from the St. Croix to the Gulf of Mexico, from the Atlantic to the Pacific, revenue is to be collected and expended, armies are to be marched and supported. The exigencies of the nation may require, that the treasure raised in the north should be transported to the south, that raised in the east, conveyed to the west, or that this order should be reversed. Is that construction of the constitution to be preferred, which would render these operations difficult, hazardous, and expensive? Can we adopt that construction (unless the words imperiously require it), which would impute to the framers of that instrument, when granting these powers for the public good, the intention of impeding their exercise by withholding a choice of means? If, indeed, such be the mandate of the constitution, we have only to obey; but that instrument does not profess to enumerate the means by which the powers it confers may be executed; nor does it prohibit the creation of a corporation, if the existence of such a being be essential, to the beneficial exercise of those powers. It is, then, the subject of fair inquiry, how far such means may be employed.

It is not denied, that the powers given to the government imply the ordinary means of execution. That, for example, of raising revenue, and applying it to national purposes, is admitted to imply the power of conveying money from place to place, as the exigencies of the nation may require, and of employing the usual means of conveyance. But it is denied, that the government has its choice of means, or, that it may employ the most convenient means, if, to employ them, it be necessary to erect a corporation. . . . The government which has a right to do an act, and has imposed on it the duty of performing that act, must, according to the dictates of reason, be allowed to select the means; and those who contend that it may not select any appropriate means, that one particular mode of effecting the object is excepted, take upon themselves the burden of establishing that exception. . . .

But the constitution of the United States has not left the right of congress to employ the necessary means, for the execution of the powers conferred on the government, to general reasoning. To its enumeration of powers is added, that of making "all laws which shall be necessary and proper, for carrying into execution the foregoing powers, and all other powers vested by this constitution, in the government of the United States, or in any department thereof." . . .

The argument on which most reliance is placed, is drawn from the peculiar language of this clause. Congress is not empowered by it to make all laws, which may have relation to the powers conferred on the government, but only such as may be "necessary and proper" for carrying them into execution. The word "necessary" is considered as controlling the whole sentence, and as limiting the right to pass laws for the execution of the granted powers, to such as are indispensable, and without which the power would be nugatory. That it excludes the choice of means, and leaves to congress, in each case, that only which is most direct and simple.

Is it true, that this is the sense in which the word "necessary" is always used? Does it always import an absolute physical necessity, so strong, that one thing, to which another may be termed necessary, cannot exist without that other? We think it does not. If reference be had to its use, in the common affairs of the world, or in approved authors, we find that it frequently imports no more than that one thing is convenient, or useful, or essential to another. . . . A thing may be necessary, very necessary, absolutely or indispensably necessary. To no mind would the same idea be conveyed by these several phrases. This comment on the word is well illustrated by the passage cited at the bar, from the 10th section of the 1st article of the constitution. It is, we think, impossible to compare the sentence which prohibits a State from laying "imposts, or duties on imports or exports, except what may be absolutely necessary for executing its inspection laws," with that which authorizes congress "to make all laws which shall be necessary and proper for carrying into execution" the powers of the general government, without feeling a conviction, that the convention understood itself to change materially the meaning of the word "necessary" by prefixing the word "absolutely." This word, then, like others, is used in various senses; and, in its construction, the subject, the context, the intention of the person using them, are all to be taken into view.

Let this be done in the case under consideration. The subject is the execution of those great powers on which the welfare of a nation essentially depends. It must have been the intention of those who gave these powers, to insure, as far as human prudence could insure, their beneficial execution. This could not be done, by confining the choice of means to such narrow limits as not to leave it in the power of congress to adopt any which might be appropriate, and which were conducive to the end. This provision is made in a constitution, intended to endure for ages to come, and consequently, to be adapted to the various crises of human affairs. To have prescribed the means by which government should, in all future time, execute its powers, would have been to change, entirely, the character of the instrument, and give it the properties of a legal code. It would have been an unwise attempt to provide, by immutable rules, for exigencies which, if foreseen at all, must have been seen dimly, and which can be best provided for as they occur. To have declared, that the best means shall not be used, but those alone, without which the power given would be nugatory, would have been to deprive the legislature of the capacity to avail itself of experience, to exercise its reason, and to accommodate its legislation to circumstances. If we apply this principle of construction to any of the powers of the government, we shall find it so pernicious in its operation that we shall be compelled to discard it. [The Court here cites the law requiring an oath of office in addition to the oath prescribed by the Constitution.]

So, with respect to the whole penal code of the United States whence arises the power to punish, in cases not prescribed by the constitution? All admit, that the government may, legitimately, punish any violation of its laws; and yet, this is not among the enumerated powers of congress. . . .

If this limited construction of the word "necessary" must be abandoned, in order to punish, whence is derived the rule which would reinstate it, when the government would carry its powers into execution, by means not vindictive in their nature? If the word "necessary" means "needful," "requisite," "essential," "conducive to," in order to let in the power of punishment for the infraction of law; why is it not equally comprehensive, when required to authorize the use of means which facilitate the execution of the powers of government, without the infliction of punishment? . . .

We admit, as all must admit, that the powers of the government are limited, and that its limits are not to be transcended. But we think the sound construction of the constitution must allow to the national legislature that discretion, with respect to the means by which the powers it confers are to be carried into execution, which will enable that body to perform the high duties assigned to it, in the manner most beneficial to the people. Let the end be legitimate, let it be within the scope of the constitution, and all means which are appropriate, which are plainly adapted to that end, which are not prohibited, but consist[ent] with the letter and spirit of the constitution, are constitutional.

That a corporation must be considered as a means not less usual, not of higher dignity, not more requiring a particular specification than other means, has been sufficiently proved. . . . If a corporation may be employed, indiscriminately with other means, to carry into execution the powers of the government, no particular reason can be assigned for excluding the use of a bank, if required for its fiscal operations. To use one, must be within the discretion of congress, if it be an appropriate mode of executing the powers of government. That it is a convenient, a useful, and essential instrument in the prosecution of its fiscal operations, is not now a subject of controversy. . . .

After the most deliberate consideration, it is the unanimous and decided opinion of this court, that the act to incorporate the Bank of the United States is a law made in pursuance of the constitution, and is a part of the supreme law of the land.

The branches, proceeding from the same stock, and being conducive to the complete accomplishment of the object, are equally constitutional. . . .

It being the opinion of the court that the act incorporating the bank is constitutional, and that the power of establishing a branch in the state of Maryland might be properly exercised by the bank itself, we proceed to inquire:

2. Whether the State of Maryland may, without violating the constitution, tax that branch?

That the power of taxation is one of vital importance; that it is retained by the States; that it is not abridged by the grant of a similar power to the government of the Union; that it is to be concurrently exercised by the two governments: are truths which have never been denied. But, such is the paramount character of the constitution that its capacity to withdraw any subject from the action of even this power, is admitted. The States are expressly forbidden to lay any duties on imports or exports, except what may be absolutely necessary for executing their inspection laws. If the obligation of this prohibition must be conceded—if it may restrain a State from the exercise of its taxing power on imports and exports; the same paramount character would seem to restrain, as it certainly may restrain, a State from such other exercise of this power, as is in its nature incompatible with, and repugnant to, the constitutional laws of the Union. A law, absolutely repugnant to another, as entirely repeals that other as if express terms of repeal were used. . . .

This great principle is, that the constitution and the laws made in pursuance thereof are supreme; that they control the constitution and laws of the respective States, and cannot be controlled by them. From this, which may be almost termed an axiom, other propositions are deduced as corollaries, on the truth or error of which, and on their application to this case, the cause has been supposed to depend. These are, 1st. That a power to create implies a power to preserve. 2d. That a power to destroy, if wielded by a different hand, is hostile to, and incompatible with these powers to create and to preserve. 3d. That where this repugnancy exists, that authority which is supreme must control, not yield to that over which it is supreme. . . .

The sovereignty of a State extends to everything which exists by its own authority, or is introduced by its permission; but does it extend to those means which are employed by Congress to carry into execution powers conferred on that body by the people of the United States? We think it demonstrable that it does not. Those powers are not given by the people of a single State. They are given by the people of the United States, to a government whose laws, made in pursuance of the constitution, are declared to be supreme. Consequently, the people of a single State cannot confer a sovereignty which will extend over them.

If we measure the power of taxation residing in a State, by the extent of sovereignty which the people of a single State possess, and can confer on its government, we have an intelligible standard, applicable to every case to which the power may be applied. We have a principle which leaves the power of taxing the people and property of a state unimpaired; which leaves to a State the command of all its resources, and which places beyond its reach, all those powers which are conferred by the people of the United States on the government of the Union, and all those means which are given for the purpose of carrying those powers into execution. We have a principle which is safe for the States, and safe for the Union. We are relieved, as we ought to be, from clashing sovereignty; from interfering powers; from a repugnancy between a right in one government to pull down what there is an acknowledged right in another to build up; from the incompatibility of a right in one government to destroy what there is a right in another to preserve. We are not driven to the perplexing inquiry, so unfit for the judicial department, what degree of taxation is the legitimate use, and what degree may amount to the abuse of the power. The attempt to use it on the means employed by the government of the Union, in pursuance of the constitution, is itself an abuse, because it is the usurpation of a power which the people of a single State cannot give. . . .

That the power to tax involves the power to destroy; that the power to destroy may defeat and render useless the power to create; that there is a plain repugnance, in conferring on one government a power to control the constitutional measures of another, which other, with respect to those very measures, is declared to be supreme over that which exerts the control, are propositions not to be denied. . . .

If the States may tax one instrument, employed by the government in the execution of its powers, they may tax any and every other instrument. They may tax the mail; they may tax the mint; they may tax patent rights; they may tax the papers of the customhouse; they may tax judicial process; they may tax all the means employed by the government, to an excess which would defeat all the ends of government. . . .

The Court has bestowed on this subject its most deliberate consideration. The result is a conviction that the States have no power, by taxation or otherwise, to retard, impede, burden, or in any manner control, the operations of the constitutional laws enacted by Congress to carry into execution the powers vested in the general government. This is, we think, the unavoidable consequence of that supremacy which the constitution has declared.

We are unanimously of opinion, that the law passed by the legislature of Maryland, imposing a tax on the Bank of the United States, is unconstitutional and void. . . .

Topic 9

NATIONAL POWER OVER THE ECONOMY

❦

The Commerce Power: A Restricted View

SCHECHTER POULTRY CORP. *V*. UNITED STATES

295 U.S. 495 (1935)

[In 1933 Congress passed the National Industrial Recovery Act. In signing the bill President Roosevelt said, "History probably will record the National Industrial Recovery Act as the most important and far-reaching legislation ever enacted by the American Congress." The purpose of the law, according to the President, was to promote re-employment, to shorten hours and increase wages, and to prevent unfair competition.

The first section of the act attempted to provide a constitutional basis for the legislation, stating:

"Section 1. A national emergency productive of widespread unemployment and disorganization of industry, which burdens interstate and foreign commerce, affects the public welfare, and undermines the standards of living of the American people, is hereby declared to exist. It is hereby declared to be the policy of Congress to remove obstructions to the free flow of interstate and foreign commerce which tend to diminish the amount thereof; and to provide for the general welfare by promoting the organization of industry for the purpose of cooperative action among trade groups, to induce and maintain united action of labor and management under adequate competitive practices, to promote the fullest possible utilization of the present productive capacity of industries, to avoid restriction of production (except as may be temporarily required), to increase the consumption of industrial and agricultural products by increasing purchasing power, to reduce and relieve unemployment, to improve standards of labor, and otherwise to rehabilitate industry and to conserve natural resources."

On May 27, 1935 the Supreme Court in a unanimous opinion declared the National Industrial Recovery Act unconstitutional on the grounds that (1), it "attempted delegation of legislative power" and (2), it "attempted regulation of intrastate transactions which affect interstate commerce only indirectly."

In the case at issue, The Schechter Poultry Corporation conducted a wholesale poultry slaughterhouse market in Brooklyn. It ordinarily purchased live poultry from commission men in New York City or at the railroad terminals and after slaughtering the poultry sold it to retail dealers and butchers. The Court stated that "New York City is the largest live-poultry market in the United States. Ninety-six per cent of the live poultry there marketed comes from other States."]

MR. CHIEF JUSTICE HUGHES delivered the opinion of the court.

Penalties are confined to violations of a code provision "in any transaction in or affecting interstate or foreign commerce." This aspect of the
case presents the question whether the particular provisions of the Live
Poultry Code, which the defendants were convicted for violating and for
having conspired to violate, were within the regulating powers of Congress.

These provisions relate to the hours and wages of those employed by
defendants in their slaughterhouses in Brooklyn and to the sales there made
to retail dealers and butchers.

(1) Were these transactions "in" interstate commerce? Much is made
of the fact that almost all the poultry coming to New York is sent there
from other states. But the code provisions as here applied do not concern
the transportation of the poultry from other states to New York, or the
transactions of the commission men or others to whom it is consigned, or
the sales made by such consignees to defendants.

When defendants had made their purchases, whether at the West Washington Market in New York City or at the railroad terminals serving the
city, or elsewhere, the poultry was trucked to their slaughterhouses in
Brooklyn for local disposition. The interstate transactions in relation to that
poultry then ended. Defendants held the poultry at their slaughterhouse
markets for slaughter and local sale to retail dealers and butchers, who in
turn sold directly to consumers.

Neither the slaughtering nor the sales by defendants were transactions
in interstate commerce. . . . The undisputed facts thus afford no warrant
for the argument that the poultry handled by defendants at their slaughterhouse markets was in "current" or "flow" of interstate commerce and was
thus subject to congressional regulation.

The mere fact that there may be a constant flow of commodities into a
state does not mean that the flow continues after the property has arrived
and has become commingled with the mass of property within the state and
is there held solely for local disposition and use. So far as the poultry here in
question is concerned, the flow in interstate commerce had ceased. The
poultry had come to a permanent rest within the state. It was not held,
used or sold by defendants in relation to any further transaction in interstate
commerce and was not destined for transportation to other states. Hence,
decisions which deal with a stream of interstate commerce—where goods
come to rest within a state temporarily and are later to go forward in interstate commerce—and with the regulations of transactions involved in that
practical continuity of movement, are not applicable here. . . .

(2) Did the defendant's transactions directly "affect" interstate commerce so as to be subject to federal regulation? The power of Congress
extends not only to the regulation of transactions which are part of inter-

state commerce, but to the protection of that commerce from injury. It matters not that the injury may be due to the conduct of those engaged in intrastate operations. Thus, Congress may protect the safety of those employed in interstate transportation "no matter what may be the source of the dangers which threaten it." . . .

Defendants have been convicted, not upon direct charges of injury to interstate commerce or of interference with persons engaged in that commerce, but of violations of certain provisions of the Live Poultry Code and of conspiracy to commit these violations. Interstate commerce is brought in only upon the charge that violations of these provisions—as to hours and wages of employes and local sales—"affected" interstate commerce.

In determining how far the federal government may go in controlling intrastate transactions upon the ground that they "affect" interstate commerce, there is a necessary and well-established distinction between direct and indirect effects. The precise line can be drawn only as individual cases arise, but the distinction is clear in principle. . . . [And] where the effect of intrastate transactions upon interstate commerce is merely indirect, such transactions remain within the domain of state power. . . .

The question of chief importance relates to the provision of the Code as to the hours and wages of those employed in defendants' slaughterhouse markets. It is plain that these requirements are imposed in order to govern the details of defendants' management of their local business. The persons employed in slaughtering and selling in local trade are not employed in interstate commerce. Their hours and wages have no direct relation to interstate commerce. . . . If the federal government may determine the wages and hours of employees in the internal commerce of a State, because of their relation to cost and prices and their indirect effect upon interstate commerce, it would seem that a similar control might be exerted over other elements of cost, also affecting prices, such as the number of employees, rents, advertising, methods of doing business, etc. All the processes of production and distribution that enter into cost could likewise be controlled. If the cost of doing an intrastate business is in itself the permitted object of federal control, the extent of the regulation of cost would be a question of discretion and not of power.

The government also makes the point that efforts to enact state legislation establishing high labor standards have been impeded by the belief that, unless similar action is taken generally, commerce will be diverted from the states adopting such standards, and that this fear of diversion has led to demands for federal legislation on the subject of wages and hours. The apparent implication is that the federal authority under the commerce clause should be deemed to extend to the establishment of rules to govern wages and hours in intrastate trade and industry generally throughout the country, thus overriding the authority of the states to deal with domestic problems arising from labor conditions in their internal commerce.

It is not the province of the Court to consider the economic advantages or disadvantages of such a centralized system. It is sufficient to say that the Federal Constitution does not provide for it. Our growth and development have called for wide use of the commerce power of the federal government in its control over the expanded activities of interstate commerce and in protecting that commerce from burdens, interferences, and conspiracies to restrain and monopolize it. But the authority of the federal government may not be pushed to such an extreme as to destroy the distinction, which the commerce clause itself establishes, between commerce "among the several States" and the internal concerns of a State. The same answer must be made to the contention that is based upon the serious economic situation which led to the passage of the Recovery Act,—the fall in prices, the decline in wages and employment, and the curtailment of the market for commodities. Stress is laid upon the great importance of maintaining wage distributions which would provide the necessary stimulus in starting "the cumulative forces making for expanding commercial activity." Without in any way disparaging this motive, it is enough to say that the recuperative efforts of the federal government must be made in a manner consistent with the authority granted by the Constitution.

[The portion of the opinion dealing with the "attempted delegation of legislative power" is omitted. The concurring opinion of Mr. Justice Cardozo is also omitted.]

The Commerce Power: An Expanded View

WICKARD *V.* FILBURN

317 U.S. 111 (1942)

[The Agricultural Adjustment Act of 1938, as related to wheat, sought to control the volume moving in interstate and foreign commerce in order to avoid surpluses and shortages and consequent abnormalities of price and obstructions to commerce. The Act, as amended, provided procedures which resulted in the fixing of a market quota applicable to each farm and laid a penalty upon any excess brought to market by the farmer. The basic provision of this law was sustained in Mulford *v.* Smith, 307 U.S. 38 (1939).

The question in the instant case is whether Congress may constitutionally regulate *production* of wheat, not intended in any part for commerce, but wholly for *consumption* on the farm.]

MR. JUSTICE JACKSON delivered the opinion of the Court. . . .

[Filburn] says that this is a regulation of production and consumption of wheat. Such activities are, he urges, beyond the reach of congressional power under the commerce clause, since they are local in character, and their effects upon interstate commerce are at most "indirect." In answer the government argues that the statute regulates neither production nor consumption, but only marketing; and, in the alternative, that if the Act does go beyond the regulation of marketing it is sustainable as a "necessary and proper" implementation of the power of Congress over interstate commerce.

The government's concern lest the Act be held to be a regulation of production or consumption rather than of marketing is attributable to a few dicta and decisions of this Court which might be understood to lay it down that activities such as "production," "manufacturing," and "mining" are strictly "local" and, except in special circumstances which are not present here, cannot be regulated under the commerce power because their effects upon interstate commerce are, as matter of law, only "indirect." Even today, when this power has been held to have great latitude, there is no decision of this Court that such activities may be regulated where no part of the product is intended for interstate commerce or intermingled with the subjects thereof. We believe that a review of the course of decision under the commerce clause will make plain, however, that questions of the power of Congress are not to be decided by reference to any formula which would give controlling force to nomenclature such as "production" and "indirect" and foreclose consideration of the actual effects of the activity in question upon interstate commerce.

At the beginning Chief Justice Marshall described the federal commerce power with a breadth never yet exceeded. Gibbons *v.* Ogden, 9 Wheat. 1, 194, 195. He made emphatic the embracing and penetrating nature of this power by warning that effective restraints on its exercise must proceed from political rather than from judicial processes. 9 Wheat. at page 197.

For nearly a century, however, decisions of this Court under the commerce clause dealt rarely with questions of what Congress might do in the exercise of its granted power under the clause and almost entirely with the permissibility of state activity which it was claimed discriminated against or burdened interstate commerce. During this period there was perhaps little occasion for the affirmative exercise of the commerce power, and the influence of the clause on American life and law was a negative one, resulting almost wholly from its operation as a restraint upon the powers of the states. In discussion and decision the point of reference instead of being what was "necessary and proper" to the exercise by Congress of its granted power, was often some concept of sovereignty thought to be implicit in the status of statehood. Certain activities such as "production," "manufacturing," and "mining" were occasionally said to be within the province of state governments and beyond the power of Congress under the commerce clause.

It was not until 1887 with the enactment of the Interstate Commerce Act that the interstate commerce power began to exert positive influence in American law and life. This first important federal resort to the commerce power was followed in 1890 by the Sherman Anti-Trust Act and, thereafter, mainly after 1903, by many others. These statutes ushered in new phases of adjudication, which required the Court to approach the interpretation of the commerce clause in the light of an actual exercise by Congress of its power thereunder.

When it first dealt with this new legislation, the Court adhered to its earlier pronouncements, and allowed but little scope to the power of Congress. United States *v.* E. C. Knight Co., 156 U.S. 1. These earlier pronouncements also played an important part in several of the five cases in which this Court later held that acts of Congress under the commerce clause were in excess of its power.

Even while important opinions in this line of restrictive authority were being written, however, other cases called forth broader interpretations of the commerce clause destined to supersede the earlier ones, and to bring about a return to the principles first enunciated by Chief Justice Marshall in Gibbons *v.* Ogden, *supra.*

Not long after the decision of United States *v.* E. C. Knight Co., *supra,* Mr. Justice Holmes, in sustaining the exercise of national power over intrastate activity, stated for the Court that "commerce among the states is not a technical legal conception, but a practical one, drawn from the course of business." Swift & Co. *v.* United States, 196 U.S. 375, 398. It was soon demonstrated that the effects of many kinds of intrastate activity upon interstate commerce were such as to make them a proper subject of federal regulation. In some cases sustaining the exercise of federal power over intrastate matters the term "direct" was used for the purpose of stating, rather than of reaching, a result; in others it was treated as synonymous with "substantial" or "material"; and in others it was not used at all. Of late its use has been abandoned in cases dealing with questions of federal power under the commerce clause.

In the Shreveport Rate Cases (Houston, E. & W. T. R. Co. *v.* United States), 234 U.S. 342, the Court held that railroad rates of an admittedly intrastate character and fixed by authority of the state might, nevertheless, be revised by the federal government because of the economic effects which they had upon interstate commerce. The opinion of Mr. Justice Hughes found federal intervention constitutionally authorized because of "matters having such a close and substantial relation to interstate traffic that the control is essential or appropriate to the security of that traffic, to the efficiency of the interstate service, and to the maintenance of the conditions under which interstate commerce may be conducted upon fair terms and without molestation or hindrance." 234 U.S. at page 351.

The Court's recognition of the relevance of the economic effects in the application of the commerce clause exemplified by this statement has made the mechanical application of legal formulas no longer feasible. Once an economic measure of the reach of the power granted to Congress in the commerce clause is accepted, questions of federal power cannot be decided simply by finding the activity in question to be "production" nor can consideration of its economic effects be foreclosed by calling them "indirect." The present Chief Justice has said in summary of the present state of the law: "The commerce power is not confined in its exercise to the regulation of commerce among the states. It extends to those activities intrastate which so affect interstate commerce or the exertion of the power of Congress over it, as to make regulation of them appropriate means to the attainment of a legitimate end, the effective execution of the granted power to regulate interstate commerce. . . . The power of Congress over interstate commerce is plenary and complete in itself, may be exercised to its utmost extent, and acknowledges no limitations other than are prescribed in the Constitution. . . . It follows that no form of state activity can constitutionally thwart the regulatory power granted by the commerce clause to Congress. Hence the reach of that power extends to those intrastate activities which in a substantial way interfere with or obstruct the exercise of the granted power." United States *v.* Wrightwood Dairy Co., 315 U.S. 110, 119.

Whether the subject of the regulation in question was "production," "consumption," or "marketing" is, therefore, not material for purposes of deciding the question of federal power before us. That an activity is of local character may help in a doubtful case to determine whether Congress intended to reach it. The same consideration might help in determining whether in the absence of congressional action it would be permissible for the state to exert its power on the subject matter, even though in so doing it to some degree affected interstate commerce. But even if appellant's activity be local and though it may not be regarded as commerce, it may still, whatever its nature, be reached by Congress if it exerts a substantial economic effect on interstate commerce and this irrespective of whether such effect is what might at some earlier time have been defined as "direct" or "indirect."

The parties have stipulated a summary of the economics of the wheat industry. Commerce among the states in wheat is large and important. Although wheat is raised in every state but one, production in most states is not equal to consumption. Sixteen states on average have had a surplus of wheat above their own requirements for feed, seed, and food. Thirty-two states and the District of Columbia, where production has been below consumption, have looked to these surplus-producing states for their supply as well as for wheat for export and carryover.

The wheat industry has been a problem industry for some years. Largely as a result of increased foreign production and import restrictions, annual exports of wheat and flour from the United States during the ten-year period ending in 1940 averaged less than 10 per cent of total production, while during the 1920's they averaged more than 25 per cent. The decline in the export trade has left a large surplus in production which in connection with an abnormally large supply of wheat and other grains in recent years caused congestion in a number of markets; tied up railroad cars; and caused elevators in some instances to turn away grains, and railroads to institute embargoes to prevent further congestion. . . .

In the absence of regulation the price of wheat in the United States would be much affected by world conditions. During 1941 producers who co-operated with the Agricultural Adjustment program received an average price on the farm of about $1.16 a bushel as compared with the world market price of 40 cents a bushel. . . .

The effect of consumption of home-grown wheat on interstate commerce is due to the fact that it constitutes the most variable factor in the disappearance of the wheat crop. Consumption on the farm where grown appears to vary in an amount greater than 20 per cent of average production. The total amount of wheat consumed as food varies but relatively little, and use as seed is relatively constant.

The maintenance by government regulation of a price for wheat undoubtedly can be accomplished as effectively by sustaining or increasing the demand as by limiting the supply. The effect of the statute before us is to restrict the amount which may be produced for market and the extent as well to which one may forestall resort to the market by producing to meet his own needs. That [Filburn's] own contribution to the demand for wheat may be trivial by itself is not enough to remove him from the scope of federal regulation where, as here, his contribution, taken together with that of many others similarly situated, is far from trivial. National Labor Relations Board *v.* Fainblatt, 306 U.S. 601, 606, *et seq.,* 307 U.S. 609; United States *v.* Darby, *supra,* 312 U.S. at page 123.

It is well established by decisions of this Court that the power to regulate commerce includes the power to regulate the prices at which commodities in that commerce are dealt in and practices affecting such prices. One of the primary purposes of the Act in question was to increase the market price of wheat and to that end to limit the volume thereof that could affect the market. It can hardly be denied that a factor of such volume and variability as home consumed wheat would have a substantial influence on price and market conditions. This may arise because being in marketable condition such wheat overhangs the market and, if induced by rising prices, tends to flow in to the market and check price increases. But if we assume that it is never marketed, it supplies a need of the man who grew it which would otherwise be reflected by purchases in the open market. Home-grown wheat in this sense competes with wheat in commerce. The stimulation of commerce is a use of the regulatory function quite as definitely as prohibitions or restrictions thereon. This record leaves us in no doubt that Congress may properly have considered that wheat consumed on the farm where grown if wholly outside the scheme of regulation would have a substantial effect in defeating and obstructing its purpose to stimulate trade therein at increased prices. . . .

[The decision of the lower court is reversed.]

GOVERNMENTAL POWER AND
LAISSEZ FAIRE

෯෯

The Police Power: A Restricted View

The provision of the Fifth Amendment that no person shall "be deprived of life, liberty, or property, without due process of law" has limited federal power, and a similar clause in the Fourteenth Amendment has proved to be an even more important restraint upon state power. "Few phrases of the law are so elusive of exact apprehension," said the Supreme Court nearly fifty years ago in Twining v. New Jersey, 211 U.S. 78. "This Court has always declined to give a comprehensive definition" of due process, added Justice Moody, "and has preferred that its full meaning should be gradually ascertained by the process of inclusion and exclusion in the course of the decisions of cases as they arise."

Before the Supreme Court was "reconstructed" by President Roosevelt, the due process clauses were the most important bases for decisions invalidating social legislation. The vicissitudes of minimum wage for women legislation under due process challenge illustrate both the Court's range of discretion and the restricted view of the police power frequently applied by the Court before 1937. In 1917 such legislation was sustained as constitutional by an evenly divided Court. Only six years later, after some changes in the Court, in Adkins v. Children's Hospital, a similar law was invalidated by a vote of five to three. In 1925 and again in 1927, without opinion, and on the authority of the Adkins decision, the Court found similar Arizona and Arkansas statutes unconstitutional. In 1936, by vote of five to four, a New York minimum wage for women law was struck down by the Court. Finally, in West Coast Hotel v. Parrish, decided the next year, such legislation was upheld when one justice altered his position. This latter decision, giving expanded scope to the police power of the state, is representative of the more liberal attitude toward social legislation which has characterized the Supreme Court since that time. The due process (and equal protection) clauses have now served chiefly as restraints upon state action in denigration of civil liberties and civil rights.

ADKINS V. CHILDREN'S HOSPITAL

261 U.S. 525 (1923)

[The question raised by appeal to the Supreme Court was the constitutionality of the Act of Congress of September 19, 1918, providing for the creation *in the District of Columbia* of a Minimum Wage Board to investigate, among others, the wages paid women in varying occupations and to declare "standards of minimum wages for women in any occupation in the District of Columbia, and what wages are inadequate to supply the necessary cost of living to any such women workers to maintain them in good health and to protect their morals." Employers were forbidden under penalty of law to employ women at wages lower than those fixed by the Board.]

MR. JUSTICE SUTHERLAND delivered the opinion of the court.

This court, by an unbroken line of decisions from Chief Justice Marshall to the present day, has steadily adhered to the rule that every possible presumption is in favor of the validity of an act of Congress until overcome beyond rational doubt. But, if by clear and indubitable demonstration a statute be opposed to the Constitution, we have no choice but to say so. . . .

The statute now under consideration is attacked upon the ground that it authorizes an unconstitutional interference with the freedom of contract included within the guaranties of the due process clause of the Fifth Amendment. That the right to contract about one's affairs is a part of the liberty of the individual protected by this clause is settled by the decisions of this Court and is no longer open to question. [Authorities.] Within this liberty are contracts of employment of labor. In making such contracts, generally speaking, the parties have an equal right to obtain from each other the best terms they can as the result of private bargaining. . . .

There is, of course, no such thing as absolute freedom of contract. It is subject to a great variety of restraints. But freedom of contract is, nevertheless, the general rule and restraint the exception; and the exercise of legislative authority to abridge it can be justified only by the existence of exceptional circumstances. Whether these circumstances exist in the present case constitutes the question to be answered. It will be helpful to this end to review some of the decisions where the interference has been upheld and consider the grounds upon which they rest. [Here follows an elaborate review of the decisions.]

If now, in the light furnished by the foregoing exceptions to the general rule forbidding legislative interference with freedom of contract, we examine and analyze the statute in question, we shall see that it differs from them in every material respect. It is not a law dealing with any business charged with a public interest, or with public work, or to meet and tide over a temporary emergency. It has nothing to do with the character, methods or periods of wage payments. It does not prescribe hours of labor or conditions under which labor is to be done. It is not for the protection of persons under legal disability or for the prevention of fraud. It is simply and exclusively a price-fixing law, confined to adult women (for we are not now considering the provisions relating to minors), who are legally as capable of contracting for themselves as men. It forbids two parties having

lawful capacity—under penalties as to the employer—to freely contract
with one another in respect of the price for which one shall render service
to the other in a purely private employment where both are willing, perhaps
anxious, to agree, even though the consequence may be to oblige one to
surrender a desirable engagement and the other to dispense with the services
of a desirable employee. . . .

The standard furnished by the statute for the guidance of the board is so
vague as to be impossible of practical application with any reasonable
degree of accuracy. What is sufficient to supply the necessary cost of living
for a woman worker and maintain her in good health and protect her
morals is obviously not a precise or unvarying sum—not even approximately so. The amount will depend upon a variety of circumstances: the
individual temperament, habits of thrift, care, ability to buy necessaries
intelligently, and whether the woman lives alone or with her family. . . .
The relation between earnings and morals is not capable of standardization.
It cannot be shown that well paid women safeguard their morals more
carefully than those who are poorly paid. Morality rests upon other considerations than wages; and there is, certainly, no such prevalent connection
between the two as to justify a broad attempt to adjust the latter with reference to the former. As a means of safeguarding morals the attempted
classification, in our opinion, is without reasonable basis. No distinction can
be made between women who work for others and those who do not; nor is
there ground for distinction between women and men, for, certainly, if
women require a minimum wage to preserve their morals men require it
to preserve their honesty. For these reasons, and others which might be
stated, the inquiry in respect of the necessary cost of living and of the
income necessary to preserve health and morals, presents an individual and
not a composite question, and must be answered for each individual considered by herself and not by a general formula prescribed by a statutory
bureau. . . .

The law takes account of the necessities of only one party to the contract.
It ignores the necessities of the employer by compelling him to pay not less
than a certain sum, not only whether the employee is capable of earning it,
but irrespective of the ability of his business to sustain the burden, generously leaving him, of course, the privilege of abandoning his business as
an alternative for going on at a loss. Within the limits of the minimum sum,
he is precluded, under penalty of fine and imprisonment, from adjusting
compensation to the differing merits of his employees. It compels him to
pay at least the sum fixed in any event, because the employee needs it, but
requires no service of equivalent value from the employee. It therefore
undertakes to solve but one-half of the problem. The other half is the establishment of a corresponding standard of efficiency, and this forms no

part of the policy of the legislation, although in practice the former half without the latter must lead to ultimate failure, in accordance with the inexorable law that no one can continue indefinitely to take out more than he puts in without ultimately exhausting the supply.

The law is not confined to the great and powerful employers but embraces those whose bargaining power may be as weak as that of the employee. It takes no account of periods of stress and business depression, of crippling losses, which may leave the employer himself without adequate means of livelihood. To the extent that the sum fixed exceeds the fair value of the services rendered, it amounts to a compulsory exaction from the employer for the support of a partially indigent person, for whose condition there rests upon him no peculiar responsibility, and therefore, in effect, arbitrarily shifts to his shoulders a burden which, if it belongs to anybody, belongs to society as a whole.

The feature of this statute which perhaps more than any other, puts upon it the stamp of invalidity is that it exacts from the employer an arbitrary payment for a purpose and upon a basis having no causal connection with his business, or the contract or the work the employee engages to do. The declared basis, as already pointed out, is not the value of the service rendered but the extraneous circumstances that the employee needs to get a prescribed sum of money to insure her subsistence, health and morals. . . . In principle, there can be no difference between the case of selling labor and the case of selling goods. If one goes to the butcher, the baker or grocer to buy food, he is morally entitled to obtain the worth of his money but he is not entitled to more. If what he gets is worth what he pays he is not justified in demanding more simply because he needs more; and the shopkeeper, having dealt fairly and honestly in that transaction, is not concerned in any peculiar sense with the question of his customer's necessities.

Should a statute undertake to vest in a commission power to determine the quantity of food necessary for individual support and require the shopkeeper, if he sell to the individual at all, to furnish that quantity at not more than a fixed maximum, it would undoubtedly fall before the constitutional test. The fallacy of any argument in support of the validity of such a statute would be quickly exposed. The argument in support of that now being considered is equally fallacious, though the weakness of it may not be so plain. A statute requiring an employer to pay in money, to pay at prescribed and regular intervals, to pay the value of the services rendered, even to pay with fair relation to the extent of the benefit obtained from the service, would be understandable. But a statute which prescribes payment without regard to any of these things and solely with relation to circumstances apart from the contract of employment, the business affected by it and the work done under it, is so clearly the product of a naked, arbitrary exercise of power that it cannot be allowed to stand under the Constitution of the United States.

We are asked, upon the one hand, to consider the fact that several States have adopted similar statutes, and we are invited, upon the other hand, to give weight to the fact that three times as many States, presumably as well informed and as anxious to promote the health and morals of their people, have refrained from enacting such legislation. We have also been furnished with a large number of printed opinions approving the policy of the minimum wage, and our own reading has disclosed a large number of the contrary. These are all proper enough for the consideration of the lawmaking bodies, since their tendency is to establish the desirability or undesirability of the legislation; but they reflect no legitimate light upon the question of its validity, and that is what we are called upon to decide. The elucidation of that question cannot be aided by counting heads. . . .

Finally, it may be said that if, in the interest of the public welfare, the police power may be invoked to justify the fixing of a minimum wage, it may, when the public welfare is thought to require it, be invoked to justify a maximum wage. The power to fix high wages connotes, by like reasoning, the power to fix low wages. If, in the face of the guaranties of the Fifth Amendment, this form of legislation shall be legally justified, the field for the operation of the police power will have been widened to a great and dangerous degree. If, for example, in the opinion of future lawmakers, wages in the building trades shall become so high as to preclude people of ordinary means from building and owning homes, an authority which sustains the minimum wage will be invoked to support a maximum wage for building laborers and artisans, and the same argument which has been here urged to strip the employer of his constitutional liberty of contract in one direction will be utilized to strip the employee of his constitutional liberty of contract in the opposite direction. A wrong decision does not end with itself; it is a precedent, and, with the swing of sentiment, its bad influence may run from one extremity of the arc to the other.

It has been said that legislation of the kind now under review is required in the interest of social justice, for whose ends freedom of contract may lawfully be subjected to restraint. The liberty of the individual to do as he pleases, even in innocent matters, is not absolute. It must frequently yield to the common good, and the line beyond which the power of interference may not be pressed is neither definite nor unalterable but may be made to move, within limits not well defined, with changing need and circumstance. Any attempt to fix a rigid boundary would be unwise and futile. But, nevertheless, there are limits to the power, and when these have been passed, it becomes the plain duty of the courts in the proper exercise of their authority to so declare. To sustain the individual freedom of action contemplated by the Constitution, is not to strike down the common good but to exalt it;

for surely the good of society as a whole cannot be better served than by the preservation against arbitrary restraint of the liberties of its constituent members.

It follows from what has been said that the act in question passes the limit prescribed by the Constitution, and, accordingly, the decrees of the court below are affirmed.

[Mr. Justice Brandeis took no part in the consideration or decision of this case.]

[The dissenting opinion of Chief Justice Taft, with which Mr. Justice Sanford concurred, is omitted.]

MR. JUSTICE HOLMES, dissenting.

The question in this case is the broad one, Whether Congress can establish minimum rates of wages for women in the District of Columbia with due provision for special circumstances, or whether we must say that Congress has no power to meddle with the matter at all. To me, notwithstanding the deference due to the prevailing judgment of the Court, the power of Congress seems absolutely free from doubt. The end, to remove conditions leading to ill health, immorality and the deterioration of the race, no one would deny to be within the scope of constitutional legislation. The means are means that have the approval of Congress, or many States, and of those governments from which we have learned our greatest lessons. When so many intelligent persons who have studied the matter more than any of us can, have thought that the means are effective and are worth the price, it seems to me impossible to deny that the belief reasonably may be held by reasonable men. . . .

I confess that I do not understand the principle on which the power to fix a minimum for the wages of women can be denied by those who admit the power to fix a maximum for their hours of work. I fully assent to the proposition that here as elsewhere the distinctions of the law are distinctions of degree, but I perceive no difference in the kind or degree of interference with liberty, the only matter with which we have any concern, between the one case and the other. The bargain is equally affected whichever half you regulate. Muller *v.* Oregon, I take it, is as good law today as it was in 1908. It will need more than the Nineteenth Amendment to convince me that there are no differences between men and women, or that legislation cannot take those differences into account. . . .

This statute does not compel anybody to pay anything. It simply forbids employment at rates below those fixed as the minimum requirement of health and right living. It is safe to assume that women will not be employed at even the lowest wages allowed unless they earn them, or unless the employer's business can sustain the burden. . . .

The criterion of constitutionality is not whether we believe the law to be for the public good. We certainly cannot be prepared to deny that a reasonable man reasonably might have that belief in view of the legislation of Great Britain, Victoria and a number of the States of this Union. The belief is fortified by a very remarkable collection of documents submitted on behalf of the appellants, material here, I conceive, only as showing that the belief reasonably may be held. In Australia the power to fix a minimum for wages in the case of industrial disputes extending beyond the limits of any one State was given to a Court, and its President wrote a most interesting account of its operation. 29 Harv. Law Rev. 13. If a legislature should adopt what he thinks the doctrine of modern economists of all schools, that "freedom of contract is a misnomer as applied to a contract between an employer and an ordinary individual employee," *ibid.* 25, I could not pronounce an opinion with which I agree impossible to be entertained by reasonable men. If the same legislature should accept his further opinion that industrial peace was best attained by the device of a Court having the above powers, I should not feel myself able to contradict it, or to deny that the end justified restrictive legislation quite as adequately as beliefs concerning Sunday or exploded theories about usury. I should have my doubts, as I have them about this statute—but they would be whether the bill that has to be paid for every gain, although hidden as interstitial detriments, was not greater than the gain was worth: a matter that it is not for me to decide.

I am of opinion that the statute is valid and that the decree should be reversed.

The Police Power: An Expanded View

WEST COAST HOTEL COMPANY *V.* PARRISH

300 U.S. 379 (1937)

MR. CHIEF JUSTICE HUGHES delivered the opinion of the court.

This case presents the question of the constitutional validity of the minimum wage law of the State of Washington.

The Act, entitled "Minimum Wages for Women," authorizes the fixing of minimum wages for women and minors Laws of 1913 (Washington) chap. 174; Remington's Rev. Stat. (1932), §§ 7623 *et seq.* It provides:

> Section 1. The welfare of the State of Washington demands that women and minors be protected from conditions of labor which have a pernicious effect on their health and morals. The State of Washington, therefore, exercising herein its police and sovereign power declares that inadequate wages and unsanitary conditions of labor exert such pernicious effect.

Sec. 2. It shall be unlawful to employ women or minors in any industry or occupation within the State of Washington under conditions of labor detrimental to their health or morals; and it shall be unlawful to employ women workers in any industry within the State of Washington at wages which are not adequate for their maintenance.

Sec. 3. There is hereby created a commission to be known as the "Industrial Welfare Commission" for the State of Washington, to establish such standards of wages and conditions of labor for women and minors employed within the State of Washington, as shall be held hereunder to be reasonable and not detrimental to health and morals, and which shall be sufficient for the decent maintenance of women. . . .

The appellant conducts a hotel. The appellee Elsie Parrish was employed as a chambermaid and (with her husband) brought this suit to recover the difference between the wages paid her and the minimum wage fixed pursuant to the state law. The minimum wage was $14.50 per week of 48 hours. The appellant challenged the act as repugnant to the due process clause of the Fourteenth Amendment of the Constitution of the United States.

[Here follows comment on Morehead *v.* New York ex rel. Tipaldo, 298 U.S. 587, and other minimum wage decisions.]

The principle which must control our decision is not in doubt. The constitutional provision invoked is the due process clause of the Fourteenth Amendment governing the States, as the due process clause invoked in the Adkins Case governed Congress. In each case the violation alleged by those attacking minimum wage regulation for women is deprivation of freedom of contract. What is this freedom? The Constitution does not speak of freedom of contract. It speaks of liberty and prohibits the deprivation of liberty without due process of law. In prohibiting that deprivation the Constitution does not recognize an absolute and uncontrollable liberty. Liberty in each of its phases has its history and connotation. But the liberty safeguarded is liberty in a social organization which requires the protection of law against the evils which menace the health, safety, morals and welfare of the people. Liberty under the Constitution is thus necessarily subject to the restraints of due process, and regulation which is reasonable in relation to its subject and is adopted in the interests of the community is due process.

This essential limitation of liberty in general governs freedom of contract in particular. More than twenty-five years ago we set forth the applicable principle in these words, after referring to the cases where the liberty guaranteed by the Fourteenth Amendment had been broadly described:

But it was recognized in the cases cited, as in many others, that freedom of contract is a qualified and not an absolute right. There is no absolute freedom to do as one wills or to contract as one chooses. The guaranty of liberty does not withdraw from legislative supervision that wide department of activity which consists of the making of contracts, or deny to government the power to provide restrictive safeguards. Liberty implies the absence of arbitrary restraint, not immunity from reasonable regulations and prohibitions imposed in the interests of the community. Chicago, B. & Q. R. Co. *v.* McGuire, 219 U.S. 549, 567.

This power under the Constitution to restrict freedom of contract has had many illustrations. That it may be exercised in the public interest with respect to contracts between employer and employee is undeniable. . . .

The point that has been strongly stressed that adult employees should be deemed competent to make their own contracts was decisively met nearly forty years ago in Holden *v.* Hardy, 169 U.S. 366, where we pointed out the inequality in the footing of the parties. We said (*Id.,* 397):

> The legislature has also recognized the fact, which the experience of legislators in many States has corroborated, that the proprietors of these establishments and their operatives do not stand upon an equality, and that their interests are, to a certain extent, conflicting. The former naturally desire to obtain as much labor as possible from their employees, while the latter are often induced by the fear of discharge to conform to regulations which their judgment, fairly exercised, would pronounce to be detrimental to their health or strength. In other words, the proprietors lay down the rules and the laborers are practically constrained to obey them. In such cases self-interest is often an unsafe guide, and the legislature may properly interpose its authority. . . .

It is manifest that this established principle is peculiarly applicable in relation to the emp.oyment of women in whose protection the State has a special interest. That phase of the subject received elaborate consideration in Muller *v.* Oregon (1908), 208 U.S. 412, where the constitutional authority of the State to limit the working hours of women was sustained. We emphasized the consideration that "woman's physical structure and the performance of maternal functions place her at a disadvantage in the struggle for subsistence" and that her physical well-being "becomes an object of public interest and care in order to preserve the strength and vigor of the race." . . .

This array of precedents and the principles they applied were thought by the dissenting Justices in the Adkins case to demand that the minimum wage statute be sustained. The validity of the distinction made by the Court between a minimum wage and a maximum of hours în limiting liberty of contract was especially challenged. 261 U.S., p. 564. That challenge persists and is without any satisfactory answer. . . .

[The court here quotes from the dissenting opinions of Justice Holmes and of Chief Justice Taft in the Adkins case.]

We think that the views thus expressed are sound and that the decision in the Adkins case was a departure from the true application of the principles governing the regulation by the State of the relation of employer and employed. Those principles have been re-enforced by our subsequent decisions. [Case references are omitted.]

With full recognition of the earnestness and vigor which characterize the prevailing opinion in the Adkins case, we find it impossible to reconcile that ruling with these well-considered declarations. What can be closer to the public interest than the health of women and their protection from unscrupulous and overreaching employers? And if the protection of women is a legitimate end of the exercise of state power, how can it be said that the requirement of the payment of a minimum wage fairly fixed in order to meet the very necessities of existence is not an admissible means to that end? The legislature of the State was clearly entitled to consider the situation of women in employment, the fact that they are in the class receiving the least pay, that their bargaining power is relatively weak, and that they are the ready victims of those who would take advantage of their necessitous circumstances. The legislature was entitled to adopt measures to reduce the evils of the "sweating system," the exploiting of workers at wages so low as to be insufficient to meet the bare cost of living, thus making their very helplessness the occasion of a most injurious competition. The legislature had the right to consider that its minimum wage requirements would be an important aid in carrying out its policy of protection. The adoption of similar requirements by many States evidences a deep-seated conviction both as to the presence of the evil and as to the means adapted to check it. Legislative response to that conviction cannot be regarded as arbitrary or capricious, and that is all we have to decide. Even if the wisdom of the policy be regarded as debatable and its effects uncertain, still the legislature is entitled to its judgment.

There is an additional and compelling consideration which recent economic experience has brought into a strong light. The exploitation of a class of workers who are in an unequal position with respect to bargaining power and are thus relatively defenceless against the denial of a living wage is not only detrimental to their health and well-being but casts a direct burden for their support upon the community. What these workers lose in wages the taxpayers are called upon to pay. The bare cost of living must be met. We may take judicial notice of the unparalleled demands for relief which arose during the recent period of depression and still continue to an alarming extent despite the degree of economic recovery which has been achieved. It is unnecessary to cite official statistics to establish what is of common knowledge through the length and breadth of the land. While in the instant case no factual brief has been presented, there is no reason to doubt that the State of Washington has encountered the same social problem that is present elsewhere. The community is not bound to provide what is in effect a subsidy for unconscionable employers. The community may direct its law-making power to correct the abuse which springs from their selfish disregard of the public interest.

The argument that the legislation in question constitutes an arbitrary discrimination, because it does not extend to men, is unavailing. This Court has frequently held that the legislative authority, acting within its proper field, is not bound to extend its regulation to all cases which it might possibly reach. The legislature "is free to recognize degrees of harm and it may confine its restrictions to those classes of cases where the need is deemed to be clearest." If "the law presumably hits the evil where it is most felt, it is not to be overthrown because there are other instances to which it might have been applied." There is no "doctrinaire requirement" that the legislation should be couched in all embracing terms. [Case references are omitted.] This familiar principle has repeatedly been applied to legislation which singles out women, and particular classes of women, in the exercise of the State's protective power. [Case references are omitted.] The relative need in the presence of the evil, no less than the existence of the evil itself, is a matter for the legislative judgment.

Our conclusion is that the case of Adkins *v.* Children's Hospital, 261 U.S. 525, should be, and it is, overruled. The judgment of the Supreme Court of the State of Washington is affirmed.

MR. JUSTICE SUTHERLAND, dissenting:

MR. JUSTICE VAN DEVANTER, MR. JUSTICE MCREYNOLDS, MR. JUSTICE BUTLER and I think the judgment of the court below should be reversed.

The principles and authorities relied upon to sustain the judgment, were considered in Adkins *v.* Children's Hospital, 261 U.S. 525, and Morehead *v.* New York ex rel. Tipaldo, 298 U.S. 587; and their lack of application to cases like the one in hand was pointed out. A sufficient answer to all that is now said will be found in the opinions of the court in those cases. Nevertheless, in the circumstances, it seems well to restate our reasons and conclusions. [The restatement is omitted.]

Section IV

What Limits on Free Speech?

THE AGE WHICH acclaimed the Declaration of Independence and added a Bill of Rights to the Federal Constitution considered freedom of expression one of the great natural rights which governments were instituted to protect. It believed that this sacred and inalienable right could not be justly impaired by any government, even with the consent of the majority. Today, many "truths" which appeared to Jefferson "self-evident" seem to have less influence on "the opinions of mankind," and the case for freedom of opinion must find a more pragmatic basis.

Most Americans would agree that freedom of speech and of the press is essential to self-government. Too few, however, adequately comprehend *why* freedom of discussion is fundamental to our democratic way of life, or why we should allow the propagation of doctrines which we regard as false, or even loathsome.

The words of the First Amendment are absolute and unqualified: "Congress shall make *no* law . . . abridging the freedom of speech, or of the press. . . ." If taken literally this would seem to prohibit *all* legislation by Congress which in any degree interferes with freedom of opinion. However, very few serious thinkers have maintained that freedom of speech should be entirely unlimited, and even many libertarian members of the Supreme Court have recognized that freedom of speech cannot be an unqualified right.

The cornerstone of most contemporary judicial discussion of freedom of speech is the so-called "clear and present" danger test first enunciated in the case of Schenck v. United States. "The question in every case," wrote Mr. Justice Holmes, "is whether the words used are used in such circumstances and are of such a nature as to create a clear and present danger that they will bring about the substantive evils that Congress has a right to prevent." Since, as Mr. Justice Holmes added, "It is a question of proximity and degree," it is not surprising that the Supreme Court justices should frequently disagree in their interpretation and application of this test.

Should freedom of speech include the right to advocate revolution and dictatorship? Should those who seek to destroy constitutional liberties be allowed to take advantage of the very liberties which they aim to destroy? To answer these questions requires an examination of the limits of freedom of discussion, an evaluation of our present loyalty-security program in public service, and related problems of individual liberties.

In the case of Gitlow v. New York, 268 U.S. 652, the majority

115

of the Supreme Court took the position that freedom of the press did not include the right to publish a manifesto which contained an "incitement" to violent revolution. In sustaining the Criminal Anarchy law of New York, Mr. Justice Sanford, writing for the majority of the Supreme Court, said in 1925:

"A single revolutionary spark may kindle a fire that, smouldering for a time, may burst into a sweeping and destructive conflagration. It cannot be said that the State is acting arbitrarily or unreasonably when in the exercise of its judgment as to the measures necessary to protect the public peace and safety, it seeks to extinguish the spark without waiting until it has enkindled the flame or blazed into the conflagration."

The dissent of Justice Holmes regarded this decision as a departure from the clear and present danger test enunciated in the Schenck case. He said:

"If what I think the correct test is applied it is manifest that there was no present danger of an attempt to overthrow the government by force on the part of the admittedly small minority who shared the defendant's view. . . . Whatever may be thought of the redundant discourse before us, it had no chance of starting a p.esent conflagration. If in the long run the beliefs expressed in proletarian dictatorship are destined to be accepted by the dominant forces of the community, the only meaning of free speech is that they should be given their chance and have their way."

Without overruling the Gitlow case, the Supreme Court in the thirties tended to return to the "clear and present danger test" as interpreted by Holmes and Brandeis. The extreme libertarian position was reached by the "Roosevelt Court" in 1941 in the case of Bridges *v.* California, 314 U.S. 252. In a 5-to-4 opinion Mr. Justice Black, writing for the majority, said: "What finally emerges from the 'clear and present danger' cases is a working principle that the substantive evil must be *extremely serious* and the degree of *imminence extremely high* before utterances can be punished." This victory for the extreme libertarian position in the Supreme Court, however, was only temporary.

The case of Dennis *v.* United States, decided in 1951, by a 6-to-2 vote, upheld the constitutionality of the Smith Act which punishes those who "knowingly or willfully advocate" the destruction of "any government in the United States by force or violence." The justices follow at least four different lines of reasoning in reaching their conclusions and none of these opinions was subscribed to by a majority of the Court.

It should be observed that in Yates *v.* United States, decided in 1957 after some changes in the composition of the Court, it took pains to emphasize that its decision was consistent with that in the Dennis case. However, it is pertinent to inquire whether the Court's narrow construction of the meaning of the word "organize" in the

Smith Act and its insistence that advocacy, to serve as a basis for conviction, must be directed toward *action,* do not, in fact suggest, a return to a somewhat more libertarian position.

We suggest, finally, that the ultimate issue is not one of constitutionality but of wisdom.

Topic 11

THE DILEMMAS OF FREEDOM

"Clear and Present Danger"

SCHENCK *V.* UNITED STATES
249 U.S. 47 (1919).

Error to the District Court of the United States for the Eastern District of Pennsylvania.

MR. JUSTICE HOLMES delivered the opinion of the court.

This is an indictment in three counts. The first charges a conspiracy to violate the Espionage Act of June 15, 1917, c. 30, § 3, 40 Stat. 217, 219, by causing and attempting to cause insubordination, &c., in the military and naval forces of the United States, and to obstruct the recruiting and enlistment service of the United States, when the United States was at war with the German Empire, to-wit, that the defendants wilfully conspired to have printed and circulated to men who had been called and accepted for military service under the Act of May 18, 1917, a document set forth and alleged to be calculated to cause such insubordination and obstruction. The count alleges overt acts in pursuance of the conspiracy, ending in the distribution of the document set forth. The second count alleges a conspiracy to commit an offense against the United States, to-wit, to use the mails for the transmission of matter declared to be non-mailable by Title XII, § 2 of the Act of June 15, 1917, to-wit, the above mentioned document, with an averment of the same overt acts. The third count charges an unlawful use of the mails for the transmission of the same matter and otherwise as above. The defendants were found guilty on all the counts. They set up the First Amendment to the Constitution forbidding Congress to make any law abridging the freedom of speech, or of the press, and bringing the case here on that ground have argued some other points also of which we must dispose. . . .

The document in question upon its first printed side recited the first section of the Thirteenth Amendment, said that the idea embodied in it was violated by the Conscription Act and that a conscript is little better than a convict. In impassioned language it intimated that conscription was despotism in its worst form and a monstrous wrong against humanity in the interest of Wall Street's chosen few. It said, "Do not submit to intimidation," but in form at least confined itself to peaceful measures such as a petition for the repeal of the act.

The other and later printed side of the sheet was headed "Assert Your Rights." It stated reasons for alleging that any one violated the Constitution when he refused to recognize "your right to assert your opposition to the draft," and went on, "If you do not assert and support your rights, you are helping to deny or disparage rights which it is the solemn duty of all citizens and residents of the United States to retain." It described the arguments on the other side as coming from cunning politicians and a mercenary capitalist press, and even silent consent to the conscription law as helping to support an infamous conspiracy. It denied the power to send our citizens away to foreign shores to shoot up the people of other lands, and added that words could not express the condemnation such coldblooded ruthlessness deserves, &c., winding up, "You must do your share to maintain, support and uphold the rights of the people of this country." Of course the document would not have been sent unless it had been intended to have some effect, and we do not see what effect it could be expected to have upon persons subject to the draft except to influence them to obstruct the carrying of it out. The defendants do not deny that the jury might find against them on this point.

But it is said, suppose that that was the tendency of this circular, it is protected by the First Amendment to the Constitution. Two of the strongest expressions are said to be quoted respectively from well-known public men. It well may be that the prohibition of laws abridging the freedom of speech is not confined to previous restraints, although to prevent them may have been the main purpose, as intimated in Patterson *v.* Colorado, 205 U.S. 454, 462. We admit that in many places and in ordinary times the defendants in saying all that was said in the circular would have been within their constitutional rights. But the character of every act depends upon the circumstances in which it is done. Aikens *v.* Wisconsin, 195 U.S. 194, 205, 206. The most stringent protection of free speech would not protect a man in falsely shouting fire in a theatre and causing a panic. It does not even protect a man from an injunction against uttering words that may have all the effect of force. Gompers *v.* Buck Stove & Range Co., 221 U.S. 418, 439.

The question in every case is whether the words used are used in such circumstances and are of such a nature as to create a clear and present danger that they will bring about the substantive evils that Congress has a right to prevent. It is a question of proximity and degree. When a nation is at war many things that might be said in time of peace are such a hindrance to its effort that their utterance will not be endured so long as men fight and that no Court could regard them as protected by any constitutional right. It seems to be admitted that if an actual obstruction of the recruiting service were proved, liability for words that produced that effect might be enforced. The statute of 1917 in § 4 punishes conspiracies to obstruct as well as actual obstruction. If the act (speaking, or circulating a paper), its tendency and the intent with which it is done are the same, we perceive no ground for saying that success alone warrants making the act a crime. Goldman *v.* United States, 245 U.S. 474, 477. Indeed that case might be said to dispose of the present contention if the precedent covers all *media concludendi*. But as the right to free speech was not referred to specially, we have thought fit to add a few words. . . .

Judgments affirmed.

"Free Trade in Ideas"

JUSTICE OLIVER WENDELL HOLMES, JR.*

Persecution for the expression of opinions seems to me perfectly logical. If you have no doubt of your premises or your power and want a certain result with all your heart you naturally express your wishes in law and sweep away all opposition. To allow opposition by speech seems to indicate that you think the speech impotent, as when a man says that he has squared the circle, or that you do not care wholeheartedly for the result, or that you doubt either your power or your premises. But when men have realized that time has upset many fighting faiths, they may come to believe even more than they believe the very foundations of their own conduct that the ultimate good desired is better reached by free trade in ideas—that the best test of truth is the power of the thought to get itself accepted in the competition of the market, and that truth is the only ground upon which their wishes safely can be carried out. That, at any rate, is the theory of our Constitution. It is an experiment, as all life is an experiment. Every

* The selection is from his dissenting opinion in Abrams *v.* United States, 250 U.S. 616, 624 (1919).

year if not every day we have to wager our salvation upon some prophecy based upon imperfect knowledge. While that experiment is part of our system I think that we should be eternally vigilant against attempts to check the expression of opinions that we loathe and believe to be fraught with death, unless they so imminently threaten immediate interference with the lawful and pressing purposes of the law that an immediate check is required to save the country.

I wholly disagree with the argument of the Government that the First Amendment left the common law as to seditious libel in force. History seems to me against the notion. I had conceived that the United States through many years had shown its repentance for the Sedition Act of 1798 by repaying fines that it imposed. Only the emergency that makes it immediately dangerous to leave the correction of evil counsels to time warrants making any exception to the sweeping command, "Congress shall make no law . . . abridging the freedom of speech." Of course I am speaking only of expressions of opinion and exhortations, which were all that were uttered here, but I regret that I cannot put into more impressive words my belief that in their conviction upon this indictment the defendants were deprived of their rights under the Constitution of the United States.

Free Speech and Self-Government

ALEXANDER MEIKLEJOHN *

The First Amendment to the Constitution, as we all know, forbids the federal Congress to make any law which shall abridge the freedom of speech. In recent years, however, the government of the United States has in many ways limited the freedom of public discussion. For example, the Federal Bureau of Investigation has built up, throughout the country, a system of espionage, of secret police, by which hundreds of thousands of our people have been listed as holding this or that set of opinions. The only conceivable justification of that listing by a government agency is to provide a basis for action by the government in dealing with those persons. And that procedure reveals an attitude toward freedom of speech which is widely held in the United States. Many of us are now convinced that, under the Constitution, the government is justified in bringing pressure to bear against the holding or expressing of beliefs which are labeled "dangerous." Congress, we think, may rightly abridge the freedom of such beliefs.

* Former President, Amherst College. Author of *The Liberal College, Freedom and the College* and other works. The selection is from Alexander Meiklejohn, *Free Speech and Its Relation to Self-Government* (New York, Harper & Brothers, 1948), *passim.* Reprinted by permission of author and publisher.

Again, the legislative committees, federal and state, which have been appointed to investigate un-American activities, express the same interpretation of the Constitution. All the inquirings and questionings of those committees are based upon the assumption that certain forms of political opinion and advocacy should be, and legitimately may be, suppressed. And, further, the Department of Justice, acting on the same assumption, has recently listed some sixty or more organizations, association with which may be taken by the government to raise the question of "disloyalty" to the United States. And finally, the President's Loyalty Order, moving with somewhat uncertain steps, follows the same road. We are officially engaged in the suppression of "dangerous" speech.

Now, these practices would seem to be flatly contradictory of the First Amendment. Are they? What do we mean when we say that "Congress shall make no law . . . abridging the freedom of speech . . . ?" What is this "freedom of speech" which we guard against invasion by our chosen and authorized representatives? Why may not a man be prevented from speaking if, in the judgment of Congress, his ideas are hostile and harmful to the general welfare of the nation? Are we, for example, required by the First Amendment to give men freedom to advocate the abolition of the First Amendment? Are we bound to grant freedom of speech to those who, if they had the power, would refuse it to us? The First Amendment, taken literally, seems to answer "Yes" to those questions. It seems to say that no speech, however dangerous, may, for that reason, be suppressed. But the Federal Bureau of Investigation, the un-American Activities Committees, the Department of Justice, the President, are, at the same time, answering "No" to the same question. Which answer is right? What is the valid American doctrine concerning the freedom of speech? . . .

When men govern themselves, it is they—and no one else—who must pass judgment upon unwisdom and unfairness and danger. And that means that unwise ideas must have a hearing as well as wise ones, unfair as well as fair, dangerous as well as safe, un-American as well as American. Just so far as, at any point, the citizens who are to decide an issue are denied acquaintance with information or opinion or doubt or disbelief or criticism which is relevant to that issue, just so far the result must be ill-considered, ill-balanced planning for the general good. *It is that mutilation of the thinking process of the community against which the First Amendment to the Constitution is directed.* The principle of the freedom of speech springs from the necessities of the program of self-government. It is not a Law of Nature or of Reason in the abstract. It is a deduction from the basic American agreement that public issues shall be decided by universal suffrage.

If, then, on any occasion in the United States it is allowable to say that the Constitution is a good document it is equally allowable, in that situation, to say that the Constitution is a bad document. If a public building may be used in which to say, in time of war, that the war is justified, then the same building may be used in which to say that it is not justified. If it be publicly argued that conscription for armed service is moral and necessary, it may likewise be publicly argued that it is immoral and unnecessary. If it may be said that American political institutions are superior to those of England or Russia or Germany, it may, with equal freedom, be said that those of England or Russia or Germany are superior to ours. These conflicting views may be expressed, must be expressed, not because they are valid, but because they are relevant. If they are responsibly entertained by any-one, we, the voters, need to hear them. When a question of policy is "be-fore the house," free men choose to meet it not with their eyes shut, but with their eyes open. To be afraid of ideas, any idea, is to be unfit for self-government. Any such suppression of ideas about the common good, the First Amendment condemns with its absolute disapproval. The freedom of ideas shall not be abridged. . . .

In the course of his argument [in Schenck *v.* United States] Mr. Holmes says, "The question in every case is whether the words used are used in such circumstances and are of such a nature as to create a clear and present danger that they will bring about the substantive evils that Congress has a right to prevent." And to this he adds, a few sentences later, "It seems to be admitted that, if an actual obstruction of the recruiting service were proved, liability for words that produced that effect might be enforced."

As one reads these words of Mr. Holmes, one is uneasily aware of the dangers of his rhetorical skill. At two points the argument seems at first much more convincing than it turns out to be. First, the phrase, "substantive evils that Congress has a right to prevent," seems to settle the issue by presumption, seems to establish the right of legislative control. If the legis-lature has both the right and the duty to prevent certain evils, then ap-parently it follows that the legislature must be authorized to take whatever action is needed for the preventing of those evils. But our plan of govern-ment by limited powers forbids that that inference be drawn. The Bill of Rights, for example, is a series of denials that the inference is valid. It lists, one after the other, forms of action which, however useful they might be in the service of the general welfare, the legislature is forbidden to take. And, that being true, the "right to prevent evils" does not give unqualifiedly the right to prevent evils. In the judgment of the Constitution, some preven-tions are more evil than are the evils from which they would save us. And the First Amendment is a case in point. If that amendment means anything, it means that certain substantive evils which, in principle, Congress has a right to prevent, must be endured if the only way of avoiding them is by the abridging of that freedom of speech upon which the entire structure of our free institutions rests. . . .

But, second, the "clear and present danger" argument which Mr. Holmes here offers, moves quickly from deliberate obstruction of a law to reasonable protest against it. Taken as it stands, his formula tells us that whenever the expression of a minority opinion involves clear and present danger to the public safety it may be denied the protection of the First Amendment. And that means that whenever crucial and dangerous issues have come upon the nation, free and unhindered discussion of them must stop. If, for example, a majority in Congress is taking action against "substantive evils which Congress has a right to prevent," a minority which opposes such action is not entitled to the freedom of speech of Article I, section 6.* Under that ruling, dissenting judges might, in "dangerous" situations, be forbidden to record their dissents. Minority citizens might, in like situations, be required to hold their peace. No one, of course, believes that this is what Mr. Holmes or the court intended to say. But it is what, in plain words, they did say. The "clear and present danger" opinion stands on the record of the court as a peculiarly inept and unsuccessful attempt to formulate an exception to the principle of the freedom of speech. . . .

Human discourse, as the First Amendment sees it, is not "a mere academic and harmless discussion." If it were, the advocates of self-government would be as little concerned about it as they would be concerned about the freedom of men playing solitaire or chess. The First Amendment was not written primarily for the protection of those intellectual aristocrats who pursue knowledge solely for the fun of the game, whose search for truth expresses nothing more than a private intellectual curiosity or an equally private delight and pride in mental achievement. It was written to clear the way for thinking which serves the general welfare. It offers defense to men who plan and advocate and incite toward corporate action for the common good. On behalf of such men it tells us that every plan of action must have a hearing, every relevant idea of fact or value must have full consideration, whatever may be the dangers which that activity involves. It makes no difference whether a man is advocating conscription or opposing it, speaking in favor of a war or against it, defending democracy or attacking it, planning a communist reconstruction of our economy or criticising it. So long as his active words are those of participation in public discussion and public decision of matters of public policy, the freedom of those words may not be abridged. That freedom is the basic postulate of a society which is governed by the votes of its citizens.

"If, in the long run, the beliefs expressed in proletarian dictatorship are destined to be accepted by the dominant forces of the community, the only meaning of free speech is that they should be given their chance and

* Article I, section 6, of the Constitution defining the duties and privileges of the members of Congress, says, ". . . and for any speech or debate in either House, they shall not be questioned in any other place."

have their way." [The quote is from Justice Holmes' dissent in Gitlow *v.* New York, 268 U.S. 652 (1925).] That is Americanism. In these wretched days of postwar and, it may be, of prewar, hysterical brutality, when we Americans, from the president down, are seeking to thrust back Communist belief by jailing its advocates, by debarring them from office, by expelling them from the country, by hating them, the gallant, uncompromising words of Mr. Holmes, if we would listen to them, might help to restore our sanity, our understanding of the principles of the Constitution. They might arouse in us something of the sense of shame which the nation so sorely needs. . . .

We Americans, in choosing our form of government, have made, at this point, a momentous decision. We have decided to be self-governed. We have measured the dangers and the values of the suppression of the freedom of public inquiry and debate. And, on the basis of that measurement, having regard for the public safety, we have decided that the destruction of freedom is always unwise, that freedom is always expedient. The conviction recorded by that decision is not a sentimental vagary about the "natural rights" of individuals. It is a reasoned and sober judgment as to the best available method of guarding the public safety. We, the People, as we plan for the general welfare, do not choose to be "protected" from the "search for truth." On the contrary, we have adopted it as our "way of life," our method of doing the work of governing for which, as citizens, we are responsible. Shall we, then, as practitioners of freedom, listen to ideas which, being opposed to our own, might destroy confidence in our form of government? Shall we give a hearing to those who hate and despise freedom, to those who, if they had the power, would destroy our institutions? Certainly, yes! Our action must be guided, not by their principles, but by ours. We listen, not because they desire to speak, but because we need to hear. If there are arguments against our theory of government, our policies in war or in peace, we the citizens, the rulers, must hear and consider them for ourselves. That is the way of public safety. It is the program of self-government.

In his study, *Free Speech in the United States,* Mr. Chafee gives abundant evidence in support of this criticism. . . . The suppression of freedom of speech, he finds, has been throughout our history a disastrous threat to the public safety. As he sums up his results, he takes as a kind of motto the words of John Stuart Mill: "A State which dwarfs its men in order that they may be more docile instruments in its hands even for beneficial purposes, will find that with small men no great thing can really be accomplished." Mr. Chafee tells the story, as he sees it, of the futility and disaster which came upon the efforts of President Wilson in World War I as he was driven, by the threat of clear and present dangers, into the suppressions of the Espionage Act.

President Wilson's tragic failure, according to Mr. Chafee, was his blindness to the imperative need of public information and public discussion bearing on the issues of war and peace. He felt bound to prevent imminent substantive evils which might arise from that discussion. In the attempt to do so, nearly two thousand persons, Mr. Chafee tells us, were prosecuted. The fruits of those prosecutions he sums up as follows: ". . . tens of thousands among those 'forward-looking men and women' to whom President Wilson had appealed in earlier years were bewildered and depressed and silenced by the negation of freedom in the twenty-year sentences requested by his legal subordinates from complacent judges. So we had plenty of patriotism and very little criticism, except of the slowness of ammunition production. Wrong courses were followed like the dispatch of troops to Archangel in 1918, which fatally alienated Russia from Wilson's aims for a peaceful Europe. Harmful facts like the secret treaties were concealed while they could have been cured, only to bob up later and wreck everything." . . .

And the final argument upon which the absoluteness of the First Amendment rests [is that] it does not balance intellectual freedom against public safety. On the contrary, its great declaration is that intellectual freedom is the necessary bulwark of the public safety. That declaration admits of no exceptions. If, by suppression, we attempt to avoid lesser evils, we create greater evils. We buy temporary and partial advantage at the cost of permanent and dreadful disaster. That disaster is the breakdown of self-government. Free men need the truth as they need nothing else. In the last resort, it is only the search for and the dissemination of truth that can keep our country safe.*

* It should be noted that, according to Meiklejohn, the word *liberty* in the due process clause of the Fifth Amendment has been "construed by the Supreme Court to include 'the liberty of speech.' The Fifth Amendment is, then, saying that the people of the United States have a *civil* liberty of speech which, *by due legal process,* the government may limit or suppress." It is Meiklejohn's view, therefore, that the Constitution recognizes "two radically different kinds of utterances." The first—relating to "discussion of public policy"—is in the realm of "absolute freedom of speech." But "the constitutional status of a merchant advertising his wares" and of similar activities "is utterly different" and subject to regulation and limitation.

Freedom to Destroy Freedom?

FREDERICK BERNAYS WIENER *

As our legislatures and courts come to closer grips with the nature—and the menace—of world communism, Americans are necessarily forced to inquire whether there is anything in the Constitution of the United States that guarantees immunity, or even possible success, for those who seek to replace the model of government fashioned at Philadelphia in 1787 with the pattern forged at Petrograd in 1917–1918 and since further developed in the Kremlin at Moscow.

To what extent, if at all, is "freedom for the thought that we hate" a principle of our Constitution? Is it the theory of our fundamental law "that the best test of the truth is the power of the thought to get itself accepted in the competition of the market"? Is there anything in the Constitution that requires the Government to stay its hand against those who would overthrow it, and to "let them stand undisturbed as monuments of the safety with which error of opinion may be tolerated when reason is left free to combat it"? . . .

FRAMERS INTENDED TO LEAVE NO SCOPE FOR ANTI-REPUBLICAN GOVERNMENT

Having fought monarchy for long and hard years in the face of terrible odds, the Framers were not quixotic enough to cast away the prize of independence by providing new sanctuaries where that hated institution might conveniently reappear. They had not turned the other cheek when George III struck at their liberties; now, having secured those liberties, they were not with the other hand preparing to endanger the hard-won prize by providing freedom for the hated thought of monarchy. Indeed, they intended to leave no scope for any antirepublican form of government. For those men of 1787, though they knew nothing of swastikas, or dictatorship of the proletariat, or fascism, or communism, were yet fully aware, good classicists that they were, of the excesses of tyranny in the days of ancient Greece and Rome. And for anti-republican ideas, whether of kings by divine right or of tyrants by irresistible force, of totalitarianism whether in the name of blood unity or in the name of economic interest, they never intended to provide a foothold. They not

* Member of the District of Columbia Bar. Professorial Lecturer in Law, George Washington University. Formerly with the Department of Justice. Author of *Effective Appellate Advocacy*. This selection is from Frederick Bernays Wiener, " 'Freedom for the Thought That We Hate': Is It a Principle of the Constitution?" *American Bar Association Journal*, Vol. 37 (March 1951). By permission.

only presupposed the orthodoxy of republicanism, they guaranteed its continuance.

At this point it will doubtless be urged, however, that the writings of Thomas Jefferson reflect the very ideas that Mr. Justice Holmes expressed, and Mr. Justice Brandeis elaborated, over a century later. Reliance is generally had on the one sentence from Jefferson's First Inaugural:

> If there be any among us who would wish to dissolve this Union or to change its republican form, let them stand undisturbed as monuments of the safety with which error of opinion may be tolerated where reason is left free to combat it.

The hard fact of the matter is, however, that Jefferson is far from being a safe guide on the issues now under consideration. He was not a member of the Constitutional Convention, being at the time Minister to France, and had no access to its records during his lifetime. His letter to Kercheval, written in 1816, in which he deprecates looking at constitutions with sanctimonious reverence, is merely an individual attitude, which is far from representative of the views of those who framed the Constitution in 1787, or of those who in 1795 decided to admit to citizenship only those aliens who were "attached to the principles of the Constitution of the United States." [1] In that connection, it is significant that Madison, then in Congress, opposed the latter requirement. "It was hard to make a man swear that he preferred the Constitution of the United States, or to give any general opinion, because he may, in his own private judgment, think Monarchy or Aristocracy better, and yet be honestly determined to support this Government as he finds it." [2] But Congress adopted the provision over Madison's objections.[3] . . .

Moreover, since Inaugural Addresses traditionally and normally have partisan connotations, Jefferson's First Inaugural must be read in the light of the political controversies of the day. It must be read with an eye to the Sedition Act, and to that measure's partisan, even virulent, enforcement by the Federalists; and pre-eminently, it must be read in the light of the vital circumstance, always overlooked by those who uncritically accept that document as constitutional gospel, that Jefferson was the real author of the Kentucky and Virginia Resolutions and hence the spiritual ancestor of nullification and of its progeny, secession.

The Southern leaders of 1860–1861 relied upon the Jeffersonian doctrine of noninterference when they left the Union. But the course of American history did not follow the Jeffersonian view. For if Jefferson was right, if those "who would wish to dissolve this Union" should "stand undisturbed as monuments of the safety with which error of opinion may be tolerated where reason is left free to combat it," then Lincoln was

[1] Secs. 1 (*Thirdly*) and 2, Act Jan. 29, 1795, c. 20, 1 Stat. 414, 414–415.
[2] 4 *Annals of Congress* 1023.   [3] *Ibid.*

128 *Basic Issues*

wrong, and the men who fought to preserve the Union were wrong, and we should now be two nations instead of one. Holmes himself asserted the error of the Jeffersonian view at the Marshall centennial in 1901, when, as Chief Justice of Massachusetts, he noted "The fact that time has been on Marshall's side, and that the theory for which Hamilton argued, and he decided, and Webster spoke, and Grant fought, and Lincoln died, is now our cornerstone." [4] Moreover, Holmes, on the United States Supreme Court, wrote the opinions upholding the convictions of Schenck [5] and Frohwerk [6] and Debs,[7] in which the "clear and present danger" test was first enunciated; if Jefferson was right, these persons should never have been convicted, they should have been permitted to stand undisturbed. Indeed, it is not amiss to point out that, much earlier, Jefferson had backtracked also; the treason prosecutions of his Administration indicated a strong disinclination to let Aaron Burr *et al.* pursue their machinations without interference.[8] . . .

WE NEED NOT FOLLOW WEIMAR EXAMPLE

These are not mere theoretical abstractions; the views herein discussed can be illustrated and illustrated by the sorry spectacle of the demise of republican governments elsewhere.

The record in the Knauer denaturalization case [9] showed that Hitler prior to 1923 "never had any intention of trying to obtain political power in Germany except by means of force, except by violence, by a *coup d'état,* or a similar direct action method." It was only after the failure of the 1923 *Putsch* "that he with his advisers decided that the way to do away with democracy in Germany was to use democracy—was to use democratic rights and privileges with the explicit aim of paralyzing democracy and the democratic procedures. . . ." [10] By allowing full "freedom for the thought that we hate," by opening its marketplaces in ideas to "the monstrous and debauching power of the organized lie," [11] the

[4] Holmes, "John Marshall," in *Collected Legal Papers* 87, 90–91.

[5] Schenck *v.* United States, 249 U.S. 47.

[6] Frohwerk *v.* United States, 249 U.S. 204.

[7] Debs *v.* United States, 249 U.S. 211.

[8] United States *v.* Burr, Fed. Case No. 14693 (C.C.D. Va.); *Ex parte Bollman,* 4 Cranch 75. See also 4 Channing, *History of the United States,* 335–343; 3 Beveridge, *The Life of John Marshall,* 274–545; Channing, *The Jeffersonian System,* 155–168.

[9] Knauer *v.* United States, 328 U.S. 654.

[10] Consolidated transcript in Knauer *v.* United States, *supra,* pages 611 *et seq.* (not printed).

[11] Gilbert Murray, quoted in Kimball, "The Espionage Acts and the Limits of Legal Toleration," 33 *Harv. L. Rev.,* 442, 447, note 36, which is an exceptionally well-reasoned defense of Abrams *v.* United States, 250 U.S. 616.

Germany of the Weimar Republic effectively signed its own death warrant. Nothing in the Constitution of the United States requires us to follow the German example.

The sad history of the second overthrow of Czechoslovakia in 1948 by the Communists illuminates the practical difficulties in the way of applying the "clear and present danger" test to the purposeful underground plottings of organized communism. Those who parrot the Holmes' formula in a vacuum of their own devising—ignoring, by the way, Holmes' warning about the consequences which follow when thoughts become encysted in fine phrases [12]—have yet to indicate the point at which, in their view, the Czechoslovak Government would have been free to move against those who eventually overthrew it. What was said in reply to a similar argument in a treason case affords an ample answer to most of the contentions drawn from a too literal application of "clear and present danger" to the machinations of the Communist Party: "And after this kind of reasoning they will not be guilty till they have success; and if they have success enough, it will be too late to question them." [13] Judge Learned Hand's Dennis opinion [14] blows a welcome breath of fresh realistic air through a good deal of abstract libertarianism. That opinion holds, in substance and effect, that nothing in the Constitution of the United States requires this country to suffer the Czechoslovak experience in the name of freedom of thought. . . .

The truth of the matter is that "freedom for the thought that we hate" is not, certainly in any absolute sense, a principle of our Constitution. And the present paper suggests that it would be well to remember that fact whenever we have occasion to deal with those who seek to use the protections of the Constitution in order to undermine the Constitution, who take advantage of American freedom only that they may be the better able to destroy it.*

[12] "It is one of the misfortunes of the law that ideas become encysted in phrases and thereafter for a long time cease to provoke further analysis." Holmes, J., dissenting in Hyde v. United States, 225 U.S. 347, 384, 391.

"To rest upon a formula is a slumber that, prolonged, means death." Holmes, "Ideals and Doubts," in *Collected Legal Papers,* 303, 306.

[13] Lord Chief Justice Treby in *Trial of Captain Vaughan,* 13 How. St. Tr. 485, 533.

[14] 183 F. (2d) 201 (C.A. 2d), decided August 1, 1950. [See next Topic.] Holmes' dissent in the Abrams case was cited by Dennis *et al.* in their brief some eleven times, Brandeis' concurring opinion in the Whitney case no less than nineteen times. Counsel for Dennis *et al.* had not progressed beyond page 14 of the transcript of his oral argument in the Second Circuit before he quoted the sentence beginning, "If there be any among us who would wish to dissolve this Union or to change its republican form," etc.

* For a reply to the above article see Arthur S. Katz, "Freedom for the Thought We Hate," *American Bar Association Journal* (December, 1951), Vol. 37, pp. 901–904.

Topic 12

FREEDOM TO ADVOCATE REVOLUTION?

❧❧❧

Democracy May Defend Itself

DENNIS ET AL. *V.* UNITED STATES

341 U.S. 494 (1951)

MR. CHIEF JUSTICE VINSON announced the judgment of the Court and an opinion in which MR. JUSTICE REED, MR. JUSTICE BURTON and MR. JUSTICE MINTON join.

Petitioners were indicted in July, 1948, for violation of the conspiracy provisions of the Smith Act, . . . § 11, during the period of April, 1945, to July, 1948. . . . We granted certiorari, 340 U.S. 863, limited to the following two questions: (1) Whether either § 2 or § 3 of the Smith Act, inherently or as construed and applied in the instant case, violates the First Amendment and other provisions of the Bill of Rights; (2) whether either § 2 or § 3 of the Act, inherently or as construed and applied in the instant case, violates the First and Fifth Amendments because of indefiniteness.

Sections 2 and 3 of the Smith Act, . . . provide as follows:

SEC. 2.
(a) It shall be unlawful for any person—
(1) to knowingly or willfully advocate, abet, advise, or teach the duty, necessity, desirability, or propriety of overthrowing or destroying any government in the United States by force or violence, or by the assassination of any officer of such government; .
(3) to organize or help to organize any society, group, or assembly of persons who teach, advocate, or encourage the overthrow or destruction of any government in the United States by force or violence; or to be or become a member of, or affiliate with, any such society, group, or assembly of persons, knowing the purpose thereof. . . .
SEC. 3. It shall be unlawful for any person to attempt to commit, or to conspire to commit, any of the acts prohibited by the provisions of . . . this title.

The indictment charged the petitioners with wilfully and knowingly conspiring (1) to organize as the Communist Party of the United States of America a society, group and assembly of persons who teach and advocate the overthrow and destruction of the Government of the United States by force and violence, and (2) knowingly and wilfully to advocate and teach the duty and necessity of overthrowing and destroying the Government of the United States by force and violence. The indictment further alleged that § 2 of the Smith Act proscribes these acts and that any conspiracy to take such action is a violation of § 3 of the Act.

The trial of the case extended over nine months, six of which were devoted to the taking of evidence, resulting in a record of 16,000 pages. . . . Petitioners dispute the meaning to be drawn from the evidence, contending that the Marxist-Leninist doctrine they advocated taught that force and violence to achieve a Communist form of government in an existing democratic state would be necessary only because the ruling classes of that state would never permit the transformation to be accomplished peacefully, but would use force and violence to defeat any peaceful political and economic gain the Communists could achieve.

But the Court of Appeals held that the record supports the following broad conclusions: By virtue of their control over the political apparatus of the Communist Political Association,[1] petitioners were able to transform that organization into the Communist Party; that the policies of the Association were changed from peaceful cooperation with the United States and its economic and political structure to a policy which had existed before the United States and the Soviet Union were fighting a common enemy, namely, a policy which worked for the overthrow of the Government by force and violence; that the Communist Party is a highly disciplined organization, adept at infiltration into strategic positions, use of aliases, and double-meaning language; that the Party is rigidly controlled; that Communists, unlike other political parties, tolerate no dissension from the policy laid down by the guiding forces, but that the approved program is slavishly followed by the members of the Party; that the literature of the Party and the statements and activities of its leaders, petitioners here, advocate, and the general goal of the Party was, during the period in question, to achieve a successful overthrow of the existing order by force and violence.

It will be helpful in clarifying the issues to treat next the contention that the trial judge improperly interpreted the statute by charging that the statute required an unlawful intent before the jury could convict. More specifically, he charged that the jury could not find the petitioners guilty under the indictment unless they found that petitioners had the intent "to overthrow the government by force and violence as speedily as circumstances permit. . . ."

The structure and purpose of the statute demand the inclusion of intent as an element of the crime. Congress was concerned with those who ad-

---

[1] Following the dissolution of the Communist International in 1943, the Communist Party of the United States dissolved and was reconstituted as the Communist Political Association. The program of this Association was one of cooperation between labor and management, and, in general, one designed to achieve national unity and peace and prosperity in the post-war period.

vocate and organize for the overthrow of the Government. Certainly those who recruit and combine for the purpose of advocating overthrow intend to bring about that overthrow. We hold that the statute requires as an essential element of the crime proof of the intent of those who are charged with its violation to overthrow the Government by force and violence. . . .

Nor does the fact that there must be an investigation of a state of mind under this interpretation afford any basis for rejection of that meaning. A survey of Title 18 of the U.S. Code indicates that the vast majority of the crimes designated by that Title require, by express language, proof of the existence of a certain mental state, in words such as "knowingly," "maliciously," "wilfully," "with the purpose of," "with intent to," or combinations or permutations of these and synonymous terms. The existence of a *mens rea* is the rule of, rather than the exception to, the principles of Anglo-American criminal jurisprudence. See American Communications Assn. *v.* Douds, 339 U.S. 382, 411 (1950). . . .

The obvious purpose of the statute is to protect existing Government, not from change by peaceable, lawful and constitutional means, but from change by violence, revolution and terrorism. That it is within the *power* of the Congress to protect the Government of the United States from armed rebellion is a proposition which requires little discussion. Whatever theoretical merit there may be to the argument that there is a "right" to rebellion against dictatorial governments is without force where the existing structure of the government provides for peaceful and orderly change. We reject any principle of governmental helplessness in the face of preparation for revolution, which principle, carried to its logical conclusion, must lead to anarchy. No one could conceive that it is not within the power of Congress to prohibit acts intended to overthrow the Government by force and violence. The question with which we are concerned here is not whether Congress has such *power,* but whether the *means* which it has employed conflict with the First and Fifth Amendments to the Constitution.

One of the bases for the contention that the means which Congress has employed are invalid takes the form of an attack on the face of the statute on the grounds that by its terms it prohibits academic discussion of the merits of Marxism-Leninism, that it stifles ideas and is contrary to all concepts of a free speech and a free press. . . .

The very language of the Smith Act negates the interpretation which petitioners would have us impose on that Act. It is directed at advocacy, not discussion. Thus, the trial judge properly charged the jury that they could not convict if they found that petitioners did "no more than pursue peaceful studies and discussions or teaching and advocacy in the realm of ideas." He further charged that it was not unlawful "to conduct in an American college and university a course explaining the philosophical theories set forth in the books which have been placed in evidence." Such a charge is in strict accord with the statutory language, and illustrates the meaning to be placed on those words. Congress did not intend to eradicate the free discussion of political theories, to destroy the traditional rights of Americans to discuss and evaluate ideas without fear of governmental sanction. Rather Congress was concerned with the very kind of activity in which the evidence showed these petitioners engaged. . . .

We pointed out in Douds, *supra,* that the basis of the First Amendment is the hypothesis that speech can rebut speech, propaganda will answer propaganda, free debate of ideas will result in the wisest governmental policies. It is for this reason that this Court has recognized the inherent value of free discourse. An analysis of the leading cases in this Court which have involved direct limitations on speech, however, will demonstrate that both the majority of the Court and the dissenters in particular cases have recognized that this is not an unlimited, unqualified right, but that the societal value of speech must, on occasion, be subordinated to other values and considerations.

No important case involving free speech was decided by this Court prior to Schenck *v.* United States, 249 U.S. 47 (1919). . . . Writing for a unanimous Court, Justice Holmes stated that the "question in every case is whether the words used are used in such circumstances and are of such a nature as to create a clear and present danger that they will bring about the substantive evils that Congress has a right to prevent." 249 U.S. at 52. But the force of even this expression is considerably weakened by the reference at the end of the opinion to Goldman *v.* United States, 245 U.S. 474 (1918), a prosecution under the same statute. Said Justice Holmes, "Indeed [Goldman] might be said to dispose of the present contention if the precedent covers all *media concludendi,* but as the right to free speech was not referred to specially, we have thought fit to add a few words." 249 U.S. at 52.

The fact is inescapable, too, that the phrase bore no connotation that the danger was to be any threat to the safety of the Republic. The charge was causing and attempting to cause insubordination in the military forces and obstruct recruiting. The objectionable document denounced conscription and its most inciting sentence was, "You must do your share to maintain, support and uphold the rights of the people of this country." 249 U.S. at 51. Fifteen thousand copies were printed and some circulated. This insubstantial gesture toward insubordination in 1917 during war was held to be a clear and present danger of bringing about the evil of military insubordination. . . .

The rule we deduce . . . is that where an offense is specified by a statute in nonspeech or nonpress terms, a conviction relying upon speech or press as evidence of violation may be sustained only when the speech or publication created a "clear and present danger" of attempting or accomplishing the prohibited crime, *e. g.,* interference with enlistment. . . .

Neither Justice Holmes (nor Justice Brandeis) ever envisioned that a shorthand phrase should be crystallized into a rigid rule to be applied inflexibly without regard to the circumstances of each case. Speech is not an absolute, above and beyond control by the legislature when its judgment, subject to review here, is that certain kinds of speech are so undesirable as to warrant criminal sanction. Nothing is more certain in modern society than the principle that there are no absolutes, that a name, a phrase, a standard has meaning only when associated with the considerations which gave birth to the nomenclature. See Douds, 339 U.S. at 397. To those who would paralyze our Government in the face of impending threat by encasing it in a semantic straitjacket we must reply that all concepts are relative.

In this case we are squarely presented with the application of the "clear and present danger" test, and must decide what that phrase imports. We first note that many of the cases in which this Court has reversed convictions by use of this or similar tests have been based on the fact that the interest which the State was attempting to protect was itself too insubstantial to warrant restriction of speech. . . .

Overthrow of the Government by force and violence is certainly a substantial enough interest for the Government to limit speech. Indeed, this is the ultimate value of any society, for if a society cannot protect its very structure from armed internal attack, it must follow that no subordinate value can be protected. If, then, this interest may be protected, the literal problem which is presented is what has been meant by the use of the phrase "clear and present danger" of the utterances bringing about the evil within the power of Congress to punish.

Obviously, the words cannot mean that before the Government may act, it must wait until the *putsch* is about to be executed, the plans have been laid and the signal is awaited. If Government is aware that a group aiming at its overthrow is attempting to indoctrinate its members and to commit them to a course whereby they will strike when the leaders feel the circumstances permit, action by the Government is required. The argument that there is no need for Government to concern itself, for Government is strong, it possesses ample powers to put down a rebellion, it may defeat the revolution with ease needs no answer. For that is not the question. Certainly an attempt to overthrow the Government by force, even though doomed from the outset because of inadequate numbers or power of the revolutionists, is a sufficient evil for Congress to prevent. The damage which such attempts create both physically and politically to a nation makes it impossible to measure the validity in terms of the probability of success, or the immediacy of a successful attempt.

In the instant case the trial judge charged the jury that they could not convict unless they found that petitioners intended to overthrow the Government "as speedily as circumstances would permit." This does not mean, and could not properly mean, that they would not strike until there was certainty of success. What was meant was that the revolutionists would strike when they thought the time was ripe. We must therefore reject the contention that success or probability of success is the criterion.

The situation with which Justices Holmes and Brandeis were concerned in Gitlow was a comparatively isolated event, bearing little relation in their minds to any substantial threat to the safety of the community. Such also is true of cases like Fiske *v.* Kansas, 274 U.S. 380 (1927), and DeJonge *v.* Oregon, 299 U.S. 353 (1937); but cf. Lazar *v.* Pennsylvania, 286 U.S. 532 (1932). They were not confronted with any situation comparable to the instant one—the development of an apparatus designed and dedicated to the overthrow of the Government, in the context of world crisis after crisis.

Chief Judge Learned Hand, writing for the majority below, interpreted the phrase as follows: "In each case [courts] must ask whether the gravity of the 'evil,' discounted by its improbability, justifies such invasion of free speech as is necessary to avoid the danger." 183 F. 2d at 212. We adopt this statement of the rule. As articulated by Chief Judge Hand, it is as succinct and inclusive as any other we might devise at this time. It takes into consideration those factors which we deem relevant, and relates their significances. More we cannot expect from words.

Likewise, we are in accord with the court below, which affirmed the trial court's finding that the requisite danger existed. The mere fact that from the period 1945 to 1948 petitioners' activities did not result in an attempt to overthrow the Government by force and violence is of course no answer to the fact that there was a group that was ready to make the attempt. The formation by petitioners of such a highly organized conspiracy, with rigidly disciplined members subject to call when the leaders, these petitioners, felt that the time had come for action, coupled with the inflammable nature of world conditions, similar uprisings in other countries, and the touch-and-go nature of our relations with countries with whom petitioners were in the very least ideologically attuned, convince us that their convictions were justified on this score. And this analysis disposes of the contention that a conspiracy to advocate, as distinguished from the advocacy itself, cannot be constitutionally restrained, because it comprises only the preparation. It is the existence of the conspiracy which creates the danger. [Citations omitted.] If the ingredients of the reaction are present, we cannot bind the Government to wait until the catalyst is added. . . .

The argument that the action of the trial court is erroneous, in declaring as a matter of law that such violation shows sufficient danger to justify the punishment despite the First Amendment, rests on the theory that a jury must decide a question of the application of the First Amendment. We do not agree.

When facts are found that establish the violation of a statute the protection against conviction afforded by the First Amendment is a matter of
law. The doctrine that there must be a clear and present danger of a substantive evil that Congress has a right to prevent is a judicial rule to be
applied as a matter of law by the courts. The guilt is established by proof
of facts. Whether the First Amendment protects the activity which constitutes the violation of the statute must depend upon a judicial determination of the scope of the First Amendment applied to the circumstances
of the case. . . .

The question in this case is whether the statute which the legislature has
enacted may be constitutionally applied. In other words, the Court must
examine judicially the application of the statute to the particular situation,
to ascertain if the Constitution prohibits the conviction. We hold that the
statute may be applied where there is a "clear and present danger" of the
substantive evil which the legislature had the right to prevent. Bearing as it
does, the marks of a "question of law," the issue is properly one for the
judge to decide. . . .

Petitioners intended to overthrow the Government of the United States
as speedily as the circumstances would permit. Their conspiracy to organize
the Communist Party and to teach and advocate the overthrow of the Government of the United States by force and violence created a "clear and
present danger" of an attempt to overthrow the Government by force and
violence. They were properly and constitutionally convicted for violation
of the Smith Act. The judgments of conviction are

Affirmed.

Mr. Justice Clark took no part in the consideration or decision of
this case.

Mr. Justice Frankfurter, concurring in affirmance of the judgment.

The First Amendment categorically demands that "Congress shall make
no law respecting an establishment of religion, or prohibiting the free
exercise thereof; or abridging the freedom of speech, or of the press;
or the right of the people peaceably to assemble, and to petition the Government for a redress of grievances." The right of a man to think what he
pleases, to write what he thinks, and to have his thoughts made available for
others to hear or read has an engaging ring of universality. The Smith Act
and this conviction under it no doubt restrict the exercise of free speech and
assembly. Does that, without more, dispose of the matter?

Just as there are those who regard as invulnerable every measure for
which the claim of national survival is invoked, there are those who find
in the Constitution a wholly unfettered right of expression. Such literalness
treats the words of the Constitution as though they were found on a piece

of outworn parchment instead of being words that have called into being a nation with a past to be preserved for the future. The soil in which the Bill of Rights grew was not a soil of arid pedantry. The historic antecedents of the First Amendment preclude the notion that its purpose was to give unqualified immunity to every expression that touched on matters within the range of political interest.

The Massachusetts Constitution of 1780 guaranteed free speech; yet there are records of at least three convictions for political libels obtained between 1799 and 1803. The Pennsylvania Constitution of 1790 and the Delaware Constitution of 1792 expressly imposed liability for abuse of the right of free speech. Madison's own State put on its books in 1792 a statute confining the abusive exercise of the right of utterance. And it deserves to be noted that in writing to John Adams' wife, Jefferson did not rest his condemnation of the Sedition Act of 1798 on his belief in unrestrained utterance as to political matter. The First Amendment, he argued, reflected a limitation upon Federal power, leaving the right to enforce restrictions on speech to the States.

The language of the First Amendment is to be read not as barren words found in a dictionary but as symbols of historic experience illumined by the presuppositions of those who employed them. Not what words did Madison and Hamilton use, but what was it in their minds which they conveyed? Free speech is subject to prohibition of those abuses of expression which a civilized society may forbid. As in the case of every other provision of the Constitution that is not crystallized by the nature of its technical concepts, the fact that the First Amendment is not self-defining and self-enforcing neither impairs its usefulness nor compels its paralysis as a living instrument. . . .

Absolute rules would inevitably lead to absolute exceptions, and such exceptions would eventually corrode the rules. The demands of free speech in a democratic society as well as the interest in national security are better served by candid and informed weighing of the competing interests, within the confines of the judicial process, than by announcing dogmas too inflexible for the non-Euclidian problems to be solved.

But how are competing interests to be assessed? Since they are not subject to quantitative ascertainment, the issue necessarily resolves itself into asking, who is to make the adjustment?—who is to balance the relevant factors and ascertain which interest is in the circumstances to prevail? Full responsibility for the choice cannot be given to the courts. Courts are not representative bodies. They are not designed to be a good reflex of a democratic society. Their judgment is best informed, and therefore most dependable, within narrow limits. Their essential quality is detachment, founded on independence. History teaches that the independence of the judiciary is jeopardized when courts become embroiled in the passions of the day and assume primary responsibility in choosing between competing political, economic and social pressures.

Primary responsibility for adjusting the interests which compete in the situation before us of necessity belongs to the Congress. The nature of the power to be exercised by this Court has been delineated in decisions not charged with the emotional appeal of situations such as that now before us. We are to set aside the judgment of those whose duty it is to legislate only if there is no reasonable basis for it. [Citations omitted.] . . .

In all fairness, the argument cannot be met by reinterpreting the Court's frequent use of "clear" and "present" to mean an entertainable "probability." In giving this meaning to the phrase "clear and present danger," the Court of Appeals was fastidiously confining the rhetoric of opinions to the exact scope of what was decided by them. We have greater responsibility for having given constitutional support, over repeated protests, to uncritical libertarian generalities.

Nor is the argument of the defendants adequately met by citing isolated cases. Adjustment of clash of interests which are at once subtle and fundamental is not likely to reveal entire consistency in a series of instances presenting the clash. It is not too difficult to find what one seeks in the language of decisions reporting the effort to reconcile free speech with the interests with which it conflicts. The case for the defendants requires that their conviction be tested against the entire body of our relevant decisions. Since the significance of every expression of thought derives from the circumstances evoking it, results reached rather than language employed give the vital meaning. . . .

[After reviewing a number of decisions of the Court, MR. JUSTICE FRANK-FURTER continued:] I must leave to others the ungrateful task of trying to reconcile all these decisions. In some instances we have too readily permitted juries to infer deception from error, or intention from argumentative or critical statements. Abrams *v.* United States; Schaefer *v.* United States; Pierce *v.* United States; Gilbert *v.* Minnesota, 254 U.S. 325. In other instances we weighted the interest in free speech so heavily that we permitted essential conflicting values to be destroyed. Bridges *v.* California; Craig *v.* Harney. Viewed as a whole, however, the decisions express an attitude toward the judicial function and a standard of values which for me are decisive of the case before us.

First.—Free-speech cases are not an exception to the principle that we are not legislators, that direct policy-making is not our province. How best to reconcile competing interests is the business of legislatures, and the balance they strike is a judgment not to be displaced by ours, but to be respected unless outside the pale of fair judgment. . .

Second.—A survey of the relevant decisions indicates that the results which we have reached are on the whole those that would ensue from careful weighing of conflicting interests. The complex issues presented by regulation of speech in public places, by picketing, and by legislation prohibiting advocacy of crime have been resolved by scrutiny of many factors besides the imminence and gravity of the evil threatened.

The matter has been well summarized by a reflective student of the Court's work. "The truth is that the clear-and-present-danger test is an oversimplified judgment unless it takes account also of a number of other factors: the relative seriousness of the danger in comparison with the value of the occasion for speech or political activity; the availability of more moderate controls than those which the state has imposed; and perhaps the specific intent with which the speech or activity is launched. No matter how rapidly we utter the phrase 'clear and present danger,' or how closely we hyphenate the words, they are not a substitute for the weighing of values. They tend to convey a delusion of certitude when what is most certain is the complexity of the strands in the web of freedoms which the judge must disentangle." Freund, *On Understanding the Supreme Court,* 27–28. . . .

Bearing in mind that Mr. Justice Holmes regarded questions under the First Amendment as questions of "proximity and degree," Schenck *v.* United States, 249 U.S. at 52, it would be a distortion, indeed a mockery, of his reasoning to compare the "puny anonymities," 250 U.S. at 629, to which he was addressing himself in the Abrams case in 1919 or the publication that was "futile and too remote from possible consequences," 268 U.S. at 673, in the Gitlow case in 1925 with the setting of events in this case in 1950.

"It does an ill-service to the author of the most quoted judicial phrases regarding freedom of speech, to make him the victim of a tendency which he fought all his life, whereby phrases are made to do service for critical analysis by being turned into dogma. 'It is one of the misfortunes of the law that ideas become encysted in phrases and thereafter for a long time cease to provoke further analysis.' Holmes, J., dissenting, in Hyde *v.* United States, 225 U.S. 347, 384, at 391." . . . It were far better that the phrase be abandoned than that it be sounded once more to hide from the believers in an absolute right of free speech the plain fact that the interest in speech, profoundly important as it is, is no more conclusive in judicial review than other attributes of democracy or than a determination of the people's representatives that a measure is necessary to assure the safety of government itself.

Third.—Not every type of speech occupies the same position on the scale of values. There is no substantial public interest in permitting certain kinds of utterances: "the lewd and obscene, the profane, the libelous, and the insulting or 'fighting' words—those which by their very utterance inflict injury or tend to incite an immediate breach of the peace." Chaplinsky *v.* New Hampshire, 315 U.S. 568, 572. We have frequently indicated that the interest in protecting speech depends on the circumstances of the occasion. See Niemotko *v.* Maryland, 340 U.S. at 275–283. It is pertinent to the decision before us to consider where on the scale of values we have in the past placed the type of speech now claiming constitutional immunity.

The defendants have been convicted of conspiring to organize a party of persons who advocate the overthrow of the Government by force and violence. The jury has found that the object of the conspiracy is advocacy as "a rule or principle of action," "by language reasonably and ordinarily calculated to incite persons to such action," and with the intent to cause the overthrow "as speedily as circumstances would permit."

On any scale of values which we have hitherto recognized, speech of this sort ranks low.

Throughout our decisions there has recurred a distinction between the statement of an idea which may prompt its hearers to take unlawful action, and advocacy that such action be taken. The distinction has its root in the conception of the common law that a person who procures another to do an act is responsible for that act as though he had done it himself. . . . We frequently have distinguished protected forms of expression from statements which "incite to violence and crime and threaten the overthrow of organized government by unlawful means." Stromberg *v.* California, 283 U.S. at 369. . . .

The object of the conspiracy before us is clear enough that the chance of error in saying that the defendants conspired to advocate rather than to express ideas is slight. Mr. Justice Douglas quite properly points out that the conspiracy before us is not a conspiracy to overthrow the Government. But it would be equally wrong to treat it as a seminar in political theory.

These general considerations underlie decision of the case before us.

On the one hand is the interest in security. The Communist Party was not designed by these defendants as an ordinary political party. For the circumstances of its organization, its aims and methods, and the relation of the defendants to its organization and aims we are concluded by the jury's verdict. The jury found that the Party rejects the basic premise of our political system—that change is to be brought about by nonviolent constitutional process. The jury found that the Party advocates the theory that there is a duty and necessity to overthrow the Government by force and violence. It found that the Party entertains and promotes this view, not as a prophetic insight or as a bit of unworldly speculation, but as a program for winning adherents and as a policy to be translated into action.

In finding that the defendants violated the statute, we may not treat as established fact that the Communist Party in this country is of significant size, well-organized, well-disciplined, conditioned to embark on unlawful activity when given the command. But in determining whether application of the statute to the defendants is within the constitutional powers of Congress, we are not limited to the facts found by the jury. We must view such a question in the light of whatever is relevant to a legislative judgment. We may take judicial notice that the Communist doctrines which these defendants have conspired to advocate are in the ascendency in powerful nations who cannot be acquitted of unfriendliness to the institutions of this country. We may take account of evidence brought forward at this trial and elsewhere, much of which has long been common knowledge. In sum, it would amply justify a legislature in concluding that recruitment of additional members for the Party would create a substantial danger to national security.

In 1947, it has been reliably reported, at least 60,000 members were enrolled in the Party. Evidence was introduced in this case that the membership was organized in small units, linked by an intricate chain of command, and protected by elaborate precautions designed to prevent disclosure of individual identity. There are no reliable data tracing acts of sabotage or espionage directly to these defendants. But a Canadian Royal Commission appointed in 1946 to investigate espionage reported that it was "overwhelmingly established" that "the Communist movement was the principal base within which the espionage network was recruited." The most notorious spy in recent history was led into the service of the Soviet Union through Communist indoctrination. Evidence supports the conclusion that members of the Party seek and occupy positions of importance in political and labor organizations. Congress was not barred by the Constitution from believing that indifference to such experience would be an exercise not of freedom but of irresponsibility.

On the other hand is the interest in free speech. The right to exert all governmental powers in aid of maintaining our institutions and resisting their physical overthrow does not include intolerance of opinions and speech that cannot do harm although opposed and perhaps alien to dominant, traditional opinion. The treatment of its minorities, especially their legal position, is among the most searching tests of the level of civilization attained by a society. It is better for those who have almost unlimited power of government in their hands to err on the side of freedom. We have enjoyed so much freedom for so long that we are perhaps in danger of forgetting how much blood it cost to establish the Bill of Rights. . . .

We must not overlook the value of that interchange. Freedom of expression is the well-spring of our civilization—the civilization we seek to maintain and further by recognizing the right of Congress to put some limitation upon expression. Such are the paradoxes of life. For social development of trial and error, the fullest possible opportunity for the free play of the human mind is an indispensable prerequisite. The history of civilization is in considerable measure the displacement of error which once held sway as official truth by beliefs which in turn have yielded to other truths. Therefore the liberty of man to search for truth ought not to be fettered, no matter what orthodoxies he may challenge. Liberty of thought soon shrivels without freedom of expression. Nor can truth be pursued in an atmosphere hostile to the endeavor or under dangers which are hazarded only by heroes. . . .

It is not for us to decide how we would adjust the clash of interests which this case presents were the primary responsibility for reconciling it ours. Congress has determined that the danger created by advocacy of overthrow justifies the ensuing restriction on freedom of speech. The determination was made after due deliberation, and the seriousness of the congressional purpose is attested by the volume of legislation passed to effectuate the same ends.

Can we then say that the judgment Congress exercised was denied it by the Constitution? Can we establish a constitutional doctrine which forbids the elected representatives of the people to make this choice? Can we hold that the First Amendment deprives Congress of what it deemed necessary for the Government's protection?

To make validity of legislation depend on judicial reading of events still in the womb of time—a forecast, that is, of the outcome of forces at best appreciated only with knowledge of the topmost secrets of nations—is to charge the judiciary with duties beyond its equipment. We do not expect courts to pronounce historic verdicts on bygone events. Even historians have conflicting views to this day on the origin and conduct of the French Revolution. It is as absurd to be confident that we can measure the present clash of forces and their outcome as to ask us to read history still enveloped in clouds of controversy. . . .

Even when moving strictly within the limits of constitutional adjudication, judges are concerned with issues that may be said to involve vital finalities. The too easy transition from disapproval of what is undesirable to condemnation as unconstitutional, has led some of the wisest judges to question the wisdom of our scheme in lodging such authority in courts. But it is relevant to remind that in sustaining the power of Congress in a case like this nothing irrevocable is done. The democratic process at all events is not impaired or restricted. Power and responsibility remain with the people and immediately with their representation. All the Court says is that Congress was not forbidden by the Constitution to pass this enactment and a prosecution under it may be brought against a conspiracy such as the one before us.

The wisdom of the assumptions underlying the legislation and prosecution is another matter. In finding that Congress has acted within its power, a judge does not remotely imply that he favors the implications that lie beneath the legal issues. Considerations there enter which go beyond the criteria that are binding upon judges within the narrow confines of their legitimate authority. . . .

Civil liberties draw at best only limited strength from legal guaranties. Preoccupation by our people with the constitutionality, instead of with the wisdom of legislation or of executive action, is preoccupation with a false value. Even those who would most freely use the judicial brake on the democratic process by invalidating legislation that goes deeply against their grain, acknowledge, at least by paying lip service, that constitutionality does not exact a sense of proportion or the sanity of humor or an absence of fear. Focusing attention on constitutionality tends to make constitutionality synonymous with wisdom. When legislation touches freedom of thought and freedom of speech, such a tendency is a formidable enemy of the free spirit.

Much that should be rejected as illiberal, because repressive and en-venoming, may well be not unconstitutional. The ultimate reliance for the deepest needs of civilization must be found outside their vindication in courts of law; apart from all else, judges, howsoever they may conscien-tiously seek to discipline themselves against it, unconsciously are too apt to be moved by the deep undercurrents of public feeling. A persistent, positive translation of the liberating faith into the feelings and thoughts and actions of men and women is the real protection against attempts to strait-jacket the human mind. Such temptations will have their way, if fear and hatred are not exorcized. The mark of a truly civilized man is confidence in the strength and security derived from the inquiring mind. We may be grateful for such honest comforts as it supports, but we must be unafraid of its uncertitudes. Without open minds there can be no open society. And if society be not open the spirit of man is mutilated and becomes enslaved.

MR. JUSTICE JACKSON, concurring.

This prosecution is the latest of never-ending, because never successful, quests for some legal formula that will secure an existing order against revolutionary radicalism. It requires us to reappraise, in the light of our own times and conditions, constitutional doctrines devised under other cir-cumstances to strike a balance between authority and liberty.

Activity here charged to be criminal is conspiracy—that defendants con-spired to teach and advocate, and to organize the Communist Party to teach and advocate, overthrow and destruction of the Government by force and violence. There is no charge of actual violence or attempt at overthrow.

The principal reliance of the defense in this Court is that the conviction cannot stand under the Constitution because the conspiracy of these de-fendants presents no "clear and present danger" of imminent or foreseeable overthrow.

Basic Issues

Communism . . . appears today as a closed system of thought representing Stalin's version of Lenin's version of Marxism. As an ideology, it is not one of spontaneous protest arising from American working-class experience. It is a complicated system of assumptions, based on European history and conditions, shrouded in an obscure and ambiguous vocabulary, which allures our ultrasophisticated intelligentsia more than our hardheaded working people. From time to time it champions all manner of causes and grievances and makes alliances that may add to its foothold in government or embarrass the authorities.

The Communist Party, nevertheless, does not seek its strength primarily in numbers. Its aim is a relatively small party whose strength is in selected, dedicated, indoctrinated, and rigidly disciplined members. From established policy it tolerates no deviation and no debate. It seeks members that are, or may be, secreted in strategic posts in transportation, communications, industry, government, and especially in labor unions where it can compel employers to accept and retain its members. It also seeks to infiltrate and control organizations of professional and other groups. Through these placements in positions of power it seeks a leverage over society that will make up in power of coercion what it lacks in power of persuasion.

The Communists have no scruples against sabotage, terrorism, assassination, or mob disorder; but violence is not with them, as with the anarchists, an end in itself. The Communist Party advocates force only when prudent and profitable. Their strategy of stealth precludes premature or uncoordinated outbursts of violence, except, of course, when the blame will be placed on shoulders other than their own. They resort to violence as to truth, not as a principle but as an expedient. Force or violence, as they would resort to it, may never be necessary, because infiltration and deception may be enough.

Force would be utilized by the Communist Party not to destroy government but for its capture. The Communist recognizes that an established government in control of modern technology cannot be overthrown by force until it is about ready to fall of its own weight. Concerted uprising, therefore, is to await that contingency and revolution is seen, not as a sudden episode, but as the consummation of a long process.

The United States, fortunately, has experienced Communism only in its preparatory stages and for its pattern of final action must look abroad. Russia, of course, was the pilot Communist revolution, which to the Marxist confirms the Party's assumptions and points its destiny. But Communist technique in the overturn of a free government was disclosed by the *coup d'état* in which they seized power in Czechoslovakia. There the Communist Party during its preparatory stage claimed and received protection for its freedoms of speech, press, and assembly. Pretending to be but another political party, it eventually was conceded participation in government, where it entrenched reliable members chiefly in control of police and information services. When the government faced a foreign and domestic crisis, the Communist Party had established a leverage strong enough to threaten civil war.

In a period of confusion the Communist plan unfolded and the underground organization came to the surface throughout the country in the form chiefly of labor "action committees." Communist officers of the unions took over transportation and allowed only persons with party permits to travel. Communist printers took over the newspapers and radio and put out only party-approved versions of events. Possession was taken of telegraph and telephone systems and communications were cut off wherever directed by party heads. Communist unions took over the factories, and in the cities a partisan distribution of food was managed by the Communist organization. A virtually bloodless abdication by the elected government admitted the Communists to power, whereupon they instituted a reign of oppression and terror, and ruthlessly denied to all others the freedoms which had sheltered their conspiracy.

The foregoing is enough to indicate that, either by accident or design, the Communist stratagem outwits the anti-anarchist pattern of statute aimed against "overthrow by force and violence" if qualified by the doctrine that only "clear and present danger" of accomplishing that result will sustain the prosecution.

The "clear and present danger" test was an innovation by Mr. Justice Holmes in the Schenck case, reiterated and refined by him and Mr. Justice Brandeis in later cases, all arising before the era of World War II revealed the subtlety and efficacy of modernized revolutionary techniques used by totalitarian parties. In those cases, they were faced with convictions under so-called criminal syndicalism statutes aimed at anarchists but which, loosely construed, had been applied to punish socialism, pacifism, and left-wing ideologies, the charges often resting on far-fetched inferences which, if true, would establish only technical or trivial violations. They proposed "clear and present danger" as a test for the sufficiency of evidence in particular cases.

I would save it, unmodified, for application as a "rule of reason" in the kind of case for which it was devised. When the issue is criminality of a hot-headed speech on a street corner, or circulation of a few incendiary pamphlets, or parading by some zealots behind a red flag, or refusal of a handful of school children to salute our flag, it is not beyond the capacity of the judicial process to gather, comprehend, and weigh the necessary materials for decision whether it is a clear and present danger of substantive evil or a harmless letting off of steam. It is not a prophecy, for the danger in such cases has matured by the time of trial or it was never present.

The test applies and has meaning where a conviction is sought to be based on a speech or writing which does not directly or explicitly advocate a crime but to which such tendency is sought to be attributed by construction or by implication from external circumstances. The formula in such cases favors freedoms that are vital to our society, and, even if sometimes applied too generously, the consequences cannot be grave. But its recent expansion has extended, in particular to Communists, unprecedented immunities. Unless we are to hold our Government captive in a judge-made verbal trap, we must approach the problem of a well-organized, nation-wide conspiracy, such as I have described, as realistically as our predecessors faced the trivialities that were being prosecuted until they were checked with a rule of reason.

I think reason is lacking for applying that test to this case.

If we must decide that this Act and its application are constitutional only if we are convinced that petitioner's conduct creates a "clear and present danger" of violent overthrow, we must appraise imponderables, including international and national phenomena which baffle the best informed foreign offices and our most experienced politicians. We would have to foresee and predict the effectiveness of Communist propaganda, opportunities for infiltration, whether, and when, a time will come that they consider propitious for action, and whether and how fast our existing government will deteriorate. And we would have to speculate as to whether an approaching Communist *coup* would not be anticipated by a nationalistic fascist movement. No doctrine can be sound whose application requires us to make a prophecy of that sort in the guise of a legal decision. The judicial process simply is not adequate to a trial of such far-flung issues. The answers given would reflect our own political predilections and nothing more.

The authors of the clear and present danger test never applied it to a case like this, nor would I. If applied as it is proposed here, it means that the Communist plotting is protected during its period of incubation; its preliminary stages of organization and preparation are immune from the law; the Government can move only after imminent action is manifest, when it would, of course, be too late.

The highest degree of constitutional protection is due to the individual acting without conspiracy. But even an individual cannot claim that the Constitution protects him in advocating or teaching overthrow of government by force or violence. I should suppose no one would doubt that Congress has power to make such attempted overthrow a crime. But the contention is that one has the constitutional right to work up a public desire and will to do what is a crime to attempt. I think direct incitement by speech or writing can be made a crime, and I think there can be a conviction without also proving that the odds favored its success by 99 to 1, or some other extremely high ratio. . . .

As aptly stated by Judge Learned Hand in Masses Publishing Co. *v.*

Patten, 244 F. 535, 540: "One may not counsel or advise others to violate the law as it stands. Words are not only the keys of persuasion, but the triggers of action, and those which have no purport but to counsel the violation of law cannot by any latitude of interpretation be a part of that public opinion which is the final source of government in a democratic state."

Of course, it is not always easy to distinguish teaching or advocacy in the sense of incitement from teaching or advocacy in the sense of exposition or explanation. It is a question of fact in each case.

What really is under review here is a conviction of conspiracy, after a trial for conspiracy, on an indictment charging conspiracy, brought under a statute outlawing conspiracy. With due respect to my colleagues, they seem to me to discuss anything under the sun except the law of conspiracy. One of the dissenting opinions even appears to chide me for "invoking the law of conspiracy." As that is the case before us, it may be more amazing that its reversal can be proposed without even considering the law of conspiracy.

The Constitution does not make conspiracy a civil right. The Court has never before done so and I think it should not do so now. Conspiracies of labor unions, trade associations, and news agencies have been condemned, although accomplished, evidenced and carried out, like the conspiracy here, chiefly by letter-writing, meetings, speeches and organization. Indeed, this Court seems, particularly in cases where the conspiracy has economic ends, to be applying its doctrines with increasing severity. While I consider criminal conspiracy a dragnet device capable of perversion into an instrument of injustice in the hands of a partisan or complacent judiciary, it has an established place in our system of law, and no reason appears for applying it only to concerted action claimed to disturb interstate commerce and withholding it from those claimed to undermine our whole Government.

The basic rationale of the law of conspiracy is that a conspiracy may be an evil in itself, independently of any other evil it seeks to accomplish. Thus, we recently held in Pinkerton *v.* United States, 328 U.S. 640, 643–644, "It has been long and consistently recognized by the Court that the commission of the substantive offense and a conspiracy to commit it are separate and distinct offenses. The power of Congress to separate the two and to affix to each a different penalty is well established. . . . And the plea of double jeopardy is no defense to a conviction for both offenses. . . ."

So far does this doctrine reach that it is well settled that Congress may make it a crime to conspire with others to do what an individual may lawfully do on his own. This principle is illustrated in conspiracies that violate the antitrust laws as sustained and applied by this Court. Although one may raise the prices of his own products, and many, acting without concert, may do so, the moment they conspire to that end they are punishable. The same principle is applied to organized labor. Any workman may quit his work for any reason, but concerted actions to the same end are in some circumstances forbidden. Labor Management Relations Act, 61 Stat. 136, § 8 (b), 29 U.S.C. § 158 (b).

The reasons underlying the doctrine that conspiracy may be a substantive evil in itself, apart from any evil it may threaten, attempt, or accomplish are peculiarly appropriate to conspiratorial Communism.

> The reason for finding criminal liability in case of a combination to effect an unlawful end or to use unlawful means, where none would exist, even though the act contemplated were actually committed by an individual, is that a combination of persons to commit a wrong, either as an end or as a means to an end, is so much more dangerous, because of its increased power to do wrong, because it is more difficult to guard against and prevent the evil designs of a group of persons than of a single person, and because of the terror which fear of such a combination tends to create in the minds of people.[2]

There is lamentation in the dissents about the injustice of conviction in the absence of some overt act. Of course, there has been no general uprising against the Government, but the record is replete with acts to carry out the conspiracy alleged, acts such as always are held sufficient to consummate the crime where the statute requires an overt act.

But the shorter answer is that no overt act is or need be required. The Court, in antitrust cases, early upheld the power of Congress to adopt the ancient common law that makes conspiracy itself a crime. Through Mr. Justice Holmes, it said: "Coming next to the objection that no overt act is laid, the answer is that the Sherman Act punished the conspiracies at which it is aimed on the common law footing—that is to say, it does not make the doing of any act other than the act of conspiring a condition of liability." Nash *v.* United States, 229 U.S. 373, 378. Reiterated, United States *v.* Socony-Vacuum Oil Co., 310 U.S. 150, 252. It is not to be supposed that the power of Congress to protect the Nation's existence is more limited than its power to protect interstate commerce.

Also, it is urged that since the conviction is for conspiracy to teach and advocate, and to organize the Communist Party to teach and advocate, the First Amendment is violated, because freedoms of speech and press protect teaching and advocacy regardless of what is taught or advocated. I have never thought that to be the law.

I do not suggest that Congress could punish conspiracy to advocate something, the doing of which it may not punish. Advocacy or exposition of the doctrine of communal property ownership, or any political philosophy unassociated with advocacy of its imposition by force or seizure of govern-

---

[2] Miller on Criminal Law, 110.

ment by unlawful means could not be reached through conspiracy prosecution. But it is not forbidden to put down force or violence, it is not forbidden to punish its teaching or advocacy, and the end being punishable, there is no doubt of the power to punish conspiracy for the purpose.

The defense of freedom of speech or press has often been raised in conspiracy cases, because, whether committed by Communists, by businessmen, or by common criminals, it usually consists of words written or spoken, evidenced by letters, conversations, speeches or documents. Communication is the essence of every conspiracy, for only by it can common purpose and concert of action be brought about or be proved. However, when labor unions raised the defense of free speech against a conspiracy charge, we unanimously said:

> It rarely has been suggested that the constitutional freedom for speech and press extends its immunity to speech or writing used as an integral part of conduct in violation of a valid criminal statute. We reject the contention now. . . .
> Such an expansive interpretation of the constitutional guaranties of speech and press would make it practically impossible ever to enforce laws against agreements in restraint of trade as well as many other agreements and conspiracies deemed injurious to society. Giboney *v.* Empire Storage & Ice Co., 336 U.S. 490, 498, 502. . . .

In conspiracy cases the Court not only has dispensed with proof of clear and present danger but even of power to create a danger: "It long has been settled, however, that a 'conspiracy to commit a crime is a different offense from the crime that is the object of the conspiracy.' Petitioners, for example, might have been convicted here of a conspiracy to monopolize without ever having acquired the power to carry out the object of the conspiracy. . . ." American Tobacco Co. *v.* United States, 328 U.S. 781, 789.

Having held that a conspiracy alone is a crime and its consummation is another, it would be weird legal reasoning to hold that Congress could punish the one only if there was "clear and present danger" of the second. This would compel the Government to prove two crimes in order to convict for one.

When our constitutional provisions were written, the chief forces recognized as antagonists in the struggle between authority and liberty were the Government on the one hand and the individual citizen on the other. It was thought that if the state could be kept in its place the individual could take care of himself.

In more recent times these problems have been complicated by the intervention between the state and the citizen of permanently organized, well-financed, semi-secret and highly disciplined political organizations.

Totalitarian groups here and abroad perfected the technique of creating private paramilitary organizations to coerce both the public government and its citizens. These organizations assert as against our Government all of the constitutional rights and immunities of individuals and at the same time exercise over their followers much of the authority which they deny to the Government. The Communist Party realistically is a state within a state, an authoritarian dictatorship within a republic. It demands these freedoms, not for its members, but for the organized party. It denies to its own members at the same time the freedom to dissent, to debate, to deviate from the party line, and enforces its authoritarian rule by crude purges, if nothing more violent.

The law of conspiracy has been the chief means at the Government's disposal to deal with the growing problems created by such organizations. I happen to think it is an awkward and inept remedy, but I find no constitutional authority for taking this weapon from the Government. There is no constitutional right to "gang up" on the Government.

While I think there was power in Congress to enact this statute and that, as applied in this case, it cannot be held unconstitutional, I add that I have little faith in the long-range effectiveness of this conviction to stop the rise of the Communist movement. Communism will not go to jail with these Communists. No decision by this Court can forestall revolution whenever the existing government fails to command the respect and loyalty of the people and sufficient distress and discontent are allowed to grow up among the masses. Many failures by fallen governments attest that no government can long prevent revolution by outlawry. Corruption, ineptitude, inflation, oppressive taxation, militarization, injustice, and loss of leadership capable of intellectual initiative in domestic or foreign affairs are allies on which the Communists count to bring opportunity knocking to their door. Sometimes I think they may be mistaken. But the Communists are not building just for today—the rest of us might profit by their example.

MR. JUSTICE BLACK, dissenting.

At the outset I want to emphasize what the crime involved in this case is, and what it is not. These petitioners were not charged with an attempt to overthrow the Government. They were not charged with overt acts of any kind designed to overthrow the Government. They were not even charged with saying anything or writing anything designed to overthrow the Government. The charge was that they agreed to assemble and to talk and publish certain ideas at a later date: The indictment is that they conspired to organize the Communist Party and to use speech or newspapers and other publications in the future to teach and advocate the forcible overthrow of the Government. No matter how it is worded, this is a virulent form of prior censorship of speech and press, which I believe the First Amendment forbids. I would hold § 3 of the Smith Act authorizing this prior restraint unconstitutional on its face and as applied.

But let us assume, contrary to all constitutional ideas of fair criminal procedure, that petitioners although not indicted for the crime of actual advocacy, may be punished for it. Even on this radical assumption, the other opinions in this case show that the only way to affirm these convictions is to repudiate directly or indirectly the established "clear and present danger" rule. This the Court does in a way which greatly restricts the protections afforded by the First Amendment. The opinions for affirmance indicate that the chief reason for jettisoning the rule is the expressed fear that advocacy of Communist doctrine endangers the safety of the Republic.

Undoubtedly, a governmental policy of unfettered communication of ideas does entail dangers. To the Founders of this Nation, however, the benefits derived from free expression were worth the risk. They embodied this philosophy in the First Amendment's command that Congress "shall make no law abridging . . . the freedom of speech, or of the press. . . ." I have always believed that the First Amendment is the keystone of our Government, that the freedoms it guarantees provide the best insurance against destruction of all freedom. At least as to speech in the realm of public matters, I believe that the "clear and present danger" test does not "mark the furthermost constitutional boundaries of protected expression" but does "no more than recognize a minimum compulsion of the Bill of Rights." Bridges *v*. California, 314 U.S. 252, 263.

So long as this Court exercises the power of judicial review of legislation, I cannot agree that the First Amendment permits us to sustain laws suppressing freedom of speech and press on the basis of Congress' or our own notions of mere "reasonableness." Such a doctrine waters down the First Amendment so that it amounts to little more than an admonition to Congress. The Amendment as so construed is not likely to protect any but those "safe" or orthodox views which rarely need its protection. I must also express my objection to the holding because, as MR. JUSTICE DOUGLAS' dissent shows, it sanctions the determination of a crucial issue of fact by the judge rather than by the jury. . . .

Public opinion being what it now is, few will protest the conviction of these Communist petitioners. There is hope, however, that in calmer times, when present pressures, passions and fears subside, this or some later Court will restore the First Amendment liberties to the high preferred place where they belong in a free society.

MR. JUSTICE DOUGLAS, dissenting.

If this were a case where those who claimed protection under the First Amendment were teaching the techniques of sabotage, the assassination of the President, the filching of documents from public files, the planting of bombs, the art of street warfare, and the like, I would have no doubts. The freedom to speak is not absolute; the teaching of methods of terror and other seditious conduct should be beyond the pale along with obscenity and immorality. This case was argued as if those were the facts. The argument imported much seditious conduct into the record. That is easy and it has popular appeal, for the activities of Communists in plotting and scheming against the free world are common knowledge.

But the fact is that no such evidence was introduced at the trial. There is a statute which makes a seditious conspiracy unlawful.[3] Petitioners, however, were not charged with a "conspiracy to overthrow" the Government. They were charged with a conspiracy to form a party and groups and assemblies of people who teach and advocate the overthrow of our Government by force or violence and with a conspiracy to advocate and teach its overthrow by force and violence. It may well be that indoctrination in the techniques of terror to destroy the Government would be indictable under either statute. But the teaching which is condemned here is of a different character.

So far as the present record is concerned, what petitioners did was to organize people to teach and themselves teach the Marxist-Leninist doctrine contained chiefly in four books: *Foundations of Leninism* by Stalin (1924), *The Communist Manifesto* by Marx and Engels (1848), *State and Revolution* by Lenin (1917), *History of the Communist Party of the Soviet Union (B)* (1939).[4]

Those books are to Soviet Communism what *Mein Kampf* was to Nazism. If they are understood, the ugliness of Communism is revealed, its deceit and cunning are exposed, the nature of its activities becomes apparent, and the chances of its success less likely. That is not, of course, the reason why petitioners chose these books for their classrooms. They are fervent Communists to whom these volumes are gospel. They preached the creed with the hope that some day it would be acted upon.

The opinion of the Court does not outlaw these texts nor condemn them to the fire, as the Communists do literature offensive to their creed. But if the books themselves are not outlawed, if they can lawfully remain on library shelves, by what reasoning does their use in a classroom become a

[3] 18 U.S.C. § 2384 provides: "If two or more persons in any State or Territory, or in any place subject to the jurisdiction of the United States, conspire to overthrow, put down, or to destroy by force the Government of the United States, or to levy war against them, or to oppose by force the authority thereof, or by force to prevent, hinder, or delay the execution of any law of the United States, or by force to seize, take, or possess any property of the United States contrary to the authority thereof, they shall each be fined not more than $5,000 or imprisoned not more than six years, or both."

[4] Other books taught were *Problems of Leninism* by Stalin, *Strategy and Tactics of World Communism* (H. Doc. No. 619, 80th Cong., 2d Sess.), and *Program of the Communist International*.

crime? It would not be a crime under the Act to introduce these books to a class, though that would be teaching what the creed of violent overthrow of the government is. The Act, as construed, requires the element of intent —that those who teach the creed believe in it. The crime then depends not on what is taught but on who the teacher is. That is to make freedom of speech turn not on *what is said,* but on the *intent* with which it is said. Once we start down that road we enter territory dangerous to the liberties of every citizen.

There was a time in England when the concept of constructive treason flourished. Men were punished not for raising a hand against the king but for thinking murderous thoughts about him. The Framers of the Constitution were alive to that abuse and took steps to see that the practice would not flourish here. Treason was defined to require overt acts—the evolution of a plot against the country into an actual project. The present case is not one of treason. But the analogy is close when the illegality is made to turn on intent, not on the nature of the act. We then start probing men's minds for motive and purpose; they become entangled in the law not for what they did but *for what they thought;* they get convicted not for what they said but for the purpose with which they said it. . . .

The vice of treating speech as the equivalent of overt acts of a treasonable or seditious character is emphasized by a concurring opinion, which by invoking the law of conspiracy makes speech do service for deeds which are dangerous to society. The doctrine of conspiracy has served divers and oppressive purposes and in its broad reach can be made to do great evil. But never until today has anyone seriously thought that the ancient law of conspiracy could constitutionally be used to turn speech into seditious conduct. Yet that is precisely what is suggested.

I repeat that we deal here with speech alone, not with speech *plus* acts of sabotage or unlawful conduct. Not a single seditious act is charged in the indictment. To make a lawful speech unlawful because two men conceive it is to raise the law of conspiracy to appalling proportions. That course is to make a radical break with the past and to violate one of the cardinal principles of our constitutional scheme.

Free speech has occupied an exalted position because of the high service it has given our society. Its protection is essential to the very existence of a democracy. The airing of ideas releases pressures which otherwise might become destructive. When ideas compete in the market for acceptance, full and free discussion exposes the false and they gain few adherents. Full and free discussion even of ideas we hate encourages the testing of our own prejudices and preconceptions. Full and free discussion keeps a society from becoming stagnant and unprepared for the stresses and strains that work to tear all civilizations apart.

Full and free discussion has indeed been the first article of our faith. We have founded our political system on it. It has been the safeguard of every religious, political, philosophical, economic, and racial group amongst us. We have counted on it to keep us from embracing what is cheap and false; we have trusted the common sense of our people to choose the doctrine true to our genius and to reject the rest. This has been the one single outstanding tenet that has made our institutions the symbol of freedom and equality. We have deemed it more costly to liberty to suppress a despised minority than to let them vent their spleen. We have above all else feared the political censor. We have wanted a land where our people can be exposed to all the diverse creeds and cultures of the world.

There comes a time when even speech loses its constitutional immunity. Speech innocuous one year may at another time fan such destructive flames that it must be halted in the interests of the safety of the Republic. That is the meaning of the clear and present danger test. When conditions are so critical that there will be no time to avoid the evil that the speech threatens, it is time to call a halt. Otherwise, free speech which is the strength of the Nation will be the cause of its destruction.

Yet free speech is the rule, not the exception. The restraint to be constitutional must be based on more than fear, on more than passionate opposition against the speech, on more than a revolted dislike for its contents. There must be some immediate injury to society that is likely if speech is allowed. The classic statement of these conditions was made by Mr. Justice Brandeis in his concurring opinion in Whitney *v.* California, 274 U.S. 357, 376–377,

> Fear of serious injury cannot alone justify suppression of free speech and assembly. Men feared witches and burnt women. It is the function of speech to free men from the bondage of irrational fears. To justify suppression of free speech there must be reasonable ground to fear that serious evil will result if free speech is practiced. There must be reasonable ground to believe that the danger apprehended is imminent. There must be reasonable ground to believe that the evil to be prevented is a serious one. Every denunciation of existing law tends in some measure to increase the probability that there will be violation of it. Condonation of a breach enhances the probability. Expressions of approval add to the probability. Propagation of the criminal state of mind by teaching syndicalism increases it. Advocacy of law-breaking heightens it still further. But even advocacy of violation, however reprehensible morally, is not a justification for denying free speech where the advocacy falls short of incitement and there is nothing to indicate that the advocacy would be immediately acted on. The wide difference between advocacy and incitement, between preparation and attempt, between assembling and conspiracy, must be borne in mind. In order to support a finding of a clear and present danger it must be shown either that immediate serious violence was to be expected or was advocated, or that the past conduct furnished reason to believe that such advocacy was then contemplated.

> Those who won our independence by revolution were not cowards. They did not fear political change. They did not exalt order at the cost of liberty.

To courageous, self-reliant men, with confidence in the power of free and fearless reasoning applied through the processes of popular government, no danger flowing from speech can be deemed clear and present, unless the incidence of the evil apprehended is so imminent that it may befall before there is opportunity for full discussion. *If there be time to expose through discussion the falsehood and fallacies to avert the evil by the processes of education, the remedy to be applied is more speech, not enforced silence.* [Italics added by Mr. Justice Douglas.]

I had assumed that the question of the clear and present danger, being so critical an issue in the case, would be a matter for submission to the jury. . . . Yet, whether the question is one for the Court or the jury, there should be evidence of record on the issue.

This record, however, contains no evidence whatsoever showing that the acts charged, *viz.,* the teaching of the Soviet theory of revolution with the hope that it will be realized, have created any clear and present danger to the Nation. The Court, however, rules to the contrary. It says, "The formation by petitioners of such a highly organized conspiracy, with rigidly disciplined members subject to call when the leaders, these petitioners, felt that the time had come for action, coupled with the inflammable nature of world conditions, similar uprisings in other countries, and the touch-and-go nature of our relations with countries with whom petitioners were in the very least ideologically attuned, convince us that their convictions were justified on this score."

That ruling is in my view not responsive to the issue in the case. We might as well say that the speech of petitioners is outlawed because Soviet Russia and her Red Army are a threat to world peace.

The nature of Communism as a force on the world scene would, of course, be relevant to the issue of clear and present danger of petitioners' advocacy within the United States. But the primary consideration is the strength and tactical position of petitioners and their converts in this country. On that there is no evidence in the record. If we are to take judicial notice of the threat of Communists within the nation, it should not be difficult to conclude that *as a political party* they are of little consequence. Communists in this country have never made a respectable or serious showing in any election. I would doubt that there is a village, let alone a city or county or state which the Communists could carry.

Communism in the world scene is no bogey-man; but Communists as a political faction or party in this country plainly is. Communism has been so thoroughly exposed in this country that it has been crippled as a political force. Free speech has destroyed it as an effective political party. It is inconceivable that those who went up and down this country preaching the doctrine of revolution which petitioners espouse would have any success. In days of trouble and confusion when bread lines were long, when the un-

employed walked the streets, when people were starving, the advocates of a
short-cut by revolution might have a chance to gain adherents. But today
there are no such conditions. The country is not in despair; the people
know Soviet Communism; the doctrine of Soviet revolution is exposed in
all of its ugliness and the American people want none of it.

How it can be said that there is a clear and present danger that this
advocacy will succeed is, therefore, a mystery. Some nations less resilient
than the United States, where illiteracy is high and where democratic traditions are only budding, might have to take drastic steps and jail these men
for merely speaking their creed. But in America they are miserable merchants of unwanted ideas; their wares remain unsold. The fact that their
ideas are abhorrent does not make them powerful. . . .

The First Amendment provides that "Congress shall make no law . . .
abridging the freedom of speech." The Constitution provides no exception.
This does not mean, however, that the Nation need hold its hand until it is
in such weakened condition that there is no time to protect itself from
incitement to revolution. Seditious conduct can always be punished. But
the command of the First Amendment is so clear that we should not allow
Congress to call a halt to free speech except in the extreme case of peril
from the speech itself.

The First Amendment makes confidence in the common sense of our
people and in their maturity of judgment the great postulate of our democracy. Its philosophy is that violence is rarely, if ever, stopped by denying
civil liberties to those advocating resort to force. The First Amendment
reflects the philosophy of Jefferson "that it is time enough for the rightful
purposes of civil government for its officers to interfere when principles
break out into overt acts against peace and good order." The political
censor has no place in our public debates. Unless and until extreme and
necessitous circumstances are shown our aim should be to keep speech
unfettered and to allow the processes of law to be invoked only when the
provocateurs among us move from speech to action.

Vishinsky wrote in 1948 in *The Law of the Soviet State,* "In our state,
naturally there can be no place for freedom of speech, press, and so on for
the foes of socialism."

Our concern should be that we accept no such standard for the United
States. Our faith should be that our people will never give support to these
advocates of revolution, so long as we remain loyal to the purposes for
which our Nation was founded.

[Most of the footnotes and many citations to cases have been omitted.]

Distinguishing Forms of Advocacy

YATES ET AL. *V.* UNITED STATES

354 U.S. 298 (1957)

MR. JUSTICE HARLAN delivered the opinion of the Court.

These 14 petitioners stand convicted, after a jury trial in the United States District Court for the Southern District of California, upon a single count indictment charging them with conspiring (1) to advocate and teach the duty and necessity of overthrowing the Government of the United States by force and violence, and (2) to organize, as the Communist Party of the United States, a society of persons who so advocate and teach, all with the intent of causing the overthrow of the Government by force and violence as speedily as circumstances would permit. . . . The conspiracy is alleged to have originated in 1940 and continued down to the date of the indictment in 1951. . . . Upon conviction each of the petitioners was sentenced to five years' imprisonment and a fine of $10,000. . . .

INSTRUCTIONS TO THE JURY

Petitioners contend that the instructions to the jury were fatally defective in that the trial court refused to charge that, in order to convict, the jury must find that the advocacy which the defendants conspired to promote was of a kind calculated to "incite" persons to action for the forcible overthrow of the Government. It is argued that advocacy of forcible overthrow as mere *abstract doctrine* is within the free speech protection of the First Amendment; that the Smith Act, consistently with that constitutional provision, must be taken as proscribing only the sort of advocacy which incites to illegal *action;* and that the trial court's charge, by permitting conviction for mere advocacy, unrelated to its tendency to produce forcible action, resulted in an unconstitutional application of the Smith Act. The Government, which at the trial also requested the court to charge in terms of "incitement," now takes the position, however, that the true constitutional dividing line is not between inciting and abstract advocacy of forcible overthrow, but rather between advocacy as such, irrespective of its inciting qualities, and the mere discussion or exposition of violent overthrow as an abstract theory. . . .

After telling the jury that it could not convict the defendants for holding or expressing mere opinions, beliefs, or predictions relating to violent

overthrow, the trial court defined the content of the proscribed advocacy
or teaching in the following terms, which are crucial here:

> Any advocacy or teaching which does not include the urging of force
> and violence as the means of overthrowing and destroying the Govern-
> ment of the United States is not within the issue of the indictment here
> and can constitute no basis for any finding against the defendants.
>
> The kind of advocacy and teaching which is charged and upon which
> your verdict must be reached is not merely a desirability but a necessity
> that the Government of the United States be overthrown and destroyed
> by force and violence and not merely a propriety but a duty to overthrow
> and destroy the Government of the United States by force and violence.

There can be no doubt from the record that in so instructing the jury
the court regarded as immaterial, and intended to withdraw from the
jury's consideration, any issue as to the character of the advocacy in
terms of its capacity to stir listeners to forcible action. Both the petitioners and the Government submitted proposed instructions which would
have required the jury to find that the proscribed advocacy was not of
a mere abstract doctrine of forcible overthrow, but of action to that end,
by the use of language reasonably and ordinarily calculated to incite persons to such action. The trial court rejected these proposed instructions
on the ground that any necessity for giving them which may have existed
at the time the Dennis case was tried was removed by this Court's subsequent decision in that case. The court made it clear in colloquy with
counsel that in its view the illegal advocacy was made out simply by
showing that what was said dealt with forcible overthrow and that it was
uttered with a specific intent to accomplish that purpose, insisting that
all such advocacy was punishable "whether in language of incitement or
not." . . .

We are thus faced with the question whether the Smith Act prohibits
advocacy and teaching of forcible overthrow as an abstract principle,
divorced from any effort to instigate action to that end, so long as such
advocacy or teaching is engaged in with evil intent. We hold that it does
not.

The distinction between advocacy of abstract doctrine and advocacy
directed at promoting unlawful action is one that has been consistently
recognized in the opinions of this Court, beginning with Fox *v.* Washington, 236 U.S. 273, and Schenck *v.* United States, 249 U.S. 47. This
distinction was heavily underscored in Gitlow *v.* New York, 268 U.S.
652, in which the statute involved was nearly identical with the one now
before us. . . . The legislative history of the Smith Act and related bills
shows beyond all question that Congress was aware of the distinction between the advocacy or teaching of abstract doctrine and the advocacy or
teaching of action, and that it did not intend to disregard it. . . .

In failing to distinguish between advocacy of forcible overthrow as an abstract doctrine and advocacy of action to that end, the District Court appears to have been led astray by the holding in Dennis that advocacy of violent action to be taken at some future time was enough. It seems to have considered that, since "inciting" speech is usually thought of as calculated to induce immediate action, and since Dennis held advocacy of action for future overthrow sufficient, this meant that advocacy, irrespective of its tendency to generate action, is punishable, provided only that it is uttered with a specific intent to accomplish overthrow. In other words, the District Court apparently thought that Dennis obliterated the traditional dividing line between advocacy of abstract doctrine and advocacy of action. . . .

In light of the foregoing we are unable to regard the District Court's charge upon this aspect of the case as adequate. The jury was never told that the Smith Act does not denounce advocacy in the sense of preaching abstractly the forcible overthrow of the Government. We think that the trial court's statement that the proscribed advocacy must include the "urging," "necessity," and "duty" of forcible overthrow, and not merely its "desirability" and "propriety," may not be regarded as a sufficient substitute for charging that the Smith Act reaches only advocacy of action for the overthrow of government by force and violence. The essential distinction is that those to whom the advocacy is addressed must be urged to *do* something, now or in the future, rather than merely to *believe* in something. . . .

Granting . . . that it was not necessary even that the trial court should have employed the particular term "incite," it was nevertheless incumbent on the court to make clear in some fashion that the advocacy must be of action and not merely abstract doctrine. The instructions given not only do not employ the word "incite," but also avoid the use of such terms and phrases as "action," "call for action," "as a rule or principle of action," and so on, all of which were offered in one form or another by both the petitioners and the Government.

What we find lacking in the instructions here is illustrated by contrasting them with the instructions given to the Dennis jury, upon which this Court's sustaining of the convictions in that case was bottomed. There the trial court charged:

> In further construction and interpretation of the statute [the Smith Act] I charge you that it is *not the abstract doctrine* of overthrowing or destroying organized government by unlawful means which is denounced by this law, but the teaching and advocacy *of action* for the accomplishment of that purpose, *by language reasonably and ordinarily calculated to incite persons to such action.* Accordingly, you cannot find the defendants or any of them guilty of the crime charged unless you are satisfied beyond a reasonable doubt that they conspired . . . to advocate and teach the duty

and necessity of overthrowing or destroying the Government of the United States by force and violence, with the intent that such teaching and advocacy *be of a rule or principle of action* and *by language reasonably and ordinarily calculated to incite persons to such action,* all with the intent to cause the overthrow . . . as speedily as circumstances would permit. (Emphasis added.) 341 U.S., at 511–512.

We recognize that distinctions between advocacy or teaching of abstract doctrines, with evil intent, and that which is directed to stirring people to action, are often subtle and difficult to grasp, for in a broad sense, as Mr. Justice Holmes said in his dissenting opinion in Gitlow, *supra,* at 673: "Every idea is an incitement." But the very subtlety of these distinctions required the most clear and explicit instructions with reference to them, for they concerned an issue which went to the very heart of the charges against these petitioners. . . .

The judgment of the Court of Appeals is reversed, and the case remanded to the District Court for further proceedings consistent with this opinion.

It is so ordered.

[Mr. Justice Burton concurred in the result and agreed with the above portion of the Court's opinion. Justices Brennan and Whittaker took no part in the consideration of this case.]

MR. JUSTICE BLACK, with whom MR. JUSTICE DOUGLAS joins, concurring in part and dissenting in part.

I agree with the Court insofar as it holds that the trial judge erred in instructing that persons could be punished under the Smith Act for teaching and advocating forceful overthrow as an abstract principle. But on the other hand, I cannot agree that the instruction which the Court indicates it might approve is constitutionally permissible. The Court says that persons can be punished for advocating action to overthrow the Government by force and violence, where those to whom the advocacy is addressed are urged "to *do* something, now or in the future, rather than merely to *believe* in something." Under the Court's approach, defendants could still be convicted simply for agreeing to talk as distinguished from agreeing to act. I believe that the First Amendment forbids Congress to punish people for talking about public affairs, whether or not such discussion incites to action, legal or illegal. See Meiklejohn, *Free Speech and Its Relation to Self-Government.* Cf. Chafee, "Book Review," 62 *Harv. L. Rev.* 891. As the Virginia Assembly said in 1785, in its "Statute for Religious Liberty," written by Thomas Jefferson, "it is time enough for the rightful purposes of civil government, for its officers to interfere when principles break out into overt acts against peace and good order. . . ."

MR. JUSTICE CLARK, dissenting. . . .

The conspiracy includes the same group of defendants as in the Dennis case though petitioners here occupied a lower echelon in the party hierarchy. They, nevertheless, served in the same army and were engaged in the same mission. The convictions here were based upon evidence closely paralleling that adduced in Dennis and in United States v. Flynn, 216 F. (2d) 354 (C.A. 2d Cir. 1954), both of which resulted in convictions. This Court laid down in Dennis the principles governing such prosecutions and they were closely adhered to here, although the nature of the two cases did not permit identical handling. . . .

I have studied the section of the opinion concerning the instructions and frankly its "artillery of words" leaves me confused as to why the majority concludes that the charge as given was insufficient. I thought that Dennis merely held that a charge was sufficient where it requires a finding that "the Party advocates the theory that there is a duty and necessity to overthrow the Government by force and violence. . . . not as a prophetic insight or as a bit of . . . speculation, but as a program for winning adherents and as a policy to be translated into action" as soon as the circumstances permit. 341 U.S., at 546–547 (concurring opinion). I notice however that to the majority

> The essence of the Dennis holding was that indoctrination of a group in preparation for future violent action, as well as exhortation to immediate action, by advocacy found to be directed to "action for the accomplishment" of forcible overthrow, to violence "as a rule or principle of action," and employing "language of incitement," *id.,* at 511–512, is not constitutionally protected when the group is of sufficient size and cohesiveness, is sufficiently oriented towards action, and other circumstances are such as reasonably to justify apprehension that action will occur.

I have read this statement over and over but do not seem to grasp its meaning for I see no resemblance between it and what the respected Chief Justice wrote in Dennis, nor do I find any such theory in the concurring opinions. As I see it, the trial judge charged in essence all that was required under the Dennis opinions, whether one takes the view of the Chief Justice or of those concurring in the judgment. Apparently what disturbs the Court now is that the trial judge here did not give the Dennis charge although both the prosecution and the defense asked that it be given. Since he refused to grant these requests I suppose the majority feels that there must be some difference between the two charges, else the one that was given in Dennis would have been followed here. While there may be some distinctions between the charges, as I view them they are without material difference. I find, as the majority intimates, that the distinctions are too "subtle and difficult to grasp."

Topic 13

LOYALTY AND SECURITY

୧୦୨

Security and Freedom

SIDNEY HOOK *

The quest for security in human life, like the quest for certainty in human knowledge, has many sources. All are rooted in man's finitude in a complex world of danger and mystery. Of the varied methods man has pursued to reduce the dangers and cope with the mysteries, the way of piecemeal knowledge and continuous experiment has been most fruitful. For it is in the fields in which human knowledge has foresworn the quest for absolute certainty, as in the scientific disciplines, that it has proved both reliable and capable of winning universal agreement. On the other hand, in the fields in which the strongest claims to certainty have been made—politics and philosophy—there is the least agreement.

Because absolute certainty in human affairs is impossible, absolute security is impossible. Unless we are aware of this, the price we pay for straining to achieve an impossible ideal may result in netting us less security than would otherwise be attainable. This is not an unusual phenomenon: it is observable in large things and small. The man who strives for absolute health may end up a valetudinarian. The man who won't venture on the highways until they are accident-proof may as well not own an automobile; and if he crawls along playing it supersafe, traffic-enforcement authorities tell us he adds to the dangers of the road.

The real problem, then, is not one of absolute security, or security in general. It is always one of achieving more and better security in meeting specific hazards in a particular area of risk and uncertainty—and meeting them in such a way that we do not lose more by the methods we use than by the disasters we would prevent. . . .

The McCarthy episode in American history was a test of political judgment and political morality. Those who dismissed him as an unimportant phenomenon or extenuated his methods in the light of his goals

---

* Chairman of the Department of Philosophy, New York University. Author of *Heresy, Yes—Conspiracy, No!; Common Sense and the Fifth Amendment;* and other books. The selection is from *Political Power and Personal Freedom* (New York, Criterion Books, Inc., 1959), pp. 235–249. By permission.

162

failed the tests of both judgment and morality. So did those who exaggerated his power, who proclaimed that he had transformed America
into a police state, and who fought McCarthy with the weapons of Mc-
Carthy instead of the weapons of truth. Even at the height of McCarthy's
power a more rational view was not impossible. . . .

"Security is like liberty," writes Mr. Justice Jackson in one of his dissenting opinions, "in that many are the crimes that have been committed
in its name." Yet he would be the first to admit that this is no more warrant for abandoning the quest for reasonable rules of security than for
relinquishing the struggle for a more humane conception of liberty. . . .

After the Seventh Congress of the Communist International, the Communists kidnaped the vocabulary of American liberalism. This "corruption of the word," as I called it then, made it easier for some sentimental
liberals to interpret sharp criticisms of Communism as oblique attacks on
liberalism, if not a first step towards Fascism. In liberal circles to be an anti-
Fascist was always honorable. But to be anti-Communist, especially during the war years, invited distrust. That liberals had a stake in the survival
of the democratic system whose defects they could freely criticize under
the ground rules of the Bill of Rights was granted, of course. That they
therefore also had a stake in preventing the ground rules from being
abused, that they had a responsibility to think about the problem, was
resolutely ignored. . . .

Instead of offering a viable alternative to eliminate or reduce these
injustices, they wrote as if the only problem was to develop more efficient
methods of detecting acts of espionage *after* they had been committed.
They thereby revealed the extent of their misunderstanding. Not the acts
prevented but those which are discovered create public disquietude, because
they give the impression that many more remain undiscovered and beyond
the reach of prosecution in virtue of the statute of limitations. . . .

Recent experience, or a study of recent history, should make it possible
for the liberal to acquire a reliable knowledge of the whole costumer's
shop of organizational masks cleverly designed by Communist technicians
to take in the unwary until the time comes for the sacrificial slaughter.
If he believes that there is a foreign threat to the survival of the liberal
community, he cannot withhold assent from the dictum of Roger Baldwin, former head of the American Civil Liberties Union, that "a superior
loyalty to a foreign government disqualifies a citizen from service to our
own." It does not disqualify the citizen from protection of the Bill of
Rights, but the right to government service is not an integral part of the
Bill of Rights.

It is the liberal *attitude,* however, which is most crucial in the reasonable administration of a security program. Just as only those who love children can be trusted to discipline them without doing psychological harm, so only those who love freedom can be trusted to devise appropriate safeguards without throttling intellectual independence or smothering all but the mediocre in blankets of regulations. No safeguards are appropriate or even efficient which impose conformity of belief or inhibit intellectual spontaneity. The fresh and unfamiliar solution to difficulties depends on a certain imaginative daring and a receptivity to such solutions by those in a position of authority. A liberal with a sense of history is aware of the possibility that in a specific situation there may be a sharp conflict between the legitimate demands of national security and the freedom of the individual. But on balance, and in perspective, he is convinced that the two are not in opposition. In the very interest of a freely expressed dissent, some security measures are required to protect the institutional processes which, however imperfectly, reflect a freely given consent. At the same time, the faith and practices of freedom, indeed, an almost religious veneration for the *élan* of the free spirit, may generate a sense of security even in the shadows of war. . . .

The argument and evidence can be put briefly. The one unshakeable dogma in the Bolshevik faith is that the Soviet Union is not safe from attack so long as the "capitalistic democracies" of the West—and not only the United States but also countries like Great Britain and France— exist. Let not those who in the past assured us that Hitler's racial myth and ideology of world conquest were "just words" tell us again that ideologies do not count in politics and history. If anything, the Kremlin has gone further than Hitler because it has publicly proclaimed that "encirclement" is a *political,* not a geographical, concept. The Communist parties of the West . . . have as their *first* function the defense of the Soviet Union. Instructions are explicit to all of them to organize secretly (as well as publicly) even in "the freest" and "most democratic" countries and to infiltrate into strategic centers. This type of activity has been extensively carried on for years especially during the days of the popular front struggle against the Nazis. Even during the war which Hitler forced on the Soviets, the Kremlin engaged in the most comprehensive types of espionage against its Allies as part of the underlying struggle which, according to their fanatical conviction, must end either with the victory of the West or the Soviet power.

Because it can count on the devotion *à outrance* of Communist nationals of other countries, many of them highly trained, intelligent and inspired by a misguided idealism which does not see under the flowers of official rhetoric the chains of Soviet control on its own people, the Kremlin possesses an incomparable advantage over the West. For one thing, it is the best informed regime in the world. . . .

Although one would hardly suspect it from present attitudes to security in many circles in those countries, it is from Canadian and British sources that we have the most incontrovertible, if not the weightiest evidence, of how Communist parties are involved in the espionage nets the Soviet Union has spun around the free world.[1]

Since the Kremlin combines this belief in the inevitablity of war with a dialectical conception according to which a sudden attack or offense, as in Korea, is the best method of defense and because of the centralized organization of western industrial life, the location of America's undispersed plants, and the evolution of thermonuclear weapons, an attempt at a sudden knockout blow cannot be ruled out as a possibility. Since Bolshevik morality is confessedly subordinate to what will further the victory of the "proletarian dictatorship"—indeed, this is *the whole* of their morality—the possession of information about strategic weakness on the part of the West, or the hope that a sudden blow may prevent instant retaliatory action, may make a decisive difference to the Kremlin in resolving to launch the Blitzkreig which will end "the final struggle." It does not require many persons to betray the key secrets of the radar defense of a nation.

The consequences of less extreme suppositions may be equally disastrous. The free world cannot deploy its defense forces everywhere. Its decisions where to stand, where to fight, once known to the Kremlin, give the latter a flexibility that it can exploit most skillfully to draw the world bit by bit into its orbit. On the other hand, there is no possibility for the free world to build up a counterweight within the Soviet sphere to redress the balance. No democratic Jeffersonian or Millsian International exists with affiliated parties in the Soviet world.

Does it follow that *every* member of the Communist party is an espionage agent ready to do the bidding of his superiors and betray his country? Is it not possible that some members of the Communist party may be loyal to their own government rather than to the Soviet Union? The best answer to these questions was made by Mr. Clement Attlee, Prime Minister at the time when Pontecorvo, scientifically a much more gifted man than Fuchs, fled from England. "There is no way," said Mr. Attlee who never chased a witch in his life, "of distinguishing such people [hypothetically loyal Communists] from those who, if opportunity offered, would be prepared to endanger the security of the state in the interests of another power. The Government has, therefore, reached the conclusion that the only prudent course to adopt is to ensure that no one who is known to be

[1] Cf. *The Report of the Royal Commission to Investigate the Facts Relating to and Circumstances Surrounding the Communication by Public Officials and Other Persons in Positions of Trust of Secret and Confidential Information to Agents of a Foreign Power* (Ottawa, 1946); also Alexander Foote's *Handbook for Spies* (London, 1949).

a member of the Communist party, *or to be associated with it in such a way as to raise legitimate doubts about his or her reliability* (my italics), is employed in connection with work, the nature of which is vital to the security of the State." It is well to remember that a clerk in a code office or even those who empty trash baskets may have access to material bearing on national security. Mr. Attlee apparently believes that if we distinguish between legal guilt and *moral* or professional guilt or unfitness, and between association by happenstance and association by cooperation, then there certainly can be and is "guilt by association." . . .

It is the gravest error to imagine that anyone in America, even Senator McCarthy who helped the Communist cause throughout the world, believed for a moment that the Communists constituted a domestic danger. But American public opinion was aroused by a series of incidents over a span of three years which seemed to show that in the international field the position of the American government was being weakened by Soviet agents.

The first was the Hiss case and the revelations that several interlocking rings of Communist conspirators had been active in high places for years. It remains mystifying that many of these individuals continued working in strategic places, one even at the Aberdeen Weapons Proving Grounds, many years after the chief operatives had been identified by former members of the Communist party. The worst of these revelations came after Mr. Truman had dismissed the Hiss case as a "red herring." Following Hiss's conviction, Wadleigh's confession, and a long line of refusals to answer questions about espionage on the ground that a truthful answer would tend to be self-incriminating, the implication was natural, and in part justified, that the government had been lax or indifferent in taking intelligent safeguards. As the Dexter White case shows, the Truman administration feared that its opponents would make political capital out of the presence of Communist espionage agents in the government and tried to hush up matters. This narrow political partisanship by no means warranted the charge of "treason" or of coddling treason hurled by some Republicans against the Democrats. There is no reason to believe that had the former been in power, they would have acted more wisely. But the country never really recovered from the shock of learning that publicly sworn testimony, some of it legally substantiated where the charges were contested, showed that persons holding the following positions were members of the secret Communist underground apparatus:

an Executive Assistant to the President of the United States
an Assistant Secretary of the Treasury
the Director of the Office of Special Political Affairs for the State
    Department
the Secretary of the International Monetary Fund

Head of Latin-American Division of the Office of Strategic Services

a member of the National Labor Relations Board

Secretary of the National Labor Relations Board

Chief Counsel, Senate Subcommittee on Civil Liberties

Chief, Statistical Analysis Branch, War Production Board

Treasury Department Representative and Adviser in Financial Control Division of the North African Board of UNRRA, and at the meeting of the Council of Foreign Ministers in Moscow

Director, National Research Project of the Works Progress Administration

These were not the only, but only the most conspicuous, positions Communists filled. The *actual* amount of damage done, however, is difficult to assess and probably will never be known. But no reasonable person can doubt the existence of a planned pattern of infiltration whose significance can be better gauged by the European reader if he draws up a comparable list of posts in his own government and fills them, in his mind's eye, with Communist espionage agents.

The second series of incidents began with the Fuchs case which broke after several outstanding scientists had dismissed the idea that atomic espionage was possible. "There are no secrets" declared the very scientists who in 1939 and 1940 had imposed upon themselves a voluntary secrecy in publications to prevent Hitler from developing nuclear power. Subsequent trials in the United States of the Communist spies associated with Fuchs produced evidence that there were others deep underground.

All this was still very much in the public mind when Truman announced that the Soviet Union had exploded its first atomic bomb, thus eliminating the monopoly of atomic power which, according to Churchill and other Europeans, had prevented the Red Army from marching west after American and British demobilization. The head of the United States Atomic Energy Commission observed that Soviet espionage had made it possible for the Soviet Union to save years of costly experiment (an observation officially repeated by President Eisenhower on October 8, 1953, after the U.S.S.R. had exploded a thermonuclear bomb).[2]

---

[2] As early as 1950 some scientists holding high official positions had charged that the Soviet Union had acquired through espionage the "know-how" to make hydrogen bombs. *The New York Times* of July 20, 1950, quoted François Perrin, Joint Commissioner for Atomic Energy in France, as saying that Russia, through its espionage network, had certainly obtained the know-how to make the hydrogen bomb. The same report appeared in *The San Francisco Chronicle* of July 23, 1950. At the time Professor Perrin's co-commissioner was Irene Joliot-Curie, wife of Frederic Joliot-Curie, later dismissed from the post as High Commissioner for Atomic Energy because of his pro-Soviet activities. Frederic Joliot-Curie subsequently charged that the U.S. was waging bacterial germ warfare in Korea and spurned the proposal of a Committee of Nobel Prize Winners to conduct an objective international inquiry into the truth of his charges.

Finally came the loss of China and the charge that some of the advisors and consultants to the State Department on Far Eastern affairs not only had long records of Communist association but had followed the twists and turns of the Party line. Some like L. Rossinger who fell back on the Fifth Amendment were identified as members of the Communist party. Although there was no legal proof of the identification by Budenz of Lattimore as a top Soviet agent, there could be no reasonable doubt that he was a fellow-traveler whose justification of the Moscow frame-up trials was very brazen. Whatever the degree of their Communism, it seemed indisputable that a group in the State Department had been urging the abandonment of all support to Chiang Kai-shek despite the absence of any alternative to Communist triumph. The defeat of Chiang may have been unavoidable, but the evidence that American Communists and their sympathizers had actively worked for his downfall by attempting to influence official channels was unmistakable.

These events, together with other trials involving Communist espionage and perjury, and the multiplication of cases of refusal to answer questions on the ground that a truthful answer would tend to be self-incriminatory, contributed to the prevalent feeling that the United States was being weakened in the cold war on whose outcome so many things, both domestic and international, depend. The Korean war exacerbated the mood. Had these events, especially the pattern of their succession, occurred in other countries, it is not likely that they would have been met with complacency.

The concern of the American people with the question of Communist penetration, in the light of the evidence, was legitimate enough. Questionable only was the character of the reaction to it on the part of the government. Buffeted by cultural vigilantes on the one side and ritualistic liberals on the other, it swung from one position to another, pleasing no one with its eclecticism. Almost all of the excesses of loyalty and security programs are attributable to the incredible political ignorance and naiveté of the personnel of the Review Boards. It was not the procedures themselves which were at fault, because oddly enough American procedures in crucial respects are fairer than the English. For example, in hearings before English boards, civil servants under investigation are rarely, if ever, told of the evidence against them. They are also denied rights of legal counsel, and even of representation. Nonetheless, American procedures worked hardship and injustices because instead of being administered by knowledgeable men and women with a little common sense who had some political experience, they were entrusted to investment bankers, corporation lawyers, army and navy officers, small town officials, or Republican or Democratic party regulars to whom Communist language was gobble-dygook, Communist ideas suspiciously like the ideas of socialists, do-gooders and even New Dealers, and Communist organizations with the distinctions between member, sympathizer, front, dupe, innocent, and honest mistaken liberal, as mysterious as the order of beings in the science of angelology.

In the light of the above, the answer to our final question regarding the relative unconcern of other nations to the problem of Communist penetration is not hard to give. The greatest Soviet effort was directed against the United States as the Kremlin's chief and strongest enemy. Since 1939 the United States has been the center of atomic weapons research and development. Its policies are more fateful for the U.S.S.R. than those of any other single nation. To make these policies miscarry, to delay, distort and abort government directives pays rich political dividends. The Kremlin is quite aware of the fact that a defeat or paralysis of the United States would mean the end of the independence of Austria, France and Italy. Further, the Communist movement in the United States is not a mass party and, in all likelihood, will never become one. But it has a solid core of some thousands of hardened "professional revolutionists." From the Soviet viewpoint they are expendable. What is more natural, therefore, than to employ them for all sorts of conspiratorial purposes from direct espionage to the capture of small but key unions, to the seeding of government services with "sleepers"? A few thousand totally dedicated persons, working underground with the help of a sympathetic periphery of several times that size, can cause a great many headaches. Countries like Austria need not worry about the problem, one is tempted to observe, because it wouldn't make a difference if they did. There isn't much the Kremlin can learn from them and an attempt at a Communist putsch on Czechoslovakian lines, so long as the United States is still strong, risks a war for which at the moment the U.S.S.R. is unready. Countries like France and Italy, on the other hand, which have mass Communist parties and where infiltration and underground organization are not inconsiderable can hardly solve the problem without facing crippling strikes and extensive public disorders. Too weak to act they sometimes pretend that there is no need for action. *They can live with the Communist menace only because the United States is free of it and only so long as the United States is strong enough to restrain the Soviet Union from overrunning the free world.*

Only those who are ignorant of the stupendous extent of Soviet infiltration and espionage over the years, the complexity of its patterns and its potential for harm, can sneer at the problems of security in the free world. It is not enough to shout slogans—whether of security or freedom. What is required is creative intelligence to devise just and effective procedures which will protect the free cultures of the world from their hidden enemies without making less free those who are not its hidden enemies.

These procedures must be flexible. They cannot be formalized into a code without inviting abuses. They must be devised and administered by civil libertarians who are familiar with Communist theory and who have studied Communist conspiratorial practice. They must be applied discreetly, without fanfare, without developing a climate of public concern. And their primary function must be effective prevention rather than exemplary punishment.

Critique of the Loyalty Program

L. A. NIKOLORIĆ *

Established by the President's Executive Order 9835 in March, 1947, the government's loyalty program . . . presents a complex problem: whether, in the name of "loyalty" and "national security," our society is justified in abusing most of the basic tenets of Anglo-American jurisprudence and legal philosophy traditional since the seventeenth century.

The purpose of the program is not to discharge employees expressly because of what they have done in the past. President Truman has stated that it is aimed at "potentially disloyal" persons who, because of attitudes and ideas they entertain today or subscribed to yesterday, might in the future undertake action contrary to the best interests of the United States. The basic concept of the program—to ferret out the "potentially disloyal" —violates a most important principle of Anglo-American law: that one cannot be punished for merely considering the commission of a crime, or for thinking in such a way that a body determines that one might undertake action contrary to the law. . . .

The loyalty program also distorts the concept of equal justice under the law. It assumes that a democratic government may exact from its employees special standards of conduct wholly offensive to constitutional guarantees of freedom and justice as applied to ordinary citizens. We deny two and a half million government employees political and intellectual freedoms in order to protect ourselves from the potentially subversive.

These innovations are spreading not only to some three and a half million state and local employees (the County of Los Angeles, among other local governments, has instituted a loyalty check), but elsewhere. The AFL and the CIO have undertaken to purge the Communists. The Army, the Navy and the Air Force pass on the loyalty of the employees of private

---

* Washington attorney associated with the firm of Arnold, Fortas and Porter. The selection is from L. A. Nikolorić, "The Government Loyalty Program," *The American Scholar,* Vol. XIX (Summer, 1950). Copyright of United Chapters of Phi Beta Kappa. By permission.

contractors who bid successfully on government jobs having to do with classified material. Congressmen have urged that all employees working for industries connected with the national security be subjected to a similar screening. Presumably this concerns the various utilities—in steel, automobile, transportation and others. Teachers and scientists have been discharged for entertaining unpopular ideas. Even veterans' organizations have pledged themselves to loyalty programs. The most liberal of these, the American Veterans Committee, has adopted resolutions directing its officers to purge the Communists.

Since we are rapidly accepting the proposition that American institutions have a right to examine their membership on the basis of their "loyalty," it is appropriate to determine what the government's loyalty program is and how it operates, its ideology, and the concrete effects of its operation. . . .

It is the duty of the [Loyalty] Boards to determine the existence of a nebulous state of mind which might lead an employee to commit in the future a disloyal act, either willfully or through an indiscretion. The most important elements of consideration are of necessity the employee's political beliefs, the organizations to which he has belonged, and the associations he has had.

Experience proves that it is not necessary for the employee to have been a member of either a Communist or Fascist organization. He will be found wanting if he has been "sympathetic" to communism or fascism, friendly to persons or organizations that are sympathetic, associated with such persons or organizations, or even "unduly talkative" in the presence of persons who are associated with sympathetic persons. The Boards do not find it necessary to prove any of these matters. They are required only to find "a reasonable doubt."

In order to assist the Boards, the Attorney General, in December, 1947, and by various supplements, designated some 150 organizations—membership in or sympathy for which is held to be indicative of disloyalty. These lists were promulgated without hearings. No explanation for the inclusion of any organization was given. . . .

Although the order provides that the employee is entitled to a charge stating the offense with some particularity, this is limited by the discretion of the agency in the interest of security considerations. Practice has shown that it has been almost impossible for an employee or his lawyer to secure a full or complete statement of the offenses.

Defending against such charges is difficult. The burden is placed on the employee to recall all the persons with whom, and organizations with which, he has ever been in contact, and to explain them. He must also prove affirmatively that he adheres to certain nebulous standards that might be construed by the Board as indicative of so loyal a state of mind that the employee will never commit a disloyal act.

The following quotation demonstrates the position in which an employee finds himself. In this case, Mr. A was faced with an unexplained action of the State Department in dismissing him "for security reasons." A asked the Board to tell him what he had done to justify the action, so that he might defend himself. The Board representative said:

> Well, we realize the difficulty you are in, in this position; on the other hand, I'd suggest that you might think back over your own career and perhaps in your own mind delve into some of the factors that have gone into your career which you think might have been subject to question and see what they are and see whether you'd like to explain or make any statement with regard to any of them. . . .

None of these things could happen in any other court or board proceeding directed against an individual in the United States. Axis Sally and Judith Coplon, who were charged with overt acts of treason and espionage, have received more procedural protection than is accorded the potentially disloyal. A common pickpocket may insist on every traditional and fundamental safeguard. A government employee may not. No one would dream of indicting Axis Sally for merely contemplating broadcasting Nazi propaganda; we would not consider putting a petty thief in jail for thinking about picking his neighbor's pocket. Yet we discharge and publicly smear government employees who have done nothing wrongful, who may not consider committing an act of disloyalty. We fire them because, on the basis of standards of the status quo, the Board suspects that they might do so in the future.

Those who would defend the program argue that the government is not required to secure to its employees procedural safeguards when it fires them. It is said that no citizen has an inherent right to government employment. Thus the government may fire arbitrarily—because it does not like the color of the employee's hair, because he is inefficient, or because the government fears that the employee may become a security risk. The procedural safeguards that are provided—charges and a hearing—are a matter of the sovereign's largess. They do not accrue to the employee as a matter of constitutional right. Therefore, the employee may not ask for other safeguards as a matter of constitutional right.

The opponents have a convincing case. Many judges, notably Mr. Justice Black, have argued that once having been hired, a government employee does secure a vested interest in his job which shall not be taken from him without cause. Cause may not be a matter of speculation; it must be a reality—such as inefficiency or overt acts of disloyalty.

Furthermore, a dismissal for disloyalty entails a permanent brand amounting to treason. Experience has shown that an employee who has been discharged under the loyalty program is unable to get another job; his career is ruined; he loses the respect of the community. Dismissal on loyalty or security grounds transcends the arbitrary right to fire. It amounts to punishment by government, which is protected by the Constitution. If this be the case, an employee who is fired on these grounds does have the constitutional right to traditional due process and safeguards.

Regardless of the coldly legal interpretation of the situation, it is obvious that a loyalty proceeding is a serious matter. On moral grounds, the government should not ruin an employee's career on a conjectural determination that he may in the future become disloyal. It must be remembered that the loyalty program was not designed or intended to punish people who have committed overt acts of disloyalty or treason. Not an employee fired has been charged with the commission of a wrongful act. During a recent public discussion with me, Mr. Seth Richardson, Chairman of the Loyalty Review Board, stated that the loyalty program has not discovered a single instance of espionage or any other overt action contrary to the best interests of the United States.

There are innumerable statutes calculated to deal with persons who are or have been acting contrary to our best interests. They include sanctions against espionage, sabotage, treason or advocacy of the overthrow of the government by force. More important to the inquiry here, any government agency may fire an employee for cause. "Cause" includes everything from simple inefficiency to disagreement with the agency's policy. Every applicant for government employment must sign, under oath, a statement that he does not subscribe to subversive doctrines and does not belong to any organization that does. Failure to make full disclosure is punishable as a criminal offense. . . .

A troublesome question is whether the loyalty program should be retained in the so-called "sensitive" agencies—the Atomic Energy Commission, the Department of Defense, and the State Department. Dr. Klaus Fuchs has done much for the proponents of the argument that in these areas, at least, we must examine employees for potential disloyalty because of the greater dangers involved.

My own view is a minority one. The proponents of the "sensitive agency" argument assume that this program is capable of catching the potentially disloyal. Even if we had the necessary instruments to accomplish this, I believe that if free institutions are to survive, they cannot be compromised in this way. A citizen in the Atomic Energy Commission should not be subjected to arbitrary treatment merely because his contribution is the more sensitive. Once the scientist or State Department official becomes a second class citizen, he will not be alone in this classification for long; he will be joined by the employee who deals in foreign trade and commerce, the expert whose concern is labor in the defense industries, and government men who deal with education and health—all fields fertile for sabotage or infiltration.

But the record speaks for itself. The loyalty program has proved to be a miserable failure as far as security is concerned. It has found no spies or security violations in sensitive areas or otherwise. Nor is it geared to; it is geared to accomplish the impossible—determine who tomorrow's spies will be. Let the FBI attend to the business of sabotage and espionage on the basis of the actual, not the potential—on the basis of acts, not possibilities. Let every agency continue to screen applicants for employment carefully; but let us not, in our fear of the police state, compromise free institutions.

The atmosphere in government is one of fear—fear of ideas and of irresponsible and unknown informers. Government employees are afraid to attend meetings of politically minded groups; they are afraid to read "liberal" publications; they screen their friends carefully for "left-wing" ideas. Government employees are in very real danger of dying intellectually and politically. Everyone knows of someone who has been accused of disloyalty—and it amounts to an accusation of treason—on ridiculous charges. Nobody wants to go through a lengthy "loyalty" investigation. The inclination and inevitable result are simply to restrict one's own freedoms.

All Americans suffer thereby. Political growth and progressive evolution depend on a vital and enthusiastic corps of government workers. Democracy can survive only upon the condition of a constant flexibility in its institutions to meet growing social and economic needs. Good government incorporates varying shades of opinion into a synthesis of action in behalf of the greatest good. Synthesis and flexibility are impossible when dissenters or the unorthodox are ruthlessly stamped out. The suppression of opposition can only mean the retention of outmoded and useless institutions, the impossibility of compromise and adjustment.

History has demonstrated again and again that freedom and the maturity of democratic processes cannot survive when the politically and economically dominant suspend traditional safeguards to the unorthodox. This is true, regardless of whether the suspension is undertaken because of fear of outside forces, or whether it is because a society has frozen in its evolutionary progress toward the fuller dignity of man. Surely it cannot be said that the United States, entering into a period of world leadership and enjoying the greatest prosperity in our history, has ceased growing. Let us not through hysteria and the uncertainty engendered by new responsibilities abdicate the basic standards of freedom which made us great. This is what we have done in the government's loyalty program; and this is what we threaten to do in the extension of that program to other segments of our society.

What Limits on the Security Program?

WALTER GELLHORN *

Wholly unrelated to the "sensitive areas," some thirty thousand civilians have professional civil-service ratings in federal agencies as chemists, physicists, meteorologists, entomologists, geologists, bacteriologists, pathologists, astronomers, and so on. To that number must be added the many thousands of supporting technical personnel and the yet further thousands of doctors, dentists, psychologists, and the like who are employed by the Veterans Administration, the Public Health Service, and other departments. Even those scientists who do have access to restricted data possess, for the most part, few real secrets—certainly far fewer than many normally self-assertive men ever permit their acquaintances to suppose. As for the scientists who will be discussed in the present piece, there is no room whatsoever for speculation on this score. They are factually, officially, and unqualifiedly barren of state secrets. They have not the slightest opportunity to deal in restricted data or to magnify their own importance by multiplying the number of hushes in hush-hush.

The inconspicuous ichthyologist of the Fish and Wildlife Service knows many secrets, to be sure, but they are the secrets of the speckled trout rather than the secrets of national defense. The mine safety engineer in the Department of the Interior peers into dark and hidden places, but the information he acquires has no element of confidentiality. The researcher at the National Cancer Institute explores the unknown, but there is certainly no disposition to conceal whatever he may discover. The Liberian scientific mission of the Public Health Service and the Agriculture Department is engaged in work of national importance, but whatever it learns about *Strophanthus sarmentosus* as a ready source of adrenocorticotrophic hormone will not be withheld from the rheumatoid arthritis sufferers of the world. . . . Yet the political views and the associations of all these men, and of others like them, have been a matter of governmental scrutiny almost as though they were entrusted with the latest developments in chemical warfare or rocket design. . . .

In the field of science, the crudities of the loyalty program discourage efforts to draw into public service the live-minded and experienced men

* Betts Professor of Law at Columbia University. Former Law secretary to Justice Harlan Fiske Stone. Author of *Individual Freedom and Governmental Restraints, American Rights,* and many other books. The selection is from *Security, Loyalty, and Science* (Ithaca, Cornell University Press, 1950), pp. 127–129, 158, 173–174. By permission.

whose talents are needed in many agencies. The distress occasioned by an unwarranted inquisition by a loyalty board is felt by a wide circle of friends and fellow-workers. Especially in the case of scientists there is a realization that even after a man has been exonerated following a hearing, he may still be subjected to a renewal of the charges and a dusting off of the same evidence if the winds of politics continue to blow strongly. On September 6, 1948, eight of America's great scientists, joining in a message to President Truman and Governor Dewey, deplored the disastrous effects upon scientific recruitment that followed the denunciatory sensationalism of the House Committee on Un-American Activities. . . . [They] concluded that the atmosphere of suspicion surrounding scientists in government was an effective deterrent to procurement and use of their services. What these men said publicly has been echoed privately by scientific men of every level of eminence.

The negative consequences of the Loyalty Order are dramatically realized when able men refuse to engage in public service or choose to leave it for less harassing occupations. All in all, however, the more serious though perhaps more subtle impact is on those who remain in federal service. . . .

Those difficulties would be diminished if we ceased searching for "disloyalty" as a general abstraction and became concerned exclusively with "security." Concededly there are positions outside the "sensitive agencies" that directly involve national safety. Occasionally an entire section or division of an organization may have occasion to deal with classified matters or may be so immediately involved in the formulation of international policy as to render it "sensitive" even though the agency as a whole may not be so. . . .

The solution here is to authorize the head of each department and agency to designate the units or particular positions in his department which he believes to be "sensitive." Persons who may be employed in these sensitive posts may properly be investigated in order that there may be full confidence in them. But as for the rest—the typists in the Veterans Administration or the Federal Housing Administration, the scientists in the Allergen Research Division or the Mycology and Disease Survey of the Bureau of Plant Industry—experience under the Loyalty Order demonstrates that constant peering over their shoulders endangers liberty without enhancing loyalty.

This is the administrative device that has been tried with reasonable success in Great Britain. There the power is lodged in each Minister to decide what parts of his ministry require the equivalent of our security clearance. In all, about 100,000 jobs were identified as having security significance. The Admiralty, as has our Department of the Army, concluded that everyone, from the highest to the lowest, must be cleared. Other ministries found no "sensitive" jobs at all. And this is as it should be, for in the variety of modern governmental activities there is room for both extremes.

If this approach be adopted, it will not mean an abandonment of interest in the probity of "nonsensitive" personnel. It will mean merely that observations will be related to behavior rather than belief. Government employees who improperly discharge their duties, whether motivated by disloyalty or mere slovenliness of habit, should of course be identified and appropriately disciplined. This, however, is a matter of administration rather than of detection. The supervisory officials of a functioning unit can more readily determine a staff member's misconduct or carelessness than can even the most vigilant agent of the FBI. The responsibility for efficiency should rest squarely on them. They cannot fulfill their responsibility if they tolerate on their staffs employees who are not actively loyal to their jobs. As for misdeeds unrelated to the direct performance of an employee's work, reliance must be placed upon the excellent counterespionage staffs of federal investigating agencies. The thorough work of the Federal Bureau of Investigation has given that bureau the place of public esteem that it occupies. The inherent absurdities of the loyalty program threaten the FBI's deservedly high reputation, for its "loyalty probers" must expend their energies in recording the often ambiguous pettinesses of political expression rather than in uncovering criminality. Releasing the FBI from the thankless and fruitless work to which it is now assigned will enhance the nation's safety. The more broadly we define the limits of our concern with personnel security, the more thinly we must spread attention to it. As has been true so often in matters of public administration, the scattershot of the blunderbuss is less effective than the aimed bullet of the rifle.

More than one hundred and fifty years ago a great friend of American democracy, Edmund Burke, argued that while restraint upon liberty may sometimes be required if liberty itself is to survive, "it ought to be the constant aim of every wise public council to find out by cautious experiments, and cool rational endeavors, with how little, not how much, of this restraint the community can subsist; for liberty is a good to be improved, and not an evil to be lessened." Burke's words are as true today as when he uttered them in 1777. The country will be the stronger for discovering that the restraints of the present loyalty program exceed the needs of national preservation.

Federalism

THE UNITED STATES is the first great experiment in federalism. Prior to the framing of the Constitution in 1787, history had witnessed the rise and fall of a number of confederacies, and the world had experienced numberless centralized or unitary states.

Our Constitution establishes a system under which, generally speaking, the federal government, subject to specific prohibitions, enjoys supremacy in the exercise of delegated sovereign powers, while the states, also subject to specific prohibitions and those inferred from grants to the federal government, exercise reserved sovereign powers. Theoretically this distribution of powers can be changed only by constitutional amendment. In actual practice, however, the elastic scope accorded by the Supreme Court to federal power, in spheres previously regarded as reserved to state action, demonstrates that the balance is a changing one.

Although some criticism of our federal structure has been far-reaching, no serious student of politics would suggest the substitution—in our vast and complex land with its long tradition of state sovereignty—of a unitary system of government. The real issues are concerned, rather, with establishing the appropriate spheres of national and state activities. To do this requires regard not only for tradition but for many other considerations including basic democratic values, experience, resources, and changing social needs.

One position that is often urged is that the emphases should be on decentralization and that ground should seldom, if ever, be yielded to the national power. Another persistently seeks to expand national control as necessary to efficiency and uniformity of social benefit. A third view would increase political centralization only when problems have clearly assumed national proportions with which the states cannot successfully cope and, at the same time, would maintain, whenever possible, administrative decentralization.

The relationship between federalism and freedom is the subject of special consideration.

Topic 14

CENTRALIZATION AND
DECENTRALIZATION

৪৩

Centralization and Democracy

PAUL STUDENSKI AND PAUL R. MORT *

Theoretically central versus local control is an issue between extreme centralization of government on the one hand, and extreme decentralization of it on the other. In actual practice, however, the issue is generally far from being so broad in character. It is limited in most cases to a consideration of whether certain functions of government should be centralized or decentralized, and of the extent to which such centralization or decentralization of them should be carried. The discussions of these narrower issues are generally carried on in much more realistic terms than the discussions of the broader theoretical issues, for they take into account particular situations and problems. . . .

The necessity of complete and direct central control over certain spheres of public affairs, such as national defense, foreign affairs, and foreign trade, is admitted by all writers. No one would seriously propose today that these functions be administered locally.

In most spheres of public affairs, however, the sharing of control by the central and local authorities is generally deemed most advisable. Central and local control are considered to possess different advantages deemed equally essential to the national welfare in the administration of public services. This sharing of control, it is noted, may take the form of (a) the exercise by the central and local governments, respectively, of independent authority over different spheres of the same functions as exemplified by the present control of most of the federal and state functions, (b) the supervision by the central government of the operations of

* Paul Studenski, former Professor of Economics, New York University. Author of *The Income of Nations, Financial History of the United States,* and other books and articles. Paul R. Mort, former Professor of Education, Teachers College, Columbia University. Author of *Principles of School Administration* and other books. The selection is from Paul Studenski and Paul R. Mort, *Centralized vs. Decentralized Government in Relation to Democracy* (New York, Bureau of Publications, Teachers College, Columbia University, 1941), *passim* as specially rearranged. By permission.

179

the local governments, as exemplified by state supervision over local educational administration and, more recently, by federal supervision over state administration of highways, social security, relief, etc., or (c) joint or cooperative management by the central government and the local authorities of certain of their affairs as exemplified by the proposals for a joint federal-state management of specific public works. . . .

MERITS OF LOCAL CONTROL

Local control (and by this is meant well-conceived local control) possesses the following principal merits, according to its advocates: (1) it promotes local unity, sense of neighborhood responsibility, spirit of self-reliance and capacity for group action; (2) it secures a close adaptation of public services to local needs; (3) it promotes and safeguards freedom, democracy, and responsible governments; (4) it promotes socially beneficial inter-community competition; (5) it permits safe experimentation with new forms and methods of government, thus fostering a gradual improvement in government throughout the country; . . . (6) it relieves the national government of congestion of business. Each one of these contentions will be reviewed below.

PROMOTION OF SELF-RELIANCE

Much emphasis is placed on the fact that overcentralization destroys civic interest, individual initiative, and the moral fiber of the nation. Citizens are discouraged from participating actively in civic affairs either as candidates for public office, or as voters, or as members of civic organizations, inasmuch as they are unable to influence materially the public policy under a system of this sort. Their freedom is restricted by the rules promulgated by the national administrative officers. Not being allowed to exercise their initiative, they become subservient subjects of a national bureaucracy. . . .

ADAPTATION TO LOCAL NEEDS

Extreme centralization, according to many writers in political science, results in a neglect of local needs. The national legislature is too absorbed with national affairs to give adequate attention to local matters. It tends to pass general laws relating to localities, which cannot possibly take care of special local situations, or else to make provision for the special conditions only of such communities as have substantial representation. . . .

The national administrative officers who dispose of the local affairs are even more inclined than the national legislature to apply uniform rules to varying situations. Uniformity of treatment simplifies their tasks. That such uniformity does violence to local development often concerns them little. They generally lack intimate acquaintance with the situations of the particular localities and therefore are unable to consider these situations even if they wished to do so. . . .

Most of the advocates of local self-government stress the fact that it secures a close adaptation of the public services to local needs. They contend that each locality has peculiar needs, predicated by its peculiar location, physical, social, and economic advantages, stage of development, historical tradition, and similar factors. In speaking of the needs of the locality, they have in mind, of course, the needs of the people inhabiting the locality. They maintain that the nation as a whole is advantaged by the intensive care which local governments are able to give to these peculiar local needs and by the close adaptation of the public services, under home rule, to peculiar local situations. They insist that the local people know best how to utilize the special advantages of their locality for their own collective benefit, and that their own self-interest prompts them to exercise their intelligence to the utmost to that end. Adequate consideration of local needs, they say, is assured under local government by the fact that the officials who formulate and execute local policy thereunder are residents of the locality and hence are interested in its welfare; that these officials are close to the citizens and susceptible to pressure on their part; and that the structure and the procedure of the local government generally become, in the course of the evolution, well adjusted to the peculiar local situation. . . .

PROMOTION OF FREEDOM AND RESPONSIBLE GOVERNMENT

The trump card of the advocates of local government, at least in England and the United States, seems to be the argument that it promotes freedom, democracy, and responsible government. This argument is developed by writers in these countries with great eloquence and conviction. The ideals of freedom, democracy, and responsible government are held by these writers to be among the highest ever conceived by man. It is contended by them that an institution that promotes these ideals deserves to be cherished and revered.

It is stated that under local self-government, local groups are free to manage their own affairs as they deem best, to venture on new undertakings, to make mistakes and to correct them in the light of experience, and that every active and interested member of the group is free to partake in this collective privilege. It is [evident] that under local self-government the individual has a wide opportunity for self-expression; that he can influence the course of public affairs in the local group much more effectively than in the national group; and that his importance in the local group is considerable, whereas in the national group it is exceedingly small. Thus, local self-government enlarges the freedom of the individual. . . .

It is pointed out by the advocates of local home rule that local public policy thereunder is determined by the people concerned, through their own democratically elected government and not by some central officials over whom they have no control. It is shown that, under local self-government, civic interest is stimulated and responsibility of the officials to the people is readily enforced. Local officials act as the servants of the people and not as their rulers. Inasmuch as each locality has its own policy-making body and its own elected officials, the opportunity for the ordinary citizen to hold public office is multiplied. Since the local government is so close at hand it tends to be responsive to the public will. The officials are accessible to the people. Although it is impossible in most of the local governments to have town meetings attended by all the citizens, an effective substitute therefor is frequently provided in the form of local referenda. All these factors help to make local government a popular government.

It is also contended that local self-government is the training school of national democracy. Local democratic processes, it is held, are simpler than the national democratic procedures. By learning how to manage democratically local affairs, it is said, a people becomes better fitted to manage democratically its national concerns. In the local democracies leaders are developed who eventually qualify for leadership in the national democracy. . . .

PROMOTION OF SOCIALLY BENEFICIAL INTER-COMMUNITY COMPETITION

Very few writers call attention to the fact that local self-government permits a healthy competition between local communities in the matter of civic improvements, and in this way promotes good government and social and economic progress. Students of government can furnish many illustrations of the fact that states and cities are trying to outdo each other in the construction of highways, development of port facilities and parks, building of schools, and similar improvements. This civic competition is due to some extent to the influence of the realtors, shopkeepers, and other commercial interests in the communities that seek to attract business and population to their localities for their own private benefit. But to some extent this competition is also due to the unselfish devotion of local civic leaders to the welfare of their respective local people. Laski says: "The only way to make municipal life an adequate thing is to set city striving against city in a consistent conflict of progressive improvement."

POSSIBILITY FOR SAFE EXPERIMENTATION WITH NEW FORMS AND METHODS OF GOVERNMENT

Many advocates of local self-government list among its merits the fact that it permits safe experimentation with new methods and forms of government, and fosters thereby a gradual improvement in government throughout the country. Groups of citizens in a locality, dissatisfied with the existing structure or procedure of their local government, may formulate programs for its reorganization along new lines and secure the consent of the local electorate to a trial of their proposals. If the experiment proves successful, it becomes established permanently in the political or administrative system of their community and is soon copied by other localities, or possibly even by the national government itself. If the experiment with a new form or method of government proves a partial or total failure, it may be reconsidered by the local people and either modified in some respects or abandoned in favor of some other, more promising arrangement. By securing a local trial for their advanced ideas, progressive citizens who enjoy a substantial local influence but have no national following may indirectly affect the course of political development in the country as a whole.

Since each experiment involves only a local area, it is held that mistakes cannot be very costly from a national point of view. Experimentation can be carried on, therefore, relatively freely. Thus, in the United States, local political experimentation has resulted in the development of the city manager form of government and the introduction in this country of the executive budget, proportional representation, the unicameral legislature, city planning, central purchasing, and a number of similar reforms.

Some writers also stress the fact that experimentation under local self-government is safe in the sense that it is carried on under conditions of a full democratic discussion and a vigilant critical observation by dissenting groups. . . .

LIGHTENING THE TASK OF THE NATIONAL AUTHORITY

It is [quite evident] that local self-government relieves the national government of the details of local administration and permits it to concentrate on the affairs which are truly national in character. National needs are better cared for as a result. Prior to the extension of the powers of local government in England during the eighties, a substantial portion of the time of Parliament was consumed annually by the consideration of local bills. There was general complaint of the congestion of the Parliamentary business which interfered with the proper consideration of national measures. The widening of the powers of self-government was urged on the ground that it would reduce this congestion. The term "specialization or division of labor" was commonly used in the English political literature of the time in the sense of a distribution of powers between the central and local governments. . . .

Excessive centralization of government, according to many scholars, promotes the rule of an irresponsible national bureaucracy and destroys democracy. The reason given is that the national legislature generally has so many measures of national importance to consider that it has no time to consider measures of only local importance. It must, therefore, delegate the local matters to the heads of the administrative departments even though those matters involve questions of public policy. Thus, in contravention of democratic principles, policy making is delegated to administrative officers. Moreover, the local questions involved are left to be decided finally, not by the heads of the departments who are responsible to the national legislature or to the elected national executive, but by the subordinate employees of the department, the permanent civil servants who are practically irremovable, and responsible to no one. Since the heads of the departments generally hold office only temporarily, they have no opportunity to acquire the expert knowledge necessary for a decision on the matters presented to them. Nor is it humanly possible for them to be acquainted with the multiple angles of the problems that are brought before them. Therefore, they must depend for advice on their subordinates—the civil servants, and sign documents which the latter present to them, even though they may not know their true implications.

The civil servants gain dominance not only over the ministers but also over the legislators, who depend on them for information, advice, and special favors. They form a closely-knit self-perpetuating group. They are bound together by common tradition and self-interest, a common distrust of the intelligence of the common citizens, and common contempt for popular government; and they shield one another. They become, in time, an entrenched and independent power in the country, in fact, its real government. Where a bureaucracy develops, democracy comes to an end. Thus runs the argument against excessive centralization.

There is wide agreement in the literature that bureaucracy lacks imagination, discourages initiative, and exercises a deadening influence on national life. It is not only oppressive, it is also slow and inefficient.

The evils of bureaucracy are so dreaded in a democratic country that the very mention of the word condemns the system of which it is a part. The argument of bureaucracy is, therefore, the most potent of all arguments advanced in American political discussion against excessive centralization. Brun, a French writer, says: [1]

> Centralization promotes bureaucracy, the dangers of which have sufficiently been demonstrated. The civil servants, greater in number from day to day, are powerful, and in practice almost irresponsible. They weigh heavily on the budget, and as if in spite of themselves, upon individual enterprises, which often appear to them suspicious . . . thus France is not a democracy; it is a bureaucracy.
>
> Bureaucracy engenders red tape, multiplies and complicates administration. The most elementary matters drag indefinitely, demanding an excessive amount of work, time, and the expenditure of money which is an actual waste.

SHORTCOMINGS OF DECENTRALIZATION

The principal shortcomings of extreme decentralization may be summarized as follows: (1) it results in an inefficient and an uneconomic management of local affairs; (2) it fosters local autocratic rule by petty officials and powerful minority groups; (3) it breeds narrow parochialism, and produces national and regional disunity and disorganization; (4) it results in extreme inequality in the standards of public service and protection of civil rights throughout the country or the region; (5) central government unifies the nation.

INEFFICIENT AND UNECONOMIC MANAGEMENT OF LOCAL AFFAIRS

Central government is in many respects more efficient and economical than are local governments, all other conditions being the same. First of all, central government generally attracts a more competent personnel for its policy-making body and its administrative departments than do local governments. The prestige attached to the holding of a national political office is far greater than that attached to the holding of a local one. The number of leading national offices in the country is smaller than the number of local ones, and the competition for them is therefore much keener. Each national legislator represents a larger area and a larger population, is concerned with more important affairs, and receives wider publicity than does a local councilman. The possibility for elevation to a higher office is greater in the case of a member of the national legislature than

[1] Charles T. Brun, *Le Regionalisme* (Paris, Bloud & Cie, 1911), pp. 15–16.

in that of a member of a municipal council. The compensation of a national representative is generally greater too. All these circumstances are responsible for the fact that capable men who are willing to devote their time to political affairs, as a rule, more readily aspire to a national political office than to a local one.

The central government has a wider choice of candidates for administrative positions than have local governments. It recruits its personnel wherever it can find suitable material. It is not obligated to employ local men for local offices. It can hire men in one locality and employ them in another. By advertising nationally the vacancies which it wishes to fill, it invites active competition for the positions from applicants all over the country. Inasmuch as the higher positions in the national administration involve greater responsibilities, enjoy greater prestige, and generally offer better pay than do the higher positions in the sphere of local government, they naturally attract more able and ambitious men. The greater opportunities which the national service offers for promotion to higher positions and also the more secure tenure of office it provides tend to secure for the national government a better personnel. In view of all these facts, the national government can afford to be more selective in its choice of employees than can the local governments.

Second, the national government has much wider sources of information than have local governments. It is in a position to collect through its local agents data on existing conditions in the various sections of the country and to base its policies on information of a comparative sort. The national service provides better opportunities to the men engaged therein to acquire wide experience than does the municipal service. The national administrators in the course of their careers are often shifted from one locality to another or travel extensively over the country and in this manner become familiar with the situations in various localities or regions.

Third, the central government can introduce much greater functional specialization in its administrative services than can local governments. It can subdivide the work into minute specialities to a much greater degree and thus can secure greater efficiency and economy of operation.

In the fourth place, the national government affords greater opportunities for centralization of administrative responsibility in a few key offices than does local government. This centralization of responsibility enables the government better to coordinate the activities of its officials. It makes possible quick and decisive action.

In the fifth place, the national government possesses the advantages of large-scale enterprise. One of these advantages, that of division or specialization of labor, has already been noted. The central government is

in a better position to employ experts to use elaborate and highly efficient equipment. Moreover, it can execute large projects affecting substantial areas, which the localities in these areas cannot possibly accomplish, separately or jointly, themselves. Large projects of this sort can be
executed more economically and are much more efficient than are the
smaller projects which local governments can undertake. The central government is able to perform, in cases of this sort, the same amount of
work as the local governments with a smaller number of employees. It
can eliminate duplicate functions and positions and use its personnel more
effectively and economically. . . .

FOSTERING LOCAL AUTOCRATIC RULE BY PETTY OFFICIALS AND POWERFUL MINORITY GROUPS

Extreme decentralization fosters local autocratic rule by petty officials
and powerful minority groups. The smaller the local area, the more static
are likely to be the social, economic, and political conditions therein.
Old-time residents cling together in an effort to preserve the traditional
policies of the community and lend loyal support to a common leader,
an old resident like themselves, who becomes the local dictator in all the
spheres of the local public life—political, economic, and the like. New-
comers who have different ideas of the development of the community
are not permitted by the dominant local clique to take active part in the
management of local affairs. The jobs in the local government are distributed by the local "boss" among his faithful followers, and a job once
granted to a follower readily becomes a sinecure. . . .

NARROW PAROCHIALISM AND NATIONAL AND REGIONAL DISUNITY AND DISORGANIZATION

Extreme decentralization results in the disorganization of government
in the country or the region. Confusing and conflicting regulations are
enacted by the various local governments. Projects conceived in the interest of the entire territory are often blocked by the refusal of a small
local area to join in the undertaking or to permit its facilities to be extended through its territory. The officials of the local government are
unwilling to cooperate. They fear that intergovernmental cooperation of
this sort may bring in its wake the unification of government, the abolition of their local independence, and a loss of their jobs; or that in some
other way it may result in the lowering of their prestige and influence
in the eyes of their own citizens. . . .

The vesting of excessively wide powers in state governments and of totally inadequate powers in the central government in this country, after the War of Independence, produced disunity and a breakdown of government. As soon as a strong central government was provided under the new constitution, the disintegrating tendencies came to an end. In like manner, in later times the exercise by the states of complete authority over the institution of slavery, over banks, railroads, monopolies and trusts, liquor traffic, and other economic and social matters produced chaos in these spheres of the national economy. With the partial or complete centralization of authority over these spheres in the national government, however, their administration became more orderly in character. The multiplication of local governments in densely populated metropolitan regions has produced serious evils. The small rural governments which, years ago, performed a useful function have become in recent times a bar to governmental and social progress.

Professor Munro refers to the shortcomings of extreme decentralization of government in this country as represented by excessive grants of power to state governments and inadequate grants of them to the Federal authority, as follows: [2]

> In their relation to the problems of American economic and social life, the states have been gradually receding as entities of political action, whether regulative or constructive, until today they are all but powerless in some of the fields ostensibly reserved to them by our scheme of government. . . . When a problem of industry or social welfare becomes too big to be handled by the authorities of the individual states, there are only two alternatives under present conditions. One is to confess our helplessness and bear the evils as best we can; the other is to demand that Washington take the problem in hand, whether it belongs there or not. It is natural that a practical people should prefer the latter alternative. They will continue to prefer it, and no theory of division of powers will stand in their way. Jurists may sob over the "vanishing rights of the states," but it is a fair guess that these rights will continue to dwindle as our problems keep growing in size. The steady erosion of state powers is bound to go hand in hand with the increasing complexity of our economic and social life. Nothing in the realm of political prophecy can be more certain than that the intrepid rear guards of the states' rights army are fighting for a lost cause. . . .

EXTREME INEQUALITY IN STANDARDS OF PUBLIC SERVICE AND PROTECTION OF CIVIL RIGHTS

Under an extremely decentralized government, the standards of public service and of the protection of civil rights, it is said, vary greatly from area to area. The maintenance by some areas of high standards benefits

[2] W. B. Munro, "Do We Need Regional Government?" *Forum* (January, 1928), p. 109.

the nation or the region. But the maintenance by others of low standards injures the neighboring communities and the country or region as a whole. For the evil conditions resulting from such low standards spread far beyond the boundaries of the areas responsible for them. The low standards maintained by these areas nullify the efforts of the other areas to maintain a high record of performance and eventually cause the latter to relax in their zeal. As a result, the quality of public services throughout the entire country or region is lowered. To prevent this eventuality, the neighboring communities and the state must take some action that would raise the standards of service in the backward areas. . . .

Swift, an American authority on education, points out that: [3]

> . . . a condition essential to democracy is equality of opportunity. . . . Inequalities of educational opportunity in the United States today are directly proportional to the degree of autonomy in matters of school support and control granted to the local communities. Any system which creates, perpetuates, and increases educational inequalities is undemocratic; and these are beyond all doubt the characteristics and results of our decentralized systems.

NATIONAL UNIFICATION AND THE SERVICE OF THE NATIONAL INTEREST

A properly conceived central government promotes national unity. It provides for the common needs of the population and for the coordinated development of all the social and economic factors upon which the welfare of the nation depends. And it obviously provides for the security of the nation. The centralized government organizes the creative forces of the nation and its resources for the achievement of these important ends. Advocates of centralization strongly emphasize the importance of these unifying functions of the central government. The need for the unification which centralization provides is admitted in many fields of public administration, even by the strongest advocates of local self-government. Thus, it is generally admitted that uniformity of regulation of interstate commerce, throughout the country, is essential for national prosperity, and that the central government, which alone can provide uniform regulation over the country as a whole, should exercise jurisdiction over this sphere of the economic life of the people. It is admitted by the advocates of modern centralization that in certain spheres of public affairs there is no need for unified administration and uniformity of regulation.

Central government equalizes the social, economic, and educational op-

[3] Fletcher H. Swift, *Federal and State Policies in Public School Finance in the United States* (New York, Ginn and Company), p. 85.

portunities available to the people in various sections of the country. It develops backward territories in accordance with national requirements. It promotes the national economy and the national culture. Well-conceived centralization enables the government to respond quickly to rapid nation-wide social and economic changes. The information which indicates occurrence of such changes and the type of adjustment required to meet them is readily available to the central government. The whole huge machinery of the government may be mobilized at a moment's notice to meet the national emergency or changed situation. Thousands of employees may be shifted from one type of activity to another or from one section of the country to another, as conditions require that this be done.

Proper centralization of government stimulates the civic interest of the people and broadens their civic outlook. It fosters broad national ideals, it gives rise to momentous political issues which profoundly stir the people, and it provides, if the people so desire, its own democratic processes for the consideration of public issues, which are just as effective as the democratic processes provided by the local government for the disposition of local affairs.

A properly conceived central government does not restrict the freedom of the individual. On the contrary, it often proves to be the most effective instrument for safeguarding the civil liberties of the people and their democratic institutions. It endeavors, in a democratic country, to guarantee fundamental civil rights to all the citizens in any portion of the country. Wherever undemocratic local pressure groups gain dominance and deny to some citizens their fundamental civil rights, the national government may intervene and may force upon these pressure groups the observance of these civil rights.

A well-conceived central government enlarges individual freedoms also by guaranteeing to the individuals freedom of enterprise over the entire national territory and by affording them an opportunity for a wider sphere of creative activity. The individual shares, in a democracy, in the determination of the large affairs with which the central government is concerned. The greater the scope of the public affairs, the greater the importance and responsibility of the individuals who share in their disposition. . . .

Some students of political science also emphasize the fact that the country which is exposed to attack requires a more centralized government than one whose natural location affords it relative security. It is significant that the tendencies toward the centralization of government become most pronounced in a country in times of war or when war is imminent.

CONCLUSION

The national interest can best be served by striking a fair balance between centralization and decentralization so that the advantages of both
of those types of control may be maintained and the disadvantages of
their extreme manifestations avoided. The exact degree of centralization
and decentralization which may be advisable in the case of different countries must necessarily depend on the size of the country, the stage of its
economic development, and the particular political, social, and economic
situation with which it may be confronted at the moment. A small country would necessarily require a more centralized government than a large
one. So, too, a country exposed to the dangers of attack requires a more
centralized organization than one that is relatively secure from external
aggression. Each country should seek to blend central control with local
control in its major public services so as best to promote its social ideals
under the particular circumstances of its life.

Federalism and Freedom: A Critique

FRANZ L. NEUMANN *

The theoretical argument for federalism revolves around the potential
of political power for evil. Federalism is seen as one of the devices to
curb the evil use of power by dividing power among a number of competing power-units.

The underlying sentiment—the corruptive influence of power—is often
not clearly formulated and the consequences thus not clearly seen. . . .

1. It is Lord Acton's statement on the corruptive effect of political
power which appears to have today the greatest influence. Three statements of his on political power are:

a. ". . . power tends to expand indefinitely, and will transcend all barriers,
abroad and at home, until met by superior forces."
b. "History is not a web woven with innocent hands. Among all the causes
which degrade and demoralize men, power is the most constant and the
most active."
c. To Creighton: "I cannot accept your canon that we are to judge Pope

* Late Professor of Public Law and Government, Columbia University. Author
of *Behemoth* and other publications. The selection is from Franz L. Neumann,
"Federalism and Freedom: A Critique," in A. W. Macmahon, ed., *Federalism:
Mature and Emergent* (New York, Doubleday & Co. Inc., 1955), pp. 45–49. By
permission of the Trustees of Columbia University.

and King unlike other men, with a favorable presumption that they did
no wrong. If there is any presumption it is the other way against holders
of power, increasing as the power increases. Historic responsibility has to
make up for the want of legal responsibility. Power tends to corrupt and
absolute power corrupts absolutely. Great men are almost always bad men,
even when they exercise influence and not authority: still more when you
superadd the tendency or the certainty of corruption by authority. There
is no worse heresy than that the office sanctifies the holder of it."

These statements have two aspects. The first one is, indeed, unobjec-
tionable and, of course, not very original. Thucydides said much the same:

> *Melians*—You may be sure that we are as well aware as you of the dif-
> ficulty of contending against your power and fortune, unless the terms be
> equal. But we trust that the gods may grant us fortune as good as yours,
> since we are just men fighting against unjust, and that what we want in
> power will be made up by the alliance of the Lacedaemonians, who are
> bound, if only for very shame, to come to the aid of their kindred. Our
> confidence, therefore, after all is not so utterly irrational.
> *Athenians*—When you speak of the favour of the gods, we may as fairly
> hope for that as yourselves; neither our pretensions nor our conduct being
> in any way contrary to what men believe of the gods, or practise among
> themselves. *Of the gods we believe, and of men we know, that by a neces-
> sary law of their nature they rule wherever they can.* And it is not as if
> we were the first to make this law, or to act upon it when made: we
> found it existing before us, and shall leave it to exist for ever after us;
> all we do is to make use of it, knowing that you and everybody else,
> having the same power as we have, would do the same as we do. (Emphasis
> supplied.)

And Montesquieu said this even more clearly. According to him power
could be checked only by power—a statement that few would be willing
to quarrel with. Not ideologies and beliefs but only a counter-power can
check power. In this he applies Cartesian principles and stands in the
tradition of Spinoza who saw no way of limiting the state's absoluteness
(which was logical consequence of his assumptions and of his geometric
method) except by a counter-power.

The Montesquieu generalization is, of course, designed to give his doctrine of the separation of powers an adequate theoretical base. But as
little as the theory of separate powers follows from his sociological observation, as little does that of the preferability of the federal state. Bentham rejected the separation of powers not only as incompatible with democracy but also because it could not really maximize freedom if the
three organs of government were controlled by the same social group.
A quite similar argument can be raised against federalism as a guarantee
for liberty. Those who assert that the federal state through the diffusion
of *constitutional* powers actually diffuses *political* power often overlook
the fact that the real cause for the existence of liberty is the pluralist

structure of society and the multi-party (or two-party) system. Federalism is not identical with social pluralism; and neither the two-party nor the multi-party system is the product of the federal state or the condition for its functioning.

2. Whether the federal state does indeed increase freedom cannot be abstractly determined. We have some evidence that the federal state as such (that is, regardless of the form of government) has not fulfilled this role. The German Imperial Constitution certainly created a federal state but there is little doubt that politically it had a dual purpose: to be a dynastic alliance against the forces of liberalism and democracy, and to secure the hegemony of Prussia. One may argue that a unitary state may even have been worse than the federal solution: that is quite possible. Nevertheless one may say, with reason, that the archaic Prussian three-class franchise could not possibly have been introduced as the system for a unitary German state. Thus a unitary German state in all likelihood would have been more progressive than the Bismarckian system. The Austro-Hungarian Dual Monarchy, after the *Ausgleich* of 1867, was an attempt to ensure the rule of the Germans and Magyars over all other nationalities. The Dual Monarchy most certainly did not maximize freedom except for the oligarchies in its two constituent states.

Perhaps more striking are the respective roles of federalism and centralism in the coming to power of National Socialism. Some believe, indeed, that the centralization under the Weimar Republic is wholly or at least partly responsible for the rise of National Socialism. But there is no evidence for this statement—nor indeed for the opposite one. It is certain that Bavaria, with the strongest states' rights tradition, gave shelter to the National Socialist movement and it is equally certain that the federal character of the Weimar Republic did not, after Hitler's appointment, delay the process of synchronization (*Gleichschaltung*) of the various state governments. Nor is there any definable relation between democratic conviction and federalist (or unitary) sympathies. The National Socialists were both centralists and reactionary, as were the Nationalists. Democrats and Social Democrats were antifederalists and committed to the preservation of political freedom. The Catholic center was not wholeheartedly committed to any position, and the Communists were, in theory, for the unitary state but did not hesitate, during the revolution of 1918, to advocate the secession of Brunswick which they believed they had in their pocket.

3. But perhaps what is meant by saying that federalism maximizes freedom is that only in a democracy does the division of constitutional power among various autonomous territorial units effect a maximum of political liberty; in other words, that democracy and the federal state go

together, even that federalism is necessary for democracy. Literally taken, this statement is most certainly untrue. The United Kingdom is a proof against it. Weimar Germany cannot be cited either for or against it. Bavaria—the most states' rights-conscious *land*—was certainly the most reactionary; Prussia, the most democratic. Insofar as the United States is concerned, it seems almost impossible to make any statement because of the extreme difficulty of attributing to the federal system—in isolation from other elements—any specific function. There are, perhaps, some tests like the protection of civil liberties. For a criminal, the federal system has obvious advantages in that it increases his margin of safety from prosecution. The need for extradition may, in isolated cases, permit a criminal to escape punishment. It is doubtful, however, that this can be taken as a compliment to federalism. Of real importance would be a study designed to prove or disprove that the federal nature of American government has strengthened civil liberties. The criminal syndicalism legislation of the post World War I period does not permit us to pass a final judgment. The "red hysteria" of that period "practically assured . . . passage (of this type of legislation) with only slight examination." The bills were passed with "breath-taking swiftness and little debate, or with a great outburst of oratory characterized more by passion, prejudice, and misinformation than by a reasoned effort to get at the facts." There seemed to be a race among the various states for the most drastic legislation, and vested interests, their influence enhanced by the makeup of the state legislatures, pushed through the bills. Simultaneously, efforts to enact a federal bill failed from 1917 to 1920. On the other hand, however, it is possible that without state laws a federal bill may have been enacted, and it is also true that in a few states no legislation was enacted. On the whole, one may perhaps say that the federal system may have speeded up inroads into the civil liberties rather than have protected them.

The same, perhaps, may be said of the present situation. The evidence is certainly too slight to be of great value in determining whether the federal system is preferable to the unitary state as an instrument to preserve or enhance civil liberties. Nor is it likely that convincing evidence can be obtained, since other factors—the plurality of the social structure, the functioning of a truly competitive party system, the strength of a favorable tradition, the intellectual level of the population, the attitude of the courts—do far more easily permit the formation of a counter-power against forces hostile to civil liberties than does the federal structure of the government.

4. Lord Acton's statements, however, are also concerned with a second aspect: namely, the corruptive influence of power. This brilliant formula

that power tends to corrupt and absolute power corrupts absolutely has attained the position of a classical remark; but, inevitably, it has also become a cliché of which neither the meaning nor the validity is ever questioned. The content of the statement is certainly not very original. While Plato's discussion of the same problem shows a much deeper insight, Lord Acton's has the undoubted merits of brevity and of quotability.

Lord Acton asserts that the character of the man who has power is corrupted by the exercise of power, or as the German adage has it: Politics corrupts the character. This is probably a valid generalization—but what is its significance for politics, in general, and for our problem, in particular? A morally evil ruler does not necessarily make a bad ruler— he may accumulate riches, indulge in all kinds of vices—and yet his rule may be beneficial; while the paragon of virtue may lead his country to destruction. But if we turn from monarchy or tyranny to representative government, the applicability of the formula to politics is quite certainly small.

However, we may well redefine the formula to mean that too much power concentrated in any organ of government has evil consequences for the people and that federalism, by dividing power among independent territorial units, checks these evil potentialities.

Thus redefined, the statement is no longer defensible because the opposite may equally be true. It is, indeed, also true: Too little power tends to corrupt and absolute lack of power corrupts absolutely; or, as Edmund Burke put it: "Nothing turns out to be so oppressive and unjust as a feeble government." One can accept Burke's assertion as absolute truth as little as one can Lord Acton's. Both are partially true generalizations, Burke's being, perhaps, a more realistic description of marginal situations than Lord Acton's. If one shares Burke's hatred of revolution, one may keep in mind that modern revolutions such as the French of 1789, the two Russian ones of 1917, and the German of 1918, had their immediate cause in the lack of power of the central governments and not in the excessive use or abuse of power.

It thus seems impossible to attribute to federalism, as such, a value; or to assert that the federal state—as contrasted to the unitary state— enhances political and civil freedom by dividing power among autonomous territorial subdivisions.

The Problem of Desegregation

OF THE MANY problems with which our country has been troubled in recent decades, few if any have assumed the great importance and engendered the deep bitterness that has been true of the controversy over racial desegregation.

Despite the unanimity of the Supreme Court in the school desegregation cases, its rulings have not been accepted nor implemented by powerful and often dominant forces in the South. A fundamental basis of objection is that the decisions are contrary to the Constitution. It may be urged by some that since these decisions are nonetheless "law of the land," they are beyond constitutional debate. However, Professor Charles L. Black, although he argues in support of the "lawfulness" of the desegregation decisions in these pages, nevertheless maintains that "if the cases outlawing segregation were wrongly decided, then they ought to be overruled." He adds, "One can go further: if dominant professional opinion ever forms and settles on the belief that they were wrongly decided, then they will be overruled, slowly or all at once, openly or silently." Under the circumstances, it seems to us that the issue of the "lawfulness" of the decisions merits consideration by the student of American politics.

We recognize that above and beyond the question of "lawfulness" lie certain moral, social and psychological arguments for and against desegregation. We believe that these, too, should be openly and seriously discussed. This is the way of democracy.

Topic 15

IS THE CONSTITUTION "COLOR BLIND"?

❦

"Separate But Equal"

PLESSY V. FERGUSON

163 U.S. 537 (1896)

[A Louisiana statute of 1890 imposed a twenty-five dollar fine on persons of Negro blood who attempted to enter railway train coaches set aside for whites. The statute also required railroads to furnish "separate but equal" railway accommodations for white and colored people. Plessy was one-eighth Negro but appeared white. He occupied a vacant seat in a railway coach reserved for white passengers, to which his ticket otherwise entitled him. He was fined as provided in the statute. On appeal, the higher state courts held the statute constitutional.]

MR. JUSTICE BROWN . . . delivered the opinion of the Court:

This case turns upon the constitutionality of an act of the General Assembly of the state of Louisiana, passed in 1890, providing for separate railway carriages for the white and colored races. . . .

The constitutionality of this act is attacked upon the ground that it conflicts both with the Thirteenth Amendment of the Constitution, abolishing slavery, and the Fourteenth Amendment, which prohibits certain restrictive legislation on the part of the states.

1. That it does not conflict with the Thirteenth Amendment, which abolished slavery and involuntary servitude, except as a punishment for crime, is too clear for argument. . . .

2. By the Fourteenth Amendment, all persons born or naturalized in the United States, and subject to the jurisdiction thereof, are made citizens of the United States and of the state wherein they reside; and the states are forbidden from making or enforcing any law which shall abridge the privileges or immunities of citizens of the United States, or shall deprive any person of life, liberty or property without due process of law, or deny to any person within their jurisdiction the equal protection of the laws. . . .

The object of the amendment was undoubtedly to enforce the absolute equality of the two races before the law, but in the nature of things it could not have been intended to abolish distinctions based upon color, or to enforce social, as distinguished from political, equality, or a commingling of the two races upon terms unsatisfactory to either. Laws permitting, and even requiring, their separation in places where they are liable to be brought into contact do not necessarily imply the inferiority of either race to the other, and have been generally, if not universally, recognized as within the competency of the state legislatures in the exercise of their police power. The most common instance of this is connected with the establishment of separate schools for white and colored children, which has been held to be a valid exercise of the legislative power even by courts of states where the political rights of the colored race have been longest and most earnestly enforced.

One of the earliest of these cases is that of Roberts *v.* City of Boston, 5 Cush. 198 (1849), in which the Supreme Judicial Court of Massachusetts held that the general school committee of Boston had power to make provision for the instruction of colored children in separate schools established exclusively for them, and to prohibit their attendance upon the other schools. "The great principle," said Chief Justice Shaw, p. 206, "advanced by the learned and eloquent advocate for the plaintiff" (Mr. Charles Sumner), "is, that by the constitution and laws of Massachusetts, all persons without distinction of age or sex, birth or color, origin or condition, are equal before the law. . . . But, when this great principle comes to be applied to the actual and various conditions of persons in society, it will not warrant the assertion, that men and women are legally clothed with the same civil and political powers, and that children and adults are legally to have the same functions and be subject to the same treatment; but only that the rights of all, as they are settled and regulated by law, are equally entitled to the paternal consideration and protection of the law for their maintenance and security." It was held that the powers of the committee extended to the establishment of separate schools for children of different ages, sexes and colors, and that they might also establish special schools for poor and neglected children, who have become too old to attend the primary school, and yet have not acquired the rudiments of learning, to enable them to enter the ordinary schools. Similar laws have been enacted by Congress under its general power of legislation over the District of Columbia . . . as well as by the legislatures of many of the states, and have been generally, if not uniformly, sustained by the courts. . . .

The distinction between laws interfering with the political equality of the Negro and those requiring the separation of the two races in schools, theatres, and railway carriages has been frequently drawn by this court. Thus in Strauder *v.* West Virginia, 100 U.S. 303, it was held that a law of West Virginia limiting to white male persons, 21 years of age and citizens of the state, the right to sit upon juries, was a discrimination which implied a legal inferiority in civil society, which lessened the security of the right of the colored race. and was a step toward reducing them to a condition of servility. Indeed, the right of a colored man that, in the selection of jurors to pass upon his life, liberty and property, there shall be no exclusion of his race, and no discrimination against them because of color, has been asserted in a number of cases. . . .

So far, then, as a conflict with the Fourteenth Amendment is concerned, the case reduces itself to the question whether the statute of Louisiana is a reasonable regulation, and with respect to this there must necessarily be a large discretion on the part of the legislature. In determining the question of reasonableness it is at liberty to act with reference to the established usages, customs and traditions of the people, and with a view to the promotion of their comfort, and the preservation of the public peace and good order. Gauged by this standard, we cannot say that a law which authorizes or even requires the separation of the two races in public conveyances is unreasonable or more obnoxious to the Fourteenth Amendment than the acts of Congress requiring separate schools for colored children in the District of Columbia, the constitutionality of which does not seem to have been questioned, or the corresponding acts of state legislatures.

We consider the underlying fallacy of the plaintiff's argument to consist in the assumption that the enforced separation of the two races stamps the colored race with a badge of inferiority. If this be so, it is not by reason of anything found in the act, but solely because the colored race chooses to put that construction upon it. The argument necessarily assumes that if, as has been more than once the case, and is not unlikely to be so again, the colored race should become the dominant power in the state legislature, and should enact a law in precisely similar terms, it would thereby relegate the white race to an inferior position. We imagine that the white race, at least, would not acquiesce in this assumption. The argument also assumes that social prejudices may be overcome by legislation and that equal rights cannot be secured to the Negro except by an enforced commingling of the two races. We cannot accept this proposition. If the two races are to meet upon terms of social equality, it must be the result of natural affinities, a mutual appreciation of each other's merits, and a voluntary consent of individuals. As was said by the Court of Appeals of New York in People *v.* Gallagher, 93 N.Y. 438, 448,

> this end can neither be accomplished nor prompted by laws which conflict with the general sentiment of the community upon whom they are designed to operate.
> When the government, therefore, has secured to each of its citizens equal rights before the law and equal opportunities for improvement and progress, it has accomplished the end for which it was organized and performed all of the functions respecting social advantages with which it is endowed.

Legislation is powerless to eradicate racial instincts or to abolish distinctions based upon physical differences, and the attempt to do so can only result in accentuating the difficulties of the present situation. If the civil and political rights of both races be equal, one cannot be inferior to the other civilly or politically. If one race be inferior to the other socially, the Constitution of the United States cannot put them upon the same plane. . . .

The judgment of the court below is, therefore, affirmed.

MR. JUSTICE HARLAN, dissenting:

In respect of civil rights, common to all citizens, the Constitution of the United States does not, I think, permit any public authority to know the race of those entitled to be protected in the enjoyment of such rights. Every true man has pride of race, and under appropriate circumstances when the rights of others, his equals before the law, are not to be affected, it is his privilege to express such pride and to take such action based upon it as to him seems proper. But I deny that any legislative body or judicial tribunal may have regard to the race of citizens when the civil rights of those citizens are involved. Indeed, such legislation as that here in question is inconsistent not only with that equality of rights which pertains to citizenship, national and state, but with the personal liberty enjoyed by everyone within the United States. . . .

It was said in argument that the statute of Louisiana does not discriminate against either race but prescribes a rule applicable alike to white and colored citizens. But this argument does not meet the difficulty. Everyone knows that the statute in question had its origin in the purpose, not so much to exclude white persons from railroad cars occupied by blacks, as to exclude colored people from coaches occupied by or assigned to white persons. Railroad corporations of Louisiana did not make discrimination among whites in the matter of accommodation for travellers. The thing to accomplish was, under the guise of giving equal accommodations for whites and blacks, to compel the latter to keep to themselves while travelling in railroad passenger coaches. No one would be so wanting in candor as to assert the contrary. The fundamental objection, therefore, to the statute is that it interferes with the personal freedom of citizens. . . . If a white man and a black man choose to occupy the same public conveyance on a public highway, it is their right to do so, and no government, proceeding alone on grounds of race, can prevent it without infringing the personal liberty of each. . . .

The white race deems itself to be the dominant race in this country. And so it is, in prestige, in achievements, in education, in wealth, and in power. So, I doubt not, it will continue to be for all time, if it remains true to its great heritage and holds fast to the principles of constitutional liberty. But in the view of the Constitution, in the eye of the law, there is in this country no superior, dominant, ruling class of citizens. There is no caste here. Our Constitution is color-blind and neither knows nor tolerates classes among citizens. In respect of civil rights, all citizens are equal before the law. The humblest is the peer of the most powerful. The law regards man as man and takes no account of his surroundings or of his color when his civil rights as guaranteed by the supreme law of the land are involved. . . .

The arbitrary separation of citizens, on the basis of race, while they are on a public highway, is a badge of servitude wholly inconsistent with the civil freedom and the equality before the law established by the Constitution. It cannot be justified upon any legal grounds.

If evils will result from the commingling of the two races upon public highways established for the benefit of all, they will be infinitely less than those that will surely come from state legislation regulating the enjoyment of civil rights upon the basis of race. We boast of the freedom enjoyed by our people above all other peoples. But it is difficult to reconcile that boast with a state of the law which, practically, puts the brand of servitude and degradation upon a large class of our fellow citizens, our equals before the law. The thin disguise of "equal" accommodations for passengers in railroad coaches will not mislead anyone, nor atone for the wrong this day done. . . .

I do not deem it necessary to review the decisions of state courts to which reference was made in argument. Some, and the most important, of them are wholly inapplicable, because rendered prior to the adoption of the last amendments of the Constitution, when colored people had very few rights which the dominant race felt obliged to respect. Others were made at a time when public opinion, in many localities, was dominated by the institution of slavery; when it would not have been safe to do justice to the black man; and when, so far as the rights of blacks were concerned, race prejudice was, practically, the supreme law of the land. Those decisions cannot be guides in the era introduced by the recent amendments of the supreme law, which established universal civil freedom, gave citizenship to all born or naturalized in the United States and residing here, obliterated the race line from our systems of governments, national and state, and placed our free institutions upon the broad and sure foundation of the equality of all men before the law. . . .

For the reasons stated, I am constrained to withhold my assent from the opinion and judgment of the majority.

"Separate Educational Facilities Are Inherently Unequal"

BROWN *V*. BOARD OF EDUCATION OF TOPEKA

347 U.S. 483 (1954)

MR. CHIEF JUSTICE WARREN delivered the opinion of the Court.

These cases come to us from the States of Kansas, South Carolina, Virginia, and Delaware. They are premised on different facts and different local conditions, but a common legal question justifies their consideration together in this consolidated opinion.

In each of the cases, minors of the Negro race, through their legal representatives, seek the aid of the courts in obtaining admission to the public schools of their community on a nonsegregated basis. In each instance, they had been denied admission to schools attended by white children under laws requiring or permitting segregation according to race. This segregation was alleged to deprive the plaintiffs of the equal protection of the laws under the Fourteenth Amendment. In each of the cases other than the Delaware case, a three-judge federal district court denied relief to the plaintiffs on the so-called "separate but equal" doctrine announced by this Court in Plessy *v.* Ferguson, 163 U.S. 537. Under that doctrine, equality of treatment is accorded when the races are provided substantially equal facilities, even though these facilities be separate. In the Delaware case, the Supreme Court of Delaware adhered to that doctrine, but ordered that the plaintiffs be admitted to the white schools because of their superiority to the Negro schools.

The plaintiffs contend that segregated public schools are not "equal" and cannot be made "equal," and that hence they are deprived of the equal protection of the laws. Because of the obvious importance of the question presented, the Court took jurisdiction. Argument was heard in the 1952 Term, and reargument was heard this Term on certain questions propounded by the Court.

Reargument was largely devoted to the circumstances surrounding the adoption of the Fourteenth Amendment in 1868. It covered exhaustively consideration of the Amendment in Congress, ratification by the states, then existing practices in racial segregation, and the views of proponents and opponents of the Amendment. This discussion and our own investigation convince us that, although these sources cast some light, it is not enough to resolve the problem with which we are faced. At best, they are inconclusive. The most avid proponents of the post-War Amendments undoubtedly intended them to remove all legal distinctions among "all persons born or naturalized in the United States." Their opponents, just as certainly, were antagonistic to both the letter and the spirit of the Amendments and wished them to have the most limited effect. What others in Congress and the state legislatures had in mind cannot be determined with any degree of certainty.

An additional reason for the inconclusive nature of the Amendment's history, with respect to segregated schools, is the status of public education at that time. In the South, the movement toward free common schools, supported by general taxation, had not yet taken hold. Education of white children was largely in the hands of private groups. Education of Negroes was almost nonexistent, and practically all of the race were illiterate. In fact, any education of Negroes was forbidden by law in some states. Today, in contrast, many Negroes have achieved outstanding success in the arts and sciences as well as in the business and professional world. It is true that public school education had advanced further in the North, but the effect of the Amendment on Northern States was generally ignored in the congressional debates. Even in the North, the conditions of public education did not approximate those existing today. The curriculum was usually rudimentary; ungraded schools were common in rural areas; the school term was but three months a year in many states; and compulsory school attendance was virtually unknown. As a consequence, it is not surprising that there should be so little in the history of the Fourteenth Amendment relating to its intended effect on public education.

In the first cases in this Court construing the Fourteenth Amendment, decided shortly after its adoption, the Court interpreted it as proscribing all state-imposed discriminations against the Negro race. The doctrine of "separate but equal" did not make its appearance in this Court until 1896 in the case of Plessy v. Ferguson, *supra,* involving not education but transportation. American courts have since labored with the doctrine for over half a century. In this Court, there have been six cases involving the "separate but equal" doctrine in the field of public education. In Cumming v. County Board of Education, 175 U.S. 528, and Gong Lum v. Rice, 275 U.S. 78, the validity of the doctrine itself was not challenged. In more recent cases, all on the graduate school level, inequality was found in that specific benefits enjoyed by white students were denied to Negro students of the same educational qualifications. Missouri ex rel. Gaines v. Canada, 305 U.S. 337; Sipuel v. Oklahoma, 332 U.S. 631; Sweatt v. Painter, 339 U.S. 629; McLaurin v. Oklahoma State Regents, 339 U.S. 637. In none of these cases was it necessary to reexamine the doctrine to grant relief to the Negro plaintiff. And in Sweatt v. Painter, *supra,* the Court expressly reserved decision on the question whether Plessy v. Ferguson should be held inapplicable to public education.

In the instant cases, that question is directly presented. Here, unlike Sweatt *v*. Painter, there are findings below that the Negro and white schools involved have been equalized, or are being equalized, with respect to buildings, curricula, qualifications and salaries of teachers, and other "tangible" factors. Our decision, therefore, cannot turn on merely a comparison of these tangible factors in the Negro and white schools involved in each of the cases. We must look instead to the effect of segregation itself on public education.

In approaching this problem, we cannot turn the clock back to 1868 when the Amendment was adopted, or even to 1896 when Plessy *v*. Ferguson was written. We must consider public education in the light of its full development and its present place in American life throughout the Nation. Only in this way can it be determined if segregation in public schools deprives these plaintiffs of the equal protection of the laws.

Today, education is perhaps the most important function of state and local governments. Compulsory school attendance laws and the great expenditures for education both demonstrate our recognition of the importance of education to our democratic society. It is required in the performance of our most basic public responsibilities, even service in the armed forces. It is the very foundation of good citizenship. Today it is a principal instrument in awakening the child to cultural values, in preparing him for later professional training, and in helping him to adjust normally to his environment. In these days, it is doubtful that any child may reasonably be expected to succeed in life if he is denied the opportunity of an education. Such an opportunity, where the state has undertaken to provide it, is a right which must be made available to all on equal terms.

We come then to the question presented: Does segregation of children in public schools solely on the basis of race, even though the physical facilities and other "tangible" factors may be equal, deprive the children of the minority group of equal educational opportunities? We believe that it does.

In Sweatt *v*. Painter, *supra,* in finding that a segregated law school for Negroes could not provide them equal educational opportunities, this Court relied in large part on "those qualities which are incapable of objective measurement but which make for greatness in a law school." In McLaurin *v*. Oklahoma State Regents, *supra,* the Court, in requiring that a Negro admitted to a white graduate school be treated like all other students, again resorted to intangible considerations: ". . . his ability to study, to engage in discussions and exchange views with other students, and, in general, to learn his profession." Such considerations apply with added force to children in grade and high schools. To separate them from others of similar age and qualifications solely because of their race generates a feeling of inferiority as to their status in the community that may affect their hearts and minds in a way unlikely ever to be undone. The effect of this separation on their educational opportunities was well stated by a finding in the Kansas case by a court which nevertheless felt compelled to rule against the Negro plaintiffs:

> Segregation of white and colored children in public schools has a detrimental effect upon the colored children. The impact is greater when it has the sanction of the law; for the policy of separating the races is usually interpreted as denoting the inferiority of the Negro group. A sense of inferiority affects the motivation of a child to learn. Segregation with the sanction of law, therefore, has a tendency to retard the educational and mental development of Negro children and to deprive them of some of the benefits they would receive in a racially integrated school system.

Whatever may have been the extent of psychological knowledge at the time of Plessy *v.* Ferguson, this finding is amply supported by modern authority. Any language in Plessy *v.* Ferguson contrary to this finding is rejected.

We conclude that in the field of public education the doctrine of "separate but equal" has no place. Separate educational facilities are inherently unequal. Therefore, we hold that the plaintiffs and others similarly situated for whom the actions have been brought are, by reason of the segregation complained of, deprived of the equal protection of the laws guaranteed by the Fourteenth Amendment. This disposition makes unnecessary any discussion whether such segregation also violates the Due Process Clause of the Fourteenth Amendment.

Because these are class actions, because of the wide applicability of this decision, and because of the great variety of local conditions, the formulation of decrees in these cases presents problems of considerable complexity. On reargument, the consideration of appropriate relief was necessarily subordinated to the primary question—the constitutionality of segregation in public education. We have now announced that such segregation is a denial of the equal protection of the laws. In order that we may have the full assistance of the parties in formulating decrees, the cases will be restored to the docket, and the parties are requested to present further argument on Questions 4 and 5 previously propounded by the Court for the reargument this Term.*

The Attorney General of the United States is again invited to participate. The Attorneys General of the states requiring or permitting segregation in public education will also be permitted to appear as *amici curiae* upon request to do so by September 15, 1954, and submission of briefs by October 1, 1954.

It is so ordered.

* These questions were designed to aid the Court to formulate specific decrees to effectuate its decision declaring segregation in public education a denial of equal protection of the laws.

BOLLING *V*. SHARPE

347 U.S. 497 (1954)

[In this case involving racial segregation in the public schools of the *District of Columbia,* the Court said, in part:]

We have this day held that the equal protection clause of the Fourteenth Amendment prohibits the states from maintaining racially segregated public schools. The legal problem in the District of Columbia is somewhat different, however. The Fifth Amendment, which is applicable in the District of Columbia, does not contain an equal protection clause as does the Fourteenth Amendment which applies only to the states. But the concepts of equal protection and due process, both stemming from our American ideal of fairness, are not mutually exclusive. The "equal protection of the laws" is a more explicit safeguard of prohibited unfairness than "due process of law," and therefore, we do not imply that the two are always interchangeable phrases. . . .

Segregation in public education is not reasonably related to any proper governmental objective, and thus it imposes on Negro children of the District of Columbia a burden that constitutes an arbitrary deprivation of their liberty in violation of the due process clause. In view of our decision that the Constitution prohibits the states from maintaining racially segregated public schools, it would be unthinkable that the same Constitution would impose a lesser duty on the Federal Government. We hold that racial segregation in the public schools of the District of Columbia is a denial of the due process of law guaranteed by the Fifth Amendment to the Constitution.

BROWN *V*. BOARD OF EDUCATION OF TOPEKA

349 U.S. 294 (1955)

[In its earlier decision in the Brown case, the Court requested further argument on the form of relief to be granted. See footnote, above. After weighing the presentations, the Court, on May 31, 1955, rendered its opinion in part, as follows.]

MR. CHIEF JUSTICE WARREN delivered the opinion of the Court.

Full implementation of these constitutional principles may require solution of varied local school problems. School authorities have the primary responsibility for elucidating, assessing, and solving these problems; courts will have to consider whether the action of school authorities constitutes good faith implementation of the governing constitutional principles. Because of their proximity to local conditions and the possible need for further hearings, the courts which originally heard these cases can best perform this judicial appraisal. Accordingly, we believe it appropriate to remand the cases to those courts.

In fashioning and effectuating the decrees, the courts will be guided by equitable principles. Traditionally, equity has been characterized by a practical flexibility in shaping its remedies and by a facility for adjusting and reconciling public and private needs. These cases call for the exercise of these traditional attributes of equity power. At stake is the personal interest of the plaintiffs in admission to public schools as soon as practicable on a nondiscriminatory basis. To effectuate this interest may call for elimination of a variety of obstacles in making the transition to school systems operated in accordance with the constitutional principles set forth in our May 17, 1954, decision. Courts of equity may properly take into account the public interest in the elimination of such obstacles in a systematic and effective manner. But it should go without saying that the vitality of these constitutional principles cannot be allowed to yield simply because of disagreement with them.

While giving weight to these public and private considerations, the courts will require that the defendants make a prompt and reasonable start toward full compliance with our May 17, 1954, ruling. Once such a start has been made, the courts may find that additional time is necessary to carry out the ruling in an effective manner. The burden rests upon the defendants to establish that such time is necessary in the public interest and is consistent with good faith compliance at the earliest practicable date. To that end, the courts may consider problems related to administration, arising from the physical condition of the school plant, the school transportation system, personnel, revision of school districts and attendance areas into compact units to achieve a system of determining admission to the public schools on a nonracial basis, and revision of local laws and regulations which may be necessary in solving the foregoing problems. They will also consider the adequacy of any plans the defendants may propose to meet these problems and to effectuate a transition to a racially nondiscriminatory school system. During this period of transition, the courts will retain jurisdiction of these cases. . . .

It is so ordered.

Topic 16

DESEGREGATION AND THE CONSTITUTION

&❧&

The "Unlawfulness" of the Decisions

EUGENE COOK AND WILLIAM I. POTTER *

The purpose of this article is to discuss without heat and, it is hoped, with some light, from a strictly legal, and not emotional, viewpoint the precedent-shattering decisions of the Supreme Court in the school segregation cases of 1954 and 1955.[1]

The decisions of the United States Supreme Court of May 17, 1954, and May 31, 1955, in the school segregation cases, Brown v. Board of Education, reported in 347 U.S. 483 and 349 U.S. 294, constitute a crisis in American constitutional law, for these reasons:

1. They are a radical departure from the doctrine of *stare decisis* firmly established in American and English jurisprudence. Moreover, the Court, as hereinafter pointed out, sustains its conclusion by a reasoning process which was heretofore unknown to jurisprudence, which conflicts with prior opinions of the same Court less than five years old, and which is sharply deprecated even by those who otherwise approve the result of the decision. If the reasoning by which the Court arrives at its conclusion is fatally defective, is not the result itself fatally defective?

2. The Court has, without any implementing act of the Congress such as is required under the terms of the Fourteenth Amendment, and by an order unprecedented in judicial history, assumed the power under that Amendment to enforce commingling of the white and colored races in state-supported schools, thus rendering a nullity state laws providing for

* Eugene Cook has been Attorney General of Georgia since 1945. He is a member of the Georgia and American Bar Associations. William I. Potter practices law in Kansas City, Missouri. He served with the F.B.I. in 1918–1919 and is a member of the Missouri Bar. The selection is from "The School Segregation Cases: Opposing the Opinion of the Supreme Court," *American Bar Association Journal*, Vol. 42 (April, 1956), pp. 313–317, 391. By permission.

[1] A brilliant and highly critical legal argument dissecting the Court's opinion in the segregation cases was made by United States Senator James Eastland, of Mississippi, in the Senate on May 26, 1955. See *Congressional Record*, pages 6068 *et seq*. The writers recommend it.

separate but equal educational facilities—an anomalous assumption of power that constitutes further encroachment by the central Government upon the rights reserved to the states and to the people by the Federal Constitution.

3. In construing segregated schools as unconstitutional and discriminatory against the Negro by reason of the equal protection clause of the Fourteenth Amendment, the Court reached the conclusion that the Negro was deprived of equal protection because the segregated school generated in him a feeling of inferiority that *may* (italics supplied) affect his heart and mind in a way *unlikely* (italics supplied) ever to be undone. To support this thesis it cited as authority college professors, psychologists and sociologists. Absent from the opinion was reference to the effect on the hearts and minds of white children and their parents because of enforced commingling with Negro children. The state, in providing segregated schools, gave heed to this preference of white parents and their children, and, desiring that state maintained free public schools should exist to educate the children of both races, solved this basic human problem by enacting laws and providing for equal educational facilities in separate schools. Reason supports the soundness and fairness of the state program, and reason supports prior decisions of the United States Supreme Court since the adoption of the Fourteenth Amendment in 1868, upholding the constitutionality of state-maintained separate-but-equal educational facilities.

The first point the Court had to resolve in the Brown case was whether the framers and ratifiers of the Fourteenth Amendment intended the equal protection clause to abolish segregation in the public schools. To this question the Supreme Court pleaded ignorance by saying that the intent of the framers and ratifiers "cannot be determined with any degree of certainty."

The Court said this, even though the briefs show that the same 39th Congress that promulgated the Fourteenth Amendment passed two bills dealing with separate schools for white and colored children in the District of Columbia. In addition, the briefs show that of the thirty-seven states in existence at that time, only five abolished segregation contemporaneously with ratification of the Fourteenth Amendment, and three of these restored segregation after the removal of federal troops.

The overwhelming majority either established or continued segregation in their public schools contemporaneously with ratification of the Fourteenth Amendment. Georgia's first public school segregation laws were enacted at the same session at which the Fourteenth Amendment was ratified. They were enacted by a Republican legislature which had thirty-three Negro members and were signed by a Republican governor.

In a recent article, Alexander M. Bikel, who was one of two law clerks to Mr. Justice Frankfurter during the segregation arguments, had this to say:

(1) The legislative history of the 14th Amendment makes clear that it was not intended to abolish segregation immediately.

(2) But it did not foreclose to a court the authority to find a different application under different circumstances years later.

We agree with his first proposition, but the latter, if correct, rules out precedent entirely and leaves the Constitution as unstable as the wind. It suggests that all constitutional amendments should include express provisions as to what they mean at different periods of time and under different circumstances. To attempt any such constitutional mechanism would be an absurdity. Why have a written constitution if the Court will not be bound by the intent of the framers and ratifiers?

In rendering its decision, the Supreme Court rejected the traditional rule of constitutional construction and substituted the intent of the Court for the intent of the people.

In its article entitled "The Supreme Court 1953 Term" the *Harvard Law Review* (68 *Harv. L. Rev.* 96) said:

In dealing with prior cases, especially Plessy *v.* Ferguson, the Chief Justice did not seek to demonstrate that the court had once blundered. His point, rather, was that these prior decisions were simply outmoded in present day society.

Thus, it is seen that a new rule of testing the constitutionality of a state's public policy as expressed in its statutes and as authorized by the Tenth Amendment has been formulated. No longer is there a question of whether there exists a conflict with precedent or whether precedent is wrong but rather whether the intent of the framers as recognized in previous decisions, is, in the opinion of the Judges, "outmoded."

The purpose of all sincere investigations is the discovery of truth. Basic truth is discoverable in the midst of external realities. It may not be manufactured by the mind. It is a tangible reality and is never new. Once found, we may seize and hold fast to it. Now let us seek and follow the truth wherever it may lead, as applied to the Brown case.

In its decision, the Supreme Court did not hold that the old "separate but equal" doctrine, laid down in Plessy *v.* Ferguson, 163 U.S. 537, was bad law. It held that it was bad sociology. It did not hold that the facts (or truths) disclosed by the records in the cases before the Court, justified a departure from the "separate but equal" doctrine. It held that "psychological knowledge," apart from these records, was of more validity than factual truths.

Without doubt there is no precedent in any recorded decision of any court, and it is hoped there will be none hereafter, reading as follows:

"Whatever may have been the extent of psychological knowledge at the time of Plessy *v.* Ferguson, this finding is amply supported by modern authority." (Citing as authority six lay textbooks, not introduced in evidence in any of the pending cases, clearly inadmissible if offered, and written, for the most part, by authors to whose affiliations and convictions the Court cannot have given the slightest investigation or attention, but which will hereafter be discussed in this article.)

The Court conceded that the records in the cases before it demonstrated equality of white and colored schools in respect to all "tangible factors." The decision could not "turn on" such "tangible factors," said the Court:

> We must look instead [not also] to the effect of segregation itself on public education.

The Court then asked:

> Does segregation . . . [alone] . . . deprive the children of the minority group of equal educational opportunities?

The answer was: "We believe that it does."
Why? Because, the Court said:

> Whatever may have been the psychological knowledge at the time of Plessy *v.* Ferguson, this finding is amply supported by modern authority. Any language in Plessy *v.* Ferguson contrary to this finding is rejected.

A judicial "finding" is, of course, supposed to be based on admissible evidence or on commonly accepted facts of which a court can take judicial notice, including congressional or state legislative declarations. In these cases the applicable congressional and state legislative declarations were to the contrary. Indeed, in 1946, Congress, in the national grants-in-aid legislation for school lunches, still in force, recognized the existence of separate school systems and merely required equal treatment, in the following language (42 U.S.C.A. 1760):

> If a state maintains separate schools for minority and for majority races, no funds made available pursuant to this chapter shall be paid or disbursed to it unless a just and equitable distribution is made within the state for the benefit of such minority races, of funds paid to it under this chapter.

Congress deliberately chose to recognize "separate but equal treatment" instead of requiring desegregation.

How did such "intangibles" become "findings" in these cases? They were not authenticated as "authority" by any method known to Anglo-Saxon jurisprudence or rules of evidence. If not in evidence, the universal rule is that it was harmful error, prejudicial to the parties defendant, for them to be considered by the Court.

We have scanned legal literature since May, 1954, in an effort to find a respectable vindication of the Supreme Court's conduct, but have found none that appeals to reason.

Under elementary and elemental law, a court may not consider treatises in a field other than law, unless the treatises themselves are the very subject of inquiry. The doctrine of judicial notice extends only to those things of common knowledge that lie without the realm of science, or to that one science in which judges are presumed to be learned or experts themselves—the science of law.

As late as 1952, Mr. Justice Frankfurter said that the Supreme Court was not competent to take judicial notice of opinions in the relatively new fields of sociology and psychology. Beauharnais *v*. Illinois, 343 U.S. 250, 263. Speaking for a majority of the Court, he wrote:

> It is not within our competence to confirm or deny claims of social scientists as to the dependence of the individual on the position of his racial or religious group in the community.

In Pinkus *v*. Reilly, 338 U.S. 269, decided November 14, 1949, Justice Black held that the use of nonlegal materials in a case was illegal, illogical and unfair. If it was illegal, illogical and unfair in 1949, what has happened since to confirm such procedure to the sense of justice of the same judges?

In the Pinkus case the parties at least had an opportunity to rebut, to disprove and to impeach by means other than cross-examination. In the integration cases, no such opportunity was afforded to parties. The intangible consideration first appeared in the secrecy of the Judge's chambers. No notice of it was given to the defendants until the judgment itself. No precedent short of Star Chamber and High Commission cases of the Stuart kings, three hundred years ago may be found for like judicial demeanor.

In National Council of American-Soviet Friendship, Inc. *v*. McGrath, 341 U.S. 123, the Supreme Court held that nonlegal materials could not be used by the Attorney General as a basis for listing an organization as communistic.

Justice Black shamed the Attorney General, calling such conduct "unfair." He said it was "abhorrent to free men." He should not now complain that we agree with him. . . .

The findings of social science are sometimes regarded as elaborate statements of what everybody knows in language that nobody can understand. While little harm can come from such an undertaking, great harm will result when a social scientist takes his deductions and generalizations into the field of judicial interpretation and treats them as the equivalent of "law."

United States Circuit Judge Jerome Frank recently wrote that these generalizations and the "inferences derived therefrom are almost certain to be importantly false. For the consequences of the operation of certain customs or group attitudes are often cancelled out by the consequences of other conflicting customs and attitudes."

Even the latest book cited by the Court itself in footnote 11 of the Brown case (Witmer and Kotinsky) states:

> Unfortunately for scientific accuracy and adequacy, thoroughly satisfactory methods of determining the effects of prejudice and discrimination on health or personality have not yet been devised, nor has a sufficient number of studies dealing with the various minority groups been made.

But the Court blandly and extrajudicially accepts as "psychological *knowledge*" what the lay experts themselves are as yet completely unsure of!

Indeed, even stronger views have been expressed of the present wholly inadequate and unscientific state of sociological knowledge of majority-minority problems.[2]

A recent writer, Edmond Cahn, who agrees with the result of the Brown case nevertheless sharply criticizes the use of sociological authority and shows its danger by saying:

> The word "danger" is used advisedly, because I would not have the constitutional rights of Negroes—or of other Americans—rest on such flimsy foundations as some of the scientific demonstrations in these records.

Since these behavioral sciences are so very young, imprecise and changeable, their findings have an uncertain expectancy of life. Today's observation may be cancelled by tomorrow's new revelation—or new technical fad.

Should our fundamental rights rise, fall or change along with the latest fashions of psychological literature? How are we to know that in the future social scientists may not present us with a collection of notions similar to those of Adolf Hitler and label them as modern science? If Mr. Justice Holmes was correct when he insisted that the Constitution should not be tied to the wheels of any economic system whatsoever, shouldn't it be similarly uncommitted in relation to other social sciences?

What of this modern authority upon which the Court based its decision? The first one cited of the six—K. B. Clark—was, at the time of the arguments before the Court, on the payroll of the National Association for the Advancement of Colored People as a so-called "social-science expert," a questionable procedure in view of the fact that the NAACP was the real party in interest waging the litigation in these cases.

---

2 "The Survival of the Moralistic-Legalistic Orientation in Sociology," a paper delivered to the Sociological Research Association, September 2, 1952, by Dr. George A. Lundberg, University of Washington, Seattle, Washington, and printed in *The Sociologist* published at the University of Colorado, Boulder, Colorado.

The book *An American Dilemma,* written by Swedish socialist Gunnar Myrdal on a grant from the Carnegie Foundation, was cited in its entirety by the Supreme Court as an authority for its ruling. . . .

It was *in this book* that Myrdal declared the United States Constitution to be "impractical and unsuited to modern conditions" and its adoption to be "nearly a plot against the common people." Furthermore, he openly avowed that liberty must be forsaken for the benefit of what he called "social equality."

Has the present Supreme Court now adopted Myrdal's view of the Constitution? In all fairness have not we Southerners good reason to be deeply disturbed over the Court's attitude toward the Constitution? Has not every citizen good reason to be deeply disturbed?

What has become of the accepted tests of the constitutionality of statutes? What of the rule that a distinction in legislation is not arbitrary and not violative of the equal protection clause of the Fourteenth Amendment "if any state of facts reasonably can be conceived that would sustain it"? New York Rapid Transit Co. *v.* New York, 303 U.S. 573. Goessaert *v.* Cleary, 335 U.S. 34.

What of the rule that "legislative determinations express or implied are entitled to great weight," and that invalidity must be shown "by things which will be judicially noticed, or by facts established by evidence," and that "the burden is on the attacking party to establish the invalidating facts"; that "being a legislative judgment, it is presumed to be supported by the facts known to the legislature unless facts judicially known, or proved, preclude that possibility"; and that "in reviewing the present determination, we examine the record not to see whether the findings of the court below are supported by evidence, but to ascertain upon the whole record whether it is possible to say that the legislative choice is without rational basis?" Weaver *v.* Palmer, 270 U.S. 402, 410; South Carolina Highway Department *v.* Barnwell Bros., 303 U.S. 177, 191-2.

What about the rule that classifications are valid under the equal protection clause unless without any rational basis on which reasonable men cannot differ? Denver *v.* New York Trust Co., 229 U.S. 123, 143. Have all of these salutary rules of constitutional adjudication gone overboard?

It is our firm opinion that the United States Supreme Court in Brown *v.* Topeka not only usurped the prerogatives of the people by amending the Federal Constitution in violation of Article V relating to amendment, but it pursued its pseudo-socio-psychological pattern by usurping the prerogatives of the United States Congress. It handed down an implementation decision on May 31, 1955, in spite of the fact that the Fourteenth Amendment itself vests in Congress the power of implementation.

The fifth section of the Fourteenth Amendment itself declares that

"Congress shall have the power to enforce by appropriate legislation the provisions of this article."

The first construction of the Fourteenth Amendment by the United States Supreme Court was in the Slaughter House Cases, 16 Wall. 36, where it was held that the main purpose of the Fourteenth Amendment was to establish the citizenship of the Negro, to give definitions of citizenship of the United States and of the states, and to protect from hostile legislation by the states the privileges and immunities of citizens of the United States as distinguished from those of citizens of the states. . . .

To protect the Negro's rights under the Fourteenth Amendment against hostile state laws and acts Congress has enacted:

Title 28, Section 1863 U.S.C.A., which prohibits exclusion from service as grand or petit juror in any court of the United States on account of race or color.

Title 42, Section 1981 U.S.C.A., which provides that all persons within the jurisdiction of the United States shall have the same right to make and enforce contracts, sue, be parties, give evidence and to full and equal benefit of all laws for the security of persons and property as is enjoyed by white citizens, and shall be subject to like punishment, pains, penalties, taxes, licenses and exactions of every kind, and to no other.

Title 42, Section 1982 U.S.C.A., which provides that all citizens of the United States shall have the same right as is enjoyed by white citizens to inherit, purchase, lease, sell, hold and convey real and personal property.

Title 42, Section 1983 U.S.C.A., which authorizes civil action for deprivation of any right, privileges and immunities secured by the Constitution and laws of the United States.

Title 42, Section 1971 U.S.C.A., which provides that all citizens of the United States regardless of race, color or previous condition of servitude, who are otherwise qualified to vote in any state, may vote at any election regardless of the constitution or laws of any state.

Title 42, Sections 1751-60 U.S.C.A., which, providing for a school lunch program by the Department of Agriculture for public and nonprofit schools, provides: "If a state maintains separate schools for minority and majority races, no funds made available pursuant to this chapter shall be paid or disbursed to it unless a just and equitable distribution is made within the state, for the benefit of such minority races, of funds paid to it under this chapter."

Since the Congress has not, pursuant to its power under Section 5 of the Fourteenth Amendment, attempted to prohibit the maintenance by the states of segregated schools, but has impliedly by the enactment of said Sections 1751-60, Title 42, U.S.C.A., aforementioned, approved them, it is apparent that the present Supreme Court has overruled both the Congress and the will of the people as expressed in state constitutions and laws. It is also apparent that the Congress has not been remiss in enacting legislation to protect the legal and political rights of the Negro under the Fourteenth Amendment, but has refused to interpret that amendment as compelling the commingling of the races in mixed schools against the wishes of the people. Moreover, the acts of Congress, Title 8, Section 1151 U.S.C.A., setting up the quota system of immigration which practically excludes immigration to the United States from geographical areas containing Negroes and Mongolians, were justified by reason of the fact that such races are not readily assimilated into the predominantly white, Caucasian race here. Such is a sound and necessary public policy to preserve the essentially Western civilization in the Continental United States. Clearly, therefore, that long-established public policy of the Congress and of the states is sought to be overturned, without their consent by a strained construction of the equal protection clause of the Fourteenth Amendment and by an apparent disregard of Article I, Section 8, Subparagraph 18, of the Constitution, which provides: "The Congress shall have power to make all laws which shall be necessary and proper for carrying into execution the foregoing powers, and all other powers vested by this Constitution in the Government of the United States or in any department or officer thereof." . . .

[At this point the authors quote excerpts from Plessy *v*. Ferguson (1896) which appear in the preceding Topic of this book.]

Until the recent decision of the present Supreme Court, that Court has adhered to the position that substantially equal educational facilities furnished by the state for white and colored was not a violation of the equal protection clause of the Fourteenth Amendment. See Sweatt *v*. Painter, 339 U.S. 629, decided in 1950; State of Missouri ex rel. Gaines *v*. Canada, 305 U.S. 337, decided in 1938.

In its singlemindedness and preoccupation in seeking to justify a radically new construction of the equal protection clause of the Fourteenth Amendment so as to outlaw state segregated schools, it by-passed and overrode the much greater constitutional principles that the people are sovereign, that the national Government has only specific powers delegated to it by the Constitution, and that all other powers reside in the states and the people. The Court has thus dealt a vital blow to the very heart and framework of our constitutional republic, which fits in with the pattern set in recent years of encroachment by the executive and judicial departments upon the rights reserved to the states and to the people by the Constitution. When, by this process, the Constitution is finally completely whittled away without a vote of the people or consent of the states, the dreams envisioned by some of the authors cited by the Court are ready for attainment, and then comes death to liberty in America.

The "Lawfulness" of the Decisions

CHARLES L. BLACK, JR. *

If the cases outlawing segregation [1] were wrongly decided, then they ought to be overruled. One can go further: if dominant professional opinion ever forms and settles on the belief that they were wrongly decided, then they will be overruled, slowly or all at once, openly or silently. The insignificant error, however palpable, can stand, because the convenience of settlement outweighs the discomfort of error. But the hugely consequential error cannot stand and does not stand.[2]

There is pragmatic meaning then, there is call for action, in the suggestion that the segregation cases cannot be justified.[3] In the long run, as a corollary, there is practical and not merely intellectual significance in the question whether these cases were rightly decided. I think they were rightly decided, by overwhelming weight of reason, and I intend here to say why I hold this belief.

My liminal difficulty is rhetorical—or, perhaps more accurately, one of fashion. Simplicity is out of fashion, and the basic scheme of reasoning on which these cases can be justified is awkwardly simple. First, the equal protection clause of the Fourteenth Amendment should be read as saying that the Negro race, as such, is not to be significantly disadvantaged by the laws of the states. Secondly, segregation is a massive intentional disadvantaging of the Negro race, as such, by state law. No subtlety at all. Yet I cannot disabuse myself of the idea that that is really all there is to the segregation cases. If both these propositions can be supported by the

* Henry R. Luce Professor of Jurisprudence, Yale Law School. Author of *The People and the Court.* The selection is from Charles L. Black, Jr., "The Lawfulness of the Segregation Decisions," *The Yale Law Journal,* Vol. 69 (January, 1960), pp. 421–430. By permission.

[1] Brown v. Board of Educ. (The School Segregation Cases), 347 U.S. 483 (1954); Bolling v. Sharpe, 347 U.S. 497 (1954); New Orleans' City Park Improvement Ass'n v. Detiege, 358 U.S. 54 (1959); Gayle v. Browder, 352 U.S. 903 (1956); Holmes v. Atlanta, 350 U.S. 879 (1955); Mayor & City Council v. Dawson, 350 U.S. 877 (1955); Muir v. Louisville Park Theatrical Ass'n, 347 U.S. 971 (1954).

[2] *Cf.* Pollak, *Racial Discrimination and Judicial Integrity: A Reply to Professor Wechsler,* 108 U. PA. L. REV. 1, 31 (1959). I am indebted throughout to this Article, though the rationale I offer in support of the decisions differs from Professor Pollak's. His, however, seems to me a sound alternative ground for the desegregation holdings.

[3] See Wechsler, *Toward Neutral Principles of Constitutional Law,* 73 HARV. L. REV. 1, 34 (1959). The present Article was immediately suggested by Professor Wechsler's questionings. It is not, however, to be looked on as formal "reply," since I cover here only one part of the ground he goes over, and since my lines of thought are only partly responsive in terms to the questions as he sees them.

preponderance of argument, the cases were rightly decided. If they cannot be so supported, the cases are in perilous condition.

As a general thing, the first of these propositions has so far as I know never been controverted in a holding of the Supreme Court. I rest here on the solid sense of The Slaughterhouse Cases [4] and of Strauder v. West Virginia,[5] where Mr. Justice Strong said of the Fourteenth Amendment:

> It ordains that no State shall make or enforce any laws which shall abridge the privileges or immunities of citizens of the United States (evidently referring to the newly made citizens, who, being citizens of the United States, are declared to be also citizens of the State in which they reside). It ordains that no State shall deprive any person of life, liberty, or property, without due process of law, or deny to any person within its jurisdiction the equal protection of the laws. What is this but declaring that the law in the States shall be the same for the black as for the white; that all persons, whether colored or white, shall stand equal before the laws of the States, and, in regard to the colored race, for whose protection the amendment was primarily designed, that no discrimination shall be made against them by law because of their color? The words of the amendment, it is true, are prohibitory, but they contain a necessary implication of a positive immunity, or right, most valuable to the colored race,—the right to exemption from unfriendly legislation against them distinctively as colored,—exemption from legal discriminations, implying inferiority in civil society, lessening the security of their enjoyment of the rights which others enjoy, and discriminations which are steps towards reducing them to the condition of a subject race.[6]

If Plessy v. Ferguson [7] be thought a faltering from this principle, I step back to the principle itself. But the Plessy Court clearly conceived it to be its task to show that segregation did not really disadvantage the Negro, except through his own choice.[8] There is in this no denial of the Slaughterhouse and Strauder principle; the fault of Plessy is in the psychology and sociology of its minor premise.

The lurking difficulty lies not in "racial" cases but in the total philosophy of "equal protection" in the wide sense. "Equal protection," as it applies to the whole of state law, must be consistent with the imposition of disadvantage on some, for all law imposes disadvantage on some; to give driver's licenses only to good drivers is to disadvantage bad drivers. Thus the word "reasonable" necessarily finds its way into "equal protec-

---

[4] 83 U.S. (16 Wall.) 36 (1873).

[5] 100 U.S. 303 (1880).

[6] *Id.* at 307–08.

[7] 163 U.S. 537 (1896).

[8] "We consider the underlying fallacy of the plaintiff's argument to consist in the assumption that the enforced separation of the two races stamps the colored race with a badge of inferiority. *If this be so, it is not by reason of anything found in the act, but solely because the colored race chooses to put that construction upon it.*" *Id.* at 551. (Emphasis added.) The curves of callousness and stupidity intersect at their respective maxima.

tion," in the application of the latter concept to law in general. And it is inevitable, and right, that "reasonable," in this broader context, should be given its older sense of "supportable by reasoned considerations." [9] "Equal" thereby comes to mean not really "equal," but "equal unless a fairly tenable reason exists for inequality."

But the whole tragic background of the fourteenth amendment forbids the feedback infection of its central purpose with the necessary qualifications that have attached themselves to its broader and so largely accidental radiations. It may have been intended that "equal protection" go forth into wider fields than the racial. But history puts it entirely out of doubt that the chief and all-dominating purpose was to ensure equal protection for the Negro. . . .

What the fourteenth amendment, in its historical setting, must be read to say is that the Negro is to enjoy equal protection of the laws, and that the fact of his being a Negro is not to be taken to be a good enough reason for denying him this equality, however "reasonable" that might seem to some people. All possible arguments, however convincing, for discriminating against the Negro, were finally rejected by the fourteenth amendment.

It is sometimes urged that a special qualification was written on the concept of "equality" by the history of the adoption of the amendment— that an intent can be made out to exclude segregation from those legal discriminations invalidated by the requirement of equality, whether or not it actually works inequality. . . . The question of the "intent" of the men of 1866 on segregation *as we know it* calls for a far chancier guess than is commonly supposed, for they were unacquainted with the institution as it prevails in the American South today. To guess their verdict upon the institution as it functions in the midtwentieth century supposes an imaginary hypothesis which grows more preposterous as it is sought to be made more vivid. They can in the nature of the case have bequeathed us only their generalities; the specifics lay unborn as they disbanded. . . .

Then does segregation offend against equality? Equality, like all general concepts, has marginal areas where philosophic difficulties are encountered. But if a whole race of people finds itself confined within a system which is set up and continued for the very purpose of keeping it in an inferior station, and if the question is then solemnly propounded whether such a race is being treated "equally," I think we ought to exercise one of the sovereign prerogatives of philosophers—that of laughter. The only question remaining (after we get our laughter under control) is whether the segregation system answers to this description.

[9] See Lindsley *v*. Natural Carbonic Gas Co., 220 U.S. 61 (1911).

Here I must confess to a tendency to start laughing all over again. I was raised in the South, in a Texas city where the pattern of segregation was firmly fixed. I am sure it never occurred to anyone, white or colored, to question its meaning. The fiction of "equality" is just about on a level with the fiction of "finding" in the action of trover. I think few candid southerners deny this. Northern people may be misled by the entirely sincere protestations of many southerners that segregation is "better" for the Negroes, is not intended to hurt them. But I think a little probing would demonstrate that what is meant is that it is better for the Negroes to accept a position of inferiority, at least for the indefinite future.

But the subjectively obvious, if queried, must be backed up by more public materials. What public materials assure me that my reading of the social meaning of segregation is not a mere idiosyncracy?

First, of course, is history. Segregation in the South comes down in apostolic succession from slavery and the Dred Scott case. The South fought to keep slavery, and lost. Then it tried the Black Codes, and lost. Then it looked around for something else and found segregation. The movement for segregation was an integral part of the movement to maintain and further "white supremacy"; its triumph (as Professor Woodward has shown) represented a triumph of extreme racialist over moderate sentiment about the Negro.[10] It is now defended very largely on the ground that the Negro as such is not fit to associate with the white.

History, too, tells us that segregation was imposed on one race by the other race; consent was not invited or required. Segregation in the South grew up and is kept going because and only because the white race has wanted it that way—an incontrovertible fact which in itself hardly consorts with equality. This fact perhaps more than any other confirms the picture which a casual or deep observer is likely to form of the life of a southern community—a picture not of mutual separation of whites and Negroes, but of one in-group enjoying full normal communal life and one out-group that is barred from this life and forced into an inferior life of its own. . . .

Segregation is historically and contemporaneously associated in a functioning complex with practices which are indisputably and grossly discriminatory. I have in mind especially the long-continued and still largely effective exclusion of Negroes from voting. Here we have two things. First, a certain group of people is "segregated." Secondly, at about the same time, the very same group of people, down to the last man and woman, is barred, or sought to be barred, from the common political life of the community—from all political power. Then we are solemnly told that segregation is not intended to harm the segregated race, or to stamp

[10] Woodward, "Capitulation to Racism," *The Strange Career of Jim Crow* (1957).

it with the mark of inferiority. How long must we keep a straight face? . . .

"Separate but equal" facilities are almost never really equal. Sometimes this concerns small things—if the "white" men's room has mixing hot and cold taps, the "colored" men's room will likely have separate taps; it is always the back of the bus for the Negroes; "Lincoln Beach" will rarely if ever be as good as the regular beach. Sometimes it concerns the most vital matters—through the whole history of segregation, colored schools have been so disgracefully inferior to white schools that only ignorance can excuse those who have remained acquiescent members of a community that lived the Molochian child-destroying lie that put them forward as "equal."

Attention is usually focused on these inequalities as things in themselves, correctible by detailed decrees. I am more interested in their very clear character as *evidence* of what segregation mans to the people who impose it and to the people who are subjected to it. This evidentiary character cannot be erased by one-step-ahead-of-the-marshal correction. Can a system which, in all that can be measured, has practiced the grossest inequality, actually have been "equal" in intent, in total social meaning and impact? "Thy speech maketh thee manifest . . ."; segregation, in all visible things, speaks only haltingly any dialect but that of inequality.

Further arguments could be piled on top of one another, for we have here to do with the most conspicuous characteristic of a whole regional culture. It is actionable defamation in the South to call a white man a Negro.[11] A small proportion of Negro "blood" puts one in the inferior race for segregation purposes;[12] this is the way in which one deals with a taint, such as a carcinogene in cranberries.

The various items I have mentioned differ in weight; not every one would suffice in itself to establish the character of segregation. Taken together they are of irrefragable strength. The society that has just lost the Negro as a slave, that has just lost out in an attempt to put him under quasi-servile "Codes," the society that views his blood as a contamination and his name as an insult, the society that extralegally imposes on him every humiliating mark of low caste and that until yesterday kept him in line by lynching—this society, careless of his consent, moves by law, first to exclude him from voting, and secondly to cut him off from mixing in the general public life of the community. The Court that refused to see inequality in this cutting off would be making the only kind of law

[11] See Mangum, Legal Status of the Negro, Ch. II, *Libel and Slander* (1940), citing and discussing cases.
[12] *Id.* ch. I.

that can be warranted outrageous in advance—law based on self-induced blindness, on flagrant contradiction of known fact.

I have stated all these points shortly because they are matters of common notoriety, matters not so much for judicial notice as for the background knowledge of educated men who live in the world. A court may advise itself of them as it advises itself of the facts that we are a "religious people," that the country is more industrialized than in Jefferson's day, that children are the natural objects of fathers' bounty, that criminal sanctions are commonly thought to deter, that steel is a basic commodity in our economy, that the imputation of unchastity is harmful to a woman. Such judgments, made on such a basis, are in the foundations of all law, decisional as well as statutory; it would be the most unneutral of principles, improvised *ad hoc,* to require that a court faced with the present problem refuse to note a plain fact about the society of the United States—the fact that the social meaning of segregation is the putting of the Negro in a position of walled-off inferiority—or the other equally plain fact that such treatment is hurtful to human beings. Southern courts, on the basis of just such a judgment, have held that the placing of a white person in a Negro railroad car is an actionable humiliation; [13] must a court pretend not to know that the Negro's situation there is humiliating?

I think that some of the artificial mist of puzzlement called into being around this question originates in a single fundamental mistake. The issue is seen in terms of what might be called the metaphysics of sociology: "Must Segregation Amount to Discrimination?" That is an interesting question; someday the methods of sociology may be adequate to answering it. But it is not our question. Our question is whether discrimination inheres in that segregation which is imposed by law in the twentieth century in certain specific states in the American Union. And that question has meaning and can find an answer only on the ground of history and of common knowledge about the facts of life in the times and places aforesaid.

Now I need not and do not maintain that the evidence is all one way; it never is on issues of burning, fighting concern. Let us not question here the good faith of those who assert that segregation represents no more than an attempt to furnish a wholesome opportunity for parallel development of the races; let us rejoice at the few scattered instances they can bring forward to support their view of the matter. But let us then ask which balance-pan flies upward.

The case seems so onesided that it is hard to make out what is being protested against when it is asked, rhetorically, how the Court can possibly advise itself of the real character of the segregation system. It seems that

[13] See *id*. at 209–10, 219–20.

what is being said is that, while no actual doubt exists as to what segregation is for and what kind of societal pattern it supports and implements, there is no ritually sanctioned way in which the Court, as a Court, can permissibly learn what is obvious to everybody else and to the Justices as individuals. But surely, confronted with such a problem, legal acumen has only one proper task—that of developing ways to make it permissible for the Court to use what it knows; any other counsel is of despair. And, equally surely, the fact that the Court has assumed as true a matter of common knowledge in regard to broad societal patterns, is (to say the very least) pretty far down the list of things to protest against.

I conclude, then, that the Court had the soundest reasons for judging that segregation violates the fourteenth amendment. These reasons make up the simple syllogism with which I began: The fourteenth amendment commands equality, and segregation as we know it is inequality.

Let me take up a few peripheral points. It is true that the specifically hurtful character of segregation, as a net matter in the life of each segregated individual, may be hard to establish.[14] It seems enough to say of this, as Professor Pollak has suggested,[15] that no such demand is made as to other constitutional rights. To have a confession beaten out of one might in some particular case be the beginning of a new and better life. To be subjected to a racially differentiated curfew might be the best thing in the world for some individual boy. A man might ten years later go back to thank the policeman who made him get off the platform and stop making a fool of himself. Religious persecution proverbially strengthens faith. We do not ordinarily go that far, or look so narrowly into the matter. That a practice, on massive historical evidence and in common sense, has the designed and generally apprehended effect of putting its victims at a disadvantage, is enough for law. At least it always has been enough.

I can heartily concur in the judgment that segregation harms the white as much as it does the Negro.[16] Sadism rots the policeman; the suppressor of thought loses light; the community that forms into a mob, and goes down and dominates a trial, may wound itself beyond healing. Can this reciprocity of hurt, this fated mutuality that inheres in all inflicted wrong, serve to validate the wrong itself?

Finally it is doubtless true that the School Segregation Cases, and perhaps others of the cases on segregation, represented a choice between two kinds of freedom of association. Freedom from the massive wrong of segregation entails a corresponding loss of freedom on the part of the whites who must now associate with Negroes on public occasions, as we

14 See Wechsler, *supra* note 3, pp. 32–33.
15 Pollak, *supra* note 2, p. 28.
16 See Wechsler, *supra* note 3, p. 34.

all must on such occasions associate with many persons we had rather not associate with. It is possible to state the competing claims in symmetry, and to ask whether there are constitutional reasons for preferring the Negroes' desire for merged participation in public life to the white man's desire to live a public life without Negroes in proximity.[17]

The question must be answered, but I would approach it in a way which seems to me more normal—the way in which we more usually approach comparable symmetries that might be stated as to all other asserted rights. The fourteenth amendment forbids inequality, forbids the disadvantaging of the Negro race by law. It was surely anticipated that the following of this directive would entail some disagreeableness for some white southerners. The disagreeableness might take many forms; the white man, for example, might dislike having a Negro neighbor in the exercise of the latter's equal right to own a home, or dislike serving on a jury with a Negro, or dislike having Negroes on the streets with him after ten o'clock.[18] When the directive of equality cannot be followed without displeasing the white, then something that can be called a "freedom" of the white must be impaired. If the fourteenth amendment commands equality, and if segregation violates equality, then the status of the reciprocal "freedom" is automatically settled.

I find reinforcement here, at least as a matter of spirit, in the fourteenth amendment command that Negroes shall be "citizens" of their States. It is hard for me to imagine in what operative sense a man could be a "citizen" without his fellow citizens once in a while having to associate with him. If, for example, his "citizenship" results in his election to the School Board, the white members may (as recently in Houston) put him off to one side of the room, but there is still some impairment of their freedom "not to associate." That freedom, in fact, exists only at home; in public, we have to associate with anybody who has a right to be there. The question of our right not to associate with him is concluded when we decide whether he has a right to be there.

I am not really apologetic for the simplicity of my ideas on the segregation cases. The decisions call for mighty diastrophic change. We ought to call for such change only in the name of a solid reasoned simplicity that takes law out of artfulness into art. Only such grounds can support the nation in its resolve to uphold the law declared by its Court; only such grounds can reconcile the white South to what must be. *Elegantia juris* and conceptual algebra have here no place. Without pretending either

[17] *Ibid.*
[18] The white inhabitants of Mobile in their corporate capacity moved to protect this particular "freedom not to associate" in 1909. See Woodward, *op. cit. supra* note 10, pp. 86–87.

to completeness or to definitiveness of statement, I have tried here to show reasons for believing that we as lawyers can without fake or apology present to the lay community, and to ourselves, a rationale of the segregation decisions that rises to the height of the great argument.

These judgments, like all judgments, must rest on the rightness of their law and the truth of their fact. Their law is right if the equal protection clause in the fourteenth amendment is to be taken as stating, without arbitrary exceptions, a broad principle of practical equality for the Negro race, inconsistent with any device that in fact relegates the Negro race to a position of inferiority. Their facts are true if it is true that the segregation system is actually conceived and does actually function as a means of keeping the Negro in a status of inferiority. I dare say at this time that in the end the decisions will be accepted by the profession on just that basis. Opinions composed under painful stresses may leave much to be desired; [19] it may be that the per curiam device has been unwisely used. But the judgments, in law and in fact, are as right and true as any that ever was uttered.

[19] I do not mean here to join the hue and cry against the Brown opinion. The charge that it is "sociological" is either a truism or a canard—a truism if it means that the Court, precisely like the Plessy Court, and like innumerable other courts facing innumerable other issues of law, had to resolve and did resolve a question about social fact; a canard if it means that anything like principal reliance was placed on the formally "scientific" authorities, which are relegated to a footnote and treated as merely corroboratory of common sense. It seems to me that the venial fault of the opinion consists in its not spelling out that segregation, for reasons of the kind I have brought forward in this Article, is perceptibly a means of ghettoizing the imputedly inferior race. (I would conjecture that the motive for this omission was reluctance to go into the distasteful details of the southern caste system.) That such treatment is generally not good for children needs less talk than the Court gives it.

Topic 17

THE SOCIAL ISSUES

❦

The Southern Case Against Desegregation

THOMAS R. WARING *

Although the Supreme Court has declared that separation of the races in public schools is unconstitutional, few white Southerners are able to accept the prospect of mingling white and Negro pupils. Resistance to the court decree is stiffening throughout the region.

Many white Northerners are unable to understand the depth of feeling in the Southern states, whose area is about a sixth of the nation and whose population is roughly a fourth of the total. The purpose of this article is to try to put before open-minded readers the point of view of the Southerner—whom the rest of the United States apparently cannot believe to be open-minded at all on the subject of race.

At the outset it is only fair to warn the Northern reader that he may be infuriated long before he reaches the end. This, I suspect, is just as inevitable as the outraged feelings of the Southerner when he reads the Northern press with its own interpretation of the American dilemma. Both sides have been shouting at each other so loudly that it is difficult any longer to hear facts through the din of name-calling. If, in the course of speaking for the South, I should raise blood pressure among some Northerners, I apologize for causing pain—with the hope that I may be able to reach Northern minds that are truly open so that some good may come along with the discomfort.

The reader outside the South may, unfortunately, react in still another way. He may find it difficult, if not impossible, to believe much of what I say. To this I can only reply that as editor of a South Carolina newspaper with a circulation of 56,000, with twenty-eight years of journalistic experience in both the North and the South, I have had to be in possession of accurate information on this as on any other subject covered in my work. Across an editor's desk pass, day by day and year after year, reports, letters, statistics—in other words, facts. By means of these facts,

* Managing Editor of the *News and Courier,* Charleston, South Carolina. The selection is from "The Southern Case Against Desegregation," *Harper's Magazine,* Vol. 212 (January, 1956), pp. 39–45. By permission.

plus personal conversations with people from all over the world, an editor manages to keep in touch with public opinion.

It is the public opinion of the South that I am about to report. That opinion is a fact. It exists, and can be demonstrated. What I am saying is documented by facts and statistics. If these should seem to the reader to add up merely to bias, bigotry, and even untruth, I shall regret it. Facts, however, remain facts.

One of the reasons these facts may be unfamiliar—and therefore incredible—is the almost unanimous attitude of the national press—daily and weekly—toward the subject of race. I read many newspapers and news magazines, and people send me clippings from others that I do not see regularly. From my observation, the testimony these publications print is almost entirely one-sided. While less violent than the Negro press—which understandably presents only the militant anti-segregation case—the metropolitan press almost without exception has abandoned fair and objective reporting of the race story. For facts it frequently substitutes propaganda.

Furthermore, with the exception of a small coterie of Southern writers whom Northern editors regard as "enlightened," spokesmen for the Southern view cannot gain access to Northern ears. . . . The South, alas, lacks a magazine or other organ with nationwide distribution.

Perhaps my first assertion of a seldom realized truth will be the most difficult to believe. This statement is that white Southerners of good will—and the percentage of decency runs about the same in the South as anywhere else—favor uplift of the Negro, and that these white Southerners are in the vast majority. If it is impossible to prove the percentage of decency among Southerners, it is equally impossible to show that people in the North—or any other region—have a monopoly of it. But the South fears, and with reason, that the uplift is being forced at too fast a pace. The vagaries of custom and race taboos have many inconsistencies. The rules of segregation, both written and unwritten, change with conditions. And the sudden rewriting by the Supreme Court of regional laws and state constitutions has stirred as much resentment in Southern breasts as would be aroused among Northerners if suddenly their own freedom from race restrictions were denied by federal fiat. (Do I hear a muffled cheer from one or two Northerners who may take a dim view of mingling the races?)

Interference with sovereignty usually produces rage. In matters of education, the states long have been sovereign—until suddenly nine men have held otherwise. Is it any wonder that the Southerner is bitter over what he believes to be a flouting of the Constitution for political reasons?

Aside from legal questions—and they are deep and broad—the Southerner believes that as a practical matter, he is better equipped by experience to cope with race problems than people from other regions, no matter what their intellectual or political attainments. One of the proofs that this belief is founded not merely on pride or emotional prejudice lies in the fact that Northerners who spend some time in the South—not tourists or weekend visitors, but people who make their homes here—come rather sooner than later to agree that this is so. These transplanted Northerners come to see that there are far more bonds of friendship and active, productive good will between the white Southerner and his Negro neighbor than they had believed—or could believe until they became eye-witnesses and partakers of this relationship.

Although the South is both willing and eager to have the Negro earn greater acceptance on many levels—especially economic—it does not consider, for reasons that I shall submit, that mixed education is the way to achieve this acceptance—certainly not at this stage of affairs.

What may lie in the distant future is more than any of us can predict with accuracy. Southerners know that race problems are as old as history. While views and philosophies may change through the ages, some basic truths stand out like the Ten Commandments. Southerners are not yet ready to accept an eleventh, "Thou shalt not protect the purity of thy race."

THE CLASH OF CULTURES

Before going into the actual reasons for the Southerner's objections to mixed education—before asking the burning question, how can the races best live together—let us examine for a moment the pattern of separation. It is a pattern that Thomas Jefferson, Abraham Lincoln, and at one time Dwight D. Eisenhower have favored as best for both races. In 1888, Henry W. Grady, Atlanta editor—described by Don Shoemaker of the Southern Education Reporting Service as a Southern "liberal" of his time—summed up the situation as follows:

> Neither "provincialism" nor "sectionalism" holds the South together but something deeper than these and essential to our system. The problem is how to carry within her body politic two separate races, and nearly equal in numbers. [Since Grady spoke, the whites in the South have come to outnumber the Negroes four to one, but the proportions vary greatly by neighborhoods.] She must carry these races in peace—for discord means ruin. She must carry them separately—for assimilation means debasement. She must carry them in equal justice—for to this she is pledged in honor and gratitude. She must carry them to the end, for in human probability she will never be quit of either.

While Grady's statements were made nearly seventy years ago and therefore are subject to the criticism that they do not reflect "modern conditions," to many Southerners they are true both now and for the future.

The presence of large numbers of Negroes—especially in the tidewater regions of Virginia, the Carolinas, and Georgia, and the plantation country of Alabama and Louisiana, Mississippi and East Texas—means that the races necessarily live in intimate daily association. Why, then, should not the children of people who live in the same community—sometimes as close neighbors—attend the same schools?

Southerners believe they have valid reasons, aside from "prejudice" about the color of skin, for their insistence on sending white children to exclusively white schools. Without debating superiority of either race, they are keenly aware of cultural differences. In some ways the standards of white people are none too high. The same economic conditions that have held back Negroes have worked against the whites. The increasing prosperity of the South is removing some of these disadvantages for both races, though not necessarily in precisely the same way.

Whether all the differences will eventually be removed, or enough of them to make mixed education acceptable to a substantial number of white people, the differences are too great *at present* to encourage white parents to permit their children to mingle freely in school. This has nothing to do with the frequent practice of children of both races of playing together when young, or with cordial relationships in many other contacts of ordinary life.

Volumes could be written on racial differences from many angles, including anthropology and sociology. I shall merely try to summarize five of the differences that most immediately come to the minds of white parents in the South. These are health; home environment; marital standards; crime; and a wide disparity in average intellectual development.

(1) *Health.* Negro parents as a whole—for reasons that white people may sympathetically deplore but which nevertheless exist—are not so careful on the average as their white neighbors in looking after the health and cleanliness of their children. The incidence of venereal disease for instance is much greater among Negroes than among whites.

Statistics to document this statement are difficult to come by, though the statement itself would be generally accepted in the South. The U.S. Public Health Service some years ago quietly stopped identifying statistics by races. South Carolina figures, available for 1952–53, give a clue to the situation in that state; it probably is much the same elsewhere in the South. Out of a population 60 per cent white and 40 per cent Negro, 6,315 cases of syphilis were reported, of which 89 per cent were among Negroes. Infection with gonorrhea was found in six Negroes to one white person, but some physicians report that many cases of gonorrhea among Negroes go unrecorded.

During the same period—1952–53—a campaign against venereal disease was carried on, county by county. A spot check of four representative counties in different parts of South Carolina showed that cases of syphilis were found among 1.3 per cent of the white persons examined. This was a fairly constant percentage. The percentage of infection among Negroes ranged in the same counties from 8.5 to 10.8 per cent, averaging more than 9 per cent.

Fastidious parents do not favor joint use of school washrooms when they would not permit it at home—and there's no use to tell them that it is unlikely that anyone will catch venereal disease from a toilet seat. They just don't want to take risks of any kind with their children.

(2) *Home environment.* For most colored children in the South the cultural background is different in many ways from that of their white neighbors—and while these differences may have various explanations, they add up in the public's mind as racial. Slavery is so long in the past that nobody thinks about it any more, but the master and servant, or boss and laborer, relationship between whites and Negroes is still the rule rather than the exception. The emergence of a middle class among the Negroes has been extremely slow—again, the reasons count for less in the minds of white parents than the fact itself. Indeed, the professional and commercial class among Negroes is so small that its members are in perhaps the most unenviable position of all. They have progressed beyond the cultural level of the vast bulk of their own people, but are not accepted among the whites, who fear to let down any dikes lest they be engulfed in a black flood.

Someone may suggest that here is an opening wedge for integration in the schools, by admitting a few well scrubbed and polished colored children of cultivated parents. In reply, let me say that this would be no more acceptable to the colored people than to the whites. The solution, perhaps—as it is among upper-bracket white people who do not send their children to public schools—might be private schools for prosperous Negroes as for prosperous whites. In any case, white people feel that cultural gaps on other levels should be filled in before discussing integrated schools.

(3) *Marital habits.* Among many Southern Negroes they are, to state it mildly, casual—even more so, in fact, than among the often-divorced personalities of Northern café society. Many Negro couples—the statistics are not readily available, for obvious reasons—do not bother with divorce because there was no actual marriage in the first place. Statistics on the results of such casual unions, however, are available. On the average one Southern Negro child in five is illegitimate. It is possible the figure may be even higher, since illegitimate births are more likely to go unrecorded. Even among Negroes who observe marriage conventions, illegitimacy has little if any stigma.

Many white persons believe that morals among their own race are lax enough as it is, without exposing their children to an even more primitive view of sex habits. Moreover, while these parents do not believe there is any surge of desire among their offspring to mate with colored people, they abhor any steps that might encourage intermarriage. They believe that lifting the racial school barriers would be such a step. Miscegenation has been on the wane of recent years. Whatever mixing of blood may have occurred—and admittedly that was due largely to lustful white men seeking out acquiescent Negro women—has been without benefit of either law or custom. On some levels of society, breaking the racial barriers might lead to mixed marriages. The mixture of races which white Southerners have observed in Latin American countries gives them a dim view of legalizing cohabitation with Negroes.

(4) *Crime.* For many years, crime in the South has been more prevalent among Negroes than among white people. Though the Northern press no longer identifies criminals by race, white Southerners have reason to believe that much of the outbreak of crime and juvenile delinquency in Northern cities is due to the influx of Negro population. They believe the North now is getting a taste of the same race troubles that the South fears would grow out of mixed schooling, on a much bigger scale. They want no "Blackboard Jungles" in the South.

Maintaining order is a first concern of Southerners. What they have heard about the fruits of integration in the North does not encourage them to adopt the Northern race pattern. In Chicago, three hundred policemen have been assigned for a year or more to guard a nonsegregated housing project, with no bigger population than a Southern village where a single constable keeps the peace. In the County of Charleston, South Carolina—with 190,000 population, nearly half Negro—the total law enforcement manpower of combined city and county forces is 175.

While the homicide rate in the South is high, it is due in large measure to knifings and shootings among the colored people. Interracial homicide is relatively rare. (One of the reasons why the ghastly killing of Emmett Till in Mississippi made hot news—and some of that news was superheated and garnished with prejudice for the Northern press—was the very fact that it *was* unusual. No lynching, as even most Northerners now realize, has occurred in years.)

With racial bars down and rowdies of both races daring one another to make something of the vast increase in daily contacts, opportunities for interracial strife are frightening. Conservative, law-abiding people— and believe it or not, they constitute the bulk of Southern whites—are deeply fearful that hatred and bloodshed would increase without separation of the races.

And they know that, in the long run, if there is riotous bloodshed it will be for the most part Negroes' blood. The thin tolerance of the ruffian and lower elements of the white people could erupt into animosity and brutality if race pressure became unbearable. Schools would be a focal point for such disturbance, first among pupils themselves and later by enraged parents. Instead of learning out of books, the younger generation would be schooled in survival—as several Northern sources have told me already is happening in some areas of New York, Philadelphia, and Washington, D. C.

(5) *Intellectual development.* Again for whatever the reasons may be, Southern Negroes usually are below the intellectual level of their white counterparts. *U.S. News and World Report*—the fairest nationally circulated publication I am acquainted with in its treatment of the race issue —has reported that in Washington, colored children are about two grades behind the whites in attainment. This discrepancy, I believe, is about par for other communities. In Washington it was found that there were even language difficulties to surmount. The children used different terms for some things.

Some advocates of integration say the way to cure these differences is to let the children mingle so that the Negroes will learn from the whites. The trouble with this theory is that even if it works, a single generation of white children will bear the brunt of the load. While they are rubbing off white civilization onto the colored children, Negro culture will also rub off onto the whites.

Few Southern parents are willing to sacrifice their own offspring in order to level off intellectual differences in this fashion. They reason that their children will get along better in later life if they have, as youngsters, the best available cultural contacts. Such an attitude is not, I understand, altogether unknown in the North. Many parents in New York City, for example, make considerable financial sacrifices to send their children to private schools, to spare them the undesirable associations and the low-geared teaching standards of most public schools.

If this sounds snobbish to a Northern reader, let me ask you to examine your own conscience. Can you honestly say that you are eager to send your own child to a classroom where the majority of other pupils will be considerably more backward in their studies, and extremely different in social background and cultural attainment? Which would you *really* put first: your theory of racial justice, or justice to your own child?

THE NEGROES' CRUSADE

In reply to objections to integration by white Southerners, someone may ask: What about the Negroes? What do they think?

At the outset, let me say that as a person who has spent most of his life in the South, has known Negroes from earliest childhood, and as a newspaperman has been dealing with race matters every day for many years, I cannot say just what goes on in the minds of the Negroes. Nor do I believe that a white man can put himself in the place of a colored man any more than he can, by taking thought, add a cubit to his stature. Until the school question became agitated in recent years, however, race relations on the whole were good. Since the agitation, relations are not yet bad in a broad sense—but they are not improving by reason of the crusade for integration.

The leadership in that crusade comes from outside the South. It is sparked by the National Association for the Advancement of Colored People. Southerners have reason to believe that this organization has a very large measure of white influence among its leaders. They recognize that both major political parties are courting the Negro vote, which holds the balance of power in key cities of populous Northern states. They are bewildered by the array of power aligned on the side of the NAACP in press, pulpit, and politics. The NAACP and its allies seem well supplied with money. They have won legal victories and they are not disposed to compromise on any front. In fact, the NAACP seems—to white Southerners—more interested in forcing the Negro into the white man's company than in equipping the Negro to qualify fully for such association.

A small but pointed illustration occurred in Charleston when a white community theater group tried to produce "Porgy" (the original play, not the opera) with a Negro cast in the city where the story is laid. There was a grave question about how the community, in a time when racial agitation was so bitter, would accept a play performed almost exclusively by Negroes. Many difficulties had to be surmounted in casting and production. But the sponsoring group, in consultation with NAACP and other Negro spokesmen, decided to proceed, and spent a sizable amount of money getting the production under way.

One of the key questions was the seating of the audience. Under South Carolina law separate seating for the races is required. The chairman of the local NAACP chapter agreed in writing, I have been informed, to an arrangement for separate seating by means of a vertical line down the center aisle, whites on one side and Negroes on the other. At the last moment, with the play already in rehearsal, the NAACP repudiated the agreement.

The Negro cast pleaded with the white sponsors to go through with the production in spite of the NAACP. By this time, however, it became obvious that the delicate circumstances had become too explosive and the production was canceled. A possible good-will gesture, opening a new line of communication, thus was halted because the NAACP would accept nothing less than complete integration—regardless of both state law and local custom.

Whether the NAACP really speaks for the rank and file of Negroes is debatable. Public expressions of opinion from Negroes in the South, other than the NAACP, are relatively few. Some white people feel that a Negro is so accustomed to telling a white man what he thinks the white man wants to hear, that they put little stock in whatever the Negro says on race. It would not be hard to believe that, given a choice, a Negro naturally would prefer all restrictions to be removed. That does not mean, however, that all Negroes want to associate with white people. Far from it; many Negroes prefer their own churches and, it stands to reason, should be equally satisfied with their own schools, so long as an equal allotment of public money is given them.

While the allotment has not always been equal—Negroes pay only a small fraction of taxes—the sums of money spent on Negro schooling have increased by leaps and bounds. On the average the South spends a greater percentage of its per capita income on schools than other regions, and nowadays the Negroes are getting their share in most areas. One thing is certain: if the schools were integrated, many a Negro school teacher would lose his or her job. Even if the white people would accept mixed pupils—and few apparently would do so—they would insist on white teachers.

Whenever a Southern Negro does object to the drive for integration, he is subject to pressure from his own people. Two Negro clergymen— what are known as "local preachers"—recently wrote letters to newspapers in lower South Carolina opposing the mixing of schools. Both were disciplined by their church superiors. Many white people on friendly terms with Negroes are convinced that as a rule, the Negroes are not eager for mixed schools so long as the schools for Negroes are adequate.

BOOTLEG SEGREGATION?

This conviction leads them to hope that a voluntary approach eventually may help to solve the problem within the Supreme Court ruling. Judge John J. Parker of Charlotte, North Carolina, senior judge of the Fourth Circuit Court of Appeals, has said:

> It is important that we point out exactly what the Supreme Court has decided and what it has not decided in this [the Clarendon County] case. . . . It has not decided that the states must mix persons of different races in the schools. . . . Nothing in the Constitution or in the decision of the Supreme Court takes away from the people freedom to choose the schools they attend. The Constitution, in other words, does not require integration. It does not forbid such segregation as occurs as the result of voluntary action. It merely forbids the use of governmental power to enforce segregation. The Fourteenth Amendment is a limitation upon the exercise of power by the state or state agencies, not a limitation upon the freedom of individuals.

The Alabama state legislature has set up a new basis for assignment of pupils which does not mention race, though its provisions might tend to keep white and Negro pupils apart. In South Carolina, a committee of fifty-two representative citizens is circulating a resolution—already signed by many thousands—asking the State Legislature to interpose its authority between the federal government and local school boards to maintain segregation. Such a move would be based on the Tenth Amendment to the U.S. Constitution, reserving to the states and the people all powers not specifically granted to the federal government.

These are only two of many tentative plans to get around the Supreme Court's decision by methods of law. Another proposal is revival of the principle of nullification, which states both in the North and South have used in years gone by. A recent example was the public disregard of Prohibition. Segregation, perhaps, may be bootlegged in some regions. How that can be done is not immediately apparent—but the resourcefulness of the rum-runners and speakeasies was not foreseen by sponsors of the Volstead Act.

As in Prohibition, there is danger that white hoodlums may enter the picture. Sporadic outbreaks of the Ku Klux Klan have been reported. To combat the lawless element, law-abiding white men—who are determined not to yield to pressures they still regard as contrary to the guarantees of the Constitution—have been forming protective organizations. These go under many names. In Mississippi, South Carolina, and some of the other states they are called Citizens Councils.

Much has been said about the adoption of "economic pressure" as a weapon by these white groups. In some instances Negroes have reported that their sharecropper contracts have not been renewed because they signed petitions to integrate schools. Other forms of pressure have been reported, and in some localities Negroes have retaliated with boycotts against white merchants who were active in the Councils. White leaders of the resistance movements repeatedly have said they were not organizing boycotts and pressures against the Negroes and that they are determined there shall be no reign of terror as predicted by some of the Negro spokesmen.

Hodding Carter—one of a handful of Southern writers granted access to the national magazines—has predicted that attempts to enforce integration in the public schools of Mississippi would be likely to create violence. White leaders are exploring many other avenues in hopes of preventing strong-arm methods from being tried. They fear also that the very existence of the public schools is in peril. Rather than accept mixed public schools, some white Southerners may seek other means of educating their children.

Even if the schools are not abandoned, it seems unlikely that the white people will submit to heavy taxation to operate schools that many of them refuse to patronize. If they are not throttled outright, the public school systems in some areas may be starved to death. The spread of resistance organizations, far from being the product of demagogues, is at the local level among ordinary people, without "big-name" leadership. School trustees and other officials are getting the message from the grass roots.

Acceptance of the Supreme Court's order in border states and lip service in some other quarters have encouraged some advocates to believe that many Southern communities soon will yield to integration. While the borders of the old Confederacy may narrow, the determination of white people in areas with heavy Negro population is not relaxing. Not only regions where Negroes predominate by ten to one are rejecting the prospect of mixed schools. Pickens County in Piedmont South Carolina has the smallest number of Negroes (about one in ten) of any county in the state; its grand jury—most fundamental of all bodies safeguarding the people's liberty—has gone on record against mixed schools. On Edisto Island, at the opposite side of the state, where a white face looks out of place, insistence on mingling would be almost academic. If any attempt were made to force white children into Negro schools, the white people would move off the island, or find other means of educating their children.

Talk about segregation may promote migration of Negroes from the South. Already thousands have left the cotton fields and villages to seek jobs in Northern cities. On the farms, machines have replaced them. With the minimum wage advancing to $1 an hour, Southern employers will demand production from their laborers that not all Negroes will be able or willing to supply. These employers also may seek ways to mechanize or to employ white labor. As industries move South, more attractive opportunities for white people are opening.

If the North continues to appeal to Negroes as a land of integration and the South continues to attract white settlers, the racial proportions may grow more nearly equal. Then the North may become more tolerant of the Southerners' view of race problems, and the South better able to handle its dwindling Negro problem. Southerners will gladly share the load.

Meanwhile, stripped of emotions, the race problem for both Southern whites and Negroes is a practical matter of daily living. The problem has been recognized by thoughtful Americans from the early days of the Republic. It would be foolish to deny that any Negro pupils ever will enter Southern white schools. (Some already have.) But it would be equally foolhardy to predict that their numbers will be significant at an early date.

Psychological Aspects of Desegregation

A REPORT BY PSYCHIATRISTS *

INTRODUCTION

School segregation has been declared illegal throughout the country. We share the widespread belief that desegregation will inevitably occur. It is already occurring, and people everywhere are aroused to the strongest emotions by the legal, economic, and social problems it entails. Some have taken firm stands for desegregation, even when this has resulted in economic sanctions and ensuing hardships. Others have openly defied the law, thereby risking arrest and punishment. In actual fact, although desegregation presents various legal, social, and economic problems, it is above all a psychological problem. Were it not for the violent feelings which are involved, it would be possible to solve the legal, economic, and social difficulties.

This report represents the pooled experience of an interracial group of psychiatrists from different parts of the country, aided by consultant social scientists. In it we shall attempt to explore some of the psychological bases for the strong personal involvement on the part of those who oppose desegregation in the hope that a better understanding of individual and group behavior will facilitate the process. We will then discuss the difficulties which retard the solution of problems connected with desegregation and the possible contribution of psychological principles for dealing with them.

Let us begin by examining the adverse psychological effects which our previous segregational policies have had on the country as a whole, on the community, and, finally, on the individual.

1. The country. For the country as a whole, the tension, ill-feeling, and disunity engendered by the segregation issue interfere with and hamper constructive activities both at home and abroad. Furthermore, segregation and racial prejudice are extremely damaging to our prestige and friendships overseas, particularly among the non-white people of the world. Finally, we have been deprived of a substantial part of our human resources because a large proportion of our population is underprivileged, economically, educationally, and socially, and is therefore unable to make its potentially valuable contribution to our nation.

* The selection is from *Emotional Aspects of School Desegregation, passim,* published by The Group for the Advancement of Psychiatry, New York, 1960. By permission.

2. The community. Segregation must inevitably lower the well-being of the community. A lack of educational and economic opportunities, high disease and death rates, crime and delinquency, sub-standard living conditions are all directly related to segregation. For example, if the local government must provide health, welfare, and educational services in duplicate, the budget for each must be lowered by the expense of the other. If sub-standard housing leads to a high rate of contagious disease among Negroes, the health of the white group is jeopardized as well. Contagiousness does not discriminate. Economic and social deprivation contribute to crime and delinquency. By limiting communication between groups, segregation promotes a social climate which is conducive to violent outbreaks of racial tension.

3. The individual. Under segregation, the Negro occupies an inferior social status. He cannot live in the neighborhood of his choice; he is not permitted to occupy certain positions; he is denied certain educational opportunities, etc. As a result of being treated as though he were unworthy, he can come to feel unworthy. These feelings of inferiority and humiliation often lead to a strong resentment of all white people, or of all Negroes, or, indeed, of all mankind. Energies which might otherwise be directed toward self-development are instead consumed by his bitterness at his lot in life.

The white person, on the other hand, may gain a false sense of superiority from the mere existence in his community of an "inferior" group. This will lead him to a self-evaluation based merely on the fact that his social, economic, and political situations compare favorably with those of the Negro. Moreover, segregation, by its very nature, is conducive to and encourages the expression of hostility and aggression, thus providing the white person with a tempting means of escape from recognizing and coping with his own problems realistically. For when feelings of self-hatred or of anger toward significant people in one's environment become too painful to face, and yet demand some outlet, they may find their target in the Negro.

We do not wish to imply that all those who believe in and advocate segregation are psychologically abnormal. There is some element of the irrational in all of us. Many people in the United States who are essentially sound psychiatrically, strongly favor segregation for many reasons, aside from obvious personal gain, including, for example, social conformity and consciously high-minded considerations. On the other hand, prejudices may be a symptom of deep emotional disorder.

By the same token, it would be an error to regard desegregation as a purely Southern issue. Anti-Negro discrimination exists in the North, and there are many segregated schools in the North. In fact, the basic issue of equal rights for Negroes and whites, and the psychological attitudes which give rise to such inequalities, exist everywhere in the United States.

OPPOSITION TO DESEGREGATION

What are some of the psychological reasons for the strong adverse response to desegregation? To begin with, it may be helpful to point out that the majority of the current generation have lived all of their lives in a segregated society. The beliefs and feelings of that society have been absorbed in their adult personalities and must, therefore, affect their attitudes toward desegregation. Some of these beliefs are related to real social and economic differences which existed in the previously segregated community. Others are associated with the racial myths that have sprung up under such conditions.

Functions of Racial Myths and Prejudices

In the myths which have grown up about the Negro he is depicted as little better than a savage animal, intellectually and normally inferior, childish and irresponsible. (Nor are such myths limited to beliefs about Negroes. For example, many people believe that all Scots are misers, all Englishmen stuffed shirts, all Frenchmen lascivious, etc.) In the case of the Negro, however, these myths serve to rationalize and justify the white person's disparaging attitudes, because he cannot clearly recognize or understand the real source of his prejudice. If we realize that myth-formation, psychologically, seeks to protect individual and group security against a sense of threat and to diminish anxiety, we can better understand why the myths of prejudice are so resistive to logic: The powerful need for safety, which the myth is created to insure, explains why it is clung to despite facts and logic to the contrary.

Myths as a Defense

During any individual's life-time, he is frequently faced with highly complicated problems which appear to him to be insoluble. At such times he may feel helpless, torn by indecision; he may not know how to solve or even approach his problem. These dilemmas provoke feelings of uneasiness that may reach proportions of extreme anxiety. In order to cope with this anxiety, he may resort to the prevailing myths to provide a seemingly rational solution to his problem. Although such myths are without objective validity, they are maintained and transmitted in the culture as a powerful influence by virtue of the fact that they have their deep roots in individual childhood experience. To illustrate: in the United States white people have had to reconcile their belief in equality and

Christian principles with their actual inhuman treatment of Negroes. In trying to solve this dilemma they have created and defended the various myths about the stereotyped Negro described above. Having created such myths, it becomes easier to justify their conduct, for principles of equality need not apply to so unworthy and inferior a group. Furthermore, through a vicious circle these myths are nourished, sustained, and perpetuated by actual present-day social and economic deprivations of Negroes.

The damaging consequences of racial myths are misconstrued as evidence to support them. American Negroes as a group are in fact multiply handicapped: socially, politically, educationally, and economically. But these handicaps are a consequence of racial discrimination rather than of racial inferiority.

The myth may serve another purpose. Individuals of any race will, from time to time, experience acute doubts about their own worth, their sexual adequacy, their acceptability. These fears and misgivings do not seem quite so intense if one focuses one's attention upon the deficiencies of others. The individual who is filled with self-contempt because of his lack of efficiency and progress on his job may turn this contempt onto the members of a racial minority, represented in myths as being stupid, lazy, irresponsible, etc. He then obtains some consolation from the thought that at least he is better than they are. But such methods of dealing with one's problems fail to reach a realistic solution of the original difficulty. Furthermore, they result in increased guilt and anxiety.

Effect on Negro-white Relationships

In addition to their effect on the psyche of the individual, these concepts of the Negro's inferiority have, of course, severely affected Negro-white relationships. Merely because of his membership in the white group, one individual is accorded certain social privileges and is regarded as "better" or higher class. Merely because of his membership in the Negro group, another is deprived of certain social privileges and is regarded as a "second-class citizen." Thus the Negro is usually expected to show deference to all white people, regardless of whether or not the white individual has reached his own stage of intellectual and social development. By contrast, the white person, with no claim to his fellow citizen's respect other than his skin color, may derive a sense of heightened worth because of this deference. This feeling of security is a fleeting one, however. The white person is well aware that the Negro has been forced to assume his attitude of deference. He cannot entirely believe his own feelings of superiority, since they are not based on actual evidence of personal growth and achievement.

This difference in social status is accompanied by differences in political and economic status. The Negro is typically a source of low-paid unskilled labor on farms, in domestic service, in industry. Because his employer or supervisor is usually white, this economic relationship has reinforced the inequities of his social situation.

The racial myth helps to maintain the Negro's political subordination. His right to vote has been curtailed, and as a result, a large part of our population has been deprived of its share in the government process.[1] He has also been excluded from governmental positions of authority and consequently almost all the positions of leadership in our society have been filled by its white members. In his deprived state, this very real lack of power and representation in community and national affairs feeds back into the Negro's feelings of inferiority to lower his self-esteem still further.

In accordance with the myth, both Negro and white are expected to assume certain roles in their relationship with each other. The Negro should be fun-loving, irresponsible, deferential, deeply loyal, dependent, afraid of whites, and capable of hard physical labor and little need for rest or relaxation. Conversely, the white person should enjoy pleasure but not live for it, plan for the future, be independent and unafraid, and utilize Negroes for the hard labor and menial tasks he considers beneath him.

The fact is, of course, that the Negro possesses the same capacities and potentialities as does the white and experiences the same basic emotions. Therefore, a relationship based on the characterizations described above must of necessity be subject to a great deal of strain and resentment. The Negro is expected to repress his ambitions, his desires for self-realization and development. In return for the Negro's acceptance of low status and dependent servility, the white offers him such advantages as freedom from responsibility and paternalistic protectiveness.

No matter how well such a Negro-white relationship may appear to function on the surface, underlying the apparent conformity and compliance are deep anger, fear, and resentment. If the myth is firmly believed, Negro-white relationships tend to become mere rituals, without genuine human significance. Even when people consciously reject the myth, there still remain deep-rooted prejudices and anxieties in Negro-white interaction.

Still another aspect of the myth derives its strength from the emotional attitudes which have come to be associated with different forms, colors, and textures of the skin. The feelings and meanings attached to different skin colors vary between cultures and subcultures in relation to patterns of emotional conditioning. For example, several studies carried

[1] Among the paradoxes of social change in the South is that Negroes are being courted for their much needed votes and purchasing power, while at the same time they are subjected to discrimination.

out in this country have indicated that most small children—both white and Negro—prefer light dolls to dark ones, even though they are not antagonistic to the dark dolls. Psychological studies of adults show that many people equate a rough, dark skin with "wrong" or with "dirtiness"; smoothness or whiteness, on the other hand, symbolize "right" or purity. Since the skin cloaks the entire body, it becomes the part of the person most accessible to superficial perception and evaluation.

In our culture yellow, brown, and black tend to be associated with ideas of evil or destructiveness; white and pink represent cleanliness, virtue, chastity. Consequently, the negative associations to his skin color may contribute and lend support to myths which have evolved about the Negro.

The Negro, in turn, long victimized as a result of the myth, may himself come to believe it. He is often as frightened as the white person by the mythical image of the dirty, aggressive Negro. Indeed, caste systems have grown up among some Negroes on the basis of how close skin color approaches white, and how close social and sexual customs approach supposed white middle-class standards. It is well known how much money and time many Negroes feel driven to spend on cosmetics, clothes, showy automobiles, etc. in an effort to break away from the devaluing self-concept fostered by the myth.

Fears Related to Sex

As a result of the myth of the Negro's sexual aggressiveness and virility, desegregation has been severely handicapped by widespread fears that the traditional barriers against sexual relationships between whites and Negroes will break down. Let us examine some of the psychological bases for such fears.

Quite apart from questions of race, unrealistic emotions and attitudes toward sex abound in our culture. In general, our attitudes toward sex are split: Sex represents the culmination of tenderness and love, but it is also regarded in our society as dirty and degrading, and as an outlet for aggressive impulses. To those who look upon another group as inferior or exploitative, sex relations with members of that group express aggression rather than love.

As part of the process of growing up we have all had to learn to give up some childish wishes, to control our impulses, to modify our sexual drives and aggressions in accordance with social prohibitions. However, these deep sexual urges do not disappear. We carry them with us into adulthood to varying degrees as conscious or unconscious fantasies. One of the prejudices learned in childhood is the belief that people of lower status groups are more primitive, aggressive, and potent sexually. According to the distortions of myths, the Negro male has great sexual prowess, the Negro female is invariably responsive. This concept of the aggressive, primitive, potent Negro represents all that is bad and forbidden, all that the white adult, when reared to conform to middle-class social mores, has been denied. Because these adults fear to allow themselves to play the leading roles in fantasies of violent primitive sexual behavior, they more readily assign such roles to the Negro.

Unacknowledged white male jealousy of the Negro male's fantasied advantage as a sexual rival for the white female is an emotional source of power behind the extreme taboo, maintained by the white-supremacy code, ostensibly to protect white womanhood. This code sanctions the most savage reprisals for Negro male violation, or even the most realistically flimsy suspicion of it, as in the Emmett Till "wolf whistle" case. The irrational emotionality of a lynch mob reveals the terrible antisocial power of racial myth. The white-supremacy code also provides immunity to the white male from Negro resistance or retaliation for the white's sexual freedom with Negro females. And so, fear and hate, founded and maintained by racial sex mythology, breeds ever more fear and hate within members of both races.

The stereotype of the sexual Negro has entered deeply into the emotions of many white people. To such people this image is very real, although objectively it is groundless. Unfortunately, certain surface facts do seem to lend it credence. Let us discuss these:

Psychiatric experience and delinquency studies have indicated that antisocial and impulsive sexual behavior is more prevalent among those persons, whether Negro or white, who have been raised under conditions of social and economic deprivation and disorganized family and community living. When statistical evidence is cited of the comparatively poor sexual restraint among Negroes, the figures may be right. However, they require interpretation. Granted that the Negro is economically underprivileged, poverty in itself does not lead to promiscuity. Such figures are actually a clue to social differences between certain Negro and white groups. There is a correlation between social disorganization and similar sexual patterns for any racial group, but in this country discrimination has caused a greater proportion of Negroes to live under such conditions. The seriousness of antisocial sex behavior cannot be minimized, but its sources should not be falsely attributed to mythological folk tales rather than to social and psychological forces which can be constructively dealt with.

Interracial Unions: Marital and Extramarital

White arguments in defense of segregation which are based primarily on the myth of Negro sexuality invariably focus on the fear of intermarriage and the desire to preserve racial purity. Do these fears stem from facts, or are they rationalizations designed to mask deep emotional confusion?

There are many people, throughout the North, as well as the South, who oppose the idea of Negro-white union. Such opposition may, of course, be attributed to biological concepts of heredity, although there is no available scientific evidence that Negro stock is genetically inferior. However, if this were really the only reason, two of its rather curious aspects would require further explanation. First, while intermarriage is prohibited by law in some states and by severe social penalties in the rest, out-of-wedlock and casual relations between the races are condoned and even expected to occur in some sections of the country. Yet genetic transmission is, of course, the same for progeny born in or out of wedlock.

Secondly, as mentioned previously, these relations are condoned only in combinations of white male and Negro female. Since the mingling of white and Negro genes occurs whether the man is white and the woman Negro or vice versa, the fear of interracial union on the basis of loss of racial purity would appear to be based on illogical rather than rational thought.

Those who oppose school desegregation on the grounds that it will encourage racial amalgamation further fail to recognize that such a process was already underway as an accomplished fact prior to the desegregation decision. Racial admixture began more than two hundred and fifty years ago with the first importation of Negro slaves, and according to several studies it has continued to increase steadily—to the same degree in segregated sections of the country as elsewhere.

As further proof of the increased white admixture to the Negro population, despite segregation one might point out the increase over the years in the practice of "passing" by light-skinned individuals of Caucasian appearance who have some fraction of Negro ancestry, but who do not identify themselves socially as Negroes. The intensity of the Negro's desire to "pass" is, of course, due to the inferior position assigned to him in American life. An individual's skin color and facial appearance, which permit his "passing," are by no means reliable indicators of his genetic endowment. Therefore, "passing" facilitates interracial union. Since discrimination provides the incentive for "passing," and "passing" increases the opportunities for admixture of white and Negro genes, this is an instance of how segregationists actually defeat their ostensible goal of preserving racial purity.

The fear that school desegregation will result in increased intermarriage, which is related to but far from identical with interracial union, expresses an emotional attitude or ignorance rather than a valid prediction.

Available data about intermarriage rates from Northern cities legally desegregated for years, is too limited and confusing for social scientists to interpret. They cannot satisfactorily account for the ups and downs of intermarriage rates in desegregated communities at different periods. Reliable predictions, therefore, as to whether, how, and when extending school desegregation to the South will influence the rate of intermarriage cannot yet be made. The readiness to predict, and with such certainty, by opponents of school desegregation would thus seem to bespeak their own bias, or be designed to arouse the emotions of others, whatever the objective facts in the matter may prove to be. Many complicated factors determine marital choice, and some of these are as yet unknown.

Perhaps, rather than focusing our attention on the effects of desegregation on intermarriage or interracial union, we might think of the over-all changes in Negro-white relationships it will bring about. As a result of school desegregation, Negroes and whites will share many experiences on an equal level. In the course of time this may lead to a great degree of interaction and mutuality in many aspects of living. Rather than leading to increased illicit, antisocial behavior, one might predict that it will lead to greater respect and responsibility in relationships between the races. . . .

ATTITUDE CHANGES

Intensification of Hostility

Among the reasons for the intense opposition of many white persons to desegregation is the fear that Negroes will gain power and use it for retaliation, physical aggression, and even role reversal—that is, the fear that the Negroes will become the dominant race and the whites the subjugated group. On the contrary, the facts show that the influential Negro leadership and organizations have conducted the struggle against discrimination through legal and other democratic means of social action. During the effective boycott of segregated buses in Montgomery, Alabama, 50,000 Negroes practiced nonviolence;[2] they refrained from retaliating to provocations ranging from insults to dynamite by white segregationists. From

[2] At present (March 1960) recent Negro student "sit-in" strikes and demonstrations against eating facilities have spread to six southern states. With few exceptions these Negroes have not retaliated with violence to verbal and physical harassment by whites. Indeed, this is their stated policy. What rioting has occurred, so far, in relation to these disciplined protests, appears to involve some members of both races whose general proneness for aggressive outbreak is triggered by the racial issue pretext. The increase of nonviolent protest techniques may reflect Negro dissatisfaction with delays in the litigation process and such anti-integration devices as pupil-placement laws which have slowed down even token desegregation.

the evidence, ideas of Negro-white role reversal seem limited to fantasies of individual Negroes and whites under conditions of segregation. . . .

Leadership

Unsettled by these inner and outer contradictions many people become very susceptible to the authority of firm and decisive leadership which can tip the scales of their opposing feelings, in either direction. We have seen this demonstrated by the power of some segregationist leaders to sway public support to "a crusade" against integrated schooling or directly or indirectly to sanction mob violence against desegregation. On the other hand, prompt, clear-cut and resolute action to uphold the Federal law by those in authority has proved effective in preventing and reducing the uncertainties stirred up by the social change-over to desegregation.

The direction in which a white person is apt to be swayed by such external authority on the issue of desegregation depends, in large part, on the development of his general attitudes by specific authority influences in his childhood. Thus, many white people conform to the practice of segregation less because of prejudice against Negroes than because of their need to conform to group patterns. These are the people who also usually require a great deal of support and approval by authority figures, however, so that typically they can readjust more readily to desegregation when it is firmly prescribed by those in authority. . . .

RESPONSES OF VARIOUS GROUPS TO DESEGREGATION

The Children

. . . The wide differences in achievement level between white and Negro children of the same age level accounts for another possible source of difficulty. Segregationists consider this further evidence of the inequality of Negroes. Actually, Negro children are at a disadvantage in this regard because the quality of schooling to which they have been exposed has been inferior, coupled with their parents' poorer educational level. Experts maintain that there is no scientific evidence of inborn differences in intelligence between Negroes and whites. Rather, the relative academic retardation of Negroes as compared to whites is due to the Negro's inferior opportunities. "I.Q." tests do not allow for the different cultural experiences of Negro children and are, therefore, inaccurate measures of Negro intelligence potential. The fact that such academic differences do exist, statistically at least, between the Negro and white groups does mean, however, that for a time the slower child will be under pressure, and that the faster child may be held back to some degree. This must be taken into account in scholastic planning. . . .

The Parents

Although children are the direct participants in school desegregation, their attitudes and behavior reflect to a great extent the attitudes and behavior of their parents. Parents in our society are immensely concerned about the welfare and future of their children. There is almost no sacrifice too great to be made for their benefit. It is because of this dedication that the threat of possible damage to the children has proved so effective a force against desegregation. Parents are concerned about the alleged dangers in intermarriage, about the psychological problems with which their children will have to cope, about the educational problems which will arise.

White parents may fear that the school their child attends will have to lower its academic standards because of the admission of Negroes. They may fear that the child, as well as the family, will lose status in the community if he attends a desegregated school, that their child will be exposed to the Negro's lower moral standards, to communicable diseases. They may also have fears with regard to future contact with Negro parents at PTA meetings, etc.

Negro parents worry about whether their children will be able to compete satisfactorily in schools with higher scholastic standards. Will they be treated fairly by their teachers? Will they be hurt physically or emotionally by the white children? Will they, as parents, be humiliated at PTA meetings, or subject to reprisals in other direct contact with whites?

CONCLUSION

In preparing this report on desegregation we have tried to bring together some facts and principles drawn from general knowledge of human behavior, as well as from our special experience in the particular aspects of prejudice and discrimination. There are inevitable strains inherent in any social change of this magnitude. We cannot hope that school desegregation will banish prejudices, but it is a step toward reversing the damage of discrimination. We believe that insight and understanding, that is, a rational approach to the profoundly irrational forces which move man, are essential and appropriate ways of dealing with desegregation issues.

Judicial Review

JUDICAL REVIEW, by which is meant the power of American courts and finally of the Supreme Court to set aside national and state legislation as unconstitutional, has served as, and remains, at least potentially, one of the most important restraints upon majority rule provided by our Constitution. (The power of judicial review with respect to federal legislation, as has been seen, was established in the case of Marbury *v.* Madison.) The question of the compatibility of judicial review with democracy has been sharply and persistently raised. And the answer, in turn, in no small part depends on how democracy is defined. Apart from its democratic or undemocratic nature, however, the issue remains whether its values to the American people have been greater than its disadvantages.

The material we have included on this issue sets forth some leading · arguments for and against judicial review. The included extract from Justice Cardozo has been characterized by D. W. Brogan, the eminent British political scientist, as "the best defense of judicial review, at any rate in the field of constitutional guarantees where its activities have been most often and most vigorously condemned." The statement of Dorothy Thompson in support of judicial review was made in 1937 in a Hearing of the Senate Committee on the Judiciary which was considering President Roosevelt's proposal to reorganize the Court.

Topic 18

JUDICIAL REVIEW EVALUATED

Is Judicial Review Necessary?

MORRIS RAPHAEL COHEN *

The power of the Supreme Court to declare acts of Congress unconstitutional does not, as a practice, exist in any other civilized country. One or two cases in Australia and Canada, under unusual conditions, are the exceptions which prove the general rule. Those who argue for its *necessity* rely on old fictions and ignore the facts. Thus, they claim that it is a necessary part of our Anglo-Saxon liberties, but Anglo-Saxon England has never allowed this power to its courts. Marshall's argument that it follows from the nature of written constitutions, is obviously refuted by the constitutions of France and of other countries where life, liberty and property are as safe, if not safer than they are here; and the argument that Federal Government is impossible without it, ignores the Swiss and other Federal states.

But the main fallacy is the argument that since the Constitution declares itself to be the supreme law of the land, therefore Congress and the Executive must accept the Court's interpretation of it, though they are supposed to be coordinate and not subordinate powers. This is the fallacy of *non sequitur*. A Constitution is adopted by the people, who ought to know what they vote for, and this cannot exclude the people's representatives in the Congress and in the Executive, mostly lawyers in any case. What the Constitution in fact does say, is that *it and the laws and treaties of the United States made in pursuance* of it, should be the supreme law of the land. Now, the members of Congress and the Executive swear to obey the Constitution, and how can they make laws and treaties under it without interpreting its meaning? And why must they disregard their own conscientious reading of the Constitution because a different opinion is held by a majority of the Supreme Court, which may not be a majority even of all the judges that

* Late Professor of Philosophy at The City College of New York. President of the American Philosophical Association, 1929. Author of *Reason and Nature, Law and the Social Order, Preface to Logic, Faith of a Liberal,* and other works. The selection is from Morris Raphael Cohen, "Is Judicial Review Necessary?", an address given at the New School Forum, April 24, 1936, and printed in slightly modified form in the *New Leader* (May 30, 1936), Vol. 19, p. 5. Reprinted with permission of the administrators of the estate of Morris Raphael Cohen and the *New Leader*.

pass on the act? The notion that the court must necessarily have the *exclusive* and final power to declare what the Constitution means is neither historically nor logically tenable. Indeed, the Supreme Court itself abandons it when it admits that the meaning of the term "republican form of government" in the Constitution must be left to Congress and to the Executive.

Let us get behind legalistic hair-splitting and look at the question in the light of common sense and the logic that is no respecter of traditional dogmas. No one really believes that the human beings who adopted the Constitution in the 18th century foresaw all our modern conditions and made unmistakable provision as to what Congress may or may not enact into law. And the notion that they laid down certain principles from which every decision of the Supreme Court is deduced with absolute rigor and without regard to the personal opinion of the judges, must be pronounced ridiculous by the logic of modern science. History shows unmistakably that decisions on constitutional issues depend upon the political, social and economic opinions of the judges. Taney differed from Marshall, Field from Waite, and McReynolds from Holmes. And who honestly doubts that if the personnel of the court were to change tomorrow, its decisions would be different?

It is certainly not through the will of the people and the express words of the Constitution that the power to regulate interstate commerce included the power to prohibit lotteries but not to regulate insurance, to prohibit the passage of liquor from some States to others or to compel railroads to install certain safety appliances, but not to prohibit them from posting notices that they will discharge their men who join trade unions. Only recently this power to regulate interstate commerce was held to include the power to order a system of workmen's compensation but not a pension system. These and a thousand other subtle distinctions are points on which well-informed men and even judges honestly differ, and how the court will rule on any actual act of Congress, is largely a matter of guess work even for lawyers. It is unbelievable that the framers of the Constitution in 1787 had settled these matters beyond a reasonable doubt. When, therefore, a mere majority of the court insists that no rational being can doubt that Congress has misread or violated the plain provisions of the Constitution, their sense of humor as well as of courtesy to their fellow judges and to the coordinate powers of the government is rather esoteric.

Consider now the practical arguments for judicial review. It has been defended as a necessary appeal from the passion and haste of Congress to the calm and deliberate judgment of the Courts; but this rests on a number of untenable assumptions. It is psychologically weird to suppose that judges are not human or free from human passions. One has only to recall Justice McReynolds' dissent in the Gold Case or the passionate outburst of Chief Justice Chase and the minority in connection with the second Legal Tender Case. Even more important is the fact that our courts are so constituted that their deliberation cannot possibly be based on adequate knowledge. For the court cannot institute investigation. It cannot hold prolonged hearings. The life of the judge does not permit him to be fully cognizant of all that is going on in our modern complicated civilization. And the fiction that judges only pass on the law and not on the actual facts makes them satisfied to decide fateful questions of public policy by listening to two lawyers argue for a few hours on submitted briefs, which is hardly an intelligent way of determining any great issue or the affairs of a nation.

Moreover, the assumption that all restraints on Congressional action are good is utterly thoughtless. One might well say that it is a good thing to tie us to stones so as to prevent us from running and possibly breaking our necks. Safety often depends upon quick action, as when our house is on fire or someone is to be rescued from danger. Indeed, this argument for the necessity of restraints on the people's representatives is precisely the one that used to be advanced in England for the House of Lords. When, however, the English people discovered that such restraints were in fact exercised in the interests of a given class, and against the popular will, they curbed that power to delay legislation.

So we may likewise curb the power of our courts to suspend Congressional legislation until the people go through the elaborate process of a Constitutional Amendment. The trouble with Congress is not only its haste but more often its cumbrous slowness. In any case, it is safer to be subject to accidental majorities of a Congress that is in touch with and responsive to popular needs than to be at the mercy of an accidental and very small majority of the Supreme Court. For the mistakes of Congress can be corrected more quickly, while to overcome the mistakes of the Supreme Court, as in the Income Tax Case of 1895, took eighteen years. Actually there have been very few acts of Congress that have been felt to be unjust or unconstitutional by a majority of our people, and from which the courts have saved us. The liberties which the courts have enforced have more often been the liberty of powerful vested interests to exploit the poor who work for a living—witness the minimum wage cases, the child labor case, the enforcement of yellow dog contracts and iniquitous injunctions, and the like. In the two cases where Congress did admittedly violate the plain command of the Constitution, to wit, in refusing from 1922 to 1932 to reapportion representation according to the latest census or to reduce representation in accordance with the plain provision of the 14th Amendment, the courts have done nothing or have been helpless. The rights and liberties of the people are safe only in the hands of a vigilant and intelligent electorate.

The power of the courts to declare legislation unconstitutional has in fact made our law uncertain and has degraded our political life. For when a law is planned no one knows with reliable certainty how the courts will rule on a Congressional enactment, and the result is that instead of discussing issues on their merits, we discuss them in terms of what a few elderly gentlemen on the Supreme Court bench will think of their constitutionality. *The worst of all possible systems of government is that which divorces power from responsibility, and that is what we do when we give the last word to judges who are not answerable to any earthly authority.*

It is vain to say the people can amend the Constitution. Not only is that process very cumbrous, requiring three-quarters of the States rather than a majority of the people, but no one knows what the courts will make of the Amendment when it is passed. Thus, when the people adopted the 11th Amendment prohibiting a foreign citizen from suing a State, it was practically nullified by Marshall permitting such suits against the officers of the State. When the people, after the Civil War, adopted the 14th Amendment to safeguard the rights of the Negroes, the latter got very little real protection from it, but it became instead an instrument to prevent the former free States from protecting their white laborers by regulating hours, wages and the like. The people recalled the court's decision of 1895 when they empowered Congress to tax incomes *from whatever source derived.* Nevertheless, the courts did not allow the taxing of incomes from child labor and other sources, thus creating a privileged class free from taxation. The words *"from whatever source derived"* are as plain as human words can be, but the courts pay more attention to obsolete political theories and Marshall's dictum that the power to tax is the power to destroy—a dictum, however, which they disregard when they allowed Congress, through heavy taxation, to drive out oleomargarine and State notes.

The arbitrary assumption that federal government cannot exist without the judicial review, ignores the fact that the harmonious adjustment between the constituent States of a federal union depends upon changing social, economic and political conditions and cannot be absolutely fixed in advance in purely legal terms. It is, therefore, properly a matter for a federal council, as Jefferson, indeed, suggested for the United States. If the distinctive virtue of a federal law is that it allows the different States to try diverse provisions for a common good, that virtue has been nearly killed by the way our Supreme Court stretched the 14th Amendment—intended by the people to protect the Negroes—to prohibit all legislation that did not appeal to elderly and conservative gentlemen who refuse to think in terms of the actual conditions of today.

It has frequently been urged that since the judicial review has been our accepted tradition since the beginning of our national life, and since we have prospered under it, it is unpatriotic to try to change it. Even if the historic facts here assumed were true, the conclusion would not follow in logic or ethics. But the history thus assumed is not quite accurate. In the early days of the Republic the matter was by no means settled, as can be seen by Chief Justice Gibson's refutation of the arguments advanced by Marshall in Marbury *v.* Madison.* The first case in which the Supreme Court undertook to set aside a Congressional enactment of general interest was really the Dred Scott case, and it was certainly not tacitly accepted. It is only since the Civil War that this power has become an active and important factor in the affairs of our country.

As a student of philosophy, I must decline the challenge to name the exact alternative to the mode prevailing today. There are many possible alternatives and we shall probably not anticipate the actual historic consequences of proposed changes any more accurately than those who adopted the 14th Amendment. But there can be no doubt that the strength of judicial review rests on the popular misconception that the Constitution is some esoteric document which in some mysterious way contains a solution to every problem, revealed only to a majority of the judges on the Supreme Court Bench. When the people at large begin to discount sanctimonious fictions and to look at the naked facts—as our advanced legal scholars and progressive jurists are already doing—they will see what all honest thinkers have seen all along, namely, that constitutional law is just what the judges make it, that our Supreme Court is, in fact, a continuous Constitutional Convention, and that the people or their elected representatives ought to have an effective way of ratifying or rejecting the results. Otherwise the will of the majority will continue to be frustrated and representative government exist in name only.

The Supreme Court and Constitutional Morality

DOROTHY THOMPSON †

I am not an expert on constitutional law, and my only justification for taking your time is that I have been for some years, as a foreign correspondent, an observer at the collapse of constitutional democracies. You might say I have been a researcher into the mortality of republics. The outstanding fact of our times is the decline and fall of constitutional democ-

* See Marbury *v.* Madison and Eakin *v.* Raub, Topic 10.

† Newspaper columnist, lecturer, radio commentator, and foreign correspondent. Contributor to many periodicals. The selection is from a statement by Miss Dorothy Thompson at a hearing before the Senate Committee on the Judiciary. Reorganization of the Federal Judiciary, Hearings before the Committee on the Judiciary, United States Senate, 75th Congress, 1st Session on S. 1392, A Bill to Reorganize the Judicial Branch of the Government. (Washington, D.C., U.S. Government Printing Office, 1937), pp. 859–867.

racy. A great need of our time is for more accurate analysis of the pathology of constitutional government, of why constitutional government perishes. A great deal of such analysis has been made, but the more thoughtful students have not made much impress on public opinion. And there are a great many people in the United States, for instance, who think . . . that constitutional democracies have fallen because they "failed to meet human needs" and pass adequate social legislation. I refer to that because that, apparently, is the President's view. That is what he said, in his first speech in support of his proposals for reforming the judiciary. He said:

> In some countries a royalist form of government failed to meet human needs and fell. In other countries a parliamentary form of government failed to meet human needs and fell. In still other countries, governments have managed to hold on, but civil strife has flared, or threats of upheaval exist.

That is what the President said, and apparently the moral of that is that unless Congress is made perfectly free to make any sort of legislation it may hit upon and then pass it on to a Supreme Court representative of the ideas of the majority, we shall see the end of democracy. Also, Mr. Harry Hopkins, in a radio address recently said, "The cure for the evils of democracy is more democracy." That is just another expression of the thought that democracies perish if they are curbed, or if they fail to respond immediately to all the economic and social demands of powerful groups of the community. . . .

The dangers that threaten democracies are two: One is that the legal pattern should be too rigid; that the dynamics in society should shatter themselves against a Chinese wall which can be broken only by revolution. That argument is constantly advanced these days by the advocates of rapid and drastic change. That argument is implicit in the President's speech at the Democratic Party rally. It is the threat of revolution. I am not impressed by that argument. I am not impressed by it, because in the past 17 years I have attended the funerals of many democracies and I have not seen one in which the cause of death could be so diagnosed. This danger confronts absolutist systems, where popular opinion is not allowed to function, where there is no representative government, where insurrection is the only outlet. Mr. Hitler faced such a danger in the summer of 1934; in Moscow we have had trials indicating that Mr. Stalin had been facing such a danger, or the danger can arise in a sudden and acute crisis such as occurred here, in 1932, when thousands of people were threatened by actual starvation, by bankruptcy, and by the complete break-down of economic life. Such emergencies from time to time hit all republics, and often, during them the constitution is tacitly suspended, by almost universal consent. Such an emergency occurred in France in 1926–27 when the franc fell catastrophically. For 2 years, Poincaré was virtually a dictator. It happened here and elsewhere during the war. But wise democracies do not attempt during such emergencies to fundamentally alter the continuing structure of the State or set precedents for new procedures, and they return as rapidly as possible to the traditional pattern of procedure.

I think the second danger to democracies is far greater: It is that reforms, often very good and much needed reforms, should be rushed through at a rate in which they cannot be digested in society. It is the danger that eager and unchecked majorities should set up new instruments of power, before they are equipped properly to administer such instruments. It is that the will of powerful pressure groups, even when such groups embrace a majority of voters, should find expression in total disregard of the feelings, apprehensions, and interests of large and important minorities. All of those things, for instance, would hold true if you analyzed the pathology of the [prewar] Austrian Republic. There is the danger that radical changes, affecting the social structure, should take place without the guidance or the check of any clear unequivocal principles. I think the greater the demand for popular franchises and rights, the greater is the need for constitutional control. Otherwise, this struggle for democratic rights—or, if you want to call it that, for new economic freedoms—can very rapidly degenerate into a chaotic redistribution of privileges. That again is what happened in Austria. There are always hundred percenters for democracy, those who want pure democracy. They want to do away with every impediment and march at high speed toward what they call a real or modern democracy, or the democracy in harmony with the times. But precisely in such revolutionary times—and we live in one—it is most necessary to have a point of reference, a warrant, an instrument which confidently assures the legitimacy of what is being done. For without such a point of reference, there ceases to be a spontaneous social cohesion and what you then get as sure as fate is social cohesion by coercion. . . .

I think the disciplines of law are particularly needed in democracies and are especially needed at any moment when a powerful majority is in temporary control of the current political situation almost to the exclusion of minority representation. . . . The men who designed the structure of this Republic realized this. They did not believe that the cure for the evils of democracy was more democracy. They believed that the prevention against a democracy running away with itself, the prevention against a powerful majority riding roughshod over the temporary minority and selling short the whole future of the country, the prevention against today's majority mortgaging tomorrow's majority, lay in a written constitution and an independent Supreme Court to interpret that constitution.

There is a reason why Supreme Court judges are appointed for life, and removable only by impeachment. That reason is obvious. It was certain that successive executives and successive Senates would seek to put upon the Supreme Court Bench men responsive to their own ideas. Everybody is human, but it was arranged that the Supreme Court, only by the merest chance, by a very remote mathematical chance, would ever coincide with the majority of the moment. It was so arranged that the Court should represent, not the momentary dominant majority, but the continuity and tradition in American life.

The difference between a regime of pure democracy, which moves from majority to majority, one often overthrowing the other and seeking to destroy all or much of what its predecessor has done—the difference between that kind of government, which I do not think has ever worked on this globe—and our own constitutional democracy is the difference between legislation which is haphazard, which is directed by powerful forces at large in society, and legislation which is somewhat checked by the will to continuity. It is true that the Supreme Court is conservative. I think it is conservative by its very nature. And that, gentlemen, is its function—to conserve. It represents, the opponents say, the past. Yes; perhaps it does. It represents continuity; it demands that today's laws shall be checked against the whole body of law and the principles governing the state, and thus it insures that new laws shall be designed in some conformity with certain long-established customs and ways of life. And just because it represents continuity, because it exerts a constant reminder on the people that they have a past, a past to which they have a duty; just because it reminds them that when they act, however radically, however drastically, they must keep an eye on long-established patterns of law and behavior—just for that reason I think it safeguards the future. For certainly those political democracies, gentlemen, have been proved safest which have the longest and most unbroken traditions. You might say that just because we have a past, we can be most confident that we have a future. . . .

The Supreme Court is essentially an instrument of the State, not of government, which is a temporary majority running the state machinery. That is to say, it is a part of the entire legal apparatus. It is not there to guarantee that the will of the majority shall be expressed but to see that the will of the majority does not infringe the basic guaranteed rights of any individual citizen who wants to appeal against that will to a higher institution of reference. In fact, the very existence of the Supreme Court is an affirmation not only that every individual citizen has equality before the law, but that any individual citizen may, at some point, assert his equality with the whole political set-up. The conception that the individual may appeal to a court of reference which is above the majority; that he can stand there, all alone, and demand a right which perhaps 99 per cent of the people do not want or cherish, is the most grandiose concept of political freedom. It was recognized as such by foreign critics and students of our system of government, such as Lord Brougham, Bryce, and Gladstone. Incidentally, 40 years ago Bryce pointed out that the power of the President to expand the Supreme

Court was the weakest point in the whole system. And it has reality only if the Court is independent of the Government, and that independence has been arranged for by a way of appointment and removal which gives every mathematical chance of success. If it becomes the instrument of the majority today, what possible guaranty have you that it will not become the instrument of another majority tomorrow? If, in our desire—a desire which I share with many members of this administration—to see a greater national consolidation, to extend the economic control of government over chaotic economic forces—an objective with which in the large sense I am in sympathy—if in order to do that, we pack the Court, what possible guaranty have we that tomorrow a government which believes that a national emergency demands the curbing of free speech, the dissolution of certain political parties, the control over the radio will not pack it again?

We have had times in our history when honest men tried to suppress all civil liberties—we have been told a lot about Supreme Court decisions that have balked social legislation and we are asked to turn back history and remember the Dred Scott case, which, they say, brought on the Civil War. But some of you gentlemen in this committee are from the South, and I wonder if you are lawyers. Do you remember the role that the Supreme Court played in the reconstruction era, in the days of the carpetbaggers, when men like Thaddeus Stevens—who were the radicals of their day— were trying to fasten a hideous tyranny forever on the South? In those days the Supreme Court alone stood between the people of the South and a black terror organized by white northerners. In those days the South was in the minority; in those days the North, in its own mind, represented all the forces of national union and solidarity, progressiveness, and enlightenment. And like lots of enlightened, progressive, world-savers in history they were ready to resort to any means whatever to make the forces of what they called justice prevail. . . .

People grow restive under the checks imposed by a regime of law. And yet all history proves that what Aristotle said is correct—that regimes tend to turn into their opposites, if the political principle which they represent is allowed to develop to the bitter end. If democracy becomes so pure and so immediate that the popular will is subjected to no standards, it rapidly moves into tyranny.

The whole world today has a new vision of freedom; economic freedom. That actually means a redistribution of wealth which will diminish the privileges of the few for the sake of the under-privileged many. From both a moral and an economic viewpoint that demand is justified and made inevitable, by our era of mass production. But that economic freedom—I do not think this can be said too often—will prove a complete mirage unless it is accomplished with the maintenance of political freedom. Political freedom is the condition of all freedom, as the people of Russia have learned, as the people of Italy have learned, and as the people of Germany have learned. They gave up political freedom to get something else which they thought at the moment was very much more important, and then they found out that there is not anything more important. And the first condition of political freedom is that we should stick to a regime of law, and not move off the path toward a regime of men. . . .

The Utility of a Restraining Power

JUSTICE BENJAMIN N. CARDOZO *

Some critics of our public law insist that the power of the courts to fix the limits of permissible encroachment by statute upon the liberty of the individual is one that ought to be withdrawn. It means, they say, either too much or too little. If it is freely exercised, if it is made an excuse for imposing the individual beliefs and philosophies of the judges upon other branches of the government, if it stereotypes legislation within the forms and limits that were expedient in the nineteenth or perhaps the eighteenth century, it shackles progress, and breeds distrust and suspicion of the courts. If, on the other hand, it is interpreted in the broad and variable sense which I believe to be the true one, if statutes are to be sustained unless they are so plainly arbitrary and oppressive that right-minded men and women could not reasonably regard them otherwise, the right of supervision, it is said, is not worth the danger of abuse. "There no doubt comes a time when a statute is so obviously oppressive and absurd that it can have no justification in any sane polity." Such times may indeed come, yet only seldom. The occasions must be few when legislatures will enact a statute that will merit condemnation upon the application of a test so liberal; and if carelessness or haste or momentary passion may at rare intervals bring such statutes into being with hardship to individuals or classes, we may trust to succeeding legislatures for the undoing of the wrong. That is the argument of the critics of the existing system.

My own belief is that it lays too little stress on the value of the "imponderables." The utility of an external power restraining the legislative judgment is not to be measured by counting the occasions of its exercise. The great ideals of liberty and equality are preserved against the assaults of opportunism, the expediency of the passing hour, the erosion of small encroachments, the scorn and derision of those who have no patience with

* Late United States Supreme Court Justice. Previously Chief Judge of the New York Court of Appeals. Author of *The Growth of Law, Law and Literature and Other Essays,* etc. The selection is from Benjamin N. Cardozo, *The Nature of the Judicial Process* (New Haven, Yale University Press, 1921), pp. 91–94. By permission of the publisher.

general principles, by enshrining them in constitutions, and consecrating to the task of their protection a body of defenders. By conscious or subconscious influence, the presence of this restraining power, aloof in the background, but none the less always in reserve, tends to stabilize and rationalize the legislative judgment, to infuse it with the glow of principle, to hold the standard aloft and visible for those who must run the race and keep the faith. I do not mean to deny that there have been times when the possibility of judicial review has worked the other way.

Legislatures have sometimes disregarded their own responsibility and passed it on to the courts. Such dangers must be balanced against those of independence from all restraint, independence on the part of public officers elected for brief terms, without the guiding force of a continuous tradition. On the whole, I believe the latter dangers to be the more formidable of the two. Great maxims, if they may be violated with impunity, are honored often with lip-service, which passes easily into irreverence. The restraining power of the judiciary does not manifest its chief worth in the few cases in which the legislature has gone beyond the lines that mark the limits of discretion. Rather shall we find its chief worth in making vocal and audible the ideals that might otherwise be silenced, in giving them continuity of life and of expression, in guiding and directing choice within the limits where choice ranges. This function should preserve to the courts the power that now belongs to them, if only the power is exercised with insight into social values, and with suppleness of adaptation to changing social needs.

Section VIII

Politics in a Democracy

THE CONSTITUTION which established the basic framework of our government did not mention political parties. The Framers, to be sure, took cognizance of the potential power of organized public opinion and political parties and attempted to curb their influence through the electoral college, the indirect election of senators, checks and balances and other devices. Yet, today, the force of both public opinion and political parties is recognized as a vital concomitant of our democratic and constitutional system.

One of the striking characteristics of our political system lies in the strength of the two-party tradition. The causes and significance of the two-party system are analyzed by E. E. Schattschneider. Within the framework of this system, there operates, according to John Fischer, an "informal, highly elastic, and generally accepted understanding" by the terms of which "all of the contending interest groups recognize and abide by certain rules of the game." This, he calls, the "Doctrine of the Concurrent Majority." The nature and implications of this "Doctrine" merit careful consideration.

Topic 19

THE AMERICAN PARTY SYSTEM

Why a Two-Party System?

E. E. SCHATTSCHNEIDER *

The rise of political parties is indubitably one of the principal distinguishing marks of modern government. The parties, in fact, have played a major role as *makers* of governments, more especially they have been the makers of democratic government. . . . The political parties created democracy and that modern democracy is unthinkable save in terms of the parties. As a matter of fact, the condition of the parties is the best possible evidence of the nature of any regime. The most important distinction in modern political philosophy, the distinction between democracy and dictatorship, can be made best in terms of party politics. The parties are not therefore merely appendages of modern government; they are in the center of it and play a determinative and creative role in it.

What are the qualities that distinguish American parties from all others? First of all, American politics is dominated and distinguished by *the two-party system*. This is the most conspicuous and perhaps the most important fact about the system. It accounts for a great variety of secondary characteristics of the parties and differentiates the major parties from all minor parties and all varieties of political organizations found in multiparty systems. . . .

THE TWO-PARTY SYSTEM

The two-party system is the most conspicuous feature of American political organization. How does it happen that party politics in the United States has been organized on this pattern? In spite of the fact that the two-party system has been explained by saying that it is a mark of the "political maturity" of Anglo-American peoples (while the multiparty systems of prewar France expressed the "national character" of Frenchmen), we are reasonably certain that definite circumstances, easily identified, make this system in-

* Foundation Professor at Wesleyan University. Author of *Politics, Pressures and the Tariff*, and *Struggle for Party Government*. The selection is from E. E. Schattschneider, *Party Government* (New York: Rinehart & Company, Inc., 1942), p. 1 and Ch. IV. By permission.

evitable in the United States regardless of the personal preferences of individual critics. We could not discard the two-party system and adopt a multi-party system in the United States, exactly as a lady might change her hat, even if we wanted to do so. What we wish for has very little bearing on what we get in the style of parties. . . .

The relation between the major and minor parties is the crucial point in the two-party system. In the United States the minor parties are excluded from power. This is done so effectively that these parties cease to be genuine parties at all and should probably be spoken of simply as educational movements. In a multi-party system the distinction between major and minor parties is not clearly marked, if it exists at all, and all parties may hope to get a fraction of the power to govern, though none hopes to get the whole of the power to govern. In practice the two-party system means that there are only two major parties, one or the other of which usually has the power to govern, though they may share power sometimes, and that no minor party is able to become a third major party permanently. The gap between the second major party and the greatest minor party is enormous and insurmountable; no minor party in American history has ever become a major party, and no major party has ever become a minor party.

The monopoly of power by the major parties is real. It means that ordinarily they will poll not less than 95 per cent of the total popular vote cast in a presidential election. They will usually win every one of the places in the electoral college, all but a handful of the seats in the House and Senate, and all but one or two of the governorships of the state; and, with the exception of two or three states, they will win all or very nearly all of the seats in both houses of the legislatures. Only in municipal elections, where nonpartisan ballots are used more extensively, is the monopoly of the major parties relaxed appreciably, and even this concession is slightly unreal. Attacks on the monopoly of the major parties have produced only the most negligible results. The two-party system is therefore the Rock of Gibraltar of American politics. How does it happen that the two-party system is one of the fixed points of the political universe? There is in fact nothing mysterious about the causes of this condition. The demonstration is mathematical and conclusive.

Causes of the Two-Party System

The American two-party system is the direct consequence of the American election system, or system of representation, which is only another way of saying the same thing. The elective process is used more extensively in the United States than it has ever been used anywhere else in the world. About 800,000 officials in the national, state, and local governments are elected by the people. This is a colossal performance, and *since parties are built around elections* it would be amazing if the form of the party system were not influenced profoundly by the nature of these elections. . . .

With certain exceptions that need not be considered here, members of the United States House of Representatives are elected from single-member districts, one district for each representative. Consequently, to elect 435 members, separate elections are held in approximately 435 districts, and in each case the candidate receiving the greatest number of votes wins, even if he does not receive a majority of the votes cast. Though this arrangement seems simple, the results from the standpoint of the parties are amazing. As far as the parties are concerned, the *geographical distribution of their electoral strength* becomes, as a consequence of this system, one of the decisive factors in determining the outcome of the election. That is, the result of the election is determined by *two* factors: (1) the size of the vote, and (2) the geographical distribution of the votes; the total vote cast for the candidates of the two parties does not alone decide the issue. . . . On the other hand, a system of proportional representation or vocational representation, by abolishing the geographical factor, would almost certainly destroy the two-party system altogether.

DISTORTION OF RESULTS BY THE SINGLE-MEMBER DISTRICT SYSTEM

We are now in a position to observe the effects on the parties of the single-member-district-system-plus-plurality-elections. First, this system tends to exaggerate the representation of the winning party. Second, the greater the victory the more will it be exaggerated proportionately. Thus a party getting 55 per cent of the vote is likely to win 60 per cent of the seats, let us say. If, however, it gets 65 per cent of the vote it is likely to win 85 per cent of the seats, and so on, though it is not asserted that these proportions are accurate, or that they can be expressed in a precise mathematical formula. The corollary of this proposition is that the smaller the percentage of the popular vote received by a given party, the more likely it is to receive less than its proportionate share of the seats. Without pretending to state an accurate formula, we can say that the tendency is about as follows: if a party receives 45 per cent of the popular vote, it is apt to get only about 40 per cent of the seats. If it gets 35 per cent of the popular vote it may get only 15 per cent of the seats, depending, of course, on the vagaries of the geographical distribution of its popular vote. If a party gets less than 25 per cent of the popular vote, it is apt to get very few seats, if any at all. Restated, the general proposition is that, other things being equal, the higher the percentage of the total popular vote cast for a party, the more cheaply (in terms of votes) will the party win seats in Congress. On the other hand, the smaller the percentage of the total popular vote cast for a party, the more expensively (in terms of votes) will seats in Congress be acquired. Obviously, the individual voter can make his own vote weigh more heavily by voting for major party candidates than by voting for minor party candidates.

Although the tendency of the single-member district system described in the preceding paragraph is not stated with the precision of a mathematical formula, it is clear that the operation of the system is to exaggerate the victory of the strongest party and to discriminate radically against lesser parties. The system discriminates *moderately* against the second party but against the third, fourth, and fifth parties the force of this tendency is multiplied to the point of extinguishing their chances of winning seats altogether. The odds against a minor party are especially great because it is certain to be no more than the third party, *unless it has strongly concentrated its strength in one section.*[1]

That the general proposition stated here is true can be demonstrated by an examination of election statistics. . . . [In the congressional election of 1958, the Democratic party with 56.6 per cent of the popular vote elected 64.9 per cent of the representatives, while the Republican party with 43.3 per cent of such vote elected 35.1 per cent of the representatives. In the presidential election of 1952, the Republican party polled 54.9 per cent of the total popular vote and received 83.2 per cent of the electoral college vote, whereas the Democratic party with 44.4 per cent of the total popular vote had only 16.8 per cent of the presidential electors. Similarly, in the presidential election of 1956 the Republican candidate with 57.3 per cent of the total popular vote received the same percentage of the electoral college vote as he did in 1952, i.e., 83.2 per cent.]

THE CRUCIAL POSITION OF THE SECOND MAJOR PARTY

The foregoing statement seems to demonstrate sufficiently that minor parties are swamped by the single-member district system, but it raises

[1] Professor Herring has observed that the most important third parties have also been *sectional* parties. See *The Politics of Democracy* (New York, W. W. Norton & Company, 1940), 182. This fact results from the single-member district system which places a great premium on geographical concentration.

a question. Why does this system not crush the second major party also? Why does it fail to produce a one-party system? This question goes to the heart of the subject. There are two answers. First, the second major party (i.e., the defeated major party) is not easily wiped out completely because it is very likely to have sufficient sectional strength to protect itself against annihilation even in a crushing defeat. Since the defeated party is the first party in some regions, it benefits by the system, to an extent. Thus the Democratic party, operating from a strong sectional base in the Solid South, is certain to win substantial representation in Congress even when all else is lost. In other words, even if disastrously defeated, a major party will still be a major party. The distribution of the popular vote is almost certain to be so irregular that the defeated major party will win *some* seats, sufficient representation to enable it to continue its agitation in the interval between elections and enough to maintain a formidable lead over all other opposition parties, i.e., to be *the* opposition.[2] The sectional base of party alignments is thus likely to enable a defeated major party to outlive electoral disasters. . . .

Even more important than congressional elections are presidential elections, which might properly be described as the focus of American politics. American parties are loose leagues of state and local party bosses for the purposes of electing a president, though this statement does not exhaust the truth. In other words, presidential elections probably influence the behavior of parties even more strongly than congressional elections do. Now it is clear that a purely sectional party can never win a presidential election. Presidents can be elected only by combinations of sections, by parties that cross sectional lines. An exclusively sectional party is doomed to permanent futility, therefore, in the pursuit of the most important single objective of party strategy. Sooner or later exclusively sectional parties are likely to lose even their sectional support in favor of a major party which has a real chance of winning the supreme prize. For this reason narrowly sectional parties cannot displace the traditional type of major party, even though the single-member district system of electing representatives might sometimes give them an advantage. We conclude that the two-party system is firmly established because the second major party is able to defend itself against purely sectional parties as well as against all other varieties of minor parties.

---

[2] Since the 52nd Congress, elected in 1890, when the Republican party won only 88 seats in the House, neither of the parties has been represented by less than 100 members and very rarely has either had fewer than 150 seats.

Government by Concurrent Majority

JOHN FISCHER *

Every now and then somebody comes up with the idea that the party system in American politics is absurd because our two great parties don't stand for clearly contrasting principles, and that we would be better off if we had a conservative party and a radical or liberal party. It is a persuasive argument, especially for well-meaning people who have not had much first-hand experience in politics. You have probably heard it; it runs something like this:

"Both of the traditional American parties are outrageous frauds. Neither the Republicans nor the Democrats have any fundamental principles or ideology. They do not even have a program. In every campaign the platforms of both parties are simply collections of noble generalities, muffled in the vaguest possible language; and in each case the two platforms are very nearly identical.

"Obviously, then, both parties are merely machines for grabbing power and distributing favors. In their lust for office they are quite willing to make a deal with anybody who can deliver a sizable block of votes. As a result, each party has become an outlandish cluster of local machines and special interest groups which have nothing in common except a craving for the public trough.

"This kind of political system"—so the argument runs—"is clearly meaningless. A man of high principles can never hope to accomplish anything through the old parties, because they are not interested in principle. Moreover, the whole arrangement is so illogical that it affronts every intelligent citizen.

"We ought to separate the sheep from the goats—to herd all the progressives on one side of the fence and all the conservatives on the other. Then politics really will have some meaning; every campaign can be fought over clearly defined issues. The Europeans, who are more sophisticated politically than we simple Americans, discovered this long ago, and in each of their countries they have arranged a neat political spectrum running from Left to Right."

This argument pops up with special urgency whenever a third party

* Editor of *Harper's Magazine*. Author of *Why They Behave Like Russians,* and many articles on politics. The selection is from John Fischer, "Unwritten Rules of American Politics," *Harper's Magazine Reader* (Chicago, Bantam Books, 1953). Original copyright, 1948, by Harper & Brothers. Reprinted by permission of author and *Harper's Magazine.*

appears—Theodore Roosevelt's in 1912, Robert LaFollette's in 1924, or Henry Wallace's in 1948. And it sounds so plausible—at least on the surface—that many people have wondered why these splinter parties have always dwindled away after the election was over. Indeed, many veteran third-party enthusiasts have been able to account for their failure only by assuming a perverse and rock-headed stupidity among the American electorate.

There is, however, another possible explanation for the stubborn durability of our seemingly illogical two-party system; that it is more vigorous, more deeply rooted, and far better suited to our own peculiar needs than any European system would be; that it involves a more complex and subtle conception than the crude blacks and whites of the European ideological parties. There is considerable evidence, it seems to me, that our system—in spite of certain dangerous weaknesses—has on the whole worked out more successfully than the European.

Perhaps it is the very subtlety of the American political tradition which is responsible for the almost universal misunderstanding of it abroad. Every practicing American politician grasps its principles by instinct; if he does not, he soon retires into some less demanding profession. Moreover, the overwhelming majority of citizens have a sound working knowledge of the system, which they apply every day of their lives—though many of them might have a hard time putting that knowledge into words. There are almost no foreigners, however (except perhaps D. W. Brogan), who really understand the underlying theory. Even the editors of the London *Economist*—probably the most brilliant and well-informed group of journalists practicing anywhere today—display their bewilderment week after week. To them, and to virtually all other European observers, our whole political scene looks arbitrary, irrational, and dangerous.

Another reason for this misunderstanding lies in the fact that surprisingly little has been written about the rules of American politics during our generation. The newspapers, textbooks, and learned journals are running over with discussions of tactics and mechanics—but no one, so far as I know, has bothered to trace out the basic tradition for a good many years.

THE DOCTRINE OF THE CONCURRENT MAJORITY

In fact, the most useful discussion of this tradition which I have come across is the work of John C. Calhoun, published nearly a century ago. Today of course he is an almost forgotten figure, and many people take it for granted that his views were discredited for good by the Civil War. I know of only one writer—Peter F. Drucker—who has paid much attention to him in recent years. It was he who described Calhoun's ideas as "a major if not the only key to the understanding of what is specifically and uniquely American in our political system"; and I am indebted to Mr. Drucker for much of the case set forth here.

Calhoun summed up his political thought in what he called the Doctrine of the Concurrent Majority. He saw the United States as a nation of tremendous and frightening diversity—a collection of many different climates, races, cultures, religions, and economic patterns. He saw the constant tension among all these special interests, and he realized that the central problem of American politics was to find some way of holding these conflicting groups together.

It could not be done by force; no one group was strong enough to impose its will on all the others. The goal could be achieved only by compromise—and no real compromise could be possible if any threat of coercion lurked behind the door. Therefore, Calhoun reasoned, every vital decision in American life would have to be adopted by a "concurrent majority"—by which he meant, in effect, a unanimous agreement of all interested parties. No decision which affected the interests of the slaveholders, he argued, should be taken without their consent; and by implication he would have given a similar veto to every other special interest, whether it be labor, management, the Catholic church, old-age pensioners, the silver miners, or the corngrowers of the Middle West.

Under the goad of the slavery issue, Calhoun was driven to state his doctrine in an extreme and unworkable form. If every sectional interest had been given the explicit, legal veto power which he called for, the government obviously would have been paralyzed. (That, in fact, is precisely what seems to be happening today in the United Nations.) It is the very essence of the idea of "concurrent majority" that it cannot be made legal and official. It can operate effectively only as an informal, highly elastic, and generally accepted understanding.

Moreover, government by concurrent majority can exist only when no one power is strong enough to dominate completely, *and then only when all of the contending interest groups recognize and abide by certain rules of the game.*

UNWRITTEN RULES OF AMERICAN POLITICS

These rules are the fundamental bond of unity in American political life. They can be summed up as a habit of extraordinary toleration, plus "equality" in the peculiar American meaning of that term which cannot be translated into any other language, even into the English of Great Britain. Under these rules every group tacitly binds itself to tolerate the interests and opinions of every other group. It must not try to impose its views on others, nor can it press its own special interests to the point where they seriously endanger the interests of other groups or of the nation as a whole.

Furthermore, each group must exercise its implied veto with responsibility and discretion; and in times of great emergency it must forsake its veto right altogether. It dare not be intransigent or doctrinaire. It must make every conceivable effort to compromise, relying on its veto only as a last resort. For if any player wields this weapon recklessly, the game will break up—or all the other players will turn on him in anger, suspend the rules for the time being, and maul those very interests he is trying so desperately to protect. That was what happened in 1860, when the followers of Calhoun carried his doctrine to an unbearable extreme. Much the same thing, on a less violent scale, happened to American business interests in 1933 and to the labor unions in 1947.

This is the somewhat elusive sense, it seems to me, in which Calhoun's theory has been adopted by the American people. But elusive and subtle as it may be, it remains the basic rule of the game of politics in this country—and in this country alone. Nothing comparable exists in any other nation, although the British, in a different way, have applied their own rules of responsibility and self-restraint.

It is a rule which operates unofficially and entirely outside the Constitution—but it has given us a method by which all the official and Constitutional organs of government can be made to work. It also provides a means of selecting leaders on all levels of our political life, for hammering out policies, and for organizing and managing the conquest of political power.

The way in which this tradition works in practice can be observed most easily in Congress. Anyone who has ever tried to push through a piece of legislation quickly discovers that the basic units of organization on Capitol Hill are not the parties, but the so-called blocs, which are familiar to everyone who reads a newspaper. There are dozens of them —the farm bloc, the silver bloc, the friends of labor, the business group, the isolationists, the public power bloc—and they all cut across party lines.

They are loosely organized and pretty blurred at the edges, so that every Congressman belongs at different times to several different blocs. Each of them represents a special interest group. Each of them ordinarily works hand-in-hand with that group's Washington lobby. In passing, it might be noted that these lobbies are by no means the cancerous growth which is sometimes pictured in civics textbooks. They have become an indispensable part of the political machine—the accepted channel through which American citizens make their wishes known and play their day-to-day role in the process of government. Nor is their influence measured solely by the size of the bankrolls and propaganda apparatus which they have at their disposal. Some of the smallest and poorest lobbies often are more effective than their well-heeled rivals. For example, Russell Smith, the one-man lobby of the Farmers Union, was largely responsible for conceiving and nursing through Congress the Employment Act of 1946, one of the most far-reaching measures adopted since the war.

Now it is an unwritten but firm rule of Congress that no important bloc shall ever be voted down—under normal circumstances—on any matter which touches its own vital interests. Each of them, in other words, has a tacit right of veto on legislation in which it is primarily concerned. The ultimate expression of this right is the institution—uniquely American—of the filibuster in the Senate. Recently it has acquired a bad name among liberals because the Southern conservatives have used it ruthlessly to fight off civil rights legislation and protect white supremacy. Not so long ago, however, the filibuster was the stoutest weapon of such men as Norris and the LaFollettes in defending many a progressive cause.

Naturally no bloc wants to exercise its veto power except when it is absolutely forced to—for this is a negative power, and one which is always subject to retaliation. Positive power to influence legislation, on the other hand, can be gained only by conciliation, compromise, and endless horse-trading.

The farm bloc, for instance, normally needs no outside aid to halt the passage of a hostile bill. As a last resort, three or four strong-lunged statesmen from the corn belt can always filibuster it to death in the Senate. If the bloc wants to put through a measure to support agricultural prices, however, it can succeed only by enlisting the help of other powerful special interest groups. Consequently, it must always be careful not to antagonize any potential ally by a reckless use of the veto; and it must be willing to pay for such help by throwing its support from time to time behind legislation sought by the labor bloc, the National Association of Manufacturers, or the school-teachers' lobby.

The classic alliance of this sort was formed in the early days of the New Deal, when most of the Roosevelt legislation was shoved onto the statute books by a temporary coalition of the farm bloc and urban labor, occasionally reinforced by such minor allies as the public power group and spokesmen for the northern Negroes. Mr. Roosevelt's political genius rested largely on his ability to put together a program which would offer something to each of these groups without fatally antagonizing any of them, and then to time the presentation of each bill so that he would always retain enough bargaining power to line up a Congressional majority. It also was necessary for him to avoid the veto of the business group, which viewed much of this legislation as a barbarous assault upon its privileges; and for this purpose he employed another traditional technique, which we shall examine a little later.

This process of trading blocs of votes is generally known as log-rolling, and frequently it is deplored by the more innocent type of reformer. Such pious disapproval has no effect whatever on any practicing politician. He knows that log-rolling is a sensible and reasonably fair device, and that without it Congress could scarcely operate at all.

In fact, Congress gradually has developed a formal apparatus—the committee system—which is designed to make the log-rolling process as smooth and efficient as possible. There is no parallel system anywhere; the committees of Parliament and of the Continental legislative bodies work in an entirely different way.

Obviously the main business of Congress—the hammering out of a series of compromises between many special interest groups—cannot be conducted satisfactorily on the floor of the House or Senate. The meetings there are too large and far too public for such delicate negotiations. Moreover, every speech delivered on the floor must be aimed primarily at the voters back home, and not at the other members of the chamber. Therefore, Congress—especially the House—does nearly all its work in the closed sessions of its various committees, simply because the committee room is the only place where it is possible to arrange a compromise acceptable to all major interests affected.

For this reason, it is a matter of considerable importance to get a bill before the proper committee. Each committee serves as a forum for a particular cluster of special interests, and the assignment of a bill to a specific committee often decides which interest groups shall be recognized officially as affected by the measure and therefore entitled to a hand in its drafting. "Who is to have standing before the committee" is the technical term, and it is this decision that frequently decides the fate of the legislation.

Calhoun's principles of the concurrent majority and of sectional compromise operate just as powerfully, though sometimes less obviously, in every other American political institution. Our cabinet, for example, is the only one in the world where the members are charged by law with the representation of special interests—labor, agriculture, commerce, and so on. In other countries, each agency of government is at least presumed to act for the nation as a whole; here most agencies are expected to behave as servants for one interest or another. The Veterans' Administration, to cite the most familiar case, is frankly intended to look out for Our Boys; the Maritime Board is to look out for the shipping industry; the National Labor Relations Board, as originally established under the Wagner Act, was explicitly intended to build up the bargaining power of the unions.

Even within a single department, separate agencies are sometimes set up to represent conflicting interests. Thus in the Department of Agriculture under the New Deal the old Triple-A became primarily an instrument of the large-scale commercial farmers, as represented by their lobby, the Farm Bureau Federation; while the Farm Security Administration went to bat for the tenants, the farm laborers, and the little subsistence farmers, as represented by the Farmers Union.

This is one reason why federal agencies often struggle so bitterly against each other, and why the position of the administration as a whole on any question can be determined only after a long period of inter-bureau squabbling and compromise. Anyone who was in Washington during the war will remember how these goings-on always confused and alarmed our British allies.

Calhoun's laws also govern the selection of virtually every candidate for public office. The mystery of "eligibility" which has eluded most foreign observers simply means that a candidate must not be unacceptable to any important special interest group—a negative rather than a positive qualification. A notorious case of this process at work was the selection of Mr. Truman as the Democrats' Vice Presidential candidate in 1944. As Edward J. Flynn, the Boss of the Bronx, has pointed out in his memoirs, Truman was the one man "who would hurt . . . least" as Roosevelt's running mate. Many stronger men were disqualified, Flynn explained, by the tacit veto of one sectional interest or another. Wallace was unacceptable to the businessmen and to the many local party machines. Byrnes was distasteful to the Catholics, the Negroes, and organized labor. Rayburn came from the wrong part of the country. Truman, however, came from a border state, his labor record was good, he had not antagonized the conservatives, and—as Flynn put it—"he had never made any 'racial' remarks. He just dropped into the slot."

The same kind of considerations govern the selection of candidates right down to the county, city, and precinct levels. Flynn, one of the most successful political operators of our time, explained in some detail the complicated job of making up a ticket in his own domain. Each of the main population groups in the Bronx—Italians, Jews, and Irish Catholics—must be properly represented on the list of nominees, and so must each of the main geographical divisions. The result was a ticket which sounded like the roster of the Brooklyn Dodgers: Loreto, Delagi, Lyman, Joseph, Lyons, and Foley.

Comparable traditions govern the internal political life of the American Legion, the Federation of Women's Clubs, university student bodies, labor unions, Rotary Clubs, and the thousands of other quasi-political institutions which are so characteristic of our society and which give us such a rich fabric of spontaneous local government.

The stronghold of Calhoun's doctrine, however, is the American party —the wonder and despair of foreigners who cannot fit it into any of their concepts of political life.

"NOT TO DIVIDE BUT TO UNITE"

The purpose of European parties is, of course, to divide men of different ideologies into coherent and disciplined organizations. The historic role of the American party, on the other hand, is not to divide but to unite. That task was imposed by simple necessity. If a division into ideological parties had been attempted, in addition to all the other centrifugal forces in this country, it very probably would have proved impossible to hold the nation together. The Founding Fathers understood this thoroughly; hence Washington's warning against "factions."

Indeed, on the one occasion when we did develop two ideological parties, squarely opposing each other on an issue of principle, the result was civil war. Fortunately, that was our last large-scale experiment with a third party formed on an ideological basis—for in its early days that is just what the Republican party was.

Its radical wing, led by such men as Thaddeus Stevens, Seward, and Chase, made a determined and skillful effort to substitute principles for interests as the foundations of American political life. Even within their own party, however, they were opposed by such practical politicians as Lincoln and Johnson—men who distrusted fanaticism in any form—and by the end of the Reconstruction period the experiment had been abandoned. American politics then swung back into its normal path and has never veered far away from it since. Although Calhoun's cause was defeated, his political theory came through the Civil War stronger than ever.

The result is that the American party has no permanent program and no fixed aim, except to win elections. Its one purpose is to unite the largest possible number of divergent interest groups in the pursuit of power. Its unity is one of compromise, not of dogma. It must—if it hopes to succeed—appeal to considerable numbers on both the left and the right, to rich and poor, Protestant and Catholic, farmer and industrial worker, native and foreign born.

It must be ready to bid for the support of any group that can deliver a sizable chunk of votes, accepting that group's program with whatever modifications may be necessary to reconcile the other members of the party. If sun worship, or Existentialism, or the nationalization of industry should ever attract any significant following in this country, you can be sure that both parties would soon whip up a plank designed to win it over.

This ability to absorb new ideas (along with the enthusiasts behind them) and to mold them into a shape acceptable to the party's standpatters is, perhaps, the chief measure of vitality in the party's leadership. Such ideas almost never germinate within the party itself. They are stolen —very often from third parties.

Indeed, the historic function of third parties has been to sprout new issues, nurse them along until they have gathered a body of supporters worth stealing, and then to turn them over (often reluctantly) to the major parties. A glance at the old platforms of the Populists, the Bull Moosers, and the Socialists will show what an astonishingly high percentage of their once-radical notions have been purloined by both Republicans and Democrats—and enacted into law. Thus the income tax, child-labor laws, minimum wages, regulation of railroads and utilities, and old-age pensions have all become part of the American Way of Life.

While each major party must always stand alert to grab a promising new issue, it also must be careful never to scare off any of the big, established interest groups. For as soon as it alienates any one of them, it finds itself in a state of crisis.

During the nineteen-thirties and -forties the Republicans lost much of their standing as a truly national party because they had made themselves unacceptable to labor. Similarly, the Democrats, during the middle stage of the New Deal, incurred the wrath of the business interests. Ever since Mr. Truman was plumped into the White House, the Democratic leadership has struggled desperately—though rather ineptly—to regain the confidence of businessmen without at the same time driving organized labor out of the ranks. It probably would be safe to predict that if the Republican party is to regain a long period of health, it must make an equally vigorous effort to win back the confidence of labor. For the permanent veto of any major element in American society means political death—as the ghosts of the Federalists and Whigs can testify.

WEAKNESSES OF THE AMERICAN POLITICAL SYSTEM

The weaknesses of the American political system are obvious—much more obvious, in fact, than its virtues. These weaknesses have been so sharply criticized for the past hundred years, by a procession of able analysts ranging from Walter Bagehot to Thomas K. Finletter, that it is hardly necessary to mention them here. It is enough to note that most of the criticism has been aimed at two major flaws.

First, it is apparent that the doctrine of the concurrent majority is a negative one—a principle of inaction. A strong government, capable of rapid and decisive action, is difficult to achieve under a system which forbids it to do anything until virtually everybody acquiesces. In times of crisis, a dangerously long period of debate and compromise usually is necessary before any administration can carry out the drastic measures needed. The depression of the early thirties, the crisis in foreign policy which ended only with Pearl Harbor, the crisis of the Marshall program all illustrate this recurring problem.

This same characteristic of our system gives undue weight to the small but well-organized pressure group—especially when it is fighting *against* something. Hence a few power companies were able to block for twenty years the sensible use of the Muscle Shoals dam which eventually became the nucleus of TVA, and—in alliance with the railroads, rail unions, and Eastern port interests—they [held] up development of the St. Lawrence Waterway. An even more flagrant example is the silver bloc, representing only a tiny fraction of the American people. It has been looting the Treasury for a generation by a series of outrageous silver subsidy and purchase laws.

The negative character of our political rules also makes it uncommonly difficult for us to choose a President. Many of our outstanding political operatives—notably those who serve in the Senate—are virtually barred from a Presidential nomination because they are forced to get on record on too many issues. Inevitably they offend some important interest group, and therefore become "unavailable." Governors, who can keep their mouths shut on most national issues, have a much better chance to reach the White House. Moveover, the very qualities of caution and inoffensiveness which make a good candidate—Harding and Coolidge come most readily to mind—are likely to make a bad President.

An even more serious flaw in our scheme of politics is the difficulty in finding anybody to speak for the country as a whole. Calhoun would have argued that the national interest is merely the sum of all the various special interests, and therefore needs no spokesmen of its own—but in this case he clearly was wrong.

In practice, we tend to settle sectional and class conflicts at the expense of the nation as a whole—with results painful to all of us. The labor troubles in the spring of 1946, for instance, could be settled only on a basis acceptable to *both* labor and management: that is, on the basis of higher wages *plus* higher prices. The upshot was an inflationary spiral which damaged everybody. Countless other instances, from soil erosion to the rash of billboards along our highways, bear witness to the

American tendency to neglect matters which are "only" of national interest, and therefore are left without a recognized sponsor.

Over the generations we have developed a series of practices and institutions which partly remedy these weaknesses, although we are still far from a complete cure. One such development has been the gradual strengthening of the Presidency as against Congress. As the only man elected by all the people, the President inevitably has had to take over many of the policy-making and leadership functions which the Founding Fathers originally assigned to the legislators. This meant, of course, that he could no longer behave merely as an obedient executor of the will of Congress, but was forced into increasingly frequent conflicts with Capitol Hill.

Today we have come to recognize that this conflict is one of the most important obligations of the Presidency. No really strong executive tries to avoid it—he accepts it as an essential part of his job. If he simply tries to placate the pressure groups which speak through Congress, history writes him down as a failure. For it is his duty to enlist the support of many minorities for measures rooted in the national interest, reaching beyond their own immediate concern—and, if necessary, to stand up against the ravening minorities for the interest of the whole.

In recent times this particular part of the President's job has been made easier by the growth of the Theory of Temporary Emergencies. All of us—or nearly all—have come around to admitting that in time of emergency special interest groups must forego their right of veto. As a result, the President often is tempted to scare up an emergency to secure legislation which could not be passed under any other pretext. Thus, most of the New Deal bills were introduced as "temporary emergency measures," although they were clearly intended to be permanent from the very first; for in no other way could Mr. Roosevelt avoid the veto of the business interests.

Again, in 1939 the threat of war enabled the President to push through much legislation which would have been impossible under normal circumstances.

ELEMENTS OF STRENGTH

Because we have been so preoccupied with trying to patch up the flaws in our system, we have often overlooked its unique elements of strength. The chief of these is its ability to minimize conflict—not by suppressing the conflicting forces, but by absorbing and utilizing them. The result is a society which is both free and reasonably stable—a government which is as strong and effective as most dictatorships, but which can still adapt itself to social change.

The way in which the American political organism tames down the extremists of both the left and right is always fascinating to watch. Either party normally is willing to embrace any group or movement which can deliver votes—but in return it requires these groups to adjust their programs to fit the traditions, beliefs, and prejudices of the majority of the people. The fanatics, the implacable radicals cannot hope to get to first base in American politics until they abandon their fanaticism and learn the habits of conciliation. As a consequence, it is almost impossible for political movements here to become entirely irresponsible and to draw strength from the kind of demagogic obstruction which has nurtured both Communist and Fascist movements abroad.

The same process which gentles down the extremists also prods along the political laggards. As long as it is in a state of health, each American party has a conservative and a liberal wing. Sometimes one is dominant, sometimes the other—but even when the conservative element is most powerful, it must reckon with the left-wingers in its own family. At the moment the Republican party certainly is in one of its more conservative phases; yet it contains such men as Senators Morse, Aiken, Flanders, and Tobey, who are at least as progressive as most of the old New Dealers.* They, and their counterparts in the Democratic party, exert a steady tug to the left which prevents either party from lapsing into complete reaction.

The strength of this tug is indicated by the fact that the major New Deal reforms have now been almost universally accepted. In the mid-thirties, many leading Republicans, plus many conservative Democrats, were hell-bent on wiping out social security, TVA, SEC, minimum-wage laws, rural electrification, and all the other dread innovations of the New Deal. Today no Presidential aspirant would dare suggest the repeal of a single one of them. In this country there simply is no place for a hard core of irreconcilable reactionaries, comparable to those political groups in France which have never yet accepted the reforms of the French Revolution.

This American tendency to push extremists of both the left and right toward a middle position has enabled us, so far, to escape class warfare. This is no small achievement for any political system; for class warfare cannot be tolerated by a modern industrial society. If it seriously threatens, it is bound to be suppressed by some form of totalitarianism, as it has been in Germany, Spain, Italy, Russia, and most of Eastern Europe.

* [This was written in 1948.]

In fact, suppression might be termed the normal method of settling conflicts in continental Europe, where parties traditionally have been drawn up along ideological battle lines. Every political campaign becomes a religious crusade; each party is fanatically convinced that it and it alone has truth by the tail; each party is certain that its opponents not only are wrong, but wicked. If the sacred ideology is to be established beyond challenge, no heresy can be tolerated. Therefore it becomes a duty not only to defeat the enemy at the polls, but to wipe him out. Any suggestion of compromise must be rejected as treason and betrayal of the true faith. The party must be disciplined like an army, and if it cannot win by other means it must be ready to take up arms in deadly fact.

Under this kind of political system the best that can be hoped for is a prolonged deadlock between parties which are too numerous and weak to exterminate one another. The classic example is prewar France, where six revolutions or near-revolutions broke out within a century, where cabinets fell every weekend, and no government could ever become strong enough to govern effectively. The more usual outcome is a complete victory for one ideology or another, after a brief period of electioneering, turmoil, and fighting in the streets; then comes the liquidation of the defeated.

Because this sort of ideological politics is so foreign to our native tradition, neither Socialists, Communists, nor Fascists have ever been accepted as normal parties. So long as that tradition retains its very considerable vitality, it seems to me unlikely that any third party founded on an ideological basis can take root. The notion of a ruthless and unlimited class struggle, the concept of a master race, a fascist élite, or a proletariat which is entitled to impose its will on all others—these are ideas which are incompatible with the main current of American political life. The uncompromising ideologist, of whatever faith, appears in our eyes peculiarly "un-American," simply because he cannot recognize the rule of the concurrent majority, nor can he accept the rules of mutual toleration which are necessary to make it work. Unless he forsakes his ideology, he cannot even understand that basic principle of American politics which was perhaps best expressed by Judge Learned Hand: "The spirit of liberty is the spirit which is not too sure that it is right."

Topic 20

"RESPONSIBLE" PARTIES

[In 1950, The Committee on Political Parties of the American Political Science Association submitted a Report titled "Toward a More Responsible Two-Party System." (It was published as a Supplement in the *American Political Science Review,* Vol. XLIV, No. 3, Part 2, September, 1950.)

The "thesis" of the Committee was stated as follows:

"Historical and other factors have caused the American two-party system to operate as two loose associations of state and local organizations, with very little national machinery and very little national cohesion. As a result, either major party, when in power, is ill-equipped to organize its members in the legislative and the executive branches into a government held together and guided by the party program. Party responsibility at the polls thus tends to vanish. This is a very serious matter, for it affects the very heartbeat of American democracy. It also poses grave problems of domestic and foreign policy in an era when it is no longer safe for the nation to deal piecemeal with issues that can be disposed of only on the basis of coherent programs."

The Committee categorically insisted that "an effective party system requires, first, that the parties are able to bring forth programs to which they commit themselves and, second, that the parties possess sufficient internal cohesion to carry out these programs." It made a number of specific recommendations designed to realize this objective.

James M. Burns' argument is in essential agreement with the philosophy of The Committee on Political Parties. On the other hand, the Stedman-Sonthoff article raises serious doubts about that philosophy and its proposed implementation.]

The Need for Disciplined Parties

JAMES M. BURNS *

OUR MULTI-PARTY SYSTEM

If the thousands of organized interests in a democracy reflect group antagonisms, it is the two-party system which, under ideal conditions, exploits the underlying solidarity among people. It is that system which, functioning properly, manages to express the concurrence of a majority.

How does the two-party system accomplish this vital task? The answer is not hard to find. In any democracy a major party seeks control of the government. To achieve that goal it bids for support throughout the community. To gain that support the party must broaden its platform through a series of compromises with organized groups and with unorganized voters. No narrow program will do the job. Constantly searching for the beliefs that bind diverse groups, the party's policy-makers define the issues that transcend the claims of special interests and find response among great masses of the people. Since the politicians attempt to attract as many "customers" as possible, the party system becomes, in the words of Lord Bryce, "the best instrument for the suppression of dissident minorities democracy has yet devised." For in a democracy the parties can hold a minority in check without stifling its creative function in the polity.

In the United States especially, a major party must find the common denominator among a large and varied group of voters, for it hopes to pluck the biggest plum of all at the next election—the Presidency. To elect a Chief Executive it must produce an electoral majority, and in doing so it forces adjustments among minority groups. As Carl Becker has said, "the fundamental compromises are, in the first instance, made not between the major parties but within them." Once having gone through this process of compromise in each of their camps, the two parties can offer the voters a relatively simple "either-or" choice rather than a confused array of alternatives. The two parties take up new ideas and attract new voters in order to survive in rigorous competition, and in doing so they display the inclusiveness that is central to democracy.

* Professor of Political Science at Williams College. Formerly Legislative Assistant, United States Congress. Author of *Roosevelt: The Lion and the Fox, John Kennedy: A Political Profile,* and co-author of *Government by the People.* The selection is from James M. Burns, *Congress on Trial* (New York, Harper & Brothers, 1949), pp. 33–44. Copyright, 1949, by Harper & Brothers. By permission.

Such, ideally, are the benefits of a two-party system. But in the United States we do not enjoy these benefits because our two-party system breaks down in the legislative branch. What we have in Congress might better be called a multi-party system. Instead of a grand encounter between the rallied forces of the two great parties in House and Senate, the legislative battle often degenerates into scuffles and skirmishes among minority groups. On matters of vital public policy the major parties fail to hold their lines. They leave the field in possession of the pressure politicians and other members of Congress who are faithful to a locality or to a special interest but not to the national platform of their party.

A glance at virtually any House or Senate roll call will demonstrate the inability of the party to enforce discipline even if it should try. In recent years the Democratic party has been especially vulnerable to the disruptive effects of bloc voting, but the Republicans too are rarely able to prevent at least a few of their adherents from crossing party lines. Party irresponsibility also affects the shaping of bills in committee and on the floor before the final roll call is reached. Indeed, it is hardly proper even to use the term "party responsibility" in discussing Congress, for the most rudimentary underpinnings of such responsibility do not exist. The party members in Congress have no common political program; as Pendleton Herring has said, "On the majority of issues the party takes no stand." And if there were such a program, little machinery exists in House or Senate to enforce it.

As a result of this situation we have in Congress, as far as public policy is concerned, a group of splinter parties. They are the Southern Democratic party, the Farmers' party, the Labor party, the New Deal party, the Liberal Republican party, the Veterans' party, the Silver party, and many others, along with the faithful adherents of the Republican and Democratic parties. A President of the United States is a Democrat or Republican, but key Senators and Representatives are more than likely to vote as members of a multi-party system.

This congressional patchwork is neither new nor accidental. It is rooted in American political organization. As national institutions, our parties are decrepit. They are coalitions of state and local party organizations, pulling together in awkward harmony every four years in an attempt to elect a President, going their own way the rest of the time.

The bosses who run the party machines are concerned more with private spoils than with public policy. The pressure groups that work through and around the parties are interested in their own designs, which may or may not coincide with the general welfare.

Lacking central control and discipline, the major party cannot hold its congressmen responsible to the broad majority of the voters in the nation who put the party into power. The national committee and chairman of the party have little control over national policy. They can do nothing for the congressman—he feels no responsibility to them.

Senators and Representatives can blithely disregard the national political platform; if they bother to pay it lip service, they usually do so because the program is so broad as to permit the widest leeway. In their states and districts the congressmen are responsible to fragments of the party—fragments that assume a variety of shapes under the impact of economic, sectional, ideological, and other forces.

BRITAIN: PARTY GOVERNMENT IN ACTION

We have much to learn from the English on this matter of political organization in a democracy. For over the course of many years they have forged a system of party government in the full sense of the term. That system serves three cardinal purposes. It unites the various branches of the government in order to carry out the will of a popular majority. It staves off the thrusts for power of minority groups. And as recent events have made clear, it offers the voters a genuine choice between two fairly distinct programs, rather than the Tweedledum-Tweedledee alternatives that often characterize political encounters in the United States. . . .

The difference between the British system and ours is not, of course, one of personality, but one of basic political organization. There the party is supreme. Its role in national life is so meaningful and decisive that most Englishmen vote in terms of the party program and record, rather than on the basis of the personality, salesmanship, and promises of the individual candidate.

On first look such a scheme might seem to bear an authoritarian stamp. But in fact the British party system is an almost ideal form of representative government. By forcing candidates for Parliament to run on the national platforms, it gives the voter a real choice between two opposing programs. And the voter expects the successful candidate to support that program once he takes his seat in the Commons, for faithfulness to that cause is part of the bargain between voter, candidate, and party. The parties make no pretense of responding to every ripple of public opinion, or to every pressure of some organized minority. They have the more vital function of expressing the broad political aspirations of a majority of the people. While in this country Congress often seems to represent every group except the majority, in Britain the major parties, operating at the highest level of political organization, give the national welfare right of way over minority interests.

Despite the omnipotence of party in Britain, the legislature is not a dead letter. On the contrary, Parliament enjoys enormous prestige in that country and throughout much of the world. "It has occupied the centre of the political stage for centuries," Jennings has written. "So much of the history of freedom is part of the history of Parliament that freedom and parliamentary government are often considered to be the same thing." . . .

How to explain the contrast between party domination of the legislative in Britain and the constant disruption of party lines in Congress? The answer, in part, lies in the greater homogeneity of the British people that permits a more cohesive political structure. But that is not the whole answer, for Britain too has her sectional rivalries that cut across parties, her special interests that would use either party in their quest for influence. The main reason for that contrast is the organization of political power in Britain as compared with America.

The Conservative Party, and to an even greater extent the Labour Party, are centralized agencies. Ample control over funds, program, and the choice of candidates is lodged in the national office of each party. Because each is responsible for judgment and action on a national scale it requires its parliamentary members to vote in national terms. In contrast to the loose decentralized party structure of the United States, continually disintegrating in Congress under the impact of organized minorities, the British parties have the means of holding their M.P.'s in line.

It is not a matter simply of enforcement machinery. Discipline in the British party rests also on the fact that, except perhaps in times of fast-moving political developments, its program is a genuine compromise among the various groups making up the party. That program is carefully devised not only to consolidate the support of the rank and file but to attract independent voters as well. On the theory that an M.P. is more easily led than driven, it may even make concessions to local and sectional interests. But those concessions are never so fundamental as to endanger seriously the party's loyalty to its national program. It is precisely in this respect—at least as far as discipline in the legislative body is concerned—that the American parties differ so drastically from their British counterparts.

MAKE-BELIEVE MAJORITIES

Lacking the party rule that invigorates the British parliamentary system, Congress is often unable to furnish majorities for even the most urgent measures. While Parliament automatically musters enough votes to enact the program of the party in power, or else must face dissolution, the majority party in Congress cannot control its own rank and file. Hence bills in Congress get stymied in committee; they survive in one chamber only to stall in the other; a few fail in conference between Senate and House. When measures become marooned somewhere in the winding legislative channels, the villain of the piece may well be a minority group holding a strong position in committee or chamber, and the majority may be powerless to come to the rescue.

How, then, do bills get passed? Partly as a result of the appeals and threats of a President acting as chief legislator as well as chief executive. The President's control of patronage, his means of mobilizing public opinion, the authority of his office often enable him to drive measures through the legislature. In many cases, too, legislation is enacted largely as a result of bi-party coalitions responding to group pressures of some sort. Such important measures as the McNary-Haugen proposals for farm surplus control in the 1920's, the Smoot-Hawley tariff of 1930, the Economy Act of 1933, the National Industrial Recovery Act of the same year, the Employment Act of 1946, the Greek-Turkish aid bill of 1947, to name only a few, were passed by Congress as a result of bi-party support.

Least significant of all in the enactment of legislation seems to be the party as such. Half a century ago A. Lawrence Lowell set out to discover how often more than nine-tenths of the party members in Congress voted on the same side of a question. He found such party cohesion in less than eight per cent of the important bills considered by the Thirty-Eighth Congress, elected in 1862; and party influence on legislation was even less in other samples he studied.

Party cohesion is still slight today. And as for straight party voting— where every Republican lines up on one side of an issue and every Democrat on the opposite side—it would be difficult indeed to find an example of such voting on an important issue (aside from "organizing" the House or Senate) in the last quarter century.

In the absence of party voting Congress at times falls back on curious methods of producing majorities. One of these might be termed the "majority by threat." It is the most primitive of all means of securing a working combination. Rather than agreeing on a common program, blocs threaten to withhold their votes from bills backed by other blocs unless support is forthcoming for their own.

It is a sort of log-rolling in reverse, with the advocates of a measure saying in effect: "If you dare to vote against our bill, we will vote against yours." Thus in 1937 the labor bloc in Congress threatened to oppose agricultural legislation unless farm representatives supported a wages and hours bill. In considering the price control bill of 1942 the majority leader issued a similar warning to the farm group. There is a vast difference between such attempts to win votes through fugitive alliances in reverse, and the effecting of agreement by intra-party action based on awareness of a broad but genuine identity of interest.

Another crude method of achieving joint action on bills is "evasion by delegation"—the consignment of broad powers of decision to the President when congressional blocs cannot agree on a closely defined policy. Not because of the need for administrative discretion but because of its own failure to find a basis for agreement, Congress passes important policy-making powers on to the Chief Executive.

An example of such delegation is found in the consideration of the National Industrial Recovery Act in 1933; protectionist and anti-protectionist Senators were at odds over an embargo provision, and as a "compromise" they left the matter to the discretion of Mr. Roosevelt. This type of delegation is a form of legislative abdication.

Such behavior by congressional majorities should not be confused with genuine majority rule. It is one thing for a party to present its platform and candidates to the voters and, when vested with power, to make specific policies in terms of the approved program. It is quite another matter when bi-party majorities, operating without the endorsement of a majority of the voters, capture the machinery of law-making. Such majorities in Congress raise hob with the representative process. They have little responsibility to the people. They may gain their ends and disappear overnight. Their actions may be good or bad, but in either case the bi-party coalitions can ignore with impunity the national party platforms which, however vague and irresolute, at least must pass some kind of public inspection. Bi-party blocs cannot long provide real majority rule. The fleeting majorities that they muster are often not truly representative of the majority of the voters.

If these coalitions do not provide real majority rule, what does? In a democracy majority rule is assumed to be the best means of discovering and satisfying the "public interest." But what kind of majority? There are many types—the majority required to pass an amendment to the Constitution, that needed to push a bill through Congress, that involved in electing a President, and others.

VIRTUES OF A POPULAR MAJORITY

The most democratic, stable, and effective type of majority, however, is a popular majority—namely, one half of all the pooled votes throughout the nation, plus one (or more). This is a different sort of majority than that represented by a coalition in Congress responding to minorities organized in the various states and districts. "No public policy could ever be the mere sum of the demands of the organized special interests," says Schattschneider; ". . . the sum of the special interests, especially the organized special interests, is not equal to the total of all interests of the community, for there are vital common interests that cannot be organized by pressure groups."

Not only do pressure groups often fail to represent fairly the interests of many of their own members. Also in the interstices of the pressure groups one finds voting fragments that see their main stake in the well-being of the community at large. The marginal members of pressure groups, those who are not members of pressure groups, and the voters who are torn between allegiance to competing pressure groups—all these have significant weight in a nation-wide popular election, but far less weight in the sum total of local elections. In short, they are far more influential in choosing Presidents (even with the electoral college) than in choosing members of Congress.

Consequently, a popular majority tends to be more representative and democratic than a "segmented" majority. It is more stable too, because it cannot be manipulated by a few pressure politicians who are able to mobilize organized interests in various states and districts. A simple, mass, nation-wide, popular majority is often feared as leading to the "tyranny of the majority." Actually it is the safest kind of majority. Building a nation-wide coalition of twenty or more millions of voters is no mean feat. It requires the presidential candidate to find a basis of harmony among diverse groups and to widen his platform to attract those groups and the millions of independent voters. A popular majority, like democratic politics in general, furnishes its own checks and balances.

The nation-wide political party is the natural vehicle for a popular majority. But it is also a rickety one. "Coalition fever" in Congress reflects the weakness of the American parties—their inertia, their slackness, their fear of assuming leadership. Organized interest groups display precisely the traits that the parties should display but do not—discipline over their representatives in office, alertness, the capacity to submerge internal differences in a united drive toward the more decisive group objectives. The special interests operate through either or both major parties with a cynical disregard for the party platform. "In a Republican district I was Republican; in a Democratic district I was a Democrat; and in a doubtful district I was doubtful," said Jay Gould, "but I was always Erie."

Similarly with the organized interests of today. It would be inconceivable for a dairy Senator from Wisconsin, a silver Congressman from Colorado, a cotton Senator from Alabama to desert their respective groups to uphold the party platform or the general welfare. In a Congress lacking sturdy party organization, many of the nation's pressure groups seem to enjoy greater representation than the majority of the voters.

Party Responsibility—A Critical Inquiry

MURRAY S. STEDMAN, JR., AND HERBERT SONTHOFF *

MAJORITY RULE OR CONSENSUS?

There may be wide agreement with the assumption in the Report of the Committee on Political Parties of the American Political Science Association [1] that *the present two party system is irresponsible,* although the precise meaning of "irresponsible" may vary greatly. Yet the essence of the assumption is that the American party system is an inadequate mechanism for translating popular wishes into action or specific policy. This charge rests on several beliefs which are open to considerable doubt. It assumes that the problem of popular responsibility is largely the mechanical one of organization, i.e., that responsibility is "effective" only when there exist clear lines of responsibility.[2] If, as the allegation presupposes, responsibility is a matter of discipline, it becomes a fairly narrow and rigid premise.

There is also an implied assumption that majority rule is preferable to consensus rule, and that anything less than majority rule is, in a technical sense, irresponsible. It is presumably held, therefore, that a majority established by consensus, either as legislative or sectional consensus, is not true majority rule and is hence irresponsible. This argument is tenable only if we identify majority rule with majority party rule. Such an identification, however, raises the central problem of popular government. Is it empirically true that all sectional interests are increasingly negligible? Is foreign policy a matter of majority party determination? Does the election of a President mean that the electoral majority approves of the

---

* Dr. Stedman formerly taught at Brown and Columbia Universities and Swarthmore College. He is co-author of *Discontent at the Polls* and *The Dynamics of Democratic Government.* Herbert Sonthoff formerly taught at Swarthmore College. The selection is from their article "Party Responsibility—A Critical Inquiry," *Western Political Quarterly,* Vol. IV (September, 1951), pp. 454–468, *passim.* By permission.

[1] "Toward A More Responsible Two-Party System." Supplement to *The American Political Science Review,* Vol. XLIV, No. 3 (September, 1950), hereafter referred to as *Report.*

[2] "Party responsibility is the responsibility of both parties to the general public, as enforced in elections. Party responsibility to the public, enforced in elections, implies that there be more than one party, for the public can hold a party responsible only if it has a choice. . . . Party responsibility also includes the responsibility of party leaders to the party membership, as enforced in primaries, caucuses and conventions." *Report,* p. 2.

platform of the winning party? And why, most importantly, is rule by compromise less efficacious and less democratic than rule by one party, even though it be the majority party? A host of problems arise here. They, as well as the charge of party irresponsibility, pose the ancient question of the meaning of majority rule. What does "majority rule" mean? Does it mean local basis of representation, method of constituting and reconstituting the lawmaker, rule of legislative procedure, agreement of and by public opinion, mandate for the executive, or government by plebiscite?

Majority rule in its strict, arithmetical sense refers to the degree rather than to the mode of agreement. It means merely opposition to the idea of minority rule, and needs by no means to be considered, therefore, as an alternative to the rule by consensus. Consensus has been the framework of American party politics, as witness most of the more significant legislative acts which were the product not of party rule but of party consensus, i.e., of agreement between major groups within the parties. In this country, therefore, "consensus" is an important procedural concept, rather than a philosophical one aiming at fundamental agreement in Mill's sense of the word. Before we undertake to streamline the party machinery to facilitate majority rule it would be wiser, and in the long run of greater benefit, to define the Constitutional task which this machinery is to serve.

CENTRALIZED PARTIES

Another assumption is that *more responsible parties would require a very high degree of centralization of the internal party structure*. It has long been noted by students of Congress that party discipline on important issues is either weak or nonexistent. . . . The advocates of party government desire not only to facilitate executive-legislative co-ordination, but also to guarantee such co-ordination through highly centralized national parties.

Such a degree of centralization would be unprecedented in American history. However, only a centralized organization could possibly commit itself to and subsequently execute a specific program. To be successful, the national party would have to control rigidly such matters as patronage, finances, the nominating processes, and local party subsidiary organizations. The locus of power would be at the national rather than at the state or local level, as is the case today.

To make this change in power relationships, the national parties would have to possess sanctions to penalize recalcitrant state and local party leaders whose faith in the national "line" might otherwise waver. Such control would go far beyond the kind envisaged, for example, by the unsuccessful "purges" of 1938, since it would not be limited merely to congressional candidates. It would affect the nominating process generally. Quite logically, therefore, the advocates of party government stress the need for great control over local party organizations, including the power to refuse to seat "disloyal" elements at national conventions, and to exclude such elements from the national committees. Furthermore, as the *Report* states, ". . . consideration should be given to the development of additional means of dealing with rebellious and disloyal state organizations."

From this line of reasoning it follows that only the closed primary could be endorsed, for only if the national party could control the local nominating process could it choose candidates loyal to itself. It is clear that such a change would require tremendous revision of existing primary statutes. For example, the four states of Pennsylvania, New York, California, and Washington all use different procedures to nominate to state-wide offices. It is hardly possible to determine objectively which of the four systems produces the best qualified candidates. Yet, most proposals for party centralization imply a drastic change of the primary, perhaps in the face of hostile public opinion.

The logic of the argument carries much further, however, than merely urging the closed primary or some particular form of it. It also implies a threat to the direct primary as an institution. If nominations are to be determined in accordance with criteria established by the national party, it is difficult to see what, if any, purpose is served by retaining the direct primary. But the abolition of the primary would have particularly serious effects in those states, counties, and cities which are essentially one-party areas. In those localities, the only meaningful choice for the voter is between candidates of the same party. This may be true not only of the choice between candidates, but also of the choice between programs. The net effect of the disappearance of primaries in such a situation would be to take from the voter his only effective weapon for registering protest. In two-party areas the ending of the direct primary would presumably have less serious results, but such an action might create more problems than it would solve.

Proponents of stronger national parties usually contend that such parties would weaken the hold of local bosses and pressure groups, thus achieving a separation of national from local issues. To be sure, if local organizations lost control of the nominating process, their power would be drastically reduced. It does not follow, however, that a greater separation of national from state and local politics would be achieved. Neither as a matter of principle nor as a matter of applied psychology is there any great support for the contention that the national parties would lose interest in local patronage. It is probable that the first of the existing national parties to reorganize itself would be able to extend its patronage power into hitherto sacrosanct areas. In passing, the question may be raised whether the whole idea of party government is compatible with any kind of nonpartisan approach to local government. If the answer is negative, one can visualize a vast new area of spoils opening up for the benefit of national organizations.

The danger of the idea of party government is not that stronger national parties per se would be created. The danger is that the national leaders, in order to build an ever more extensive base for their own operations, might take over, so far as possible, all existing state and local organizations. Such a development would clearly imply more than the death of the direct primary. To propose it raises very serious challenges to the federal pattern itself and to many real advances made in state and local governments during the past half century. Quite possibly, because of its widespread character the centralized type of bossism, even under the name of "party government," might be even more objectionable than the existing local bossism.

In view of the almost proverbial contempt in which many professional students of politics hold party machines, a word in their defense may appear unusual. Still, we need to reflect on the positive services they perform in terms of the organization of local voter interest; and we should also consider the extent to which the usual connotation of the term "politician," which has become almost an expletive, impedes a realistic understanding of the functional role the politician plays in the crystallization of political opinion and in the political process on the grass roots level generally. It is an open question whether greater responsibility of the political party to the voter is obtained by strengthening the internal chains of party command through closer adherence to an obligatory party platform. The role of the local leader also requires examination; for another belief seemingly held by the proponents of stronger parties is that the public will abandon the idea of the politician as a broker. It is urged that the public will prefer an automaton committed beyond all else to the party program, and thus will cast aside the traditional politician's role of middleman. The implications of this line of thought are far-reaching. What is being urged is nothing less than a revolutionary transformation in the role and function of the party, of the candidates, and of the electorate. . . .

"MEANINGFUL" PARTY PROGRAMS

Advocates of stronger parties also assume that pressure group activity is inferior to activity taken within the party itself. Strong parties are held to be the natural foes of pressure groups. But is the transference of pressure group activity into the party fundamentally compatible with the idea of *two* strong parties? There can be no doubt that such transference of influence is logically compatible with the existence of many *small* relatively fanatical parties. The farmers could organize a farmers' party; the veterans, educators, labor unions, and small businessmen could do the same. Such a development, however, is the antithesis of the strong *two-party* system which the proponents of more centralized parties are urging. The real choice is between a relatively weak two-party system with many outside interest groups or a very strong multi-party system with few nonpartisan interest groups. The latter development involves a fundamental reconstruction and reorientation of American socio-economic life which might easily threaten the stability of the Republic. This would be too high a price to pay for the subjugation of pressure groups. . . .

The proposal for greater party centralization is further justified by its proponents with the argument that public policy, both on the legislative and executive levels, is becoming increasingly national in character. It is held, therefore, that party policy, to be effective and responsible, must comply with this trend; that, as sectionalism as a conscious political interest is dying out in national life, party interest must follow the same trend. No one will deny the increasingly national scope of government responsibilities and obligations. Yet that does not necessarily mean an automatic and corresponding decline either of sectional interests or of regional and local political problems. If that were so, regional and local political concerns and interests would long since have declined in American life, spurred on during the last two wars when considerations of national strength and survival were paramount.

The question therefore arises whether the insistence upon greater national party organization and a more "national" scope of party platforms is based on the assumption (which the *Report* seems clearly to suggest) that party programs will be the more "meaningful" as they become more national in scope. It is perhaps this assumption which is the ultimate justification for the call for greater party discipline. Hypothetically, national party programs need not conflict with sectional interests. A program which is the result of compromise between sectional interests, or even between interest groups, is not necessarily less "meaningful" than a program aimed exclusively at the level of national policy. A foreign policy program *is* meaningful because it is concerned only with the national interest; but even and particularly there, we are conscious of the strength of domestic regional and group interests and of their influence upon the determination of policy. Does the strength of that influence *necessarily* make for national weakness? That it may contribute to an indeterminate foreign policy with lamentable frequency cannot be denied. But does the answer then lie in as radical a change of domestic political processes as is suggested? A growth of general political intelligence may well be a better and more convincing answer.

Perhaps the central question is simply whether democracy is best realized through strong parties ("strong" meaning highly disciplined) or by a strong electorate organized in a variety of ways, including political parties. Such a variety of organization may be an expression of democratic strength of a different kind, representing and expressing the variety of ideas and desires of a people as diverse and as active as are Americans. A further, if subsidiary and tactical, question which should not be ignored is whether *legislative* responsibility, which in this country is responsibility by *both* parties, would be actually increased by greater internal party responsibility and by two party programs. The latter may be sufficiently distinct to offer a "meaningful" choice, but would be bound to impede the kind of interparty agreements upon which the smooth functioning of Congress and of the state legislature depends. For "on its official side, the party is unitary; on its unofficial side, it is pluralistic. It is consensus while it tries *to create* consensus. Its success in America has depended on its maintaining the double role. . . ."

CHANGE IN VOTING BEHAVIOR?

The similarity between major party platforms has led many to believe that there is no difference between the major parties. The electorate, they argue, has no real choice; and, in any event, whatever choice a majority of the voters may make has little significance. However, various studies of voting behavior attest to a marked difference in social composition of the major parties in two-party areas. It would seem reasonable, in view of this difference, to expect that the performance of Congress would differ according to the party in control. In actual fact, the qualitative output in Congress varies considerably *over a period of time*. The Congresses of the Wilsonian and New Deal eras passed numerous great regulatory acts; yet few such acts were placed on the statute books during the period of "normalcy." In short, while the electorate may show a fairly high degree of party consistency, a sufficient percentage of the electorate changes its views from time to time so that legislative changes do, in fact, occur.

If the voters can influence changes in the tenor of congressional legislation at intervals, what may be said for the success of party leaders in attempting to accelerate such change through control over party personnel? Here again the comparative consistency of voting habits is relevant. The failure of the famous 1938 "purge" showed that Democratic voters generally preferred the primary candidate who was opposed by

President Roosevelt. The preference of the electorate for the present major parties *as they are,* is another important factor when considering the possibility of change in voting behavior. Public opinion polls show no great dissatisfaction with the present party system. The public generally adopts a negative attitude when the questions of reconstruction along liberal versus conservative lines or the creation of new parties are raised.

Proponents of stronger parties usually assume further that the public may be easily induced to prefer programs to personalities in particular elections. Both for the parties in and out of power, the prime objective is held to be the creation of specific programs. This assumption runs counter to existing practice. The fact that, over a period of time, the *tenor* of legislative acts will vary does not indicate that in specific elections the public supports or desires to support a specific *party* program. A study by Woodward and Roper [3] implies that personality is a very strong factor in determining the outcome of a given election. From the long-range point of view, Louis Bean [4] concludes that the trend of the business cycle is the most significant single factor in determining party control of the presidency and of Congress. Bean's study is concerned, of course, with party control, and not with qualitative differences in program. Yet both studies show how relatively insignificant is specificness of party program as a factor in existing voting behavior.

The demands upon the parties for more specific commitments to the electorate, the call for more definite national programs, for a perpetual state of preparedness to assume the burden and responsibility of the government, appear at first glance to be nothing but common sense. They are the heart of every criticism of the American party system. They imply, however, nothing short of a complete change of voting behavior. They may be "realistic" so far as efficiency in policy determination is a criterion, yet they are illusory as regards the disposition of the electorate. The question is how anxious are we to alter this disposition, even if such alteration were possible by some formula of social psychology. That disposition of the average voter has made possible the present system of constituent-representative relationship, which is one of remarkable closeness considering the size of the country and of the electoral districts. It has kept the voter close to and interested in the Government. It is that disposition which has made for a more tangible basis of popular government in this country—for a more "personal" basis, in several senses of the word—than would be possible by a system of increased

[3] Julian Woodward and Elmo Roper, "Political Activity of American Citizens," *The American Political Science Review,* Vol. XLIV:4 (December, 1950), pp. 872–885.
[4] Louis Bean, *How To Predict Elections* (New York, Alfred A. Knopf, 1948).

party control. The greater the party control, the more the legislator is bound to the "boys in the back room" rather than to the "boys on the front lawn."

DISCIPLINED PARTIES AND BIPARTISAN POLICY

Criticisms of the existing party system often imply that under a reconstructed and centralized system *the same party would normally control both executive and legislative departments*. The idea of fusion of executive and legislative departments through the instrumentality of party is basic to cabinet government. Such advocates of cabinet government as Elliott [5] and Hazlitt [6] have built a case largely upon the alleged unworkability of any system of a separation of powers. But in this study our concern is not with the case presented by the avowed advocates of cabinet government; it is rather with those who argue that greater party responsibility and centralization can be achieved without reckoning conclusively with the separation of powers principle.

Such an argument necessarily assumes that normally the same party will control both Congress and the presidency. Whether this is to be accomplished through the establishment of national party councils, coincidence of terms of office, or some other means, is not important. What is important is that, short of Constitutional amendment, there is no *guarantee* that the President and either house might not be of different parties. In terms of representation, the distinction between President and Congress is similar to that drawn by Rousseau in his comparison of the general will and the will of all. It is, of course, the latter which Congress now often represents. In any case, the proposals to establish party government would alter this pattern.

Let us hypothesize a very strong, disciplined party system in this country. Furthermore, let us imagine that for one reason or another the President and one or both houses represent different parties. What might be expected to occur in the highly important area of foreign affairs? Bipartisanship on foreign policy is often criticized on three principal grounds: First, that it is undemocratic in that the minority party by its acquiescence may contribute to its own demise; second, that it is immoral in that a totally false and misleading impression of national unity may be created; third, that it is incompatible with party government.

[5] William Y. Elliott, *The Need for Constitutional Reform* (New York, Whittlesey House, 1935).

[6] Henry Hazlitt, *A New Constitution Now* (New York, Whittlesey House, 1942). An excerpt from this book appears in *Basic Issues* under the title "Irresponsible Government."

It is the last charge which concerns us here and needs examination. Under our present party arrangement, with one or two exceptions the major parties have always co-operated in periods of external crisis. Co-operation was never a hundred per cent complete; but a working majority of each major party usually agreed with its counterpart as to the basic policies to be followed. Whatever opposition existed was likewise usually bipartisan; that is, it was not confined to a single party. A most significant demonstration of approval of bipartisan foreign policy, so obvious as often to be overlooked, occurred in the 1948 elections. Whatever else the presidential election of that year showed, it conclusively demonstrated support for Truman's "bipartisan" foreign policy by repudiating the proposals of Henry A. Wallace.

In principle, the proponents of party government are driven to the position that bipartisanship is per se an evil. They condemn the present practice where, instead of aligning themselves solidly on different sides of great policy issues, Senators and Representatives split into pro and con bipartisan blocs. Party allegiance becomes subordinate to sectional and regional interests.

Few would argue that such an arrangement is an unmixed blessing. On the credit side, however, it offers the tremendous advantage of very great flexibility. It does not suffer from the rigidity which the existence of a really strong, well-organized opposition party would entail. The basis of consensus is broad enough to allow for compromise and thus, among other things, plays down any process of aggrandizement by the President at the expense of Congress. Some critics of the existing system express the fear that our traditional form of government may break down as the result of a series of crises in which congressional inability to co-operate with the executive is followed by presidential dictatorship. These fears appear grossly exaggerated. Nevertheless, in the absence of cabinet responsibility under a parliamentary type of government, the prospect of a breakdown in democratic procedures would surely be aggravated rather than lessened by the existence of strongly disciplined and highly dedicated parties. If such a doctrinaire congressional-presidential impasse would be unfortunate in domestic affairs, it could conceivably be disastrous in the area of foreign policy.

President and Congress

THE OFFICE OF the president is now the most powerful, responsible, and difficult in the democratic world. Yet, the author of a classic study of the American party system, after observing our convention method of nominating candidates for the presidency and the considerations which controlled its action, characterized the process as "a colossal travesty of popular institutions." The correctness of M. Ostrogorski's appraisal is clearly a matter of importance. The issue is discussed by James Bryce, Harold Laski, and Pendleton Herring.

The gap between the Congress and the President has to some extent been bridged by political parties intent upon controlling all the branches of government. Nevertheless, as recent experience has shown, our system makes possible a President of one party and a Congress dominated by another. The result may be stalemate on important issues with responsibility difficult to establish. Furthermore, the role of the president in the legislative process, even when Congress is composed predominantly of members of his own party, is uncertain and varying.

Under these circumstances various measures to improve or even drastically alter legislative-executive relations have been advocated. Some critics of our form of government, like Henry Hazlitt, wish to create a system in America similar to British parliamentary government in order to concentrate power and responsibility, and minimize the possibility of stalemate. This view is challenged by Don K. Price, who emphasizes the great advantages of the American presidential system.

In specific relation to the powers of Congress, two issues which have commanded considerable attention in recent years are discussed: the uses and abuses of (1) the filibuster and (2) congressional investigations, particularly in regard to alleged subversion.

CHOOSING A PRESIDENT

※

Why Great Men Are Not Chosen President

JAMES BRYCE *

Europeans often ask, and Americans do not always explain, how it happens that this great office, the greatest in the world, unless we except the Papacy, to which any one can rise by his own merits, is not more frequently filled by great and striking men. In America, which is beyond all other countries the country of a "career open to talents," a country, moreover, in which political life is unusually keen and political ambition widely diffused, it might be expected that the highest place would always be won by a man of brilliant gifts. But from the time when the heroes of the Revolution died out with Jefferson and Adams and Madison, no person except General Grant, had, down till the end of last century, reached the chair whose name would have been remembered had he not been President, and no President except Abraham Lincoln had displayed rare or striking qualities in the chair. Who now knows or cares to know anything about the personality of James K. Polk or Franklin Pierce? The only thing remarkable about them is that being so commonplace they should have climbed so high.

Several reasons may be suggested for the fact, which Americans are themselves the first to admit. One is that the proportion of first-rate ability drawn into politics is smaller in America than in most European countries. This is a phenomenon whose causes must be elucidated later: in the meantime it is enough to say that in France, where the half-revolutionary conditions that lasted for some time after 1870 made public life exciting and accessible; in Germany, where an admirably-organized civil service cultivates and develops statecraft with unusual success; in England, where many persons of wealth and leisure seek to enter the political arena, while burning questions touch the interests of all classes and make men eager observers of the combatants, the total quantity of talent devoted to parliamentary or administrative work has been larger, relatively to the population, than in

* British Ambassador to the United States, 1907–1913. Formerly President of the American Political Science Association. Author of *The Holy Roman Empire, Modern Democracies, The American Commonwealth*, etc. The selection is from James Bryce, "Why Great Men Are Not Chosen President," *The American Commonwealth* (New York, The Macmillan Co., 1922–23), Vol. 1, Ch. 8. By permission.

America, where much of the best ability, both for thought and for action, for planning and for executing, rushes into a field which is comparatively narrow in Europe, the business of developing the material resources of the country.

Another is that the methods and habits of Congress, and indeed of political life generally, give fewer opportunities for personal distinction, fewer modes in which a man may commend himself to his countrymen by eminent capacity in thought, in speech, or in administration, than is the case in the free countries of Europe. . . .

A third reason is that eminent men make more enemies, and give those enemies more assailable points, than obscure men do. They are therefore in so far less desirable candidates. It is true that the eminent man has also made more friends, that his name is more widely known, and may be greeted with louder cheers. Other things being equal, the famous man is preferable. But other things never are equal. The famous man has probably attacked some leaders in his own party, has supplanted others, has expressed his dislike to the crochet of some active section, has perhaps committed errors which are capable of being magnified into offences. No man stands long before the public and bears a part in great affairs without giving openings to censorious criticism. Fiercer far than the light which beats upon a throne is the light which beats upon a presidential candidate, searching out all the recesses of his past life. Hence, when the choice lies between a brilliant man and a safe man, the safe man is preferred. Party feeling, strong enough to carry in on its back a man without conspicuous positive merits, is not always strong enough to procure forgiveness for a man with positive faults.

A European finds that this phenomenon needs in its turn to be explained, for in the free countries of Europe brilliancy, be it eloquence in speech, or some striking achievement in war or administration, or the power through whatever means of somehow impressing the popular imagination, is what makes a leader triumphant. Why should it be otherwise in America? Because in America party loyalty and party organization have been hitherto so perfect that any one put forward by the party will get the full party vote if his character is good and his "record," as they call it, unstained. The safe candidate may not draw in quite so many votes from the moderate men of the other side as the brilliant one would, but he will not lose nearly so many from his own ranks. Even those who admit his mediocrity will vote straight when the moment for voting comes. Besides, the ordinary American voter does not object to mediocrity. He has a lower conception of the qualities requisite to make a statesman than those who direct public opinion in Europe have. He likes his candidate to be sensible, vigorous, and, above all, what he calls "magnetic," and does not value, because he sees no need for, originality or profundity, a fine culture or a wide knowledge. Candidates are selected to be run for nomination by knots of persons who, however expert as party tacticians, are usually commonplace men; and the choice between those selected for nomination is made by a very large body, an assembly of nearly a thousand delegates from the local party organizations over the country, who are certainly no better than ordinary citizens. . . .

It must also be remembered that the merits of a President are one thing and those of a candidate another thing. An eminent American is reported to have said to friends who wished to put him forward, "Gentlemen, let there be no mistake. I should make a good President, but a very bad candidate." Now to a party it is more important that its nominee should be a good candidate than that he should turn out a good President. A nearer danger is a greater danger. As Saladin says in *The Talisman,* "A wild cat in a chamber is more dangerous than a lion in a distant desert." It will be a misfortune to the party, as well as to the country, if the candidate elected should prove a bad President. But it is a greater misfortune to the party that it should be beaten in the impending election, for the evil of losing national patronage will have come four years sooner. "B" (so reason the leaders), "who is one of our possible candidates, may be an abler man than A, who is the other. But we have a better chance of winning with A than with B, while X, the candidate of our opponents, is anyhow no better than A. We must therefore run A." This reasoning is all the more forcible because the previous career of the possible candidates has generally made it easier to say who will succeed as a candidate than who will succeed as a President; and because the wirepullers with whom the choice rests are better judges of the former question than of the latter.

After all, too, a President need not be a man of brilliant intellectual gifts. His main duties are to be prompt and firm in securing the due execution of the laws and maintaining the public peace, careful and upright in the choice of the executive officials of the country. Eloquence, whose value is apt to be overrated in all free countries, imagination, profundity of thought or extent of knowledge, are all in so far a gain to him that they make him "a bigger man," and help him to gain over the nation an influence which, if he be a true patriot, he may use for its good. But they are not necessary for the due discharge in ordinary times of the duties of his post. Four-fifths of his work is the same in kind as that which devolves on the chairman of a commercial company or the manager of a railway, the work of choosing good subordinates, seeing that they attend to their business, and taking a sound practical view of such administrative questions as require his decision. Firmness, common sense, and most of all, honesty, an honesty above all suspicion of personal interest, are the qualities which the country chiefly needs in its first magistrate.

So far we have been considering personal merits. But in the selection of a candidate many considerations have to be regarded besides the personal

merits, whether of a candidate, or of a possible President. The chief of
these considerations is the amount of support which can be secured from
different States or from different "sections" of the Union, a term by which
the Americans denote groups of States with a broad community of interest.
State feeling and sectional feeling are powerful factors in a presidential
election. The Middle West and Northwest, including the States from Ohio
to Montana, is now the most populous section of the Union, and therefore
counts for most in an election. It naturally conceives that its interests will
be best protected by one who knows them from birth and residence. Hence
prima facie a man from that section makes the best candidate. A large State
casts a heavier vote in the election; and every State is of course more likely
to be carried by one of its own children than by a stranger, because his
fellow-citizens, while they feel honoured by the choice, gain also a substantial advantage, having a better prospect of such favours as the administration can bestow. Hence, *cæteris paribus,* a man from a large State is
preferable as a candidate. The problem is further complicated by the fact
that some States are already safe for one or other party, while others are
doubtful. The Northwestern and New England States have usually tended
to go Republican; while nearly all of the Southern States have, since 1877,
been pretty certain to go Democratic. *Cæteris paribus,* a candidate from a
doubtful State, such as New York and Indiana have usually been, is to be
preferred.

Other minor disqualifying circumstances require less explanation. A
Roman Catholic, or an avowed disbeliever in Christianity, would be an
undesirable candidate. For many years after the Civil War, any one who
had fought, especially if he fought with distinction, in the Northern army,
enjoyed great advantages, for the soldiers of that army rallied to his name.
The two elections of General Grant, who knew nothing of politics, and
the fact that his influence survived the faults of his administration, are
evidence of the weight of this consideration. . . .

These secondary considerations do not always prevail. Intellectual ability
and strength of character must influence the choice of a candidate. When
a man has once impressed himself on the nation by force, courage, and
rectitude, the influence of these qualities may be decisive. They naturally
count for most when times are critical. Reformers declare that their weight
will go on increasing as the disgust of good citizens with the methods of
professional politicians increases. . . .

We may now answer the question from which we started. Great men
have not often been chosen Presidents, first because great men are rare in
politics; secondly, because the method of choice may not bring them to the
top; thirdly, because they are not, in quiet times, absolutely needed. Let us
close by observing that the Presidents, regarded historically, fall into three

periods, the second inferior to the first, the third rather better than the second.

Down till the election of Andrew Jackson in 1828, all the Presidents had been statesmen in the European sense of the word, men of education, of administrative experience, of a certain largeness of view and dignity of character. All except the first two had served in the great office of secretary of state; all were known to the nation from the part they had played. In the second period, from Jackson till the outbreak of the Civil War in 1861, the Presidents were either mere politicians, such as Van Buren, Polk, or Buchanan, or else successful soldiers, such as Harrison or Taylor, whom their party found useful as figureheads. They were intellectual pigmies beside the real leaders of that generation—Clay, Calhoun, and Webster. A new series begins with Lincoln in 1861. He and General Grant, his successor, who cover sixteen years between them, belong to the history of the world. Even the less distinguished Presidents of this period contrast favourably with the Polks and Pierces of the days before the war, if they are not, like the early Presidents, the first men of the country. If we compare the twenty Presidents who were elected to office between 1789 and 1900 with the twenty English prime ministers of the same period, there are but six of the latter, and at least eight of the former whom history calls personally insignificant, while only Washington, Jefferson, Lincoln, and Grant can claim to belong to a front rank represented in the English list by seven or possibly eight names. It would seem that the natural selection of the English parliamentary system, even as modified by the aristocratic habits of that country, had more tendency to bring the highest gifts to the highest place than the more artificial selection of America.

Crises Produce Great Presidents

HAROLD J. LASKI *

The big problem that is raised by the American method of nominating presidential candidates is whether it puts a premium, as Lord Bryce argued, against the opportunity of first-rate men to receive consideration. I do not think his case is proved by making a list of first-rate men, Clay and Calhoun and Webster, for example, who missed nomination. The answer to that

* Late Professor of Political Science at The London School of Economics. Formerly Chairman of the British Labor Party Executive Committee. Author of numerous books on politics including *Grammar of Politics, Democracy in Crisis, State in Theory and Practice,* and *The American Democracy.* This selection is from Harold J. Laski, *The American Presidency* (New York, Harper & Bros., 1940), pp. 49–53. Copyright, 1940, by Harper & Bros.

argument is, first, that many first-rate men have become president by reason of the system; and second, that the reasons which stopped others would have been powerful reasons against their elevation in any representative democracy. . . .

Granted, this is to say, the greatness of the prize, and the necessity of popular election, it is difficult to see what other method than the nominating convention is available; more, it is true to say that, on balance, it has worked well rather than badly. The criticisms that are brought against it are rather, in their real substance, criticisms of the place of the presidency in the American constitutional scheme than of the method whereby the president is chosen. It is regrettable that an inexperienced man may come to reside in the White House; the answer is that few of those who have reached it have been inexperienced men. If it be said that men like Harding and Coolidge were unfit for the great post they secured, the answer is that the first had considerable experience both in the Ohio legislature and in the Senate, while the second had been a successful Massachusetts politician, twice occupying the governorship, for twenty years. If we take the presidents of the twentieth century, there is not one who had not been prepared for presidential office by a long experience of politics. . . .

It must be remembered that, in making the choice, there are two fundamental considerations in the background of which the meaning of "availability" must be set. The first is that the party choosing a candidate wants, if it can, to win; and second, it knows that if it does win, and its nominee becomes president, there is great likelihood of its having to adopt him a second time, since not to do so is to condemn an Administration for which it has to bear responsibility. While, therefore, it is quite true that a party convention provides an opportunity for the art of such a dubious wire-puller as Mr. Daugherty, it is also true that the managers of a great party are anxious to avoid, if they can, the consequences of success in that type of manipulation. . . .

All in all, I doubt whether the methods of the system are very different from those of other countries. They are, perhaps, more open and crude than in Great Britain. There is no generosity in the fight for power. There is a passionate determination on the part of organized interests to get the "safe" man who can be relied upon to live up to the commitments exacted from him. There is the fierce conflict of rival ambitions. There is the organization of every sort of cabal to win a victory for its man. Press and radio and platform are vigorously manipulated to this end. Immense promises are made, pretty ugly deals are effected. Yet I suggest that anyone who knows the life of a political party from within Great Britain will not feel inclined to cast a stone at the American system. It fits, well enough, the medium in which it has to work. It achieves the results that the needs of the people require.

For there is at least one test of the system that is, I think, decisive. There have been five considerable crises in American history. There was the need to start the new republic adequately in 1789; it gave the American people its natural leader in George Washington. The crisis of 1800 brought Jefferson to the presidency; that of 1861 brought Abraham Lincoln. The War of 1914 found Woodrow Wilson in office; the great depression resulted in the election of Franklin Roosevelt. So far, it is clear, the hour has brought forth the man. It is of course true, as Bagehot said, that "success in a lottery is no argument for lotteries." I agree that no nation can afford a succession of what Theodore Roosevelt termed "Buchanan Presidents"—men whose handling of the issues is uncertain and feeble. But the answer is that the nation has never had that succession; an epoch of Hardings and Coolidges produces, by the scale of the problems to which it gives rise, its own regeneration. The weak president, as I have argued, comes from the fact that a strong predecessor has set the feet of the nation on level ground. He is chosen because, after a diet of strong occasions, a nation, like an individual, turns naturally to the chance of a quiet time. "Normalcy" is always certain to be popular after crises. The issue is whether, when crisis comes, the system can discover the man to handle it. On the evidence, this has so far been very remarkably the case. To urge that it is chance is, I think, a superficial view. It is the outcome of the national recognition that energy and direction are required, and the man chosen is the party response to that recognition. . . . The more deeply we penetrate the working of the system the more clearly does it emerge that the result is inherent in its nature.

The Uses for National Conventions

PENDLETON HERRING *

The usefulness of our national nominating conventions has at times seemed obscure. Most of the criticism of party conventions grows out of the belief that they are held to discuss policy as well as to nominate candidates. Such a belief misinterprets the structure of our party system. . . . The behavior of any organization must be interpreted in the light of the elements that compose it if any understanding is to be achieved. To expect bands of local chieftains and their henchmen to come together and act as

* Director Social Science Research Council. Formerly Professor of Government, Harvard University, and Professor, Harvard Graduate School of Public Administration. Author of *Group Representation Before Congress, Public Administration and the Public Interest, Presidential Leadership,* and other works. The selection is from Pendleton Herring, *The Politics of Democracy: American Parties in Action* (New York, Rinehart & Co., Inc., 1940), Ch. 16. By permission of the publisher.

a deliberative national unit once every four years is to expect the impossible.

Our conventions could be orderly if they were the apex of a well-organized hierarchy. The most dignified, orderly, and impressive assembly for selecting an individual for a high office is the College of Cardinals. Even this august assembly is not without its political undercurrents, but it can function with its unexampled success because it is the final expression of a remarkably well-disciplined body. . . .

Our political parties are built not on the rock of faith but rather on the broad mud flats of popular desires and individual ambitions. The party convention is no better than the loose and undisciplined local and state organizations that send their delegates to bargain. If we cannot do much to change these underlying factors the question then is to consider anew what can be done with the materials at hand.

Judged as strictly rational and intellectual performances, these huge assemblies are flat failures; but are they to be measured by such standards?

Let us first hear some of the critics. No recent writer is more outspoken than Herbert Agar. He states that "the position of the average delegate at a national convention has neither dignity nor sense." "Never a wholly adequate device, the nomination convention," he says, "is now an anachronism." He deplores the absence of serious discussion of public problems and the "atmosphere of lightminded carousal." This comes in for heartiest condemnation. "The delegates even showed signs of being ashamed of their own immoderate antics. They wondered whether the way to run a great political party is to get drunk and ride donkeys into hotel lobbies. . . . They knew they ought to be doing serious work. Yet there was no serious work to do, so they took refuge in idiocy." The author quotes Milton on the noises of Hell and concludes that conventions are worse. Agar's reaction is that of a cultured and sensitive man who evidently does not enjoy rough-housing. He would feel equally ill at ease at an American Legion convention or a conclave of the Elks.

Many of us would certainly prefer to see conventions less noisy, more thoughtful and "full of argument and heart-searching and high seriousness." My purpose here, however, is not to exhort delegates to be sober and meditative, but rather to raise the question as to whether a convention is primarily an intellectual activity. . . .

The attention of commentators has been focused most eloquently on sins of omission. The following views of Lord Bryce serve as a classic critique upon the shortcomings of the party convention:

> It goes without saying that such a meeting is capable neither of discussing political questions and settling a political programme, nor of deliberately weighing the merits of rival aspirants for the nomination. Its programme must be presented to it cut and dry, and this is the work of a small committee. In

choosing a candidate, it must follow a few leaders. And what sort of leaders do conventions tend to produce? Two sorts—the intriguer and the declaimer. . . . For men of wisdom and knowledge, not seconded by a commanding voice and presence, there is no demand, and little chance of usefulness, in these tempestuous halls. . . . Large popular gatherings . . . are excitable in virtue of their size. . . . A national convention . . . is the hugest mass meeting the world knows of. . . . The struggle in a convention is over men, not over principles.

Such a sweeping denunciation hardly stands close scrutiny. The men influential in "these tempestuous halls" are the same men who serve as political leaders in Congress and the state governments. A huge mass meeting cannot be judged by its incapacity to perform tasks appropriate to a small committee. Unless we are to substitute for the convention a small executive council, we must accept the characteristics resulting from size. Moreover, its positive qualities are worthy of our respect. It is an indigenous institution and can be best evaluated with respect to our own peculiar needs.

What has our experience with national party conventions demonstrated their basic purpose to be? It is to find a man whom a majority of the voters will agree to support.

Farley has given us a perfect picture of the professional politician's attitude toward the selection of a candidate. On his way to the Elks' convention Farley called upon the national Committeeman of South Dakota, Bill Howe. Farley relates:

> . . . We sat in a lunchroom at Aberdeen on a roasting-hot day. Bill was a canny politician who had been in the game for years; he knew it backward and forward. We sat there for some time, exchanging generalities, without disclosing what either of us really had in mind. Just before it was time to go, Bill plumped his fat fist on the table and growled in a deep voice, "Farley, I'm damn' tired of backing losers. In my opinion, Roosevelt can sweep the country, and I'm going to support him."

The desire to find a winner and thereby help the ticket back home is a force of no small importance. The primary task of the delegates is to find a winning candidate. The convention is designed to unite diverse sections and rival leaders behind a man, and to whip up the enthusiasm of party workers to fight for his election. This involves not questions of public policy but problems of party strategy. In view of the rivalries, the frank self-seeking, and the bitter jealousies arising in our party conventions, the ultimate adjustment almost invariably reached is a triumph of popular government.

The value of the convention lies in its permitting the rank and file of the party to participate physically and emotionally in a common enterprise. Here are the men who must carry the brunt of the campaign. Here they have their chance to meet, to shout together, to act together, to feel together. The excitement and the turmoil of the convention fulfill a useful purpose. The relationship of follower and leader is seldom an intellectual bond. A common bond of sympathy, a common symbol, is easily grasped and equally binding.

The party convention places a premium on party harmony. It reveals in a beating glare of publicity any thin spots and holes in the party fabric. Hence the impetus of the whole procedure is toward agreement. Prolonged dispute is greatly feared. As William G. McAdoo explained to the 1932 convention, when shifting the California delegation to Roosevelt: "Sometimes in major operations where skillful surgery is required, the life of the patient may be destroyed if there is unnecessary delay. We believe, therefore, that California should take a stand here tonight that will bring this contest to a swift and, we hope, satisfactory conclusion—a stand, we hope, which will be promotive of party harmony." A convention must try to unify a party not inherently unified. Its purpose is not to examine intellectual differences but to seek terms of agreement. When differences cannot be reconciled, the politicians seek unity in the face of disagreement. A party convention offers them the opportunity to negotiate and human materials with which to work.

As just noted, the basic function of the convention is to focus national attention upon the task of selection that is going forward, and then to align the regular party politicians behind a man who will lead them to victory. To do this the methods must be such as to attract and hold the attention of the great mass of citizens. Experience indicates that prizefights, football games, and similar sporting spectacles have characteristics that please the populace. Debating societies have a more limited following. The intellectually inclined may view this as an unfortunate situation. If a political spectacle is the way to arouse public attention, that is reason enough for the average politician.

The party convention may likewise be viewed as an excellent implement for compromise. Compromise in politics is not achieved simply through argumentation. The process entails bargaining and manipulation as well. There are various levels and types of compromise. To reach such peaceful adjustments of interest requires an area for movement and something with which to trade and barter. The party convention creates a human situation and provides scope under general rules of the game for elaborate inter-relationships. Here concessions of many types can be made and victories in various terms are possible. The range of satisfactions is great, and disappointment on one count may be compensated for on another. There must be something wherewith to compromise. . . .

No one would think of planning an industrial development, an army campaign, or an educational program by devices similar to a party convention. No one can accurately regard our conventions as deliberative or planning agencies. Our conventions are a romantic and flamboyant attempt to get a high degree of popular participation in the high drama of democracy. It is not an institution to be dismissed contemptuously because of its noise and apparent confusion. It is characteristic of our free political system; the Nazis had pageantry of a different sort. Those who prefer order found it at Nuremberg.

There is much that is not heroic in our system. The heroic mold has seemed ill suited to the peaceful routine of minding one's own business and working for a living. If we are approaching more dangerous times we will have less use for negative candidates selected because they came from the tactically important states with large electoral votes. Our easygoing, rough-and-tumble politics of compromise and barter may give way to a more efficient and effective control from the top. The demands made upon government may force our political parties to attempt a more authoritarian line. There would be no point in carefully devising a program unless the party leaders were determined to carry it through. This would entail sanctions to make such power effective. Our party conventions have sought not the strongest or wisest candidate but rather the man who would best serve to unite the party and attract the voters. This is one consequence of treating the presidency as a symbol as well as a job.

A party convention is a parley of state bosses accompanied by their henchmen carrying with them local jealousies and favoritisms. A convention might possibly become a meeting dominated by a clique of politicians in command of a national machine. Instead of selecting a compromise candidate, they might decide to put before the country their strong man who would—through all the arts of persuasion—be sold to the public as the leader.

The party convention is not an inappropriate device for serving our present purposes. In fact, it is admirably suited to testing the talents of our politicians. It demands organizational skill and manipulative genius—both of which qualities are exceedingly useful in democratic government. . . .

Much more can and should be done to give men of reason and knowledge a more strategic position within the party structure. Parties can aid in the political education of their own membership. Questions of public policy must now be thought of in national and even international terms. This means that the inadequacies of the local politician become more evident. Social and economic necessities push us forward in demanding more intelligence in the conduct of political affairs. Yet we would be shortsighted indeed if we placed our faith in the expert as the only man with the answer. The party convention is one institutional expression of human beings competing by their wits and emotions for some of the prizes available under popular government.

Topic 22

CAN PRESIDENTIAL GOVERNMENT DO THE JOB?

❧

The Solitary President

HERMAN FINER *

The constitutional convention desired to secure an unmistakable focus of responsibility and avoid confusion; and to encourage vigor and despatch in judgment and decision. The weak colonial governors were in disfavor. Hence no plural or collective executive, like a cabinet or council of ministers, was established, though it must never be forgotten that a multiple executive was proposed only to be dropped for reasons not fully reported in the records of the convention.

All constitutional responsibility is focused on one man and one man alone. The constitution even provides for his impeachment. The consequences are interesting and dangerous.

No collective responsibility in a group of men equal in status, with perhaps some ascendency in a prime minister, was sought. None has developed. Something called the President's cabinet, always including the ten departmental heads and usually others, was evolved. Yet, in reality, no cabinet exists, in the sense of a constitutionally responsible multiheaded council for the exercise of the chief executive's power. The cabinet is a mere collection of Presidential minions, "clerks" as they have been called. The President's will is supreme, whatever they may advise, because his responsibility is sole and plenary. Indeed, it is rare that the cabinet is called together; rarer still that it discusses major issues; and practically never that it makes a corporate decision. The President makes up his own mind, whatever the votes—when, indeed, votes are taken.

The talk of a cabinet, then, is specious: it is a cabinet at a meeting to hold conversations, perhaps at times to deliberate, but hardly ever to create a collective will that shall govern all including the President. The President

* Professor of Political Science, University of Chicago. Formerly Lecturer on Political Science, London School of Economics. Author of *British Civil Service, America's Destiny, Theory and Practice of Modern Government,* and many other works. The selection is from Herman Finer, *The Theory and Practice of Modern Government,* Revised Edition, pp. 671–681, 703. By permission of Henry Holt & Co., Inc. Copyright, 1949.

floats above it, and aloof. He is not merged in a team; he is detached.

Though business may be distributed, partly by the Presidential wish and his general executive power, and partly by statutes of Congress which vest various administrative powers in the several heads of departments, no real sharing of authority occurs. . . .

Every President is personally liable to be smitten in conscience, self-respect, and political reputation, by the boomerang of his own delegation of authority; responsibility—that is, punishability—is inescapable. He distributes business, or Congress does, but, whoever acts, he alone takes political responsibility. He therefore is careful not to devolve authority, which still attaches to him. It is always only a distribution of business. For whatever may be the actual demonstrable errors of his cabinet heads, political blame will come back to him. The President takes the greatest political risk in surrendering some of his authority into the keeping of others. If he is a conscientious man, this is a painful strain on him. He is torn between the impulse not to share power with others, though he has so crushing a burden himself, and the impulse to give it and then feel that unless he watches its use closely, Congress and public opinion will make him smart with blame. Congress may have given power and responsibility to a departmental chief, provided him with funds, instructed and encouraged him at its hearings, yet, since the President bears responsibility for executive competence, he cannot find relief from departmental concern, for he cannot cut the knot the constitution has tied.

It is an impossible burden. And, in fact, it cannot be borne in a governmental system so widely and deeply active as the American of the twentieth century is obliged to be. Too much responsibility paralyzes the will, for the imagined consequences are too fearful. An excessively concentrated accountability causes incomplete devolution of work to subordinate agencies, and a process of frantic intrusions and exits, by the chief executive, in the alternations between relief and accumulating anxiety. When the President is a weak man—which by the bargaining, contractual, almost casual, nature of the forces producing a nomination, he is liable at any moment to be—the pitiable man is reduced to a frightened whistling for courage, and policy to collapse.

The constitution and its conventional apparatus have provided him with no one he can fully trust; no one to lend him acceptable and dependable counsel; no one to encourage him with the sincerity that comes when a colleague's political fate is bound up with the results of the encouragement he gives. How much easier is the British cabinet minister's task, and how much lighter the prime minister's, even though the latter's power is not reduced and limited by any federal division of power, or checks and balances, or the exclusion of some matters from governmental jurisdiction altogether, as under the United States constitution.

It is not to be wondered that Presidents have been obliged to set up "kitchen cabinets" and "brain trusts" and "Assistant Presidents." . . . Instead of decision by cabinet, we have decision by tête-a-tête. Notice how on the death of one President, and the succession of the Vice-President of that same party, the former's departmental chiefs flee Washington, while the new chief executive brings in his own "gang." Frances Perkins's description of the Roosevelt cabinets fits the stories of previous Presidencies and corroborates that given verbally to the present author by other members of Roosevelt administrations.

> But as the years went on, Roosevelt's cabinet administration came to be like most previous ones—a direct relationship between a particular cabinet officer and the President in regard to his special field, with little or no participation or even information from other cabinet members. Certainly almost no "cabinet agreements" were reached. . . .

The effect of the last man in to see the President is most often decisive. The disputant who appears at the White House, as contrasted with the other man who stayed away, wins a superior influence. Cabinet members take deliberate care to safeguard their departmental concerns from cabinet discussion, with mutual understandings for suppression. One of those especially trusted by the President lunches with him weekly. Here is a fortuitous assemblage of regional, local, sectional, vocational, and "party" chieftains, each with his own fief; some, but few, with broad views of policy; some, but not all, loyal to the President's person and comprehending the import of his policy. They have come into politics for a time; they do not expect to stay; they will retire soon because they are sick or disagree with the President or are merely unwilling to shoulder an unprofitable burden or wish to repair their fortunes in their private business. Or they will cling to office, despite disagreement with the President, useful or not to the public welfare, and the President will not eject them as early as the public good demands because he may offend the chieftain's followers or clients, and so lose support in Congress or popular votes if he contemplates a second term.

Yet there is still a drawback: the President cannot wholly trust them. For they may involve him in trouble, and they are behind-the-scenes operators. In that case, what becomes of the Philadelphia Convention's desire to secure an indubitable locus of responsibility? The President is still "responsible," but it is a nominal responsibility. His backstairs mentors have not been tracked down and punished, or pilloried before an electorate which may make him or them or his party suffer for misgovernment at the next election. A cabinet on the British and even on the Continental model constitutes the principal part of the executive: there is little in the kitchen (I do not say "nothing"): there are enough advisers to render a "kitchen" unnecessary: the overt cabinet is the group, as a group, to be held to responsibility.

This element of solitary, and not plural, responsibility is the plague spot of the American constitution in the twentieth century. All remedial gadgets must break against its insidious obstinacy. For above all, it destroys from the beginning to the end the possibility of coordinating the work of policy making and administration that has been distributed, and the various work of the agencies and departments and commissions set up by statute. No one man can coordinate so much with so little. Nor can one man, with this unique responsibility, take advantage of the technical and personal devices which from time to time have been proposed and even established to assist him to coordinate the vast proliferation of executive bodies. For we revert always to *his* responsibility, his pride, and his conscience. . . .

When a President is swamped with responsibility he is, paradoxically, tempted to "off-the-cuff" decisions, for how can he genuinely let his duty invade him? The amount of business is beyond one man's capacity or conscience. One solitary man must, surely, look for short cuts. The President needs help, as the Committee on Administrative Management declared; but he needs the help of a dozen or fifteen men, good and true, who bear a direct responsibility *with* him (not *to* him) to the public and the party and the Congress. . . .

The Presidency needs to be put into commission. It needs distribution among fifteen equals, each of whom is fully the master and the servant of his own portion of responsibility and of all common policy which comes to them as a collective unity. You can coordinate if you have divided; you can divide if you can trust; you can trust if you alone are not saddled with all responsible decision. To apply a famous dictum of de Tocqueville's, used by him to describe the centralization of the *ancien régime* in France: when you centralize in a solitary President, you risk apoplexy at the center and anæmia at the extremities, or a red face and palsied hands. Nor is that all: if no full authority can be granted a departmental chief, how is one to induce men of stature to seek office and stay there?

All these proposed administrative gadgets may well help a little on lesser matters, and even that is to be much applauded. But every gadget calls for another gadget to stop up the still-existing leak, *ad infinitum*. Still, the reservoir of responsibility is so high and heavy that it will flood the channels made for it: what is needed is one collective reservoir and its sharing among a dozen or more interconnected basins, with free circulation among them all. The proposed reforms still leave the President high and dry, for they still leave him responsible for too much.

Nor is this all. The heads of departments are granted authority and are saddled with responsibility for their department by laws made in Congress. It has been found impossible to stop them from appealing to Congress for the funds and the legislation to implement their departmental policy, whether or not that conflicts with the President's. Close observers admit in desperation that independent staff work for the President (for example, especially through the Bureau of the Budget) may do much to enforce regulations and controls and prepare long-range plans, but *cannot* build up a unified program of policy and legislation.

Indeed, as one contemplates the collection of incongruous personalities in American cabinets from the beginning, but more especially since the end of the nineteenth century, it is ridiculous to mention the word "party." They are usually appointed because they have or are supposed to have some special interest or expertness in the field of that department—Henry Wallace in Agriculture, and then in Commerce; Jesse Jones in the Reconstruction Finance Corporation; Clinton Anderson in Agriculture; Henry Morgenthau, Jr., in the Treasury (because Mr. Roosevelt had a personal faith in him); Chester Bowles in price administration; Frances Perkins in labor welfare; or Wilson Wyatt as housing administrator, and so on. They are opinionated men; their natural pride is not moderated by party loyalty and solidarity with their chief executive. Their loyalties are divided between the President and their own department; they may sway between the President and Congress; they are torn between their own personal ideas and those of the President.

The memoirs of Sumner Welles, Raymond Moley, and Cordell Hull combined throw an authentic and tragic light on incoherence and mismanagement of foreign policy from 1933 to Pearl Harbor. The Pearl Harbor Report reveals a want of alert coherence between White House, the Secretaries of State, War, and Navy, and the Chiefs of Staff, with some proper blame on the first, or, more reasonably, on the system. Other studies throw light on the lack of solidarity at the center—fumbling in the formation of policy, and stumbling and staggering in its fulfillment.

Even with so potent and clever a President as Franklin Delano Roosevelt as compared with . . . Harry S. Truman, the President needs twelve or fifteen men of his own stature, of equal responsibility with him, equal in accepting party leadership and loyalty. And he and they need the ever-operative assistance of some sixty career men, heading the departments permanently, under the political secretaries—the cream of the crop of an "administrative group" of perhaps 10,000 or 12,000 at all ages on the scale from cadets to mature men and women, to be their advisers, their staff, their arms of administration. All need a Congress organized for, and alert regarding, its function of making collective and unified the policy of the scattered elements of the administration, by everyday, regular, organized, public criticism. Pearl Harbors, domestic as well as foreign, may be avoided where a collective fifteen are responsible, and where the Congressional five hundred badger them with relentless questions. . . .

The lack of a central *thinking,* focusing body of advisers at the top is acknowledged by observer after observer of the Washington apparatus of government, however reluctant in the beginning they may be to admit any deficiencies in the American constitution. . . .

In the British system of government, and even perhaps in the French, though it is weaker, the unintermittent merging of executive and legislature, the ever-continuing life in each other's physical presence, is some assurance of the unison of mind which leads to a unison of guesswork, and therefore to a sharing of responsibility for policy. It enables a measured trust in the executive that purges a peevish demand for "all the facts." The United States President is, on the other hand, compelled to face the task of correct inference from uncertain premises alone—this is a burden of all governments, everywhere, and at all times in human history. It is a dreadful burden for a solitary man, even if assisted by a few faithful friends, to bear alone. Accompanying it is a twin burden: that the knowledge of the facts and the consequent guesses must be carried forward in a state of tentativeness and uncertainty, in a condition merely of temporary probability and yet of possible final certainty, in face of a clamant people anxious to learn what sacrifices, what burdens, what happiness or unhappiness the future holds in store for them, and a people also, to whom the President owes an accounting. Particularly when the horror of war or the misery of depression is being faced is it difficult, as electorates now are, to release the secrets of fact and conjecture, when this may mean undeliberate, emotional behavior by popular groups, which would not occur later when time and events have ripened and made concrete the surmises which the statesman is obliged to nurse. The President is in a position where he can see much further than most people in the nation, even than the most enlightened publicists, but he is in a position where he must not talk as much as undutiful ones. He must bide his time, suffer the criticism until the day of reckoning, and hope that his prophetic thinking is sound enough to redeem his repute because it served his people.

Irresponsible Government

HENRY HAZLITT *

Once we have recognized the vices of our form of government, we must act to remove them. This does not mean a generation hence, or in the next

* Associate Editor of *Newsweek.* Formerly editorial writer for *The New York Times.* Author of *Thinking as a Science, Instead of Dictatorship, Economics in One Lesson,* etc. The selection is from Henry Hazlitt, *A New Constitution Now* (New York, Whittlesey House, 1942), Ch. XIV, pp. 277–286. Reprinted by permission of the publisher.

decade, or next year. We must begin *now*. . . . We cannot afford deliberately to handicap ourselves by adhering to a form of government that
we recognize to be dangerously inefficient or unreliable in a crisis.

What is the central vice of our form of government? In a single word,
it is *irresponsible*. All its chief defects come back to this. Either they are
forms of irresponsibility, or they promote it. We arbitrarily separate the
legislature and the executive. We choose each in such a way that there is
no assurance that they will want the same policies—indeed, often in such
a way that it is almost certain that they will want different policies. Congress can prevent the President from doing what he wishes, but cannot
make him do what it wishes. The President, through his veto power, can
usually prevent Congress from doing as it wishes unless its desired policy
is almost unanimous. He needs only the support of "a third plus one" in
one House of the legislature to stop Congress from adopting a policy.
Moreover, if he does not like a law that Congress adopts, he may enforce
it either very feebly or in such a way as to make it seem obnoxious. If the
President wishes any positive action from Congress, he must usually get his
way, as Harold Laski has put it, "very largely by the use of patronage—
about as undesirable a method of persuasion as the imagination can conceive." The Senate, again—indeed, a single Senate committee chairman
unknown to the public—may through negative vote or mere inaction absolutely veto even the unanimous will of the House of Representatives.

The result is hopelessly to confuse the public regarding whom to hold
responsible for a policy or for failure to adopt a policy. The public must
wait perhaps through years of deadlock and paralysis to decide the question by its vote; and assuming even then that it knows *how* to decide, it may
be powerless to decide. It cannot change whom it wishes when it wishes.
It cannot change the government, or the government's policies, at any one
election. At one election it can change the House of Representatives but
not the President; so that even if it strongly disapproves of the President's
policies it must nevertheless either endorse those policies or create a stalemate. At no election can it change more than one-third of the Senate. And
if the voters of the whole country are almost unanimous in their opposition,
say, to the influential foreign policies of the chairman of the Senate Foreign
Relations Committee (who gets his position, not by the free choice of his
colleagues, but by seniority), they are powerless to do anything about it.
Only the voters of a single State—the State from which the Senator comes
(at the moment of writing, Texas, representing less than 5 per cent of the
total voting population), are ever consulted on that question, and then only
once in six years.

All this makes for government irresponsibility of the most shocking kind.
The only cure is the adoption of the principle of *concentration of responsibility*. This, as Ramsay Muir has pointed out, is the essential principle of

the British Constitution, as contrasted with the *separation of powers* which is still the basic principle of the American Constitution.

Since the attack on Pearl Harbor the American public has been brought to recognize how disastrous can be the consequences of failure to fix and concentrate responsibility, even in the lower echelons of command. The Pearl Harbor disaster itself, in which the war was nearly lost in a day, was in large part owing, as the Roberts Commission report made clear, to the failure to concentrate responsibility for the defense of Pearl Harbor. Authority was divided between the Army and Navy commanders there; neither seemed to know exactly where his responsibility began or ended: neither was under obligation to consult with the other regarding the question; and so neither, apparently, condescended to consult the other. When the *Normandie,* the greatest shipping prize in the hands of the American Government, was burned at its pier through inexcusable carelessness, an investigation by Congress revealed no one whose authority had been so unmistakably fixed in advance that he could be held clearly responsible for the disaster. When Congress tried to find who was responsible for the Government's failure to build up a great stock pile of rubber and to begin effective steps to encourage synthetic production, it was confronted by more efforts to shift responsibility. At the time of writing there is no way to determine who was responsible for the failure to have sufficient air power at the Philippines or to protect that air power from almost instant destruction. Even the broadest facts necessary to form a judgment have been withheld from the public.

If these are the results of failure to fix and concentrate responsibility at lower levels, what must be said of our national failure to fix and concentrate responsibility at the very top? American officeholders are in the habit of using the word "responsibility" very loosely. They often declare roundly that they "take full responsibility" for this or that step; but they fail to recognize the implications of their statement. Responsibility implies, in public life, *accountability;* and real accountability implies *immediate removability*. There is no other political way in which responsibility can be made effective. We make a general in the field responsible in two ways: we give him the men, the equipment, the help and the full authority he asks for; we honor him for his success; and we remove him for his failure. So it should be with our political leaders. We should not place in power with them other men who conceive it to be their duty or function to obstruct them at every turn. We should clothe them with real authority for positive as well as negative action. But if they fail to carry out the wishes of the people, then the people, without long or disastrous delays, should be able to remove them.

Because America does not follow this policy, its public thought is hopelessly and chronically confused. We sink into endless argument over points that in England could not be the subject of argument at all. Who was responsible for American unpreparedness? This was a subject of dispute in the Presidential election of 1940 and has been since. We "analyze" the votes of Republicans and Democrats on a score or more of bills. In practically no case do we find a solid vote of Republicans opposed to a solid vote of Democrats; we decide in each case by comparing the percentage division of the vote within each party. (The Republicans alone, in fact, could not at any time have blocked a single [Roosevelt] "Administration" measure. Whenever the majority of Republicans was successful, it was through the aid of recalcitrant Democrats.) Who was responsible for the original Neutrality Bill? Was the President "forced" to sign this against his judgment? Who blocked the proposal for the fortification of Guam? What defense appropriations were the Republicans mainly responsible for blocking? What of the defense appropriations that the President never even asked for? What attitude *would* the Republicans have taken, or would "Congress" have taken, if these appropriations *had* been asked for?

Few questions of this sort could ever arise in England, or in any country with a sound cabinet government. The Prime Minister or a member of his Cabinet would state his preparedness policy and ask for his appropriation. If Parliament refused that appropriation, or attempted to cut it down, or tried to pass any neutrality bill in spite of "the Government's" wishes, the Prime Minister could announce that the vote was a vote of confidence and could resign or dissolve Parliament if it failed to meet his wishes. The public would never have the slightest doubt as to where responsibility lay. It might have the opportunity then and there, in fact, to decide between the Prime Minister and the parliamentary majority, if the two disagreed, and to make unmistakably known its own ideas of what the proper policy should be. *That* is responsible government.

It is a defect of the presidential system not merely that it scatters responsibility within the government itself among separate agencies insulated from each other, but that it has no organized opposition. This may seem a strange defect to complain of; nevertheless, it is a real and a serious one. "He who wrestles with us," wrote Burke, "strengthens our nerves, and sharpens our skill. Our antagonist is our helper." A good opposition forces a government to improve itself.

When there is no organized opposition, the criticism of the government's policies is the random and sporadic criticism of individuals as such. They are all saying different things; most of them are ill informed; they are only a babble of voices; they are likely to sound like mere carpers and scolders; and the public is confused. One criticism is often the opposite of another. The government seizes upon this fact, argues that the two criticisms cancel out, and that they prove it must be doing a good job. When individual Congressmen of the opposite party speak only for themselves, each says only those particular things that he thinks will help toward his own reelection in his own district. Criticism under presidential government is commonly aimless, moreover, because except at fixed intervals of four years no immediate result can follow from it.

But under a cabinet form of government the opposition is as organized as the government itself. It has a chosen leader. That leader is its spokesman. That leader must consult his colleagues, just as the premier must, and formulate a responsible program of criticism. The criticism is that of a party eager to prove that it is itself able to take over the government, if need be, at once. The leader of the opposition must therefore forego trivial and carping criticisms, which merely confuse the public, and concentrate on those issues that are centrally important. He must propose some constructive alternative to the course that he condemns. The criticism by an organized opposition, in brief, is not scattered and self-contradictory, but unified and consistent. The public is educated by this clarity. The opposition can itself help to frame issues. It can force the government to take a position on them. In Britain these vital functions are acknowledged. "His Majesty's Opposition" is recognized to be an integral part of the governmental system.

Responsibility, I have said, implies immediate removability. By that I mean immediate removability either of the chief executive himself, or of those in the legislature whose votes have effectively opposed him. It is not difficult to see why this must be so. If the executive's opponents in the legislature cannot be immediately removed by the people, they can continue to oppose his will and make it impossible for him fully to carry out his policies. In that case he cannot be held clearly responsible if the results are bad. If the chief executive himself, on the other hand, cannot be immediately removed when he is unable or unwilling to carry out the popular will, then the people in the interim before removal have a government that is not responsible to them because they cannot reach it. The absence of this immediate removability perverts public thought, for when the people know in advance that they cannot change their executive even when they are dissatisfied with him, they hesitate to hold him clearly responsible for his errors lest they discredit him at home and abroad and bring about a situation of mere chaos.

So difficult has it been under our system to fix responsibility, and so reluctant has the public been even to try to fix responsibility for disaster on men in high places whom it has no means of removing, that a strange doctrine has been preached in America. This doctrine tells us that we were "all of us responsible" for our general unpreparedness, for the loss of the Philippines, or for the disaster at Pearl Harbor. It is not necessary here to try to weigh elaborately the pros and cons of this remarkable contention. It is sufficient to notice that the notion of *universal* responsibility in such a context is a "non-operational" concept. That is to say, it is meaningless for practical action; nothing can be done with it.

The dictionary tells us that responsible means *answerable;* this implies answerable *to* someone. A whole people cannot be operationally answerable to themselves. They cannot replace themselves. They cannot resign, if only because they do not know what to resign *from.* The notion of universal responsibility, in short, is in this context operationally meaningless. It is a vague rhetorical mumble jumble in place of realistic analysis. The notion of the responsibility of specific officials, on the other hand, makes sense. It is an operational concept: one can act on it. If a specific official does well, he can be applauded, promoted or reelected; if he does badly, he can be removed and replaced by someone else who we hope will do better. That is what responsibility really means.

We Americans are usually acknowledged to be the most efficient people in the world as individuals. But we allow ourselves to be organized, or, rather, disorganized, at the top by one of the most miserably inefficient forms of government that it would be possible to conceive. This inefficiency is dangerous always; in time of war it may prove fatal. Our form of government will become increasingly dangerous to our national welfare and security until we reform it in accordance with the principle of Concentration of Responsibility.

Advantages of the Presidential System

DON K. PRICE *

To keep the administration of government under the control of the people, to invigorate it for effective action in their behalf, and to adjust national policy and its administration to the needs of various regions and institutions—these are urgent problems in this time of crisis.

While in Great Britain as well as in the United States new political and administrative institutions are being worked out to meet the needs of the hour, it is curious that much of the academic and journalistic criticism of government in America is based on a desire to imitate the classic parliamentary system of government. This is all the more curious since the British long ago abandoned the classic parliamentary system as definitely as they abandoned the classic theories of political economy.

* Dean of Graduate School of Public Administration, Harvard University, and Associate Director of Public Administration Clearing House. *Co-author of City Manager Government in the United States, The British Defense Program and Local Government.* The selection is from Don K. Price, "The Parliamentary and Presidential Systems," *The Public Administration Review,* Vol. III (Autumn, 1943), pp. 317–334. By permission of *The Public Administration Review.*

Perhaps only a psychoanalyst could explain America's peculiar nostalgia for the obsolescent political institutions of the mother country, but the persistence of her obsession with the parliamentary system makes it not only an interesting theoretical problem but a practical political and administrative issue. . . .

In the British system the nice balance between the Cabinet and the Commons has long since been upset. A half-century ago it was not too unreasonable to argue that the power of the House to dismiss the Cabinet, balanced against the power of the Cabinet to dissolve the House, would always result in a perfect balance of democratic control and executive authority. Within limits, the system worked that way; the Cabinet could never outrage public opinion for fear of losing the support of the House, the members of which went home every week end to get the opinion of the county families if not of the people; the House would never yield to minority interests, for the Cabinet would have the House dissolved if defeated on a policy question, and the members, not wishing to risk their seats in a general election, would not vote against the Cabinet. The equation balanced until a new factor— the electorate—became continuously instead of only potentially effective.

The British in effect did to the House of Commons what the Americans did much earlier to their Electoral College: they made it an automatic machine for registering the vote of the people, as organized into parties, for a Prime Minister. Once the Prime Minister is in office, with the Cabinet that he selects, the House remains in session to enact the bills proposed by the Cabinet, to vote the funds requested by the Cabinet, and to serve as the place where Cabinet ministers make speeches for the newspapers to report to the public but rarely remain to listen to the speeches of other members.

In theory, the House has the power to turn the Cabinet out of office or to refuse to enact the laws it proposes. But that constitutional power seems to be going the way of the King's power to appoint ministers and to veto legislation. Theoretically it exists, but politically it is rarely exercised. Since 1895 only two Cabinets have been refused a vote of confidence and turned out of office by the House, and neither of them had majority support to begin with. A political machine does not elect men to vote against its boss, and the Prime Minister is leader of the party and boss of the machine.

By invading and taking over the executive power the House of Commons destroyed its own independence. The very privilege of holding the Cabinet responsible makes it impossible for the House to think independently. No members of the House will accept office and serve in the Cabinet if the House will not support them. After taking office they will not accept defeat by the House without dissolving the House, calling for a new election, and appealing to the voters to return members who will support them. Because this is constitutionally possible, the members of the House who select and support a Cabinet put the desire to keep their men in office ahead of all minor considerations. The party machinery therefore controls the members fairly rigidly; if the Cabinet wants a measure passed, it will be passed, according to the schedule of debate which the Cabinet considers expedient. As soon as the House of Commons took away the power of the House of Lords by the Parliament Act of 1911 it had to surrender its independence to its leaders; in the cautious words of Sir William Anson, on that date "legislative sovereignty may be said to have passed to the Cabinet." . . .

This control by party machines over the political fortunes of members is a corollary of the similar control by the Cabinet over the legislative procedure. The Cabinet takes for its legislative program just as much of the time of the House as it needs, and during the 1920's and 1930's that was about seven-eighths of the total. The remainder went to consideration of measures proposed by private members (private members are all those except the seventy-odd members who are a part of the "Government" as ministers or assistants to ministers), who drew lots for the privilege of getting their bills considered by the House. No private member's bill could be passed if the Cabinet opposed it, and in practice private members who drew the right to introduce a bill would often ask the Cabinet (or its Whips) for a bill to introduce. . . .

The House of Commons has no committees, in the sense that Congress understands that term. At one stage a bill is referred to a committee—one of several large committees which do not deal with any specialized subject matter, which do not have any fixed membership, and which have no initiative or influence whatever of their own, being little more than devices to permit interested parties to testify. Funds are appropriated and statutes enacted without any independent review, and as the Cabinet requests.

The House votes the funds requested by the Cabinet; it does not have the constitutional power to vote more money for any purpose than the Cabinet asks for, and it has never during this century voted any less. In theory the private member may offer amendments to legislation proposed by the Cabinet, but in practice, as Mr. W. Ivor Jennings puts it, "Members appeal to the minister to accept amendments; they do not compel."

In short, through the party machinery the Cabinet controls the House of Commons on every question that is important enough to be called policy, and it *must* control the House as long as it is "responsible" to the House. The British short-cut the House of Commons to elect their executives as effectively as American voters short-cut the Electoral College. But between elections, since they have reduced their legislature to a voting machine under the control of the Cabinet, they have to rely on the executive to take complete charge of legislation, restrained and guided effectively only by public opinion as it is expressed through the press and through a multitude of private organizations as well as in the House. This is what Mr. Lloyd George meant when he told a Select Committee on Procedure on Public Business in 1931 that "Parliament has really no control over the Executive; it is a pure fiction." . . .

From one point of view, this system brings about an admirable coherence of policy; if a Cabinet is engaged in carrying out a certain program, it has a right to insist that its responsibility not be hampered by the enactment of measures that are inconsistent with it. But, from another point of view, the issue whether certain policies are consistent with each other is the most important issue to be decided, and the most important issue ought to be decided by the supreme authority. . . .

In practice, a legislature cannot exercise control or take an independent line unless it can set up committees to make investigations and recommendations. Under the parliamentary system, the Cabinet is the committee to end all committees; it can tolerate no rivals. It can let other committees conduct investigations and hearings or propose minor amendments, but on any question that a minister chooses to consider policy the House must fall into line. This lets the Cabinet define the scope of "policy," and it is not inclined to leave any controversial issue of importance outside the definition that it formulates. . . .

Thus the House cannot itself make decisions on the several major issues of policy that exist at any one time; constitutionally it can only choose which Cabinet to entrust those decisions to, and as a matter of practical politics it can only keep in office the men it is elected to keep in office.

What is true of policy is even more true of administration. The outlines of departmental organization are fixed by Cabinet action, without legislation, and so are the principal procedures of management, such as budgeting, planning, and personnel. The Cabinet itself now operates through a hierarchy of committees and subcommittees which have no hard-and-fast membership and no formalized existence; any decision on which agreement cannot be reached by common consent is passed on up the line . . . to be settled in the last analysis by the Prime Minister. The freedom of the Cabinet to handle administrative questions with this degree of independence undoubtedly makes for a high degree of coordination. . . .

Congress, since it has not taken over control of administration, has not had to feel responsible as an organization for getting the work of government accomplished. For that reason it has not had to organize itself into a tightly disciplined body, controlled by a single small committee that can act in a businesslike way. If it should do so, the individual members would have to surrender to their organization the individual freedom of action and decision that now enables them to criticize and restrain at their discretion even an administration that they generally propose to support.

During the Napoleonic war, according to Lord Mountararat in *Iolanthe,*

> The House of Lords throughout the war
> Did nothing in particular
> And did it very well.

The House of Commons, which was forced by the bombing of its own quarters to move into those of the House of Lords some years ago, has succeeded to the role which Mr. W. S. Gilbert described with his usual precision of language. The House of Commons has influence, it does an important job, and it does it very well. But it does not control things "in particular." Its control has become so general, it is exercised through so rarefied a medium, that the Commons seem to be following the Lords into the status of one of the "theatrical elements" of the British constitution. . . .

But under the presidential system the public official is under no such restraint. The popular control of the executive is a double control: the people elect the President and the President holds his appointees responsible, retaining the power to discharge them at his discretion; and the people elect the Congress, which controls the executive by statutes, by appropriations, and by investigations. For failing to comply with congressional legislation, a public official is subject to legal penalties; for being so zealously opposed to administration policy that his administrative usefulness is ended, he is subject to removal by his administrative superiors. But since the advocacy of policy by the administrative official does not threaten the tenure of Congressmen, it does not need to be prohibited. Unlike the House of Commons, the Congress retains the power to regulate and control the executive in detail, without putting at stake on any issue the tenure of office of its own members or the President or (generally speaking) subordinate executives. For this reason, it largely divorces questions of policy from questions of party politics in its own proceedings, and executive officials are therefore free to participate in discussions of policy as much as they like—if they are willing to risk their jobs by making themselves no longer useful to the President or his successor. In public discussions of policy they are no more bound as a matter of democratic principle by the restrictions that apply to the British civil service than the President is bound by the restrictions that apply to the King—and for exactly the same reason. . . .

The presidential system, although it unifies responsibility for the execution of a program, does not unify responsibility for the preparation and enactment of a legislative program, as does the parliamentary system. Thus the voters are less able to hold a party clearly responsible for its administration of the program as a whole. On the other hand, the voters have a double check on their government—administratively through the President, their only national representative, and legislatively through the

Congress. And they know that, however poorly the President and the Congress are carrying out their responsibilities, they are not kept from exercising their controls by a system of mutual deference that results from the fear of disturbing each other's tenure of office.

CONSTITUTIONAL FEDERALISM

It is easy to arrange complete harmony between executive and legislature by unifying them. But that only covers up the problem; any differences then appear within the legislature itself, and if they are serious enough the several factions, merely by refusing to cooperate, can simply bring government to a standstill. There is nothing automatic in the process by which various political groups combine in a two-party system. That process has to be impelled by a positive community of interest and a positive loyalty to a central symbol. If even a significant minority has different interests and no loyalty and wishes only to make the existing system of government impossible, there can be no orderly opposition, no gentlemanly alternation of "ins" and "outs."

During the nineteenth century there was little friction in the British parliamentary system because it reflected accurately the concentration of political influence. The two previous centuries had been different. . . . A federal constitutional republic needs a separation of powers to keep its federalism adjusted to the wishes of the people. If a single national representative body is omnipotent, it is likely to disregard subordinate loyalties in carrying out its program. Much of the friction that arises between the President and Congress grows out of the conflict between the national program as planned by the executive branch and the impulse of the legislators who modify it in the interests of their constituencies. Since the American executive is not a part of Congress, members of Congress have no institutional incentive to nationalize our system and to ignore the rights and interests of state and local governments. Their lack of individual responsibility for the administration of any federal program enables them to protect local interests and often to overemphasize them.

Senators and Representatives alike may be called to account more effectively by state and local interests than by their national party organizations. The existence of equal representation in the Senate, which the Constitution provides shall be permanent except by the consent of the states, would make it almost impossible to adopt a parliamentary system; it is difficult to imagine the more powerful of the two houses giving control over the executive to the lower house alone, and it is equally fantastic to imagine them acting jointly on every question.

Neither house of Congress has yet been willing to handle legislation by a committee system which is immediately responsible to the wishes of the house as a whole. If the isolationist Senator Reynolds heads the Military Affairs Committee during a world war, the Senate simply puts up with him. The advocates of "responsible" government will know they are making progress when either house decides to remove the chairman of any committee that differs with the house as a whole on a question of policy. And when both houses agree to hold each other's committees mutually responsible, and to discharge their chairmen whenever they disagree with each other, then we shall really be well along toward minimizing local differences and adopting the tightly knit system of parliamentary government.

But in the meantime, the flexibility of the presidential system has its advantages. We can make progress piecemeal, without waiting for a whole program to get approval in principle. The chief executive can get a majority from these groups on one issue, from those groups on another. The party discipline can be relatively loose; groups that oppose the administration on one issue for local or special reasons need not oppose it on the next. A parliamentary cabinet, by tending to command the same majority on all issues (since that majority wants to keep its administration in office) also tends to keep the opposition always against it. If that minority is concentrated in national or regional or social groups that appeal strongly enough to the loyalty of their members, such opposition is apt to become uncompromising and irreconcilable.

The kind of flexibility that the presidential system permits may be useful in dealing with various types of institutions, as well as with various regions or political groups in the state.

The neat logic of the parliamentary system requires the legislature to hold the executive responsible for a little issue in the same way as for a big one, for a technical detail or a subordinate's error in judgment in the same way as for a major policy decision. This was tolerable enough when government had very little to do with the daily lives of people. But now the dividing line between governmental and other institutions has become very shadowy, all sorts of hybrid agencies and corporations exist, and many private corporations and institutions carry on functions for governmental agencies. In such a situation, if a legislature is to keep the whole organism working in the public interest, it cannot depend mainly on a power to hire and fire the head of it, but it must approve one action and condemn another, encourage here and reprove there, expand this agency and restrict that one.

Under the parliamentary system the legislature must always hold a sword over the head of the executive and cannot stoop to slap his hand. To keep a discussion of the British Broadcasting Corporation from bringing up a vote along party lines on which the Cabinet might be ousted, the Cabinet had to set it up by a statute that makes it generally impossible for the

House to control its detailed operations or even to ask questions about them. If an executive and a legislature have a degree of mutual independence, the legislature may review the budget of a government corporation and force it to change its policy without conflicting with the chief executive at all.

In their system of legislative control over the executive the British have let the Americans outdo them in refusing to conform to an abstract theory. The omnipotence of the House of Commons, the absolute responsibility of the ministers to Parliament—these ideas are so mystical that they can be explained only in terms of nostalgia for the nineteenth century. They are corollaries to other absolutes of the nineteenth century that we now see melting away—the idea of the absolute sovereignty of each nation, the idea of the complete freedom of private business from governmental interference. In the years that lie ahead, we shall probably work out a great many compromise adjustments between the world program and the interests of nations and their component parts; between governmental policy and the freedom of private corporations and institutions. If a legislative body is going to play an active role in such developments, it will need to be able to make up its collective mind coherently and responsibly, as the parliamentary system has been supposed to require it to do. But it will also need freedom to be inconsistent, to restrain the executive even when it wishes to support him, and to keep people and institutions from being fitted to the Procrustean bed of unified policy. Every step toward unification with the executive is a step toward the loss of that freedom. . . .

It is odd enough to find Americans who seek to increase legislative control over the executive arguing for the system that in Britain has given the executive control over the legislature; or Americans who seek to remove unpopular department heads arguing for a system that in Britain keeps the administrative heads from being known, much less responsible, to the people. But it is even more peculiar, at a time when people are thinking about the creation of international federal institutions, to find Americans proposing to discard the presidential system that has been associated with constitutional federalism, in favor of a system that has never proved its ability to accommodate the interests of diverse areas and populations in a federal republic.

America is a federation that is becoming a nation; the institutional system that has helped her do so will be of interest to the whole world as it moves toward greater unity. She gets her job of government done by popular control over two cooperating branches—an executive that provides unity and enterprise, a legislature that furnishes independent supervision and the restraining influence of local interests. Members of her public service are as varied in their origins and experience as the mixture of public and private institutions in her society itself; the leading members of that service come from private life and return to it freely, looking on the government as the people's agency open to their participation.

The assumptions that the legislature alone represents the people and that the administrative officials and departments are responsible to the people only through the legislature served the cause of democratic government well when the executive departments were under a hereditary monarch. They are the classical assumptions of the parliamentary system. Under the presidential system they can only set up an impossible relationship as the ideal to be attained and handicap the legislative and executive branches alike in their efforts to work together to meet the demands of a new age.

Topic 23

THE FILIBUSTER

❦

The Public Business Must Go Forward

JACOB K. JAVITS *

[At the opening of the 1959 session of Congress, some Democratic and Republican Senators, including Senator Javits, proposed a substantial change in Senate Rule XXII so that debate could be shut off by a simple majority of the whole Senate membership. The Senate rejected this proposal and adopted a plan by which cloture could be made operative by vote of two-thirds of the senators on the floor. While Javits' argument and that of Lindsay Rogers were addressed to the old Rule, they have retained their essential force insofar as the prevailing Rule still requires an extraordinary majority to impose an end to debate, and remains a source of continuing controversy.]

After careful study of the hearing testimony and of the historic conceptions of the function of the Senate, I am convinced that rule XXII needs amendment to end its veto power on behalf of a small minority; while at the same time assuring the opportunity for full debate and discussion of any subject in the Senate, which has been called the greatest deliberative body on earth.

I do not believe that the present rule XXII serves the purpose of deliberation within the Senate or of education of the public generally. No one questions those two objectives. What I do question is a delegation of the power and responsibility of the majority to a determined minority, which has been and can be again and again an arbitrary block to action, contrary to the will of the majority of this body and of the people to whom they are responsible. Indeed, it seems to me prophetic that this report is filed at an hour of basic crisis in the defense of our country when the weapons which challenge us are precisely so mortally dangerous because of the speed with which they may be effectively used to destroy us. In such a time—and there is nothing temporary about this new frame of reference—there is a justifiable demand for making our organs of decision conform to the challenge. How appropriate, then, to consider now a rule of debate which can and has paralyzed decision in the Sen-

* United States Senator from New York. The selection is from *Proposed Amendments to Rule XXII of the Standing Rules of the Senate* (Senate Report No. 1509, 85th Congress, 2d Session), pp. 9–19. By permission.

ate and which can be used by a determined minority to paralyze it on any subject—not alone civil rights. Rule XXII as now written was archaic long before the first Russian earth satellite was launched and is even more so now.

Careful research on the development of the United States Government from its initial period under the Articles of Confederation, through the Constitutional Convention of 1787, when studied in the light of the contemporaneous writings of the Founding Fathers, convinces me that the power which now stems from rule XXII was not even contemplated at the time. On the contrary, from the expressed views of Madison, Hamilton, and others, a method of parliamentary procedure premised on rule XXII would have been violently opposed had it been suggested.

For the premise of rule XXII violates fundamental parliamentary law. It is at odds with early Senate procedures, British Parliamentary practice, and, almost without exception, is contrary to all our State legislative rules of procedure.

In the early Senate, simple majority cloture was used and the "previous question" as a parliamentary device was available under Senate rules and in Jefferson's Senate Manual to close debates. Even after reference to the "previous question" was dropped from the standing rules (in 1806), the presiding officer's power to rule on questions of relevancy and order could have prevented abuse through unrestrained irrelevancies. The conjunction of the lack of cloture and the lack of enforcement of a rule of relevancy (after 1872) made possible the modern veto-type filibuster.

Its fullest development and its most flagrant abuses have occurred following the Civil War in opposition to civil rights legislation—mostly in the last 35 years. While rule XXII did not prevent enactment of the Civil Rights Act of the last session, I believe it did profoundly affect its final formulation. . . .

The realistic effect of [both the old and new rule XXII] is that a small minority of Senators, if sufficiently determined, can by use of a filibuster absolutely prevent the Senate from taking action (in the only way it can—by voting) even though a great majority of Senators desires to come to a vote. Voting is the final method of resolution of national issues contemplated in the Constitution. Protracted speaking which is not intended to illuminate that decision, but to prevent its occurrence, makes a mockery of freedom of speech by confusing it with freedom to obstruct. It does not require great imagination to grasp the significance of this potential power in the hands of Members bent on influencing enactment or the course of particular proposals, without the necessity for persuasion.

The basic issue underlying the problem of cloture is whether we shall permit the Senate, resting as it does on the premise of majority rule, to function at all; to fulfill its legislative purpose; or whether we shall permit the Congress to be stultified by the undemocratic and, in essence, unparliamentary device of filibuster in the Senate—even though cloaked in the senatorial toga of rule XXII. . . .

THE POWER OF THE FILIBUSTER AS A VETO, WITH A CASE HISTORY OF THE CIVIL RIGHTS BILL OF 1957

The *ability* to carry on a filibuster can affect the kind of legislation passed by the Senate even though no actual filibuster is undertaken. The incidence of a filibuster or the certain knowledge that a filibuster would be organized has made the majority come to terms before. The mere threat that a filibuster of great length would be undertaken against some proposal or unless amendment to a bill was accepted has in effect resulted in the majority of the Senate acquiescing in changes in legislation which otherwise they would probably not have considered wise or desirable.

Careful study of the legislative background and history of the civil rights bill of 1957 and the changes that occurred during the long Senate debate bears out this conclusion and illustrates the pervasive and subtle effect of rule XXII. . . . It became apparent that a bloc of Senators had selected part III as the most objectionable feature of the bill from their viewpoint; and that they were prepared to use every parliamentary device to prevent the enactment of a law which would contain the authorization for the Attorney General on his own motion to enforce through civil action (as an alternative to criminal prosecutions in existing law) the provisions of the 14th amendment to the Constitution. I believe that a number of Senators, among whom were some who favored the retention of part III, felt that insistence on part III would inevitably force the Senators from the South into a filibuster, with the ensuing possibility that no bill at all might be passed. . . .

I have no doubt that if part III had been retained in the bill the Senate would have faced the necessity of a long filibuster which could be blocked only if a large majority were sufficiently determined to sit out the long dreary months that would have been involved. In that interim, no other business could have been transacted and Congress would have been at a standstill. In these times, with important pending legislation, this was a risk to which, naturally, Members of the Senate should give thoughtful consideration. The determined proponents of part III were fully aware of the consequences of insisting upon it. Schedules were worked out for around-the-clock coverage of the Senate floor, Members had beds installed in their offices, the staff details were worked out for a 24-hour operation. Senator Russell of Georgia, the leader of the southern bloc of Senators, was interviewed on a nationwide television program, Face the Nation, on July 21, 1957. Pertinent excerpts of the interview transcript inserted in the Congressional Record of July 22, 1957, indicate clearly the position of the minority:

> Mr. SHADEL. But, Senator, is there any feeling in the Senate that this bill is going to go through, as is, without modifications?
> Senator RUSSELL. Not on my part because I will certainly die fighting it in my tracks before this vicious bill could go through, and I would feel the same way if it were aimed at any section of the country. . . .
> Mr. LAWRENCE. Well, would it be the intention of the South, under the circumstances that I can foresee and that you can foresee at the moment, to talk this bill to death?
> Senator RUSSELL. I can't say that, Mr. Lawrence, without seeing the bill and if it has these very vicious provisions in it, well, you may be sure that we will use every means at our command to fight it to the very death because it is a very vicious piece of legislation in its present form.

Decision by ordeal was imminent.

No one who participated in the Senate's deliberations could escape the sense of drama, or the mounting tension and concern over the threat inherent in a filibuster. It was in this atmosphere that crucial decisions were made resulting in a number of changes in the legislation, including the elimination of part III. In closing on this point, I should like to add that Little Rock has demonstrated that the decision taken by the Senate to eliminate part III was unwise and that the risk of a stubborn filibuster should have been faced. . . .

Close observers of the legislative process in Congress are aware of this force—of the filibuster—in other legislative compromises which have been adopted, and could cite other examples of the effect of the filibuster on legislation. Vice President Charles G. Dawes, a keen student of Senate proceedings, described the effect of the filibuster in the following words:

> The right of filibuster does not affect simply legislation defeated but, in much greater degree, legislation passed, continually weaving into our laws, which should be framed in the public interest alone, modifications dictated by personal and sectional interest as distinguished from the public interest.

It is no answer to say, as some do say, that such power prevents or softens bad legislation. Of course, it may do that; because legislative proposals subject to a successful filibuster do not get enacted. If any specific action is bad, inaction may be preferred. If all change were bad, then whatever inhibited it would be wise. But the millennium is not here and events do not wait, even if governments do. This built-in stalemate as a permanent method of procedure is opposed to our American spirit and genius.

If the men who conceived our Constitution had thought we needed the concurrence of the majority of two Houses, the assent of the President, and in addition the forbearance of 33 Senators to make law, I assume they would have said so. If this additional check on governmental action is necessary, let us amend the Constitution. The standing rules of the Senate were not drafted in Philadelphia in 1787. The American people neither concurred in them nor agreed to be bound by them—nor did the States. In each Congress, as adopted or acquiesed in, and, to the extent they are constitutional, they bind our Senate procedure so long as they remain unchanged, but they are not the supreme law. They are not the bulwark of free speech and States rights; nor are they immutable. . . .

One may, of course, argue that the existence of rule XXII by which any substantial group of Senators can conduct a filibuster so as to act as a veto, constitutes a "power" which may be exercised on behalf of the States represented by the filibustering Senators; but it is the power neither of persuasion nor of public education. It is an arbitrary power unsanctioned by the Constitution and indeed in direct conflict with its spirit.

Far from securing any constitutional balance, rule XXII seriously disturbs it. The Constitution, in article I, section 5, clause 1, states that—

A majority of each [House] shall constitute a quorum to do business.

That is, 49 Senators are sufficient for the transaction of legislative business. A majority of this quorum is required to assent to the passage of a normal bill. Yet cloture may not be invoked unless at least 64 Members are present and vote for cloture. Legislation of the most profound national effect requires the assent of fewer than half of those required to bring a filibuster to a reasonable close so that that very legislation may be acted upon. I fail to see what balance is here maintained by continuance of the present rule. Alexander Hamilton in arguing, in the Federalist Papers, for the adoption of the Constitution he had helped frame, set forth the need for a totally different balance (Federalist Papers No. 22):

To give a minority a negative upon the majority (which is always the case where more than a majority is requisite to a decision), is, in its tendency, to subject the sense of the greater number to that of the lesser. . . . This is one of those refinements which, in practice, has an effect the reverse of what is expected from it in theory. The necessity of unanimity in public bodies, or of something approaching toward it, has been founded upon a supposition that it would contribute to security. But its real operation is to embarrass the administration, to destroy the energy of the Gov-

ernment, and to substitute the pleasure, caprice, or arifices of an insignificant, turbulent, or corrupt junto, to the regular deliberations and decisions
of a respectable majority. . . . The public business must, in some way or
other, go forward. If a pertinacious minority can control the opinion of a
majority respecting the best mode of conducting it, the majority, in order
that something may be done, must conform to the views of the minority;
and thus the sense of the smaller number will overrule that of the greater,
and give a tone to the national proceedings. Hence, tedious delays; continual negotiation and intrigue; contemptible compromises of the public
good, and yet, in such a system, it is even happy when such compromises
can take place: for upon some occasions things will not admit of accommodation: and then the measures of government must be injuriously suspended, or fatally defeated. It is often, by the impracticability of obtaining
the concurrence of the necessary number of votes, kept in a state of inaction. Its situation must always savor of weakness, sometimes border upon
anarchy. . . .

When the concurrence of a large number is required by the Constitution
to the doing of any national act, we are apt to rest satisfied that all is
safe, because nothing improper will be likely to be done; but we forget
how much good may be prevented, and how much ill may be produced,
by the power of hindering the doing what may be necessary; and of keeping affairs in the same unfavorable posture in which they may happen to
stand at particular periods.

. . . There was a great question of the proper balance of State representation in the Congress in 1787. A study of the debates of the Constitutional Convention shows very clearly that the decision to establish 2
Houses, one to be based on a reference to population, and the other to
have 2 Senators from each State regardless of size or population, was
the compromise between the delegates from big States and the delegates
from the small States. This was the only basis on which the small States
would agree to join the Federal Union. This was the great compromise
that gave the small States an equal measure of legislative power with the
more populous States in this body.

As far as the big States are concerned, according to Madison and
others devoted to the principle of proportional representation, they had
given enough and more than enough when they finally agreed that each
State should have two votes in the Senate. No one then dreamed that
in the future Senators would want to upset this balance and add an additional check by a small minority of one-third upon the power of a
majority of the Senate as so constituted. This, of course, was long prior
to the time when John C. Calhoun developed his theory of concurrent
majorities under which legislation favored by a majority in the country
as a whole or in the Congress would be subject to the veto of a majority
of each and every sectional interest in the country.

This kind of balance, which the opponents of civil-rights legislation wish to retain in the Senate, is a modern version of Calhoun's "concurrent majorities." It was such a sectional right of veto and interposition that Calhoun and other States-rights advocates urged during the debates, in and out of Congress, that led up to the Civil War. This type of imbalance, however, finds no support in the Constitution nor in current practice outside of rule XXII.[1]

Senator Underwood of Alabama said, with respect to the filibuster against the Dyer anti-lynching bill, as follows:

> We are not disguising what is being done on this side of the Chamber. It must be apparent, not only to the Senate but to the country, that an effort is being made to prevent the consideration of a certain bill, and I want to be perfectly candid about it. It is known throughout the country generally as a "force" bill. . . .
> *I do not say that captiously. I think all men here know that under the rules of the Senate when 15 or 20 or 25 men say that you cannot pass a certain bill, it cannot be passed.* . . .
> I want to say right now to the Senate that if the majority party insists on this procedure they are not going to pass the bill, and they are not going to do any other business. . . .
> You know you cannot pass it. Then let us go along and attend to the business of the country. [Emphasis supplied.]

Shortly thereafter he posed the dilemma which the Senate faced even more concisely:

> There is but one way for the Senate now to get down to work and transact the business of the Government before the 4th of March, and that is to get a final disposition of this force bill before anything else is done. Pass it if you can; abandon it if we force you to do so. . . .
> So long as the Senate has the rules that it has now, you know just as well as I know that I am standing here that you cannot pass it; and, more than that, the country does not want you to pass it.

The reality of the use of the filibuster as a veto has been borne out by the experience of the intervening years. As my colleague, Senator Kuchel, of California, put it last summer in the hearings before this subcommittee:

> How can any reasonable person uphold such tactics as those which occurred some years ago when the Senate ludicrously debated for 2 weeks a motion to amend the Chaplain's prayer?

Permitting a Senator or a group of Senators to talk for hours and days on any conceivable subject or on no subject in order to consume time and prevent the Senate from voting, affords no dignity to the Senate and

---

[1] The paralyzing effect of the minority veto is clearly evident in the deliberations of the United Nations Security Council.

adds nothing to its deliberative function. Reading recipes for "pot licker," "fried oysters," quoting from Aesops Fables,[2] and otherwise talking in utter irrelevancies does nothing to enhance the Senate's standing as a great deliberative body.

Senators have a right—and freely exercise it—to express their views on any question before the Senate or before the country. Without doubt it would be a violation of the letter and the spirit of the Constitution to deny or even seriously abridge the right of debate. But, it is also a most flagrant violation of the spirit of the Constitution to clothe this body with forms of procedure by which it may be blocked in the exercise of the legislative powers, and thereby suspended of every other function except that of speaking. The Senate has a duty to debate, but it is likewise a constitutional duty of a majority of this body to act, and with some reasonable expedition. We are obligated not only to pass laws, but also to pass them in time to meet the public need and the general welfare of the country.

Some observers have declared that, far from enhancing the Senate's deliberative function, the right to filibuster has all but destroyed it. Vice President Dawes, for example, said of the veto power of the filibuster:

> The Senate is not and cannot be a properly deliberative body, giving due consideration to the passage of all laws, unless it allots its time for work according to the relative importance of its duties, as do all other great parliamentary bodies. It has, however, through the right of unlimited debate surrendered to the whim and personal purposes of individuals and minorities its right to allot its own time. Only the establishment of majority cloture will enable the Senate to make itself a properly deliberative body. This is impossible when it must sit idly by and see time needed for deliberation frittered away in frivolous and irrelevant talk, indulged in by individuals and minorities for ulterior purposes.

Yet, the Senators who argue that rule XXII should be retained in its present form support this retention as necessary to its deliberative character. I certainly agree that the Senate is a forum of great debate, deliberation, and revision; but I submit that it owes nothing to rule XXII for achieving this distinction. It has achieved that eminence despite the rule.

---

[2] During the filibuster against the extension of a skeletonized NRA, Senator Long discussed various recipes at great length. This talk continued for 15½ hours and included the reading of long passages from works of Victor Hugo and a reading and discussion of the United States Constitution, article by article, without any necessary reference to the pending business. (See *Congressional Record,* vol. 79, pt. 8, pp. 9122 et seq.)

On June 20, 1936, Senator Rush D. Holt of West Virginia successfully filibustered against passage of a coal conservation bill by reading Aesops Fables to the Senate. The Senate finally adjourned, sine die, without ever voting on the bill.

Barrier Against Steamrollers

LINDSAY ROGERS *

"The Senate of the United States is the only legislative body in the world which cannot act when its majority is ready for action." Thus Woodrow Wilson early in 1917 when a Senate filibuster killed his proposal to arm American merchant ships. The "little group of willful men" were successful only because we then had "short sessions" of Congress that had to come to an end on March 4. The check was not a catastrophe. The ships were armed under authority conferred by an old statute that had been forgotten.

In 1917 the Senate was powerless to end a debate so long as any senator insisted on holding the floor, but debate can now be ended by a vote of two-thirds of the "Senators duly chosen and sworn." It is this much-debated Rule XXII that the Northern liberals hope to change in order to prevent Southern senators from using a filibuster to prevent the passage of drastic civil-rights legislation.

The Northern liberals propose two amendments. The first of these is that two days after a petition has been filed to end debate, two-thirds of the Senate present and voting may so decree. This is not very important; if such a cloture resolution were up, practically all of the "Senators duly chosen and sworn" would be present and vote. But the Northern liberals have a further proposal: that fifteen days after the filing of a petition to end debate, a majority of the entire Senate may so decree. Garrulity would still be permitted; each senator could speak for an hour, but under such circumstances only the filibusterers would do so. Then a vote. No longer could a filibuster interpose a veto as it has sometimes done in the past.

Such a change in the rule would, I think, be a mistake. Not so, says [former] Senator Irving M. Ives (R., New York), who maintains that "the principle of majority rule is at stake." It is only in the Senate of the United States, exclaims Senator Clifford P. Case (R., New Jersey), that an opposition must be beaten down by "physical exhaustion" and where "the medieval practice of trial by ordeal still survives."

With great respect to Senator Ives, the term "majority rule" is meaningless as he uses it. Does he want to amend the Constitution so that the Senate would advise and consent to the ratification of a treaty by a

* Consultant to the Senate Committee on Foreign Relations and former Professor of Public Law at Columbia University. Author of *The American Senate, Crisis Government, The Pollsters,* and other works. The selection is from "Barrier Against Steamrollers," *The Reporter,* Vol. 20 (January 8, 1959), pp. 21–23. By permission.

majority instead of a two-thirds vote? Is he uneasy because of the theoretical possibility that the minority which defeats a treaty (or a proposed Constitutional amendment) might come from the seventeen smallest states with a total population less than that of New York? Or that a Senate majority might be drawn from twenty-five states with a population of less than twenty-nine millions? We elect Presidents not by a national popular majority or even plurality, but by counting the ballots federally; each state's Presidential electors do the choosing. Fifty-one per cent may be a numerical majority, but in many cases it is not the majority that our Constitutional practices contemplate. Our Federal arrangements take account of what has been called "the gravity and the impact of the decision." Thus, when one great section of our country opposes a proposed decision, attention may well be paid to "gravity" and "impact."

And when Senator Case brands the Senate as the only legislative assembly in which verbal avoirdupois plays a role along with numbers, so what? The Northern liberals have sometimes insisted on "trial by ordeal." Senator Paul H. Douglas (D., Illinois) boasts that in 1954 he "spoke for three days against the offshore oil bill and in 1956 for four days against the natural gas bill. In each case, with my colleagues of the so-called liberal group, we kept the discussion going for approximately a month." Mr. Douglas applauds "stunts such as Senator Morse's record-breaking, 22½-hour speech delivered without sitting down or leaving the Chamber." The stunters were not attempting "to prevent a vote from being taken." They simply "believed that in these cases many of our colleagues were not fully acquainted with the real issues which were at stake." This is not a veto, Mr. Douglas insists, but only an endeavor to educate senators who were poorly informed. I would allow a substantial group of senators who are well informed, who come from a great section of the country, and who are united in purpose, to impose a veto unless two-thirds of their colleagues are prepared to overrule them.

BLOCKING THE STEAMROLLER

Gladstone called the Senate "the most remarkable of all the inventions of modern politics," and it has remained remarkable in that, contrary to the fate of practically every other upper chamber, it has not become secondary and suffered a loss of authority either by Constitutional amendment or by custom. It is the only legislative body in the world made up of representatives from commonwealths no one of which without its consent can be deprived of its equal representation and whose rights, even though steadily dwindling, still remain substantial. Where in other assemblies is there anything resembling our Senate's rule that its members must not "refer offensively to any State of the Union"?

The filibuster is a weapon that the Constitutional framers who constructed the Senate failed to anticipate but one that they would view with favor. "A dependence on the people is, no doubt, the primary control on the government," Number 51 of *The Federalist* tells us; "but experience has taught mankind the necessity of auxiliary precautions." The framers sought to have "in the society so many separate descriptions of citizens as will render an unjust combination of the majority of the whole very improbable, if not impracticable." The filibuster is no more than a modern "auxiliary precaution" against what one more than one-third of the senators may consider an "unjust combination" of the majority; and I am not impressed when I am told that no other legislative body in the world allows a minority to have such a formidable weapon of defense.

With us the Executive holds office for a fixed term and never appears before the legislature to account for his actions. Hence, it is "an auxiliary precaution" that there be some place in the congressional system at which a party steamroller will meet an effective barrier. The House of Representatives cannot serve this purpose. There, debate is often more severely limited and freedom of decision is more restricted than in any other legislative chamber in the world. A two-thirds majority can suspend the rules, and after forty minutes of discussion, it can pass a measure with no opportunity to offer amendments. A special order from the Rules Committee can allocate time for debate between the majority and minority and require that the House can say only "Yes" or "No." Since the senators number only ninety-eight and show more qualities of prima donnas than do representatives, they would refuse to shackle themselves as do members of the House when they approve a special order from the Committee on Rules; senators would insist that they be permitted to vote on amendments. But without the possibility of parliamentary obstruction —that is, filibustering—a party steamroller, driven by a President and party leaders, could on occasion move almost as ruthlessly on the Senate side as it does on the House side of the Capitol.

Thirty-odd years ago in a book called *The American Senate,* which now occasionally enjoys what William James called the immortality of a footnote, I argued the case for the filibuster. I began the book during the Harding administration and finished when Coolidge was in the White House—the era of the Teapot Dome scandals. The Republican Party machine was then powerful enough to prevent any investigation by a House committee, and Republicans in the Senate were not anxious to uncover wrongdoing. The Republican leaders knew that Senator Thomas J. Walsh of Montana and other Democrats could hold up important business; hence they had to consent to the thoroughgoing inquiry that was demanded. As to whether the threatened filibuster that brought about this result was in the public interest, it is sufficient to remark that three out of ten cabinet members were permitted or pressed to resign, and that there were several indictments and two suicides.

Those desiring Federal civil-rights legislation talk a great deal about the high-handed behavior of a minority. The Southern senators, it is charged, are able to defy "not only a majority in the Senate, but a majority in the country at large." Probably a majority in the country at large is willing for more civil-rights legislation to be passed, but we must not forget that one of the main reasons the framers of the Constitution provided two senators for each state, large or small, was precisely in order to protect the rights of sections against a majority in the country at large.

December 5, 1958, marked the twenty-fifth anniversary of an event on which the Northern liberals might pause to reflect: the end of national prohibition, which was, perhaps, in President Herbert Hoover's phrase, an experiment "noble in motive" but which was certainly a spectacular and disastrous failure. In 1918, when the state legislatures began to vote on the proposed prohibition amendment, saloons were illegal in approximately ninety per cent of the area of the nation, which contained nearly two-thirds of the population of the country. Temperance societies and the Anti-Saloon League (the most powerful pressure group that ever worked on Congress and state legislatures) insisted that aridity be complete. The "drys" marched to a battle that they won. Then they lost the war.

One concluding observation. Ours is the only major country with a two-party system where the laws that get on the Federal statute books, or that fail to get there, usually have bipartisan support and bipartisan opposition. In academic quarters one sometimes hears laments that American political parties are not "disciplined"; that their leadership is sometimes shadowy or undiscoverable, and that they do not present to the electorate clashing bodies of doctrine. But in a country as vast as the United States, with different sectional interests, a political providence has been good in seeing to it that a party majority does not pass party legislation which is opposed by a powerful and determined party minority; that on policies our parties prefer concessions to Pyrrhic victories. The filibuster is undemocratic if "democracy" means that anywhere, and particularly in a federal system, any majority should be able to do what it wishes on any issue at any time. Do the Northern liberals thus define "democracy"? Federalism was the means of forming the nation and it remains the means of preserving it. Congress, as well as the Supreme Court, is the Federal system's manager, and a Senate filibuster is well worth while if, on occasion, it prevents the Congressional manager from being tyrannical.

CONGRESSIONAL INVESTIGATIONS

〖◇〗

A Defense of Investigations

JAMES BURNHAM *

In the past, congressional investigations have been intermittently and sometimes sharply attacked. The 1923–24 investigations into the oil industry and the Departments of the Navy and Justice were condemned by Owen J. Roberts, speaking before the American Bankers' Association, as mere "propaganda for nationalization." The *Wall Street Journal* dismissed them as a "political smokescreen." The *New York Times* declared that Congress was "investigation-mad," and was trying to introduce "government by clamor [and] hole in corner gossip." The *Times* (in February, 1924) upheld Attorney General Daugherty as a sturdy patriot who was defending "decency [and] honor . . . , the honor which ought to prevail among gentlemen, if not among politicians." [1] In the same month the Communist *Daily Worker* created the label, "smelling committees."

A few years earlier Walter Lippmann, in his book, *Public Opinion,*[2] had described investigations as "that legalized atrocity . . . where Congressmen starved of their legitimate food for thought, go on a wild and feverish man-hunt, and do not stop at cannibalism." In 1925 the influential legal authority, J. H. Wigmore, characterized the investigators as "on the level of professional searchers of the municipal dunghills." The investigators to whom Wigmore was thus referring (Senators Walsh, Wheeler, Borah and LaFollette) were also termed, in the contemporary press, "scandal-mongers," "mud-gunners," "assassins of character." Their inquiries were described as "lynching bees," "poisoned-tongued partisanship, pure malice, and twittering hysteria," and "in plain words, contemptible and disgusting."

A decade later the New Deal inquiries into investment, banking, utilities,

---

* Editor of the *National Review*. Author of *The Managerial Revolution, The Machiavellians,* and *Web of Subversion*. The selection is from *Congress and the American Tradition* (Chicago, Henry Regnery Company, 1959), pp. 236–252. By permission.

[1] Within six months Daugherty had resigned in disgrace, after the investigators had shown that during his two and a half years in Washington on a $15,000 salary, his personal holdings had shifted from a $19,000 debt to a $100,000 fortune.

[2] Published in 1922.

and munitions were the targets for denunciations comparable in content though less colorful in rhetoric. Long before, congressional investigating methods had been eloquently criticized even from the floor of Congress itself. In 1860, during the course of the Senate inquiry into John Brown's raid on Harper's Ferry, Senator Charles Sumner defended a contumacious witness, Thaddeus Hyatt, who had been "incarcerated in the filthy jail" for having refused to answer the committee's questions: [3] "To aid a committee of this body merely in a legislative purpose, a citizen, guilty of no crime, charged with no offense, presumed to be innocent, honored and beloved in his neighborhood, may be seized, handcuffed, kidnapped, and dragged away from his home, hurried across State lines, brought here as a criminal, and then thrust into jail." . . .

Generally speaking, as these prominent instances suggest, it has been the gored ox that has bellowed. Whether well-grounded or not, vigorous congressional inquiries usually threaten institutionalized as well as individual interests. The spokesmen and friends of these interests, along with the individuals directly involved, fight back as best they are able. Usually the best defense, in a public polemic, is to drop the question of one's own private concern out of sight, and to counterattack either with *ad hominem* grapeshot or with seemingly general considerations of propriety, morals and political philosophy.

It was natural enough that the *Wall Street Journal,* the American Bankers Association, the *New York Times* (as edited in the 1920's) and the Hearst press (with large Hearst mining interests in the background) should look with initial disfavor on a probing of oil leases by a partisan and already suspect Public Lands Committee. The established banking and investment interests, the utility holding companies, and the great industrial corporations that had armed the nation for the first world war could not, even though cowed by the long depression, welcome the inquiries of the 1930's into their carefully unpublic ways. John Brown was a martyred hero of the abolitionists, who had provoked and financed his raid on Harper's Ferry. The abolitionist Senators from New England could hardly have been expected to further an investigation, headed by a Senator from Virginia, which was likely to confirm the formal case against Brown and to uncover the links in the conspiracy. . . .

Hugo L. Black, writing in 1936 when he was an investigator and not a Supreme Court Justice, summed up the natural response: "The instant that a resolution [authorizing an investigation] is offered, or even rumored, the call to arms is sounded by the interest to be investigated." [4]

[3] Here and below, the quotations of the Harper's Ferry debate are taken from *Congressional Globe,* 36th Congress, 1st session, March 12, 1860, pp. 1100–09; and Part 4, June 15, 1860, pp. 3006–7.

[4] Hugo L. Black, "Inside a Senate Investigation" (*Harper's,* February, 1936).

II

I do not mean to suggest that all of these past criticisms of inquiries have been subjectively biased or hypocritical. It may be presumed that Dean Wigmore was concerned primarily with the investigative procedures that are too coarse and unrestrained for so judicially oriented a mind as his was. Mr. Lippmann has been long and persistently critical of investigations differing widely in subject-matter and political direction. For that matter, most of the critics have doubtless been sincere enough when they voiced their criticisms.

At the same time we may note that until recent years, most of the attacks on the investigations, like the defending replies, seem to be part of the general political struggle in the nation over issues and problems that have successively arisen. The impetus of the attacks has been specific: against this particular inquiry or related set of inquiries. The legislative inquiry as an accredited institution of the American political system has not been in dispute. The critics did not question Congress' autonomous right to investigate, with adequate compulsory sanctions, in its own way and on its own sovereign authority. . . .

During the past decade the attack on the investigations has assumed a very different character. Although it has arisen primarily out of inquiries dealing with Communism and other forms of subversion, it is no longer specific or limited. In fact, it is no longer an attack on investigations, but on the investigatory power, and it has come in waves from all directions: from journalists, cartoonists, publicists and academicians; from the courts; from the executive; and even from within Congress itself.

As pictured by the most influential liberal cartoonists, led by Herblock and Fitzgerald, the typical congressional investigator is either a gangster, a Star Chamber hanging-judge, or a rubber-truncheoned fascist. Thousands of editorials, articles, monographs, lectures and sermons have condemned the investigating committees, their methods, their results and their most prominent members. In 1955 two general books—Alan Barth's *Government by Investigation* and Telford Taylor's *Grand Inquest*—broadened the adverse critique that had been undertaken by such preliminary studies as Robert K. Carr's *The House Committee on Un-American Activities*. A number of organizations—among them Americans for Democratic Action, the American Civil Liberties Union and the Committee for an Effective Congress—have in these recent years made the defects of investigations and investigators a principal element of their public agitation. For several years prior to his death in 1957, the figure of Senator Joseph R. McCarthy of Wisconsin became the symbolic target for this massive campaign against the investigatory power—a campaign which began, however, before McCarthy's entry on the national stage, as it continues after his exit.

III

The opponents and critics of congressional investigations do not explicitly call for the abolition of the investigatory power; that is, they do not state that Congress should be altogether deprived of the right and power to make investigations. They argue, rather, that the investigations should be curbed, limited and controlled in such ways as to prevent violations of rights, demagogic exploitation, encroachments on the executive or judiciary, and other excesses. The restrictive proposals go along such lines as the following:

(A.) *Some topics should be outside the purview of investigations.* These prohibited subjects would include all private affairs, rather broadly defined.[5] It has also been urged that all the varied matters included under "espionage" and "subversion" should be put under the exclusive jurisdiction of the Federal Bureau of Investigation and other security agencies: that is, should be shifted wholly out of the legislative into the executive branch.

(B.) *Investigating committee proceedings should be governed by detailed rules for the protection of the rights and privileges of witnesses, similar to the rules governing judicial actions.* Witnesses should have right to counsel, to confront accusers, to cross-examine, to call rebuttal witnesses and submit rebuttal evidence, to obtain full transcripts, and so on.[6]

It should perhaps be added that many of the rules proposed by the critics—such as the requirement of a committee quorum for all hearings and for all decisions in preparation of hearings—are virtually impossible under the real conditions of congressional activity. Others, drawn from courtroom practice, are inappropriate to an investigation, which by the nature of the case, is partly a "fishing expedition" in which the issues are not known fully in advance—unlike a court action, where the issue is defined in the indictment. And it is seldom remarked that the loose investigatory procedures, though they undoubtedly sometimes violate what would generally be regarded as individual rights and are often

[5] Thus extending a principle recognized by the Supreme Court in Kilbourn v. Thompson (1881).

[6] Actually, many such procedural rules have in fact been adopted by the committees, either through customary practice or on formal action. The House Committee on Un-American Activities—to cite one of the most controversial instances —operates in accordance with a printed list of fourteen rules in addition to the governing rules of the House itself.

disturbing to individual pleasure and convenience, at the same time frequently offer witnesses unusual liberties that they do not possess in the courtroom: to make long statements; to argue with interlocutors; to bring in hearsay, subjective motivation, mitigating circumstances; to delay and repeat; to become the accuser and to counterattack.

(C.) *The self-incrimination clause of the Fifth Amendment should have total application to inquiry proceedings.* That is, a witness, without any motivating explanation on his part or any objective indication that the refusal is well-grounded, should have the right to refuse to answer any question whatever on the ground that by answering it he risks possible incrimination. This blanket restraint on the investigatory function seems to be accepted at present by the courts and by Congress. It is further and persistently being proposed that the grounds for a refusal to testify should also include the First Amendment guarantees of freedom of belief and speech. Historically there is no foundation for applying these amendments to congressional inquiries. "These guarantees," observe Messrs. Kelly and Harbison, "were historically associated almost entirely with the business of the courts. And the substantive guarantees of the Bill of Rights—freedom of speech, press, and the like—appeared to apply to the content of congressional legislation, not to the mode of enacting it." [7]

(D.) *All phases of congressional investigations should be subject to review and adjudication by the courts.* For a hundred and fifty years the Supreme Court shied as far away as it could from intervention in the legislature's investigatory power, finally summing up its traditional recognition of legislative autonomy therein by its sweeping decision in McGrain *v.* Daugherty (1927). In the late 1940's, by refusing to review three lower court decisions that reasserted congressional autonomy in investigations,[8] the Court held fast to McGrain *v.* Daugherty against the rising liberal clamor. Then, in a series of decisions that began with Christoffel *v.* United States (1950) and reached a high point in Watkins *v.* United States (1957), the Supreme Court asserted what would be by implication its general right to define the rules, limits, methods, scope and sanctions of the investigatory power. On the meaning of the Watkins case, which reversed the decision of both the District Court and the Court of Appeals, dissenting Justice Tom C. Clark wrote that the Supreme Court was appointing itself "Grand Inquisitor and supervisor of congressional investigations."

[7] Alfred H. Harbison and Winfred A. Kelly, *The American Constitution* (New York, Norton & Co., 1955), p. 908.

[8] United States *v.* Bryan (1947), United States *v.* Josephson (1948), Barsky *v.* United States (1948). In the latter two decisions there had been a sharp division in the Court of Appeals.

(E.) *Congressional investigators who get out of bounds should be disciplined.* This proposal, a frequent exhortation of the critics of Congress, is difficult to apply, because of the explicit words of Article I, Section 6 of the Constitution: "[Senators and Representatives] shall in all Cases, except Treason, Felony and Breach of the Peace, be privileged from Arrest during their Attendance at the Session of their respective Houses, and in going to and returning from the same; and for any Speech or Debate in either House, they shall not be questioned in any other Place." Since these words seem to put members of Congress, so far as their official acts go, out of reach of the courts, traditional doctrine has left their due punishment to the ballot. As a disciplinary supplement, the new critics urge—though so far unsuccessfully—that too savage investigators might be tamed by being deprived of committee chairmanships, or even of membership on committees that conduct investigations.

The temporary focusing of the problem in Senator Joseph McCarthy provoked a novel, and momentous sanction. In 1954, through combined pressure from a liberal-led public opinion and the executive branch, Congress was induced to turn its investigatory power against itself; and then, by the Senate vote of an unprecedented censure against one of its own members, to make common cause with its critics.

[The fact is] that a true investigatory power cannot exist unless the investigator (individual or institution) is equipped with immunity, autonomy, and the power of compulsion. The public critique and the Supreme Court decisions since 1950, though not openly directed against the investigatory power itself, have attacked and much weakened these three conditions of its effective operation.

The power of compulsion is meaningless unless there is assured, speedy punishment for contumacious witnesses. Such punishment, under the now prevailing court rulings and congressional practice, is neither sure nor speedy. It can be postponed indefinitely when it is not avoided altogether, by legal technicalities, the plea of civil rights, or Congress' own unwillingness to pursue the matter vigorously. Thus, with very little personal hazard, witnesses may defeat the ends of a current inquiry: there will be a new Congress with new interests, before the question of punishment is decided one way or the other.

The investigator's immunity and autonomy do not mean that he can properly do anything that he wishes, but that the major decisions about what he can properly do will be his. More specifically applied to congressional investigation: that Congress shall itself decide when an investigation has a legislative purpose, what sort of evidence is relevant to that purpose and from whom, how evidence and information may be most fruitfully gathered. Quite possibly this is too great a license to be granted without restriction to any single institution. That is not here at issue, but merely the historical observation that in recent years the investigatory power of Congress, at the same time that it has emerged as the first among the remaining congressional powers, has been shorn and blunted by a many-sided and continuing attack. The public controversy over the investigatory power has often failed to distinguish between two types of inquiry that are profoundly different in their political meaning: investigations into the activities of private citizens, associations and institutions, on the one hand; and on the other, investigations of the administration of the government—that is, of the executive branch and the bureaucracy. A particular inquiry may bridge the two types (as in a study of the relation between a government regulatory agency and the industry it is supposed to regulate), but the functional distinction remains clear.

Most of the formal arguments that are advanced against investigations concern, primarily or exclusively, the first type. It is alleged that the civil rights or personal life of private citizens who appear as witnesses are violated, and that the protection of these private rights is a duty that takes precedence over the possible public gains from investigating this or that subject-matter. That is to say, the argument is cast in the form of: individual liberty *vs.* despotism.

For Americans, an argument in this form has roots in both tradition and rhetoric. It is persuasive to many citizens even apart from their opinion on the particular content of the investigations which provoke the controversy. And it is a fact that an unchecked investigatory power always threatens and sometimes subverts what Americans wish to regard as inviolable individual rights.

But inquiries into the doings of the executive and the bureaucracy are of a different order, in which private and individual rights are only coincidentally at stake. By making an artificial amalgam between the two types of investigation, we smear the second with the doubtful or negative feelings attached to the first. Objectively, the principal similarity between the two is the mere fact that both express the investigatory power of the legislature.

Traditionally it has never been questioned, either in doctrine or practice, that the legislature possesses the power, as it was put in early years, "to inquire into the honesty and efficiency of the executive branch." Under the American system it is this that is the heart of the investigatory power. It is conceivable that, without a major constitutional transformation, Congress could cede all investigations of the affairs of private citizens to the executive and judiciary. But if it lost the power to investigate the executive, Congress would retain only the name of legislature.

The late Senator George Norris, once the dean of liberals, accurately remarked during the controversies of 1924: "Whenever you take away from the legislative body of any country in the world the power of investigation, the power to look into the executive department of the government, you have taken a full step that will eventually lead into absolute monarchy [9] and destroy any government such as ours."

Woodrow Wilson's distaste for the practices of Congress did not lead him to obscure the basic relations:

> Quite as important as legislation is vigilant oversight of administration. . . . An effective representative body [ought] to serve as [the nation's] eyes in superintending all matters of government. . . . There is some scandal and discomfort, but infinite advantage, in having every affair of administration subjected to the test of constant examination on the part of the assembly which represents the nation. . . . Congress is the only body which has the proper motive for inquiry. . . . It is the proper duty of a representative body to look diligently into every affair of government and to talk much about what it sees. It is meant to be the eyes and the voice and to embody the wisdom and will of its constituents. Unless Congress have and use every means of acquainting itself with the acts and the dispositions of the administrative agents of the government, the country must be helpless to learn how it is being served. . . . The only really self-governing people is that people which discusses and interrogates its administration.[10]

Professor McGeary has put the situation still more bluntly: "An administrator's knowledge that at some future time he and his activities might be subjects of congressional investigation has probably been the principal external deterrent to wrong-doing in the executive branch." [11]

Scholars who have taken refuge in the United States from totalitarian regimes have been still more deeply impressed with the crucial role of legislative investigations into the operations of the executive. Dr. Henry W. Ehrmann, a refugee from Nazism, concludes that a lack of this power was a prime factor both in the failure of German pre-Nazi parliamentarism and in the bureaucratic sclerosis of the French political system.[12] He recalls the judgment of Germany's great sociologist, Max Weber: "In his criticism of the political situation in Imperial Germany, [Weber] attributed greater responsibility for the unsatisfactory results of constitutional life to the lack of parliamentary investigation than to any

[9] In the traditional American vocabulary, "absolute monarchy" was the term often used to refer to "despotism."

[10] Woodrow Wilson, *Congressional Government*, pp. 277–303 *passim*.

[11] N. Nelson McGeary, "Historical Development," a contribution to the symposium on congressional investigations in *University of Chicago Law Review*, Vol. 18, No. 3, Spring 1951; p. 430.

[12] Henry W. Ehrmann, "The Duty of Disclosure in Parliamentary Investigation: A Comparative Study" (*Univ. of Chicago Law Review*, Vol. 2, No. 2, Feb. 1944), pp. 117–53.

other single factor. The German parliament was condemned to dilettantism as well as ignorance."

Under Weber's influence, a right of parliamentary inquiry was introduced into the Weimar Constitution, but, as in the case of the inquiry function in France, there was no real power of compulsion to back it up. In both countries it could therefore have only minor political significance. "The unsatisfactory results in both France and Germany can easily be explained by the insufficient powers obtained by the parliamentary committees."

It is against this background that we may evaluate the progressive undermining of the investigatory power during the past decade by the executive as well as by liberal publicists and the courts. The executive under Presidents Franklin Roosevelt, Truman and Eisenhower has challenged the investigatory power in the most direct of ways: with respect to an ever expanding mass of data, it has simply refused to supply information to the investigating committees.

These refusals have been formally motivated by: the doctrine of "the separation of powers"; the need for secrecy; various laws, and in particular a "housekeeping act" of 1789 originally passed to authorize executive departments to set up files and records; an alleged traditional practice within the American system. These considerations were systematically stated in a memorandum submitted in May, 1954 by Attorney General Herbert Brownell to President Eisenhower, and countered by a Staff Study of the House Committee on Government Operations, dated May 3, 1956.

The executive's argument from tradition is undoubtedly specious. It is true that a number of Presidents, beginning with the first, have denied the universal right of Congress to call for testimony and documents from the executive branch. Among them have been Presidents otherwise so various as Andrew Jackson, John Tyler, Abraham Lincoln, Grover Cleveland and Calvin Coolidge. Washington would seem to have declared—in theory—a complete executive immunity to the investigatory power: "The executive ought to communicate such papers as the public good would permit and ought to refuse those, the disclosure of which would injure the public." Jackson, when Congress wished to look more closely into the working of his Spoils System, replied indignantly: "For myself, I shall repel all such attempts as an invasion of the principles of justice, as well as of the Constitution; and I shall esteem it my sacred duty to the people of the United States to resist them as I would the establishment of a Spanish inquisition." Even Calvin Coolidge denounced with unwonted sharpness the investigatory feelers directed by the Couzens committee at Secretary Andrew Mellon's administration of the Treasury Department. . . .

This earlier occasional practice—which like so much in the older American tradition commends itself to ordinary common sense—has now been blown up into a polished routine. By an administrative fiction, the "confidential" relation between President and subordinates—which in the past meant a literal personal relation between man and man—has been extended to the entire bureaucracy, so that the executive now claims a right to order any official or employee of the bureaucracy to refuse to testify to an investigating committee, or to withhold almost any sort of document or record pertaining to any department or agency.

In explaining Congress' 1958 attempt to restore the traditional interpretation of the 1789 housekeeping act as a mere authorization to preserve public records, Representative John E. Moss of California commented:

> The "housekeeping act" has been twisted and tortured by federal officials seeking to withhold information from the public and from the Congress. . . .
>
> A few of the recent examples of misuse of the act include the withholding by the Treasury Department of information about imports and exports; the attempt by the Agriculture Department to impose censorship as the price for cooperation in the making of newsreel and television films about agricultural subjects; the withholding of information by the Farmers' Home Administration and the Rural Electrification Administration on loans of public money.

Mr. Moss added a revealing datum: "Each of the ten Cabinet departments opposed this amendment to restore the traditional interpretation." [13]

With the shibboleths of secrecy, security and "classification," the executive has still further darkened the screen constructed out of the claims of constitutional privilege and separation of powers. Whenever the executive (or the bureaucracy) wishes to hide information from congressional scrutiny, it is only necessary to declare it "classified." Sometimes, granted the conditions of our age, this procedure is justified—as, for example, in the case of advanced military experiments, or the Federal Bureau of Investigation's "raw" (*i.e.,* unevaluated) security files on individuals [14]—but the secrecy labels have been extended over a considerable portion of the nation's ordinary business, which thus becomes removed from congressional (and thereby also from public) scrutiny.

The results are sometimes curious, from a traditional point of view.

[13] *New York Times,* Aug. 17, 1958.

[14] Common sense would agree that it would be improper to turn over such files to a large and factionally minded congressional committee. But even in this case there are solutions other than total executive immunity: *e.g.,* the British practice of showing the confidential material to a small parliamentary committee of authoritative and trusted members. Something of this sort was done in Washington during the 1953 conflict over the appointment of Charles Bohlen as Ambassador to Moscow.

The executive, for example, will call on Congress to vote appropriations for foreign aid, but will decline to furnish the information about what has been, is being and is intended to be done with the forign aid. On the basis of a special commission study, like the 1957 "Gaither report," the executive will demand certain armament funds; but will not show Congress the report which supplies the motivation. The executive will insist on Senate confirmation of a military treaty, like those establishing the North Atlantic or the Southeast Asia treaty organizations, without disclosing the commitments that the treaty entails. Thus, inevitably, the weakening of the congressional investigatory power leads to a correlated further weakening of the congressional share in the power of the purse, the war power and the treaty power.

It would be wrong to exaggerate the stage that the contest has reached. The investigatory power is bruised and shaken, but it is still vigorous. In fact, it is just because the investigatory power is so vigorous, because it retains more vitality than any other of the congressional powers, that it is so sharply under attack. It becomes easier to see why Dr. Ehrmann, reflecting on the experiences of many nations, concluded the study to which we have made reference with the summary judgment: "Certainly 'government by investigation is not government,' but government without investigation might easily turn out to be democratic government no longer."

A Threat to Civil Liberties?

LLOYD K. GARRISON *

Congressional investigations are a peculiarly American invention, born of the separation of the executive and legislative branches. They have served the country well and we could not do without them; but in recent years some of them have developed excesses which have caused their friends both in and out of Congress much concern.

In the way they treat witnesses and persons accused by witnesses, the committees may be likened to a poker, cool at one end and hot at the other. At the cool end, we see them performing their earliest historical function of checking up on the executive branch, seeking information and scrutinizing this or that activity. Congress has been at this salutary

* Noted New York lawyer and part-time Professor of Law at New York University. Former dean of the University of Wisconsin School of Law. The selection is from "Congressional Investigations: Are They a Threat to Civil Liberties?" *American Bar Association Journal,* Vol. 40 (February, 1954), pp. 125–128. By permission.

task since 1792, and in the course of it questions of civil liberties have seldom been presented.

At the cool end also are those investigations where the object is to get facts needed for the shaping of legislation. It was not till 1827 in the House and 1859 in the Senate that investigations of this sort, backed by the subpoena power, were instituted, but they have grown apace with the increasing complexity of legislative problems. In these inquiries, private citizens have been witnesses more often than government employees, and private rather than official acts more often the subject of examination; but where Congress has had a clear legislative end in view and the committees have sincerely sought light on defined and specific problems, questions of civil liberties have rarely arisen.

In both the executive and the legislative fields the process of investigation may shift toward the warmer end of the poker where the committees' motives are less simple and direct than those which have just been described. The bias against particular agencies or private groups has at times been so strong that their representatives or members have been treated less than fairly. Liberals and conservatives alike have complained of this sort of treatment.

The hot end of the poker begins to burn when the committee's target is no longer an agency or group but a single individual. There the individual, on trial for his actions, associations or beliefs, stands isolated and virtually defenseless. He may contend that no legislative purpose can be served by the investigation, or that given questions are not relevant to the subject matter of the inquiry, or that a subpoena of his private records is too broad; but these defenses are for practical purposes worthless (see the illuminating analysis by Judge Wyzanski in the March, 1948, issue of the *Record of The Association of the Bar of the City of New York*).

The witness may of course claim his privilege against self-incrimination and suffer the inferences which the public generally, and it may be justifiably, draws from such a plea. Apart from this he is substantially at the mercy of the committee. In extreme cases, where the investigation may destroy his livelihood, regardless of the truth of the charges, and the committee knows this or even encourages such a result, the committee's action may come close to being a bill of attainder. "A bill of attainder" said the Supreme Court in the post-Civil War case of Cummings *v.* Missouri, 4 Wall. (U.S.) 277, 323, "is a legislative Act which inflicts punishment without a judicial trial"; and a similar pronouncement was made in the companion case of *Ex parte* Garland, 4 Wall. (U.S.) 333. In those cases the Court reversed the convictions of Cummings, a Roman Catholic priest, and of Garland, a lawyer, for practicing their callings without swearing that they had never taken arms against the United States or abetted its enemies.

These cases were reaffirmed in 1945 in United States *v.* Lovett, 328 U.S. 303, where the Court said at page 318 that "When our Constitution and Bill of Rights were written, our ancestors had ample reason to know that legislative trials and punishments were too dangerous to liberty to exist in the nation of free men they envisaged. And so they proscribed bills of attainder." The Court accordingly held unconstitutional an act of Congress prohibiting salary payments to three named employees charged by a Committee with disloyalty. The Court said that: "What is involved here is a Congressional proscription of Lovett, Watson and Dodd, prohibiting their ever holding a government job. Were this case to be not justiciable, Congressional action, aimed at three named individuals, which stigmatized their reputation and seriously impaired their chance to earn a living, could never be challenged in any court. Our Constitution did not contemplate such a result" (page 314).

PERSONS UNDER INVESTIGATION SHOULD NOT BE DENIED RIGHTS

When a congressional committee in an investigation aimed at particular individuals "stigmatizes their reputation" and "seriously impairs their chance to earn a living," to use the language of the Court, the action is not far in effect as well as in spirit from the action condemned by the Constitution, even though the committee does not directly inflict the punishment but leaves that task to others, having reason to expect its due performance. The very fact that the committee's action, though close to a bill of attainder, is not literally one, emphasizes the need of affording defendants in these "legislative trials," to the fullest possible extent, the basic protections extended to accused criminals by the Bill of Rights.

And not to defendants only. Innocent outsiders may be, and in late years frequently have been, accused by witnesses in the course of particular investigations without an opportunity to appear and be heard in their own defense; and even where that opportunity has been given the defense has never yet caught up with the accusation.

In the light of these abuses numerous reforms have been proposed in recent years by leaders of the Bar, law teachers, The Association of the Bar of the City of New York, students of government, and members of Congress from both sides of the aisle. The proposals are of three sorts.

The first would bring the executive and legislative branches closer together in knowledge and understanding, so as to lessen the number of investigations and to improve their temper and narrow their scope. Outstanding is Senator Kefauver's bill for a question period in Congress comparable to that in the House of Commons, but adapted to the American scene. It seems to me wholly admirable in concept and in detail. It would not, however, affect investigations of individuals unconnected with the government, where the most severe abuses have occurred.

The second type of proposal relates to the all-important question of personnel. One measure, for example, would concentrate investigations in the hands of the standing committees and their subcommittees. This was intended by the Legislative Reorganization Act of 1946, but has not been fully accomplished. The great objection to special committees is that the person who proposes the resolution invariably is appointed chairman and then runs the show, whatever his qualifications.

Another set of proposals relating to personnel would sharply (and I think rightly) curtail the power of the chairman. Thus it is suggested that a majority of the committee should be required to authorize certain important steps, such as initiating an investigation, defining its scope, issuing subpoenas, finding a witness in contempt, deciding whether a given hearing should be public or in executive session, releasing or making use of testimony given in executive session, and approving the text of interim and final reports. Plainly there is need of a greater assumption of responsibility by committee members in spite of the heavy pressure for time under which all members labor. There is general agreement that all investigating committees should be provided with expert staff and counsel. It has also been proposed, with obvious justification, that committeemen and staff members should be precluded from speaking or writing about the committee's work for compensation, and that predictions and conclusions, which have so frequently prejudiced individuals, ought not to be publicly aired in advance of the report.

The third type of proposal has to do with procedural rules, of whose importance we as lawyers are particularly aware. The rules most frequently advocated are that a person who believes he has been injured by the testimony of another should have the right to appear and be heard, to call witnesses on his own behalf and to cross-examine his accusers, with the aid of counsel and of committee subpoenas if need be. These elementary rights, the core of our Anglo-Saxon system of discovering the truth, are long overdue in congressional investigations. They are needed not merely to protect the individual but even more importantly to bring out the truth in the public interest. They must obviously be subject to limitations and controls, lest the time of committees be unduly wasted and the proceedings get out of hand. These limitations and controls will not be easy to work out, and some degree of flexibility and room for experimentation seems desirable, But the practical problems, such as they may be, ought not to be allowed to delay action where the principle at stake is so clear.

At least one committee has successfully conducted an investigation in which all parties were given the right to examine and cross-examine witnesses and to rebut adverse testimony. This was the House Judiciary Committee's subcommittee on the study of monopoly power, under the chairmanship of Representative Celler. Concededly it operated in the cooler zone of seeking light on specific legislative problems and did not have to cope with the emotions and tensions that are aroused where a committee's object is to expose the activities, associations or beliefs of a particular individual. But even in investigations of the latter sort, where the rights in question are so essential to the ascertainment of the truth, there is no reason to suppose that the successful experience of the Celler committee could not be duplicated, given a competent chairman and rules of reasonable limitation.

WHAT SHOULD BE THE SCOPE OF INVESTIGATIONS

Now I turn to the question of the scope and reach of congressional investigations. This is of basic importance because even if rights of the sort just discussed are granted, they will necessarily fall short of those prevailing in courts of law, given the practical requirements of committee operation. Moreover the existence of these rights will not prevent the mere making of an accusation from irretrievably injuring the reputation of the person accused, however innocent he may later prove himself to be. This difficulty might be cured if it were possible to establish some closely safeguarded procedure, comparable to that of a grand jury, where charges could be sifted in private before any person was subjected to the humiliation of being publicly interrogated or denounced. But it is doubtful whether such a procedure could be worked out. Probably the nearest thing to it is the frequent practice of examining witnesses in executive session before a decision is reached as to whether to call them publicly; but this procedure in turn is unsatisfactory: because of time pressure, the attendance at executive sessions is generally meager and but little attention can be given to weighing the evidence after it is in; leaks to the watchful and sometimes prying press may occur, to the prejudice of the witness; and, particularly if the witness is a well-known person, the fact that he has been called is almost sure to become public knowledge and in and of itself is harmful to him. Finally—and this applies of course to public as well as executive sessions—the triers of the facts are politicians, of whom it can be said with certainty that they are neither juries nor judges.

These difficulties are inherent in trying to convert legislative investigations of individuals into the semblance of judicial trials. The judicial safeguards against falsehood and harassment which we so rightfully revere simply cannot, in full measure, be adapted to investigating committees. It follows from this that Congress should exercise the utmost restraint in launching investigations of individuals where by the very nature of the process, even after all practical procedural reforms have been made, full justice cannot be done and truthful conclusions cannot be assured. It does not follow, however, that there are any areas of American life which should permanently and under all circumstances be blocked off from the scrutiny of committees. Congress would not stand for such a limitation and the public interest would not be served by it. We need only recall a few of those investigations in which the careers of individuals were shattered but the country was the gainer: Teapot Dome, for example, and the King Committee's recent investigation of the Bureau of Internal Revenue, and other inquiries into alleged frauds upon the government. Similarly, some of the exposures of Communist infiltration into government, illustrated by examples of particular individuals, helped to illuminate the nature and objectives of the Communist Party and the steps that the government must take in self-defense.

What is needed is not a fixed limitation upon the scope of congressional investigations, but the assumption of a greater degree of responsibility by Congress as a whole for what is done in its name. Even the Supreme Court upon occasion has had to be admonished to exercise self-restraint within its sphere of power. The time is surely ripe for a congressional stock-taking of that which it is permitting its committees to do, particularly in the field of alleged subversion, where because of the natural anxieties of our citizens and the dazzling glare of publicity committee activities are heavily concentrated.

In this most sensitive field of inquiry, the investigations have proliferated out into the community in an ever-widening circle, embracing all manner of people unconnected with the government or with the defense effort, in walks of life far removed from any possibility of sabotage, espionage or interference with the economy, and far removed also from any serious likelihood of federal regulation. It is in these investigations that the maximum harm can be done to innocent individuals with the least gain to the country. I suppose that wherever in private life a Communist member is made to suffer from public exposure some damage, potential or actual, is done to the Party, and this may be chalked up as a gain; but we must measure the cost on the other side of the ledger. There is, to begin with, the injury to those who, having been called to testify, are not shown to have had any connection with the Party, or whose connection with it was at some time in the past. More seriously, the spreading ambit of these inquiries into men's beliefs and associations, past and present, contributes to the general state of timidity and conformity that is creeping over the land and sapping our vitality as a nation. Nothing is more un-American than timidity and conformity. And nothing is more risky in the age in which we live.

We are living as Toynbee puts it, in a "time of troubles." In such a time it is above all things important that we, the people of the United States, should remain clear-headed, unafraid, resourceful in our thinking as in our actions, and ready to change old policies, and, if need be, invent new ones, as circumstances may require. The censorship of books, attacks upon schools, colleges, newspaper editors and clergymen, the browbeating of those both in and out of government who dare to criticize the conduct of investigations, the multiplication of loyalty oaths and tests for various kinds of private employment, the building up of multitudinous dossiers on the private lives of citizens, the use against individuals of the undisclosed contents of reports prepared by secret agents, the increasingly intolerant treatment of immigrants and aliens, the excessive encroachments upon executive functions, and the spreading abroad of fear, suspicion and confusion—in these developments lie serious risks to our national sanity and our capacity to deal boldly and creatively with a world in ferment.

It would be unfair to ascribe to congressional investigations all of these threats to our true security. Many of them stem from state and municipal actions, and many are initiated or furthered by private groups. But what Congress does affects the whole body politic more powerfully than any other influence; the dramas of the committee rooms radiate outward to a watching and listening public and profoundly affect for good or evil the patterns of thought and emotion which in the end will shape our destinies.

So I say that there is no more urgent need than for Congress to assume responsibility not merely for improving the procedures of its committees but for passing upon the scope and reach and aims of their investigations.

What, then, specifically should be done? Two possible courses, among many which have been proposed, suggest themselves. The first would be for Congress to establish a joint standing Committee on Investigations, composed of leading members of both houses, to which all requests for investigations would be referred for study and recommendation. The joint Committee would first consider whether or not there was need of the investigation, balancing gains and risks from an over-all national standpoint. The joint committee would also consider how the investigation could best be conducted, whether by a standing committee or a special committee, or (as has often been suggested) by outside experts or officials together with Senators and Representatives, or by officials or outside experts alone, with or without the grant of particular powers. The joint committee would also consider whether any special procedures or safeguards should be adopted, consistent with the practical requirements of the task to be done, and having in mind the extent to which the rights of individuals might be adversely affected. The joint Committee would be required to report within a stated time, and its report would be recommendatory only, final responsibility being borne by the particular house involved.

A second step forward could be taken by Congress's adoption of minimum standards for the conduct of all investigating committees, defining the functions of chairmen and the duties of members, and the rights of witnesses and persons accused by witnesses. The makings of these minimum standards already exist in various pending bills introduced by Senators and Congressmen who have given long and patient study to the matter. Several committees have, in addition, adopted rules of procedure of their own which mark a real step forward. Common agreement should be possible, and the standards when adopted could from time to time be improved by particular committees and by Congress itself after adequate experimentation.

There will of course be many difficulties in the way of any reform: the vested interests of particular committees, the ambitions of individual Senators and Congressmen. But Congress is responsive to the will of an informed people. . . .

The Welfare State

IN AN AGE of vast and proliferating government regulation and enterprise, an issue of persistent and increasing importance is: What are
the economically efficient and politically democratic limits of what
has come to be known as the welfare state? This issue receives the
attention of three scholars in the pages that follow.

Topic 25

THE DEMOCRATIC LIMITS OF THE WELFARE STATE

৪৩

The Limits of Intervention

LOUIS M. HACKER *

The current debate on the limits of intervention (Is the welfare state inevitable? Can we stop short of socialism?) is taking place in a fog through
which light shines only occasionally. In consequence, voices seem disembodied and values unreal as historical experience and political and economic
truths are sacrificed to the demands of urgency. It has been said, for example,
by a recent writer, that our modern world is unique because of "the decline
of competition, the recurrence of periods of depression and the persistence
of demands for basic economic reforms," [1] and that first call upon economic
and political statesmanship is the resolution of our "pressing immediacies"

* Professor of Economics and former Dean of the School of General Studies at
Columbia University. Author of *The Shaping of the American Tradition* and *The
Triumph of American Capitalism*. The selection is from Louis M. Hacker, "The
Limits of Intervention," *The American Scholar*, Vol. 19 (Autumn,, 1950), pp. 481–
486. By permission.
[1] K. William Kapp, "Economic Planning and Freedom" in *Weltwirtschaftliches
Archiv*, Band 64, Heft 1 (Hamburg, 1950).

—to wit, stability, security and full employment. National planning stands high on any agenda.[2]

Why urgency? These analyses, or reproaches, are almost as old as historical man himself. The Gracchi talked in the same vein; so did the rebels and popular leaders of the early fourteenth and sixteenth centuries. The complaints against monopoly and depression fill the pages of our first economic literature; the demands for "basic economic reform"—to mention only the best known of the viewers-with-alarm—go back as far as Harrington in the seventeenth century, and their number is legion in the nineteenth (Saint-Simon, Owen, Fourier, Proudhon, Cabet, Marx, Morris, Bellamy).

Another question: Dare a democracy ever yield to a sense of urgency? If we believe in unlimited debate, the examination of choices, and the peaceful persuasion and full support of a majority of the electorate—as well as the conversion of the majority by a minority—can we at any time say that emergency measures are in order? A fair charge against Lincoln was that he suspended habeas corpus and imposed martial law in Northern districts that were not even threatened by invasion. Even when Britain was so threatened, after the fall of France, its government never abridged the constitutional guarantees of the British people.

These questions, however, are not my immediate interest here. I am addressing myself to that of intervention: Are there limits to it? In fact, how far can public authority legitimately go before it changes our world entirely from the one we have to another with completely different codes of behavior, morality and welfare? . . .

The middle-of-the-roaders, the faint of heart, Mr. Arthur M. Schlesinger, Jr.'s "vital centrists," hope we can stop in midcareer and that "the welfare state" will be a working compromise between no-intervention and full-intervention. But the fox has been flushed, the hounds are in full cry, and away we go over hill and dale, not meaning to pull up until we are in at the kill. "Kill" is the wrong word, of course, except to the cynical. The happy huntsmen are convinced we can plan for stability and security, and at the same time maintain full consumer choices, a free market, and the right to invest—which means to take risks. *Our* welfare state will not be dominated by the police.

The British Labor government has formally declared that its grand plan encompasses only these three ideas: direction over investment, location of industry, and foreign exchange. It does not mean to nationalize entirely, and never without compensation. No policeman here—certainly as far as the Englishman's fundamental rights are concerned. But let us see.[3]

---

[2] J. B Condliffe, *The Commerce of Nations* (New York, 1950).

[3] Mr. Harold Wilson, President of the British Board of Trade, reported in The London *Times,* Jan. 20, 1950: "Basic controls, such as those of the location of industry, foreign exchange and the volume of investment, will be maintained as permanent in-

You want to start a newspaper and you begin making your rounds of the very many public offices involved. You learn, in time, that your investment plans, for share capital to erect buildings and furnish equipment, cannot have top priority ("More important to build houses for workers"); that paper shortages forbid the launching of new publishing ventures ("Purchases from the dollar area must be rigorously controlled by import licenses"); that all trained workers already have jobs and trade-union contracts ("A planned economy is based on high employment"). Socialism has a job to be done; first things come first, and dissent—which has always been a luxury— must wait its turn. There is no open attack on liberty. It is only that the sustenance it requires for survival simply becomes more difficult, if not impossible, to obtain. . . .

And as regards the brave challenge: "The art of political economy . . . must take account of criteria other than wealth"—this has been the stand of every Utopian from Plato up to and beyond William Morris. Without wealth —achieved not through privilege but by starting risky ventures—how can men launch new and cheaper ways of making goods and creating services? And unless we do so. will the cruel poverty which plagues so large a part of the population of the earth's surface, causing disease, starvation and early death, ever be abolished? Only a fool will deny that great deficits everywhere exist in the areas of health, education, child care—all the social services. The point is a simple one: Unless we continue to expand and create new engines of production—tearing down obsolescent plants, erecting more efficient factories and mills, building hydroelectric irrigation and flood-control projects, laying out more systems of communication—and make it possible, in consequence, to turn out more and cheaper hard and soft goods, we cannot pay for social security. The fascinating and frightening lesson of Britain's National Health Act is that its people need health services, but that the British economy will go bankrupt if its socialist leaders continue trying to pay for the health program at the expense of plant modernization. At this point in our development we simply cannot afford socialism—at any rate, Christian socialism, which is a morality and not a method for organizing production.

All this being so, how far may we expect the state to go? It has traditional roles which all of us in a democratic society are accustomed to see performed. It provides for the national defense; it maintains and upholds an incorruptible judiciary guided by the Rule of Law; it encourages and safeguards freedom of religion, communication and association; it gives minority groups protection and permits them to be heard; it employs the police power to defend and improve the life, health and morals of its people. The state can and should

---

struments to ensure the maintenance of our economic position and the fulfillment of our full employment programme."

go further; and, having said this, one should also be prepared to say: There are other functions which are the proper concerns, but also the limits, of state intervention. I record them here, not necessarily in the order of their importance.

1. The protection of private property is an important function of the state. If we are committed to the encouragement of innovation in order to increase production; if we are ready to agree that capital formation in a poor world is still a crying need; if we concede that the maintenance of unequal wage and salary scales is one of the ways through which savings can occur; if, from historical experience, we are prepared to recognize that unless risks can be taken—and fortunes made by the successful—the idea of economic progress must be abandoned, then private property and private business decision must be assured. In a free society, the existence of free consumer choices always will keep resources scarce. Unless we build our foundations on the vision of an ideal Spartan world—Plato's and More's and Marx's Utopias—there will always continue to be a relative dearth of goods. It is idle to talk of the abolition of wages as an ultimate goal, for the surfeit of plenty of which all well-intentioned romanticists have dreamed (Marx was the worst of the lot!) can never be realized.

The existence of unequal wages is one of the great social incentives: in fact, unequal wage scales are further developed in the Soviet Union than in most capitalist countries. Unequal wage and salary scales—leading to private fortunes—are a great spur to innovation. Short of a war period (the caterpillar tractor, the jet plane, atomic energy), it still is to be demonstrated that a planned and regulated economy is a more favorable climate for innovation than capitalism. The very nature of socialism—the timidity of functionaries, the vested interests of labor unions and cooperatives, the curious cost-accounting procedures—stifles innovation. Capitalism is not on trial here; its achievements, as far as production is concerned, have been magnificent. If the state means to concern itself with social welfare, it must permit adventurers to invest, take risks, and save for further investments from their successful ventures.

2. All this does not mean that privilege is to be tolerated. Tariffs that have outlived their usefulness (encouraging infant industries) must be abolished; monopolies and unfair trade practices are to be fought; patents are proper, but they should not be privately suppressed; excessive fortunes and idle funds should be regarded with suspicion. Every political thinker worthy of the name, from Aristotle to John Stuart Mill, was aware of the fact that no society could endure for long, or ward off social discontent, unless it constantly preoccupied itself with the question of the redistribution of wealth and income. There was always a wealthy group in the top layer and a poor one in the bottom. In between was to remain that broad sector of the middle class

which had the fluidity and opportunity to reach above or—if unsuccessful —to fall below.

Redistribution, through taxation, keeps opportunity alive and makes possible the regular emergence of new adventurers or innovators. So does the maintenance of the luxury industries, although in a minor way. Mandeville, in part, was right: the luxury industries are useful—not, of course, because they give employment, but because they help the profligate and stupid to speed the processes of redistribution. (J. M. Keynes was either cynical or entirely despairing when he applauded Mandeville.) Taxation, of course, is a two-edged sword: it always threatens the life of incentive.

3. Given the possession of that awful weapon, fiscal power, the state has a great responsibility: the protection of society's credit structure is in its hands. The state cannot be heedless in the management of its own finances. So completely—for good or ill—does it dominate central banking today that any recklessness on its part must have a blighting effect on enterprise at once. A sound monetary and credit system and a manageable public debt are the first concerns of virtuous lawmakers; otherwise, economic chaos inevitably follows. The history books are filled with too many familiar examples to require their recital here.

This warning, particularly, must be taken to heart by new or underdeveloped nations. The formula of inflation (or repudiation) and price and exchange controls seems such a simple and magical one; but only one's own people—and not for long—can be bemused by it. Certainly the stranger— the foreign investor and trader—will smell danger at once. That great and wise young man, Alexander Hamilton, America's first secretary of the Treasury, knew how vital it was that the young republic's public and private credit be built on an indestructible foundation. He paid off the revolutionary foreign and domestic debts; the prewar commercial claims of English merchants were to be honored; the new public debt was to be secured by a sinking fund; a central bank was established to regulate the currency; and long-term foreign funds and short-term financing flowed into the United States, to make its formative years secure.[4]

It would be idle to maintain that lawmakers must ever close their minds to the occasional necessity for unbalanced budgets. The experiences of the 1930's and the teachings of Keynes and his disciples are valuable here: deficit financing in bad years, surpluses in good ones. But what shall we say of a government which, during the greatest peacetime period of prosperity in its history, complacently draws up a budget calling for a deficit of five billions of dollars?

I am arguing for fiscal integrity; but I am not saying that state fiscal intervention should never take place. In a young or growing economy, there are

[4] See my own *England & America: The Ties that Bind. An Inaugural Lecture* (Oxford, 1948) for a fuller exposition of this point.

many areas where private capital cannot enter because it is not powerful enough. Indeed, in the underdeveloped countries—in the new nations of India and Israel, for example, and in Latin America—public investment will undoubtedly occur. Private investment, with foreign funds, however, is more efficient, and because it is willing to take risks is less likely to be badgered by the cautious or the foolish. An illuminating contrast is that between the building of the railroads by foreign private capital in the United States after the Civil War, on the one hand, and, on the other, the current efforts of the British Labor government to push its great groundnuts project in Africa. In both cases, financial failure initially took place. In the United States, the railroads were built despite the losses suffered by British, German and Swiss investors; in Britain, the plans for the development of Africa have come under such sharp criticism that the government has been forced to narrow and limit its outlays.[5]

4. Up to this point, I have mentioned the economic responsibilities of the state; there remains to be discussed an important social one. All cultures have had dependent or unemployable persons. Their care becomes a public duty in a world such as ours which advances in medical knowledge and develops a more refined social conscience, prolongs the age of child dependency, increases life expectation and therefore the numbers of the old, and has large numbers of the chronically and permanently ill. A distinction should be drawn between the sick and those chronically and permanently ill; between the unemployed and the unemployables. Invalidity, dependent mothers and children, and the aged (where there do not exist adequate pension programs) are a public concern and should be budgeted for.

On the other hand, the sick can be taken care of more efficiently and at less cost by private-insurance and group-medicine devices. And the unemployed can be protected by pension funds and schemes. There is a large area of joint enterprise, participated in by industry and labor, which we are beginning to explore in the United States. This, it seems to me, is a more fruitful experimentation than state programs. The welfare funds currently being set up in many of our industries place administration and responsibility where they belong; and they have the great virtue of preserving the independence of the unions.

If we mean what we say about our liberties, then pluralistic loyalties need encouraging: devolution of power, and not its concentration, is the key to proper political thinking. The welfare state (or socialism) produces the reverse, and sooner or later, because it has fiscal authority over all the social services, as well as over credit, production and exchange, it must

---

[5] Because I favor foreign investments, I know I will be charged with "imperialism." Two of the greatest troublemakers of modern times have been Hobson and Lenin, who popularized, and cast obloquy on, this concept. See my *England & America,* heretofore referred to.

weaken the independence of associations (trade unions, trade associations) and convert them into pale satellites without lives of their own.

5. Finally, I wish to mention what may be called the psychological duty of the state: the preservation of opportunity. There will not be an active and contented citizenry unless opportunity flourishes, unless people can climb up and down the ladder of economic success and social recognition. The founder of the Medicis began as a wool comber; the first Astor was a butcher boy; the first Vanderbilt, a ferryman. Innovators must have the chance to start, and their talents demand social acceptance. In our world of great institutional organization—the guidance of public offices, corporations, trade unions—the surest way to maintain opportunity is through the creation and defense of full educational facilities.

The state must educate, therefore, because education is expensive and should be universal. Plato's Academy, the Stoics, Peter Abelard, could meet their pupils over a covered walk or in a room; the gathering together of teachers and scholars for discourse constituted early education. But when education requires libraries, laboratories and elaborate equipment; when education begins with infancy and does not end until death; when it tries to reach whole populations to train for the effective citizenship of all rather than the leadership of the few—then we cannot escape public outlays.

Outlays are one thing; supervision is another. This is not the place to examine closely the complicated question of educational policy. The elimination of privately-administered educational institutions would be a tragedy, if we really mean what we say about wanting to uphold a democratic society and to produce free men. Authority does not start in the schools; it begins in the family, probably. But certainly the perversion of young minds can be effectively completed, and their thought forever controlled, by those who dominate education.

The state undoubtedly will have to subsidize higher education (scholarships would be the best way), but educational administration should be in the hands of local agencies (where the schools are public) and in the hands of faculties (where the schools are private). If the schools can be kept independent, the Big Policeman will be kept cut down to size.

The preservation of liberty is no longer an abstract question. Political theorists, up to now, have always assumed that threats to it came from irresponsible authority. But liberty can be put in jeopardy equally by a state which starts out with benevolent intentions. Socialism's aim is not power but welfare; yet in striving to achieve welfare it threatens innovation, sacrifices fiscal integrity, and dries up opportunity. The state has positive functions; but, if we are interested in economic progress and the maintenance of liberty, there should be specific limits on intervention. To define functions is also to limit them.

Empirical Problems and Particular Goals

CHARLES E. LINDBLOM *

Mr. Hacker asks: "Is the welfare state inevitable? Can we stop short of socialism?" But these factual questions he chooses not to answer. Instead he defines the *proper* limits of government intervention, and we can only guess whether the inevitable is improper.

For present purposes, I am inclined to believe that he has asked the wrong questions, but answered the right ones (though wrongly). Leaving prediction aside, I shall comment on his proposals for proper policy.

To ask how far government should go is something like asking how fast an automobile should be driven. I think Mr. Hacker is, in effect, saying that he cannot agree that fifty miles per hour is a proper maximum, even if it was once so considered. But he cannot, on the other hand, approve speeds of much over seventy miles per hour because he knows the hazards of high velocity.

As ordinarily asked and answered, such questions come close to being nonsense. Ninety miles per hour is no further from an optimum than forty or sixty. It all depends on traffic, weather, the effectiveness of brakes, the vision and reaction time of the driver, the technical characteristics of the automobile, and a number of other variables which not only can be changed, but are, in fact, always changing.

Similarly, the proper limits on government in economic life depend on a number of changeable and ever-changing conditions about which Mr. Hacker says almost nothing. Limits on intervention should depend on at least the following variables:

1. *The community's objectives or values.* These objectives change frequently, and the functions of government ought to change with them.

2. *The specific kinds of problems with which the community must deal.* It is incredible that the common prescriptions for the limits of government intervention have not been rewritten since Hiroshima. While national security has dictated a government monopoly of a potential major source of industrial energy, we idiotically turn out the same old slogans.

3. *The degree to which power in government can be held responsible.* This, in turn, depends upon such factors as the degree of consensus in the com-

* Professor of Economics, Yale University. Author of *Unions and Capitalism* and other books and articles. The selection is from Charles E. Lindblom, "Empirical Problems and Particular Goals," *The American Scholar,* Vol. 19 (Autumn, 1950), pp. 486–488. By permission.

munity, the level of party responsibility, and the extent of citizen participation in politics. Again, these are not only varying but variable.

4. *The effectiveness of alternative nongovernmental techniques for reaching individual and community objectives.* Would it have been sensible, for example, to debate the ambitious extension of government power involved in the establishment of the Federal Reserve System without first diagnosing the performance of private banking as of 1913?

If we first become reasonably clear about our values and objectives, the determination of the proper limits on government power then becomes a technical problem, largely empirical rather than moral—approached in the same way that we determine optimum driving speeds by examining, among other things, night blindness among drivers.

The converse of this proposition is that the limits of intervention cannot successfully be discussed with terms which reduce complicated empirical questions to relatively simple problems of morality. . . .

It is high time we stopped talking about socialism. Mr. Hacker is against socialism, but this assurance gives me very little idea of what he is actually against. If socialism means increased government intervention in economic life, he is not opposed. If it means more equality—social and economic —he is not opposed. If it means democratization of industrial life, I infer that he is not opposed to that either. If his objection to socialism simply reflects his belief that too much is too much, we can dispense with the term and get down to the job of defining "too much."

On the other hand, if Mr. Hacker's repeated objections to socialism record his opposition to nationalization of industry, I suggest that he is beating a dead horse. We in the United States have long ago agreed that nationalization was a suitable specific organizational technique in certain limited circumstances. Among democratic socialists here and abroad, this is about all that is today being claimed for nationalization. What specific industries are well suited to nationalization is a technical question on which sweeping generalizations are worthless.

I would therefore conclude that social policies should be designed neither to "save" capitalism from socialism, nor to substitute socialism for capitalism. We live in an economy as much socialist as capitalist—and I can say this easily because neither of the terms means anything in particular. Policy should now be directed to choosing and developing the best of specific alternative social techniques, public and private, to achieve particular social goals. My guess is that policy so designed would be less timid than Mr. Hacker's.

Defense of the Welfare State

MAX LERNER *

I find Professor Hacker less persuasive in his introductory remarks than he is when he tackles the main matter at hand. He asks, to start with, "why the urgency" about economic reform, and points out that the reformist analyses and reproaches "are almost as old as historical man himself." It is a little as if a writer on medicine were to ask "why the urgency" in the efforts to improve medical science, and were to point out that the diagnoses of disease and the calls for cure "are almost as old as historical man himself."

More than a decade ago I wrote a book called *It Is Later Than You Think*. I would not in today's crisis diminish in the slightest degree the sense of urgency implied in that title. I am certain that Professor Hacker will not deny the reality of the contemporary struggle between an all-out totalitarianism, which aims to put the whole economy, and with it the whole human mind and personality, under rigid public direction, and, on the other hand, the effort to find a way of organizing the economy effectively without destroying freedom. The problem is at once economic, political and moral. When Professor Hacker says with disdain that "socialism—at any rate, Christian socialism . . . is a morality and not a method for organizing production," he does it less than justice by denying its economic and political aspect; yet its moral emphasis—the effort at a greater economic security and stability, the effort to meet the threat of corporate power-aggregates, the effort to create access to opportunity for all—is not in our day a negligible emphasis. In most areas of the world the problem that Professor Hacker is inclined to dismiss with an air of tiredness as old stuff of the utopian brand is a problem as real as livelihood and freedom. If we ignore it or abdicate it, we may find soon that we have lost the battle for the allegiance of men, and with it the chance to explore further the best ways of organizing an economy for common ends through democratic means.

Professor Hacker gets some telling effects from the English dilemma by pointing out that if your choice is between paying for social security or using the same limited funds to renovate obsolescent machinery, it is no solution to let the machinery go on obsolescing. What he does not add is that America, with a national income approaching three hundred billion dollars a year, is not faced by anything like so cruel a choice. I have noted a tendency

* Professor of American Civilization at Brandeis University. Author of *It Is Later Than You Think, American Civilization,* and other books; newspaper columnist. The selection is from Max Lerner, "State Capitalism and Business Capitalism," *The American Scholar,* Vol. 19 (Autumn, 1950), pp. 488–491. By permission.

on the part of many of the critics of the New Deal and Fair Deal to use the case of England as a whipping boy. They attribute to socialism all the present ills of England, and by a transposition they imply that Americans, too, will have to live under austerity, and ration orange juice and gasoline, if they move further toward socialism. On the other hand, they attribute to pure capitalism all the productive achievements and material prosperity of America today, and by a transposition they imply that if contemporary Britain had not followed after the strange gods of socialism, the British, too, would have today a bull market, roads crowded with burnished autos, shop windows crammed full of luxuries, the highest living standards in history, a Byzantine lushness of life, and money to burn.

It should be pointed out for the historical record that there is a difference in the resources of the two countries, both natural and human. It should also be pointed out that the obsolescence of British machinery, British railway equipment, British coal mining equipment, was notorious long before the labor governments were even heard of. Writing in 1915, Thorstein Veblen, in his *Imperial Germany and the Industrial Revolution,* gave a classic analysis of Britain's lag in terms of "the penalty for taking the lead." Whether he was right or wrong in his analysis, the fact of the British lag was recognized thirty-five years ago. Professor Hacker, who has had a first hand acquaintance with Britain as exchange professor at Oxford, should know that the bankruptcy of Britain is not the consequence of the labor government, but that the labor government is the consequence of the bankruptcy of Britain. That bankruptcy came under capitalist auspices, and was nourished by the fearful material and human expenditures of two world wars. British socialism, to the extent that it exists, is a particular kind of socialism that comes in the wake of a deficit economy. That is why Aneuran Bevan was so roundly cheered at a British Labor party conference when he said that "the language of priorities is the religion of socialism." Because the British problem was one of priorities, it does not follow that it is—or would be—the American problem as well.

The case of America presents, not the problem of deficits, but the problems of distribution, stability, security. What Professor Hacker calls deficits in the areas of health, education, child care, and the social services are (for the case of America) deficits not for all the people but only for some of the people. The New Deal and Fair Deal have already gone a considerable distance toward wiping them out, and the Cassandra-like prophecies which have dogged us since 1934—that we could do so only by eating into risk capital and investment capital—have proved utterly empty. Always we were asked the question: "Where will the money come from?"—the question that Professor Hacker is still asking. Would it be acrimonious to suggest that not only has the community found the money to establish these services, but that in the process both the volume of capital and the profits of private enterprise have been increased? And I would suggest also that to go farther along the same road, and wipe out wholly the deficits in the areas of health, education, child care and all the social services would, far from destroying the private sectors of the economy, build an even stronger base under their prosperity.

I hope I am not unfair to Professor Hacker when I say that he seems to miss the dynamic elements in the American economy. Like other critics of the Welfare State, his thinking seems to go back to the presuppositions of the wage-fund economic theorists—that there is a static fund of income upon which the society can draw as upon a bank account, and that if you withdraw it for social security, for public medical services, for farm subsidies, for public-housing construction, for hydroelectric dams, you may overdraw your account. What we have found in the case of America since the beginning of the New Deal is that the psychological factors are the crucial ones in an economy, as in all human living. John Maynard Keynes understood this, and that is why he evolved a new—if still crude—psychological language of the "propensities" to save and spend and consume. Given a strong base of resources, managerial ability, technology and labor power, as we have in America, the extent of potential national product and national income in the calculable future is such as to stagger the imagination. In that sense, the most recent report of the Committee of Economic Advisers to the President was not a utopian or a whimsical report, but a realistic assessment of what can be accomplished in the next fifty years, based upon what we have accomplished in the past twenty years. The psychological atmosphere of confidence, employment and social construction achieved by the New Deal gave a fillip to the managerial group, as well as to the workers and the consumers. That is why America has managed at once to move toward a Welfare State and to increase its national income.

But the psychological factor is only one of a complex of factors that made this possible. It would be as foolish to attribute the results to government intervention as it would be to insist that America's current prosperity is due to the boldness and imaginativeness of "risk taking capital." The wealth of a nation lies in the state of its industrial arts, its technological advance, its managerial skills, its labor force. All of these may be called "socialist" in the sense that they are all community possessions. They come from social sources and they should pay a social dividend. To an extent they are doing so in America. Wages and living standards are high, profits are unexampled, new industries and new millionaires are being created. And all of this is being done within what has been called the "strait jacket" of the New Deal and the Fair Deal.

But there are lumps in the porridge. Professor Hacker, I am sure, will agree with me when I enumerate them. The biggest lump is the fact that much of our present prosperity is the result of armament economics.

Second, there is the glaring fact of corporate monopoly. Since the 1880's the free American economy has been growing less free. The path of monopoly is strewn with the graves of small enterprises. Every year the area of concentrated corporate power gets greater; the area of small business enterprise shrinks. The monopolies are governments in themselves and bureaucracies in themselves. They levy their toll, as Thurman Arnold has pointed out, not only on their rivals, but also on the consumer. They are the American form of feudalism.

The third lump is boom-and-bust. The American economy has gone periodically through fevers and chills. To the extent that we carry over the planlessness of the past, to that extent we shall continue the alternation of boom-and-bust.

The fourth lump is that so-called "risk taking capital" has tended to stay out of the areas of risk, and to play it safe. It has not pushed with boldness into the possibilities of large scale investment with low profit margins. Some of the critics of American capitalism from inside have pointed out that it has not taken advantage of doing a larger volume of business on a lower margin of profit. It has tended to charge what the traffic will bear. The replacement of Commonwealth and Southern by the TVA has shown that the government is sometimes in a better position to take risks than private capital is. In the entire field of housing today there is very little risk left. The risks are all guaranteed by public funds, and the profits are the reward, not of risk, but of capital.

It is to correct these still crucial defects of our economy that we must continue along the path of economic reform.

This means exploring further what John Stuart Mill called the "limits of the province of government." Professor Hacker has mapped out with considerable cogency the five major duties of the state, and then he has drawn a line as with a flaming sword, with the injunction: "thus far and no farther at your mortal peril."

I cannot have his certitude about how definite these limits are. I think it is a matter for many decades of further experience and further experiment and the further use of the inquiring mind.

Western Europe, especially Britain, has been experimenting with the socialism of the deficit economy. America alone, as I have said, has the resources for experimenting with a better organization of a surplus economy.

It will not do to debate the issue as if it were a clear one between "capitalism" and "socialism." The fact is that in the modern Western State, whether in Britain or America, whether in Israel or India (both of which have become Western states), there are elements both of capitalism and of socialism. Perhaps it would be better to say that there are elements of business capitalism and of state capitalism. The problem is how to form an amalgam of them which will achieve the best form of welfare economy.

Britain has moved reluctantly toward a larger public sector—that is, a sector of state capitalism. It has done so from necessity in the interest of sheer survival, although the Marxist tradition of the Labor party has given the new developments a dogmatic welcome. America has moved, also under the spur of necessity, toward enlarged sectors of public action in the economy. Dogmatically we abhor every such step. We call it "socialism" and many worse names as well. But under the spur of the great depression, and the thrust of the democratic welfare impulse, which is very strong in the American tradition, we have nevertheless kept moving. Our problem has been, not sheer survival, as in the case of Britain, but stability and security.

I don't think that Professor Hacker is justified in ridiculing the concept of a mixed economy, such as will be found in Professor Schlesinger's *Vital Center* and in Irwin Ross's book on the mixed economy, *Strategy for Liberals*. Our whole historic instinct has been to cling to the private sector wherever we can, to move toward the public sector only when we must. There is no danger within the American tradition and the American psychology that we will embrace socialism either out of dogmatic enthusiasm or subservience to the state. The greater danger lies in the fact that the great power structures in America are the aggregates of corporate power; that they function very much as governments function; that, more than ever, they control the agencies of public opinion and influence the direction of education and belief; that the business system in America is invested with power, and that property is invested with sanctity and with grace. My own anxiety is not that we will slip unaware into socialism, but that we will not have the courage to challenge those who fear the valid extensions of the public sector.

Section XI

Democracy Evaluated

THAT GOVERNMENTS derive "their just powers from the consent of the governed" appears to many Americans so self-evident as to require no demonstration. But in a world in which democracy as understood and valued in the West is under challenge, it is essential to subject this premise to continuing examination.

This section begins with a selection from Edward Sait who maintains that there are serious weaknesses in traditional democratic theory and practice. It follows with the Leninist-Stalinist critique of capitalist democracy. [It may be asked why a book on American government should include excerpts from Lenin's *State and Revolution* and Stalin's speech on Soviet "Democracy." An excellent answer can be found in John Stuart Mill's famous essay "On Liberty": "They [who] have never thrown themselves into the mental position of those who think differently from them and considered what such persons may have to say . . . do not, in any proper sense of the word, know the doctrine which they themselves profess," or, at best their conclusion is held "in a manner of a prejudice, with little comprehension or feeling of its rational grounds." It must be borne in mind, too, that the most serious challenge to American democracy today is being made in the name and under claim of a superior form of Soviet "democracy"—a claim that demands critical evaluation.]

A reply to the Communist challenge and a defense of democracy are from the writings of H. B. Mayo and others who emphasize the fundamental values which democracy promotes. [In earlier topics consideration was given to the value and limits of free expression. The case for free speech is obviously an integral part of the case for democracy and arguments which support one will ordinarily support the other.]

371

Topic 26

WHITHER DEMOCRACY?

The Decline of Democracy

EDWARD MCCHESNEY SAIT *

The triumphs of democracy in the nineteenth century bred a strange mystical faith that did not allow itself to be disturbed by facts. . . . The fundamentalist holds fast to the original creed by lifting it above the plane of reason and argument. It is revealed truth. No matter what strange anomalies confront him in its practical application, he must keep this precious inheritance whole and undefiled. The cure for the shortcomings of democracy, he always maintains, is more democracy. If he is confronted with facts, with the contradiction between those facts and his theory, he replies that "democracy must not be judged by its yesterday, or by its to-day, but by its to-morrow"—its always receding to-morrow; and that, as Chesterton says of Christianity, it has not been tried and found wanting, but found hard and not tried.

The fundamentalist takes a sanguine view of human nature and of average human capacity. He believes that, notwithstanding the evil propensities of individuals, men taken in the mass spontaneously generate the truth, or at least, by some mysterious power of divination, recognize the truth and resolutely follow it. The voice of the people is the voice of God. . . .

Now, since the voice of the people is the voice of God, a peculiar spiritual quality attaches to the ballot, through which the people speak. The ballot has magical properties. A century ago, the English fundamentalists embodied their aspirations—universal suffrage, annual elections, vote by ballot, etc.—in the People's Charter and took Feargus O'Connor as their prophet. Deploring the misery of the masses, O'Connor said: "Laws made by all would be respected by all. . . . Universal Suffrage would, at once, change the whole character of society from a state of watchfulness, doubt, and suspicion, to that of brotherly love, reciprocal interest, and universal confidence. . . . Away, then, with the whole system at once: The wound is too deep to be healed by partial remedies; the nation's heart's blood is

* Late Professor of Government, Pomona College. Author of *American Parties and Elections* and of *Democracy*. The selection is from Edward McChesney Sait, *Political Institutions: A Preface* (New York, Appleton-Century-Crofts, Inc., 1938), Ch. XIX. By permission.

flowing too rapidly to be stopped by ordinary stypticks. . . . Give us, then, the only remedy for all our social ills and political maladies; make every man in his artificial state as he might be in his natural state, his own doctor, by placing the restorative in his hand, which is UNIVERSAL SUFFRAGE!!! . . . Six months after the Charter is passed every man, woman, and child in the country will be well fed, well housed, and well clothed." . . .

According to the Greek view—the view of Plato and Aristotle and Polybius—forms of government perpetually change and succeed each other in some definite cycle; but, according to the fundamentalist, democracy is the perfect and permanent flower of a completed evolution. It is an everlasting flower which, without the help of the watering-can, will keep its bloom through the ages. No matter if it is neglected utterly: never will a petal fall.

This belief in the permanence of democracy does not harmonize well with an age that has the facts of history at its command and which prates about a scientific attitude. Yet quite a few educated persons entertain it. A Socialist, like Franz Oppenheimer, may be forgiven; he must not look outside his Marxian bible, being intellectually free, as the medieval schoolmen were, only within rigidly-set limits. Perhaps Woodrow Wilson may be forgiven; he wrote at the end of the nineteenth century, before the symptoms of democratic decay had become manifest. Less lenience can be shown to college professors of the present day. Harold J. Laski says: "Democratic government is doubtless a final form of political organisation in the sense that men who have once tasted power will not, without conflict, surrender it." This opinion is all the more curious in view of the fact that it was expressed several years after the Italian people had cheerfully surrendered their power to Mussolini.

Robert M. MacIver says: "If we are right in our interpretation of the state as an organ of community, we must regard all states in which the general will is not active as imperfect forms. This view seems to be confirmed by a study of the historical process, for it appears to be true that, in spite of reversions, the main trend of the state, *after it has finally emerged as a state,* is toward democracy. . . . No institutions are secure, but those which rest on the sustaining power of the community are the strongest. A people can overthrow every form of government but its own—then it finds no alternative. A republic may be destroyed from without, but it is as nearly invincible from within as anything human." On this statement it is enough to say for the moment that the people are not like an individual; they divide in opinion; and, if they divide on fundamental issues, chaos supervenes and opens the way for monarchy.

SYMPTOMS OF DECLINE

Is democracy the final flower of political evolution? Perhaps, to scientific minds, it appears rather as a system which, in a world of ceaseless change, has shown itself best adapted to a certain set of temporary conditions. Yesterday the rule of One was all but universal; to-day the rule of the Many has supplanted it. There is no reason to suppose that to-morrow will be as to-day. Institutions are set up and modified and abandoned, sometimes by the caprice of man or what seems like it, sometimes by the stern pressure of circumstances. Will democracy still fit our circumstances twenty-five, fifty, or one hundred years from now? There are obscure, underlying forces that act quite independently of the human will and shape the social structure. These forces may be exerting an influence that will ultimately undermine the foundations of democracy. . . .

Hilaire Belloc, analyzing a different set of social forces and proceeding along a different route, arrives at a position incompatible with democracy. His argument appears in *The Servile State*. That brilliant and ingenious essay, which was published in 1912, seeks to prove that the capitalist régime—unstable in equilibrium, incapable of guaranteeing sufficiency and security to the mass of the wage-earners—is moving toward something quite different from the socialist solution and quite at variance with the democratic ideal. The future society will be a servile society. "We are," says Belloc, "rapidly coming nearer to the establishment of compulsory labour among an unfree majority of non-owners for the benefit of a free minority of owners." The very legislation that is designed to improve the lot of the masses—employers' liability, insurance against sickness and unemployment, old-age pensions, the minimum wage—carries with it the implication of servitude. The State guarantees to the proletarian, as the master did to his slave, sufficiency and security; and the next step, the fatal corollary of the first—already foreshadowed in the attitude of the State toward its employees—will lead it to impose the obligation to work. Belloc believes that, except for the active and adventurous few, men like slavery when they experience it; they get the things most valued in life: sufficiency, security, and relief from responsibility. The people of the U.S.S.R. have had experience of something akin to it latterly; and, whether they really like it or not, they seem quiescent.

LOSS OF FAITH

No human institution can stand still; the process of transformation goes steadily forward. . . . The late Lord Bryce was unrivaled in his acquaintance with political affairs and unsurpassed in sobriety and penetration of judgment. His sympathies were strongly democratic. Yet at the close of his life his optimism faltered. The time had come for men to face the facts and be done with fantasies. "Few are the free countries," he wrote, "in which freedom seems safe for a century or two ahead. . . . When the spiritual oxygen which has kept alive the attachment to liberty and self-government in the minds of the people becomes exhausted, will not the flame burn low and perhaps flicker out?" No one thought of trying to revive popular government when it disappeared in Greece and Rome. "The thing did happen: and whatever has happened may happen again. People that had known and prized political freedom resigned it, did not much regret it, and forgot it." These lines were written before the March on Rome by Mussolini's Black Shirts.

Unquestionably the growing skepticism about democracy must be attributed in part to the excesses committed in its name. The franchise has been given to all adults, women as well as men; special privileges or immunities have been granted to organized labor and other interests; the rich have been taxed for the benefit of the poor. Let us remember the warning of Montesquieu: Governments decline and fall as often by carrying their principles to excess as by neglecting them altogether. . . . Evidence of popular disillusionment, of declining faith in democracy, can be found in many different places. Within the last twenty years, for example, the critical literature has assumed formidable proportions. . . .

The most obvious of all the disquieting phenomena is the fallen prestige of representative assemblies. Cynicism is not, of course, peculiar to our own time. Carlyle, after taking Emerson to "the national talk-shop," the House of Commons, asked him if he did not now believe in a personal devil; Lavelaye observed that Italy was fortunate in the situation of her capital, since the Roman malaria effectively abridged the sessions of parliament. . . . Ridicule and contempt [of Congress] are the familiar language of the Press and of men prominent in the business world. The country feels safest, according to the New York *Times,* when Congress is not in session. The worst thing we have, according to E. H. Gary, is our American Congress. "There has never been a time," says Representative Robert Luce, whose scholarly books and long service in the House give his words some authority, "when the legislative branch of the government, both national and state, has been held in such low esteem." Even the British House of Commons—doubtless regarded more highly, both at home and abroad, than any other representative body—suffers from a perpetual bombardment of derisory missiles. . . .

That representative assemblies have sunk low in prestige will probably be admitted without the submission of more evidence. However, our state constitutions offer cogent proof. In pre-democratic days these constitutions went no farther than to lay down a few principles and describe the framework of government. They were brief documents, running to no more than

ten or twelve pages in Thorpe's collection. What influence was at work,
then, to produce monstrosities like the Oklahoma constitution of 1907,
which—though not now the longest—spreads itself over seventy-odd pages?
If one glances through those dreary pages, the answer becomes apparent:
the legislature had to be put under restraint. . . . Our state legislatures,
with half a dozen exceptions, are permitted to meet only once every two
years, and, even so, are limited in more than half the states to a session of
sixty days or less. According to the *New Republic,* business associations
wish "to reduce the sessions of the state legislatures, which are supposed
to safeguard American social welfare, to once every four years." May we
not expect in the future some still more drastic curtailment of power? The
popular attitude suggests it. When the legislature completes its little span
of active life, a sigh of relief shakes the atmosphere. The newspapers busily
set to work estimating the damage that the "people-chosen" have done.

The typical product of popular rule is the politician. Since it is his
function to make the laws and guide the destinies of the community, he
must be chosen, one would suppose, because of his outstanding qualifications. Yet the politician, far from commanding respect, is the perpetual
butt of sarcasms. H. G. Wells describes him as "an acutely humiliating
caricature of the struggling soul of our race." He is, says Émile Faguet,
"a man who, in respect of his personal opinions, is a nullity, in respect of
education, a mediocrity; he shares the general sentiments and passions of
the crowd. . . . He is precisely the thing of which democracy has need.
He will never be led away by his education to develop ideas of his own; and
having no ideas of his own, he will not allow them to enter into conflict
with his prejudices. His prejudices will be, at first, a feeble sort of conviction, afterwards, by reason of his own interest, identical with those of
the crowd. . . ."

It is absurd to blame the politician because he is not a superman. In
order to become a politician, he had first of all to be a mediocrity.

The masses resent superiority as reflecting upon their own condition, and
fear it as subversive of the democratic régime. . . . Democracy loves a
crowd, but, fearing the individuals who compose it, tries to blot out human
prestige and minimize the influence of personality. "Democracy has achieved
its perfect work," says Ralph Adams Cram, "and has now reduced all
mankind to a dead level of incapacity, where great leaders are no longer
wanted or brought into existence, while society itself is unable, of its own
power as a whole, to lift itself from the nadir of its own uniformity. . . .

COMPLEXITY OF GOVERNMENT

To-day everybody is impressed with the complexity of our economic,
and consequently of our social, life. In place of the simple conditions of the

frontier, which gave President Jackson the idea that, without preliminary training or special aptitudes, any one was competent to hold public office, we are confronted now with the most baffling and intricate problems. How striking the change has been may be gathered by comparing the national party platforms of the present era with the platforms of the forties or even the seventies. The problems have grown highly technical, transcending the capacities of ordinary citizens and requiring the attention of experts. Can democracy, with its belief in the average man and its distrust of the specialist, endure this new strain?

Bismarck said quite truly that institutions must be judged by what is accomplished through them. Democracy will be judged—and is being judged—by its success or failure in supervising a highly specialized economic mechanism. According to Bryce: "Neither the conviction that power is better entrusted to the people than to a ruling One or Few, nor the desire of the average man to share in the government of his own community, has in fact been a strong force inducing political change. Popular government has been usually sought and won and valued, not as a good thing in itself, but as a means of getting rid of tangible grievances or securing tangible benefits, and when these objects had been attained, the interest in it has gradually tended to decline. If it be improbable, yet it is not unthinkable that, as in many countries impatience with tangible evils substituted democracy for monarchy or oligarchy, a like impatience might some day reverse the process."

The task of government has become vastly more difficult during the past generation. Have the people acquired a corresponding increase in competence? We are sometimes told, if public affairs have grown terribly complicated, terribly hard to penetrate, the capacity of the masses to control them has, like the efficiency of the naval gun, increased at a higher ratio. The masses are educated, enlightened. How could it be otherwise when we spend more than two billion dollars yearly on our public schools in the United States and at the same time diffuse the highest forms of culture through the moving pictures, the radio, and the Sunday supplement?

What the average citizen has obtained is the rudiments of knowledge. He can write a letter; he can read a book. But, unfortunately, his smattering of education has made him arrogant and bold in situations that call for modesty and caution in expressing a judgment. The more remote things are from his experience and the less he knows about them, the more definite his opinions seem to be. It is doubtful that bigger doses of education would do him any good. Education can train, but not create, intelligence. When Dr. Joseph Collins tells about the prevalence of adult-infantilism and when the testers fix the average mental age of the electorate at fourteen, there may be some excuse for regarding the electorate as incurably stupid.

Wyndham Lewis, master of devastating satire and picturesque phrase,

. . . says: ". . . Although we have called this prodigious mass of people 'infantile,' they are of course outwardly grown up. They do not call themselves infantile as a community. They claim to be treated as responsible, accomplished, intelligent beings. They want to have official bulletins every morning of all accidents, fires, murders, rapes that have occurred throughout the night and part of the preceding day. They wish a detailed account of how their agents and ministers of state have 'fulfilled their trust,' as they call it, in the conduct of that great and sacred affair, the commonwealth. And they wish to be informed punctually of the results of all racing, ball-games, paper-chases, bull-fights, and other similar events."

The potentialities of education have been exaggerated grotesquely. Education can only "lead forth" inborn talents, not create them; and many biologists believe that the germ-plasm of Western peoples is deteriorating. Not only is warfare dysgenic,—it "but straws the wheat and saves the chaff with a most evil fan,"—but the best stock, rising to the top in the social scale, resorts to birth-control or becomes sterile. It is the Infant Class . . . that is setting the future tone of the human species. This tendency has been confirmed by the growth of a somewhat indiscriminate humanitarian spirit in the West. Help is extended prodigally to those who cannot or will not help themselves. The doctrine of equality, which justifies the raising of the low and the leveling of the high, becomes a doctrine of inequality in practice, when the energetic and thrifty Few are called upon to provide housing, food, medical care, education, amusements, and much besides for the slothful and improvident Many, the very dregs of society. The worst specimens are coddled, and encouraged to breed, as if they were the best. They are even maintained at public expense without the necessity of working. From the standpoint of heritable qualities, the political competence of the people as a whole declines, while the complexity of the problems of government increases.

Political interest is declining. Apathy is attested not only by the bewildered complaints of democratic fundamentalists, but by the statistics of elections. . . . By way of generalization, it is enough to say of the American situation that half the potential voters ignore the election and that three-quarters ignore the primary. The diagnostician, as he observes the pallid countenance of democracy, the wasting-away of a once robust physique, recognizes the symptoms of a fatal malady: there is no hope for the patient; this is persistent anemia. What has become of the devotion and enthusiasm that marked the democratic crusade in the nineteenth century or the suffragette movement of the early twentieth? The crusading spirit is gone now. . . .

The ordinary voter is ill-informed, apathetic, and indolent. Political issues do not touch him closely. He is preoccupied, first of all, with the task of making a living and, then, with his home and family. If he is a religious man, the church attracts him more than the polling booth. And can we be surprised that, after the exhausting labors of the day, he wants to keep his few hours of leisure for recreation and amusement? Now that political issues have grown so complicated as to be unintelligible to the average voter, civic duty does not attract his jaded mind. He will not listen to the pious doctrine that, in addition to being wise about his own personal affairs, he must now be wise about everybody else's as well. "When the private man has lived through the romantic age," says Walter Lippmann, "and is no longer moved by the stale echoes of its hot cries, when he is sober and unimpressed, his own part in public affairs appears to him a pretentious thing, a second-rate, an inconsequential. You cannot move him with a good straight talk about service and civic duty, nor by waving a flag in his face, nor by sending a boy scout after him to make him vote. He is a man back home from a crusade to make the world something or other it did not become. . . ."

EXPERTS AS A MENACE

There is no use blinking the fact: democracy everywhere is on trial. On all sides the gospel of efficiency is being preached. . . . Here lies the dilemma: democracy without experts—and it has a justifiable fear of them—faces the danger of collapse; with experts—they being a lean and hungry crowd—it faces the danger of being devoured by its own offspring. It is on the latter horn of the dilemma that democracy is being impaled.

More than twenty-five years ago Ramsay Muir came to the pessimistic conclusion that Englishmen, gradually ceasing to feel a sense of personal responsibility for public affairs, were losing, in consequence, the habit of self-government. He attributed this tragic condition to the steady, persistent, and powerful influence of the great permanent officials, whose actions are never submitted to the judgment of the electorate and whose names are never—or very seldom—mentioned by newspapers. . . . Parliament has delegated a vast range of legislative power to the departments. Delegation has gone so far that, in one statute at least, the minister (in practice, his technical advisers) was empowered to do anything "which appears to him necessary or expedient" for the purpose named, even to the point of modifying the provisions of the Act. Most of the departmental rules and orders do not require any affirmative action by Parliament. What we encounter, therefore, is parliamentary abdication in the interest of efficiency. In the second place, there has been an equally marked tendency to confer upon the administrative experts judicial or quasi-judicial power, without allowing appeal to the ordinary courts. The expert makes the law, applies it, and penalizes offenders. Yet he lives somewhere in the shadows, beyond the range of the light that beats upon Parliament, the police, and the courts. . . .

All thoughtful Englishmen must now be aware that a "new despotism" is taking shape. Americans should recognize a similar phenomenon in their own country. Long before the danger was made obvious by the New Deal, the note of alarm had been sounded.

THE COLLAPSE OF CONSENSUS

Democracy implies in one sense the rule of all, and in another sense the rule of the majority. We speak of all as ruling when all respect the right of the majority to rule. Since unanimous decisions are rare, whether in the popular choice of representatives or in the passing of laws, it has been the practice of democracies from time immemorial to accept the voice of the majority as the voice of all. Without such a compromise, little business could be transacted. But such a compromise is possible only when the disagreements between majority and minority touch upon matters of secondary importance and when there is a coincidence of interest in matters of primary concern, unless the latter have been removed from the arena of normal party conflict by some artificial contrivance such as a constitutional bill of rights. The accord between majority and minority goes by the name of consensus.

Democracy cannot exist without consensus, or a near approach to it. . . . The twentieth century witnesses a sudden growth of social cleavages and violent class hatreds, such as kept Spain in turmoil for years and at last plunged her into a savage civil war. Russia, Italy, and Germany found a way out through the suppression of irreconcilable minorities and the creation of an artificial uniformity. . . . At any rate, the collapse of consensus will always and everywhere entail the collapse of democracy. On that point there can be no doubt whatever. . . .

In Great Britain, notwithstanding the rise of a Socialist party and the deleterious effect of urban life upon the masses, the native inclination to compromise still runs strong, as does also the respect for law. Yet Professor Laski says:

> The success of the British Parliamentary system has been built upon the fact that the major parties in the state could agree to accept each other's legislation, since neither altered the essential outlines of that social-economic system in which the interests of both were involved. With the emergence of the Labor party as the alternative government, a different position has come into view. The Labor party aims at the transformation of a capitalist into a socialist society. It seeks, therefore, directly to attack, by means of Parliament, the ownership of the means of production by those classes which constitute the foundation of Tory and Liberal strength. Its principles are a

direct contradiction of those of its rivals. It denies the validity of the whole social order which the nineteenth century maintained. Is it likely that it can obtain its objectives in the peaceful and constitutional fashion which was characteristic of the Victorian epoch? . . .

Such are the views of a prominent British socialist.

In the United States the situation is, in some respects, more reassuring. It is true that the urban population now exceeds the rural and that class-consciousness has spread among the ranks of the proletariat, especially with the growth of industrial unionism since 1936. These factors will make themselves felt in the partisan realignment that seems to be impending. The proletariat is far from being a class-conscious unit, however; the skilled trades—constituting a sort of aristocracy of labor—incline to something like a middle-class mentality; and, with the middle-classes, they stand in the way of a clear-cut social division in party politics. Far more effective as an obstacle to such a division are the agricultural interests, which cannot be harmonized with those of the wage-earners. As long as agriculture retains anything like its present character and importance, there is no good prospect for the formation of a major party that openly advocates a Marxian solution. There still seems to be a vast reservoir of moderate opinion that makes itself heard in time of crisis. But that alone does not guarantee the survival of consensus.

Topic 27

COMMUNISM AND DEMOCRACY

❦

State and Revolution

V. I. LENIN *

Marx's doctrines are now undergoing the same fate, which, more than once in the course of history, has befallen the doctrines of other revolutionary thinkers and leaders of oppressed classes struggling for emancipation. During the lifetime of great revolutionaries, the oppressing classes have invariably meted out to them relentless persecution, and received their teaching with the most savage hostility, most furious hatred, and a ruthless campaign of lies and slanders. After their death, however, attempts are usually made to turn them into harmless saints, canonizing them, as it were, and investing their name with a certain halo by way of "consolation" to the oppressed classes, and with the object of duping them; while at the same time emasculating and vulgarizing the real essence of their revolutionary theories and blunting their revolutionary edge. At the present time the bourgeoisie and the opportunists within the Labor Movement are co-operating in this work of adulterating Marxism. They omit, obliterate, and distort the revolutionary side of its teaching, its revolutionary soul, and push to the foreground and extol what is, or seems, acceptable to the bourgeoisie. . . .

THE STATE AS THE PRODUCT OF THE IRRECONCILABILITY
OF CLASS ANTAGONISMS

Let us begin with the most popular of Engels' works, *The Origin of the Family, Private Property, and the State*. Summarizing his historical analysis Engels says:

> The State in no way constitutes a force imposed on Society from outside. Nor is the State "the reality of the Moral Idea," "the image and reality of Reason" as Hegel asserted. The State is the product of Society at a certain stage of its development. The State is tantamount to an acknowledgment that the given society has become entangled in an insoluble contradiction with

---

* Outstanding leader of the Russian Bolshevik Revolution. First Chairman of the Council of People's Commissars, U.S.S.R. Author of *Imperialism: The Highest Stage of Capitalism* and numerous other books and articles. *State and Revolution*, written in 1917, is presented here in abridged and rearranged form.

itself, that it has broken up into irreconcilable antagonisms, of which it is powerless to rid itself. And in order that these antagonisms, these classes with their opposing economic interests, may not devour one another and Society itself in their sterile struggle, some force standing, seemingly, above Society, becomes necessary so as to moderate the force of their collisions and to keep them within the bounds of "order." And this force arising from Society, but placing itself above it, which gradually separates itself from it— this force is the State.

Here, we have, expressed in all its clearness, the basic idea of Marxism on the question of the historical role and meaning of the State. The State is the product and the manifestation of the irreconcilability of class antagonisms. When, where and to what extent the State arises, depends directly on when, where and to what extent the class antagonisms of a given society cannot be objectively reconciled. And, conversely, the existence of the State proves that the class antagonisms *are* irreconcilable. . . .

According to Marx, the State is the organ of class *domination,* the organ of oppression of one class by another. Its aim is the creation of order which legalizes and perpetuates this oppression by moderating the collisions between the classes. But in the opinion of the petty-bourgeois politicians, the establishment of order is equivalent to the reconciliation of classes, and not to the oppression of one class by another. To moderate their collisions does not mean, according to them, to deprive the oppressed class of certain definite means and methods in its struggle for throwing off the yoke of the oppressors, but to conciliate it. . . .

But what is forgotten or overlooked is this:—If the State is the product of the irreconcilable character of class antagonisms, if it is a force standing above society and "separating itself gradually from it," then it is clear that the liberation of the oppressed class is impossible without a violent revolution, and without the destruction of the machinery of State power, which has been created by the governing class and in which this "separation" is embodied. . . .

What does this force consist of, in the main? It consists of special bodies of armed men who have at their command prisons, etc. We are justified in speaking of special bodies of armed men, because the public power peculiar to every State "is not identical" with the armed population, with its "self-acting armed organization." . . .

BOURGEOIS DEMOCRACY

In capitalist society, under the conditions most favorable to its development, we have a more or less complete democracy in the form of a democratic republic. But this democracy is always bound by the narrow framework of capitalist exploitation, and consequently always remains, in reality, a democracy only for the minority, only for the possessing classes, only for the rich. Freedom in capitalist society always remains more or less the same as it was in the ancient Greek republics, that is, freedom for the slave owners. The modern wage-slaves, in virtue of the conditions of capitalist exploitation, remain to such an extent crushed by want and poverty that they "cannot be bothered with democracy," have "no time for politics"; that, in the ordinary peaceful course of events, the majority of the population is debarred from participating in public political life. . . .

Democracy for an insignificant minority, democracy for the rich—that is the democracy of capitalist society. If we look more closely into the mechanism of capitalist democracy, everywhere—in the so-called "petty" details of the suffrage (the residential qualification, the exclusion of women, etc.), in the technique of the representative institutions, in the actual obstacles to the right of meeting (public buildings are not for the "poor"), in the purely capitalist organization of the daily press, etc., etc.—on all sides we shall see restrictions upon restrictions of democracy. These restrictions, exceptions, exclusions, obstacles for the poor, seem slight—especially in the eyes of one who has himself never known want, and has never lived in close contact with the oppressed classes in their hard life, and nine-tenths, if not ninety-nine hundredths, of the bourgeois publicists and politicians are of this class! But in their sum these restrictions exclude and thrust out the poor from politics and from an active share in democracy. Marx splendidly grasped the *essence* of capitalist democracy, when, in his analysis of the experience of the Commune, he said that the oppressed are allowed, once every few years to decide which particular representatives of the oppressing class are to represent and repress them in Parliament! . . .

In a democratic Republic, Engels continues "wealth wields its power indirectly, but all the more effectively," first, by means of "direct corruption of the officials" (America); second, by means of "the alliance of the government with the stock exchange" (France and America). At the present time, imperialism and the domination of the banks have reduced to a fine art both these methods of defending and practically asserting the omnipotence of wealth in democratic Republics of all descriptions.   . .

We must also note that Engels quite definitely regards universal suffrage as a means of capitalist domination. Universal suffrage, he says (summing up obviously the long experience of German Social-Democracy), is "an index of the maturity of the working class; it cannot and never will, give anything more in the present state." The petty-bourgeois democrats such as our Socialist-Revolutionaries and Mensheviks and also their twin brothers, the Social-Chauvinists and opportunists of Western Europe, all expect a "great deal" from this universal suffrage. They themselves think and instil into the minds of the people the wrong idea that universal suffrage in the "present state" is really capable of expressing the will of the majority of the laboring masses and of securing its realization. . . .

Take any parliamentary country, from America to Switzerland, from France to England, Norway and so forth; the actual work of the State is done behind the scenes and is carried out by the departments, the chancelleries and the staffs. Parliament itself is given up to talk for the special purpose of fooling the "common people." . . .

Two more points. First: when Engels says that in a democratic republic, "not a whit less" than in a monarchy, the State remains an "apparatus for the oppression of one class by another," this by no means signifies that the *form* of oppression is a matter of indifference to the proletariat, as some anarchists "teach." A wider, more free and open form of the class struggle and class oppression enormously assists the proletariat in its struggle for the annihilation of all classes.

Second: only a new generation will be able completely to scrap the ancient lumber of the State—this question is bound up with the question of overcoming democracy, to which we now turn.

DICTATORSHIP OF THE PROLETARIAT

The forms of bourgeois States are exceedingly various, but their substance is the same and in the last analysis inevitably the *Dictatorship of the Bourgeoisie*. The transition from capitalism to Communism will certainly bring a great variety and abundance of political forms, but the substance will inevitably be: the *Dictatorship of the Proletariat*. . . .

The State is a particular form of organization of force; it is the organization of violence for the purpose of holding down some class. What is the class which the proletariat must hold down? It can only be, naturally, the exploiting class, i.e., the bourgeoisie. The toilers need the State only to overcome the resistance of the exploiters, and only the proletariat can guide this suppression and bring it to fulfillment, for the proletariat is the only class that is thoroughly revolutionary, the only class that can unite all the toilers and the exploited in the struggle against the bourgeoisie, for its complete displacement from power. . . .

But the dictatorship of the proletariat—that is, the organization of the advance-guard of the oppressed as the ruling class, for the purpose of crushing the oppressors—cannot produce merely an expansion of democracy. *Together* with an immense expansion of democracy—for the first time becoming democracy for the poor, democracy for the people, and not democracy for the rich—the dictatorship of the proletariat will produce a series of restrictions of liberty in the case of the oppressors, exploiters and capitalists. We must crush them in order to free humanity from wage-slavery; their resistance must be broken by force. It is clear that where there is suppression there must also be violence, and there cannot be liberty or democracy. . . .

The replacement of the bourgeois by the proletarian State is impossible without a violent revolution. . . . There is [in *Anti-Dühring*] a disquisition on the nature of a violent revolution; and the historical appreciation of its role becomes, with Engels, a veritable panegyric on violent revolution. . . . Here is Engels' argument:

> That force also plays another part in history (other than that of a perpetuation of evil), namely a *revolutionary* part; that, as Marx says, it is the midwife of every old society when it is pregnant with a new one; that force is the instrument and the means by which social movements hack their way through and break up the dead and fossilized political forms—of all this not a word by Herr Dühring. Duly, with sighs and groans, does he admit the possibility that for the overthrow of the system of exploitation force may, perhaps, be necessary, but most unfortunate if you please, because all use of force, forsooth, demoralizes its user! And this is said in face of the great moral and intellectual advance which has been the result of every victorious revolution! And this is said in Germany where a violent collision—which might perhaps be forced on the people—should have, at the very least, this advantage that it would destroy the spirit of subservience which has been permeating the national mind ever since the degradation and humiliation of the Thirty Years' War. And this turbid, flabby, impotent, parson's mode of thinking dares offer itself for acceptance to the most revolutionary party which history has known!

In the *Communist Manifesto* are summed up the general lessons of history, which force us to see in the State the organ of class domination, and lead us to the inevitable conclusion that the proletariat cannot overthrow the bourgeoisie without first conquering political power, without obtaining political rule, without transforming the State into the "proletariat organized as the ruling class"; and that this proletarian State must begin to wither away immediately after its victory, because in a community without class antagonisms, the State is unnecessary and impossible.

WHAT IS TO REPLACE THE SHATTERED STATE MACHINERY?

In 1847, in the *Communist Manifesto,* Marx was as yet only able to answer this question entirely in an abstract manner, stating the problem rather than its solution. To replace this machinery by "the proletariat organized as the ruling class," "by the conquest of democracy"—such was the answer of the *Communist Manifesto*. . . .

Refusing to plunge into Utopia, Marx waited for the experience of a mass movement to produce the answer to the problem as to the exact forms which this organization of the proletariat as the dominant class will assume and exactly in what manner this organization will embody the most complete, most consistent "conquest of democracy." Marx subjected the experiment of the [Paris] Commune, although it was so meagre, to a most minute analysis in his *Civil War in France*. Let us bring before the reader the most important passages of this work. . . .

> The Commune was the direct antithesis of the Empire. It was a definite form . . . of a Republic which was to abolish, not only the monarchical form of class rule, but also class rule itself.

What was this "definite" form of the proletarian Socialist Republic? What was the State it was beginning to create? "The first decree of the [Paris] Commune was the suppression of the standing army, and the substitution for it of the armed people," says Marx. . . . But let us see how, twenty years after the Commune, Engels summed up its lessons for the fighting proletariat. . . .

> Against this inevitable feature of all systems of government that have existed hitherto, viz., the transformation of the State and its organs from servants into the lords of society, the Commune used two unfailing remedies. First, it appointed to all posts, administrative, legal, educational, persons elected by universal suffrage; introducing at the same time the right of re-calling those elected at any time by the decision of their electors. Secondly, it paid all officials, both high and low, only such pay as was received by any other worker. The highest salary paid by the Commune was 6,000 francs (about £240).
> Thus was created an effective barrier to place-hunting and career-making, even apart from the imperative mandates of the deputies in representative institutions introduced by the Commune over and above this. . . .

The lowering of the pay of the highest State officials seems simply a naive, primitive demand of democracy. One of the "founders" of the newest opportunism, the former Social-Democrat, E. Bernstein, has more than once exercised his talents in the repetition of the vulgar capitalist jeers at "primitive" democracy. Like all opportunists, like the present followers of Kautsky, he quite failed to understand that, first of all, the transition from capitalism to Socialism is impossible without "return," in a measure, to "primitive" democracy. How can we otherwise pass on to the discharge of all the functions of government by the majority of the population and by every individual of the population. And, secondly, he forgot that "primitive democracy" on the basis of capitalism and capitalist culture is not the same primitive democracy as in pre-historic or pre-capitalist times. Capitalist culture has created industry on a large scale in the shape of factories, railways, posts, telephones, and so forth: and *on this basis* the great majority of functions of "the old State" have become enormously simplified and reduced, in practice, to very simple operations such as registration, filing and checking. Hence they will be quite within the reach of every literate person, and it will be possible to perform them for the usual "working man's wage." This circumstance ought to and will strip them of all their former glamour as "government," and, therefore, privileged service.

The control of all officials, without exception, by the unreserved application of the principle of election and, *at any time,* re-call; and the approximation of their salaries to the "ordinary pay of the workers"—these are simple and "self-evident" democratic measures, which harmonize completely the interests of the workers and the majority of peasants; and, at the same time, serve as a bridge leading from capitalism to Socialism. . . .

The dictatorship of the proletariat, the period of transition to Communism, will, for the first time, produce a democracy for the people, for the majority, side by side with the necessary suppression of the minority constituted by the exploiters. Communism alone is capable of giving a really complete democracy, and the fuller it is the more quickly will it become unnecessary and wither away of itself. In other words, under capitalism we have a State in the proper sense of the word: that is, a special instrument for the suppression of one class by another, and of the majority by the minority at that. Naturally, for the successful discharge of such a task as the systematic suppression by the minority of exploiters of the majority of exploited, the greatest ferocity and savagery of suppression is required, and seas of blood are needed, through which humanity has to direct its path, in a condition of slavery, serfdom and wage labor.

Again, during the *transition* from capitalism to Communism, suppression is *still* necessary; but in this case it is suppression of the minority of exploiters by the majority of exploited. A special instrument, a special machine for suppression—that is, the "State"—is necessary, but this is now a transitional State, no longer a State in the ordinary sense of the term. For the suppression of the minority of exploiters, by the majority of those who were *but yesterday* wage slaves, is a matter comparatively so easy, simple and natural that it will cost far less bloodshed than the suppression of the risings of the slaves, serfs or wage laborers, and will cost the human race far less. And it is compatible with the diffusion of democracy over such an overwhelming majority of the nation that the need for any *special machinery* for *suppression* will gradually cease to exist. The exploiters are unable, of course, to suppress the people without a most complex machine for performing this duty; but *the people* can suppress the exploiters even with a very simple "machine"—almost without any "machine" at all, without any special apparatus—by the simple *organization of the armed masses* (such as the Councils of Workers' and Soldiers' Deputies, we may remark, anticipating a little).

Finally, only under Communism will the State become quite unnecessary, for there will be *no one* to suppress—"no one" in the sense of a *class,* in the sense of a systematic struggle with a definite section of the population. We are not utopians, and we do not in the least deny the possibility and inevitability of excesses by *individual persons,* and equally the need to suppress such excesses. But, in the first place, for this no special machine, no special instrument of repression is needed. This will be done by the armed nation itself, as simply and as readily as any crowd of civilized people, even in modern society, parts a pair of combatants or does not allow a woman to be outraged. And, secondly, we know that the fundamental social cause of excesses which violate the rules of social life is the exploitation of the masses, their want and their poverty. With the removal of this chief cause, excesses will inevitably begin to "wither away." We do not know how quickly and in what stages, but we know that they will be withering away. With their withering away, the State will also wither away.

THE "WITHERING AWAY" OF THE STATE

Engels' words regarding the "withering away" of the State enjoy such a popularity, are so often quoted, and reveal so clearly the essence of the common adulteration of Marxism in an opportunist sense that we must examine them in detail. Let us give the passage from which they are taken.

> The proletariat takes control of the State authority and, first of all, converts the means of production into State property. But by this very act it destroys itself, as a proletariat, destroying at the same time all class differences and class antagonisms, and with this, also, the State.

Engels speaks here of the *destruction* of the capitalist State by the proletarian revolution, while the words about its withering away refer to the remains of a *proletarian* State *after* the Socialist revolution. The capitalist State does not wither away, according to Engels, but is *destroyed* by the proletariat in the course of the revolution. Only the proletarian State or semi-State withers away after the revolution. . . .

A general summary of his views is given by Engels in the following words:—

> Thus, the State has not always existed. There were societies which did without it, which had no idea of the State or of State power. At a given stage of economic development which was necessarily bound up with the break up of society into classes, the State became a necessity, as a result of this division. We are now rapidly approaching a stage in the development of production, in which the existence of these classes is not only no longer necessary, but is becoming a direct impediment to production. Classes will vanish as inevitably as they inevitably arose in the past. With the disappearance of classes the State, too, will inevitably disappear. When organizing production anew on the basis of a free and equal association of the producers, Society will banish the whole State machine to a place which will then be the most proper one for it—to the museum of antiquities side by side with the spinning-wheel and the bronze axe.

FIRST PHASE OF COMMUNIST SOCIETY: SOCIALISM

It is this Communist society—a society which has just come into the world out of the womb of capitalism, and which, in all respects, bears the stamp of the old society—that Marx terms the first, or lower, phase of Communist society.

The means of production are now no longer the private property of individuals. The means of production belong to the whole of society. Every member of society, performing a certain part of socially-necessary labor, receives a certificate from society that he has done such and such a quantity of work. According to this certificate, he receives from the public stores of articles of consumption, a corresponding quantity of products. After the deduction of that proportion of labor which goes to the public fund, every worker, therefore, receives from society as much as he has given it.

"Equality" seems to reign supreme. . . . But different people are not equal to one another. One is strong, another is weak; one is married, the other is not. One has more children, another has less, and so on.

> With equal labor [Marx concludes] and, therefore, with an equal share in the public stock of articles of consumption, one will, in reality, receive more than another, will find himself richer, and so on. To avoid all this, "rights," instead of being equal, should be unequal.

The first phase of Communism, therefore, still cannot produce justice and equality; differences and unjust differences in wealth will still exist, but the *exploitation* of one man by many, will have become impossible, because it will be impossible to seize as private property the *means of production,* the factories, machines, land, and so on. . . .

"He who does not work neither shall he eat"—this Socialist principle is *already* realized. "For an equal quantity of labor an equal quantity of products"—this Socialist principle is also already realized. Nevertheless, this is not yet Communism, and this does not abolish "bourgeois law," [for Communism] gives to unequal individuals, in return for an unequal (in reality) amount of work, an equal quantity of products.

This is a "defect," says Marx, but it is unavoidable during the first phase of Communism; for, if we are not to land in Utopia, we cannot imagine that, having overthrown capitalism, people will at once learn to work for society *without any regulations by law;* indeed, the abolition of capitalism does not *immediately* lay the economic foundations for such a change. . .

The State is withering away in so far as there are no longer any capitalists, any classes, and, consequently, any *class* whatever to suppress. But the State is not yet dead altogether, since there still remains the protection of "bourgeois law," which sanctifies actual inequality. For the complete extinction of the State complete Communism is necessary.

THE HIGHER PHASE OF COMMUNIST SOCIETY: COMMUNISM

Marx continues:

In the higher phase of Communist society, after the disappearance of the enslavement of man caused by his subjection to the principle of division of labor; when, together with this, the opposition between brain and manual work will have disappeared; when labor will have ceased to be a mere means of supporting life and will itself have become one of the first necessities of life when with the all-round development of the individual, the productive forces, too, will have grown to maturity, and all the forces of social wealth will be pouring an uninterrupted torrent—only then will it be possible wholly to pass beyond the narrow horizon of bourgeois laws, and only then will society be able to inscribe on its banner: "From each according to his ability; to each according to his needs."

Only now can we appreciate the full justice of Engels' observations when he mercilessly ridiculed all the absurdity of combining the words "freedom" and "State." While the State exists there can be no freedom. When there is freedom there will be no State.

The economic basis for the complete withering away of the State is that high stage of development of Communism when the distinction between brain and manual work disappears; consequently, when one of the principal sources of modern *social* inequalities will have vanished—a source, moreover, which it is impossible to remove immediately by the mere conversion of the means of production into public property, by the mere expropriation of the capitalists.

This expropriation will make it possible gigantically to develop the forces of production. And seeing how incredibly, even now, capitalism *retards* this development, how much progress could be made even on the basis of modern technique at the level it has reached, we have a right to say, with the fullest confidence, that the expropriation of the capitalists will result inevitably in a gigantic development of the productive forces of human society. But how rapidly this development will go forward, how soon it will reach the point of breaking away from the division of labor, of the destruction of the antagonism between brain and manual work, of the transformation of work into a "first necessity of life"—this we do not and *cannot* know.

Consequently, we are right in speaking solely of the inevitable withering away of the State, emphasizing the protracted nature of this process, and its dependence upon the rapidity of development of the *higher phase* of Communism; leaving quite open the question of lengths of time, or the concrete forms of this withering away, since material for the solution of such questions is not available.

The State will be able to wither away completely when society has realized the formula: "From each according to his ability; to each accord-

ing to his needs"; that is when people have become accustomed to observe the fundamental principles of social life, and their labor is so productive, that they will voluntarily work *according to their abilities*. "The
narrow horizon of bourgeois law," which compels one to calculate, with
the pitilessness of a Shylock, whether one has not worked half-an-hour
more than another, whether one is not getting less pay than another—
this narrow horizon will then be left behind. There will then be no need
for any exact calculation by society of the quantity of products to be distributed to each of its members; each will take freely "according to his
needs." . . .

The scientific difference between Socialism and Communism is clear.
That which is generally called Socialism is termed by Marx the first or lower
phase of Communist society. In so far as the means of production become
public property, the word Communism is also applicable here, providing
that we do not forget that it is not full Communism. . . .

Democracy implies equality. The immense significance of the struggle of
the proletariat for equality and the power of attraction of such a battlecry
are obvious, if we but rightly interpret it as meaning the *annihilation of
classes*. But the equality of democracy is *formal* equality—no more; and
immediately after the attainment of the equality of all members of society
in respect of the ownership of the means of production, that is, of equality
of labor and equality of wages, there will inevitably arise before humanity
the question of going further from equality which is formal to equality
which is real, and of realizing in life the formula, "From each according to
his ability; to each according to his needs." By what stages, by means of
what practical measures humanity will proceed to this higher aim—this we
do not and cannot know. But it is important that one should realize how
infinitely mendacious is the usual capitalist representation of Socialism as
something lifeless, petrified, fixed once for all. In reality, it is only with
Socialism that there will commence a rapid, genuine, real mass advance, in
which first the majority and then the *whole* of the population will take part
—an advance in all domains of social and individual life.

Soviet "Democracy"

JOSEPH STALIN *

The complete victory of the socialist system in all spheres of the national
economy is now a fact. This means that exploitation of man by man is
abolished—liquidated—while the socialist ownership of the implements and

* Late Secretary-General of the Communist Party of the Soviet Union and Chairman
of the Council of Ministers, U.S.S.R. Author of *Foundations of Leninism, Problems of*

means of production is established as the unshakable basis of our Soviet society.

As a result of all these changes in the national economy of the U.S.S.R., we have now a new socialist economy, knowing neither crises nor unemployment, neither poverty nor ruin, and giving to the citizen every possibility to live prosperous and cultured lives. Such, in the main, are the changes which took place in our economy during the period from 1924 to 1936. Corresponding to these changes in the sphere of the economy of the U.S.S.R., the class structure of our society has also changed. As is known, the landlord class had already been liquidated as a result of the victorious conclusion of the Civil War.

As for the other exploiting classes, they shared the fate of the landlord class. The capitalist class has ceased to exist in the sphere of industry. The kulak class has ceased to exist in the sphere of agriculture. The merchants and speculators have ceased to exist in the sphere of distribution. In this way, all exploiting classes are proved to have been liquidated. . . .

How are these changes in the life of the U.S.S.R. reflected in the draft of the new Constitution? In other words, what are the main specific features of the draft Constitution submitted for consideration at the present congress? . . .

Our Soviet society succeeded in achieving socialism, in the main, and has created a socialist order, *i.e.,* has achieved what is otherwise called among Marxists the first or lower phase of communism, that is, socialism. It is known that the fundamental principle of this phase of communism is the formula: "From each according to his abilities; to each according to his deeds." . . . But Soviet society has not yet succeeded in bringing about the highest phase of communism where the ruling principle will be the formula: "From each according to his abilities; to each according to his needs," although it sets itself the aim of achieving the materialization of this higher phase, full communism, in the future.

Unlike the bourgeois constitutions, the draft of the new Constitution of the U.S.S.R. proceeds from the fact that antagonistic classes no longer exist in our society, that our society consists of two friendly classes: the workers and peasants, that precisely these toiling classes are in power, that the state guidance of society (dictatorship) belongs to the working class as the advanced class of society, that the Constitution is needed to consolidate the social order desired by and of advantage to the toilers. . . .

The draft of the new Constitution of the U.S.S.R. is . . . profoundly international. It proceeds from the premise that all nations and races have

---

Leninism and numerous articles on Communism. The selection is from the report of Joseph Stalin to the Special Eighth All-Union Congress of Soviets, delivered November 25, 1936.

equal rights. It proceeds from the premise that color or language differences, differences in cultural level or the level of state development as well as any other difference among nations and races, cannot serve as grounds for justifying national inequality of rights. It proceeds from the premise that all nations and races irrespective of their past or present position, irrespective of their strength or weakness, must enjoy equal rights in all spheres, economic, social, state and the cultural life of society. Such is a feature of the draft of the new Constitution. [Another] specific feature of the draft of the new Constitution is its consistent and fully sustained democracy. For it all citizens are equal in their rights. Neither property status nor national origin, nor sex, nor official standing, but only the personal capabilities and personal labor of every citizen determine his position in society.

A specific feature of the draft of the new Constitution is that it does not limit itself to recording formal rights of citizens, but transfers the center of gravity to questions of the guarantee of these rights, to the question of the means of exercising them. It does not merely proclaim the equality of the rights of citizens but ensures them by legislative enactment of the fact of liquidation of the regime of exploitation, by the fact of liberation of citizens from any exploitation. It not only proclaims the right to work, but ensures it by legislative enactment of the fact of non-existence of crises in Soviet society, and the fact of abolition of unemployment. It not merely proclaims democratic liberties but guarantees them in legislative enactments by providing definite material facilities.

It is clear, therefore, that the democracy of the new Constitution is not the "usual" and "generally recognized" democracy in general, but socialist democracy. . . .

BOURGEOIS CRITICS OF THE CONSTITUTION

A few words about bourgeois criticism of the draft Constitution. . . . Whereas [one] group charges that the draft Constitution renounced the dictatorship of the working class, [another] group, on the contrary, charges that the draft makes no change in the existing position of the U.S.S.R.; that it leaves the dictatorship of the working class intact, does not provide for freedom of political parties, and preserves the present leading position of the Communist Party of the U.S.S.R. And, at the same time, this group of critics believes that the absence of freedom for parties in the U.S.S.R. is an indication of the violation of the fundamental principles of democracy.

I must admit the draft of the new Constitution really does leave in force the regime of the dictatorship of the working class, and also leaves unchanged the present leading position of the Communist Party of the U.S.S.R. If our venerable critics regard this as a shortcoming of the draft Constitution, this can only be regretted. We Bolsheviks, however, consider this as a merit of the draft Constitution. As for freedom for various political parties, we here adhere to somewhat different views.

The party is part of the class, its vanguard section. Several parties and consequently freedom of parties can only exist in a society where antagonistic classes exist whose interests are hostile and irreconcilable, where there are capitalists and workers, landlords and peasants, kulaks and poor peasants. But in the U.S.S.R. there are no longer such classes as capitalists, landlords, kulaks, etc. In the U.S.S.R. there are only two classes, workers and peasants, whose interests not only are not antagonistic but, on the contrary, amicable. Consequently there are no grounds for the existence of several parties, and therefore for the existence of freedom of such parties in the U.S.S.R. There are grounds for only one party, the Communist Party, in the U.S.S.R. Only one party can exist, the Communist Party, which boldly defends the interests of the workers and peasants to the very end. And there can hardly be any doubt about the fact that it defends the interests of these classes.

They talk about democracy. But what is democracy? Democracy in capitalist countries where there are antagonistic classes is in the last analysis the democracy for the strong, democracy for the propertied minority. Democracy in the U.S.S.R., on the contrary, is democracy for all. And from this it follows that the principles of democracy are violated not by the draft of the new Constitution of the U.S.S.R. but by the bourgeois constitutions. That is why I think that the Constitution of the U.S.S.R. is the only thoroughly democratic constitution in the world.

Topic 28

REPLY TO THE COMMUNIST CHALLENGE

❧

Analysis of the Communist Critique

H. B. MAYO *

Marxism may be studied today for at least two good reasons. In the first place, Marx was one of those pioneers, like Darwin or Freud, who changed the tenor of man's thought; and every student of history and society must sooner or later come to terms with him. His work may be riddled with ambiguities and inconsistencies, but it remains one of the landmarks of human thought, and the critical appraisal of any great system is one way of extending our knowledge. Marx's insight was never so constructive as it was analytic and critical; and certainly his influence has not been wholly beneficial. Yet much the same could be said of the founders of many other systems.

There is a second, but no less important, reason for studying Marxism. Marx's theories have often been refuted, but they are now the official beliefs of a third of the world's population. Hence to discuss them systematically is no mere academic diversion: urgent questions of domestic and international policy compel us to inquire into what the communist part of the world believes, or professes to believe. The democrat ought to know the case of his chief opponent, its strength and its weakness. To reject communism is not enough; it must be rejected soberly, and on the right grounds, with knowledge of what it does and does not contain.

To explain Marxism has naturally involved an examination of the writings of both Marx and Engels, since it is from these two men, joint authors of the *Communist Manifesto* in 1848, that the ideas of modern communism are largely derived. If our study stopped with Marx, however, we could hardly understand modern communism, which differs in many important respects from what Marx taught. Communism today is firmly cast in the Russian mold, and it has thus been necessary to examine also the additions and alterations to Marx's thought made by Lenin and Stalin. Marx once

* Professor of Political Science, University of South Carolina. The selection is from H. B. Mayo, *Democracy and Marxism* (New York: Oxford University Press, 1955), from the Preface and Chs. III and IX with some rearrangement. By permission.

wrote that Russia always runs after the most extreme ideas the West has to offer. In some particulars, indeed, Russian communism, although paying tribute to Marx, flatly contradicts some of his theories.

Marxism as a grand-scale philosophy of history has obvious anti-democratic implications. The theory of an inevitable law of history, a dialectical economic process to which mankind can only conform, is stultifying to a free society. Democracy involves a faith in a future which is open and which can be, in time, what man chooses to make it, whereas Marxism casts the immediate future in an iron mold. So far as the Marxist philosophy of history is believed, even though it is false, to that extent it tends to weaken the will to democracy, encourages a fatalistic submission to communist movements, and postpones freedom of choice for mankind until the far future and the arrival of the classless society. Anyone who really believes in the inevitable victory of communism is lost as a democrat.

But the big guns of the Marxist attack are aimed more directly against democracy. . . . Marxist political theory describes the state as a class state, a mere instrument of exploitation in the hands of the bourgeoisie. Legal and political systems are called forceful instruments of class rule, with the moral code cunningly devised to operate by persuasion to serve the same class interests. . . .

There is no possible way of operating a constitutional democracy smoothly if this kind of theory is widely believed by the citizens, and Lenin's advice to communists to get into a parliament in order to disrupt it is a natural deduction for anyone who regards bourgeois democracy as a sham. . . .

Nevertheless the Marxist critique may usefully be examined. Marxists can of course find real instances in all democracies of class pressures upon government, and the farther back one goes into history the more numerous the instances become; naturally so, since democracy did not spring full-fledged into being, but has been steadily developing through the years. For that reason, too, Marxists are fonder of citing the past, as revealed in the works of Marx and Engels, than of making fresh analyses of contemporary society.

A plausible case for the Marxist critique can very easily be made. Who can deny on the one hand the tender solicitude of government for business, and on the other, the shorter shrift which labor has so often got as its portion? Who can deny the enormous influence of money and a monied press in molding public opinion and influencing elections and legislatures? Who would feel so confident of receiving justice under the law even today if he were destitute?

Yet even when one has selected all the class elements within the democracies—conditions so much better documented by others than by Marxists —such a case is slowly but surely becoming obsolete. The redeeming feature of the democracies is that they are aware of the existing anomalies and are steadily reducing them; so that to say with the Marxist that the liberal democratic state of today is only a class dictatorship, or that "formal" freedom exhausts the content of democracy for the mass of the population, is a farcical exaggeration which scarcely calls for refutation. One comment suffices. Civil servants are not lackeys of the capitalists, as Lenin thought; their increasing number shows how the welfare state is growing, not how the bourgeoisie is grinding the faces of the poor.

One may go deeper with the inquiry. If Marx's general theory is right, and the economic foundation is all-important, can politics matter at all? Two conclusions are possible. One is that drawn by non-revolutionary socialists such as the Fabians: the political system can be consciously and flexibly adapted to changing economic conditions, and as long as that is done there need never be a violent break with the past. But such a conclusion is distasteful to Marxists and instead their conclusion is that under capitalism the chief purpose of the struggle for political power is to strengthen the class consciousness of the proletariat. Democratic politics has merely an instrumental and temporary function, to enable the proletariat to capture the state machinery in order to "smash" it. The Marxist theory thus reduces democracy to a mere stage before the inevitable dictatorship.

It was of course only too easy in early nineteenth-century England to believe in the ineffectual state and the harsh realities and power of economic life. The state that Marx analyzed was, in truth, grossly class-biased, as was the Russian state against which Lenin inveighed. But historically it is political action that has come in to redress the balance and to make wealth and economic power more and more responsible for public welfare. And every partial political control has also enlarged the area of man's freedom by lessening dependence on purely unplanned and unregulated economic forces. It is, among other reasons, just because the conscious social controls have increased steadily in number and scope since Marx's day that his predictions have proved to be so wide of the mark. . . .

What makes dogmatic Marxism an enemy of *contemporary* democracy is the denial of the autonomy and efficacy of politics *here and now* in any of the liberal democracies. Democracy can be stretched to mean many things, but when it ceases to mean that through political action a free people can shape the policies they desire, including the economic policies, then with Marx we must lapse into sheer economic determinism. This is only another way of saying that the difference between Marxist and democrat is that the latter believes it is possible to achieve economic change by peaceful political means, but that nothing short of revolution will satisfy the Marxist.

The "revisionists" had a keener understanding here than Marx and Lenin. Lenin had written that "the toiling masses are *barred* from participation in bourgeois parliaments . . ." The statement was nonsense, based upon the working example of no capitalist democracy, and in convenient forgetful-ness of Engels' observation that communists thrived on legal methods. Marx was indignant at the Gotha Program, since, although not saying so in as many words, it amounted to a rejection of his theory of the class state, and an affirmation that the state could be used for the benefit of all classes including the workers. The leaders of the Social Democratic party in Ger-many were aware that they could reasonably expect substantial reforms once the workers were enfranchised. The Social Democratic party, it is true, continued to suffer from a split personality: in practice its program was one of reform, but a section of its membership continued to profess adherence to Marxist theory. Nevertheless the party remained firmly grad-ualist and democratic in its conduct until the Russian revolution. In the end doctrinaire Leninism drove a section of the proletariat (the communist party) into open hostility toward democracy, while under the influence of revisionist leaders the rest of the workers rallied to the support of constitu-tional government.

The idea that government is conducted by a ruling class, whose interests are always identified with the national interest, was not invented by Marx but had been an accepted commonplace long before the nineteenth century. Sir Thomas More had defined government as "nothing more than a certain conspiracy of rich men procuring their own commodities under the name and title of a Commonwealth." James Harrington had taken it for granted (in 1656) that "power follows property." Even with the rise of modern democracies, the idea that political power *should* follow property took a long time a-dying, and for that matter still lingers on at the municipal level of government, in the remnants of property qualifications sometimes at-tached to the vote. But the Marxist accusation that government is merely another arm of the bourgeoisie or, in Lenin's words, "the millionaires" na-tional committees called governments, has become a less and less adequate description of democratic government.

The one thing which Marxism cannot explain in modern democracies is the hostility of business toward its alleged puppet, the state. On ordinary empirical grounds, however, the explanation is easy: the enmity arises be-cause the democratic state is used to benefit all classes, to weight the scales in favor of the weak, and to subject the economy to political direction. . . .

To Marx, the economic forces worked themselves out through the class struggle. Now, the sharpening of the class struggle and the increasing im-poverishment which Marx expected have not in fact come about, and there is consequently no sign that the capitalist democracies will ever pass through the period of revolution predicted by Marx. . . .

Perhaps the great depression during the 1930's was the period when, if ever, the danger of proletarian revolution was most to be apprehended, yet nowhere did the revolution occur. In Britain the number of votes cast for the communist party remained negligible, while in the United States the communist vote actually declined. If there is such a thing as a consensus, it is that never again will depressions be allowed to become really severe. The United States and Canada have both officially adopted the Keynesian principles, the former in the Employment Act of 1946, and the latter in the 1945 White Paper on Employment and Income. The specific measures so far proposed are not likely, in themselves, to avert another slump, yet nevertheless once the state has assumed responsibility for a high level of employment, income, and prosperity, more than half the battle has been won. Citizens will rightly expect their government to take adequate remedial measures, and no democratic government will be able to refuse, especially now that the economists are widely publicizing the view (perhaps a little too confidently) that they know how to avert a serious slump, and how to keep on increasing the real income per capita.[1] Should the economic situation require drastic measures, as it may well do, these could lead very far indeed away from the kind of capitalist society we have had in the past. Lord Keynes himself foresaw that prospect and did not dodge it.[2]

Marxism is here, again, at sharp odds with democracy, since it teaches that the democracies cannot prevent the crises of boom and slump. Engels was eloquent on the subject:

> Bourgeois economics can neither prevent crises in general, nor protect the individual capitalists from losses, bad debts and bankruptcy, nor secure the individual workers against unemployment and destitution. It is still true that man proposes and God (that is, the extraneous force of the capitalist mode of production) disposes.

All later Marxists have constantly chanted the same refrain: ". . . capitalist society is always an endless horror." [3] Within the framework of capitalism, crises can never be abolished, but will continue to get worse and worse, until the final catastrophic collapse.

As capitalist society changes its character, however—and it is changing all the time—many of the worst objections to it tend to disappear, in particular those stemming from unemployment and gross inequality. "Prosperity demoralizes the workers," as Marx noted, and since increasing impoverishment and the "industrial reserve army" are nowhere in evidence, Marxism loses its trump card. Political action then becomes a matter of degree, a little more or less of public ownership, social security, or piecemeal planning, in the interest of equality and the general welfare. Revolutions are not made by this pragmatic approach to the problems of society.

Since industrial society is nothing if not dynamic and experimental it

---

[1] E.g. Benjamin Higgins, *What Do Economists Know?*, Melbourne, 1951.
[2] *General Theory of Employment, Interest and Money*, Ch. 24.
[3] Engels, *Anti-Duhring, Handbook,* p. 301; *Lenin, Selected Works,* 1951, I, Part 2, p. 574.

would be more than remarkable, it would be miraculous, if subsequent development had fitted into the iron prognosis drawn up by Marx a century ago. (The society which Marx studied was moreover largely that of the *early* nineteenth century; that is, many of the Reports and Blue Books which he used referred to the past, and not to the second half of the century, when he studied and wrote.) The increasing economic influence and the growing political influence of the "working class," and of the organized farmers, are two of the outstanding features of the modern world, especially in the more industrialized countries. And these are not revolutionary groups. As we know well, one of the best innoculations against revolution is a flourishing trade-union movement which can see that it is making substantial gains. Marx would no doubt take the stand that all these things do not really lead to a change of system per se, but that is only a matter of definition. What matters is that the going economic and social system under which we now live, whatever it may be called, is quite unlike the society analyzed by Marx and even more unlike the future which he anticipated. . . .

Marx turned to the study of economic history to find the proof for his class-struggle theory. The social scientist of today, however, turns to society not with a thesis to prove but with a question: are the rigidities arising from property relations so serious that industrial society cannot adapt its institutions and ideas to the changing modes of production quickly enough to make a peaceful transition to the future? In less Marxist language: is the social lag between technology on the one hand, and institutions and beliefs on the other, capable of being reduced peacefully? . . .

The functions of the state have always been to provide internal order and protection from external enemies. But they have never been confined to these, and there is no mystery about the process by which the democratic state has gone beyond them to concern itself deeply with the economy. . . . No sharp line can in fact be drawn between politics and the economy. As Adam Smith astutely noted, property and wealth depend upon society and law as well as upon individual effort; and this is especially true in the present highly interdependent society. Business itself has set the example for state intervention by its readiness to seek government protection whenever the chill winds of competition have become too biting. The United States, like all democracies, has always had an empirically collectivist tradition.[4] Modern advertising, too, by its emphasis on "service to the community"—which makes so many advertisements read as though put out by philanthropists—encourages the citizen to judge the performance of business by the test of public welfare. The relief of depressions and the planning of a wartime economy have accustomed the public to state action for the achievement of specific objectives. The logic of democracy

[4] George H. Sabine, "Two Democratic Traditions," *Philosophical Review,* October 1952, pp. 451ff.

and the spread of humanitarianism have generated new demands and, contrary to the Marxist assumption, it has been possible to appeal successfully to reason and conscience in all democratic states, and (equally important) the increasing productivity has assured that the demands could be met.

The ghost of the Great Depression haunts every democracy, and although there may be no great confidence in the ability of private enterprise alone to maintain economic stability and rising living standards, there is every confidence in a partnership of government and business that offers a middle way between rugged competition and total collectivism. One of the reasons why this "middle way" is not better understood is that it changes so fast that theory cannot keep up with it. Nor have we yet discovered a satisfactory word to describe it. (The term "neo-mercantilism" has been suggested, but has some drawbacks.)

As the public interest instead of private profit becomes more and more the criterion of economic action, as taxation regulates income in order to influence demand and promote equity, and as regulation of many kinds becomes a normal concomitant of business, the essentially private nature of the economy is slowly but steadily altered, and the social character of freedom and property is increasingly recognized. What is remarkable about this historic development is not the amount of opposition to trade unions, state regulation, government enterprise, progressive and rising taxation, and the welfare state; what is much more surprising is that private enterprise should put up such a comparatively weak fight as it finds itself taxed, controlled, hampered, and sometimes eliminated by the responsible public authorities. So far has the process gone that it becomes ever more difficult to see any point at which a stand in defense of the past could be made.

The mixed economy we have at present is partly "socialized" and partly in private hands, partly free and partly controlled. Anyone who fails to recognize this, and to make it the very basis of his analysis, is looking at the world through glasses as opaque as those worn by the Marxist. A system and an age are passing away and the resulting conflicts in society are being resolved in other ways than by means of a sharpening class struggle. Nor is it accurate to describe present society as socialist, for the kind of society that is coming about in the Western democracies is a long way removed from socialism as it has traditionally been understood. In Britain many an old-time socialist has been disillusioned by the course of events, while many a younger conservative finds the changed social climate quite congenial. The same process goes on in nearly every country regardless of the political party in power, and serves to show how free societies can adapt themselves peacefully to meet changing conditions. Democracy today is not merely liberalism but liberalism with something added, which may be described as social welfare and the public interest.

We are thus justified in saying that whatever kind of economic society is evolving (regardless of the label pinned on it) is bound to be collectivist to some large degree, and subject to political planning in a number of spheres, if it is to be based on modern technology with its possibilities of a high standard of living. How large the private sector of the economy will remain, and whether it will be a *free* society, preserving and extending the best in our heritage, we do not know. But we can keep a free society if enough people want it strongly enough. We need not be slaves of technology or of social trends.

Lenin and Stalin have extended Marx's theory of the class state to justify the existence of only one political party, a system that has been established in the U.S.S.R. In doing so they have used several arguments. One of these is that only one party is possible, "the Communist Party, which does not share and cannot share the guidance of the state with any other party." [5] Nor is this merely while the revolution is in progress—which would be excusable (after all, revolutionists usually tend to treat all opposition as treason)—but it is meant to apply as long as the Soviet state endures; until the never-never land of the classless society and plenty is reached, when "the Party will die out."

That there must be only one party is an assertion, not an argument. It can hardly be profitably discussed, since there is simply no way of proving or disproving it; and in any case the communists never try the alternative to see whether it would or would not work. There is little use in pointing out that the democratic socialist countries disprove the necessity for a one-party state, since the stock communist reply consists in a denial that they are socialist at all. The British Labour Government, for instance, was labeled a reactionary capitalist regime—an impression not shared by Mr. Churchill or by the North American press. The communist annoyance with countries like Britain arises because these countries flout the Marxist thesis that capitalism can be transformed only by violence. The American annoyance, on the other hand, is derived from the businessman's myth that any overhaul of capitalism must be communism.

But the real communist argument for the single party is a matter of Marxist definition. Political parties are regarded merely as representative of economic classes and since—when reduced to the simplest terms—there are only two classes, the proletariat and the bourgeoisie, therefore there are only two real parties: the communist party represents the working class while all other parties represent the interests of the bourgeoisie. After the revolution, since there will be only one class (more strictly, no class) there will then be no need for more than one party. It is a typical piece of rigid and deductive Marxist reasoning.

Following the same line of thought, Lenin used to argue that in the democ-

[5] Stalin, *Leninism, Selected Writings,* p. 42; Burns, ed., *Handbook of Marxism,* p. 851.

racies there is really only one party (excluding communists where they exist, and they do exist, contrary to Lenin's belief) since there is agreement by all the so-called parties on fundamentals. If Lenin were right, then reasoning by analogy we could expect a number of parties to appear in the communist proletarian state; all of them agreeing on, say, the principle of public ownership but differing on such "nonessentials" as the relative proportions of consumer or capital goods to be produced by the Five Year Plans. But there are as yet no signs of any such open differences within the U.S.S.R. (The Nazis, so it is said, predicted that ultimately, when all were in agreement, two parties would be permitted.)

The charge that democracies contain only one party divided into the "ins" and the "outs" deserves some attention. Others besides Marxists have declared that party differences are purely artificial, as meaningless as the struggles between the Big Enders and the Little Enders in Lilliput.

In the first place, even if it were true, and party platforms scarcely mattered, the existence of a number of parties led by different persons engaged in a fight for office would still be of high value. If power tends to corrupt —about which there can be little doubt—it is wise to shift "office holders" from time to time.

In the second place, the communist charge ignores all party divisions except the economic. Now it was true that before the advent of socialist parties the older parties did not challenge the principle of private ownership of the means of production. The case is usually made, for example, that the Liberals and Conservatives in nineteenth-century Britain did not differ on "fundamentals," in the sense that they agreed upon private ownership and enterprise, and that the same is true of similar parties today in Canada and the United States. Even here, however, doubt arises. It all depends on what is regarded as fundamental. These parties *feel* their differences to be vital, and would strongly resent being forced into one party. And if they feel that way it seems foolish to argue that parties do not matter. Once more we see that only by assuming that economic differences alone are important can the Marxist case be sustained. But to do that is to beg the whole question.

A third and more important objection, however, is that democracies do in fact contain parties and other minorities, which do not subscribe even to the most fundamental beliefs of the great majority, and the existence of such critical opposition is one of the tests of democracy. Parliament may be something of a distorting mirror, in reflecting all opinions and group interests in the country, but it is a counsel of despair and cynicism to smash it on that account, and to ignore all the other channels by which public opinion influences legislation.

A democracy becomes endangered whenever frustrated minorities put their principles before the "rules of the game." That is why, in the last analysis, every democratic socialist must, if he is a democrat, put the democratic method before his socialist objectives should he ever be placed in the invidious position where he is forced to choose between the two. A democracy becomes more stable as its opposing parties approach each other in outlook and come to share the moral premises of democracy (or, alternatively, as they agree to keep strongly felt differences outside of politics); but that is a long way from proving that party differences are of no great importance. As a common religious faith is not required by different countries before they can agree on international law, so uniformity is not required within any particular country before it can become democratic. The only concensus that is indispensable to the working of the democratic method is the agreement to differ, and not to persecute. And it is at this very point that the one-party system differs so profoundly from the democracies and creates the strong presumption, which is confirmed by all experience, that no democracy—in any ordinary non-communist sense of the word—is possible without at least two political parties and a wide range of civil liberties.

The special case of socialist and non-socialist governments alternating in power may be mentioned. It hardly seems possible to socialize a country under one regime and to "de-socialize" it under another, although it is not impossible to "de-nationalize" specific undertakings. Yet that is to express the general problem in an unreal and extreme form, since no democratic socialist government has gone very far with a socialist program. All democratic governments are both socialist and capitalist nowadays, depending on one's yardstick, and the difference is hardly more than a question of degree. During the tenure of office of one party the rate of socializing is more rapid, while under another there is a period of consolidation, not of a complete unscrambling of the eggs. As the argument in the preceding section has shown, much of the welfare and regulating program is almost forced upon a society based upon specialization, interdependence, and modern technology, and subject to all the moral pressures engendered in a democracy.

[We have seen] many points at which the Marxist theory conflicts with the theory of democracy, but for the sake of convenience the chief points may be summarized here.

The Marxist philosophy of history is in contradiction to the democratic theory that a free society has an open future. The Leninist theory of imperialism makes impossible almost any trading or other economic relations of capitalist democracies with poorer parts of the world because it teaches that these relations are invariably "exploitive." The Marxist theory of truth teaches the class-partisan nature of all ideas, including those of economic theory. The ethical theory of Marxism is that whatever serves the interests of the proletarian struggle is right—and it easily follows that any methods, even the most undemocratic, are justified so long as they promote this end. The Marxist theory that economic forces determine all the other institutions and ideologies of society is at odds with the democratic use of political action to build the free and just society.

The Marxist diagnosis of the liberal state as merely the political arm of the bourgeoisie, if accepted by large numbers of people, tends to hamper the smooth working of constitutional democracy. Marxism teaches that the class struggle is everything, that class differences are irreconcilable; yet the one thing calculated to destroy democracy is the existence of bitterly hostile class parties that put their objectives before the maintenance of democracy.

Marxism teaches that since liberal democracy is a sham, it must be over-thrown by the class-conscious proletariat (or, in later communist theory, by the party, on behalf of the proletariat); that the overthrow can only be by violent revolution (or perhaps today by a *coup d'état*); and that the communist party will then proceed to suppress all other parties and set up a dictatorship instead. Early Marxism had presupposed an element of de-mocracy in the "dictatorship" phase, but modern communist practice by subordinating the proletarian state to the party has violated every demo-cratic belief in the dignity and moral responsibility of free men. And to make matters worse it has done this behind the moral façade of its ultimate utopianism.

Marxism teaches all this as scientific truth, and that those who oppose it are class enemies of the proletariat. These are the chief issues on which the Marxist social theory conflicts most openly with the theory of democracy. They establish the case beyond dispute that the two theories are quite irreconcilable. Only on two important issues could the Marxist and the democrat find themselves in agreement, the first being that of the ultimate goal of the classless society of "plenty." But this in turn is so universal an ideal, and so remote from realization in any near future, and hence so utopian, that it is of no practical importance in helping to bring Marxist and democrat into the same camp.

The second issue arises because in one sense the Marxist professes not to be anti-democratic at all, but to be in favor of democracy, while asserting that it is impossible under capitalism. A recent study of the theoretical foundations of democracy, to which both Marxists and non-Marxists con-tributed, turned up an astonishing amount of seeming agreement:

> Probably for the first time in history, "democracy" is claimed as the proper ideal description of all systems of political and economic organization ad-vocated by influential proponents.[6]

[6] *Democracy in a World of Tensions* (A symposium prepared for UNESCO, Paris, 1951), p. 527.

Although one side was talking of "proletarian democracy," the other was talking of Western democracy, whether in its capitalist or socialist variety. Yet both sides were also agreeing upon an ideal democracy, while disagreeing only on the economic foundation required to support it. The dispute over the necessary and sufficient conditions for democracy could theoretically be settled by an appeal to empirical evidence, but it cannot be so settled as long as the Marxist stand is one of definition and dogmatic assertion. In practice, therefore, it is precisely the doctrinal position which drives the Marxist into implacable enmity to capitalist democracy—and most of the democracies of the world are still far more capitalist than socialist. The Marxist wants all or nothing, and thus rejects the piecemeal changes, the mixed economy, the agreement to work within the constitutional framework. To him these are not good in themselves, but are useful only as preliminaries to the dictatorship of the proletariat.

> [Editors' Note: The student should note that Professor Mayo uses "Marxism" as a shorthand term for Lenin's and Stalin's interpretation of "Marxism." Although Soviet leaders regard their doctrines as "Marxism in the epoch of imperialism and of the proletarian revolution," this claim has been contested by certain socialist as well as non-socialist schools of thought.
>
> Specifically important in relation to democracy was the difference between Marx and Lenin on the nature and organization of the Party which was to seize power. As Professor Mayo points out elsewhere, "Marx seems to have had in mind a mass party, officered by communist intellectuals who would provide the advanced theory and the leadership, yet with the rank and file sharing actively in the discussion and the decisions; a party, in brief, rather like the type of political party usually found in the democracies." Lenin, on the other hand, maintained that "the communist party must be small, 'narrow,' 'unified,' 'a professional organization of revolutionists,' to *direct* and *dominate* the proletariat; not a party democratically controlled by the workers, but instead one that controlled the workers. Membership was to be confined to those who played an *active* part in the organization. A close watch must be maintained over doctrine, and those who dissented even on minor points of tactics must be expelled."
>
> Another significant difference is that while both Marx and Engels conceived of the possibility that socialism might be realized in countries with a developed democratic tradition "by peaceful means," Lenin said that "this exception made by Marx is no longer valid" and insisted that "the replacement of the bourgeois by the proletarian state is impossible without a violent revolution."]

Why I Am Not a Communist

MORRIS RAPHAEL COHEN *

What distinguishes present-day Communists is not . . . their professed ultimate goal or their analysis of our economic ills, but their political remedy or program—to wit, the seizure of power by armed rebellion [1] and the setting up of a dictatorship by the leaders of the Communist Party. To be sure, this dictatorship is to be in the name of the *proletariat,* just as the fascist dictatorship is in the name of *the whole nation.* But such verbal tricks cannot hide the brute facts of tyrannical suppression necessarily involved in all dictatorship. For the wielders of dictatorial power are few, they are seldom if ever themselves toilers, and they can maintain their power only by ruthlessly suppressing all expression of popular dissatisfaction with their rule. And where there is no freedom of discussion, there is no freedom of thought.

This program of civil war, dictatorship, and the illiberal or fanatically intolerant spirit which war psychology always engenders may bring more miseries than those that the Communists seek to remove; and the arguments to prove that such war is desirable or inevitable seem to me patently inadequate.

Communists ignore the historic truth that civil wars are much more destructive of all that men hold dearest than are wars between nations; and all the arguments that they use against the latter, including the late "war to end war," are much more cogent against civil wars. Wars between nations are necessarily restricted in scope and do not prevent—to a limited extent they even stimulate—co-operation within a community. But civil wars necessarily dislocate all existing social organs and leave us with little social capital or machinery to rebuild a better society. The hatreds which fratricidal wars develop are more persistent and destructive than those developed by wars that terminate in treaties or agreements.

Having lived under the tyranny of the Czar, I cannot and do not condemn all revolutions. But the success and benefits of any revolution depend on

* Late Professor of Philosophy, The City College of New York. President of the American Philosophical Association, 1929. Author of *Reason and Nature, Law and the Social Order, Faith of a Liberal,* and other works. The selection is from Morris Raphael Cohen, "Why I Am Not a Communist," *Modern Monthly* (April, 1934), Vol. 8, No. 3; reprinted in *The Meaning of Marx. A Symposium,* by Bertrand Russell, John Dewey, Morris Cohen, Sidney Hook, and Sherwood Eddy (New York, Rinehart & Co., Inc., 1934). Reprinted with permission of the administrators of the estate of Morris Raphael Cohen.

[1] Since this article was written armed intervention seems to have largely replaced armed rebellion as a technique for the seizure of power.

the extent to which—like the American Revolution of 1776, the French Revolution of 1789, and the anti-Czarist Revolution of March 1917—it approximates national unanimity in the co-operation of diverse classes. When armed uprisings have been undertaken by single oppressed classes, as in the revolt of the gladiators in Rome, the various peasant revolts in England, Germany, and Russia, the French Commune of 1871, or the Moscow uprising of 1905, they have left a deplorably monotonous record of bloody massacres and oppressive reaction. The idea that armed rebellion is the only or the always effective cure for social ills seems to me no better than the old superstition of medieval medicine that blood-letting is the only and the sovereign remedy for all bodily ills.

Communists may feel that the benefits of their Revolution of 1917 outweigh all the terrific hardships which the Russian people have suffered since then. But reasonable people in America will do well to demand better evidence than has yet been offered that they can improve their lot by blindly imitating Russia. Russian breadlines, and famine without breadlines, are certainly not *prima facie* improvements over American conditions. At best a revolution is a regrettable means to bring about greater human welfare. It always unleashes the forces that thrive in disorder, the brutal executions, imprisonments, and, what is even worse, the sordid spying that undermines all feeling of personal security. These forces, once let loose, are difficult to control and they tend to perpetuate themselves. If, therefore, human well-being, rather than mere destruction, is our aim, we must be as critically-minded in considering the consequences of armed revolution as in considering the evils of the existing regime.

One of the reasons that lead Communists to ignore the terrific destruction which armed rebellion must bring about is the conviction that "the revolution" is inevitable. In this they follow Marx, who, dominated by the Hegelian dialectic, regarded the victory of the proletariat over the bourgeoisie as inevitable, so that all that human effort can hope to achieve is "to shorten and lessen the birth pangs" of the new order. There is, however, very little scientific value in this dialectic argument, and many Communists are quite ready to soft-pedal it and admit that some human mistake or misstep might lead to the triumph of fascism. The truth is that the dialectic method which Marx inherited from Hegel and Schelling is an outgrowth of speculations carried on in theologic seminaries. The "system" of production takes the place of the councils or the mills of the gods. Such Oriental fatalism has little support in the spirit and method of modern science. Let us therefore leave the pretended dialectic proof and examine the contention on an historical basis.

Historically, the argument is put thus: When did any class give up its power without a bloody struggle? As in most rhetorical questions, the questioner does not stop for an answer, assuming that his ignorance is conclusive as to the facts. Now, it is not difficult to give instances of ruling classes giving up their sovereignty without armed resistance. The English landed aristocracy did it in the Reform Bill of 1832; and the Russian nobility did it in 1863 when they freed their serfs, though history showed clearly that in this way not only their political power but their very existence was doomed (for money income has never been so secure as direct revenue from the land, and life in cities reduced the absolute number of noble families). In our own country, the old seaboard aristocracy, which put over the United States Constitution and controlled the government up to the Jacksonian era, offered no armed resistance when the backwoods farmers outvoted them and removed church and property qualifications for office and for the franchise.

But it is not necessary to multiply such instances. It is more important to observe that history does not show that any *class* ever gained its enfranchisement through a bloody rebellion carried out by its own unaided efforts. When ruling classes are overthrown it is generally by a combination of groups that have risen to power only after a long process. For the parties to a rebellion cannot succeed unless they have more resources than the established regime. Thus the ascendancy of the French bourgeoisie was aided by the royal power which Richelieu and Colbert used in the seventeenth century to transform the landed barons into dependent courtiers. Even so, the French Revolution of 1789 would have been impossible without the co-operation of the peasantry, whose opposition to their ancient seigneurs was strengthened as the latter ceased to be independent rulers of the land. This is in a measure also true of the supposedly purely Communist Revolution in Russia. For in that revolution, too, the peasantry had a much greater share than is ordinarily assumed. After all, the amount of landed communal property (that of the crown, the church, etc.) which was changed by the peasants into individual ownership may have been greater than the amount of private property made communal by the Soviet regime. Even the system of collective farms is, after all, a return to the old *mir* system, using modern machinery. The success of the Russian Revolution was largely due to the landlords' agents who, in their endeavor to restore the rule of the landlords, threw the peasantry into the arms of the Bolshevists. Indeed, the strictly Marxian economics, with its ideology of surplus-value due to the ownership of the means of production, is inherently inapplicable to the case of the peasant who cultivates his own piece of ground.

Even more important, however, is it to note that no amount of repetition can make a truth of the dogma that the capitalist class alone rules this country and like the Almighty can do what it pleases. It would be folly to deny that, as individuals or as a class, capitalists have more than their proportionate share of influence in the government, and that they have exercised it unintelligently and with dire results. But it is equally absurd to maintain that they have governed or can govern without the co-operation of the farmers and the influential middle classes. None of our recent constitutional amendments—not the income-tax amendment, not the popular election of the United States Senators, not woman suffrage, neither prohibition nor its repeal—nor any other major bit of legislation can be said to have been imposed on our country in the interests of the capitalist class. The farmers, who despite mortgages still cling to the private ownership of their land, are actually the dominant political group even in industrial states like New York, Pennsylvania, and Illinois.

The Communist division of mankind into workingmen and capitalists suffers from the fallacy of simplism. Our social structure and effective class divisions are much more complicated. As the productivity of machinery increases, the middle classes increase rather than decrease. Hence a program based entirely on the supposed exclusive interests of the proletariat has no reasonable prospect. Any real threat of an armed uprising will only strengthen the reactionaries, who are not less intelligent than the Communist leaders, understand just as well how to reach and influence our people, and have more ample means for organization. If our working classes find it difficult to learn what their true interests are and do not know how to control their representatives in the government and in the trade unions, there is little prospect that they will be able to control things better during a rebellion or during the ensuing dictatorship.

If the history of the past is any guide at all, it indicates that real improvements in the future will come like the improvements of the past—namely, through co-operation among different groups, each of which is wise enough to see the necessity of compromising with those with whom we have to live together and whom we cannot or do not wish to exterminate.

I know that this notion of compromise or of taking counsel as the least wasteful way of adjusting differences is regarded as hopelessly antiquated and bourgeois, but I do not believe that the ideas of so-called Utopian socialists have really been refuted by those who arrogate the epithet "scientific" to themselves. The Communists seem to me to be much more Utopian and quite unscientific in their claims that the working class alone can by its own efforts completely transform our social order.

I do not have very high expectations from the efforts of sentimental benevolence. Yet I cannot help noticing that the leaders of the Communists and of other revolutionary labor movements—Engels, Marx, Lassalle, Luxemburg, Liebknecht, Lenin, and Trotsky—have not been drawn to it by economic solidarity. They were not workingmen nor even all of workingmen's families. They were driven to their role by human sympathy. Sympathy with the sufferings of our fellow men is a human motive that cannot be read out of history. It has exerted tremendous social pressure. Without it you cannot explain the course of nineteenth-century factory legislation, the freeing of serfs and slaves, or the elimination of the grosser forms of human exploitation. Though some who regard themselves as followers of Karl Marx are constantly denouncing reformers who believe in piecemeal improvement and hope rather that things will get worse so as to drive people into a revolution, Marx himself did not always take that view. Very wisely he attached great importance to English factory legislation which restricted the number of hours per working day, for he realized that every little bit that strengthens the workers strengthens their resistance to exploitation. Those who are most oppressed and depressed, the inhabitants of the slums, do not revolt—they have not energy enough to think of it. When, therefore, Mr. Strachey and others criticize the socialists for not bringing about the millennium when they get into power, I am not at all impressed. I do not believe that the socialists or the Labor Party in England have been free from shameful error. But neither have the Communists, nor any other human group, been free from it. Trite though it sounds, it is nevertheless true that no human arrangement can bring about perfection on earth. And while the illusion of omniscience may offer great consolation, it brings endless inhumanity when it leads us to shut the gates of mercy. Real as are our human conflicts, our fundamental identity of interest in the face of hostile nature seems to me worthy of more serious attention than the Communists have been willing to accord it.

If liberalism were dead, I should still maintain that it deserved to live, that it had not been condemned in the court of human reason, but lynched outside of it by the passionate and uncompromisingly ruthless war spirit, common to Communists and Fascists. But I do not believe that liberalism is dead, even though it is under eclipse. There still seems to me enough reason left to which to appeal against reckless fanaticism.

It is pure fanaticism to belittle the gains that have come to mankind from the spirit of free inquiry, free discussion, and accommodation. No human individual or group of individuals can claim omniscience. Hence society can only suffer serious loss when one group suppresses the opinions and criticisms of all others. In purely abstract questions compromise may often be a sign of confusion. One cannot really believe inconsistent principles at the same time. But in the absence of perfect or even adequate knowledge in regard to human affairs and their future, we must adopt an experimental attitude and treat principles not as eternal dogmas, but as hypotheses, to be tried to the extent that they indicate the general direction of solution to specific issues. But as the scientist must be ever ready to modify his own hypothesis or to recognize wherein a contrary hypothesis has merits or deserves preference, so in practical affairs we must be prepared to learn from those who differ with us, and to recognize that however contradictory diverse views may appear in discourse they may not be so in their practical applications.

Thus, the principles of Communism and individualism may be held like theologic dogmas, eternally true and on no occasion ever to be contaminated one by the other. But in fact, when Communists get into power they do not differ so much from others. No one ever wished to make everything communal property. Nor does anyone in his senses believe that any individual will ever with impunity be permitted to use his "property" in an antisocial way when the rest of the community is aroused thereby. In actual life, the question how far Communism shall be pushed depends more upon specific analyses of actual situations—that is, upon factual knowledge. There can be no doubt that individualism à la Herbert Hoover has led millions to destruction. Nevertheless, we must not forget that a Communist regime will, after all, be run by individuals who will exercise a tremendous amount of power, no less than do our captains of industry or finance today. There is no real advantage in assuming that under Communism the laboring classes will be omniscient. We know perfectly well how labor leaders like John Lewis keep their power by bureaucratic rather than democratic methods. May it not be that the Stalins also keep their power by bureaucratic rather than democratic methods?

Indeed the ruthless suppression of dissent within the Communist Party in Russia and the systematic glorification of the national heroes and military objectives of Czarist days suggest that the Bolshevik Revolution was not so complete a break with the Russian past as most of its friends and enemies assumed in earlier days. In any event we have witnessed in the history of the Communist movement since 1917 a dramatic demonstration of the way in which the glorification of power—first as a means of destroying a ruling class, then as a means of defending a beleaguered state from surrounding enemies, and finally as a means of extending Communism to neighboring lands—comes imperceptibly to displace the ends or objectives which once formed the core of Communist thought. Thus, one by one, the worst features of capitalist society and imperialism, against which Communism cut its eye teeth in protest—extreme inequality in wages, speed-up of workers, secret diplomacy, and armed intervention as a technique of international intercourse—have been taken over by the Soviet Union, with only a set of thin verbal distinctions to distinguish the "good" techniques of Communism from the corresponding "bad" techniques used by capitalism. As is always the case, the glorification of power dulls the sense of righteousness to which any movement for bettering the basic conditions of human living must appeal.

The Communist criticism of liberalism seems to me altogether baseless and worthless. One would suppose from it that liberalism is a peculiar excrescence of capitalism. This is, however, not true. The essence of liberalism—freedom of thought and inquiry, freedom of discussion and criticism—is not the invention of the capitalist system. It is rather the mother of Greek and modern science, without which our present industrial order and the labor movement would be impossible. The plea that the denial of freedom is a temporary necessity is advanced by all militarists. It ignores the fact that, when suppression becomes a habit, it is not readily abandoned. Thus, when the Christian Church after its alliance with the Roman Empire began the policy of "compelling them to enter," it kept up the habit of intolerant persecution for many centuries. Those who believe that many of the finer fruits of civilization were thereby choked should be careful about strengthening the forces of intolerance.

When the Communists tell me that I must choose between their dictatorship and Fascism, I feel that I am offered the choice between being shot and being hanged. It would be suicide for liberal civilization to accept this as exhausting the field of human possibility. I prefer to hope that the present wave of irrationalism and of fanatical intolerance will recede and that the great human energy which manifests itself in free thought will not perish. Often before, it has emerged after being swamped by passionate superstitions. There is no reason to feel that it may not do so again.

The Effects of Dictatorship

HAROLD J. LASKI *

Marx has assumed the seizure of power, and a period of rigorous control until the people are prepared for communism. But he has not shown what approximate length that period is to be, nor what certainty we have that those who act as controllers of the dictatorship will be willing to surrender their power at the proper time. It is a commonplace of history that power is poisonous to those who exercise it; there is no reason to assume that the Marxian dictator will in this respect be different from other men. And, *ex hypothesi,* it will be more difficult to defeat his malevolence since his regime will have excluded the possibility of opposition. No group of men who exercise the powers of a despot can ever retain the habit of democratic responsibility. That is obvious, for instance, in the case of men like Sir

* Late Professor Political Science at London School of Economics. The selection is from Harold J. Laski, *Karl Marx: An Essay,* pp. 43–45, published in England by the Fabian Society, 1921; and in America by the League for Industrial Democracy, 1933. Reprinted by permission of the late author and the League for Industrial Democracy.

Henry Maine and Fitzjames Stephen, who, having learned in India the habit of autocratic government, become impatient on their return to England of the slow process of persuasion which democracy implies.

To sit continuously in the seat of office is inevitably to become separated from the mind and wants of those over whom you govern. For the governing class acquires an interest of its own, a desire for permanence, a wish, perhaps, to retain the dignity and importance which belong to their function; and they will make an effort to secure them. That, after all, is only to insist that every system of government breeds a system of habits; and to argue as a corollary therefrom that the Marxian dictatorship would breed habits fatal to the emergence of the régime Marx had ultimately in view. The special vice of every historic system of government has been its inevitable tendency to identify its own private good with the public welfare. To suggest that communists might do the same is no more than to postulate their humanity. And it may be added that if they surrender power at a reasonable time, the grounds for so doing, being obviously in their nature non-economic, would thereby vitiate the truth of the materialistic interpretation of history.

All this, it is worth noting, is to omit from consideration the ethical problems that are involved. It is obvious, for example, that it involves the complete erosion of the whole historic process. But the erosion of responsibility in the governing class is the destruction of personality in their subjects. In such a regime notions of liberty and equality are out of place. Yet it is obvious that the two main defects of capitalism are its failure to produce liberty and equality for the mass of humble men and women. Marx, that is to say, contemplated a condition which reproduces exactly the chief vices of capitalism without offering any solid proof of their ultimate extinction. For, after all, the chief effort that is worth making is toward a civilization in which what Mr. Graham Wallas has termed, "the capacity of continuous initiative," is implied in the fact of citizenship. It is clear enough that the possibility upon which the existence of that capacity turns is a wide distribution of power. A man whose thought and acts are at the disposal of other men is deprived of his personality, and that deprivation is implied in the rigorous centralization to which Marx looked forward.

Topic 29

DEFENSE OF DEMOCRACY

⚜

Justification of Democracy

H. B. MAYO *

In this discussion, I propose to examine the values which are inherent in or implied by *any* democracy; those values which follow logically or emerge from the actual working of a democratic system. Those values will then constitute a large part of the justification for democracy. . . .

DEMOCRACY IS "FOR" THE PEOPLE

One broad implication of democracy almost inevitably follows from the system: government by the people is likely to aim also at government *for* the people, and not only because democracy is partly so defined, as in Lincoln's well-known phrase. . . .

Of itself, this does not take us very far—it merely puts the emphasis on the *people*. In some way, what is done to and for them is most important of all; the sights are trained on them, and not upon a collectivity, an organic state, a divine monarch, a particular class, or the like. The utilitarians in their emphasis on the happiness of the greatest number, and all democratic politicians in stressing the welfare or service of the people, belong in some sense to the same tradition of government for the people. Some of the support for democracy, and the opposition too, has come from those who hoped or feared, as the case might be, that it would turn out to be *for* the people.

So much has the idea of government *for* the people sunk into the modern mind that dictators nowadays profess to rule for the benefit of their people, a method of justification for despotism used far less often in earlier days. The definition of democracy given by Soviet spokesmen usually follows this line: if the policies of a government are for the benefit of the people, instead of for "their most bitter enemies," then the

* Professor of Political Science, University of South Carolina. Author of *An Introduction to Marxist Theory*. The selection is from *An Introduction to Democratic Theory* by Henry B. Mayo. © 1960 by Oxford University Press, Inc. Reprinted by permission.

government is a democracy. But this definition will not do. It abolishes the distinction entirely between benevolent despotism and democracy, while in the absence of the political freedoms and effective choice—which are distingushing features of democracy—we have only the dictator's word for it that his policies are in fact for the people.

The Soviet definition leads into two ancient errors: one is that the wishes of the people can be ascertained more accurately by some mysterious methods of intuition open to an elite rather than by allowing people to discuss and vote and decide freely. The other error goes deeper: that in some way the rulers know the "real" interest of the people better than the people and their freely chosen leaders would know it themselves. All fanatics believe the same.

When Aristotle spoke of the state continuing that men might live well and said that the purpose of the *polis* was to promote the "good" life, he too laid the democrat's emphasis on "*for* the people" (though in this case on a concept of their virtue). Historical experience shows, I think, a rather high positive correlation between rule *by* and *for* as representative democracy has broadened. After votes for women were secured, more women's-rights legislation of all kinds followed; with every widening of the franchise, more legislation followed to benefit the enfranchised voters. Common sense and a knowledge of political methods would confirm this: after all, a politician comes to office by bidding for votes, by offering something he believes the voters want. He has room for "statesmanship" in the debate and competition, which give him the chance to persuade them to want what he thinks they need. The cynic might call this mass bribery, but it scarcely rivals the class bribery of the earlier limited franchise. There is too much evidence that special-interest legislation was a corrupt and delicate art, brought to a much finer flower of perfection in the days before universal suffrage.

Yet this first implication—that democracy works out for (or is designed for) the people—is undeniably vague. What sectional interest or policy, after all, is not defended on the ground that it is *for* the people? Yet vague as it is, it is not useless, and may be said to constitute one of the values of democracies, a value which many people rate highly. In this context, however, I shall treat it as a highly general, preliminary value, and proceed to identify more specific values of democracy.

THE SPECIFIC VALUES OF A DEMOCRATIC SYSTEM

The values of democracy are two-fold: (a) those underlying the principles considered separately; and (b) the values of the system as a whole. The task is to identify the values in both cases, so that, these being isolated, we may see what values we are committed to when we embrace democracy. In isolating these values we are not, of course, committing ourselves to every institution in every democracy, since obviously any actual democracy contains much that is unique and adventitious derived from its particular history. . . .

(1) *The first value is the peaceful voluntary adjustment of disputes.* Life in any human society contains a perpetual conflict of interests and opinions, whether the conflict is suppressed or conducted openly. If anyone doubts this, let him look around him or read history. A democracy is unique in recognizing the political expression of such conflicts as legitimate, and in providing for their peaceful adjustment through the negotiations of politics, as an alternative to their settlement by force or fiat. Every political theory either provides means for this peaceful settlement within a political system, or else it must call upon a *deus ex machina* to impose order, an authority from outside the system of conflict, as Hobbes expected the monarch of the Leviathan to rule, as Bolingbroke looked to his Patriot King, as Plato looked to his Guardians, as the Germans looked to the Führer and as Marx once or twice spoke of the state as standing "above society."

Democracy makes unique provision for the peaceful adjustment of disputes, the maintenance of order, and the working out of public policies, by means of its "honest broker" or compromise function. The policy compromises are worked out as the representatives bid for electoral support, amid the constant public debate, agitation, and politicking that go on in the context of political liberties, until in time many policies pass from dispute to virtual unanimity in settled law; . . .

Democracy is thus institutionalized peaceful settlement of conflict (ballots for bullets, a counting instead of a cracking of heads), a settlement arrived at *pro tem* with the widest possible participation because of the adult suffrage and the political freedoms. It is distinguished from elite systems or borderline cases (with *some* freedoms, *some* choice, etc.) by the difference in degree, by the recognition of the legitimacy of many diverse political interests and the extent of public participation in the settlement of disputes.

Here, then, is a value, characteristic of democracy, which will be prized by all who prefer voluntary to imposed adjustment and agreement. It is not a value, however, to those (if there are any such) who believe that force is preferable; nor would democracy be valued by those who believe that the ideally best policies are always preferable even if they have to be imposed from above.

(2) *The second value is that of ensuring peaceful change in a changing society.* This is so closely related that it may be regarded as an application of the first to the special circumstances of the modern world.

The value makes a stronger appeal today than in earlier, more static, periods, that is, it has a greater element of plausibility now, because we accept the normality, even inevitability, of rapid technological change. Tomorrow the stars. (In suggesting that technology is an independent variable, initiating social and political changes though not fully determining their extent or direction, we need not ignore other determinants such as population changes or such mechanisms as the entrepreneurial function.)

We know from experience that social changes of many kinds inevitably follow the technological. The democratic political method—flexible, responsive to public opinion and to the influence of leadership, open to controversy—ensures political adaptation to this determinant of change. Almost by definition, because of the electoral changes of policy-makers, there is less "political lag" in the many adjustments which are required in law and policy to meet rapidly changing circumstances. . . .

(3) *The third value is the orderly succession of rulers.* Democracy not only presides over social conflict and change, but at the same time solves an even older political problem: that of finding, peacefully, legitimate successors to the present rulers. Hobbes, for instance, thought that the problem of succession was the chief difficulty with a monarchical system. Democracy is pre-eminently an answer to the question which no alternative system can answer convincingly in the modern climate of opinion: how to find and change the rulers peaceably and legitimately. The methods of self-appointment, of hereditary succession, of co-option by an elite, and of the *coup d'état* are not contemporaneously plausible in their philosophic justifications, apart altogether from the practical difficulties inherent in them, to which abundant historical experience testifies.

It was with these three social values in mind—peaceful adjustment, change, succession—that Judge Learned Hand could write of democracy and free elections:

> It seems to me, with all its defects our system does just that. For, abuse it as you will, it gives a bloodless measure of social forces—bloodless, have you thought of that?—a means of continuity, a principle of stability, a relief from the paralyzing terror of revolution.[1]

(4) *The fourth value is that of the minimum of coercion.* A fourth value may be constructed by reference to the extent and quality of coercion involved in a democracy. . . . It is not only that almost by definition the greater number approves of the policy decisions, so that always the smaller number is coerced. This is the least of the argument, which depends much more on the existence of political freedoms and the way in which policies are made. For one thing there is great value

[1] Learned Hand, *The Spirit of Liberty,* ed. Irving Dillard, New York, 1952 and 1959, p. 76.

in a safety valve, in being able to let off steam and to contribute to the debate and the politicking even though one is finally outvoted. We may follow the fashion and call it a catharsis, a working-off harmlessly of buried feelings of aggression, guilt, or the like. An ill-treated minority does normally feel differently—less coerced—if political equality is recognized and if it has to give only conditional obedience to policies which it may criticize and which it can entertain a reasonable hope of altering either by persuasion or by political influence. (This does not, however, always satisfy "permanent" minorities. . . .)

We may go further. The normal democratic policy is in a sense a decision which gives no claimant everything he asks for; is not a mere mechanical compromise but a new policy, shaped from the continuing dialogue and struggle of the political process. Some go so far as to call the method "creative discussion." From this it is only a short step to saying that there is more value in decisions which we make, or help to make, than in having "wiser" decisions made *for* us, and which we must be compelled to obey.

> To try to force people to embrace something that is believed to be good and glorious but which they do not actually want, even though they may be expected to like it when they experience its results—is the very hall mark of anti-democratic belief.[2]

One might plausibly assume then that nearly everybody would accept this value—that *ceteris paribus,** it is better to coerce fewer people than more, to get voluntary observance rather than coerced obedience, to substitute what Wordsworth called the "discipline of virtue" for the "discipline of slavery": "order else cannot subsist, nor confidence nor peace." The notion of willing obedience reasonably, freely, and conditionally given would also agree with ideas of self-discipline, responsibility, and the like, of which we hear so much.

(5) *The fifth value is that of diversity.* The argument here depends initially on whether diversity of beliefs and action, and a wider area of choice, are of themselves good. Many will dispute their value, since diversity and variety can result in more of both the good and the bad, and free choice implies the freedom to choose badly. Ruskin thought that liberty of choice destroyed life and strength, and hence democracy was destructive. Human freedom has destructive as well as creative possibilities. But is there not at least some prima facie case for diversity and variety per se, as there is for freedom?

In the first place there is always diversity in any society, even if not to the extent of as many opinions as there are men. Democracy merely

---

[2] Cf. A. D. Lindsay, *The Modern Democratic State,* Oxford, 1943, pp. 45, 241, 275. Schumpeter, *Capitalism, Socialism and Democracy* (New York, 1950), p. 237.

* Other things being equal.

recognizes its existence, and legitimatizes the different opinions and interests. . . .

In the second place, the value of open channels and political liberties is that by implication an inevitable variety will result. Here, too, as far as ideas are concerned, we may fall back upon the arguments used by Mill in his defense of liberty of opinion. We do rightly, on grounds of experience, to be suspicious of man's ability to know beforehand what new idea or proposal or way of behaving should be strangled at birth by the authorities and what allowed to live. The true and the good often repel in their very novelty.

In the third place, however, we can only say that "other things being equal," a wider choice is *ipso facto* good; it is a necessary condition for moral improvement, for reaching closer to the truth (so long as we assume we have not already reached perfection or the *summum bonum*). . . .[3]

By maintaining an open society, democracy may then be called good because its freedoms give flexibility and a wide variety of choice. The argument may rest not only on the formal principles of democracy, but also on the empirical tendency for the political freedoms to extend beyond the purely political. The tendency is strong and ever present since political discussion includes the very topic of what is political, and because in their bidding for votes, parties and candidates tend to compete in granting substantive favors, including repeal of restrictive laws in some fields, and promotion of positive policies in others, e.g., on behalf of education, the arts and sciences. It is partly because of this tendency that democracy is sometimes called a "way of life." . . .

(6) *The sixth value is the attainment of justice.* Justice has been rated highly by political philosophers as a value to be attained in many societies. Its achievement is often regarded as the central core of political morality, and the defense of democracy on this ground must be that it is the system best able to produce justice. There are several relevant points in the case.

First, let us grant that the best we can hope for in any practicable political system is not that injustice will never be committed (a perfectionist ideal) but that it can be seen, corrected if possible, and avoided the next time beforehand. (The dilemma could perhaps be avoided if democracy were by definition, or could be in practice, unanimous rule.

[3] A subsidiary value from diversity may be formulated: a wider range of temptations gives more opportunities of strengthening the character. For this reason Morris Cohen could write: "the very essence of civilization [is] that we should increase the temptation and with it the power of self-control." *Reason and Law,* Glencoe, Ill., 1950, p. 52. Rousseau started from the same point: morality for the individual implies liberty of choice. Unfortunately, he tended to merge individual liberty in the community, though in this he was not far from one of the ideals of the Greek city-state.

There would then be no others within the system to judge the decisions to be unwise or unjust. But even then, a later generation could pass such judgment, as could persons in other states. Unanimity or universality is no guarantee of rightness or justice.) The link with democracy lies in the political liberties—the procedures, the publicity, and possibilities of redress. What the U.S. Supreme Court once said of liberty may be true of justice too: "the history of liberty has largely been the history of the observance of procedural safeguards."

No political system, lacking perfection, can be entitled to unconditional allegiance. There may come a time when any individual may feel bound in conscience to withhold his obedience; and it comes to much the same thing to say that no political system can lay down, beforehand, the institutional rules for justified disobedience or rebellion. In this respect, democracy again makes perhaps the best claim for obedience to an unjust law because of the political freedoms, provisional obedience, and chances of redress. It is certainly not illogical to obey a particular bad law if it is part of a general system of which we approve, and where we have the liberty of protest and persuasion, and the reasonable hope for redress. We must beware of posing the problem of obeying bad laws too sharply, and on this we may look to Locke for some sensible observations. Allegiance and obedience are never explainable on the ground that the political system gives us, as individuals, everything that we want.

Second, the likelihood of injustice under democracy is much less than where the political freedoms are suppressed, and where none of the usual political safeguards exist. Democracy provides some representation of all substantial groups and interests (though not always strictly in proportion to their numbers, and still less to their "importance"); injured interests, being vocal and able to muster power through influencing votes and through many other recognized and legitimate ways, are seldom likely to be ignored when policy decisions are being made. . . .

Third, democracy involves political compromise or harmony by the adjustment of conflicting claims. This may fairly enough be called "relative" justice, even though it does not approach the kind of harmony or "right relationship" of classes which constituted so much of Plato's idea of justice. In any case "absolute" justice is an ideal beyond the reach of democratic politics, partly because it involves less than full satisfaction of some claims (or "rights") but also partly because absolute justice in any other sense is beyond any system of government. Only relative justice, the relative attainment of any of our highest ideals, is feasible in any political system. The best word to use perhaps is equity, with its connotation of both justice and flexibility. . . .

(7) [*Another*] *value consists of the freedoms found in a democracy.* . . .

The case for democracy, on the ground that it promotes freedoms, is chiefly in terms of the political freedoms. Whether freedoms will be extended to other spheres is not guaranteed by the logic of the democratic system, but is merely a likelihood or probability, a tendency for the political freedoms to carry over into other spheres. The presumption is extremely strong that they will do so, as they did in Athens if we may take the word of Pericles on the social freedom which the citizens enjoyed. It is the same sort of (weaker) tendency by which equality tends to be carried over from the political to other spheres. As Duverger puts it:

> The history of the development of civil rights in France shows a link between the existence of a liberal regime and that of a democratic regime with free elections. This same link is to be found in most of the countries in the world, so that the following general statement may be formulated: civil rights in a country exist in direct proportion to the degree of democracy to be found there. This is not a logical connection but one based on actual fact.[4]

The case can go somewhat deeper. The inescapable conditions of social life impose restrictions on one's freedom of action: freedoms conflict with other goods which we value highly, and sometimes with one another. The essential function of co-ordinating freedoms with one another and with other goods is performed by all governments, but the claim on behalf of democracy is that democratic co-ordination maximizes freedoms. And—paradoxical though it may sound—the maximizing of freedoms does not necessarily mean that the laws are few. To protect and even extend freedoms may demand an elaborate network of laws. We may start with Hobbes's dictum about the silence of the law, but a political theory cannot end there.

It is perhaps worth mentioning again that the political freedoms of a democracy may be valued highly in their own right, and not only for the instrumental reason that they give citizens a share in political power, or are necessary to promote social welfare. There is eloquent testimony that such freedoms may be valued intrinsically, given by many refugees from Nazi Germany and from the Soviet Union and its satellites. Those of us living in democracies, having been born free, and never having been deprived, must often make a greater effort in order to appreciate our birthright. To those who value political freedoms, for whatever reason, the justification for democracy is strong; to those who place a higher intrinsic value upon *other* freedoms, it can at least be said that democracy has a marked tendency to extend the freedoms from the political to other spheres if only because there are channels for the political extension of freedoms.

(8) *Finally, a value may be constructed for democracy from the de-*

[4] Maurice Duverger, *The French Political System* (Chicago, 1958), p. 161.

ficiencies of alternative systems. Any alternative is inevitably a system in which some kind of minority makes the policy decisions—always of course a properly qualified minority, since no one advocates that the numerical minority should rule merely *because* they are a minority.

In the contemporary world there is a strong, almost universal aversion to the idea that any kind of minority has any right or title to rule. Not only are the almost unrecognized postulates of our political thinking against it, but also the rational objections: What minority? What credentials? Who will judge the credentials? Nor must we make the mistake of merely assuming that because democracy is imperfect, any minority alternative is better because it is made so by definition. We cannot get from a definition to a feasible and perfect political system.

COMMENTS ON THE JUSTIFICATION

Obviously, only those who prize those values listed above, and who believe they are inseparable from or most likely to be promoted by a democracy, will find the values cogent arguments for a democratic system. Thus, apart altogether from considerations of the social and other empirical conditions necessary for democracy, we have not proved that democracy is logically always and everywhere the best political system. I do not think it can be proved, in any logical sense of proof, and that is why I have not attempted it. Instead we may agree with Aristotle that the best form of government is relative to circumstances. The case for democracy is a case, not a demonstration like a Euclidean theorem. By taking this attitude we avoid making a political system itself into an absolute value, as well as the mistake of completely identifying any existing democracy with the theoretical model.

Again, all the values noted are not always and only found in actual democratic systems. Political systems do not always work as their distinguishing principles might lead us to think. Absolute monarchies, for instance, may occasionally be noted for the freedoms and diversity which they permit, as in the rich literary, artistic, and scientific life of eighteenth-century France. But those values noted above follow from the logic of a democratic system, whereas they do not follow from the logic of other systems. . . .

SOME CRITICISMS OF DEMOCRACY

A common opinion has it that democracy has lost much of its appeal in the modern world because its attitudes or character are thought not to agree with the findings of psychology. At any rate, there is a substantial corpus of pessimistic writing to that effect.

For one thing, it is alleged that a whole body of psychological doctrine, starting with Freud, has undermined belief in the rationality of man by showing that much of our behavior is determined at the unconscious mental level. If political decisions cannot be partly rational—in both the economic sense of means to ends and the sense of choosing ends—it is hard to see how we can justify democracy. Another fashionable school of thought purports to show that people are "naturally" and not "culturally" afraid of what Gide called the "anguish of freedom"— of choice, self-discipline, and the responsibility that the democratic method presupposes.

Then, again, so it is said, sociology and the discovery of "iron laws of oligarchy" in virtually every type of large-scale social organization including political parties tend to the same pessimistic conclusion of the inherent unsuitability of democratic principles and attitudes for any large-scale organization, and *a fortiori* for one as large as a political system. This kind of social determinism is seen at its most determinist and pessimistic in the classic by Michels on *Political Parties:* the iron law of oligarchy is "the fundamental sociological law of political parties." No remedy can be found: all organizations in time will become oligarchic. The charge of inevitable oligarchy, or something very similar, is brought not only by Michels but also by writers such as Pareto, Mosca, and Burnham, and is supported by much empirical evidence drawn from the study of political parties, trade unions, and business organizations. The charge is based on different concepts such as that of the "managerial elite," the inevitable trends to bureaucracy, the "organization man," the nature of large-scale technology, and so forth. The concept of the "sociology of knowledge" has contributed also to the same end—e.g., here and there in the works of Karl Mannheim—by suggesting that social factors determine man's beliefs and actions.

What are we to say to these impressive arguments? For myself, I do not find that they support the anti-democratic conclusions so often drawn. Take the "iron law of oligarchy." There is nothing in democratic theory which cannot come to terms with leadership in organizations, political or any other kind. It is no great news that large-scale organizations are led by the leaders. This sociological finding, for which so many—sometimes conflicting—causes are given and from which different conclusions are drawn, is only devastating to a primitive or direct type of democratic system, and scarcely affects a representative system. A democracy does not require everyone to be politically active, or show all the democratic attitudes, and can make full allowance for the realities of leadership and parties. (A democracy does, however, presuppose that political action is not determinist, but that human choice and attitudes do count, causally; that human choice can control and mold the impersonal forces at work in society, and within limits shape them to human ends.)

A fuller answer may be attempted to the charge based upon psychology. We can, in the first place, readily admit that any democracy may contain a proportion of undemocratic personalities, judged by the standards set forth above or by other standards. How high the proportion can get before a democracy becomes unworkable, we simply do not know. Doubtless the proportion will vary with the kind of political circumstances at different times, including the urgency and magnitude of the policies to be made, the quality of political leadership, and so forth. We do know, however, that democracy need not presuppose any large proportion of the politically active, or even a high proportion of voters. Despite Aristotle, not every man is (or need be) a political animal.

Then, too, we can point to the going democracies, some of which have been successful for a considerable time; and to the many attempts at self-government—even those that have failed—all of which must be explained away by the psychological pessimists. Those who assert that man is not psychologically able to work democracy often forget that full representative democracy is, for all practical purposes, a comparatively new political system. It takes time for the masses of men to adjust to new political forms, and to adapt to the ideas and the moral climate which accompanies democracy—the autonomy, the discussion, the political equality and freedoms, and the majority principle—until they become "second nature." Life in the past seems to have been lived more by "instinct" (or custom) and government has been more readily accepted with resignation, instead of approached with the idea that it can be popularly created and controlled. Every democracy trails clouds of these older traditions into the present. Democracy, as Morley said, "stands for a remarkable revolution in human affairs." Then, too, there is still the cogent point that so much of man's "unfitness" for democracy may be simply his "unfitness" for, or painful adjustment to, a scientific and industrial urban way of living.

In pointing thus to experience with democracy and self-government, we do not need to posit any primitive "instinct to freedom," nor yet to assume any universal psychological or other needs which only democracy can satisfy. There is a set of psychological *wants* that are democratic, but they are a function of the values of democracy, i.e., they are culturally learned and (as yet) certainly not universal. Men may come to democracy to fulfill different needs—as they go to religion for different reasons. It is enough if the needs thus fulfilled, in their overt expression as wants, are compatible with democracy. (Those who have been led to take a pessimistic view of man's capacity for democracy have, I think, been led astray by making two additional mistakes: first, by founding their psychological theory upon clinical experience with the unfit; and second, by assuming that democracy presupposes that all, or even a large proportion of, citizens need be politically active. They have been better at their psychology, their technical expertise, than in their understanding of politics.)

We can also point to the psychological evidence in *favor* of man's capacity for democracy—including those persons who value the procedures of democracy more highly than any of its substantive objectives. While it may be true that "every man bears within himself a dormant fascist," it is equally true that we are all animals in our unconscious. It is what is in our consciousness that counts, and the business of any society is to make a civilized consciousness.

Our conclusions can be modest. We need conclude only that there is nothing in the demands which democracy makes upon men, or in the kind of personality which it requires and promotes, that is at variance with what we know with a fair degree of reliability of psychology. This may not be saying much, because we may not know much for certain; most psychology is local and western and not universal. On the other hand, if we do not know much, it is hard to feel that arguments drawn from psychological theories are very damaging to democracy. We must assume, however, that the democratic character "does not form against the grain" in enough people [to make it impossible] to work the system successfully. Compatibility, then, is a justifiable assumption, and a quite sufficient one. "Man has no nature: what he has is . . . history." (And it may help to recall that anthropology finds something very like democracy in some early primitive societies, whence some assert that democracy is the oldest form of government, while some make the cheerful assumption that democracy is the norm at which the political animal most naturally will arrive.) . . .

THE CHARGE OF INCOMPETENCE

The second class of contemporary criticism, commanding a wide following, may for convenience be grouped under the head of "incompetence." A host of such specific charges used to be directed at the existing democracies before World War II, most of them being associated with Fascism and Nazism, both of which despised democracy but avoided the Marxist diagnosis of putting the blame on the capitalists and the economic system. The charges were focused instead around the allegation that democracy is incompetent and inefficient—in dealing with serious economic problems, in its unstable domestic and foreign policies, and in its inability to prepare for war. The breakdown of democracy in Germany and Italy, and its relative economic failure everywhere in the depression of the 1930's, was usually adduced as supporting evidence of incompetence. (The Marxist criticism is almost the opposite, that democracy *is* efficient in terms of its own "real" underlying principles—giving the *bourgeoisie* their way, and maintaining class rule for the time being.)

The alleged incompetence of democracy is accounted for in several ways. For one thing, the democratic system is inevitably slow—taking too long to act, to hammer out a policy in the endless debates, electioneering, and politicking. This slow method is quite unsuited for dealing with emergencies requiring quick decision. Nothing gets done, except during a war, and then only at the cost of suspending democracy.

For another, the political system of democracy is said to be inherently unsuited to the complexities and large scale of the modern world, whatever may perhaps have been its usefulness in a simpler age, when political units were small or when *laissez faire* prevailed and the services provided by government were few. When a government does a few things, mistakes hardly matter; but when many things, failures are always serious and may be calamitous. This particular criticism is indeed made the basis of pessimistic predictions of the prospects of democracy by both its friends and its enemies: by its friends who fear that "increasing" government may destroy democracy, and by its enemies who hope that it will do so.

Then again, democracy is said to fail on the score of leadership. The talents for vote-getting are not those of ruling—of making "wise" decisions. Democracy emphasizes and rewards the former, and bonuses opportunism of parties and politicians as they have the money or cunning to influence the votes. But good government, wise policies, are needed to ensure the success of any system, and only good leaders can provide these desiderata.

Moreover, even if competent leaders should occasionally find themselves in office—combining the roles of politicians and statesmen—they are hopelessly handicapped by the methods of democratic politics. Democracy diffuses responsibility for policies, whereas responsibility must be concentrated in order to "get things done," i.e., to decide policies, to make them into a consistent pattern, and to see they are carried out efficiently. A casual reference to the near-chaos or deadlock in some multi-party systems—usually that of France—is taken to be enough to document the case against democratic leadership.

The very principle of compromise which is, so to speak, built into the democratic system further militates against efficiency, consistency, and "good" government. Compromise is also made the basis of the charge that democracy lacks "principle" (compromise is said to be the exaltation of "no principle"), while in addition it stands for and invites unlimited sectionalism, pressures, and group selfishness. Alternatively, democracy is sometimes accused of being organized deceit and hypocrisy

—professing high principles and the public interest but always deviating from them in the compromises of politics—an inevitable tendency (so it is said), since, not being able to accomplish anything important, politicians must pretend that the trivial things they actually do are important.

Democracy is also confusing to the citizens, who cannot understand the complexities and subtleties of its policy-making or methods of operation. It has, moreover, no ideology, no body of agreed and simple doctrine, no great aims or purposes, by which to inspire devotion and sacrifice and to command the enthusiastic loyalty, if not the understanding, of the masses. The result is bound to be disillusion and apathy among the public, and in the end a collapse of the system from its own defects —to give way to more militant, inspiring, and demanding faiths, supporting other newer systems which are the "wave of the future." Where the democratic system has worked, after a fashion, its success is accounted for by extraneous or fortuitous factors which have, as it were, managed to keep a bumbling and incompetent system afloat in spite of its defects.

The case is familiar and at first sight formidable. (I pass over the virtues sometimes grudgingly granted to democracy, e.g., that it solves the problem of peaceful succession of rulers.) And it would obviously be foolish to deny an element of truth here and there in these criticisms. Before coming to grips with the main charge of incompetence, two oft-forgotten points of considerable importance should be recalled.

(a) Much of democratic government—though by no means all—is conducted in the white glare of publicity, and faults are exaggerated. The very function of an opposition is to oppose, and to do so as noisily and as effectively as possible. Because of the political liberties allowed, every democracy produces critics of the system and of its most fundamental principles. Mistakes of policy and abuses of the system, both real and imaginary, are freely ventilated—often to loud and profitable applause. By contrast, only praise and flattery are allowed in a dictatorship, and since the mistakes and evils go uncriticized, one tends to assume they are nonexistent. The old observation is still true that under a popular government everyone speaks ill of the people with freedom and without fear; whereas no one speaks of an absolute prince without a thousand fears and precautions.

(b) The critics of democracy all too often fail to apply the same standards to democracy as to its rivals. The very highest, often perfectionist, standards are used to judge democracy—as when moral purists attack the United States for the mote and make generous excuses for the Soviet beam, or denounce the scandals of democratic politics, forgetting the institutionalized corruption of other political systems. (This kind of criticism also subtly shifts the ground of attack from incompetence to moral turpitude.)

Nevertheless, even when due allowance has been made for the exaggeration of faults and the use of the double standard, the charge of incompetence raises a question which goes to the very root of the theory of democratic politics. Incompetence, or the lack of political wisdom, constitutes in fact the gravamen of the most serious charge (other than the Marxist) and is also the oldest of the criticisms against democracy —modern versions being seldom more than glosses on Plato, with a few topical illustrations added. In the end, the quasi-Platonic criticism is directed against the principle of political equality, and rests upon a particular view of the nature of politics. This principle of political equality, so it is said, is based on the assumption of equality of political wisdom among the citizens—which is absurd. Political wisdom is distributed unequally, and some obviously know more than others. The masses of the citizens are ignorant, and even if most of them can be made technically literate, their judgment on public policy (if it can be called judgment) is necessarily incomplete and faulty.

Whatever validity Plato's critique of the assumption of equal political wisdom had against Athenian democracy, the modern version has far less force against the indirect, representative democracy with which we are familiar. Political wisdom of a high order on every complex issue is not required of all citizens in a system where the people do not make the policy decisions, but instead elect and authorize representatives to do this for them. The wisdom is needed by the leaders (though there is admittedly the problem of how the leaders may persuade the citizens to follow them). The modern criticism ought, then, to be directed against the democratic method of choosing its leaders (politicians). And often it is in fact so directed—as when it becomes an attack upon the universal suffrage, which is alleged to have been responsible for the rise of Hitler, to make the conduct of enlightened foreign policy impossible, to lower and destroy moral and cultural values alike.[5]

Democracy, like any other political system, must produce "adequate" leaders, adequate to ensure the continuance of the system, and thus to realize its values; adequate to meet the short- and long-term problems, whether economic or international or whatever they may be. Democracy obviously stands or falls by its method of selecting its leaders, and rests on the explicit assumption that elections are the best, or least bad, method of choosing the wisest and best. Behind the elections there is, of course, the pre-selection of candidates by parties—using all the polit-

[5] For a survey of the criticisms of democracy on cultural grounds by Carlyle, Ruskin, Arnold, Stephen, Maine, and Lecky see Benjamin E. Lippincott, *Victorian Critics of Democracy*, Minneapolis, 1938. Tocqueville and Henry Adams should also be consulted.

ical criteria of "availability," electoral appeal, and so forth; an elaborate and severely competitive pre-selection process that is usually ignored by the critics.

Let us grant that we need more investigations into democratic leadership: how it is in fact found and brought forward; in what political "talent" consists; whether there is a large stock of "talent"; whether the system does in fact make good use of its "talent"; whether a traditional ruling class is necessary (as Schumpeter argued); whether businessmen as a class are inherently poor political leaders (as Adam Smith believed); whether democratic leadership tends to compare unfavorably with leadership in other systems, and many similar questions. H. L. Mencken was much more severe than Adam Smith on what he called the plutocracy. Bryce too, a friendly critic, thought that the chief fault of democracy was "The power of money to pervert administration or legislation."

The theoretical argument against democratic wisdom is not, however, to be turned aside by empirical studies of leadership, even if their results should happen to be favorable to democracy. Questions of philosophy and principle are also at stake. Plato, it will be recalled, supported his critique by extended argument on the kind of knowledge required, and hence on the difficulty of acquiring wisdom, and on the training and qualifications of the guardians. The philosopher-rulers were to be an aristocracy in the better sense of the word, who by a combination of experience and knowledge received their title to rule just because they *were* qualified.

Fundamentally, two quite different views of the nature of politics and government—the question of what politics and political leadership are *about*—are involved. In the one case, the "proper end" and the implementing policies can only be known with difficulty, by the philosophers; in the democratic view the ends and policies are many and conflicting, the task of ruling is not conceived as holding society, willy-nilly, to the highest ideals, but of achieving the tolerable and the acceptable for the time being, of permitting progress to whatever ideals may be cherished and which the public may be persuaded to accept. Knowledge of the *summum bonum* is not excluded from a democracy, but it must be married to political persuasion in the politician or pressure group.

It is, however, when we come to consider practical minority-rule alternatives to democracy that the nature of the elite critique is more clearly revealed. Not only do all such critiques start by assuming differences in political capacity and wisdom—so much is admitted to exist—but they go on to assert that the "wise elite" can be identified and their rule validated. This is precisely the insuperable difficulty, since there are no accepted credentials for such wisdom.

Nor will I forsake the faith of our fathers in democracy, however I must transmute it, and make it unlovely to their eyes, were they here to see their strangely perverse disciple. If you will give me scales by which to weigh Tom and Dick and Harry as to their fitness to rule, and tell me how much each shall count, I will talk with you about some other kind of organization. Plato jumped hurdles that are too high for my legs. . . .[6]

Even if an elite is once selected, methods of continuing its recruitment and training must be invented. (The nearest approach to a dominant elite today is the self-selected communist party in some countries.)

The selection of an elite cannot be done by mass voting, or else we should be back again at democracy, yet somehow the whole of the citizens must be able to recognize the presence of such wisdom and the rulers who have it; and must accept and continue to accept the validity of their rule, i.e., its legitimacy. It is no wonder that even Plato flinched at this task, and resorted to his "myths" and "conditioning" once the initial philosopher-kings were installed. Nor can it be seriously maintained today that we can accept the rule of some kind of aristocracy based on and validated by wealth, blood, intellect, military prowess, or priestly power. (Think of the difficulty of getting an I.Q. rating accepted as conferring a right to rule.) We know that none of these is necessarily accompanied by political wisdom.

Further, the elite alternative assumes that the wisest and best, once found, will accept rule and responsibility, and will continue to exercise it wisely, their virtue and judgment alike remaining incorruptible by power. These are large assumptions, for which we are not in the market. Architects of Utopia may ignore the peril, but we know too much today about the corrupting influence of power upon those aloof from and out of touch with the governed, exacting obedience, yet unaccountable to anyone except their consciences or their God. It is for this reason that it seems so true that "Great men are nearly always bad men." In the end such rulers can only reduce the stature of their subjects, and they are left trying vainly— as Mill put it—to "do great things with little people." Only a democracy provides institutional safeguards against the corruption of power in an elite, by its freedoms and elections answering the old question *quis custodiet ipsos custodes?* * Elites and dictators both good and bad, are shrewd enough not to take chances by asking for a free renewal of their mandate. They fall a prey to all the evils of the "cult of the individual," having "no remedy for the personality defects which they may bring into their exalted station."[7]

---

[6] Learned Hand, *op. cit.* p. 77. See also Charles E. Merriam, *Systematic Politics,* Chicago, 1945, pp. 187ff.

* Who will watch over the rulers?

[7] F. Hermens, *The Representative Republic,* Notre Dame, 1958, p. 83.

Section XII

The Bases of American Foreign Policy

PARTICIPATION IN two world wars in one generation suggests that the survival of America as an independent and democratic nation is inextricably linked with developments abroad.

On what premises and assumptions should American foreign policy be based? Should we agree with Wilson that "we dare not turn from the principle that morality and not expediency is the thing that must guide us, and that we will never condone iniquity because it is most convenient to do so."? Or, must we distinguish between "moral sympathies and the political interests which [we] must defend"? Or, should we seek a "coincidence between national self-interest and supranational ideals."? The issue is discussed by Professors Hans J. Morgenthau, Robert E. Osgood, and H. B. Mayo.

Topic 30

IDEALS AND NATIONAL INTEREST

❧❦❧

The Primacy of the National Interest

HANS J. MORGENTHAU *

Moral principles and the national interest have contended for dominance over the minds and actions of men throughout the history of the modern state system. The conduct of American foreign affairs in particular has from

* Professor of Political Science, University of Chicago. Author of *Scientific Man vs. Power Politics, Politics Among Nations, In Defense of the National Interest,* and of

its very beginning been deeply affected by the contest between these two principles of political action. Perhaps never before or after have the practical alternatives which flow from these two principles been stated with greater acumen and persuasiveness than in the Pacificus articles of Alexander Hamilton, and it is for the light which Hamilton's arguments shed upon our problem—as well as for the analogy between the situation to which they apply and some of the situations with which American foreign policy must deal in our time—that we might dwell at some length upon the situation which gave rise to the Pacificus articles, and upon the philosophy which they express.

In 1792 the War of the First Coalition had ranged Austria, Prussia, Sardinia, Great Britain and the United Netherlands against revolutionary France, which was tied to the United States by a treaty of alliance. On April 22, 1793, Washington issued a Proclamation of Neutrality, and it was in defense of that proclamation that Hamilton wrote the Pacificus articles. Among the arguments directed against the Proclamation were three derived from moral principles. Faithfulness to treaty obligations, gratitude toward a country which had lent its assistance to the colonies in their struggle for independence, and the affinity of republican institutions, were cited to prove that the United States must side with France. Against these moral principles, Hamilton invoked the national interest of the United States:

> There would be no proportion between the mischiefs and perils to which the United States would expose themselves, by embarking in the war, and the benefit which the nature of their stipulation aims at securing to France, or that which it would be in their power actually to render her by becoming a party.
>
> This disproportion would be a valid reason for not executing the guaranty. All contracts are to receive a reasonable construction. Self-preservation is the first duty of a nation; and though in the performance of stipulations relating to war, good faith requires that its ordinary hazards should be fairly met, because they are directly contemplated by such stipulations, yet it does not require that extraordinary and extreme hazards should be run. . . .
>
> The basis of gratitude is a benefit received or intended which there was no right to claim, originating in a regard to the interest or advantage of the party on whom the benefit is, or is meant to be, conferred. If a service is rendered from views relative to the immediate interest of the party who performs it, and is productive of reciprocal advantages, there seems scarcely, in such a case, to be an adequate basis for a sentiment like that of gratitude. . . . It may be affirmed as a general principle, that the predominant motive of good offices from one nation to another, is the interest or advantage of the nation which performs them.

many articles in the field of international relations. The selection is from Hans J. Morgenthau, "The Primacy of the National Interest," *The American Scholar,* Vol. 18 (Spring, 1949), pp. 207–210 and from "Another 'Great Debate': The National Interest of the United States," *The American Political Science Review,* Vol. XLVI (December, 1952), pp. 961–988. Reprinted by permission of *The American Scholar* and of *The American Political Science Review.*

Indeed, the rule of morality in this respect is not precisely the same between nations as between individuals. The duty of making its own welfare the guide of its actions, is much stronger upon the former than upon the latter; in proportion to the greater magnitude and importance of national compared with individual happiness, and to the greater permanency of the effects of national than of individual conduct. Existing millions, and for the most part future generations, are concerned in the present measures of a government; while the consequences of the private actions of an individual ordinarily terminate with himself, or are circumscribed within a narrow compass. . . .

The philosophy of this discussion provided the guiding principles of American foreign policy for more than a century. That philosophy has found expression in the *Federalist* and Washington's Farewell Address, no less than in many diplomatic documents. It was eclipsed by a conception of foreign policy whose main representatives were McKinley, Theodore Roosevelt and Admiral Mahan. In that second period, moral principles were invoked side by side with the national interest to justify American expansion within and outside the Western hemisphere. Yet, as before with Gladstone's similar emphasis upon the moral obligations of British foreign policy, it so happened that by a felicitous coincidence what the moral law demanded of the United States was always identical with what its national interest seemed to require.

It is a distinctive characteristic of the third conception of American foreign policy, propounded by Woodrow Wilson, that this identity between the national interest and moral principles is consciously abandoned, and that the sacrifice of the national interest for compliance with moral principles is made the earmark of a worthy foreign policy. In his address at Mobile on October 27, 1913, Wilson declared: "It is a very perilous thing to determine the foreign policy of a nation in the terms of material interest. It not only is unfair to those with whom you are dealing, but it is degrading as regards your own actions. . . . We dare not turn from the principle that morality and not expediency is the thing that must guide us, and that we will never condone iniquity because it is most convenient to do so."

"Only a free people . . ." he said in his message of April 2, 1917, "prefer the interest of mankind to any interest of their own. . . . We have no selfish ends to serve. . . . We are but one of the champions of the rights of mankind." And in his message of January 22, 1917, he had opposed "a peace that will serve the several interests and immediate aims of the nations engaged."

It stands to reason that no statesman in actual performance could have lived up to such principles without ruining his country. Whenever, therefore, Wilson had to apply these moral principles to situations, especially in the Western hemisphere, where the national interest was of long standing and well-defined, he applied them in actions which might as well have been justified in terms of the national interest. Where, however, the national interest was new and not yet clearly defined—as with regard to Europe at the end of the First World War—Wilson started with the assumption, which was a subtly isolationist one, that no specific national interest of the United States was affected by any particular settlement of European issues, and ended up with half-hearted, uneasy compromises between moral principles and the national interests of the more influential European states. Such compromises could not fail to shock the adherents of the Wilsonian principles, to disappoint the nations whose interests had not been fully satisfied, and to remain unintelligible to those sectors of the American public which, following the Federalist tradition of the national interest, had not been affected by the idealism of Wilson's "new diplomacy."

Thus the twenties witnessed a revival of the conception of the national interest, however erroneously defined. Under Franklin D. Roosevelt, Wilsonianism was revived in the foreign policy of Cordell Hull, while the President came closest to identifying the national interest with moral principles, the characteristic of the second period of American foreign policy. It is with the Truman Doctrine that a fourth conception of foreign policy has come to dominate the conduct of American foreign affairs. The Truman Doctrine is Wilsonian in that it proclaims universal moral principles—such as promotion of free and democratic governments everywhere in the world —as standards of American foreign policy. It is within the Federalist tradition in that it finds the containment of Russian power at some point required by the national interest. Yet, by defining that point in terms of its moral principles and not in those political and military terms which the national interest would demand, it vitiates its consideration of the national interest and cannot help being eclectic and immature as a philosophy, and half-hearted, contradictory and threatened with failure in actual operation. . . .

The man in the street, unsophisticated as he is and uninformed as he may be, has a surer grasp of the essentials of foreign policy and a more mature judgment of its basic issues than many of the intellectuals and politicians who pretend to speak for him and cater to what they imagine his prejudices to be. During the recent war the ideologues of the Atlantic Charter, the Four Freedoms, and the United Nations were constantly complaining that the American soldier did not know what he was fighting for. Indeed, if he was fighting for some utopian ideal, divorced from the concrete experiences and interests of the country, then the complaint was well grounded. However, if he was fighting for the territorial integrity of the nation and for its survival as a free country where he could live, think, and act as he pleased, then he had never any doubt about what he was fighting for. Ideological rationalizations and justifications are indeed the indispensable concomitants of all political action. Yet there is something unhealthy in a craving for ideological intoxication and in the inability to act and to see merit in action except under the stimulant of grandiose ideas and far-fetched schemes. Have our intellectuals become, like Hamlet, too much beset by doubt to act and, unlike Hamlet, compelled to still their doubts by renouncing their sense of what is real? The man in the street has no such doubts. It is true that ideologues and demagogues can sway him by appealing to his emotions. But it is also true, as American history shows in abundance and as the popular success of Ambassador Kennan's book demonstrates, that responsible statesmen can guide him by awakening his latent understanding of the national interest.

Yet what is the national interest? How can we define it and give it the content which will make it a guide for action? This is one of the relevant questions to which the current debate has given rise.

It has been frequently argued against the realist conception of foreign policy that its key concept, the national interest, does not provide an acceptable standard for political action. This argument is in the main based upon two grounds: the elusiveness of the concept and its susceptibility to interpretations, such as limitless imperialism and narrow nationalism, which are not in keeping with the American tradition in foreign policy. The argument has substance as far as it goes, but it does not invalidate the usefulness of the concept.

The concept of the national interest is similar in two respects to the "great generalities" of the Constitution, such as the general welfare and due process. It contains a residual meaning which is inherent in the concept itself, but beyond these minimum requirements its content can run the whole gamut of meanings which are logically compatible with it. That content is determined by the political traditions and the total cultural context within which a nation formulates its foreign policy. The concept of the national interest, then, contains two elements, one that is logically required and in that sense necessary, and one that is variable and determined by circumstances.

Any foreign policy which operates under the standard of the national interest must obviously have some reference to the physical, political and cultural entity which we call a nation. In a world where a number of sovereign nations compete with and oppose each other for power, the foreign policies of all nations must necessarily refer to their survival as their minimum requirements. Thus all nations do what they cannot help but do: protect their physical, political, and cultural identity against encroachments by other nations.

It has been suggested that this reasoning erects the national state into the last word in politics and the national interest into an absolute standard for political action. This, however, is not quite the case. The idea of interest is indeed of the essence of politics and, as such, unaffected by the circumstances of time and place. Thucydides' statement, born of the experiences of ancient Greece, that "identity of interest is the surest of bonds whether between states or individuals" was taken up in the nineteenth century by Lord Salisbury's remark that "the only bond of union that endures" among nations is "the absence of all clashing interests." The perennial issue between the realist and utopian schools of thought over the nature of politics, to which we have referred before, might well be formulated in terms of concrete interest *vs.* abstract principles. Yet while the concern of politics with interest is perennial, the connection between interest and the national state is a product of history.

The national state itself is obviously a product of history and as such destined to yield in time to different modes of political organization. As long as the world is politically organized into nations, the national interest is indeed the last word in world politics. When the national state will have been replaced by another mode of organization, foreign policy must then protect the interest in survival of that new organization. For the benefit of those who insist upon discarding the national state and constructing supranational organizations by constitutional fiat, it must be pointed out that these new organizational forms will either come into being through conquest or else through consent based upon the mutual recognition of the national interests of the nations concerned; for no nation will forego its freedom of action if it has no reason to expect proportionate benefits in compensation for that loss. This is true of treaties concerning commerce or fisheries as it is true of the great compacts, such as the European Coal and Steel Community, through which nations try to create supranational forms of organization. Thus, by an apparent paradox, what is historically relative in the idea of the national interest can be overcome only through the promotion in concert of the national interest of a number of nations.

The survival of a political unit, such as a nation, in its identity is the irreducible minimum, the necessary element of its interests vis-à-vis other units. Taken in isolation, the determination of its content in a concrete situation is relatively simple; for it encompasses the integrity of the nation's territory, of its political institutions, and of its culture. Thus bipartisanship in foreign policy, especially in times of war, has been most easily achieved in the promotion of these minimum requirements of the national interest. The situation is different with respect to the variable elements of the national interest. All the cross currents of personalities, public opinion, sectional interests, partisan politics, and political and moral folkways are brought to bear upon their determination. In consequence, the contribution which science can make to this field, as to all fields of policy formation, is limited. It can identify the different agencies of the government which contribute to the determination of the variable elements of the national interest and assess their relative weight. It can separate the long-range objectives of foreign policy from the short-term ones which are the means for the achievement of the former and can tentatively establish their rational relations. Finally, it can analyze the variable elements of the national interest in terms of their legitimacy and their compatibility with other national values and with the national interest of other nations. . . .

We have said before that the utopian and realist positions in international affairs do not necessarily differ in the policies they advocate, but that they part company over their general philosophies of politics and their way of thinking about matters political. It does not follow that the present debate is only of academic interest and without practical significance. Both camps, it is true, may support this same policy for different reasons. Yet if the reasons are unsound, the soundness of the policies supported by them is a mere coincidence, and these very same reasons may be, and inevitably are, invoked on other occasions in support of unsound policies. The nefarious consequences of false philosophies and wrong ways of thinking may for the time being be concealed by the apparent success of policies derived from them. You may go to war, justified by your nation's interests, for a moral purpose and in disregard of considerations of power; and military victory seems to satisfy both your moral aspirations and your nation's interests. Yet the manner in which you waged the war, achieved victory, and settled the peace cannot help reflecting your philosophy of politics and your way of thinking about political problems. If these are in error, you may win victory on the field of battle and still assist in the defeat of both your moral principles and the national interest of your country.

Any number of examples could illustrate the real yet subtle practical consequences which follow from the different positions taken. We have chosen two: collective security in Korea and the liberation of the nations that are captives of Communism. A case for both policies can be made from both the utopian and realist positions, but with significant differences in the emphasis and substance of the policies pursued.

Collective security as an abstract principle of utopian politics requires that all nations come to the aid of a victim of aggression by resisting the aggressor with all means necessary to frustrate his aims. Once the case of aggression is established, the duty to act is unequivocal. Its extent may be affected by concern for the nation's survival; obviously no nation will commit outright suicide in the service of collective security. But beyond that elemental limitation no consideration of interest or power, either with regard to the aggressor or his victim or the nation acting in the latter's defense, can qualify the obligation to act under the principle of collective security. Thus high officials of our government have declared that we intervened in Korea not for any narrow interest of ours but in support of the moral principle of collective security.

Collective security as a concrete principle of realist policy is the age-old maxim, "Hang together or hang separately," in modern dress. It recognizes the need for nation A under certain circumstances to defend nation B against attack by nation C. That need is determined, first, by the interest which A has in the territorial integrity of B and by the relation of that interest to all the other interests of A as well as to the resources available for the support of all those interests. Furthermore, A must take into account the power which is at the disposal of aggressor C for fighting A and B as over against the power available to A and B for fighting C. The same calculation must be carried on concerning the power of the likely allies of C as over against those of A and B. Before going to war for the defense of South Korea in the name of collective security, an American adherent of political realism would have demanded an answer to the following four questions: First, what is our interest in the preservation of the independence of South Korea; second, what is our power to defend that independence against North Korea; third, what is our power to defend that independence against China and the Soviet Union; and fourth, what are the chances for preventing China and the Soviet Union from entering the Korean War?

In view of the principle of collective security, interpreted in utopian terms, our intervention in Korea was a foregone conclusion. The interpretation of this principle in realist terms might or might not, depending upon the concrete circumstances of interest and power, have led us to the same conclusion. In the execution of the policy of collective security the utopian had to be indifferent to the possibility of Chinese and Russian intervention, except for his resolution to apply the principle of collective security to anybody who would intervene on the side of the aggressor. The realist could not help weighing the possibility of the intervention of a great power on the side of the aggressor in terms of the interests engaged and the power available on the other side.

The Truman administration could not bring itself to taking resolutely the utopian or the realist position. It resolved to intervene in good measure on utopian grounds and in spite of military advice to the contrary; it allowed the military commander to advance to the Yalu River in disregard of the risk of the intervention of a great power against which collective security could be carried out only by means of a general war, and then refused to pursue the war with full effectiveness on the realist grounds of the risk of a third world war. Thus Mr. Truman in 1952 was caught in the same dilemma from which Mr. Baldwin could extricate himself in 1936 on the occasion of the League of Nations sanctions against Italy's attack upon Ethiopia only at an enormous loss to British prestige. Collective security as a defense of the *status quo* short of a general war can be effective only against second-rate powers. Applied against a major power, it is a contradiction in terms, for it means necessarily a major war. Of this self-defeating contradiction Mr. Baldwin was as unaware in the 'thirties as Mr. Truman seemed to be in 1952. Mr. Churchill put Mr. Baldwin's dilemma in these cogent terms: "First, the Prime Minister had declared that sanctions meant war; secondly, he was resolved that there must be no war; and thirdly, he decided upon sanctions. It was evidently impossible to comply with these three conditions." Similarly Mr. Truman had declared that the effective prosecution of the Korean War meant the possibility of a third world war; he resolved that there must be no third world war; and he decided upon intervention in the Korean War. Here, too, it is impossible to comply with these three conditions.

Similar contradictions are inherent in the proposals which would substitute for the current policy of containment one of the liberation of the nations presently the captives of Russian Communism. This objective can be compatible with the utopian or realist position, but the policies designed to secure it will be fundamentally different according to whether they are based upon one or the other position. The clearest case to date for the utopian justification of such policies has been made by Representative Charles J. Kersten of Wisconsin who pointed to these four "basic defects" of the "negative policy of containment and negotiated coexistence":

> It would be immoral and unchristian to negotiate a permanent agreement with forces which by every religious creed and moral precept are evil. It abandons nearly one-half of humanity and the once free nations of Poland, Czechoslovakia, Hungary, Rumania, Bulgaria, Albania, Lithuania, Latvia, Estonia and China to enslavement of the Communist police state.
>
> It is un-American because it violates the principle of the American Declaration of Independence, which proclaims the rights of all people to freedom and their right and duty to throw off tyranny.
>
> It will lead to all-out World War III because it aligns all the forces of the non-Communist world in military opposition to and against all the forces of the Communist world, including the 800,000,000 peoples behind the Iron Curtain.
>
> The policy of mere containment is uneconomic and will lead to national bankruptcy.

This statement is interesting for its straightforwardness and because it combines in a rather typical fashion considerations of abstract morality and of expediency. The captive nations must be liberated not only because their captivity is immoral, unchristian, and un-American, but also because its continuation will lead to a third world war and to national bankruptcy. To what extent, however, these considerations of expediency are invalidated by their utopian setting will become obvious from a comparison between the utopian and the realist positions.

From the utopian point of view there can be no difference between the liberation of Estonia or Czechoslovakia, of Poland or China; the captivity of any nation, large or small, close or far away, is a moral outrage which cannot be tolerated. The realist, too, seeks the liberation of all captive nations because he realizes that the presence of the Russian armies in the heart of Europe and their cooperation with the Chinese armies constitute the two main sources of the imbalance of power which threatens our security. Yet before he formulates a program of liberation, he will seek answers to a number of questions such as these: While the United States has a general interest in the liberation of all captive nations, what is the hierarchy of interests it has in the liberation, say, of China, Estonia, and Hungary? And while the Soviet Union has a general interest in keeping all captive nations in that state, what is the hierarchy of its interests in keeping, say, Poland, Eastern Germany, and Bulgaria captive? If we assume, as we must on the historic evidence of two centuries, that Russia would never give up control over Poland without being compelled by force of arms, would the objective of the liberation of Poland justify the ruin of western civilization, that of Poland included, which would be the certain result of a third world war? What resources does the United States have at its disposal for the liberation of all captive nations or some of them? What resources does the Soviet Union have at its disposal to keep in captivity all captive nations or some of them? Are we more likely to avoid national bankruptcy by embarking upon a policy of indiscriminate liberation with the concomitant certainty of war or by continuing the present policy of containment?

It might be that in a particular instance the policies suggested by the answers to these questions will coincide with Representative Kersten's proposals, but there can be no doubt that in its overall character, substance, emphasis, and likely consequences a utopian policy of liberation differs fundamentally from a realist one.

The issue between liberation as a utopian principle of abstract morality *vs.* the realist evaluation of the consequences which a policy of liberation would have for the survival of the nation has arisen before in American history. Abraham Lincoln was faced with a dilemma similar to that which confronts us today. Should he make the liberation of the slaves the ultimate standard of his policy even at the risk of destroying the Union, as many urged him to do, or should he subordinate the moral principle of universal freedom to considerations of the national interest? The answer Lincoln gave to Horace Greeley, a spokesman for the utopian moralists, is timeless in its eloquent wisdom. "If there be those," he wrote on August 22, 1862,

> who would not save the Union unless they could at the same time save slavery, I do not agree with them. If there be those who would not save the Union unless they could at the same time destroy slavery, I do not agree with them. My paramount object in this struggle *is* to save the Union, and is *not* either to save or to destroy slavery. If I could save the Union without freeing *any* slave I would do it, and if I could save it by freeing *all* the slaves, I would do it; and if I could save it by freeing some and leaving others alone I would also do that. What I do about slavery, and the colored race, I do because I believe it helps to save the Union; and what I forbear, I forbear because I do *not* believe it would help to save the Union. I shall do *less* whenever I shall believe what I am doing hurts the cause, and I shall do *more* whenever I shall believe doing more will help the cause. I shall try to correct errors when shown to be errors; and I shall adopt new views so fast as they appear to be true views.

I have here stated my purpose according to my view of *official* duty; and I intend no modification of my oft-expressed *personal* wish that all men everywhere could be free.

The foregoing discussion ought to shed additional light, if this is still needed, upon the moral merits of the utopian and realist positions. . . .

The realist recognizes that a moral decision, especially in the political sphere, does not imply a simple choice between a moral principle and a standard of action which is morally irrelevant or even outright immoral. A moral decision implies always a choice among different moral principles, one of which is given precedence over others. To say that a political action has no moral purpose is absurd; for political action can be defined as an attempt to realize moral values through the medium of politics, that is, power. The relevant moral question concerns the choice among different moral values, and it is at this point that the realist and the utopian part company again. If an American statesman must choose between the promotion of universal liberty, which is a moral good, at the risk of American security and, hence, of liberty in the United States, and the promotion of American security and of liberty in the United States, which is another moral good, to the detriment of the promotion of universal liberty, which choice ought he to make? The utopian will not face the issue squarely and will deceive himself into believing that he can achieve both goods at the same time. The realist will choose the national interest on both moral and pragmatic grounds; for if he does not take care of the national interest nobody else will, and if he puts American security and liberty in jeopardy the cause of liberty everywhere will be impaired.

Finally, the political realist distinguishes between his moral sympathies and the political interests which he must defend. He will distinguish with Lincoln between his *"official* duty" which is to protect the national interest and his *"personal* wish" which is to see universal moral values realized throughout the world. . . .

The contest between utopianism and realism is not tantamount to a contest between principle and expediency, morality and immorality, although some spokesmen for the former would like to have it that way. The contest is rather between one type of political morality and another type of political morality, one taking as its standard universal moral principles abstractly formulated, the other weighing these principles against the moral requirements of concrete political action, their relative merits to be decided by a prudent evaluation of the political consequences to which they are likely to lead.

These points are re-emphasized by the foregoing discussion. Which attitude with regard to collective security and to the liberation of the captive nations, the utopian or the realist, is more likely to safeguard the survival of the United States in its territorial, political, and cultural identity and at the same time to contribute the most to the security and liberty of other nations? This is the ultimate test—political and moral—by which utopianism and realism must be judged.

Ideals and Self-Interest

ROBERT ENDICOTT OSGOOD *

There is no virtue in a nation's being able to achieve its ends if those ends are not worth achieving. Obviously, I am not just interested in the stability and effectiveness of America's foreign relations as one might be interested in the adjustment of the Hopi Indians to their social and physical environment, without passing any judgment on the moral purpose and consequence of such an adjustment. . . .

SELF-INTEREST WITHOUT IDEALS IS SELF-DEFEATING

Fundamentally, there is no justification for ideals beyond the ideals themselves. They are matters of faith, not empirical propositions. But, if one assumes the worth of the Christian-liberal-humanitarian ideals, as this essay does, then it is relevant to understand that the calculation and pursuit of national self-interest without regard for universal ideals is not only immoral but self-defeating. Any assessment of the conditions for achieving a nation's international ends which ignores this fact is unrealistic.

If one believes that the enrichment of the individual's life, and not the aggrandizement of the state, is the ultimate goal of politics, if one believes that the object of survival is not mere breathing but the fulfilment of the liberal and humane values of Western civilization, then the preservation and the promotion of American power and interests cannot be an end in itself; it is but a means to an end. This is not just a theoretical consideration. It has practical implications for the conduct of America's foreign relations, and for her domestic affairs too, in the present time of troubles.

National security, like danger, is an uncertain quality; it is relative, not absolute; it is largely subjective and takes countless forms according to a variety of international circumstances. Under the complex circumstances of a world-wide power conflict the bounds of self-preservation are vastly extended, until there is scarcely any aspect of foreign policy that does not involve the nation's safety. Under the impact of persistent fear and tension

* Associate Professor of Political Science, University of Chicago. This selection is from Robert Endicott Osgood, *Ideals and Self Interest in America's Foreign Relations* (Chicago, University of Chicago Press, 1953), pp. 20, 442–444, 446–451, & 23.

national security becomes even more protean and nebulous, so that the notion of self-defense tends to become absorbed in the notion of self-assertion, and the assertion of national pride, honor, prestige, and power tends to become an end in itself. But when the preservation or aggrandizement of national power becomes an end in itself, the search for security will have defeated its very purpose; for according to the values which America professes to exemplify, power is meaningless unless it is a means to some ultimate goal.

If American power becomes an end in itself, American society, no less than international society, will suffer; for unless American security is measured by ideal standards transcending the national interest, it may take forms that undermine the moral basis of all social relations. If the Christian, humanitarian, and democratic values, which are the basis of America's social and political institutions, are valid at all, they are as valid outside American borders as within. Consequently, if they cease to compel respect in America's foreign relations, they will, ultimately, become ineffective in her domestic affairs. The resulting destruction of America's moral fiber through the loss of national integrity and the disintegration of ethical standards would be as great a blow to the nation as an armed attack upon her territory.

I do not mean that the standard of conduct in America's internal affairs varies in direct proportion with her standard in foreign relations. Clearly, this is not the case, for the relative anarchy of international society imposes severe limitations upon human morality, which, fortunately, do not apply to relations among groups and individuals within the structure of American society. Nevertheless, since the validity of the moral and ethical principles which form the bonds of American society is derived from their universal applicability, it would be unrealistic to suppose that the American people can maintain the vitality of these principles within their national borders while they are allowed to languish outside. If national self-interest becomes an all-consuming end in America's outlook upon international relations, it will necessarily jeopardize the strength and stability of liberal and humane values within the United States.

Woodrow Wilson and other American idealists understood the profound moral and psychological bond between America's international and her national behavior. Their mistake was in confusing what was ideally desirable with what was practically attainable. To expect nations to conform to the moral standards obeyed by groups and individuals within nations is not only utopian but, as Theodore Roosevelt asserted, ultimately destructive of both universal principles and the national advantage. But it is equally true that to reduce what is ideally desirable to what is practically attainable is to deprive the popular conscience of a standard of moral judgment which is indispensable to the progress and stability of all social relations, whether within or among nations. This is the moral dilemma posed by the impact of man's egoism upon his desire for perfection. In the past, American Realists have been too prone to ignore this dilemma by investing the unpleasant realities of national egoism with the character of normative principles. . . .

HUMAN NATURE DEMANDS THAT IDEALS SUPPLEMENT REASON

A view of international relations which imagines that nations can in the long run achieve a stable and effective foreign policy solely by a rational calculation of the demands of national self-interest is based upon an unrealistic conception of human nature, for it is certainly utopian to expect any great number of people to have the wit to perceive or the will to follow the dictates of enlightened self-interest on the basis of sheer reason alone. Rational self-interest divorced from ideal principles is as weak and erratic a guide for foreign policy as idealism undisciplined by reason. No great mass of people is Machiavellian, least of all the American people. Americans in particular have displayed a strong aversion to the pursuit of self-interest, unless self-interest has been leavened with moral sentiment.

A genuine realist should recognize that the transcendent ideals expressed in the traditional American mission, no less than America's fundamental strategic interests, are an indispensable source of stability in America's foreign relations. The vitality and the persistence of the liberal strain of American idealism—whether manifested in anti-imperialism, the peace movement, internationalism, the search for disarmament, or anti-fascism—is evidence of this fact. However naive or misguided the proponents of this central strain of American idealism may have been during the last half-century, they have, nevertheless, tenaciously preserved its vital core, which constitutes its universal validity; and their continual reassertion of that vital core of moral purpose—a reassertion kindled by a lively conscience and a profound faculty for self-criticism—has been one of the strongest, most consistent, and most influential aspects of America's international conduct. If American idealism has, at times, been an unsettling influence upon foreign policy, it is because it has lacked the discipline of political realism; but this is largely due to America's relative isolation and security in the past, not to any fatal antithesis between realism and idealism. One can well imagine American idealism being moderated by a less utopian view of international politics—indeed signs of this development are already apparent—but a steady and effective foreign policy devoid of moral appeal is scarcely conceivable.

If the present international tension puts a premium upon a rational comprehension of the thrust of national power and self-interest in world politics, it equally demands an unwavering devotion to ideal ends transcending the national interest in order that reason be given direction and purpose. For example, we have observed that, according to a realistic view of international relations, the American people must be prepared to compromise their ideals in the short run in order to preserve and promote them in the long run. We have stated that compromise will become increasingly necessary, the longer the polarized power struggle persists; and that, therefore, the need for clear, calm reason will become correspondingly great. However, unless the people realize that reason is only the instrument for effecting compromises and not the standard for judging their effectiveness, some anxious citizens, in their growing concern for the national security, may become so habituated to compromise that they will lose sight of the ideal criteria of judgment which determine whether a compromise achieves its purpose. They may blindly settle upon the half-loaf or reject the loaf altogether, when three-quarters of the loaf is available. As fear may constrict ideals to an inflexible pattern, reason may so continually stretch ideals to suit expediency that they will lose all shape and elasticity. The end result will be the same: the undermining of that idealistic element of stability in foreign relations, which reason alone cannot supply. . . .

A preoccupation with expediency leads men to seek the minimum risk and effort in the expectation of a limited return; it dulls imagination and saps initiative. A purely selfish attitude tends to confine attention to those manifestations of power which bear directly and immediately upon the national interest; it tends to obscure those positive, constructive measures which cope with the basic social and psychological conditions behind such manifestations. Rational self-interest, by itself, fails to inspire boldness or breadth of vision. It may even corrode the national faith and paralyze the will to resist. In a sense, the collapse of France was the collapse of pure rational expediency, as expressed in the popular slogan "Why die for Danzig?" It is no accident that those American isolationists in the period preceding Pearl Harbor who were most insistent that the United States shape its foreign relations strictly according to its selfish interests were also the ones who were most blind to the real requirements of American self-interest, and the least willing to take measures that recognized the dependence of American security upon the survival of Great Britain and France; whereas those idealists who were most sensitive to the Fascist menace to Western culture and civilization were among the first to understand the necessity of undertaking revolutionary measures to sustain America's first line of defense in Europe.

In other words, a realistic conception of human nature must recognize that national egoism unenlightened by idealism may lead men to view America's self-interest too narrowly to achieve or preserve security itself, for idealism is an indispensable spur to reason in leading men to perceive and act upon the real imperatives of power politics. It limbers the imagination and impels men to look beyond the immediate circumstances of the power struggle. It places the status quo in the perspective of ultimate goals. It frees the reason to examine broadly and perceptively the variety of means for adjusting the instruments of national purpose to the ever-changing international environment. Idealism illuminates the basic human aspirations common to all people and thus sharpens men's insight into the psychological sources of national power. It excites the human sympathies which inspire men to enlarge the area of mutual national interest among peoples sharing common values. Idealism is the driving force, the dynamic element, which can dispel the inertia of habit and move men to adopt the bold, constructive measures necessary for surmounting the present crisis and the crises beyond. In the long run, it is the only impulse that can sustain the people's willingness to make the personal and national sacrifices that are indispensable for sheer survival.

THE EXPEDIENCY OF IDEALISM

A true realist must recognize that ideals and self-interest are so closely interdependent that, even on grounds of national expediency, there are cogent arguments for maintaining the vitality of American idealism.

Ideals are as much an instrument of national power as the weapons of war. All manifestations of national power, including the threat of coercion, operate by influencing the thoughts and actions of human beings, whether by frightening them or by converting them. Since men are motivated by faith and moral sentiment as well as by fear and the instinct of self-preservation, the strength of America's moral reputation and the persuasiveness of the American mission are as vital a factor in the power equation as planes, ships, and tanks. One has only to recall the consequences of the rise and fall of America's moral reputation during and after World War I to understand the force of American idealism among foreign peoples.

The persuasiveness of the American mission is especially significant under the present circumstances, when the competition of ideologies is such a conspicuous feature of the power struggle between the Russian and the American orbits and when the effectiveness of American policy depends so heavily upon winning the moral and intellectual allegiance of vast numbers of people in the throes of social and nationalistic revolution. If in the eyes of millions of people living in underdeveloped areas of the world the United States ceases to stand for a positive and constructive program of social and material progress, if American ideals no longer mean anything beyond smug generalities and hypocritical rationalizations of selfish national advantage, then all the wealth and military power the United States can muster will not render these people an asset to the free world. If the nations within the Western Coalition conclude that America has lost all passion for improving the lot of common people for the sake of the people themselves, if they believe that Americans have lost interest in the vision of world peace in their overriding concern for their national self-interest, then no display of shrewd power politics will win for the United States the popular trust and admiration which American leadership requires.

Moreover, no coalition can survive through a common fear of tyranny without a common faith in liberty. If the leader of the Western Coalition ceases to sustain that faith, then who will sustain it? Because the United States is unavoidably thrust into a position of global leadership, her standards of conduct must, inevitably, have a great influence in setting the moral tone of international relations in general. Consequently, it behooves America to conduct its foreign relations in a way that will encourage the kind of international environment compatible with its ideals and interests.

That kind of environment cannot exist apart from a widespread respect for the universal ideals of peace, brotherhood, and the essential dignity of the individual. To perceive this one has but to imagine the unmitigated anarchy that would ensue if every nation identified the interests of all nations with its own interests and pursued its own independent security as a self-sufficient end without relation to universal goals; for if every nation made expediency its sole guide in foreign relations, and if every nation anticipated that every other nation was motivated solely by the improvement of its own welfare, the only bond among nations would be the concurrence of their interests. But there is no automatic harmony of interests among nations, and unadorned reason is a weak instrument for achieving the tolerance and fair play indispensable to a contrived harmony. If national self-interest were the sole standard of conduct common to nations, an improvement in the power position of one nation would set off a wave of distrust among the rest; and, eventually, the pressure of international conflict would loosen what moral and ethical restraints man has succeeded in placing on his collective behavior; international society would disintegrate into a Hobbesian state of anarchy. In the light of this prospect, it is apparent that America's moral leadership is an indispensable instrument of her survival.

We may admit the expediency of America's reputation for idealism, but we should not imagine that America's ability to gain the moral and intellectual allegiance of foreign peoples is merely a problem in the technique of propaganda. To be sure, skilful propaganda can make a vast difference in the effectiveness of America's leadership. American ideals must be interpreted with resourcefulness and imagination, according to the particular needs and aspirations of different peoples. But, no matter how clever American propaganda may be, if it is not consistent with American actions, it will be of little value as an instrument of policy and may well alienate its intended converts. At the same time, the actions of the United States must, in the long run, reflect the actual state of American opinion; for no foreign program, least of all one of international benevolence, will survive long in a democracy if it is contrary to public opinion, and it would be extremely unrealistic to expect Americans to support such a program for its propagandistic worth if they did not also believe in its moral worth. It follows that a sincere and widespread devotion to positive ideals of human betterment is a prerequisite for effective propaganda, for Americans cannot pretend to be idealists without being truly idealistic. American idealism cannot be exported like American machinery and weapons. The United States is a democracy, and, therefore, official propaganda, in its broad outlines, must be believed to be effective. Otherwise, it will be undermined at home, foreign peoples will see that it is undermined, and American idealism will be marked down as deception and hypocrisy. Therefore, genuine conviction becomes necessary in order to sustain the appearance of idealism demanded by sheer national expediency. It is fortunate for the survival of democratic government that this paradox exists. . . .

To recognize the points of coincidence between national self-interest and supranational ideals is one of the highest tasks of statesmanship. The last half-century of Anglo-American relations demonstrates that men can recognize and even multiply the points of coincidence by patiently building upon a foundation of mutual self-interest to enlarge the area of international confidence and respect. It seems likely that the greatest advances in international morality in the foreseeable future will be brought about by men with enough vision and good will to temper the more immediate or extreme demands of national self-interest with the superior demands of a long-run interest in international compromise and the rational, peaceful settlement of differences. In this imperfect world it is neither too much nor too little to expect that man's recognition of the coincidence of ideals with national self-interest may mitigate and enlighten the thrust of national egoism. . . .

What Unites the West?

H. B. MAYO *

We are often told that behind the conflict of power between Russia and the West there is an irreconcilable ideological conflict; that two fundamentally different philosophies and ways of life are at stake; and that the tension can be resolved only when one or the other ideology is stamped out by war. On the one side, obvious to all, is the philosophy of communism,

* Professor of Political Science, University of South Carolina. The selection is from H. B. Mayo, *Democracy and Marxism* (New York: Oxford University Press, 1955), from Ch. IX. By permission.

the confused and odious ideology upon which the U.S.S.R. and its satellites are, or profess to be, united. On the other there is something called "Western civilization." Exactly what kind of *Weltanschauung* the West stands for is not easy to say; and no wonder, since within it there is something to everyone's taste. It is a rich *smorgasbord* of philosophies, religions, political, economic, and social systems. Is there, behind this surface diversity, agreement among the Western allies upon any kind of fundamental principles?

Private enterprise or free competition is often said to be the basic principle that unites the West. Yet Yugoslavia and Norway are dissenters, and several other countries in the Western camp have had socialist governments at one time or another, and may have them again at the next election; while almost everywhere the capitalist countries have diluted the pure milk of private enterprise and competition. Western Europeans, for the most part, have no intention of fighting an atomic war in defense of private enterprise; and still less is this slogan (or principle) likely to attract support from the masses in the uncommitted countries of the Far East.

Is the West united on the principle of national sovereignty? Curiously enough it is the communist countries which have become notorious for their beating of the nationalist drums, whether in Russia, Yugoslavia, or China. But even more important is the fact that the really strong popular support for a merging of national sovereignties, for schemes of federalism, and for eventual world government comes from within the Western countries themselves. To say that the West stands for complete national sovereignty and the Soviet Union for internationalism is not only to distort the truth but also to invite Western democrats to desert their own side *en masse*.

Is religion something that unites the Western allies? Hardly any part of the globe is more secular in outlook than the Western world. Secularism is often associated with the enjoyment of creature comforts, the good things of this world. In our day the emphasis is on a constantly rising standard of living, measured in such terms as more leisure and a larger output of goods and services. If judged by their actions (and their advertising) the Western peoples seem to attach paramount importance to these material standards. But on this very point the West and the Soviet Union are, for once, in agreement, since both make a fetish of higher productivity and standards of living.

An even more difficult question arises. On which religion are we united —the Jewish, the Moslem, or the Christian? Is Turkey not in the alliance? Is Israel not a friendly neighbor? And if the Christian, which of the innumerable bodies into which Christendom is divided? No doubt if we all belonged to the same church it would unite us; but we do not.

There has been a strong move afoot to put up a fourth uniting principle called "Western values." But as one philosopher has said:

> These western values are supposed to consist of toleration, respect for in-
> dividual liberty, and brotherly love. I am afraid this view is grossly un-
> historical. If we compare Europe with other continents, it is marked out as the
> persecuting continent.[1]

Western history has often shown us the opposite qualities: intolerance, blind
obedience to authority, and ruthless self-interest. Values of all kinds can be
found in our blood-stained past, but which ones we select depends entirely
on our *present* beliefs, and it is precisely the unity of these present beliefs
which may be questioned.

Are we bound together by a belief in peaceful change as opposed to
violence and revolution? Peaceful political change is a principle adhered
to only in the democracies—how does one get a change of government or
policy in Spain or the Argentine?—and so is included within the wider principle of democracy. The claim that democracy is the unifying principle of the
West, although stronger than the others, is not without weaknesses. A number of democracies stand aloof from the Western alliance, while one of the
allies (Yugoslavia) adheres to an ideology similar to that of the Soviet Union;
one is authoritarian in a clerico-Fascist way (Spain); and South Africa—
which must also be counted in the Western camp—introduces an embar-
rassing racial complication. Clearly we cannot, without qualification, equate
the West with democracy.

Nevertheless, the more powerful of the Western nations *are* democracies.
The United States, Britain, Canada, for example, do substantially believe in
and practice the democratic principles of constitutionalism, political freedom,
toleration, and maintain the traditional cultural and civil liberties. Enough
other countries are with them on these matters to justify the claim that in a
broad general sense the Western cause is the cause of democracy. If the
Western allies should triumph, democracy would gain enormously in prestige
and influence, and communism in turn would suffer the ignominious fate of
Nazism and Fascism.

The agreement is not unanimous, however, by all the nations in the alliance, but is only a kind of majority-nation opinion; and even that does not
extend beyond political democracy. One should not, like the Marxists, decry
political democracy merely because one believes it is not enough, but it is
as well to realize that the Western world differs widely on how far democracy
should be extended into the economic and social sphere. Any one interpretation, if pushed too far, may endanger the solidarity of the alliance.

What, then, does unite the West? The answer is simple. It is fear of a
possible enemy, the threat of possible aggression, and so the Western nations
have allied and armed for self-protection. This may seem a negative sort of
union, and of course it is negative to those who favor liberating crusades on
behalf of great principles, and the enthusiasm which belief in cosmic ulti-

[1] B. Russell, *New Hopes for a Changing World,* London, 1951, p. 118.

mates can give. What is often forgotten, however, is that resistance to a common enemy has usually been the chief bond between allies, a classic example having occurred in the Second World War, when the democracies and the Soviet Union fought together against the Nazis.

Such an alliance also has its positive side, since when all the exceptions are allowed for, the Western cause remains, broadly speaking, the cause of democracy. Moreover, each nation within the alliance is also protecting its independence, its way of life, its own ideals, however these may be defined. And while defending what is our own we defend also the essential principle of diversity.

A great deal of nonsense is talked about the need for a faith to unite the West against communism. Many people are frantically looking around for a faith or an idea that can command general assent and inspire the West to the fervor of enthusiasm formerly displayed by the Nazis, and now by communists. But it is more than doubtful whether such an ideal set of values or ultimate principles can be found to command general agreement. Nor is it possible to adopt beliefs merely because they would be useful in the cold war: beliefs on such a scale can be manufactured to order only in the totalitarian states. The very search for a Western faith is a tacit admission that we are not already agreed upon our ideology. The common impression that an ideological conflict has lead to international friction is probably mistaken. It seems nearer the truth that the friction and fears came first and the clash of ideologies has been called upon in order to bolster morale.

If the preceding argument is sound, then it is misleading and self-deceptive to speak of ideological Western unity where none exists, because such talk tends to gloss over the differences within the Western alliance, and to assume that all are democratic, or share some other common philosophy, solely because they are anti-Soviet and reject communism. It is also dangerous, because it leads to a fanaticism and a warlike spirit which can make war more likely. Inflammatory crusading talk may not easily be deflected from the rash aim of liberation to the proper but humdrum job of defense. And if an ideological war should come it will be a war of extermination, not of mere defeat, since the only thorough way to extinguish a heresy (for the time being) is to kill off the heretics. Christian Europe tried this barbarous method long ago, and there are more heretics today than ever. Heresies rarely stay dead. Moreover, an uncompromising ideological attitude will keep us fighting forever all over the globe, since as soon as one "bad" principle or philosophy is destroyed another is bound to spring up and offend us. Already there has been friction among the allies, caused by this talk of "our" ideology. Even the total preparation for an ideological war, and the atmosphere of conformity created, are giving rise to a tendency which, if carried far enough, could convert the West into military states indistinguishable from military tyrannies.

But the most serious immediate danger is this: for the West to adopt the language and attitude of Russia, with constant emphasis on a messianic message, is to make it almost impossible to come to any sort of peaceable *modus vivendi*. Questions of moral principle should not be ignored in international relations; but if it is a mistake to ignore them, it is an even worse mistake to elevate every clash of interest into a conflict of sacred principles. In that way we become intransigent, publicly committed beforehand on every issue, until every compromise, every trivial concession, every negotiation is interpreted as surrender, betrayal, or appeasement.

What we tend to forget is that it is not necessary to agree on our metaphysics first in order to live together without fighting. Differences on ultimates divide Jew from Gentile, Catholic from Protestant, Moslem from Hindu, atheist from believer. And none of these differences is likely to be settled in any foreseeable future. But the slumbering volcanoes need not erupt. We have learned to live together within the democracies, despite the gulfs that divide us, united in our common humanity, in the desire for law and order, and in the procedural agreement to differ.

So in the international sphere. An international community does not necessarily presuppose that we all think alike on fundamentals. We are all united in our will to survive, and it is (or ought to be) perfectly possible to live in a world at peace without deciding whose ultimates are right. War will settle not which side is right but merely which is the more powerful; although victory will no doubt lend prestige to the ideas of the winner. . . .

Section XIII

Freedom and Survival in the Atomic Age

HAVING GIVEN consideration to the appropriate roles of "national interest" and of moral or ideological principles in the formulation of American foreign policy, our inquiry turns, more specifically, to the contemporary issue of whether "coexistence" between the U.S.S.R. and the U.S. is a sound and realistic objective. What are the implications, risks, advantages of, and alternatives to, such a policy? The discussion between Nikita S. Khrushchev and George F. Kennan on "coexistence" first appeared in *Foreign Affairs*. It is reproduced here in its entirety.

A complementary issue of compelling importance concerns the appropriate policies for America in light of the development of nuclear weapons of incredibly destructive power. In this connection, we present the viewpoints of three eminent scholars.

Topic 31

HOW TO ENSURE PEACEFUL COEXISTENCE

๛

On Peaceful Coexistence

NIKITA S. KHRUSHCHEV *

I have been told that the question of peaceful coexistence of states with different social systems is uppermost today in the minds of many Ameri-

* Chairman of the Council of Ministers of the Union of Soviet Socialist Republics and First Secretary of the Central Committee of the Communist Party of the Soviet Union. The selection is from "On Peaceful Coexistence," *Foreign Affairs*, Vol. 38 (October, 1959), pp. 1–18. Copyright by the Council on Foreign Relations, Inc., New York. By permission.

cans—and not only Americans. The question of coexistence, particularly in our day, interests literally every man and woman on the globe.

We all of us well know that tremendous changes have taken place in the world. Gone, indeed, are the days when it took weeks to cross the ocean from one continent to the other or when a trip from Europe to America, or from Asia to Africa, seemed a very complicated undertaking. The progress of modern technology has reduced our planet to a rather small place; it has even become, in this sense, quite congested. And if in our daily life it is a matter of considerable importance to establish normal relations with our neighbors in a densely inhabited settlement, this is so much the more necessary in the relations between states, in particular states belonging to different social systems.

You may like your neighbor or dislike him. You are not obliged to be friends with him or visit him. But you live side by side, and what can you do if neither you nor he has any desire to quit the old home and move to another town? All the more so in relations between states. It would be unreasonable to assume that you can make it so hot for your undesirable neighbor that he will decide to move to Mars or Venus. And vice versa, of course.

What, then, remains to be done? There may be two ways out: either war—and war in the rocket and H-bomb age is fraught with the most dire consequences for all nations—or peaceful coexistence. Whether you like your neighbor or not, nothing can be done about it, you have to find some way of getting on with him, for you both live on the same planet.

But the very concept of peaceful coexistence, it is said, by its alleged complexity frightens certain people who have become unaccustomed to trusting their neighbors and who see a double bottom in each suitcase. People of this kind, on hearing the word "coexistence," begin to play around with it in one way and another, sizing it up and applying various yardsticks to it. Isn't it a fraud? Isn't it a trap? Does not coexistence signify the division of the world into areas separated by high fences, which do not communicate with each other? And what is going to happen behind those fences?

The more such questions are piled up artificially by the cold-war mongers, the more difficult it is for the ordinary man to make head or tail of them. It would therefore be timely to rid the essence of this question of all superfluous elements and to attempt to look soberly at the most pressing problem of our day—the problem of peaceful competition.

II

One does not need to delve deeply into history to appreciate how important it is for mankind to ensure peaceful coexistence. And here it may be said parenthetically that the Europeans might have benefited a great deal in their day if, instead of organizing senseless crusades which invariably ended in failure, they had established peaceful relations with the differently-minded peoples of the Moslem East.

But let us turn to facts concerning the relatively recent past when the watershed between states no longer consisted of different religious creeds and customs, but of much deeper differences of principle relating to the choice of social systems. This new situation arose on the threshold of the 1920's when, to the booming of the guns of the Russian cruiser *Aurora* which had joined the rebellious workers and peasants, a new and unprecedented social system, a state of workers and peasants, came into the world.

Its appearance was met with disgruntled outcries of those who naïvely believed the capitalist system to be eternal and immutable. Some people even made an attempt to strangle the unwanted infant in the cradle. Everybody knows how this ended: our people voted with their arms for Soviet power, and it came to stay. And even then, in 1920, V. I. Lenin, replying to the question of an American correspondent as to what basis there could be for peace between Soviet Russia and America, said: "Let the American imperialists not touch us. We won't touch them."

From its very inception the Soviet state proclaimed peaceful coexistence as the basic principle of its foreign policy. It was no accident that the very first state act of the Soviet power was the decree on peace, the decree on the cessation of the bloody war.

What, then, is the policy of peaceful coexistence?

In its simplest expression it signifies the repudiation of war as a means of solving controversial issues. However, this does not cover the entire concept of peaceful coexistence. Apart from the commitment to non-aggression, it also presupposes an obligation on the part of all states to desist from violating each other's territorial integrity and sovereignty in any form and under any pretext whatsoever. The principle of peaceful coexistence signifies a renunciation of interference in the internal affairs of other countries with the object of altering their system of government or mode of life or for any other motives. The doctrine of peaceful coexistence also presupposes that political and economic relations between countries are to be based upon complete equality of the parties concerned, and on mutual benefit.

It is often said in the West that peaceful coexistence is nothing else than a tactical method of the socialist states. There is not a grain of truth in such allegations. Our desire for peace and peaceful coexistence is not conditioned by any time-serving or tactical considerations. It springs from the very nature of socialist society in which there are no classes or social groups interested in profiting by war or seizing and enslaving other people's territories. The Soviet Union and the other socialist countries, thanks to their socialist system, have an unlimited home market and for this reason they have no need to pursue an expansionist policy of conquest and an effort to subordinate other countries to their influence.

It is the people who determine the destinies of the socialist states. The socialist states are ruled by the working people themselves, the workers and peasants, the people who themselves create all the material and spiritual values of society. And people of labor cannot want war. For to them war spells grief and tears, death, devastation and misery. Ordinary people have no need for war.

Contrary to what certain propagandists hostile to us say, the coexistence of states with different social systems does not mean that they will only fence themselves off from one another by a high wall and undertake the mutual obligation not to throw stones over the wall or pour dirt upon each other. No! Peaceful coexistence does not mean merely living side by side in the absence of war but with the constantly remaining threat of its breaking out in the future. *Peaceful coexistence can and should develop into peaceful competition for the purpose of satisfying man's needs in the best possible way.*

We say to the leaders of the capitalist states: Let us try out in practice whose system is better, let us compete without war. This is much better than competing in who will produce more arms and who will smash whom. We stand and always will stand for such competition as will help to raise the well-being of the people to a higher level.

The principle of peaceful competition does not at all demand that one or another state abandon the system and ideology adopted by it. It goes without saying that the acceptance of this principle cannot lead to the immediate end of disputes and contradictions which are inevitable between countries adhering to different social systems. But the main thing is ensured: the states which decided to adopt the path of peaceful coexistence repudiate the use of force in any form and agree on a peaceful settlement of possible disputes and conflicts, bearing in mind the mutual interests of the parties concerned. In our age of the H-bomb and atomic techniques this is the main thing of interest to every man.

Displaying skepticism about the idea of peaceful competition, Vice President Nixon, in his speech over the Soviet radio and television in August 1959, attempted to find a contradiction between the Soviet people's professions of their readiness to coexist peacefully with the capitalist states and the slogans posted in the shops of our factories calling for higher labor productivity in order to ensure the speediest victory of Communism.

This was not the first time we heard representatives of the bourgeois countries reason in this manner. They say: The Soviet leaders argue that they are for peaceful coexistence. At the same time they declare that they are fighting for Communism and they even say that Communism will be victorious in all countries. How can there be peaceful coexistence with the Soviet Union if it fights for Communism?

People who treat the question in this way confuse matters, wilfully or not, by confusing the problems of ideological struggle with the question of relations between states. Those indulging in this sort of confusion are most probably guided by a desire to cast aspersions upon the Communists of the Soviet Union and to represent them as the advocates of aggressive actions. This, however, is very unwise.

The Communist Party of the Soviet Union at its Twentieth Congress made it perfectly clear and obvious that the allegations that the Soviet Union intends to overthrow capitalism in other countries by means of "exporting" revolution are absolutely unfounded. I cannot refrain from reminding you of my words at the Twentieth Congress: "It goes without saying that among us Communists there are no adherents of capitalism. But this does not mean that we have interfered or plan to interfere in the internal affairs of countries where capitalism still exists. Romain Rolland was right when he said that 'freedom is not brought in from abroad in baggage trains like Bourbons.' It is ridiculous to think that revolutions are made to order."

We Communists believe that the idea of Communism will ultimately be victorious throughout the world, just as it has been victorious in our country, in China and in many other states. Many readers of [this article] will probably disagree with us. Perhaps they think that the idea of capitalism will ultimately triumph. It is their right to think so. We may argue, we may disagree with one another. *The main thing is to keep to the positions of ideological struggle, without resorting to arms in order to prove that one is right.* The point is that with military techniques what they are today, there are no inaccessible places in the world. Should a world war break out, no country will be able to shut itself off from a crushing blow.

We believe that ultimately that system will be victorious on the globe which will offer the nations greater opportunities for improving their material and spiritual life. It is precisely socialism that creates unprecedentedly great prospects for the inexhaustible creative enthusiasm of the masses, for a genuine flourishing of science and culture, for the realization of man's dream of a happy life, a life without destitute and unemployed people, of a happy childhood and tranquil old age, of the realization of the most audacious and ambitious human projects, of man's right to create in a truly free manner in the interests of the people.

But when we say that in the competition between the two systems, the capitalist and the socialist, our system will win, this does not mean, of course, that we shall achieve victory by interfering in the internal affairs of the capitalist countries. Our confidence in the victory of Communism is of a different kind. It is based on a knowledge of the laws governing the development of society. Just as in its time capitalism, as the more progressive system, took the place of feudalism, so will capitalism be inevitably superseded by Communism—the more progressive and more equitable social system. We are confident of the victory of the socialist system because it is a more progressive system than the capitalist system. Soviet power has been in existence for only a little more than 40 years, and during these years we have gone through two of the worst wars, repulsing the attacks of enemies who attempted to strangle us. Capitalism in the United States has been in existence for more than a century and a half, and the history of the United States has developed in such a way that never once have enemies landed on American territory.

Yet the dynamics of the development of the U.S.S.R. and the U.S.A. are such that the 42-year-old land of the Soviets is already able to challenge the 150-year-old capitalist state to economic competition; and the most farsighted American leaders are admitting that the Soviet Union is fast catching up with the United States and will ultimately outstrip it. Watching the progress of this competition, anyone can judge which is the better system, and we believe that in the long run all the peoples will embark on the path of struggle for the building of socialist societies.

You disagree with us? Prove by facts that your system is superior and more efficacious, that it is capable of ensuring a higher degree of prosperity for the people than the socialist system, that under capitalism man can be happier than under socialism. It is impossible to prove this. I have no other explanation for the fact that talk of violently "rolling back" Communism never ceases in the West. Not long ago the U.S. Senate and House of Representatives deemed it proper to pass a resolution calling for the "liberation" of the socialist countries allegedly enslaved by Communism and, moreover, of a number of union republics constituting part of the Soviet Union. The authors of the resolution call for the "liberation" of the Ukraine, Byelorussia, Lithuania, Latvia, Estonia, Armenia, Azerbaijan, Georgia, Kazakhstan, Turkmenistan and even a certain "Ural Area."

I would not be telling the full truth if I did not say that the adoption of this ill-starred resolution was regarded by the Soviet people as an act of provocation. Personally I agree with this appraisal.

It would be interesting to see, incidentally, how the authors of this resolution would have reacted if the parliament of Mexico, for instance, had passed a resolution demanding that Texas, Arizona and California be "liberated from American slavery." Apparently they have never pondered such a question, which is very regrettable. Sometimes comparisons help to understand the essence of a matter.

Travelling through the Soviet Union, leading American statesmen and public figures have had full opportunity to convince themselves that there is no hope of sowing strife between the Soviet people and the Communist Party and the Soviet Government, and of influencing them to rebel against Communism. How, then, are we to explain the unceasing attempts to revive the policy of "rolling back" Communism? What do they have in mind? Armed intervention in the internal affairs of the socialist countries? But in the West as well as in the East people are fully aware that under the conditions of modern military technique such actions are fraught with immediate and relentless retaliation.

So we come back to what we started with. In our day there are only two ways: peaceful coexistence or the most destructive war in history. There is no third choice.

III

The problem of peaceful coexistence between states with different social systems has become particularly pressing in view of the fact that since the Second World War the development of relations between states has entered a new stage, that now we have approached a period in the life of mankind when there is a real chance of excluding war once and for all from the life of society. The new alignment of international forces which has developed since the Second World War offers ground for the assertion that a new world war is no longer a fatal inevitability, that it can be averted.

First, today not only all the socialist states, but many countries in Asia and Africa which have embarked upon the road of independent national statehood, and many other states outside the aggressive military groupings, are actively fighting for peace.

Secondly, the peace policy enjoys the powerful support of the broad masses of the people all over the world.

Thirdly, the peaceful socialist states are in possession of very potent material means, which cannot but have a deterring effect upon the aggressors.

Prior to the Second World War the U.S.S.R. was the only socialist country, with not more than 17 percent of the territory, 3 percent of the population, and about 10 percent of the output of the world. At present, the socialist countries cover about one-fourth of the territory of the globe, have one-third of its population, and their industrial output accounts for about one-third of the total world output.

This is precisely the explanation of the indisputable fact that through-out the past years, hotbeds of war breaking out now in one and now in another part of the globe—in the Near East and in Europe, in the Far East and in Southeast Asia—have been extinguished at the very outset.

What does the future hold in store for us?

As a result of the fulfillment and overfulfillment of the present Seven Year Plan of economic development of the U.S.S.R., as well as of the plans of the other socialist countries of Europe and Asia, the countries of the socialist system will then account for a little more than half of the world output. Their economic power will grow immeasurably, and this will help to an even greater extent to consolidate world peace: the material might and moral influence of the peace-loving states will be so great that any bellicose militarist will have to think ten times before risking going to war. It is the good fortune of mankind that a community of socialist states which are not interested in new war has been set up, because to build socialism and Communism the socialist countries need peace. Today the community of socialist countries which has sprung up on the basis of complete equality holds such a position in the development of all branches of economy, science and culture as to be able to exert an influence to-wards preventing the outbreak of new world wars.

Hence we are already in a practical sense near to that stage in the life of humanity when nothing will prevent people from devoting themselves wholly to peaceful labor, when war will be wholly excluded from the life of society.

But if we say that there is no fatal inevitability of war at present, this by no means signifies that we can rest on our laurels, fold our arms and bask in the sun in the hope that an end has been put to wars once and for all. Those in the West who believe that war is to their benefit have not yet abandoned their schemes. They control considerable material forces, as well as military and political levers, and there is no guarantee that some tragic day they will not attempt to set them in motion. That is why it is so much the more necessary to continue an active struggle in order that the policy of peaceful coexistence may triumph throughout the world not in words but in deeds.

Of much importance, of course, is the fact that this policy has in our day merited not only the widest moral approval but also international legal recognition. The countries of the socialist camp in their relations with the capitalist states are guided precisely by this policy. The principles of peaceful coexistence are reflected in the decisions of the Bandung Conference of Asian and African countries. Furthermore, many countries of Europe, Asia and Africa have solemnly proclaimed this principle as the basis of their foreign policy. Finally, the idea of peaceful coexistence has found unanimous support in the decisions of the twelfth and thirteenth sessions of the United Nations General Assembly.

In our view, peaceful coexistence can become lasting only if the good declarations in favor of peace are supported by active measures on the part of the governments and peoples of all countries. As far as the Soviet Union is concerned, it has already done a good deal in this respect, and I am able to share some experiences with you.

As far back as March 12, 1951, the Supreme Soviet of the U.S.S.R. adopted a "Law on the Defense of Peace," stating:

> (1) Propaganda for war, in whatever form it may be conducted, undermines the cause of peace, creates the menace of a new war and therefore constitutes the gravest crime against humanity.
> (2) Persons guilty of war propaganda should be brought to court and tried as heinous criminals.

Further, the Soviet Union has in recent years unilaterally reduced its armed forces by more than 2,000,000 men. The funds released as a result have been used to develop the economy and further raise the material and cultural living standards of the Soviet people.

The Soviet Union has liquidated its bases on the territories of other states.

The Soviet Union unilaterally discontinued the tests of atomic weapons and refrained from conducting them further until it became finally clear that the Western powers refused to follow our example and were continuing the explosions.

The Soviet Union has repeatedly submitted detailed and perfectly realistic proposals for disarmament, meeting the positions of the Western powers halfway. But to solve the disarmament problem it is necessary for our Western partners to agree and desire to meet us halfway too. This is just what is lacking.

When it became clear that it was very difficult under these conditions to solve the complex disarmament problem immediately, we proposed another concrete idea to our partners: Let us concentrate our attention on those problems which lend themselves most easily to a solution. Let us undertake initial partial steps on matters concerning which the views of the different parties have been brought closer together.

It is perfectly clear that one of these questions today is the question of discontinuing atomic and hydrogen weapon tests. The progress achieved in this matter justifies the hope that an agreement on the discontinuation of nuclear weapon tests will shortly be reached. Implementation of this measure will, of course, be an important step on the way to the solution of the disarmament problem and the banning of nuclear weapons in general.

Attributing much importance to contacts and intercourse between statesmen of all countries, the Soviet Government a few years ago proposed that an East-West heads of government conference be convened in order to come to terms—taking into account present-day realities and guided by the spirit of mutual understanding—on concrete measures, the realization of which would help to relax international tension.

We also proposed that this conference consider those international questions for the settlement of which realistic prerequisites already existed. As a first step toward such a settlement, we proposed to the powers concerned that a peace treaty be concluded with Germany and that West Berlin be granted the status of a demilitarized free city. I want to emphasize particularly that we were guided primarily by the desire to put a final end to the aftermath of the Second World War. We regard the liquidation of the consequences of the Second World War and the conclusion of a peace treaty with the two German states—the German Democratic Republic and the German Federal Republic—as the question of questions.

Indeed, 14 years have already passed since the war ended, but the German people are still without a peace treaty. The delay has afforded wide scope for renewed activities of the West German militarists and revanchists. They have already proclaimed their aggressive plans, laying claim, for instance, to lands in Poland and Czechoslovakia. Of course, the German revanchists are thinking not only of a march to the East; they also know the way to the West. In the Second World War the Hitlerites occupied Western Europe before advancing against the Soviet Union.

Will the direction chosen by the modern German revanchists for their aggression be any consolation to the peoples of Europe if a global war breaks out on that continent? The lessons of history should not be ignored. To do so often ends in tragedy.

Some say: The Soviet people are unduly sensitive. Can one assume that Western Germany is now in a position to precipitate another world war? Those who put the question thus forget that Western Germany is at present acting in the world arena not alone but within the military North Atlantic bloc. She plays a paramount role in this bloc. And more than that, life has shown that the North Atlantic Alliance is being gradually converted into an instrument of the German militarists, which makes it easier for them to carry out aggressive plans. It is not at all impossible, therefore, that Western Germany, taking advantage of her position in the North Atlantic Alliance, might provoke hostilities in order to draw her allies into it and plunge the whole world into the chasm of a devastating war.

All this indicates how timely and realistic are the proposals of the Soviet Government for the conclusion of a peace treaty with Germany and for bringing the situation in West Berlin back to normal.

And yet, some of the Western opponents of the Soviet proposals say that if the Soviet Union really stands for peaceful coexistence it should even be asked to commit itself to the preservation of the existing status quo. Others argue that if the Western powers agree to the conclusion of a peace treaty with the two German states that would amount to a retreat on their part, and the Soviet Union should make some compensation for this "retreat."

There are no grounds whatever for these assertions, in our opinion. The task before us is to do away with the aftermath of the Second World War and to conclude a peace treaty. And any possibility of someone gaining and others losing, of someone acquiring and others making concessions, is out of the question here. All the parties concerned acquire a stronger foundation for the maintenance of peace in Europe and throughout the world in the shape of a peace treaty. Does this not accord with the interests of all the peoples?

At times, and of late especially, some spokesmen in the West have gone so far as to say that the abolition of the aftermath of the Second World War is a step which would allegedly intensify rather than ease international tension. It is hard to believe that there are no secret designs behind allegations of this kind, especially when attempts are made to present in a distorted light the policy of the U.S.S.R., which is intended to secure a lasting and stable peace, by alleging that it all but leads to war. It seems to us, on the contrary, that the Soviet position on the German question corresponds most of all to the present-day reality.

It now seems that no sober-minded leader in the West is inclined any longer to advance the unrealistic demand for the so-called reunion of Germany before the conclusion of a peace treaty, in as much as more and more political leaders are becoming aware of the fact that reunion in the conditions now obtaining is a process which depends upon the Germans themselves and not upon any outside interference. We should start from the obvious fact that two German states exist, and that the Germans themselves must decide how they want to live. In as much as these two states, the German Democratic Republic and the German Federal Republic, do exist, the peace treaty should be concluded with them, because any further delay and postponement of this exceptionally important act tends not only to sustain the abnormal situation in Europe but also to aggravate it still further.

As for Germany's unity, I am convinced that Germany will be united sooner or later. However, before this moment comes—and no one can foretell when it will come—no attempts should be made to interfere from outside in this internal process, to sustain the state of war which is fraught with many grave dangers and surprises for peace in Europe and throughout the world. The desire to preserve the peace and to prevent another war should outweigh all other considerations of statesmen, irrespective of their mode of thinking. The Gordian knot must be cut: the peace treaty must be achieved if we do not want to play with fire—with the destinies of millions upon millions of people.

IV

In this connection it is impossible to ignore also the question of West Berlin. It is commonly known that the German revanchists have made West Berlin the base for their constant undermining and subversive activity directed towards the provoking of war. We resolutely reject any attempts to ascribe to the Soviet Union the intention of seizing West Berlin and infringing upon the right of the population in this part of the city to preserve its present way of life. On the contrary, in demanding the normalization of the situation in West Berlin, we have proposed to convert it into a free city and to guarantee, jointly with the Western states, the preservation there of the way of life and of the social order which suits the West Berlin inhabitants best of all. This shows that the positions of the Government of the Soviet Union and the Governments of the Western states, judging by their statements, coincide on this question. We, and so do they, stand for the independence of West Berlin and for the preservation of the existing way of life there.

It is, therefore, only necessary to overcome the difficulties born of the cold war in order to find the way to an agreement on West Berlin and on the wider question of the conclusion of a peace treaty with the two German states. This is the way to ease international tensions and to promote peaceful coexistence. It would strengthen confidence between states and assist in the gradual abolition of unfriendliness and suspicion in international relations.

Implementation of the Soviet proposals would not injure the interests of the Western powers and would not give any one-sided advantages to anybody. At the same time, the settlement of the German question would prevent a dangerous development of events in Europe, remove one of the main causes of international tension and create favorable prospects for a settlement of other international issues.

The proposals of the Soviet Union were discussed at the Foreign Ministers' Conference in Geneva. The Ministers did not succeed in reaching an agreement, but the Geneva conference did accomplish a great deal of useful work. The positions of the two sides were positively brought closer together and the possibility of an agreement on some questions has become apparent.

At the same time, we still have substantial differences on a number of questions. I am deeply convinced that they are not fundamental differences on which agreement is impossible. And if we still have differences and have not reached agreement on certain important questions, it is, as we believe, with adequate grounds—a result of the concessions made by the Western powers to Chancellor Adenauer, who is pursuing a military policy, the policy of the German revanchists. This is a case of the United States, Britain and France dangerously abetting Chancellor Adenauer. It would have been far better if the NATO allies of Western Germany would persuade Chancellor Adenauer, in the interest of the maintenance of peace, that his policy imperils the cause of peace and that it may ultimately end in irreparable disaster for Western Germany. All this emphasizes again that the representatives of the states concerned must do some more work in order to find mutually acceptable decisions.

I believe that my trip to the United States and the subsequent visit of President Eisenhower to the Soviet Union * will afford the possibility for a useful exchange of opinions, for finding a common tongue and a common understanding of the questions that should be settled.

V

We are prepared now as before to do everything we possibly can in order that the relations between the Soviet Union and other countries, and, in particular, the relations between the U.S.S.R. and the U.S.A., should be built upon the foundation of friendship and that they should fully correspond to the principles of peaceful coexistence.

I should like to repeat what I said at my recent press conference in Moscow: "Should Soviet-American relations become brighter, that will not fail to bring about an improvement in the relations with other states and will help to scatter the gloomy clouds in other parts of the globe also. Naturally, we want friendship not only with the U.S.A., but also with the friends of the U.S.A. At the same time we want to see the U.S.A. maintain good relations not only with us, but with our friends as well."

What, then, is preventing us from making the principles of peaceful coexistence an unshakable international standard and daily practice in the relations between the West and East?

Of course, different answers may be given to this question. But in or-

* The visit did not materialize.

der to be frank to the end, we should also say the following: *It is necessary that everybody should understand the irrevocable fact that the historic process is irreversible.* It is impossible to bring back yesterday. It is high time to understand that the world of the twentieth century is not the world of the nineteenth century, that two diametrically opposed social and economic systems exist in the world today side by side, and that the socialist system, in spite of all the attacks upon it, has grown so strong, has developed into such a force, as to make any return to the past impossible.

Real facts of life in the last ten years have shown convincingly that the policy of "rolling back" Communism can only poison the international atmosphere, heighten the tension between states and work in favor of the cold war. Neither its inspirers nor those who conduct it can turn back the course of history and restore capitalism in the socialist countries.

We have always considered the Americans realistic people. All the more are we astonished to find that leading representatives of the United States still number in their midst individuals who insist on their own way in the face of the obvious failure of the policy of "rolling back" Communism. But is it not high time to take a sober view of things and to draw conclusions from the lessons of the last 15 years? Is it not yet clear to everybody that consistent adherence to the policy of peaceful coexistence would make it possible to improve the international situation, to bring about a drastic cut in military expenditures and to release vast material resources for wiser purposes?

The well known British scientist, J. Bernal, recently cited figures to show that average annual expenditures for military purposes throughout the world between 1950 and the end of 1957 were expressed in the huge sum of about 90 billion dollars. How many factories, apartment houses, schools, hospitals and libraries could have been built everywhere with the funds now spent on the preparation of another war! And how fast could economic progress have been advanced in the underdeveloped countries if we had converted to these purposes at least some of the means which are now being spent on war purposes!

VI

It is readily seen that the policy of peaceful coexistence receives a firm foundation only with increase in extensive and absolutely unrestricted international trade. It can be said without fear of exaggeration that there is no good basis for improvement of relations between our countries other than development of international trade.

If the principle of peaceful coexistence of states is to be adhered to, not in words, but in deeds, it is perfectly obvious that no ideological differences should be an obstacle to the development and extension of mutually advantageous economic contacts, to the exchange of everything produced by human genius in the sphere of peaceful branches of material production.

In this connection it may be recalled that soon after the birth of the Soviet state, back in the early 1920's, the Western countries, proceeding from considerations of economic interest, agreed to establish trade relations with our country despite the acutest ideological differences. Since then, discounting comparatively short periods, trade between the Soviet Union and capitalist states has been developing steadily. No ideological differences prevented, for instance, a considerable extension of trade relations between the Soviet Union and Britain and other Western states in recent years. We make no secret of our desire to establish normal commercial and business contacts with the United States as well, without any restrictions, without any discriminations.

In June of last year the Soviet Government addressed itself to the Government of the United States with the proposal to develop economic and trade contacts between our two countries. We proposed an extensive and concrete program of developing Soviet-American trade on a mutually advantageous basis. The adoption of our proposals would undoubtedly accord with the interests of both states and peoples. However, these proposals have not been developed so far.

Striving for the restoration of normal trade relations with the United States, the Soviet Union does not pursue any special interests. In our economic development we rely wholly on the internal forces of our country, on our own resources and possibilities. All our plans for further economic development are drawn up taking into consideration the possibilities available here. As in the past, when we outline these plans we proceed only from the basis of our own possibilities and forces. Irrespective of whether or not we shall trade with Western countries, the United States included, the implementation of our economic plans of peaceful construction will not in the least be impeded.

However, if both sides want to improve relations, all barriers in international trade must be removed. Those who want peaceful coexistence cannot but favor the development of trade, economic and business contacts. Only on this basis can international life develop normally.

VII

Peaceful coexistence is the only way which is in keeping with the interests of all nations. To reject it would mean under existing conditions to doom the whole world to a terrible and destructive war at a time when it is fully possible to avoid it.

Is it possible that when mankind has advanced to a plane where it has proved capable of the greatest discoveries and of making its first steps into outer space, it should not be able to use the colossal achievements of its genius for the establishment of a stable peace, for the good of man, rather than for the preparation of another war and for the destruction of all that has been created by its labor over many millenniums? Reason refuses to believe this. It protests.

The Soviet people have stated and declare again that they do not want war. If the Soviet Union and the countries friendly to it are not attacked, we shall never use any weapons either against the United States or against any other countries. We do not want any horrors of war, destruction, suffering and death for ourselves or for any other peoples. We say this not because we fear anyone. Together with our friends, we are united and stronger than ever. But precisely because of that do we say that war can and should be prevented. Precisely because we want to rid mankind of war, we urge the Western powers to peaceful and lofty competition. We say to all: Let us prove to each other the advantages of one's own system not with fists, not by war, but by peaceful economic competition in conditions of peaceful coexistence.

As for the social system in some state or other, that is the domestic affair of the people of each country. We always have stood and we stand today for non-interference in the internal affairs of other countries. We have always abided, and we shall abide, by these positions. The question, for example, what system will exist in the United States or in other capitalist countries cannot be decided by other peoples or states. This question can and will be decided only by the American people themselves, only by the people of each country.

The existence of the Soviet Union and of the other socialist countries is a real fact. It is also a real fact that the United States of America and the other capitalist countries live in different social conditions, in the conditions of capitalism. Then let us recognize this real situation and proceed from it in order not to go against reality, against life itself. Let us not try to change this situation by interferences from without, by means of war on the part of some states against other states.

I repeat, there is only one way to peace, one way out of the existing tension: peaceful coexistence.

A Western View

GEORGE F. KENNAN *

In the public debate that has marked the progress of what is called the cold war, no term has been used more loosely, and at times unscrupulously, than the word "coexistence." In the article under his name, published in *Foreign Affairs* [reprinted above], Mr. Khrushchev has given us an interesting definition of what he understands by this term. Peaceful coexistence, he says, signifies in essence the repudiation of war as a means of solving controversial issues. It presupposes an obligation to refrain from every form of violation of the territorial integrity and sovereignty of another state. It implies renunciation of interference in the internal affairs of other countries. It means that political and economic relations must be put on a basis of complete equality and mutual benefit. It involves, he says, the elimination of the very threat of war. It is something which "should develop into peaceful competition for the purpose of satisfying man's needs in the best possible way."

Not only has Mr. Khrushchev given us this definition but he has made it plain that he considers that the Soviet Union abides by these principles, has abided by them ever since the revolution of the autumn of 1917 and cannot help but abide by them in view of its social foundation; whereas there are still important elements in the Western countries who, in his view, do not abide by these principles, who "believe that war is to their benefit," who want to inflict "capitalism" by violent means on unwilling peoples and whose opposition must be overcome before peaceful coexistence can really be said to prevail.

II

There could be few propositions more amazing than the assertion that the Soviet state "from its very inception . . . proclaimed peaceful coexistence as the basic principle of its foreign policy," and that the initial

* Member of the Institute for Advanced Study, Princeton. Former U.S. Ambassador to the Soviet Union and head of the Policy Planning Staff in the Department of State. Author of *Soviet-American Relations, 1917–1920; Realities of American Foreign Policy;* and *Russia, the Atom and the West*. The selection is from "Peaceful Coexistence: A Western View," *Foreign Affairs*, Vol. 38 (January, 1960), pp. 171–190. Copyright by the Council on Foreign Relations, Inc., New York. By permission.

Communist leaders in Russia were strong partisans of the view that peaceful coexistence could and should prevail among states with different social systems.

One returns reluctantly to the record of those early years of Soviet power. One can well believe that authoritative circles in Moscow assess somewhat differently today the prospects for violent social revolution in the main industrial countries of the West, and perhaps even its necessity. One can imagine that they have a concept of the obligations of Russian Communists to the workers of those Western countries which is also somewhat different from that which prevailed in Moscow in 1917 and 1918. If this is so, then it would surely be better to let bygones be bygones, rather than permit the problem of coexistence in the present to be complicated by altercation over the attitudes of the past. The years 1917 and 1918 were, after all, a time of tremendous turmoil and tragedy in world affairs. Men acted, everywhere, in the spirit of violence and passion. Many things were done by both Communist and non-Communist sides which today, from the perspective of 40 years, appear clearly regrettable. Surely there could be very few people in the non-Communist world who would wish now to revive the controversies of that day or to associate themselves indiscriminately with the outlooks and prejudices of the period of World War I and its aftermath.

But if reference is to be taken prominently on the Communist side to the attitudes of Soviet leaders in 1917, as proof of the inviolable and inevitable attachment of Russian Communism to such principles as the repudiation of violence as a means of solving controversial political issues, the renunciation of interference in the internal affairs of other countries and the predominance of peaceful competition as between states of different social systems, then the Western scholar cannot refrain from registering his amazement and protest. It is surprising that there should be so little respect for the true history of the Russian revolutionary movement on the part of those who profess today to be its custodians and protagonists that they are willing to pervert it in this way for the sake of their own tactical convenience. One shudders to think what Lenin would have said to these preposterous distortions. Do the present leaders of the Russian Communist Party really profess to have forgotten that Lenin regarded himself outstandingly as an *international* socialist leader? Who was it wrote, on October 3, 1918, "The Bolshevik working class of Russia was always internationalist not only in words, but in deeds, in contrast to those villains—the heroes and leaders of the Second International. . . ."? Who was it said, in that same document, "The Russian proletariat will understand that the greatest sacrifices will now soon be demanded of it for the cause of internationalism. . . . Let us prepare ourselves at once. Let us prove that the Russian worker is capable of working much more energetically, and of struggling and dying in a much more self-sacrificing way, when it is a matter not of the Russian revolution alone but of the international workers' revolution. . . ."?[1]

This is, as every good Communist in Russia knows, only a single quotation out of literally thousands that could be adduced to illustrate the devotion of the Bolsheviki in Lenin's time to socialism as an international cause—the devotion, that is, precisely to the duty of interfering in the internal affairs of other countries with the object of altering their system of government and mode of life.

The proposition that the political power dominant in the Soviet Union has always been on the side of coexistence, as defined by Mr. Khrushchev, also calls upon us to forget the long and sinister history of the relationship between Moscow and the foreign Communist Parties in the Stalin era. There is ample documentation to show for what purposes foreign Communist Parties were used during those years, by whom, and by what methods. There are many of us in the West who, again, would be happy to disregard these recollections when it comes to the political discussion of the present day. But it is another thing to suffer insult to one's intelligence; and if people in Moscow wish this unhappy history to be forgotten outside Russia, they must not blandly turn the facts of history upside down and ask that the resulting configuration be accepted as proof of the inevitable commitment of Russian Communism to the principles of coexistence.

Over a hundred years ago a distinguished Western visitor, the Marquis de Custine, wrote from Petrograd that: "Russian despotism does not only count ideas and feelings as nothing, but it remakes the facts, it enters the lists against the evident, and triumphs in the struggle."

People cannot hope to triumph in such a cause today. The very cultivation of these distortions, seeking as it does the obfuscation of public understanding of the historical development of the relations between the Soviet Union and the West, is itself a grievous disservice to any truly hopeful form of coexistence.

These statements of mine are not to be taken as implying a disposition to believe that the attachment of Mr. Khrushchev and certain of his colleagues to the principles of coexistence, as he has now defined them, is insincere and conceals sinister motives. This does not necessarily follow. The purpose is merely to point out that people in Moscow are not likely to strengthen belief outside Russia in the sincerity of their attachment to liberal and tolerant principles of international life by distort-

[1] V. I. Lenin, *Sochineniya* (Fourth Edition). Moscow, 1952, v. 28, p. 83.

ing the history of the Lenin or Stalin eras or by pleading that such an attachment flows inevitably from the nature of the social and political system prevailing in the Soviet Union. It is possible to conceive that the Soviet attitude in such questions may have changed; it is not possible to accept the proposition that it did not need to change in order to meet the requirements of peaceful coexistence, as Mr. Khrushchev has defined them.

III

In the statement of the Soviet view of coexistence, much stress has been laid on the attachment of people in the West to capitalism and on their alleged desire to see it triumph as a world system.

The Westerner of this day experiences a certain bewilderment when he hears the term "capitalism" used in this way. What is it that is meant by this expression? One notices that whatever the reality may be which it purports to symbolize, it is one which in Russian Communist eyes has not changed appreciably since the Russian Social Democratic Party came into being at the turn of the century. If there is any recognition in official Soviet thought of the fact that changes in the economic practices and institutions of non-Communist countries over this past half-century have been such as to affect in any way the elements of the classic Marxist view of Western capitalism, I am not aware of the place where this has found expression. Contemporary Soviet ideological material seems to suggest that there exists outside the Communist orbit a static and basic condition—a set of practices known as "capitalism" and expressed primarily in the private ownership of the means of production—which has undergone no essential alteration over the past 50 years, or indeed since the lifetime of Karl Marx; which continues to be the dominant reality of Western society; belief in which constitutes the essence of all non-Communist political philosophy; and to which the Western governments and "ruling circles," in particular, remain, as a matter of pride and tenacious self-interest, profoundly committed. It would presumably be to "capitalism" in this sense that Mr. Khrushchev was referring when he wrote that many readers of *Foreign Affairs* would perhaps think that capitalism will ultimately triumph.

It is hardly necessary to emphasize how far this seems, to many of us outside Russia, from the reality of this day. The principles of free economic enterprise and private ownership of the means of production have indeed had a prominent part to play in the economies of non-Communist countries everywhere over this past half-century. But in no two countries has this part been quite the same. Elements of public and social control have come in, everywhere, to challenge and modify the operation of these principles. The resulting balance between private control on the one hand and social or public control on the other now varies greatly from country to country. There is today not *one* social and economic system prevailing outside the Communist orbit: there are almost as many such systems as there are countries; and many of them are closer to what Marx conceived as socialism than they are to the laissez faire capitalism of his day. In each of them, furthermore, the balance between private and social influences is everywhere in a state of flux and evolution which makes it quite impossible to predict from the aspect it assumes today what aspect it is going to assume tomorrow.

This means that in the non-Communist world, where it is customary to attempt to relate the meaning of words to objective phenomena, the term "capitalism" no longer has any generic and useful meaning. It is only in Russia, where theoretical concept can still be spared the test of relevance to objective reality, that a meaning for this term still exists. Not only this, but there are numbers of issues of public life which today appear to most people in the non-Communist world as having a higher importance, from the standpoint of their general effect on the human condition, than the issues of the ownership of the means of production and the distribution of wealth with which the Marxist doctrine was preoccupied.

How absurd, in the light of these facts, to picture Western non-Communists as the passionate protagonists and devotees of something called "capitalism," and to suggest that there are influential people in the West who desire to bring upon the earth the miseries of another world war in the hope of being able to inflict the capitalist system on great masses of people who do not desire it. The question of who owns the machines is not the one that today dominates the thoughts and discussions of Western society and Western "ruling circles"; it is primarily the question of human freedom—of the right of people to choose and alter their own social and political systems as they like, to select those who shall govern them within the framework of those systems, and to enjoy, within that same framework, the civil liberties which relieve them of the fear of arbitrary injustice, permit them to practice freedom of the mind and enable them to walk with their heads up.

I am aware that Communists have long professed to see no value in either the parliamentary or judicial institutions of the liberal West. The classical Communist position has dismissed these institutons as frauds perpetrated on the helpless workers by the monopolists who exploit them. Is it too much to hope that people in the Communist world will now manifest their interest in coexistence by abandoning cynical and ridiculous extremism, in the face of which the whole development of British and American society over these last centuries becomes historically unintelligible?

That these liberal institutions are imperfect, most Englishmen or Americans would, I think, readily concede; but the overwhelming majority of us believe them to embody something that lies close to the essence of human dignity, as we have learned to see it, and something which is one of the most precious attainments of civilized man. It is to this, not to the system governing ownership and control of the industries of our country, that our deepest pride and loyalties relate. If, by the fair operation of these parliamentary institutions, and with preservation of all basic civil liberties, the arrangements governing ownership or control of the means of production should be drastically changed (and some already have been), most of us would view this as no final tragedy and would not see ourselves as defeated. But if it were the other way round, and if such changes had to be purchased at the price of the sacrifice of the rights and privileges which our parliamentary and judicial institutions now generally, if imperfectly, provide—then, and only then, would we consider ourselves to have suffered an irreparable defeat—only then would it seem to us that what was most essential had been lost.

We decline, therefore, to be depicted as the passionate protagonists of something called "capitalism" waging an ideological competition with the protagonists of something called "socialism." Least of all can we in America accept the charge of wishing to impose something called capitalism on other peoples. Several European countries have changed their social and economic institutions over the course of recent decades in ways that carry them very far from those prevailing in the United States. In this, they have not encountered the slightest opposition or hindrance from the American side. The basic ideological issue, as seen in the United States today, is not capitalism versus socialism but freedom versus its opposite. The disagreement between Moscow and the "leading circles" of the non-Communist world is not really a disagreement about which form of social system is most productive; it is rather a disagreement about what is most important, in the first place, in the lives of peoples.

IV

The fact that an ideological disagreement of this nature exists is in itself no reason why peaceful coexistence, as Mr. Khrushchev defines it, should not prevail. There is nothing new in the prolonged peaceful residence, side by side, of ideologically antagonistic systems. Many of the present peaceful relationships of international life, outside the Communist orbit, have evolved from ones which were originally relationships of profound ideological antagonism. There was, for that matter, no ideological affinity but rather a sharp ideological conflict between the Tsarist system in Russia and the world of American political thought. This did not prevent the two powers from existing in the same world, without hostilities, for more than a hundred years.

There are no doubt individuals scattered here and there throughout the Western countries who find intolerable this present antagonism of outlook as between the Soviet Government and the Western peoples and who cannot see how it can be either resolved or endured by means short of a world war. If one searches, one can even find, for quotation, public utterances of this view. But it would be generally agreed, I think, that these people are few and not very influential. The general attitude throughout the West would unquestionably be—and this goes for governments as well as for individuals—that while the social and political system now dominant in Russia is one that may not commend itself to us, its existence and prevalence there is not our responsibility; it is not our business to change it; it constitutes in itself no reason why a relationship of peaceful coexistence should not prevail.

The cold war, let it be said most emphatically, does not exist because people in the West object to the Russian people having socialism or any other system they wish. If, in fact, it were only a matter of ideologies, and only a matter of the relationship between the West and Russia proper, there would be no reason why the Soviet demand for "peaceful coexistence" should not be accepted without reservation.

But the Soviet Union is not only an ideological phenomenon. It is also a great power, physically and militarily. Even if the prevailing ideology in Russia were not antagonistic to the concepts prevailing elsewhere, the behavior of the government of that country in its international relations, and particularly any considerable expansion of its power at the expense of the freedom of other peoples, would still be a matter of most serious interest to the world at large.

And it is, let us recall, precisely such an expansion that we have witnessed in recent years. So far as Europe is concerned, this expansion had its origin in the advance of Soviet armies into Eastern and Central Europe in 1945. This advance was not only accepted at the time—it was generally welcomed in the West as a very important part of the final phase of the struggle against Hitler. But it has had a consequence which few people in the West foresaw in 1945 and which fewer still desired: the quasi-permanent advancement of the effective boundaries of Moscow's political and military authority to the very center of Europe.

The discussion of the question of coexistence on the Communist side is cast in terms which take no account of this situation and which ask us, by implication, either to ignore it or to pretend that it does not exist. The problem, we are told, is to "liquidate the consequences of the Second World War"; but this particular consequence, we are left to infer, is one which is neither to be liquidated nor to be spoken about.

Is this a realistic demand? One cannot agree that it is. The position of preëminence which the U.S.S.R. enjoys among the countries of the Communist bloc is not a secret. The Communist leaders of various countries do not ignore it when they themselves assemble to discuss international affairs. What people in the West should or should not do to change or affect this situation is another problem; but to demand that a situation which is perfectly well recognized *within* the Communist world as a significant factor in world affairs should be effectively ignored when it comes to the discussion of coexistence between East and West is surely neither reasonable nor helpful. The fact is that this extension of Russia's political and military power into the heart of Europe represents a major alteration in the world strategic and political balance, and one that was never discussed as such with Western statesmen, much less agreed to by them.

It is not just the *fact* of this situation which is of importance to the Western peoples; there is also the question as to *how* it came into existence and *how* it is being maintained. The truth is that it did not come into existence because the majority of the people in the region affected became convinced that Communism, as Mr. Khrushchev has put it, was "the more progressive and equitable system." This peaceful competition for the minds of men which the Communists today ask us to accept as the concomitant and condition of peaceful coexistence had precious little to do with the means by which socialist governments, on the pattern approved by Moscow, were established in the countries of Eastern Europe in 1944 and 1945 or with the means by which their rule was subsequently consolidated there. In the view of the West, formed on the strength of overwhelming historical evidence, these régimes were imposed by the skillful manipulations of highly disciplined Communist minorities, trained and inspired by Moscow, and supported by the presence or close proximity of units of the Soviet armed forces. They have been maintained in power by similar means.

It is not the intention here to attempt to judge these happenings from a moral standpoint. I do not mean to challenge the proposition that Russia has political interests in Eastern Europe and that these deserve the respect of Western governments as a matter of elementary political realism. Nor do I wish to deny that the present situation, whatever we may think of its origin, represents today a heavy commitment of the Soviet

Government, which the latter cannot reasonably be asked to alter in any abrupt or drastic manner dangerous to its own political security.

There are, as Mr. Khrushchev knows, people in the West who have not despaired of finding ways to reconcile Soviet interests in this area both with the interests of the Western powers and of the respective peoples, and who have done what they could to pave the way for reasonable and moderate solutions of these difficulties. But the efforts of such people are bound to remain fruitless if the Soviet Government continues to give the impression that, having quietly pocketed this region, it is now saying to the West: "Coexistence begins at this point, and any curiosity on your part about the fate of these peoples will be a violation of it."

It was indicated above that the existence of the Soviet brand of socialism in *Russia itself* may well be regarded in the West as Russia's own business and need not be a barrier to peaceful coexistence. The Soviet régime is, after all, an indigenous régime throughout the greater part of the area of the Soviet Union. The processes in which it had its origin were not democratic ones in the Western sense, but they were deeply Russian ones, reflecting some very basic realities of the Russian political life of that day. It is indeed not the business of Americans to interfere with such a régime.

But when it comes to the governments of the Communist bloc in Eastern and Central Europe, then the problem is inevitably more complicated. These governments are not, in the main, truly indigenous. All this is of course relative; for seldom, if ever, is there *no* area of identity between the interests and sentiments of a people and the régime, however despotic, that governs it. But these régimes represent, in Western eyes, the fruits of a species of conquest and subjugation which was not less real for the fact that it did not generally involve hostile military invasion in the usual sense. And the thought inevitably presents itself: if such a thing could be done to *these* peoples, by means short of overt military aggression, and if we are now asked to accept it as something not to be discussed in connection with peaceful coexistence, to how many other peoples could this also be done, within the very framework of coexistence we are being asked to adopt?

The fact is (and it is one we have had impressed upon us in painful ways over these past four decades) that there are more ways than outright military aggression or formal political intervention by which the fate of smaller peoples may be brought under subjection to the will of larger ones, and more devices than those of the classic nineteenth century colonialism by which peoples can be kept in that state. There does exist, after all, such a thing as the science of insurrection—the science of the seizure of power by conspiratorial minorities, of the conquest of the vital centers of power, of the control of the streets, of the manipulation of civil conflict. Who would deny that this science had a part, and a very basic one, in the Communist thinking and training of an earlier day? Revolutions may not be "made to order"; but that they normally flow only from the spontaneous impulses of the masses and are never influenced by the organizational and military activities of political "vanguards" is something that would scarcely be reconcilable with Communist doctrine of an earlier day, and something we certainly cannot be asked, in the light of historical evidence, to accept.

Mr. Khrushchev gives the impression that all this is not an important part of *his* thinking today. It would be wrong to assume automatically that there is no sincerity in this claim. (He has a point when he says that we should not look for the double bottom in *every* suitcase.) But even if this should be true in his particular case, it would scarcely be true of all of his present associates in the Secretariat and Presidium of the Communist Party of the Soviet Union; nor is there any reason to believe it to be true of the leaders of Russia's principal associate in the family of nations: Communist China.

Again, one must stress the fact that the historical record cannot be suddenly ignored. If the capitalist countries have, in Mr. Khrushchev's view, a past record to be explained away (he accuses us of having organized "senseless crusades" against Soviet Russia), so does Soviet Russia. In particular, it will be a long time before the foreign policies and methods of Joseph Stalin cease to be a determining factor in the consciousness of the West. In one sense, we are all, like Mr. Khrushchev himself, Stalin's pupils. It is from him that we learned a great deal of what we know about such things as ruthlessness and consistency and deception in international politics. Mr. Khrushchev must not now ask us to forget too quickly—certainly not more quickly than some of his own Russian and Chinese associates—the lessons we have learned from this eminent political teacher.

These reflections have an important bearing on the words "peace" and "peaceful" which are used so frequently on the Communist side in connection with the problem of coexistence. What is it that is meant by these terms?

The word "peace" has no meaning outside of the concrete conditions by which it is marked. Peace is not the mere absence of overt hostilities. We have peace today, in that sense. There is "peace," for that matter, in any well-disciplined prison. Peace is not an abstraction. Lenin understood this well. Thus he wrote in 1915: "The slogan of peace may be advanced either in connection with specific conditions of peace, or without any conditions at all—by way of struggle, that is, not for any specific peace but for peace in general (Frieden ohne weiters). It is clear that in the latter case we have to do not only with a slogan which is not a socialist one but is in general a senseless one, devoid of content." [2]

What content are we then to assign to the term "peace" in Communist usage? It is unreasonable to ask Lenin's pupils to make this plain and to specify, when they use this term, precisely what sort of peace they are talking about: peace in whose interests? on what conditions? at what cost?

There is one kind of peace that is compatible with the true security of peoples; and this is one which is based on the principles of genuine national freedom. There is another kind of peace which represents the silence that reigns where the instruments of coercion are simply too formidable to be challenged by those against whom they are aimed.

The bandying about of the word peace as an abstraction evades, once more, the fact that there are ways in which peoples can be oppressed which do not necessarily involve at any given time the visible exertion of force across international frontiers—that sometimes the mere threat of force is enough. And it evades the fact that there have been instances, as in Hungary in 1956, where the Soviet attachment to "peace" did not inhibit the use of Soviet armed forces to determine the political situation in a neighboring country. Is it seriously supposed that people outside Russia can overlook these facts when the question of "peaceful" coexistence is discussed?

V

Much is made, in Communist discussion of coexistence, of the military dispositions of the Western countries, particularly the United States. The United States Government is reproached for maintaining bases in various parts of the world; for being unwilling to agree to a total abolition and renunciation of atomic weapons and to a final ban on nuclear tests; for failure to match unilateral measures of reduction of conventional armaments which the Soviet Government claims (without very adequate proof) to have taken; for rearming the Germans within the framework of NATO, etc. All these facets of behavior on the part of the United States Government are cited as inconsistent with a true disposition to abide by the principle of peaceful coexistence.

The writer of these lines has had his own differences with the military policies of the Western coalition in recent years. These policies have suffered, in his opinion, from several distortions. They have often reflected a certain mis-estimation of the true nature of the problem with which they were designed to deal. They seem sometimes to have been predicated on a

[2] *Ibid.*, v. 21, p. 262.

view of Soviet intentions which, to anyone familiar with the history and psychology of Soviet power, can only appear crude and one-sided, drawn rather from the memories of past adversaries than from a dispassionate study of Russian-Communist principles and tactics. They have at times involved one-sided and unsound commitments to individual categories of weapons. They seem sometimes to have reflected an exaggerated confidence in the device of military alliance as a sort of panacea for all political ills, as though there were no dangers other than those of direct military aggression. They have on more than one occasion led to military dispositions which, however defensive in motivation, could well appear to a possible opponent as the reflection of an intention to initiate hostilities at some stage or other.

All this is true; yet none of it taken separately nor all of it taken together justifies the extreme interpretation Moscow has placed upon it. The Soviet leaders seem either unwilling or unable to take any proper account of the true measure of the shock wrought to the Western public by their exploitation, for purposes of political aggrandizement, of their military position in Eastern and Central Europe in the period 1945 to 1948; by their failure to match the demobilization of the Western armies; by the political attack launched by the Communists in Western Europe in the years 1947 and 1948; by the imposition of the Berlin stockade, and above all by the launching of the Korean War. To people in the West these actions seemed to reflect a hostility no less menacing in intent than would have been threats of overt military aggression by Soviet forces. Coming as they did on the heels of the Second World War, affecting as they did nerves already frayed and minds already prone to anxiety as a result of these fresh experiences, it is not surprising that they produced on a great many people in the West the impression that the security of Western Europe, having just withstood one fearful challenge, was now confronted by another one of scarcely smaller dimensions. Neither is it surprising that peoples' reaction to this impression should have been the intensive effort to re-create, within the framework of a Western alliance, something of the armed force which had been so hastily and trustingly demobilized in the immediate aftermath of the war. The history of Europe has been such that danger to the nation, within the period of historical memory, has generally been associated with the movement of armies over land frontiers. It is probably only natural that the peoples of the Continent should be obsessed with the *manie d'invasion* and should look to the creation of defensive military power as a means of protection even against pressures which are actually much more subtle and refined than those of regular military action.

In the questions raised from the Soviet side about the military rivalry there is room for discussion and room for compromise. But no useful purpose will be served by the willful misinterpretation and distortion of this subject in which people in Moscow stubbornly persist. The suggestion that there is a sizable or serious body of people in the West who, in the immediate aftermath of the horrors of 1939–1945, wish for new orgies of bloodshed and slaughter is too absurd to be entertained for a moment. The suggestion, in particular, that Chancellor Adenauer would be one of these people is so patently absurd, so wildly remote from the entire fabric of political realities in Germany today, and so mischievous in its obvious intent and implications, that its continued reiteration in Moscow is a grievous discouragement to those who hope for better understanding.

Mr. Khrushchev is right in viewing the weapons race of this day as inconsistent with any satisfactory form of coexistence. But the prospects for bettering this situation will not be promising so long as Moscow persists in viewing the military policies pursued in the Western coalition in recent years as solely the products of the lust of Western financiers and manufacturers thirsting for another war in the hopes of greater profits, and refuses to recognize that these policies, however misconceived or overdrawn, represent in large measure the natural and predictable reactions of great peoples to a situation which Moscow itself did much to create.

VI

A further component of the demand which is made from the Communist side in the name of peaceful coexistence relates to what Mr. Khrushchev has called an "increase in extensive and absolutely unrestricted international trade." Ideological differences, it is argued, should not be an obstacle to the development of trade. Without such trade, international life cannot be expected to develop normally.

This is, from the Western standpoint, an odd and somewhat puzzling requirement. If trade between the Soviet Union and non-Communist countries were of such a nature as to bring with it the normal incidental advantages of economic contact—extensive reciprocal travel and residence of businessmen in the other country, the establishment of close personal contacts and associations, the intermingling, in short, not only of the economic life but also of the peole of two countries at least in a certain limited area of activity—then one would be able to see some relevance of the question of trade to the question of peaceful coexistence. But the Soviet Government, as is known, maintains a monopoly of foreign trade, conducts most of its transactions abroad, denies generally to foreign businessmen the privilege of residing and doing business on Soviet soil and takes most elaborate and unusual measures of precaution to see that

Soviet citizens do not form permanent relationships of personal confidence or friendship with any foreigners whatsoever, whether through business contacts or otherwise.

In these circumstances, one might suppose, the virtues of increased international trade would of necessity be confined to the direct benefits such trade might bring to the economies of the respective partners. That there are such benefits to be obtained, at least in modest measure, cannot be disputed. But Mr. Khrushchev has himself denied that these benefits are of any vital significance to the Soviet Union. "In our economic development," he writes, "we rely wholly on the internal forces of our country, on our own resources and possibilities. . . . Irrespective of whether or not we shall trade with Western countries . . . the implementation of our economic plans . . . will not in the least be impeded."

In the case of the United States, it is hard to believe that trade with Russia could have a much greater significance than it has for the Russians. Except in time of war, trade between Russia and the United States has never assumed very large dimensions, either in the Tsarist or the Soviet period. The things which Russia normally has to sell are not such as to have any very sensational implications for the American economy; and the same would be true of the possibilities presented by the purchasing programs of the Soviet Foreign Trade Monopoly, to date.

In addition to this, the Western governments have to consider not just the possible advantages of trade with a foreign trade monopoly but also its possible dangers. Such trade is controlled and shaped at the Soviet end by a great government which has political as well as economic interests to pursue. This being so, one cannot look to a mere mutual economic advantageousness, as one does in the case of trade between countries with a free enterprise system, to provide the guarantee of stability. This is particularly the case when the government in question goes out of its way to emphasize how little dependent it is on this trade, how well it can get along without it. The non-Communist governments have always to reckon with the possibility that exchanges carefully built up over the course of the years and involving important commitments on the part of Western firms may be suddenly terminated by a switch in the purchasing policy of the other party, for reasons into which considerations of economic advantage do not enter at all. These things have happened in the past. Even if they had not happened in the past, there would be no guarantee that they could not happen in the future. This precariousness, arising from the absence on one side of the normal balance wheel of international trade—commercial self-interest—does not mean that trade with the Soviet Union is never safe or desirable; but it does place definite limitations on its possibilities.

One can well imagine that the emphasis laid on this factor by Mr. Khrushchev and other Soviet spokesmen rests on the fact that the expression of a desire for expanded trade relations has often (and particularly in Soviet diplomatic history) constituted the prelude to a political rapprochement or entente between two powers. But it would be difficult to persuade Americans to accept this view of the significance of commercial policy. In the American tradition, trade is a means of meeting real economic needs, not of expressing political feelings.

There have been in recent years, in the American position on questions of East-West trade, certain features which have been widely regarded by people in countries allied with the United States, and by some Americans, as distortions: as the expression of an undue timidity in the face of domestic criticism or of an exaggerated conception of the effect of such trade on Soviet military preparations. If a reëxamination of these attitudes would have, in Soviet eyes, a significance which would really be helpful in relaxing international tensions, then the suggestion is one that should not be lightly dismissed in Washington.

But even if this reëxamination were undertaken, we would still be faced with the fact that the existence in Moscow of a governmental monopoly of foreign trade creates a set of conditions for trade quite different from those to which people in the West are accustomed. This does not exclude the possibility of commercial exchanges; it does not even exclude the possibility of a considerable increase of Soviet-American trade over its present levels. It does place a ceiling on what can, from the Western standpoint, reasonably be expected. And this ceiling is such that it is difficult to see how foreign trade could enter very importantly into the problem of peaceful coexistence.

VII

One last reflection. Again, the values to which it relates are relative ones; but the difficulties which lie at the heart of the tensions between the Communist and non-Communist worlds will never be overcome if relative distinctions are to be ignored.

The reference here is to the concept of truth that prevails in Moscow (not to mention Peking) as opposed to that which prevails in most other parts of the globe.

We are all accustomed to hearing not only from the Communist propaganda machine but from the lips of senior Soviet statesmen propositions which are either so patently absurd or so flatly in contradiction to known facts that no child could believe them. If we were to take seriously what comes to us from the Soviet side we should have to believe, for example, that Russia has been governed for over 40 years by a group of men who differ so profoundly from all mortals who have existed before or elsewhere that they have—over this entire period—never made a mistake, never analyzed a problem incorrectly, never been guided by any sentiments other than those of most selfless dedication to the welfare of others. This we are asked to believe despite the fact that at one time or another over the course of these years numbers of these people, theretofore a part of this supposedly all-wise leadership, have been suddenly denounced by their associates as treacherous criminals and dealt with accordingly. Simultaneously we are asked to accept the thesis that with one or two possible exceptions the Western countries have been led—through an equally remarkable coincidence—exclusively by people who were unmitigated villains: either bloodthirsty, greedy capitalists or the spineless stooges of such capitalists. One could go on citing such examples at any length. One has only to think of the bland distortions of the historical record that enter constantly into the Soviet statements on foreign policy: the claims with respect to such matters as the outbreak of the Korean War, the origin of the difficulties in Southeast Asia, the nature of the Soviet action in Hungary, etc.

A characteristic but particularly serious extrapolation of this irresponsible attitude toward objective fact will be found in the anti-American campaign of recent years. While this campaign reached its apotheosis before Stalin's death, it did not, unfortunately, cease entirely with that event. The Western public generally is little aware of the fantastic distortion of the image of the United States which has been purveyed to the Soviet public, and particularly to the Soviet intelligentsia, over the course of the past ten years by those who control the informational media of the Communist Party of the Soviet Union. An image of America continues to be cultivated in which even those Americans who are critically inclined towards many manifestations of American life would not recognize the country they know—an image in which the real faults of American civilization find as little recognition as its real virtues.

Propaganda is propaganda; but surely, like everything else in life, it has its limits. What are we to conclude from the propagation of these fantastic misapprehensions about the United States?—that the Soviet leaders really believe them? or that, knowing them to be misapprehensions, they nevertheless find it in order that Soviet citizens should be encouraged to accept them as true? Either variant would have most questionable implications from the standpoint of the prospects for peaceful coexistence.

Nor is it much comfort to people in the West to be assured that if only tensions would be reduced and military preparations relaxed this stream of deliberate detraction would dry up as miraculously and suddenly as it once burst forth. People in the United States have much to correct in their civilization, but little to hide. They are as little interested in being artificially spared by others in the critical appraisal of American life as they are in being artificially disparaged. Let this appraisal be as critical and as skeptical as it will, provided only that it is honest.

Can one ignore, in the discussion of the problem of coexistence, the implications of this attitude toward objective reality—an attitude that characterizes not just the professional Soviet propagandist but the Communist Party of the Soviet Union as a whole, and the statesmanship which that Party inspires? It will always be difficult to know how much confidence can be placed in people who appear to be deliberately deceiving either themselves or others. Is it too much to ask the Soviet leaders to drop today this Byzantine dogmatism of political thought and utterance, for which a case might have been made in the early days of the revolutionary militancy of the Party, when it was still fighting for its ascendancy in Russia, but which is out of place on the part of a great government which asks for acceptance as a mature and responsible force in world affairs? Scarcely anyone, surely, is deceived today by these absurd extremisms. But there are many people in the non-Communist world to whom these recurring evidences of irresponsibility in the attitude toward truth are a constant source of misgiving about the prospects of any sound and enduring coexistence between Communist and non-Communist worlds. What can be the value of specific understandings, these people ask, if the underlying assumptions and beliefs are so grotesquely different? If the Soviet leaders really think us to be as evil as they depict us to their own people, how can they seriously believe in the possibility of coexisting peacefully with us? If, on the other hand, they are deliberately misleading their own people, how can we, on our side, have confidence in them?

The demand that must be made on Moscow is not in any sense a demand for the uncritical acceptance of other points of view. What we would like would be to see in the statements of Soviet leaders, and in the propaganda material produced under their direction, at least a reasonable effort to reconcile the picture they paint of world realities with the objective evidence they have before them. So long as the leaders of the Communist Party of the Soviet Union continue to hold that truth is what it is useful to the interests of the Party that people should believe, regardless of how preposterous or absurd this may be in the light of objective evidence—so long as they continue to deny the very existence of an objective reality and, accordingly, any obligation on their part to understand and respect it —even those people in other parts of the world who might most earnestly wish for coexistence as Mr. Khrushchev has defined it will have to put restraints on their hopes and expectations. The road to peaceful coexistence lies, admittedly, through many gates; but one of these is the abandonment by Russian Communists of the absurd contention that theirs is a party which has always had a perfect understanding of the human predicament and has never made a mistake.

VIII

If Moscow is sincere in the quest for peaceful coexistence, and if to this end it is prepared to envisage a *general* revision, on both sides, of the attitudes and practices that have produced, or have been produced by, this dangerous state of world affairs known as the cold war, there will then be no lack of people in the countries outside the Communist orbit prepared to lend their influence to this process, and if need be, at considerable personal cost; for it is not in Russia alone that the extent of the danger is apparent. But if it is conceived in Moscow that the adjustment has all to be made on the Western side, there will be little that anyone on this side of the line can usefully do to advance coexistence beyond its present uncertain status.

Could we not, all of us, now put aside the pretense of total righteousness and admit to a measure of responsibility for the tangled processes of history that have brought the world to its present dangerous state? And could we not, having once admitted this, drop the argument about whose responsibility is greatest and address ourselves at long last, earnestly and without recrimination, to the elimination of the central and most intolerable elements of the danger?

Topic 32

WORLD COMMUNISM AND
NUCLEAR WAR

රැ3

A Policy for Survival

SIDNEY HOOK *

American foreign policy has been in a state of crisis ever since the end
of World War II. The crises have been partly of this country's own making. It has made error upon error, all based on a failure to understand
the nature of the Communist threat. . . .

No one knows whether the use of tactical atomic weapons can be
limited and the use of the ultimate weapons with thermonuclear warheads
avoided. During the last war, despite all the prewar Cassandras, poison
gas was not used because of the certainty that it would be employed by
the other side in retaliation. The same might be true for hydrogen bombs
in the next war. Nonetheless, it seems to me to be true that the ultimate
weapon can be a deterrent only if the Kremlin believes it will be used.
*This means that the ultimate weapon of the West is not the hydrogen bomb
or any other super-weapon but the passion for freedom and the willingness
to die for it if necessary.* Once the Kremlin is convinced that we will use this
weapon to prevent it from subjugating the world to its will, we will have
the best assurance of peace. Once the Kremlin believes that this willingness
to fight for freedom at all costs is absent, that it has been eroded by
neutralist fear and pacifist wishful thinking, it will blackmail the free
countries of the world into capitulation and succeed where Hitler failed.

Shortly after the first atomic bomb was exploded, Elmer Davis responded
to the call for one world with the retort: "No world is better than some
worlds." It is possible to panic the West by a picture of the universal
holocaust a nuclear world war would bring, to panic the West to a point
where survival on any terms seems preferable to the risks of resistance.
The pages of history show that moral integrity in extreme situations is

* Chairman of the Department of Philosophy, New York University. Author
of *From Hegel to Marx, Marx and the Marxists,* editor of *Determinism and Freedom.* The selection is from "A Foreign Policy for Survival," *New Leader* (April 7,
1958), pp. 8–12. By permission.

often the highest political wisdom. The struggle against totalitarianism is not only a political struggle but also a moral one, which limits the extent to which we can carry appeasement. If Hitler had commanded the weapon resources of the Soviet Union, would we have yielded to one Munich after another until the world was one vast concentration camp? I hardly think so. Those who are prepared to sacrifice freedom for peace and for mere life will find after such sacrifice no genuine peace and a life unfit for man. Paradoxical as it may sound, life itself is not a value. What gives life value is not its mere existence but its quality. Whoever proclaims that life is worth living under any circumstances has already written for himself an epitaph of infamy. For there is no principle or human being he will not betray; there is no indignity he will not suffer or compound.

Sometimes those who should know better seem to ignore this. Bertrand Russell recently declared in an interview with Joseph Alsop that, if the Communists could not be induced to agree to reasonable proposals for controlled nuclear disarmament, he would be in favor of unilateral disarmament even if this meant Communist domination of the entire world.

Bertrand Russell's career as a counselor to mankind, here as in some of his observations about the United States as a police state, proves that all the mathematical logic in the world is not a substitute for common sense. In so many words, he says: "I am for controlled nuclear disarmament, but, if the Communists cannot be induced to agree to it, then I am for unilateral disarmament even if it means the horrors of Communist domination." When they listen to sentiments like this, why *should* the Soviets consent to controlled nuclear disarmament? All they need do is wait and the world will be given to them on a platter to do with as they will. Why *should* they compromise? Not knowing whether they will survive *our* resolution to fight if necessary for freedom, they may be tempted to accept reasonable proposals. But words like Russell's tell them that all they need do is sit tight, make threats and wait for us to come crawling to them disarmed. . . . Russell's words express a dubious political morality and a bad strategy. They bring about the very intransigence among the Communists which he uses as the justification for capitulation.

We do not, however, need to strike an heroic stance in shaping a viable foreign policy. Intelligence must be our guide. If we can keep the free world from falling into the trap set by the Kremlin and preserve peace by increasing the power and readiness of the free world, we can then rely upon the processes of education, the force of example, the contagion of free ideas, the cultural osmosis of the great traditions of the West gradually to soften, to liberalize, to round off the edges of the totalitarian regimes of the world until their own peoples rally their energies to overthrow their oppressors and establish the democratic governments necessary to establish one free world republic.

The Greater Disaster

BERTRAND RUSSELL *

Dr. Sidney Hook's article contains much with which I am in agreement —more, I think, than Dr. Hook realizes. . . . Where he and I disagree is as to the advisability of an ultimate resort to nuclear war if the Communist powers cannot be contained by anything less. Both Dr. Hook and I are concerned with possibilities which we respectively think improbable. Dr. Hook maintains that, even if his policy led to the extinction of human life, it would still be better than a Communist victory. I maintain, on the contrary, that a Communist victory would not be so great a disaster as the extinction of human life. He admits that his policy *might* lead to the one disaster, though he does not think that it would. I admit that the policy which I advocate *might* lead to the other disaster, though I, again, do not think that it would do so. We are agreed that both these extreme consequences are somewhat hypothetical, and we are also agreed that both of them would be disasters. We differ only as to which of them would be the greater disaster.

There are here two quite distinct matters to be discussed: First, what is the likelihood that the policy which I advocate would lead to the universal domination of Communism? And, second, if it did, would this be worse than the ending of human life? It is the second question that I wish to examine, since the first involves difficult political and psychological considerations as to which differences of opinion will inevitably persist.

Dr. Hook asserts that "Bolshevism is the greatest movement of secular fanaticism in human history." I will not dispute this, but is there not also fanaticism in the attitude of Dr. Hook and of the powerful men who agree with him? Human history abounds in great disasters. One civilization after another has been swept away by hordes of barbarians. The Minoan-Mycenaean civilization was destroyed by savage warriors whose descendants, after a few centuries, became the Greeks whom we still revere. When the Mohammedans swept over the greater part of the Eastern Roman Empire, it seemed to Christian contemporaries that the civilization of the regions which they conquered was being destroyed, and yet, before long, it was the Arabs who mainly preserved the heritage of an-

* Lord Russell was the recipient of the Nobel Prize for literature in 1950. Author of *Principia Mathematica* (with A. N. Whitehead), *The Analysis of Mind, Human Knowledge,* and numerous books and articles. The selection is from "World Communism and Nuclear War," *New Leader* (May 26, 1958), pp. 9–10. By permission.

tiquity. Genghis Khan was quite as bad as Stalin at his worst, but his grandson Kublai Khan was a highly civilized monarch under whom Chinese culture flourished.

The men who think as Dr. Hook does are being un-historical and are displaying a myopic vision to which future centuries are invisible. A victory of Communism might be as disastrous as the barbarian destruction of the Roman Empire, but there is no reason to think that it would be more disastrous than that event. While the human race survives, humaneness, love of liberty, and a civilized way of life will, sooner or later, prove irresistibly attractive. The progress of mankind has always been a matter of ups and downs. The downs have always seemed final to contemporaries, and the ups have always given rise to unfounded optimism. Western Europe in the year 1000 gave no promise of the renaissance that began some centuries later. The human spirit throughout Western Christendom was as narrowly imprisoned as it was in Russia under Stalin. Any person who supposes that the evils of Communism, if it achieved a supremacy, would last forever is allowing himself to be so limited by the heat of present controversies as to be unable to see their similarity to equally virulent controversies in the past or to realize that a dark age, if it is upon us, like the dark ages of the past will not last forever.

Dr. Hook says quite truly that life, in itself, is not of value. It gives, however, the only possibility of any value. I cannot applaud the arrogance of those who say: "If the next century or so is to be such as I (if I were alive) would find unpleasant, I shall decide that not only this period but all future time shall be destitute of life." Nor can I wholly admire the kind of "courage" which is advocated by Dr. Hook and others who think like him, which has, in large part, a vicarious character somewhat detracting from its nobility. I have nothing to say against the man who commits suicide rather than live under a regime which he thinks evil, but I do not feel much approval of the man who condemns everybody else to death because he himself does not find life worth living.

A Free Man's Choice

SIDNEY HOOK *

The issues between us are two. The first Russell wholly avoids, even though it is my main point and by far of greater political weight. Russell has declared to the entire world that, if the Soviet Union refuses to ac-

---

* This selection is from "A Free Man's Choice," *New Leader* (May 26, 1958), pp. 10–12. By permission.

cept reasonable proposals for international disarmament, the West should disarm unilaterally—even at the cost of the universal reign of Communist terror. I criticized this view as helping to produce the very situation in which we may have to choose between capitulation to Communist tyranny or war. . . .

Arguments from history are rarely decisive, but I think it is fairly well established that the appeasement of Hitler—not only Munich but the mood that nothing could be worse than war—encouraged Hitler in his aggression. I go further. Even if in my heart I agreed with Russell (as I do not) that in the ultimate event, capitulation to Communism was a lesser evil than the risks of war, I should regard it as a piece of unmitigated political foolishness to proclaim it. We live in a contingent world. What we do, even sometimes what we say, counts. Especially important are the policies we advocate. For, to the extent that they influence human action, they influence future events. Russell's proposal is tantamount to playing with all cards face up against a shrewd and ruthless gambler with a hidden hand. When the stakes are human freedom, it is irresponsible to play a game which invites the Kremlin to bluff us into submission with threats of atomic blackmail. The Soviets are just as vulnerable to us as we are to them.

The Soviet leaders belong to the human race, too. For them, survival is an even more important value than for many in the West. That is why I am convinced that ultimately they are more likely to consent to reasonable proposals for a peaceful settlement once they are persuaded that we will fight rather than surrender, than if they are persuaded by Russell and others that we will surrender rather than fight. *This* is the crucial point which Russell has completely ignored. . . .

It seems to me today that the probability of Communism destroying human liberty everywhere is considerably greater than the probability, if it comes to war, of human life being destroyed everywhere—particularly if we keep up scientific inquiry into defense. . . .

It may be that today, if the scientists of the free world rally to the cause of freedom's defense and not to the cause of Russell and unilateral Western disarmament, discoveries will be made which will counteract some of the lethal after-effects of weapons. In that case, even if the Kremlin forces a war on the West, it may be repelled without the destruction of all human life or even the whole of Western Europe. It is an error to assume that a balance of armaments or even an armaments race inevitably makes for war. Else we would never be at peace. Unpreparedness also may lead to war. There is a risk, of course. The important thing, therefore, is to see to it that the potential aggressor never is certain that he can win. But this is precisely what Russell's policy prevents us from doing.

Suppose now we were confronted with the limiting case: choice between the horror of Communism for some hundreds of years and the end of human life. Here every lover of freedom and of life is on uncertain and tragic ground. One cannot be sure that at the decisive moment the situation will look the same. Yet every compassionate person, including Russell, feels that there is a limit in suffering and ignominy beyond which the whole human enterprise comes into moral question. The problem is where to draw the limit. At present, I cannot, like Russell, find grounds in history for reconciling myself to the first of the above alternatives. Some of my reasons are:

1. In the past, the triumphs of barbarism were local, not universal. Today, a Communist world would be a tightly knit despotism of fear without sanctuaries, without interstices to hide, without possibilities for anonymity.

2. In the past, tyrants ruled with a primitive technology. The possession today of refined scientific techniques increases immeasurably the extent and intensity of terror ruthless men can impose on those they rule. A Communist world could easily become a scientific Gehenna—something incomparably worse than the destruction of the Roman Empire by the barbarians.

3. I cannot regard the achievement which in the past has sometimes followed the triumph of cruel tyrants as worth the price in torture and agony that preceded it. To me, the splendor and glory of the Court of Kublai Khan were not worth even one of the many pyramids of human skulls his grandfather, Genghis Khan, heaped up in carving out his empire. And a few years ago I believe Bertrand Russell would have agreed with me. If the triumph of Hitler were a necessary condition for a new renaissance, what anti-Fascist would be willing to pay the price?

4. It is not at all unlikely that factional struggle will break out again either at the Communist center or periphery among the political gangsters who rule the Communist world. In such an event, thermonuclear weapons of even more destructive power than those we know may be used to end men's miserable lives, and all the additional agony and terror would have been in vain.

5. It is no arrogance on my part to propose to the generation of the free that they follow a policy of resistance rather than of surrender, any more than it is arrogant for Russell to propose surrender rather than resistance. But perhaps he means it is arrogant for any generation of men to make a decision which will prevent the future generations of the yet unborn to have their chance and make their choice. I must confess that I have some difficulty with this notion of obligation, as if it implied there were millions of souls extending into eternity waiting to be born.

I do not share this theology. If there are such souls, they may perhaps become embodied elsewhere.

Communists have always argued that it is justified to bury several generations, if necessary, in order to fertilize the soil of history for a glorious future to be enjoyed by the still unborn. In some respects, Russell's argument is similar except that, as an opponent of Communism, he puts the glory much further into the future. Cosmic optimism, however, seems no more credible to me than historical optimism.

Morally, those who are unborn cannot reproach us for denying them the bliss of birth in a Communist world but those who already exist, our children and grandchildren, may curse us for turning them over to the jailors of a Communist 1984 in which, brainwashed and degraded, they are not even free to die until their masters give them leave. There are more horrors in the Communist heaven or hell than Russell seems aware of.

Freedom to Survive

BERTRAND RUSSELL *

The argument that you cannot negotiate successfully if you announce in advance that, if pressed, you will yield, is entirely valid. If I were the government of either A or B, I should make no such an announcement. But this has no bearing on the purely academic question of what it would be wise to do if the completely desperate situation arose. I must, however, once more insist that the view in favor of avoiding nuclear warfare even at great cost is one which applies to both sides equally and which, as far as I can judge, is no more likely to be adopted by one side than the other. It is entirely unjust to regard the opinions that I have expressed as more useful to the one side than to the other. . . .

Dr. Hook's reasons for supposing that, if Communism conquered the world, its bad features would persist indefinitely are, to my mind, completely untenable. The worst features of Communism have been developed under the influence of fear and would almost certainly grow less if fear were removed. He points out that "in the past, tyrants ruled with a primitive technology." But it was no less effective for being primitive. He alludes to Genghis Khan's pyramids of heads, which were just as thorough-going as Auschwitz. It is an example of his slippery methods of controversy when he says that "the splendor and glory of the court

* This selection is from "Freedom to Survive," *New Leader* (July 7–14, 1958), pp. 23–25. By permission.

of Kublai Khan were not worth even one of the many pyramids of human skulls his grandfather, Genghis Khan, heaped up." I had never maintained that they were. What I had said was that they gave reason for hope that a bad regime might improve—which is a very different thing. . . .

Dr. Hook is guilty of curious inconsistencies which are an indication of his fanaticism. He says: "Communists have always argued that it is justified to bury several generations, if necessary, in order to fertilize the soil of history for a glorious future to be enjoyed by the still unborn." His own position is that it is justified to bury not several generations but *all* future generations, not in order that they may enjoy a glorious future, but in order that they may have no future at all. This is an immeasurable exaggeration of the very fault for which he criticizes the Communists.

I should like to correct a misunderstanding promoted, I think, by a report of an interview in which only a small part of my thought was expressed. I think that, with wise statesmanship on the part of the West, it will not be at all difficult to avoid both nuclear war and surrender. What I advocate in practice, and not as the outcome of an artificial logical dilemma, is a conclusion of agreements between East and West admitting the inevitability of coexistence and the disastrous futility of war. I wish both sides to realize that war cannot achieve anything that either side desires, and that, in consequence, points in dispute can only be settled by negotiation.

The Need to Resist

SIDNEY HOOK *

Is there any doubt that belief in Russell's "theoretical" proposition, that capitulation and the risk of Communist domination with all its barbarity should be preferred to war and the risk to human survival, *tends* to undermine the will to resist Communist aggression? Russell is so absolutely convinced of the validity of his proposition in theoretical ethics that he believes that only the insane can disagree with him. Why, then, does he not accept the responsibility for its practical effects?

Russell asserts that "The question at issue between Dr. Hook and myself arises only if all attempts at negotiation [between the West and the USSR] fail." He is wrong again. The primary issue between us is whether

* This selection is from "Bertrand Russell Retreats," *New Leader* (July 7–14, 1958), pp. 25–27. By permission.

Russell's position will contribute to the failure of those negotiations and whether mine will contribute to their success. Russell's belated second thoughts indicate that he, too, now believes it was not practically wise to declare what he did in his interview. The inferences I and others drew from his interview were perfectly legitimate. Further thought, I hope, will convince him that the Kremlin is less likely to risk aggression if it believes the West will resist to the end than if it is persuaded that Russell's proposition in "theoretical ethics" will guide the West's action. Only if Russell admits this are our remaining differences minor. . . .

As I read the evidence, Russell's recent efforts to diminish East-West tensions have helped disarm psychologically only the West and strengthened the position of the Communist world as well as the resolution of the Kremlin to pursue its present tack. Some of the atomic scientists of West Germany have cited his position as justifying their abandonment of defense research in nuclear weapons. Russell should know that the absence of a free press and of any possibility of freely expressed dissent makes it impossible for him to have any appreciable influence in the Communist world the Kremlin is not willing to let him have. . . . There is no public opinion in the Soviet Union except the opinion of the Kremlin. . . .

Russell brings in the hope of the future and reminds us that the agony of present generations may be followed by improvement. "Genghis Khan," he wrote, "was quite as bad as Stalin at his worst, but his grandson Kublai Khan was a highly civilized monarch under whom Chinese culture flourished." In my criticism I did not contest the possibility of improvement. I denied, *what is essential to Russell's argument,* that it was necessarily worth the price. . . .

I am puzzled to explain Russell's failure to see that in order to justify submission to Moscow, he cannot stop short with believing that there may be improvements in the distant future but must also believe that the expectation of these improvements is worth the cruelties and indignities which will follow submission in the present. (*Mutatis mutandis,* the same logic holds in relation to Genghis and Kublai Khan.) I suspect his lapse at this point flows from a natural and creditable reluctance to drain the cup of appeasement to its bitter dregs.

Russell may retort (1) that in time Communism may be followed by much greater glories than those of the court of Kublai Khan, and that *these* glories are worth the price of submission to Moscow; and (2) that, as he actually says, "the worst features of Communism have been developed under the influence of fear and would almost certainly grow less if fear were removed."

Let us consider the second point first. If the worst features of Communism have developed under the influence of fear of the outside world, how account for the fact in the early years, when seven invading armies stood on Soviet soil, political and cultural terror was not as widespread or severe as when the Soviet Union was subsequently free of invaders and at peace? The entire history of Communist Russia (and China!) makes Russell's generalization dubious. Cruelty and arbitrariness are indigenous to the very system of totalitarian Communism, and the fear in the hearts of the Soviet rulers is not so much of the free world as of their own oppressed people. Further, Russell ignores my argument that it is likely that future Titos and Maos and Stalins will war on each other and use the existence of differences in Communist states as pretexts for their organized cruelties. I grant that some things may grow better, but I am not sanguine that the worst features of Communism will grow less, or sufficiently less to justify Russell's recommendation to surrender to universal torture rather than to resist. Perhaps under Communism, in time, greater glories will develop than those of the court of Kublai Khan. But the probability is just as great that greater infamies will also develop. . . .

I justify my choice of resistance rather than of surrender *only in terms of the experiences of the existing generations,* not future generations. And the ground of my choice is not that existing generations will escape any future but that they will escape a future of torture and infamy which Russell admits will be theirs if they submit to "the horrors of Communism." The error in logic arises from Russell's failure to note that, since on my argument there are no future generations whose desires need be considered, I cannot sensibly be criticized for trying to bury them. I have not returned to the ontology of Plato and the early Russell. My argument is addressed only to the present generations. *They* must make the choice—only *their* desires, wishes, fears and hopes count. This is as far away as anyone can get from the Communist position, Russell to the contrary notwithstanding.

Even more misleading is Russell's statement that I am denying to those who prefer life under Communism, whether in Communist and neutralist countries, freedom to choose the alternative they prefer. I have no quarrel with those who live in Communist countries—only with their dictators who seek to impose the yoke of bondage on other peoples. To say that because I urge resistance to aggression I do not believe in freedom for those who wish to live under Communism, is as absurd as to charge Russell, because he urged resistance to Hitler, with not believing that those who preferred a peaceful life under Fascism should be free to make their choice. Hitler was morally responsible for the fate of the victims of the resistance against him. The rulers of the Kremlin are morally responsible for the consequences of the resistance to their aggression. . . .

Granted the need for continuous effort to negotiate a reasonable settlement with the Kremlin, the troublesome questions arise when we ask: If the Communists seize West Berlin, should the free world resist? Or if West Germany is invaded? Or the rest of Western Europe? Or England? As distinct from Russell, I believe the free world should declare it will resist wherever the Communist world resorts to force, and to declare it in such a way that the Kremlin has no doubts it *will* resist. There will then be no war.

No man can win freedom and peace unless he conquers his fear of death. No nation can preserve its freedom unless it is willing to risk destruction in its defense. To do otherwise is to break faith with those who died to keep it free.

The free society from Pericles to the present has survived because it has valued some things more than survival, because its vision of human excellence, dignity and joy has made some kinds of life unworthy of man. Bertrand Russell is one of the great moulders of the traditions of the free society. In disagreeing with him strongly on a matter of policy, we nonetheless honor the values and visions he has served during a long life and which he has taught us to cherish.

Policy of Balance

JOHN H. HERZ *

COLLECTIVE SECURITY, BIPOLARITY, AND THE "NEW BALANCE"

"Nuclear stalemate," that is, equilibrium, by and large, in nuclear weapons and forces on the part of the two blocs, is in one way the military aspect of this precarious world balance. In another way, however, the nuclear factor tends to destroy the functioning of the bipolar system altogether. What use are bases, satellites, security pacts and security zones, when intercontinental missiles with nuclear warheads reach from center to center and render any "walls" meaningless? Total permeability disarms even the global blocs, and in a situation where not even two halves of the earth prove big enough to assume the security function of the traditional nation, the logic of things seems to press to-

* Professor of Government, The City College of New York. Author of *Political Realism and Political Idealism, International Politics in the Atomic Age,* and other books. The excerpt is from "Balance System and Balance Policies in a Nuclear and Bipolar Age," *Journal of International Affairs,* Vol. XIV, No. 1 (1960), pp. 35–48. By permission.

ward only one further and ultimate solution: world control by one single power. For only the elimination of the nuclear opponent could give a nuclear power that feeling of security from annihilation which the advent of the nuclear age has placed in jeopardy. A certain logic of history likewise points to such a final outcome, for if we glance at developments over the last 1,500 years or so, we discover that the trend has been going from smallest and small to ever larger political units, and the logic of things would appear to involve the ultimate step: substituting one all-comprehensive, global unit for the existing two major ones. But at this very point, reflection on the implications of the nuclear weapon makes it clear that even this way out has become blocked. Since it is hardly imaginable that one of the nuclear powers could be eliminated by the other except through total nuclear war, the attempt to attain this final objective in all likelihood would entail mutual, not one-sided, destruction. The application of the means to attain the end by itself precludes the attainment.[1]

Thus we are thrown back to continuing nuclear competition, and the prospect of an era of increasing insecurity and fear, where death of all or most, and destruction of everything of value, are possible at any moment; . . .

POLICY AND CHOICES

Must we then despair, or resign ourselves to a fate from which there is no escape? Viewing the situation in this light explains the advocacy of policies of despair, for instance, that of unilateral disarmament or surrender. Faced with the alternative: "rather dead than red," or: "rather red than dead," it might indeed, under nuclear conditions, not be mere cowardice to choose the latter and give up liberty and way of life so that mankind can at least continue to exist. For, while in times past the heroic choice, with individuals or groups sacrificing themselves for the sake of their ideals, was meaningful, it is at least questionable whether a present generation so determined would have the right, by sacrificing its own existence, to doom perhaps all future generations as well. Those in favor of capitulation (and it would, of course, be capitulation by the West, Communism not being likely to be so considerate) can claim with some plausibility that theirs is the advocacy of life, or at least the possibility

---

[1] What is not precluded is the eventual attainment of world-control by "peaceful" means, that is, by the reduction, step by step, of the sphere of one superpower through penetration and expansion on the part of the other. There is little doubt that such is the ultimate objective of, at least, Soviet "coexistence" policy. Such policy is still fraught with danger of mutually suicidal nuclear clashes, as will be detailed below.

of life's continuance on earth, with the hope that even a global Communism, like all systems and regimes before, would some time pass.

If there really was no alternative but to choose between the nuclear holocaust and such policies as the unilateral disarmament of the West, we all would have to make our choice, and it would be an agonizing one. Fortunately, it would not seem that at this point we have attained the stage where no other alternative remains. Indeed, there is an opposite view, one that sins through as excessive an optimism as the one mentioned before sins through over-pessimism. I refer to the view which holds that the existing balance of nuclear power among the two blocs, through the effect of mutual deterrence, has come to guarantee permanent peace, a world situation in which the possibility of a mutually suicidal nuclear war can be written off for all practical purposes. As Churchill once put it (but this was many years ago), we would "by a process of sublime irony have reached a stage in this story where safety will be the sturdy child of terror, and survival the twin-brother of annihilation." [2]

I am afraid that such reliance would be unrealistic. We have become all too familiar with the recurring instances of crisis where, sooner or later, one or the other side threatens that, in the words of our opponent, "the rockets will fly"; this has been so at the off-shore islands of China, at Suez, and most recently at Berlin. And who can say that it would always remain bluff or bluster, that a policy of nuclear blackmail will not one final day, by intention or inadvertence, have to be implemented by the deed? Here are a few of those numerous cases in which deterrence might quite conceivably fail.

There is, first, the possibility of miscalculation, technical error (for instance, in the interpretation of some radar signal), human failure, and so forth, especially with ever-shorter time available between discovery of a suspicious phenomenon and decision. SAC's so-called "fail-safe" system, for instance, is, I believe, a dangerous illusion and anything but safe.

Second, technological developments may cause one or the other side to believe (probably erroneously) that it has a chance to destroy the opponent by surprise attack (pre-emptive war, as the newfangled term goes) without risking effective retaliation. Even now, when avoidance of the retaliatory blow is hardly imaginable, we can hear from time to time voices advocating such pre-emption.

Third, mutual misunderstanding concerning the circumstances under which aggression, or a similar serious step on the part of one side, would cause the other side to react by nuclear force; misunderstanding, that is,

[2] Speech in Commons, March 1, 1955.

concerning how far one can go without running into massive retaliation.

Finally, there are the nuclear dangers involved in polycentrism, the concentration of nuclear power in many centers, where some irrational leader, some future Hitler, in madness, despair, out of spite, or for reasons of domestic policy, could pull mankind into the abyss.

POLICY OF BALANCE FOR COEXISTENCE

If, then, the "new balance" of power based on a nuclear "balance of terror" is so shaky and at the same time so menacing in its consequences, can anything be done to render it more stable while simultaneously reducing the nuclear threat?

Certain objectives emerge as matters of urgent and immediate concern. All too often, since the dawn of the atomic age, we have missed opportunities—for instance, for supervised arms destruction or arms control—simply by allowing that moment to pass when such things were still technically feasible. But to do nothing—the characteristic of bipolar policy so far—means perpetuation of arms competition and cold war with all their menace. Such unimaginative policy deserves rejection as strongly as one of integral pacifism and surrender. It is, in a way, understandable that the enormity of the threat which Communism poses to what we consider the free world induces many to emphasize "preparedness" to the exclusion of any kind of negotiation and accommodation. But the enormity of this threat to us is matched by that of the weapons to all—the threat of genocide by that of omnicide—and the chief goal of policy must therefore be to avoid getting oneself into a situation where the choice lies between annihilative war and surrender. I submit that only a stabilization of the present balance of power, unsatisfactory though it is in many ways, can give some assurance of such avoidance, and that only a new type of determined and consistent balance policy can render the *de facto* balance more stable. Merely a few suggestions can be presented here.

In the armaments field, first: stabilize the "nuclear club," that is, prevent the emergence of additional nuclear powers. An agreement on the definitive, supervised, world-wide cessation of nuclear tests would be an important step toward this aim. It may be too late already for France * and, possibly, China; but it is obvious that only while keeping the number of nuclear units small can one inaugurate a policy of diminishing the danger of nuclear war and of reducing international tension in general.

Second: clearly define the *casus belli nuclearis;* that is, state under

---

* France has already joined the "nuclear club."

but greater stability of conditions can only be reached by policy in the non-armament field.

Here, it is in my opinion of prime importance to realize that under present nuclear and bipolar conditions all that diplomacy can hope to achieve is a provisional stabilization of conditions based by and large on the present bipolar *status quo*. Since the present power positions of the antagonistic blocs could be changed unilaterally only by the use of force, it is only through mutual accommodation which recognizes the overall spheres of power and influence as they exist that issues can be settled in the more concrete instances.

As the case of Hungary has shown so tragically, actual policy оι the West is already based on the more or less conscious realization that force is no longer usable to change the present hard shell of the blocs. And it is my impression that at least one thing in Soviet advocacy of peaceful coexistence is not more propaganda but concern with unalterable facts: its insistence that war should be ruled out in the interest of both sides. An earlier illusion that Communism would somehow emerge without mortal injury from nuclear war between the systems, and inhabitants of Communist countries prove less killable than those in capitalist regimes, seems to have yielded to recognition of the nuclear facts of life. Thus, concern for survival, that concern which both sides have in common, must become the basis of a common policy of survival, a policy where each side must at all times be concerned with the opponent's policy as well and, if necessary, prevent him from committing mistakes which might plunge not only him but the entire world into the abyss. So interwoven is the fate of all of us today that that which once was a cherished objective of national foreign policy, namely, to have one's opponent commit vital mistakes, today must yield to a policy of a minimal security interest.

Thus, a delimitation of spheres, a drawing of lines of *de facto* control, which, far from implying moral sanction or political approval, would merely be expressive of the prevailing power status,[3] seems to be the first prerequisite of the "holding operation" or stopgap policy here suggested. But how to achieve even this much? There are innumerable problems of tactics and approach, of procedures and institutional devices (such as that concerning the role the United Nations system might play in this operation) which might be taken up here, but only a few can be mentioned.

How, for instance, should one deal with those problems and areas

[3] As Eugene Rabinowitch has recently said: "It is an accident of scientific progress, achieved in our time, not the justice or adequacy of the present distribution of world power, that calls for a freeze" ("Status Quo With a Quid Pro Quo," *Bulletin of the Atomic Scientists*, September 1959, p. 290).

which circumstances the opponent must expect nuclear retaliation. Only by doing this can one hope to avoid the danger of total war breaking out through misunderstanding. The simplest way would be for the powers to declare or promise not to use the nuclear weapon first; that is, to agree to use it only in retaliation against the opponent's first using it. This implies foregoing the use and the threat of the use of nuclear weapons in response to non-nuclear attack; but in view of the likelihood of effective nuclear counter-retaliation to such retaliation, this threat has become—or, at least, is bound soon to become—implausible anyway. And as long as it is still plausible, the greatest value of the renunciation here suggested would lie in the prevention of further nuclear blackmail. For so long as the powers consider themselves bound by their declaration, they will not be in a position to bring about nuclear war scares. Of course, the weapon must still be held in readiness to discourage abuse of the promise. Under viewpoints of Western strategy and security, moreover, the doubt arises whether renouncing the nuclear threat would not put the West in a decisive disadvantage *vis-à-vis* the East because of its patent inferiority in conventional armaments. This certainly is true for today, though not necessarily forever. The West will have to seek a better balance in conventional forces anyway so as to be able to face emergencies with other than the alternative of big war or surrender. It will have to achieve this balance either by increasing its preparedness in conventional arms and manpower, or by inducing the East to reduce its establishment to an equilibrium level. It may thus be necessary to rearm conventionally in order to reduce the danger of nuclear war. *Si vis pacem, para bellum non-atomicum.*

But even conventional war, once it becomes general and involves the superpowers directly, may not stay non-atomic. What about a nuclear "war of desperation" on the part of one side engaged in conventional war when it faces the likelihood of defeat? And "limited nuclear war," fought with "mere" tactical atomic weapons, is even more likely to degenerate into total war. It seems that only by keeping operations strictly localized and fighting it out by proxy, as it were, can the major powers escape the risk of eventual all-out war. Diplomacy will have to look more and more for substitutes of the threat of military force to defend what heretofore has been known as the national interest. This leads to the question of policy in the non-armament field. While additional steps in the armament field, such as control of the military uses of outer space and, indeed, gradual reduction of nuclear armament and installations as such, are vital, no policy limited to this field alone makes sense. Tension arising from the peril of nuclear war can possibly be reduced here,

proach can hardly be called entirely unrealistic. Prior to our age of radical newness, it is true, advocacy of a policy substituting the observance of universal interests for national interests was correctly considered utopian, because national interests could still, and only, be safeguarded by nations as units of power, while most internationalist ideals ran counter to what nations could afford. But now the former dichotomy of interests and ideals has become one of two sets of interests, with the former ideal now constituting a compelling interest itself. While formerly the lives of people, their goods and possessions, their hopes and their happiness were tied up with the affairs of the country in which they lived and which protected them, now that destruction threatens everybody in every one of his most intimate, personal interests, national interests are bound to compete with, and eventually to recede behind, the common interests in sheer survival. If we add to this the universal interest in the solution of other world problems—those posed by the exhaustion of soil and other vital natural resources, the "population explosion," and many more—it is perhaps not utopian to expect that the ultimate spread of a universalist attitude through rational foreign policies would at last become possible.

Right now, of course, this is still "music for the future." Realism compels us to set more modest standards and goals for present policy. Quite apart from the ideological and political gulf that separates two worlds, the security dilemma as such, the dilemma of mutual fear and mutual suspicion about aims and intentions in which both sides find themselves entangled, would appear to make a provisional standstill agreement the most we can hope for at this juncture. So frightful is the predicament in which a runaway science and technology has placed the human race that not the attainment of some better "new balance" but the mere preservation of the ever so unsatisfactory old one must now be our prime endeavor. For this way only may we pass through the valley of deadly peril to the heights of survival in safety.

where the boundary between the two worlds is contested or ill-defined and serious crises have arisen or are bound to arise? Obviously, mutual accommodation and compromise must be the means of settlement, and a concrete attack upon each situation as it presents itself from case to case seems preferable to trying general and overall solutions. In this connection, checking one's ideological preoccupations at the entrance door to the conference hall would be helpful, but, on the other hand, there do exist interest, values, ideals on both sides which appear so vital to the respective systems that bargaining where they are affected would seem out of the question. In other words, one always has to distinguish between the negotiable and the non-negotiable, that which, for one or the other side, is a matter of principle. Thus, for the West, permitting populations now free and to whose freedom the West has committed itself, to pass under Communist control (even though it might be a compromise *quid* for a corresponding Communist *quo*), would truly be betrayal, and one that would undermine its whole moral position. West Berlin comes to mind.

But the same goes for Communism, where yielding back to capitalism what in Eastern eyes constitutes "socialist achievements" might be similarly impossible. East Germany, perhaps, is a case in point. Arriving at a concrete solution may prove extremely difficult in such instances, and policies of delay, of procrastination, may be the only "solutions" which are for the time being available. Thus, in the case of Berlin, where both sides have invoked rules of international law to bolster their respective views on the status of West Berlin and on Western rights of access, the West might consider "Fabian" tactics, such as utilizing the International Court of Justice, either by asking it for a verdict on the legal questions involved, or, in case of a Soviet refusal to accept the Court's jurisdiction, by having the General Assembly of the United Nations request an advisory opinion. Even though the latter would not be legally binding, it might become a basis for renewed negotiations, conceivably even giving Khrushchev a chance to extricate himself from his advanced position. In any event, time would be gained, it being unlikely that unilateral steps would be taken while the matter was *sub judice*.

In other instances, solutions of substance may be possible, provided the right moment is grasped to initiate negotiations. That moment, obviously, is not when a crisis has reached its culmination and concessions are impossible for prestige reasons, but when that particular crisis, as it so far has always happened sooner or later, simmers down. At this point, for instance, the Far Eastern situation, where the issue of world war or peace several times in recent years has revolved around the ridiculously petty question of the off-shore islands, might well be tackled in its larger connotations. Granting diplomatic recognition to the Peiping regime and yielding the off-shore islands (after evacuation of those unwilling to stay) in return for Chinese recognition of Nationalist control over Taiwan would seem to be the kind of compromise that would provide for a clearer delimitation of spheres; and neither side would yield anything of value it possesses now. But it is easy to see how ideological obsessions on both sides would stand in the way of a rational settlement of this kind.

Another problem, one raised inevitably when freezing an existing status, be it ever so temporary and provisional, is proposed, concerns the "dynamics" of international affairs ("no status can be supposed to last forever"), and the dynamic nature of Communism in particular. Is not Communism, a pseudo-religious faith and movement, by its very nature expansionist? But the suggestion here made was based entirely on the assumption that a minimal rationality will continue to govern the policies of the East as well, and that this rationality will cause it to forego military means of expansion in favor of trying "peaceful penetration." And as far as the latter is concerned, it would seem up to the non-Communist world to create conditions in which Communism finds no chance to establish itself. We know that in advanced, industrialized societies Communism has never attained control by peaceful means. And where it seems to have opportunities today, in that part of the world which we call backward or underdeveloped, it would seem to be a policy of hardheaded interest and idealist sacrifice all in one for the West to assist in creating conditions which would lift these areas to a standard of living worthy of human beings. If the developed nations of the West prove unable or unwilling to make the necessary sacrifices, Communism would deserve outcompeting them.

THE OUTLOOK

Beyond this, one may continue to hope for liberalization of conditions and regimes now in the opponent's camp. The case of Poland comes to mind. Lifting the threat or pressure involved in a so-called policy of liberation might even make it easier for Moscow or Peiping to reduce some measure of restrictiveness in regard to subject populations, possibly even within their own countries. Without indulging in facile optimism, one might then perhaps envisage a more remote future where tension will have abated to such an extent that radically new attitudes would gradually be substituted for exclusive concern with national interests. I have called this approach a universalist one and defined universalism as "that comprehension of mankind as one group which imposes itself on those aware of the absolute peril in which the new weapons have placed mankind."

If one takes into consideration this peril, on the one hand, and the manifold "one-world" trends in the present world, on the other hand, such an ap-